Handbook of Management Consulting Services

Handbook of Management Consulting Services

Sam W. Barcus III, Editor
Partner
Barcus Britt Leiffer Consulting
Nashville, Tennessee

Joseph W. Wilkinson, Editor
Professor of Accounting
Arizona State University
Tempe, Arizona

Second Edition

McGraw-Hill, Inc.
New York   San Francisco   Washington, D.C.   Auckland   Bogotá
Caracas   Lisbon   London   Madrid   Mexico City   Milan
Montreal   New Delhi   San Juan   Singapore
Sydney   Tokyo   Toronto

Library of Congress Cataloging-in-Publication Data

Handbook of management consulting services / Sam W. Barcus III,
    editor, Joseph W. Wilkinson, editor — 2nd ed.
        p.   cm.
    Includes index.
    ISBN 0-07-003686-1
    1. Business consultants.   I. Barcus, Sam W.   II. Wilkinson,
Joseph W.
HD69.C6H36   1994
001'.068—dc20   94-23359
                                                          CIP

    4 5 6 7 8 9 0   DOC/DOC   9 0 9 8 7

ISBN 0-07-003686-1

*The sponsoring editor for this book was Jim Bessent, the editing supervisor was
Peggy Lamb, and the production supervisor was Donald F. Schmidt. This book
was set in Palatino. It was composed by McGraw-Hill's Professional Book Group
composition unit.*

Printed and bound by R. R. Donnelley & Sons Company.

This book is printed on recycled, acid-free paper containing a
minimum of 50% recycled, de-inked fiber.

McGraw-Hill books are available at special quantity discounts
to use as premiums and sales promotions, or for use in corporate training programs. For more information, please write to
the Director of Special Sales, McGraw-Hill, Inc., 11 West 19th
Street, New York, NY 10011. Or contact your local bookstore.

Contents

Part 1. Introduction to Management Consulting

Part 2. Client-Consultant Relationships

Part 5. Practice Management

Part 6. Business Consulting Services

Part 7. Specialized Consulting Services

Contributors

Sam W. Barcus III received his B.B.A. degree from the University of Texas and his M.B.A. degree from the University of Houston. He joined Price Waterhouse in Memphis as a consultant, working on a variety of computer-related projects, including system design. He joined Touche Ross in Nashville to establish a management consulting practice serving businesses throughout the Southeast. Today he is a partner in Barcus Britt Leiffer Consulting, which provides information management consulting, education/training, and technology implementation. Mr. Barcus is a certified public accountant and has held leadership positions in a number of professional and community organizations. He conducts workshops and seminars in North America, Latin America, Asia, Europe, and South Africa. (CHAPTERS 9 & 19)

Brian Beiles is a consultant and trainer who works with organizations and their managers to enable them to deal effectively with strategic change. He designs and delivers workshops that integrate the disciplines of leadership, empowerment, teamwork, and service quality and are perceived by clients as especially relevant to succeeding in today's highly competitive, customer-driven environment. Mr. Beiles is a C.A., M.B.A., and a principal of The Cadence Group. He has more than 20 years of business and consulting experience, particularly in the financial services, real estate, and retail industries where he has held a number of senior positions. This gives him a broad perspective in addressing strategic business issues, and enables him to relate effectively with management at all levels. In addition to his work with a number of organizations internationally, Mr. Beiles is on faculty with the Division of Executive Development at York University and the Banff School of Management. (CHAPTER 26)

Victor M. Bond is president of ChangeNet, a network of applied psychologists, social anthropologists, communications specialists, and other professionals whose expertise is focused on diagnosing, planning, and implementing major change in large organizations. Mr. Bond's specialties are individual and group intervention and facilitation, organizational communications, and video production. He has recently led the development of a worldwide change management training curriculum for one of the largest high-technology companies, and personally intervened with individuals and groups in one of the largest mergers in U.S. business history. He has also produced a weekly cable television program *The Change Network*. Mr. Bond founded ChangeNet after a 15-year career with IBM. During that period, he was a director of marketing and director of strategy, and, in those capacities, was responsible for over $1 billion in revenue and for the development of IBM's U.S. and worldwide strategies, particularly in the areas of services and consulting. He was also, during that time, responsible for serving the financial services and insurance industries in New England and the Mid-Atlantic states. He holds a B.S. in Mathematics from Harvard College. (CHAPTER 28)

Lamar Bordelon is president and CEO of Pound International, Inc., a consulting company with clients in the United States and across the Pacific Rim, providing services in areas which include project management, professional development, process control, data security, total quality management, business system planning, and business continuation planning. Mr. Bordelon's career began in his native Houston, Texas, where he studied physics and mathematics at the University of Houston after serving in the U.S. Marine Corps during the Korean War. He started with Honeywell, Inc., as associate application engineer. After a variety of assignments he became project manager for their Southwest Region projects, including the Manned Spacecraft Center for NASA and the Astrodome. He moved to Robertshaw Aeronautical & Electronic Controls and became district manager for sales and service, then acting regional manager for the Central U.S. Region. Mr. Bordelon then became a data acquisition and control systems specialist for IBM, with responsibility for nationwide support for process control systems for IBM's process industry customers headquartered in Houston. That led to the position of national account manager for EXXON's process-related operations, then to international account manager for ESSO Eastern account, responsible for IBM's marketing activities to their offices across Asia—from Japan to Australia to Pakistan.

He then moved to Paris, France as IBM's process industry representative to the USSR. He returned to the United States for a variety of assignments, culminating in the position of Team Leader for IBM SE Professional Development Department, which required developing, organizing, and conducting customized training courses throughout the United States, Asia, and the Americas (both North and South). IBM next moved Mr. Bordelon to Sydney, Australia, to establish and manage a professional development department serving IBM branches and customers across Australia, New Zealand, and S.E. Asia. IBM decided to also establish a Systems Integration function to serve the same geographical area and Mr. Bordelon's assignment was extended as consulting project manager. He retired early after 22 years with IBM, and returned to Dallas, Texas, where he founded Pound International, Inc. (CHAPTER 15)

J. Owen Cherrington is a professor of accounting at Brigham Young University. He earned his Ph.D. in accounting at the University of Minnesota in 1972. Prior to his present positio, Dr. Cherrington served as assistant professor at Pennsylvania State University and associate professor at Utah State University. He is the author of several textbooks and journal articles. He also serves as consultant for several business organizations. He holds memberships in the American Accounting Association, American Institute of Certified Public Accountants, and Utah Association of Certified Public Accountants. (CHAPTER 4)

Dwight W. Clark has been a Justice Consultant with IBM Corporation since 1989. He is acknowledged nationwide as a leader in the implementation, design, and analysis of automated court and criminal justice systems. Clark has achieved national recognition as a project manager, instructor, facilitator, advisor, and consultant to courts and justice agencies. He received his J.D. from California Western Law School in 1974, a masters in public administration from USC, School of Public Administration in 1976, and is a certified specialist in judicial administration. Mr. Clark came to IBM after 13 years with the San Francisco Municipal Court, where for 5 years he managed court operations and more than 200 employees as clerk-administrator. Previously, he worked with the U.S. Probation Department in Los Angeles.

A professional background with the American legal system, combined with a comprehensive technical knowledge of automation, data processing, and computer performance analysis, makes Mr. Clark a leading advisor to justice agencies. He addresses the specific operational requirements of selecting, designing, and implementing appropriate technology. Mr. Clark's expertise has led to speaking engagements at seminars, conferences, executive briefings, and planning sessions, both at customer sites throughout the United States and Asia Pacific, as well as at the Advanced Business Institute in New York. Mr. Clark serves as faculty for the College of Professional Studies, University of San Francisco and the National Judges College in Reno, Nevada. He served as a faculty member at The Future and The Courts Conference in San Antonio, Texas, in 1990. He is currently a member of the National Association for Court Management, the California Bar Association, the American Bar Association, the American Judicature Society, and the National Association for Justice Information Systems. He has been selected as guest speaker for the National Court Technology Conferences, the National Reporter Conference, and the California, Colorado, and Oregon Court Clerks Associations. Mr. Clark was the 1984 recipient of the Technology Achievement Award from the Public Technology Inc. Consortium, Washington, D.C. (CHAPTER 34)

Scott Cosman is a consultant with Andersen Consulting. He has been with the consulting firm since 1988 and specializes in systems integration. He obtained a B.B.A. and an M.S. in finance form Texas A&M University in College Station, Texas. He currently resides in Scottsdale, Arizona. (CHAPTER 13)

Paula Dawson is a consulting manager at Midrange Systems Solutions (MSS), a Phoenix-based firm. MSS provides business application solutions to clients on the IBM S/3X and AS/400 midrange platforms. Their scope of services include information systems planning, application software development, and customization using a wide-range of CASE and other application development productivity tools. (CHAPTERS 22 & 24)

Charles E. Day, CMC, is a management consultant specializing in the application and integration of telephone and automated computer system technologies. He has successfully developed strategic and technical plans as well as managed the implementation of hundreds of telephone- and computer-related systems and voice/data network projects. As a chief telecommunications officer for the nation's largest airline, he managed the design and implementation of both national and international projects. Mr. Day is active in numerous professional and technical organizations and holds a B.S. degree in mathematics and physics and a Master of Science in administration/computer science from The George Washington University. (CHAPTER 30)

Elaine Dickson, since 1983, has been president of Corporate Transitions, Inc., a consulting firm specializing in strategic planning, organizational development, and performance management. She also serves as executive director of the Center for Nonprofit Management, a joint venture of the HCA Foundation and United Way of Middle Tennessee. Ms. Dickson has broad management experience. She was dean of student affairs in higher education, an internal consultant and transition manager for a major reorganization project in a national organization, and start-up manager of a national direct sales business. Her in-depth experience includes managing in rapidly changing environments. Ms. Dickson has a doctor's degree in education with specializations in management and the behavioral sciences. (CHAPTER 25)

Valerie Norton Downs if a senior consultant in the Skills Management and Transformation practice of IBM. She consults in human performance analysis and skills management, specializing in the human aspects of change management and implementation. Prior to joining the education company, she developed and led IBM's national health care consulting and services practice. Her practice consulted with clients in business transformation and total quality management (TQM), information technology strategy and planning, and systems implementation. She has held a variety of marketing, staff, and management positions in IBM in which she developed a broad-based industry background. Prior to joining IBM in 1978, she spent 3 years with Castle & Cooke, Inc., in San Francisco as a budget analyst. She received her MBA in International Business from Golden Gate University and her BA in French and humanities from the College of St. Benedict. She is a member of the American Society for Quality Control and the American Society for Training and Development. Ms. Downs wishes to thank her collaborators on this chapter, all of whom are former or current members of IBM's health care group: Katie Asplin, Doug Bartee, Nancy Discher, Carolyn Jackson, Robert Niebergall, Betty Oliver, and David Ramzy. Without them this chapter would not have been possible. (CHAPTER 33)

David J. Dyda, IBM Corporation, Sacramento, Calif., has 14 years' experience in the information systems and technology industry with IBM, primarily with organizations in the health care and public sector industries. The primary focus of his consulting is in providing clients with assistance in identifying and evaluating business and work processes and analyzing and recommending various technology alternatives for enabling the management of business processes. (CHAPTER 27)

Bruce A. Esposito is a management consultant and senior faculty member of IBM's Executive Consulting Institute. He specializes in management consultant development and its associated techniques, tools, and frameworks. He has strong skills in the areas of problem solving, creativity, team building, professional practices, and the linkage of business plans with information and telecommunications plans. He developed his expertise working with a broad spectrum of consulting practices in the Americas, Europe, and Asia Pacific and with clients varying in size and industry, with a focus on the financial services and process arenas.

In addition, he has responsibility for the engagement management curriculum and problem solving frameworks across multiple curricula. Prior to joining the Institute, Mr. Esposito worked as a management consultant in an IBM Applications Solutions practice, where he was involved in addressing client business problems through the use of information integration and rapid application development techniques. He was also a member of a consulting group whose focus was to work with clients to develop information systems investment strategies. He has a broad background in telecommunications and computer networking design and implementation and has also served as the manager of management communications for an IBM division president, with responsibility for all major communications vehicles including a management journal, a trade press function, and speeches. As a graduate of IBM's Systems Research Institute, he was a frequent guest lecturer in their "Computer Networking Series." Mr. Esposito holds a Ph.D. in applied mathematics from Courant Institute, New York University, and a bachelors of arts in mathematics from Queens College. (CHAPTER 20)

Steven P. Golen is associate professor of accountancy at Arizona State University. He received his B.S. and M.A. degrees from Western Kentucky University and his Ph.D. degree from Arizona State University. He previously taught at Louisiana State University. Professor Golen has published articles on accounting communications in such journals as *Advances in Accounting* and *The CPA Journal.* Also, he was co-author of two monographs, *Developing the Internal Auditors' Leadership Skills* and *Conducting Internal Audit Interviews,* published by the Institute of Internal Auditors. He is a member of the American Accounting Association, Institute of Internal Auditors, and the Institute of Management Accountants. (CHAPTER 5)

Gary Grudnitski is professor of accountancy at San Diego State University. He earned his Ph.D. at the University of Massachusetts in 1975. Prior to his present position, Dr. Grudnitski held positions as systems analyst with Bell Telephone (Canada) and the Government of

Saskatchewan, as associate professor of accounting at the University of Texas at Austin, and as resident academic with Arthur Young's information technology consulting group in Reston, Virginia. He has instructed in a variety of professional programs, including the AICPA National MAS training program and the University Education for Management Consulting. He is co-author of the second through fifth editions of *Information Systems: Theory and Practice.* He has also published articles in a variety of journals, including the *Journal of Management Consulting.* (CHAPTER 11)

Gordon L. Hornbaker is an independent small business consultant, specializing in business and marketing planning. His company, Grand Designs, Inc., is based in Paradise Valley, Arizona. Hornbaker received a bachelor's degree in biological sciences and a masters in business at Indiana University. Since then, he has worked for 10 years with Baxter International in several sales and marketing functions. He has started several new businesses, including a multimillion dollar custom manufacturing company in Scottsdale, Arizona. For the past 5 years, he has served as a planning and development consultant to small businesses in the Phoenix/Scottsdale area. (CHAPTERS 22 & 24)

Charlotte A. Jenkins is a manager within the management consulting services area of Price Waterhouse. Jenkins has worked with Price Waterhouse since 1980. She transferred from the Nashville office to Los Angeles, where she specializes in health care consulting. Her background and experience have been with information systems, procedures, and organization analysis. Some specific projects that she has conducted and managed address: business planning; information system feasibility studies; computer system hardware and software evaluation, selection, and implementation; productivity improvement studies and procedures; job descriptions and specifications; and organization reviews. (CHAPTER 16)

Ira Kasdan recently accepted a position as vice president of performance improvement for the Carlson Travel Group, a multibillion dollar global travel company. He was founder and president of the Management Institute for Better Working Teams and Individuals (BWTI), an educational and performance services company with 1993 sales approaching $2 million. He developed curricula for professional and technical development programs used to train more than 300,000 people on topics ranging from sales and sales management to customer satisfaction, quality, risk management, new products, and technical skills. He also created training programs and materials used in a wide range of industries including construction, heavy equipment, automotive, information systems, financial services, health care, hospitality, public utilities, transportation, and travel. He designed a consulting skills training program for systems engineers and technical professionals conducted for more than 5,000 people in five countries and has directed major organizational improvement efforts in areas including reduction and quality and sales improvement. Mr. Kasdan is listed in *Who's Who in U.S. Executives* in 1990 and is a member of the National Speakers Association. (CHAPTER 14)

Jeff Kasschau is the president and CEO of 1st Approach, Inc., a Carlsbad, California, consulting firm that specializes in software development and engineering services. He has been practicing in the public utility sector since 1979, emphasizing the development of computer-based solutions supporting administrative, financial, engineering, plant operations, and maintenance activities. Prior to his present position, Mr. Kasschau held the positions of vice president with RJC Energy Consultants and manager, management information systems, with Arthur Andersen & Co. and was on the faculty of Saddleback College. He is a graduate of Arizona. Mr. Kasschau holds industry memberships with the Electric Power Research Institute, American Nuclear Society, Nuclear Information Records Management Association, Project Management Institute, and Data Processing Management Association, while he holds professional memberships with the American Institute of Certified Public Accountants, Arizona Society of Certified Public Accountants, and Institute of International Business Planning. (CHAPTER 32)

James C. Kinard is an associate professor of accounting and MIS at The Ohio State University. He earned his Ph.D. in accounting from Stanford University in 1969. Dr. Kinard served as assistant professor of accounting and management information systems at Cornell University from 1968 to 1972. He has served with three different public accounting firms. He has directed the AICPA National MAS training program and served as a member of the AICPA MAS Executive Committee. He has published articles in several academic journals and holds memberships in the American Accounting Association, the Institute of Management Sciences, the Decision Sciences Institute, and the Association for Computing Machinery. (CHAPTER 2)

Mary Ann Kipp is a partner with Kipp & Associates, a Nashville-based consulting firm with an emphasis in strategic management, organization development, and executive coaching. She conducts counseling in career and life transitions and carries out interventions dealing with team dysfunction, group communication, and organizational change. Ms. Kipp is also a frequent speaker for trade and professional groups. Ms. Kipp's prior achievements include managerial responsibilities within two of the major human service organizations in the United States. More recently, she has focused extensively on family owned businesses and the unique challenges they present to family members and external managers alike. Ms. Kipp holds a B.A. from St. Anselm's College in Manchester, New Hampshire, and a Masters degree from Syracuse University. She is also a member of The American Society for Training and Development, The Planning Forum, and the Organization Development Network. (CHAPTER 35)

Michael F. Kipp is a partner in Kipp & Associates, a Nashville-based consulting form focused on strategic management, organization development, and executive coaching. A skilled facilitator and experienced chief executive officer, he advises executives and their teams through planned change and corporate transformation. Mr. Kipp has consulted in a variety of operating environments throughout North America and has worked with the American Foundation for Management Research, conducting engagements for clients in strategic planning and management development, and held senior managerial roles in both government and business. He was principal in a start-up venture and President of Signature, Inc., a specialty insurer. Earlier, he served as marketing director with Hospital Corporation of America, senior vice president with Health Industries, Inc., and deputy commissioner for the State of New York. He has lectured on the adjunct graduate faculties at Syracuse University and the State University of New York. A member of the National Speakers Association, the Organization Development Network, and The Planning Forum, Mr. Kipp has appeared frequently at business, trade, and professional gatherings and on the platform for American Management Association's President's Course. Mr. Kipp is a graduate of St. Anselm's College, Syracuse University, and the Columbia University Advanced Program in Organization Development. (CHAPTER 23)

Stuart Kliman is a principal with Conflict Management, Inc. CMI is a consulting firm that works with its clients to help them achieve better returns (more substantive and relationship "value") on their significant internal and external negotiations. Mr. Kliman's practice focuses on a wide variety of negotiation issues, including those involving information systems, banking, and marketing. Mr. Kliman also plans, coordinates, and teaches negotiation and relationship management workshops, and has done so for attorneys, business executives, accountants, law students, and other graduate students in North America, Europe, and the Far East. Before joining CMI, Mr. Kliman worked as a member of the Harvard Negotiation Project and was an associate with the law firm of Arent, Fox, Kintner, Plotkin & Kahn in Washington, D.C. Mr. Kliman is a member of the Maryland Bar and received his J.D. from from Harvard Law School and his B.A. from Franklin & Marshall College. (CHAPTER 31)

Edward J. Koplos is the creator and manager of IBM's Executive Consulting Institute, which was established to provide education and development for the recently formed IBM Consulting Group. Based on Mr. Koplos's research into consulting firm training methods a series of intensive training programs were developed. To date more than 2500 IBM consultants have been trained world-wide. Mr. Koplos was also part of the team which formulated IBM's entry into Management Consulting.

Additionally, Mr. Koplos has worked extensively in the area of strategy creation and implementation and has held a variety of management and marketing positions in both the United States and Asia. He co-published a series of books on strategy and planning methodologies and models. These books have significantly upgraded the skills of IBM consultants and allowed clients to realized improved results from their planning efforts. He was recognized for his work Asia with an Outstanding Contribution award from the IBM Asia Pacific Group.

Mr. Koplos is a distinguished graduate of Purdue University, with a degree in industrial economics and areas of concentration in finance and accounting, industrial labor relations, and psychology. (CHAPTER 20)

Larry Kuhlken has spent 23 years serving clients as a management consultant, information technology consultant, project manager, and a professional services practice executive. He has been a key participant in over 400 engagements and an engagement leader of such diversified business subjects as auto parts and food distribution, retail merchandise processing, life and health insurance, land sales, and information systems conversions. Larry is an expert in project management and the business and financial management of people services businesses. He teaches regularly in management training on these subjects, is the author of *Expanding Professional Services: A Manager's Guide To A Diversified Business.*

Mr. Kuhlken is a graduate of Stanford University and has worked for GE as an engineer and for IBM as a consultant, project manager, marketing representative, and systems integration practice branch manager. Additionally, he has been in both staff and executive management positions in IBM's internal information systems organizations. He was an author of the IBM Managing the Application Development Process series. (CHAPTER 18)

Patricia McCracken, Director of Olympics Communications, IBM, Armonk, N.Y., is responsible for building worldwide communications strategy to leverage IBM's investment as a long-term International Olympic sponsor.

Earlier, as director of internal communications, she designed a worldwide employee communications strategy, revamped an employee magazine as role model for new corporate culture which in 1994 received IABC's Award for Communications Excellence (ACE) and an IABC Silver Quill Award, created a tightly knit international network to help implement communications plan in support of corporate strategy, and added new media channels to reach and influence highly diverse employee audiences.

As program director, world-class communications, she devised and facilitated an international total quality management program for IBM Communications. Quality councils comprised top international practitioners in foremost public relations practices. Through research, teamwork, and internal and external benchmarking, councils analyzed, defined, and recommended tools and methodologies for IBM Communications professional community. As strategy and issue manager, she developed worldwide public relations strategies driving key business issues, including technology leadership, innovation, and market-driven quality. Ms. McCracken worked closely with top executives and international teams to identify audiences, objectives, messages, and media mix to achieve goals, and directed staff, public relations agencies, and consultants in strategy implementation.

She earned her B.A. in English literature at St. Mary's College, South Bend, Indiana, and her M.S. in Communications and Public Relations at Boston University. Ms. McCracken is a member of the International Association of Business Communicators (IABC), the Council of Communication Management, and the Public Relations Society of America (PRSA). (CHAPTER 21)

Brian MacDonald is a director, Western U.S., for Lotus Consulting Services group, a division of Lotus Development Corporation. Within Lotus, he acts as a specialist on large extended-enterprise technology implementations based on Lotus Notes and complementary technologies. His current focus is on the hosting of global Notes networks on public data services. Earlier he was CEO of Database Management Sciences (DMS), one of the UK's leading client-server development firms, which he sold to Lotus in 1993. Before DMS, he worked for several years in Europe designing client-server architectures for some of the world's largest finance and telecommunications companies. Before moving to Europe, Mr. MacDonald worked in Washington, D.C., as a program manager with the Defense Advanced Research Projects Agency (DARPA), served as an architecture specialist with the Strategic Defense Initiative Organization, and consulted to several other defense-related agencies. He holds a B.A. degree from the University of California at Santa Barbara and an M.A. from Georgetown University and has completed a post-graduate fellowship at Oxford University. He is the author of several articles on client-server systems development, system architectures, and the management of distributed systems. (CHAPTER 29)

Lynn I. McKell is a professor of accounting at Brigham Young University. He earned his Ph.D. in management science at Purdue University in 1973. Prior to his present position, Dr. McKell served as visiting professor of management science and information systems at the University of Minnesota. He also held several positions in private industry. Currently, he is a member of the board of directors of the Sterling Wentworth Corporation of Provo, Utah. Dr. McKell has also served as the principal investigator for the MASPACK 85 study conducted under the auspices of the American Institute of Certified Public Accountants, as well as chairman of the MAS section of the American Accounting Association and member of the MAS Education and Professional Development Subcommittee of the AICPA. He has received a patent for an improvement on a signal generator and has published articles in a variety of professional journals. He holds memberships in the Institute of Management Science, American Institute for Decision Sciences, American Accounting Association, and International Association for Financial Planning. (CHAPTER 12)

Charles Margerison is co-author of Team Management Systems' family of tools. He is also chief executive of MCB Publications, an organization which publishes management books and journals. Dr. Margerison was previously professor of management development at the Cranfield School of Management, UK, and at the University of Queensland. Prior to that he worked both in the manufacturing industry and public organizations. A graduate of the University of London School of Economics and Liverpool University, UK, he gained a doctorate at Bradford University, UK. He has worked with a number of global organizations. Dr. Margerison's various books include *Managerial Consulting Skills* (Gower Press) and *Management Development* (McGraw-Hill). (CHAPTERS 6 & 7)

Frederic Margolis is an internationally known consultant in training and development. He has designed over 400 courses for organizations such as DuPont, Price Waterhouse, Chrysler, and World Bank. He has made major presentations at 10 ASTD national conventions. He is the author of many articles and several books including: *Understanding*

Training: Perspectives and Practices, and *Instructing for Results,* both published by University Associates, San Diego, California. (CHAPTER 8)

Martha Andrews Nord is founder and president of Nord Consultants, a consortium of communication specialists based in Nashville, Tennessee. The group provides customized communication training, coaching, assessments, and document development to improve productivity, support quality initiatives, implement business strategies, and develop leadership. While building Nord Consultants, she also served 16 years on the faculty of the School of Engineering and the Owen Graduate School of Management at Vanderbilt University. As associate professor of the practice of management and technical communication, she developed and directed the Communication for Engineers Program and the Management Problem Solving and Communication core course for MBAs. She co-authored the award-winning, "Design that Delivers: Formatting Documents for Print and Online" in *Techniques for Technical Communicators,* Macmillan, 1993. Nord has been recognized with a national program award from the Association of Professional Writing Consultants for writing training designed for Vanderbilt University staff and has been elected an Associate Fellow of the Society for Technical Communication as a tribute to her pioneering efforts in developing communication programs for engineers and managers. She earned her Ph.D. from Vanderbilt University. She is immediate past national president of the Association of Professional Writing Consultants and chair of the Consultants Committee of the Association for Business Communication. (CHAPTER 17)

Mary Pilney earned a B.A. and Masters in professional accounting from the University of Texas at Austin. Currently an independent consultant, she specializes in small businesses and not-for-profit entities. Prior to 1988, Ms. Pilney worked as a consultant with Arthur Andersen & Co., and later as the executive director of Automation Services with the Texas State Treasury. (CHAPTER 11)

Dennis R. Togo is assistant professor of accounting at the University of New Mexico. He earned his Ph.D. from Arizona State University in 1986. Prior to his present position, Dr. Togo served as a visiting assistant professor at Arizona State University, an assistant professor at Brigham Young University–Hawaii Campus, and a certified public accountant with Ernst and Ernst in Honolulu, Hawaii. He has published articles in academic journals on computer usage for managerial decision making. He holds memberships in the American Accounting Association and the Institute of Management Accountants. (CHAPTER 10)

Jeff A. Weiss is a principal of Conflict Management, Inc. CMI is a consulting firm that works with its clients to help them achieve better returns (more substantive and relationship "value") on their most significant internal and external negotiations. Much of Mr. Weiss's work has been for clients in the information systems, pharmaceutical, and manufacturing industries, with an emphasis on developing strong intercorporate ventures and alliances. Mr. Weiss also develops and conducts negotiation training workshops for clients throughout the world. Prior to joining Conflict Management, Inc., he worked at the Harvard Negotiation Project, collaborating with Professor Roger Fisher (one of the co-authors of the best-selling book *Getting to Yes: Negotiating Agreement without Giving In*) and others in designing tools and techniques for practitioners of negotiation. He was also one of the original organizers of Conflict Management Fund (now, Conflict Management Group), a nonprofit corporation designed to facilitate the mediation and negotiation of issues of international public concern. Mr. Weiss has assisted in teaching negotiation courses at the Harvard Law School and at Harvard's Program on Instruction for Lawyers. He is a member of the Massachusetts Bar and is a graduate of Harvard Law School and Dartmouth College. (CHAPTER 31)

Joseph W. Wilkinson is professor of accounting at Arizona State University, where he teaches courses in accounting information systems, systems analysis and design, financial modeling, and management consulting. Before earning his doctorate at the University of Oregon, Dr. Wilkinson worked as an industrial engineer, systems analyst, and accountant in such organizations as Price Waterhouse and Hughes Aircraft. Dr. Wilkinson is the author of numerous articles and four textbooks, including *Accounting and Information Systems*. He also was the founding editor of the *Journal of Information Systems.* (CHAPTERS 1, 3, & 24)

Preface

Consulting services are in great demand among businesses and not-for-profit and governmental organizations. Every year many individuals join the management consulting profession to provide such services. Perhaps you have taken this step or are planning to do so in the near future. If so, this handbook is intended to help you succeed in this most demanding profession.

The handbook consists of many parts. The first introduces you to consulting and the consulting profession. It also describes the attributes and skills that you need as a consultant, such as the ability to communicate effectively. The second part covers client-consultant relationships, including ideas for collaborating with clients. The third part clearly outlines the major phases of the consulting process, including problem definition, fact finding and analysis, solution development, and implementation. The fourth part describes engagement management, including proposal preparation, engagement planning and documentation, and the presentation of results. The fifth part discusses the management of a consulting practice. Among the matters discussed are practice planning and administration, marketing of professional services, and the selection and development of staff. The sixth part discusses business consulting services and includes chapters on timely topics such as communications, team building, process improvement, and change management. The seventh part, on specialized consulting services, includes chapters on emerging consulting opportunities such as technology planning, telecommunications, negotiations, and health care.

Even from this brief summary of the handbook's contents, you can comprehend its broad scope and direct relevance to the world of management consulting. We believe that it can serve you as both (1) a tutor and (2) a reference work. We also believe that you will find its contents especially useful if you perform management consulting services as:

1. A member of a public accounting firm
2. A member of a management consulting firm
3. An individual practitioner
4. A member of the services function in a technology company
5. A member of an organization's internal consulting group

It can also be useful if you are a university student or working professional who has an interest in a management consulting career.

We wish to acknowledge the numerous contributors, who are listed in the pages preceding this preface. Their efforts and expertise have provided the main value of this handbook. In addition we want to express appreciation for the support and guidance provided by two McGraw-Hill editors. Jim Bessent and Margaret Lamb have added to the value and quality of the handbook.

In conclusion, we hope that this handbook will help in some small way to further the practice of management consulting.

Sam W. Barcus III
Nashville, Tennessee

Joseph W. Wilkinson
Tempe, Arizona

Part 1
Introduction to Management Consulting

1

What Is Management Consulting?

Joseph W. Wilkinson
School of Accountancy
Arizona State University
Tempe, Arizona

Management consulting is a profession whose members provide extremely useful services to managers. In fact, many of its practitioners are called management advisory services specialists. The profession of management consulting is growing at an accelerating rate, and the end of this growth trend is not in sight. Every day new organizations join the ranks of management consulting clients. The overwhelming majority of these organizations appear to be satisfied with the range of services that they receive.

This introductory chapter explores the meanings of management consulting, the reasons for using management consultants and the roles that they perform, and the types of organizations that draw upon the services of management consultants. It also reviews the history and evolution of the management consulting profession, as well as the relationships and responsibilities of management consultants to a variety of parties. The chapter concludes by discussing the pros and cons of a management consulting career.

Definition of Management Consulting

The term *management consulting* is so broad that its definition has defied the efforts of experienced management consultants themselves. In fact, a committee of management consultants, formed under the auspices of the Arizona Society of Certified Public Accountants, recently concluded that the term cannot be defined. In spite of this pessimistic conclusion, a wide variety of authors and other authorities have offered their interpretations of the term. Thus, the following definition is suggested, based on the deliberations of another group of consultants:

> Management consulting is an independent and objective advisory service provided by qualified persons to clients in order to help them identify and analyze management problems or opportunities. Management consultants also recommend solutions or suggested actions with respect to these issues and help, when requested, in their implementation. In essence, management consultants help to effect constructive change in private or public sector organizations through the sound application of substantive and process skills.[1]

The stock-in-trade of a management consultant is

> advice and technical assistance, where the primary purpose is to help the client improve the use of its capabilities and resources to achieve its objectives. For the purpose of illustration, "helping the client improve the use of its capabilities and resources" may involve activities such as
>
> 1. Counseling management in its analysis, planning, organizing, operating, and controlling functions
> 2. Conducting special studies, preparing recommendations, proposing plans and programs, and providing advice and technical assistance in their implementation
> 3. Reviewing and suggesting improvement of policies, procedures, systems, methods, and organization relationships
> 4. Introducing new ideas, concepts, and methods to management[2]

These activities of management consultants involve two types of encounters with clients: consultations and engagements.

A *consultation* normally consists of providing advice and information in a short time frame. This advice and/or information is provided orally during one or more discussions with the client. Sometimes the advice and/or information will be represented as definitive by the consultant, as when he or she is fully aware of the situation and possesses sufficient expertise to require no recourse to references. Often, however, such advice and/or information will be qualified by stated limitations. These limitations may be due to lack of firsthand observation of the problem situation, to lack of familiarity with underlying technical aspects, and so on.

An *engagement* consists of that form of management advisory or consulting service

> in which an analytical approach and process is applied in a study or project. It typically involves more than an incidental effort devoted to some combination of activities relating to determination of client objectives, fact-finding, opportunity or problem definition, evaluation of alternatives, formulation of proposed action, communication of results, implementation, and follow-up.[3]

Reasons for Using Consultants

Management consultants are generally engaged by key managers and administrators of client organizations. Why do such managers and administrators need the services of consultants? Consultants, after all, cannot be expected to be as familiar with the organizations as are the managers and administrators. Also, consultants are generally much more costly for each day of service than would be a newly hired manager or employee.

Benefits Provided by Consultants

A management consultant can provide at least three valuable benefits:

1. *Independent viewpoint:* Precisely because a management consultant is not a member of the organization, he or she brings objectivity and detachment to problems faced by the organization. That is, the consultant is sufficiently removed to see the true nature of the problems and to distinguish between feasible and infeasible solutions. In addition, an experienced consultant can introduce new ideas into the organization that were gleaned from other engagements. Also, because the consultant is customarily neither involved in the internal politics of the informal organization nor associated with cliques within it, his or her suggestions tend to be accepted as unbiased.

In some cases, this independent viewpoint may be put to a less justifiable purpose. For instance, a manager may be involved in a struggle with another manager in the organization over the best course of action. The first manager may engage a consultant to support his or her point of view. If the consultant is expected to prepare a supporting report solely on the basis of that manager's conclusions, and is not given the opportunity to form an objective view, then the engagement is not professional.

2. *Special qualifications:* An experienced management consultant possesses special knowledge and skills and a variety of personal attributes.

These qualifications tend to establish the consultant as the most desirable candidate to undertake an engagement involving his or her area of expertise. Although success in any engagement cannot be guaranteed, the consultant with the most suitable qualifications should have the greatest chance of achieving a successful conclusion.

3. *Temporary professional service:* Organizations sometimes find themselves short of critical professional resources. For instance, a manager may have an accident or take a short leave of absence to attend a graduate management program. Alternatively, a short-term problem may arise, such as the need to train managers in computer modeling, and there may be no one available in the organization to provide the instruction. In such cases management consultants can fill in as temporary professional help. Calling in consultants will probably be less expensive in the long run than hiring new managers or employees.

Roles Performed by Consultants

In providing the above-mentioned services to clients, consultants can be seen to perform the following roles.

1. *Professional adviser and counselor:* A consultant is a professional, in that he or she meets the standards of a profession. That is, the consultant has mastered an established body of knowledge, has completed educational requirements, and is governed by a code of conduct. (In reality, not all practicing management consultants currently meet these standards. But in our view, only those consultants who do so are worthy of the name.)

In addition to being a professional, a management consultant provides management advisory and consulting services. These services are rendered to managers and are intended to assist in the management and administration of organizations.

2. *Qualified resource:* A management consultant is a resource upon which managers and administrators of organizations can draw as needed. In this sense, the management consultant is akin to a vendor of a computer system. However, the management consultant provides services consisting of advice and managerial consulting assistance.

3. *Change agent:* A management consultant is a catalyst for change. In the process of solving problems for clients, the consultant must consider means by which solutions can be effected. These solutions often consist of changes within the client organizations. For instance, changes may be made to organizational structures, to procedures, and to job responsibilities. Unless these changes are understood and accepted by the affected employees and managers, the recommendations of the consultant will have little value.

Roles to Be Approached with Caution

While all consultants would probably agree on the above roles, other, less clear-cut roles are sometimes performed by members of the consulting profession. These latter roles include the following.

1. *Decision maker:* In providing management advice and consulting services, a management consultant may be asked to recommend preferable courses of action. Most consultants stop short of actually making the decisions for managers of client organizations. The moment a consultant assumes authority for making and implementing decisions, he or she ceases to provide a truly independent viewpoint.

2. *Salesperson of proprietary products:* The stock-in-trade of a management consultant is management advisory and consulting services. Some consultants offer, as an adjunct to such services, proprietary products. For instance, certain public accounting firms (large as well as small) espouse specific computer hardware and software products. Although the consultants may believe that these computer-related products will improve their clients' information systems, a question arises concerning the independence of the consultant if he or she receives monetary benefits from the manufacturers of such products. Even if the consultant can in fact perform a fair evaluation, the client may have concerns about the fairness of the evaluation, and the appearance of bias might undermine the value of the consulting service.

3. *Packager of standard services:* Some management consultants offer "prepackaged" services, such as 1-day seminars on database software systems or 1-week installations of spreadsheet software systems. Consultants may legitimately be involved in training programs and systems installations, in that such projects normally involve analytical and creative activities. However, once a training program or installation has become so standardized that the analytical and creative aspects no longer exist, it is generally viewed as no longer being a consulting service. A consultant who insists upon handling such packaged services is not likely to be viewed as performing a consultant role during such activities.

Types of Clients Served

Who uses the services of management consultants? While the mix of clients will vary from one consultant to another, the types of clients served by the management consulting profession as a whole include the following.

1. *Privately owned business firms:* Every firm organized for the purpose of earning profits through commerce and industry is a potential client. Thus, a consultant might have clients that are involved in merchandising, manufacturing, banking, transportation, insurance, food services, education, and other industries. These firms may exhibit such varied characteristics as:

   a. Major activities consisting of providing products or services to others
   b. Ownership structures consisting of single proprietors, partners, or stockholders
   c. Organizational sizes ranging from a few employees to many thousands of employees
   d. Physical sizes ranging from a single building in one location to numerous buildings in scattered geographical locations
   e. Organizational structures ranging from a high degree of centralization to a high degree of decentralization
   f. Resource structures ranging from labor-intensive requirements to capital-intensive requirements

2. *Government agencies and organizations:* Most if not all government organizations engage management consultants at one time or another. The clients may be government agencies at the local, state, national, or international level. For instance, management consultants have been engaged by the following clients:

   a. Parks and Recreation Department of Mesa, Arizona
   b. Department of Transportation of Arizona
   c. Rural Electrification Administration, U.S. Department of Agriculture
   d. International Labor Organization, United Nations

Occasionally, management consultants are engaged directly by countries. For instance, consultants have been engaged by Venezuela and Egypt to aid in their economic planning and development.

3. *Not-for-profit nongovernment organizations:* Organizations such as hospitals, universities, research institutes, and charitable institutions are increasingly using management advisory and consulting services. Many such organizations are under private ownership. In recent years, private not-for-profit organizations have been faced with problems of raising funds and revenues while reducing costs; in attempting to solve such problems, they often turn to consultants for advice and assistance.

4. *Professional associations:* Numerous groups and associations that provide professional services are private and organized for profit; medical, legal, accounting, and engineering practices are examples. Others are not for profit, such as the National Association of Accountants and the American Medical Association. Even though such groups and associ-

ations generally include highly trained and skilled personnel, they often need advice and assistance with management and organizational problems and issues.

5. *Other types:* Although every potential client will probably fit into one of the above categories, it is useful to include a catchall category. This category might contain such groups as labor unions, sports organizations, and religious organizations.

History and Evolution of Management Consulting

Although management consulting has its origins in biblical times, its modern-day history dates from the mid-eighteenth century. This section traces the history and evolution of management consulting since that time. Our focus will be upon the evolutionary thread that weaves through the accounting profession.

Before the Twentieth Century

As far as we know, management advisory and consulting services were applied for the first time by an English accountant in 1744. In that year Alexander Chalmers prepared an interest table and planned the keeping of books for the Fund of Widows and Orphans. In 1788 a Scottish merchant asked his accountant to provide advice concerning business matters. Otherwise, the eighteenth century and much of the nineteenth century found British accountants generally performing bookkeeping tasks.

The English corporation laws (the Companies Act of 1879 and the Bankruptcy Act of 1883) changed the dominant role of professional accountants from bookkeepers to auditors. However, in the United States accountants still served primarily as bookkeepers until the first decade of the twentieth century.

1900–1918

During the first decade of the twentieth century, the role of accountants in the United States shifted from bookkeepers to auditors. With the passage of the income tax laws in 1913, accountants also began to provide tax services. On the other hand, very few management advisory and consulting services were provided. Perhaps the most prominent engagement involved the survey of Westinghouse's East Pittsburgh plant by the public accounting firm of Marwick and Mitchell in 1910. This survey consisted of reviews of the organization, cost and general accounting system, production methods, and premium pay scales.

Science and engineering also contributed to the development of management consulting methods during the early years of the century. Perhaps the best-known pioneer from this era was Frederick Taylor, who applied the scientific method to the solving of production problems. By careful observation and study of every step and operation in a manufacturing process, followed by correlation and analysis of the data, Taylor was able to establish fair work standards for workers and machines. His achievements laid the foundations for methods analysis, work simplification, and time and motion studies. Others such as H. L. Gantt, Frank Gilbreth, and Harrison Emerson continued Taylor's efforts and achievements.

1919–1945

As income tax rates increased after World War I, the role of the accountant as tax adviser grew accordingly. Tax services, together with auditing services, effectively occupied most of the professional accountant's attention.

In the meantime, management consulting firms were beginning to flourish. These firms generally had an engineering orientation that dated back to the work of the pioneers in scientific management and industrial engineering. However, they also tended to be broader-gauged, since business firms were becoming larger and more complex. Ed Booz, George Fry, and Carl Hamilton, among others, recognized the importance of the human resource in the organization. Thus, their consulting firm led the way with a "people-oriented" approach, focusing on such areas as organizational planning, management development and training, administrative policies, and personnel administration.

As the movement toward general business management consulting intensified, American public accounting firms awoke to the potentialities of management advisory and consulting services. They realized that such consulting was within the capabilities of accountants, especially with respect to financial management and control. They also recognized that accountants who perform audits possess important advantages when they undertake consulting engagements:

1. Auditors already have a familiarity with clients and their organizations, operations, and problems.

2. Auditors maintain continued contact with client firms, thereby providing warranties (in effect) for clients.

3. Auditors function in accordance with professional rules of conduct, thus helping to ensure their clients of high-quality work and ethical conduct.

Just as public accounting firms began to move diligently into management advisory and consulting services, events conspired to derail their expansion temporarily. The Great Depression of the 1930s reduced the ability of clients to purchase such services, and World War II depleted the accounting firms of consulting employees.

However, World War II showed public accounting firms that the demand for consulting services was strong and apt to grow. Numerous firms in war industries employed those accountants who were available and qualified to develop cost accounting systems and to perform other, related services.

After World War II

In the years since World War II, the management consulting profession has mushroomed and matured. A number of management consulting firms have been formed and have grown immensely. Among the non-accounting consulting firms are Booz, Allen & Hamilton; McKinsey & Company; Cresap, McCormick & Paget; and Theodore Barry & Associates. These firms vary widely in the services that they emphasize, though all stress the primacy of providing personalized management advisory and consulting services.

The postwar history of the public accounting firms reflects the severity of the changes that have taken place throughout the management consulting profession. Shortly after the war, the firms formally acknowledged the growing importance of management advisory and consulting services. Nearly every large firm established a separate division, on an equal standing with the audit and tax divisions, for management advisory services. Large firms also began to perform consulting engagements that were completely separated from the audit and tax engagements.

In addition to these organizational steps, the firms considered the services that they would provide. In 1946 the American Institute of Certified Public Accountants (AICPA) published a list of services that were reasonable for public accounting firms to provide, and many firms decided to offer some or all of these services. Among the services provided were operational budgeting, forecasting, and cost controls.

During the remainder of the 1940s and into the 1950s, the public accounting firms continued to add services. Certain of these services, such as computer systems analysis and inventory management, were added in response to developments in information and computer technology. Other services, such as capital budgeting and computer system auditing and acquisition analysis, were added in response to the demands of clients. As the services expanded beyond the areas of basic accounting competence, the firms began to employ nonaccountants.

Thus, computer systems analysts, programmers, and management scientists began to intermingle with auditing and tax specialists.

Management advisory and consulting services have grown at an ever-increasing rate during the past four decades. In the 1990s, the management advisory and consulting services division of the typical large public accounting firm, and of many smaller local accounting firms, is growing more rapidly than the audit and tax divisions. In some firms small business and/or microcomputer service divisions have been added. These divisions are essentially offshoots of the management advisory and consulting services division.

Continuing Trends

The practice of management consulting has changed dramatically since the early days of this century. As the above history has indicated, one trend has been in the direction of greater scope and specialization of services. The "efficiency engineer" and the generalist of past decades have been supplemented by multivaried specialists. Management consultants now specialize in information systems, automated offices, financial analysis and modeling, budgetary and cost controls, organizational structures, personnel compensation, strategic planning, and a host of other areas.

A second trend has been the improving quality of business education. Numerous universities throughout the United States and other developed countries are providing sound graduate-level education in such fields as accounting, management, marketing, and statistics. Many of these universities offer programs leading to a master's degree in business administration. These high-quality undergraduate and graduate programs are bringing a supply of better-trained entrants into the ranks of the management consulting profession. As a result of this infusion, management consulting is becoming a catalyst for the advancement of better management concepts and techniques.

A third trend concerns the changing management culture. Before World War II, many business firms were relatively small, family-owned enterprises managed by individuals with extensive experience and limited education. Since World War II, managers and management consultants alike have become more educated. More managers are employed by large or moderate-sized firms and organizations. These managers tend to view themselves as members of a profession. Consequently, they exhibit a decreasing degree of loyalty to individual firms and an increasing degree of mobility between firms. They also are showing an increasing understanding of the roles and benefits of management consultants in the business world.

A related trend is the growth in size and complexity of institutions that function in the business world. Many business firms have become conglomerates. A firm that some years ago might have been called a chemistry company is now an energy complex. Many not-for-profit organizations have also become large and diversified. For instance, some hospitals have become nationwide health-care chains. Furthermore, an increasing number of firms and organizations have become multinational.

On the other hand, there has been a concurrent upward trend in the number of business start-ups each year. Most of these start-ups are small business firms in a service or high-technology area.

A final trend pertains to modern technology. Technological developments have occurred at a breathtaking pace in such areas as information sciences and decision sciences. Computer hardware and software, together with data communications and robotics, represent powerful tools for business management. These tools are spawning automated offices, superproductive factories, real-time information systems, and interactive decision support systems. Managers now have the means to control far-flung operations, to develop sounder plans, and to make faster decisions than ever before.

Future Prospects

What do these trends portend for the future of management consulting? A veteran management consultant made the following predictions about a decade ago, and they still appear to be valid.[4]

First, management consulting will become even more specialized. Consulting specialists will need to be ever diligent to avoid obsolescence. Consulting firms will need to continually add new specialties, just as producing firms add new products.

In recent years, a number of firms have developed or strengthened several areas of specialization. One area is financial modeling, using spreadsheet software packages on microcomputers. Another area is "one stop shopping" service for small business firms. This service, which often is administered by a separate division in the consulting firm, involves the assignment of a single consultant to each small business client. This single consultant provides advice across the entire array of the client's activities. In effect, the consultant becomes a member of the client's management team. A third area is assistance on large projects involving perhaps a year or longer. A typical project is the design and implementation of a complex computer-based information system.

Second, practicing consultants will interact more closely with the faculties of business schools. They will draw upon the results of research performed at such academic institutions. In turn, they will provide academic researchers with the materials for performing research and preparing case studies.

Third, management consulting firms will tend either to remain small or to become quite large. Small practitioner firms will prosper by focusing on narrow areas of specialization. Large firms will more easily sustain the high costs of developing and offering a wide range of specialties.

Fourth, the number of internal consultants—those who are employees of nonconsulting firms—will continue to grow, since they provide beneficial services at less cost. However, they will never replace external consultants, who provide an essential service through their objectivity.

Fifth, as consultants grow in number, they will develop more sophisticated means of marketing their services.

Sixth, the bright graduates of management and business schools will continue to be attracted to careers in management consulting. The reasons for this continuing interest in the profession are discussed at the end of the chapter.

Relationships to Other Parties

A management consultant must maintain close relationships with a variety of parties. Here is a partial list of such parties:

- Managers who contact the consultant on behalf of clients
- Managers and employees of clients who will need to be interviewed and otherwise dealt with during the course of engagements
- Employees of clients who are assigned to work under the consultant's direction
- Managers and employees of clients who will be affected by results of consulting engagements
- Managers of prospective clients
- External auditors, lawyers, and other professionals who represent clients or perform services for them
- Competing management consultants
- Professional consulting associations, such as the Institute of Management Consultants
- Communities within which the consultant and client reside

As a professional, the consultant must always strive to act responsibly and ethically toward all these parties. In return for the faith and trust that these parties place in the consultant, he or she accepts an obligation to behave in a manner that reflects a high level of public service.

Pros and Cons of Management Consulting

In concluding this opening chapter, let us consider the benefits and drawbacks of being a management consultant.

A career in management consulting offers interesting challenges. Your work assignments tend to be varied. They encourage you to employ your talents, abilities, and skills to the fullest. They often allow you to avoid the 8-to-5 routine.

Management consulting can bring intangible as well as tangible rewards. You gain considerable satisfaction from helping others solve tough problems and seeing the fruits of your efforts emerge in the form of successful information systems or strategic plans. At the same time, you are generally paid handsomely for your efforts. The salaries and bonuses of consultants in both large and small firms compare favorably with those of other professionals.

As a management consultant, you will probably be offered enticing opportunities. You may be asked to join the management team of a client, perhaps even to assume the top position in the client firm. As an employee of a large management consulting firm, you may see that your specialty is in such demand that you could start your own consulting practice.

The drawbacks relate primarily to the lifestyle and risks that every management consultant faces. On occasion you must expect to endure irregular living conditions, such as lengthy workdays and stays away from home. You will sometimes be placed under tremendous job pressures and stresses. These conditions can put severe strains on your health, peace of mind, and family harmony. If you decide to go into practice on your own, you are also likely to encounter strains on your pocketbook and self-confidence while waiting for clients to appear.

If you have the personal qualities and education that a management consultant needs, as well as an intense interest in the challenge and rewards of the profession, these drawbacks need not represent insurmountable hurdles.

Notes

1. This definition was developed by directors of the management consulting professional associations (AICPA/MAS, ACME, IMC), together with practi-

tioners and academics, at the Conference on University Education and Management Consulting, held in Salt Lake City, February 21–22, 1985.

2. "Statement on Standards for Management Advisory Services No. 1," par. 4, *Definitions and Standards for MAS Practice.* Copyright 1981, American Institute of Certified Public Accountants, New York. Reprinted with permission.

3. *Ibid.*

4. Richard M. Paget, "The Future of Management Consulting," *MAS Communication,* March 1982, pp. 59–61.

2

The Management Consulting Profession and Consulting Services

James C. Kinard

*Department of Accounting and Management
Information Systems
The Ohio State University
Columbus, Ohio*

The management consulting profession consists of a large, diverse collection of individuals, firms, and associations. All members of the profession should have one common interest—to provide professional advice and assistance to clients with respect to the management and operation of their organizations.

This chapter examines both the profession and the array of services that it provides. It begins by identifying the attributes that bestow the status of a profession upon management consulting. Then the chapter surveys the composition of the profession, including the major professional associations that unify and serve the member consultants and their firms. Next it presents the consulting process, the types of consulting engagements, and the various services offered by consultants. Finally, the chapter identifies the ways in which consultants organize to render their services.

Why Management Consulting Is a Profession

The term *profession* is defined as a calling or vocation in which members, possessing certain attributes, provide beneficial services to clients under strictly specified conditions. Management consulting qualifies as a profession, since its members:

1. Possess a variety of skills and qualities, the acquisition of which requires extensive education, training, and/or experience
2. Provide services that are based on technical proficiency, which in turn is recorded in an appropriate body of knowledge
3. Abide by a code of ethics and practice standards in the delivery of services to clients and in relationships with competitors and with the public
4. Establish fees that are fixed with respect to amount and type of work to be performed and that are not contingent on an outcome of some event (e.g., a legal suit)

In addition, certain management consultants, such as those employed by public accounting firms within some jurisdictions, are expected to hold certificates to practice issued by states or other government bodies.

Composition of the Management Consulting Profession

The management consulting profession is growing rapidly. This growth is due in part to the intense demand for management consulting services by all types and sizes of organizations in all countries around the globe. It is also due to the relatively small amount of capital needed to start a management consulting practice.

Because the profession is growing in diversity as well as numbers, authorities cannot agree on its boundaries at any point in time. Thus, its overall size cannot be easily estimated. Perhaps as many as 100,000 full-time consultants are currently practicing in the United States, while many more thousands are practicing in other countries (principally those of Western Europe). Additionally thousands of part-time consultants must be included as members of the profession.

In spite of the diversity of the profession, its basic structural composition is readily apparent. The following categories reflect this structure.

1. *Generalist management consulting firms:* This category consists of several thousand large, medium-sized, and small firms. Practices in these firms range from several thousand full-time consultants down to two consultants. The services they provide can be extremely varied. Some firms offer engineering and scientific consulting as well as management consulting. Examples of generalist firms are Booz, Allen & Hamilton, Inc.; McKinsey and Company; Towers, Perrin, Forster, and Crosby; Authur D. Little, Inc.; Boston Consulting Group; A. T. Kearney; Temple, Barker, and Sloane; and Theodore Barry & Associates. Many of the firms in this category hold memberships in the Association of Management Consulting Firms (ACME).

2. *Public accounting firms:* This category constitutes the largest identifiable segment of the management consulting profession, including as many as 6000 firms. While most public accounting firms provide some management consulting services, their practices consist primarily of auditing and tax services, which yield most of the revenues. Some of the largest firms in this category maintain separate divisions for providing management consulting services. Typically, these divisions are staffed with full-time consultants, many of whom are not accountants by training. Most public accounting firms, however, do not maintain separate management consulting divisions. In such firms, accountants, usually those with auditing responsibilities, typically serve as part-time consultants on occasions when clients ask for consultations or contract for consulting engagements.

The public accounting firms that perform the greatest amount of consulting work are the Big Six: Price Waterhouse & Co.; Coopers & Lybrand; Deloitte & Touche; Ernst & Young; KPMG Peat Marwick; and Arthur Andersen & Co. In fact, the largest management consultancy in the world, Andersen Consulting, is a division of Arthur Andersen & Co. Even though it does not offer a complete range of consulting services, Andersen Consulting has had an average annual growth rate of 15 percent since its inception about 40 years ago.

Most of the Big Six firms experienced spectacular growth during the 1980s, partly as a result of reorganizations and partly as a result of their aggressive targeting of expanding markets. Today, these firms rank among the top ten consulting practices in terms of billings.

3. *Specialized management consulting firms:* As noted in Chapter 1, increasing specialization has been one of the notable trends in the man-

agement consulting profession. Indeed, the majority of management consulting firms may be classified as specialized firms. Specialized firms range from organizations having extremely large practices to organizations having two or three partners. Andersen Consulting, the largest firm in this category, specializes in information systems consulting, although it also provides generalized services spanning the entire systems development life cycle from planning to implementation. Computer Sciences Corporation and Electronic Data Systems are two other examples of very large specialized organizations. Both provide information systems consulting services (and thus compete directly with Andersen Consulting). Smaller specialized firms include Cambridge Energy Research Associates, which serves the petrochemicals industry, and Kaplan, Smith, which serves the financial services industry. These examples merely suggest the variety of specialized services currently available.

4. *Individual practitioners:* Individual management consultants are unaffiliated with consulting firms in the above-mentioned categories. Individual practitioners generally operate their practices full time. However, this category also includes two groups who function as consultants on a part-time or occasional basis: university professors and retired professionals. The latter group has increased significantly in recent years, partly because many middle and senior managers have been forced into early retirement.

Individual practitioners, who number in the thousands, offer in the aggregate as wide a range of services as the consulting firms. A typical individual practitioner, however, provides services in the limited areas with which he or she is familiar and in which he or she is skilled. Typically, individual practitioners serve relatively small clients that cannot afford the fees of fully staffed consulting firms. However, some practitioners with special qualifications are engaged by large clients.

Individual practitioners offer their clients a number of benefits that management consulting firms cannot provide. First, because their overhead is relatively low, they can charge lower hourly fees. Second, they can maintain closer ties with each client and thus gain a greater familiarity with the client's particular situation. Third, many individual practitioners possess rare skills and knowledge or considerable experience or both. For instance, a professor who is conducting research in organizational behavior can bring the latest research findings to a troubled client firm. Also, many professor-consultants network within their own universities and within their academic disciplines, so that they can draw on a larger pool of ideas and subcontract portions of larger engagements.

5. *Internal consulting groups:* Consultants listed in the four above categories may be characterized as *external consultants,* since they provide services to clients who are external to their firms or practices.

Consultants who are employees of a nonconsulting firm are known as *internal consultants*. This latter group of consultants consists primarily of specialists who are assigned to specific service departments or functions, such as the industrial engineering department, the information systems function, or the long-range planning department. In some firms, however, they are attached to more broadly based organizational units. Two examples are the Management Services Group within W. R. Grace & Company and the Corporate Consulting Service within General Electric.

Internal consultants provide consulting services to the other departments of the organization that employs them. Although they lack the fully independent status of external consultants, they have a more thorough knowledge of the complex relationships within the organization than external consultants can hope to attain. Thus, they tend to be assigned to problem situations that require thorough organizational knowledge but not the independent outlook of external consultants. Since the services of internal consultants are less expensive than those of external consultants, internal consultants are also more often involved in projects that are expected to be quite lengthy and detailed. For instance, an internal consultant is more likely than an external consultant to be assigned to implementation projects, which are relatively long-lived.

Internal consultants tend not to be independent and their experience is often limited. Thus, external consultants are preferable for assignments requiring (a) independent perspectives or (b) broad experience gained from solving similar problems faced by other organizations.

Certain assignments, such as the development of new information systems, may suitably be performed jointly by internal and external consultants. Each may have specified tasks and responsibilities. For example, the external consultants may be assigned to define the problem, the internal consultants to gather facts and opinions from employees, and both to analyze the findings and develop feasible solutions. In some engagements, the main task of internal consultants may be to observe the activities and techniques of external consultants, so that they can complete the projects or be able to perform similar projects on later occasions.

6. *Research-oriented organizations:* A small number of institutes and other organizations undertake engagements that look beyond specific short-range internal problem situations. Certain organizations in this category (a) perform studies of broad economic and social problems or (b) aid in developing and implementing public-sector programs. Government agencies, the customary clients of such organizations, award contracts (often on a competitive basis) for the above-mentioned consulting services. An example of a public-sector consulting organization is Planning Resources Corporation (PRC). Other organizations in

this category are research institutes, or *think tanks,* that perform research studies and provide advice in technical, military, and economic areas. Their clients may be government agencies, business firms, industry associations, or universities. Examples of research institutes are the Rand Corporation and SRI International.

The monthly newsletter *Consultant's News* reports on the entire management consulting profession. This publication also maintains a bookstore that fills mail orders for books, studies, directories, and other management consulting materials.

Professional Management Consulting Associations

Associations have been formed to provide a variety of services to the management consulting profession. Through the efforts of such associations, the management consulting services sector has moved from being a heterogeneous collection of firms and individuals toward becoming a relatively cohesive profession. Most of the associations are organized to serve the consulting firms of a particular nation. An example of a national association is the Institute of Certified Management Consultants of Canada. Some professional associations are international. The membership of Accounting Firms Associated, Inc., for example, consists of public accounting firms located in countries throughout the world. Perhaps the most important international association is the International Council of Management Consulting Institutes, which has more than 10,000 members affiliated with institutes in twelve countries. The major associations in the United States are described below.

Institute of Management Consultants (IMC)

The IMC was founded in 1968 for the purpose of ensuring the public "that members possess the ethical standards and the professional competence and independence necessary to be qualified management consultants."[1] To achieve the first part of its objective—to enhance the reputation of management consultants among the public and among potential clients—the IMC has established a code of ethics. To achieve the second part, the IMC administers a certification program for management consultants. A consultant earns the coveted professional designation of certified management consultant (CMC) when he or she satisfies the following requirements:

1. Devotes current activity (over half of working hours) to the public practice of management consulting, serving clients on a fee basis

2. Has at least 5 years of experience in the full-time practice of management consulting, including 1 year with major responsibility for client projects, in addition to a bachelor's degree from an accredited college or university

3. Submits written summaries of five client assignments in which a major role was played

4. Passes a qualifying interview by demonstrating professional competence in areas of specialization, application of experience, and understanding of the current state of the art

5. Obtains six references, three of them from officers or executives served during the past 5 years

Approximately 1700 consultants have qualified for the CMC designation.

To enhance members' professional competence on a continuing basis, the IMC sponsors a broad program of professional development activities. The program ranges from orientation courses for newer consultants to advanced consulting skills workshops for senior consultants. The IMC also publishes the *Journal of Management Consulting,* the most authoritative American practitioner periodical in the field of management consulting.

The several thousand members of the IMC are primarily independent individual consultants, small consulting firms, and partnerships. Many of the members are also affiliated with other professional associations. The IMC recently absorbed two smaller associations: the Association of Management Consultants (AMC) and the Society of Professional Management Consultants (SPMC).

Association of Management Consulting Firms (ACME)

ACME was founded in 1929 as the Association of Consulting Management Engineers and then incorporated in 1933 as ACME, Inc. ACME represents the body of middle-sized management consulting firms.

Like IMC, ACME has established a code of ethics. It enforces the code, with respect to its members, by investigating all complaints of code violation and taking disciplinary action against members whose conduct clearly falls below the standards set forth in the code. ACME also serves as a central clearinghouse and research center for a major segment of the management consulting profession. It fulfills this purpose by maintaining a complete management consulting library and extensive files of current information on several hundred areas of specialization and thousands of management consulting firms, sponsoring research (including publication of the biannual *Annotated Bibliography on Management*

Consulting and assorted monographs) as well as seminars and training programs.

Membership is limited to about 50 medium-sized consulting firms. However, membership has undergone some turnover, as firms have gone out of business, merged, or resigned.

In 1989 ACME and IMC formed the Council of Consulting Organizations, Inc. Each is now a semi-independent division of the council. In addition to the traditional New York City offices, the council maintains a Brussels office.

American Institute of Certified Public Accountants (AICPA)

The AICPA is a professional association whose voting members are CPAs in the 50 states and other jurisdictions. Also, the AICPA has approved associate membership in some of its divisions, including the Management Consulting Services (MCS) Division (formerly the Management Advisory Services Division). Associate members are non-CPAs who are employed by a CPA firm and are sponsored by an AICPA member. Both associate members and voting members are entitled to receive the association's newsletter and practice aids.

Only a minority of the accountants who are AICPA members provide full-time management consulting services. The MSC Division administers the services provided by both full-time and part-time management consultant practitioner members, who number in excess of 5000.

The executive committee of the MSC Division has issued a code of ethics, called Standards for Management Consulting Services, that covers all professional services provided by members. Consultants who violate these standards are subject to disciplinary actions.[2]

The MSC Division publishes several series of practice aids on specialized subjects to guide consultants in assisting clients. Separate series pertain to technical issues, small business consulting, and practice administration. Examples of Technical Consulting Practice Aids are *Conversion to a Microcomputer-Based Accounting System* (No. 11), *Microcomputer Training* (No. 14), and *Disaster Recovery Training* (No. 15). Examples of Small Business Consulting Practice Aids are *Assessing Franchising Opportunities* (No. 13), *Developing Management Incentive Programs* (No. 15), and *Improving Organizational Structures* (No. 16). An example of a Practice Administration Aid is *Human Resources and Management for a MAS Practice* (No. 6). Recently, the MSC Division began publishing a series of Industry Consulting Practice Aids. An example is Consulting Services Practice Aid 92-4, titled *Law Firms.*

Through its structure of subcommittees, the MSC Division conducts a variety of activities of interest to consultants. The committee structure for the 1992–1993 year consisted of the MSC executive committee and sub-committees on business valuations and appraisals, computer applications, litigation services, practice standards and administration, small business consulting practices, and technical and industry consulting practices. Through the efforts of the business valuation and appraisals subcommittee, the AICPA has approved a specialist accreditation program in CPA business valuation services that will accompany a similar program in personal financial planning.

Other Consulting Associations

The Association of Internal Management Consultants (AIMC) is an association of individuals engaged in internal management consulting. In addition to promoting the role of the internal consultant, its purpose is to provide a forum for the exchange of information among members and to raise the standards of the profession.

The Management Consultancy Division of the Academy of Management is an association of about 1000 academics who teach management consulting courses in schools of business and/or practice consulting on a part-time basis.

The Association of Systems Management (ASM) is an association of information systems analysts. Although the majority of ASM members are employees of business firms and nonbusiness organizations, a significant number are external consultants who engage in information systems analysis, design, and implementation.

The Information Systems/Management Advisory Services (IS/MAS) section of the American Accounting Association consists of almost 1000 members. Half are university professors of accounting and the other half are management consulting practitioners in public accounting firms. The IS/MAS section coordinates presentations of topics of interest to consultants at meetings of the American Accounting Association. It also publishes the *Journal of Information Systems*, which includes articles concerning research and practice in information systems development and management and management consulting.

The Consulting Process

A management consultant engages in a clearly defined process when he or she performs a management consulting service. Since the service is performed for the purpose of solving a problem facing a client, it can be labeled a problem-solving process. Since it is performed by a consultant, it can also be called a consulting process. Both labels will be employed throughout the following chapters.

A consulting or problem-solving process takes place during the course of an engagement. The process encompasses three perspectives: analytic, administrative, and communicative. Each is discussed below.

Analytic Elements of the Consulting Process

The analytic elements of the consulting process consist of (1) identifying the objectives to be achieved, (2) defining the problem or opportunity for improvement, (3) ascertaining and then analyzing the facts, (4) determining and evaluating solution alternatives and then formulating a preferred solution or proposed action, (5) communicating the results of the formulation, and (6) implementing the solution or proposed action, if appropriate.

These elements may be combined, their scope expanded or contracted, and their sequence altered to fit specific problem situations. All must be completed for a satisfactory resolution of a problem. It is not necessary, however, for the consultant to perform all the elements personally. In fact, it is usually preferable (with respect to costs and benefits as well as to concerns of user involvement) for the client to participate in performing most if not all of the elements.

A recent AICPA consulting standard emphasizes the contractual agreement between the client and the consultant as the basis for the scope of work in an engagement.[3] Third-party concerns, which are central to the audit and attestation services provided by CPA firms, do not arise in consulting services.

The analytic elements are extremely important in the performance of consulting services and are discussed extensively in Chapters 10–13.

Administrative Elements of the Consulting Process

"A consulting engagement, regardless of its technical nature, requires sound and effective managing if the engagement is to accomplish its objective."[4] Most consulting engagements include the following managing or administrative activities:

1. Engagement planning, including a work plan, that leads to a letter of understanding or a contract with a client

2. Engagement operations and control, including productively following the work plan, preparing working papers and interim reports, and controlling time and expenses

3. Engagement reporting and evaluation, including documenting the conclusions, preparing the final report, and assessing the performance of participants and effectiveness of the result

Administrative elements are discussed extensively in Chapters 14–17.

Communicative Elements of the Consulting Process

Ineffective communication during a consulting engagement—and especially at the end of an engagement—can impair the final result. In fact, proficiency in communication is essential to the successful completion of every phase of the consulting process. A management consultant must be able to speak, write, and listen effectively. These elements of communication are discussed in Chapter 5.

Types of Consulting Engagements

Management consultants apply the consulting process to engagements that have widely varying characteristics. Thus, it is useful to classify the key dimensions of a consulting engagement. The six relevant dimensions are: the nature of the problem, the service delivery area, the elements or phases of the analytic process, the technical skills used, the nature of the client's organization, and the geographical area(s) where the engagement takes place. These dimensions of an engagement are displayed in Figure 2-1.

Each dimension, and its possible categories, is discussed separately below. However, it should be noted that every engagement involves all six dimensions. Thus, although an engagement may briefly be described as a financial management engagement (i.e., in accordance with the service delivery area), it also takes place at one or more specific locations,

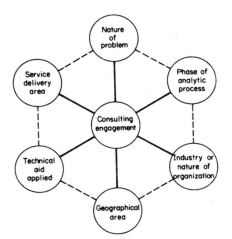

Figure 2-1 Dimensions of a consulting engagement.

involves a client that is a member of a particular industry (e.g., the banking industry) or of a particular form of organization (e.g., a corporation), and so on.

Furthermore, the categories within each dimension may be coded, so that an engagement may be concisely but fully and clearly characterized. Coding is particularly useful if a management consulting firm desires to file reports of the various engagements for later reference by staff consultants.

Nature of the Problem

A problem may be classified as corrective, progressive, or opportunistic, according to the situation in which it arises.

Corrective Problem.   A corrective problem arises in a situation in which conditions have suddenly worsened. The consultant is expected to suggest corrective action(s) that will return the situation to its normal condition. A corrective problem usually demands urgent action. Essentially, the process consists of "putting out a fire." Defining the problem is often easier than determining the recommended course of action. An example of a corrective problem is a sudden drop in productivity in a critical manufacturing department.

Progressive Problem.   A progressive problem arises in a situation that has deteriorated. For instance, a firm may have grown appreciably while its procedures have remained unchanged; meanwhile, the firm's competitors may have acquired advanced technology. This type of situation is commonly encountered with information systems. If a firm has continued to employ manual procedures in spite of considerable growth in transaction volumes and developments in information technology, the consultant may determine that computer-based transaction-processing systems are likely to provide significant improvements.

Opportunistic Problem.   An opportunistic problem arises in a situation in which a future opportunity exists. For instance, a firm might have excessive available cash and short-term investments that are not earning a desirable rate of return. As the firm's consultant, your responsibility is to search out and recommend opportunities for more effective long-term use of the funds. Your recommendations may range from investing in longer-term securities to marketing new products to training up-and-coming managers. Obviously, opportunistic problems are likely to lead to more risky, as well as potentially more rewarding, courses of action than are corrective and progressive problems.

Service Delivery Area

Perhaps the most common means of describing engagements is in terms of *service delivery areas*—that is, the functions or activities in which the problems reside. Service delivery areas are classified in various ways. A typical classification plan might use the following principal service delivery areas:[5]

1.0	General management
2.0	Manufacturing
3.0	Personnel
4.0	Marketing
5.0	Finance and accounting
6.0	Procurement
7.0	Research and development
8.0	Packaging
9.0	Administration
10.0	International operations

Within each principal service delivery area might be several narrower areas. Thus, the finance and accounting area might include:[6]

5.1	General accounting
5.2	Cost accounting
5.3	Long-range financial planning
5.4	Short-term planning, budgeting, and control
5.5	Credit and collections
5.6	Capital investment
5.7	Marginal income analysis
5.8	Financial information and reporting
5.9	Financial planning
5.10	Valuations and appraisals
5.11	Taxes

The AICPA classification plan includes the following service delivery areas in which consultants, especially CPAs, from public accounting firms are likely to be qualified to provide assistance:[7]

Budgeting

Business planning

Business valuation

Cash and inventory management

Computer applications

Financial ratio analysis

Securing of loans

New areas of consulting services constantly arise as clients discover new problems or opportunities. The following service delivery areas have seen the most rapid growth in recent years:

Activity-based costing

Information management

Human resources management

Institutional infrastructure development and diffusion

Management succession

Acquisitions, mergers, and joint ventures

Corporate downsizing

Strategic planning, including competitive strategies

The recently issued AICPA consulting standards, described earlier in the chapter, considerably broaden the accounting profession's view of the scope of consulting services. At the same time, the standards recognize the conflict between some of these services and the audit service.[8] Periodically the scope of consulting services provided by the accounting profession is affected by regulations established by the Securities and Exchange Commission (SEC) or questioned by congressional oversight committees. The Big Six accounting firms are on record as favoring a broad scope of services.[9]

Phases of the Analytic Process

As noted earlier, the analytic phases of the consulting process consist of identifying objectives, defining the problem, finding out the facts, determining the recommended solution or proposed course of action, communicating the recommendation, and implementing the solution or action. An engagement could involve one, some, or all of these phases. For instance, it might focus primarily on defining the problem situation. Or it might consist of assisting in the implementation of a course of action on which the client has decided. Or it might involve all the phases up to, but not including, implementation.

Because the analytic phases of the process are dynamic and interrelated, all must be performed by either the client or the consultant in order for the process to be completed. This assertion is true whether the problem involves routine internal operations or product acceptance and customer attitudes. For instance, defining a problem related to manufacturing operations will probably involve the identification of manufacturing objectives and the determination of at least the pertinent facts underlying the problem.

Technical Skills

Most consulting engagements can be aided by technical models or methodologies. For instance, capital investment planning can be aided by a discounted cash flow model such as the present-value model or the internal rate of return model. Information systems development can be aided by structured methodologies such as business information systems analysis and design (BISAD) and business systems planning (BSP).[10]

An increasing number of technical aids are being incorporated into computer programs to facilitate management consulting engagements. Examples of such technical aids include structured analysis and design technique (SADT),[11] computer-aided software engineering (CASE), spreadsheet software packages such as Lotus 1-2-3 and Excel, and financial modeling software packages such as the interactive financial planning system (IFPS).[12] Examples of budget models developed using software packages are given in later chapters.

Nature of Organization

As described in Chapter 1, the client—the subject of an engagement—may be a privately owned business firm, a government agency, a not-for-profit nongovernment organization, a professional association, or some other type of organization. A client organization may be further classified by industry group. For example, a privately owned business firm may belong to one of the following industry groups:

Agriculture

Forestry

Fishing

Mining

Construction

Manufacturing

Transportation

Communications

Electric and gas utility

Sanitary services

Wholesale trade

Retail trade

Finance

Insurance

Each industry group in turn may be subdivided into specific industries. For example, mining includes gold mining, bituminous coal mining, oil production, and so on.

Geographical Area

An engagement may be restricted to a single location, such as the only location of a small firm or the home office of the client. Alternatively, it may involve multiple locations, such as the several production plants and warehouses of a large manufacturing firm. An engagement may also include locations in foreign countries.

Approaches to Management Consulting Practices

A management consultant who is establishing a practice can choose from a variety of approaches. Four basic approaches are discussed below: the generalist approach, the specialist approach, the process-oriented approach, and the content-oriented approach. Each approach has its pros and cons with respect to a particular type of problem or to a particular client organization. In addition to the four above-mentioned approaches, several other approaches are briefly described. It should be emphasized, however, that many individual practitioners and consulting firms offer a blend of approaches, modifying the blend to suit the needs of each engagement.

Generalist Approach

The *generalist approach* relies on and applies the basic principles of business management to problem situations. It maintains that these principles are equally relevant to and dominant in every industry and in most if not all types of organizations. This approach is helpful in discovering and defining the underlying causes of problems and conditions relating to opportunities, as well as in detecting feasible solutions. The generalist approach requires that the consultant has a sound training in the principles of business management, obtained via a graduate program in business management or equivalent experience in business management.

Specialist Approach

The *specialist approach* is an outgrowth of the tremendous expansion of knowledge and the complexity of modern-day organizations.

Consultants have found it increasingly difficult to maintain sufficient expertise in the variety of skills required to handle the problems of many types of complex organizations. Thus, both individual consultants and consulting firms have tended to limit the services they provide to a manageable subset of the universe of consulting services and clients. For instance, an individual consultant might specialize in the selection, evaluation, and application of microcomputers. A consulting firm might specialize in information systems development or executive compensation.

The practice specialization established by an individual or a consulting firm may be based on service delivery area, technical skill, organization type, or geographical area.

Service Delivery Area Specialization. Individual practitioners and consulting firms may choose to specialize in one or more service delivery areas. Service delivery areas are often defined by a function such as marketing, human resources, finance, accounting, information systems, operations, or strategic management. Some areas are so broad that the consultant could specialize in serving a segment within a function, such as pension administration within the accounting function.

Technical Specialization. Individual practitioners and consulting firms may specialize in a technical skill or methodology, such as optimization modeling, software development, financial planning, or marketing research methodologies. An example of a firm that has developed a successfully marketed new technique is Boston Consulting Group, which specializes in product matrix charts and experience curve models.[13]

Type of Organization Specialization. Specialization also relates to types of organizations. For instance, a consulting firm might specialize in banking institutions, municipal governments, steel manufacturers, or educational institutions.

Geographical Specialization. Many consulting firms specialize in limited geographical areas close to their offices. This type of specialization conserves resources and enables the consultants to become very familiar with local conditions, practices, and personnel. On the other hand, a large number of firms have expanded the area they serve to an entire nation, such as the United States. The number of larger firms expanding their operations to serve clients in global markets is growing. American firms such as A. T. Kearney and Andersen Consulting have truly global practices, with offices in many foreign countries. Cap Gemini (based in France) has expanded its practice into the United States and a number of other countries.

Process-Oriented Approach

A *process-oriented approach* helps clients employ the consulting process described earlier. A consultant using this approach works closely with key members of a client's organization, conveying his or her understanding of the process to the members. The consultant encourages the client's personnel to formulate solutions to problem situations and facilitates their efforts, rather than his or her own solutions. Thus, a process-oriented consultant believes that his or her primary responsibility is to teach or train a client's personnel in a sound problem-solving procedure. When this approach is skillfully employed, it can lead to a deeper understanding of a problem situation and a sounder solution than the consultant could develop independently. It also tends to instill process skills into the client's personnel, so that they can tackle future problems on their own. However, this approach can be more time-consuming than the content-oriented approach. If it is not applied skillfully, or if the client's personnel are not sufficiently attentive and diligent, the process-oriented approach could lead to undesirable solutions.

Content-Oriented Approach

The *content-oriented approach*, which focuses on the problem situation itself, is also called a task-oriented or project-oriented approach. The consultant personally performs all the phases in the consulting process, relying on his or her experience and skills. Eventually the consultant develops a preferred solution and presents it as a recommendation to the client.

In a pure application of the content-oriented approach, the client's personnel do not participate except to provide needed facts about the problem situation. They do not, therefore, gain the benefits of learning how to solve their own problems. Many consultants advocate a blend of the process- and content-oriented approaches. The extent to which the client's personnel are involved depends on the knowledge and attitude of the client's personnel, the complexity of the problem, and the skill and patience of the consultant.

Other Approaches

Consulting practices that emphasize the *diagnostic approach* focus on the phases of the consulting process that end with a recommended solution to the problem. Advocates of the diagnostic approach believe that advisory service is the best and most professional use of the consultant's time and expertise.

Other consulting practices emphasize the *full-process approach*, which includes the implementation phase in addition to the earlier phases of the consulting process. Depending on the type of engagement, implementation may involve making changes in the client's operational system, management system (organization), or information system. Advocates of the full-process approach believe that implementation is difficult for a client to perform unassisted and that the consultant has a responsibility to aid the client in effecting a change. Two large firms that specialize in information systems consulting—Andersen Consulting and Computer Sciences Corporation—provide consulting services that range from planning information systems to implementing the systems. They employ computerized CASE tools to aid in integrating planning with implementation.[14] It should be noted that certain so-called strategy management firms have historically not included implementation within the scope of their engagements.

Two approaches that are related to the above-mentioned services are the *advisory approach* and the *action-oriented* approach. The advisory approach is similar to the diagnostic approach, whereas the action-oriented approach involves "hands on" activity, such as the implementation of an information system. Consultants who take the action-oriented approach may be involved in what the AICPA calls *transaction services.* Examples of transaction services are establishing the valuation of a client's business, obtaining financing for a client, performing litigation support, and aiding in matters relating to a client's insolvency or bankruptcy.[15]

Two final approaches that should be considered focus on deliverables. The *customized approach* emphasizes the uniqueness of each engagement and attempts to tailor a solution to the particular circumstances encountered in the engagement. The *packaged approach* emphasizes the similarities among problems faced by all clients and attempts to apply a packaged methodology and, when suitable, a packaged solution that has been developed for the generic category of problems in which the defined problem seems to fit. Andersen Consulting tends to use a series of packages, including Method/1 and Design/1, when developing an information system for a client. Although the packaged approach may be the most cost-efficient, it may not provide the best solution in nonroutine problem situations.

Practice Management by Management Consulting Firms

In addition to selecting suitable approaches to a consulting practice and to individual engagements, a management consulting firm must decide on its own management policies and procedures. Among the topics that must be considered are:

Practice planning

Marketing of consulting services

Practice economics

Development of management consultants

These topics are discussed extensively in Chapters 18–20.

Notes

1. This quotation and the requirements listed in this section are based on the brochure *IMC Purposes, Programs, and Benefits of Membership,* published by the Institute of Management Consultants, Inc. Chapters 3 and 4 of this handbook discuss the areas of knowledge and skills needed for professional competence, as well as the ethical standards and independence that management consultants should maintain at all times.

2. AICPA Management Advisory Services Executive Committee, "Statement on Standards for Consulting Services No. 1," *Definitions and Standards for MAS Practice,* November 1991.

3. Monroe S. Kuttner, "CPA Consulting Services: A New Standard," *Journal of Accountancy,* November 1991, pp. 38–41.

4. MAS University Education Task Force, *University Education for Management Consulting: Position Paper and Conference Report,* ed. Monroe S. Kuttner. New York: AICPA, 1978, p. 7.

5. Jerome H. Fuchs, *Making the Most of Management Consulting Services.* New York: American Management Association, 1975, pp. 143–46.

6. *Ibid.*

7. "Statement on Standards for Consulting Services No. 1," *op. cit.*

8. Roger E. Muns, Robert S. Roussey, and William E. Whitmer, "Practical Definitions of Six Consulting Functions," *Journal of Accountancy,* November 1991, pp. 43–45.

9. Arthur Andersen & Co., Coopers & Lybrand, Deloitte & Touche, Ernst & Young, KPMG Peat Marwick, and Price Waterhouse, *The Public Accounting Profession: Meeting the Needs of a Changing World,* January 1991.

10. BISAD is marketed by Honeywell Information Systems, Inc.; BSP is marketed by International Business Machines Corporation.

11. SADT is marketed by Sof Tech, Inc.

12. LOTUS 1-2-3 is marketed by Lotus Development Corporation; EXCEL is marketed by Microsoft Corporation; IFPS is marketed by EXECUCOM.

13. Robert O. Metzger, *Profitable Consulting: Guiding America's Managers into the Next Century,* Reading, Mass.: Addison-Wesley, 1989, p. 75.

14. David A. Ludlum, "Consultants Regroup: Shift Focus as Clients Seek One-Stop Shopping," *Computerworld,* March 21, 1988, pp. 99, 101.

15. Kuttner, "CPA Consulting Services: A New Standard," *op. cit.*

3

Body of Knowledge for Consultants

Joseph W. Wilkinson
School of Accountancy
Arizona State University
Tempe, Arizona

As noted in earlier chapters, consultants need a variety of technical skills. At the core of these technical skills must be a body of knowledge that enables a consultant to:

1. Be competent in the delivery of high-quality consulting services
2. Fulfill at least one requirement relating to professional status
3. Provide the foundation for future growth in the consultant's practice
4. Develop one or more specialties within the consulting field

Consultants normally acquire the requisite body of knowledge through formal education. Because few colleges and universities offer degrees in consulting, however, a one-time formal education is generally not sufficient. To keep abreast of new concepts and techniques, consultants must upgrade and update their underlying knowledge through additional courses at colleges and universities. In addition, consultants should supplement their learning through such avenues as self-directed study, professional development programs, conferences, and on-the-job training.

Body of Knowledge Frameworks

Several management consulting associations have developed frameworks relating to a requisite body of knowledge. Three such frameworks will serve as the basis for the composite body of knowledge that is reviewed in this chapter.

The organization formerly known as the Association of Consulting Management Engineers (ACME) proposed a common body of knowledge for management consultants, consisting of the following:[1]

1. Basic understanding of general management, including its major objectives and activities

2. General understanding of the overall environment in which consultants operate, including:

   - The legal, economic, political, social, and physical environments of business and nonbusiness entities
   - The major characteristics, similarities, and differences of the institutional forms known as businesses, nonprofit organizations, and government organizations
   - The major subclassifications of these three institutional forms
   - The impact of technology on these institutional forms

3. General knowledge of the functional areas within business entities, including:

   - Each function's standard definition, purposes, subfunctions, and relationships to other functions
   - Problems involved in each function's direction
   - Conditions affecting each function's importance and nonimportance
   - Methods of conducting the operations of each function

4. General understanding of the principles and practices of management consulting, including the consulting process and the conduct of consulting engagements

The Institute of Management Consultants (IMC) proposed a body of knowledge that consists of the following:[2]

1. Management consulting as a process and a profession

2. General knowledge, including the nature and environment of a business, the major elements of law relevant to business, aspects of macro- and microeconomics, the managerial process, and the attributes of government and nonprofit institutions

3. General or entity management, including top management and the board of directors, organizational principles and their application,

selection and evaluation and compensation of executives, goals and objectives, control of regular operations and special projects, and special management problems

4. Operations, including manufacturing and manufacturing management, quality control, inventory management, and production planning and control

5. Marketing, including market planning and strategy, market research, product development, distribution channels, product distribution, advertising and promotion, public relations, packaging, sales force operations, sales analysis, financial and cost controls, and management science applications

6. Logistics, materials management, and physical distribution, which includes physical distribution and systems planning, transportation and traffic management, warehousing, site selection, materials handling, materials management, production and inventory control, customer service, package design, and distribution

7. Research and development, including research organization, long-range planning, technological forecasting, technological innovation and technology transfer, selection of new projects or products, project planning and control, economics, personnel administration, patents and licenses, public policy, and incentives

8. Finance and accounting, including financial and accounting organization, design and operation of financial and accounting subsystems, financial and management accounting, financial management of assets and liabilities, taxes, insurance, pensions, securities, and government and nonprofit institutions

9. Human resources, including planning and organization, procurement, staffing, appraisal, training, management development, compensation, executive selection, health and safety, people management, employee relations, special employee groups and problems, government requirements and controls, records, reports, and communications

10. Information systems, including organization, skill requirements, information concepts, systems selection strategies, computer-based processing concepts and equipment, systems life cycle, programming and software engineering, data-processing operations, data control, and applications

11. Management science, including role and function of management science, statistics and mathematics, forecasting, mathematical programming and networks, inventory models, simulation models, and management science models

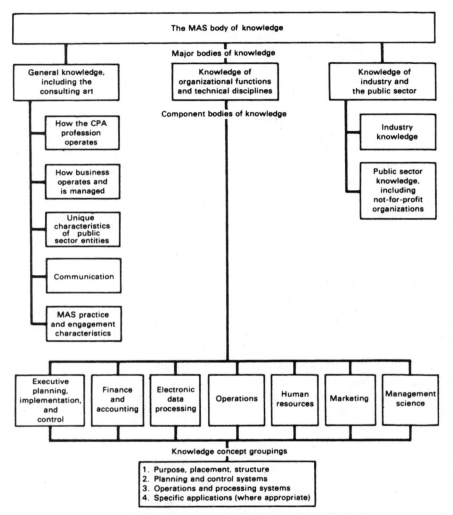

Figure 3-1 The body of knowledge needed by consultants who perform management advisory services (MAS). (*Source:* Edward L. Summers and Kenneth E. Knight, *Management Advisory Services by CPAs,* American Institute of CPAs, New York, 1976, p. 82. © 1976 by the American Institute of CPAs, Inc.)

The body of knowledge proposed by the American Institute of Certified Public Accountants (AICPA) is diagramed in Figure 3-1.[3] The three major areas of knowledge identified are general knowledge, knowledge of organizational functions and technical disciplines, and knowledge of private industry and the public sector. These major areas are further subdivided as shown in the figure.

A composite body of knowledge based on the three frameworks would include the following categories:

1. General management of organizations

2. Characteristics and environment of business entities within varied industries

3. Public-sector entities (including not-for-profit organizations)

4. Functional areas within entities:
   - Finance and accounting
   - Logistics
   - Marketing
   - Human resources
   - Research and development
   - External affairs
   - Information systems

5. Technical disciplines:
   - Mathematics and statistics
   - Quantitative and management science techniques
   - Information technology
   - Communications techniques

6. Principles and practices of management consulting, including techniques for data collection, problem definition, and solution development

The first five categories within the composite body of knowledge are discussed briefly in following sections. Several of the categories are also discussed in later chapters of this book. The sixth category (management consulting principles and practices) is extensively described in Chapters 10–13. Furthermore, numerous textbooks are available concerning each of the topics listed in the composite body of knowledge.

General Management of Organizations

General management encompasses a variety of activities, including setting goals and objectives, organizing operations and tasks, planning future operations, monitoring and controlling current operations, supervising employees, and communicating objectives and decisions. These activities can be subdivided to reflect more precise processes.

Setting Goals and Objectives

Setting goals and objectives should be the first activity. Until the founding managers decide what business their firm is in, the firm is not likely to survive in a competitive environment. Goals provide the broad aims that are to guide the firm's overall activities. Two commonly stated goals are (1) to achieve a growing level of sales and maintain adequate profitability and (2) to provide satisfactory service to (a specified category of) customers. Objectives follow from goals and are generally stratified into long-term, medium-term, and short-term objectives. To be operational, each objective should express a desired result in quantitative terms and for a specified time horizon. For example, an objective might be to capture 20 percent of the microcomputer market within 2 years.

Organizing Operations and Tasks

An organization is the framework through which management achieves its tasks. A formal organizational structure is generally a hierarchical arrangement of the tasks of a firm and the authority to see that the tasks are carried out. Operations and tasks can be segmented according to functions, product lines, projects, geographical territories, markets served, or some combination of these. For instance, a matrix structure blends functions and projects. An organizational structure is typically diagramed by means of an organization chart that depicts a collection of boxes at several managerial levels. Each box represents a responsibility center that is headed by a manager—for example, a credit department that is headed by a credit manager.

Two trends concerning organizations have become apparent in recent years. First, organizational structures are being decentralized to a greater degree; that is, considerable authority is being delegated to the middle and lower managerial levels. Second, flexible and innovative organizational arrangements are being increasingly employed, with the net effect that hierarchical arrangements are losing their dominance. For instance, firms may form temporary organic work groups to undertake various tasks or projects and then disband the groups when the tasks or projects are completed.

Planning Future Operations

Planning can be subdivided into strategic planning and tactical planning. Strategic planning is the process of deciding which strategies and resources are necessary to achieve a firm's objectives. Sound strategic planning can provide clear competitive advantage for a firm. It employs a long-range perspective, focusing on a firm's major strengths and weaknesses as well as the problems and opportunities in the environment.

Tactical planning is the process of translating strategic decisions into specific operational programs, plans, and instructions—for instance, translating strategic decisions concerning advertising into more detailed advertising programs and budgets.

Monitoring and Controlling Current Operations

Control consists of monitoring, measuring, and evaluating the performances of ongoing activities. Thus, it is essentially a regulatory process. In organizations, control can be subdivided into management control and operational control. Management control is the process by which managers ensure that resources are acquired and used efficiently and effectively. Operational control, by contrast, is the process that promotes efficiency in operational tasks. For instance, management control may control the use of production-related resources by comparing the actual costs incurred in each production department against budgeted costs and, in the process, evaluating the performance of each department manager. Operational control may control the task of manufacturing products by monitoring and measuring the percentage of rejected units. Both types of control generally lead to corrective actions.

Planning and control are related through the decision processes by which managers provide direction to a firm. A decision process consists of the following steps: (1) recognize and define a problem that needs a decision, (2) determine alternative courses of action, (3) evaluate the alternatives by means of a decision model, (4) select the best alternative according to an established model criterion (e.g., least costs), (5) carry out the decision choice, and (6) follow up the decision results.

Supervising Employees

A vital activity of managing is motivating and directing employees. Various theories have been developed concerning effective styles by which managers can perform these human-oriented activities. According to the needs hierarchy described by management theorist Abraham Maslow, managers can motivate employees by satisfying their basic needs. These range from physiological needs such as food, rest, and freedom from illness to needs for security, belonging, self-esteem, social recognition, and self-actualization. These needs can best be met if employees are consulted before decisions are made and if employees are allowed to participate in the decision process to the greatest feasible extent. A complementary theory proposed by Douglas McGregor suggests that replacing Theory X (the traditional view of direction and control) with Theory Y (the integration of individual goals with organizational goals) will encourage employees to direct their efforts to achieving the success of their firm. Another complementary theory contrasts the mechanistic management style with the organic management style. The mechanistic style focuses on the hierarchical organizational structure and the traditional view of employees as pay-driven time servers. The organic style is humanistic, in that it views employees as wanting to perform challenging work and to be partners with management. As noted earlier, the organic approach encourages the use of groups or teams in undertaking tasks and projects.

Communicating Objectives and Decisions

Communication within an organization is critical to the achievement of a firm's goals and objectives. Employees as well as lower-level managers must be informed of decisions that affect them and their jobs. They need to be provided with information promptly and fully, both to enable them to perform effectively and to give them a sense of belonging within the organization.

Business Entities in Varied Industries

Any business entity—corporation, partnership, or proprietorship—has key characteristics. These characteristics include, in addition to objectives, the variety of processes that a business entity employs and their required inputs and outputs. Inputs include such resources as humans, materials and supplies, facilities, funds, and data. Outputs consist of information plus products and/or services. Other key characteristics are the entity's principal subsystems (the organizational structure, the information system, and the operational system) and their subsystem's subsystems—for example, sales processing and general ledger processing. Every business entity encounters constraints, such as those pertaining to its area of operations and its budget; it also employs feedback controls that regulate its subsystems and internal controls to ensure the reliability of its information outputs. Furthermore, the business entity serves a variety of users, ranging from customers to owners and prospective owners.

A business entity functions within an environment that is economic, technical, social, and political. The environment provides opportunities, such as entry into a new market. On the other hand, it presents constraints and problems, such as shortages of critical raw materials or rapid rises in interest rates. Consultants should be able to identify each client's opportunities, constraints, and problems, as well as determine the significant influences on each client. Three categories of influences worth noting are those stemming from needed resources, the industry of which the client is a member, and the legal obligations and social responsibilities facing the client.

As noted earlier, the resources needed by a business entity consist of humans, materials, facilities, funds, and data. The needed mix of resources depends on the types of activities conducted by the entity. For example, the critical need of a grocery chain is a wide variety of merchandise for sale. Although space in which to house and sell the merchandise is needed, the store facilities are secondary in importance and are typically leased. On the other hand, a steel manufacturer employs materials that are few and simple in nature. However, because it needs massive steel-producing facilities on a long-term continuing basis, the manufacturer normally acquires these facilities by purchase. The mix of resources and the manner in which the resources are employed become quite important considerations when designing an entity's information system, since a primary function of the system is to monitor the resources and aid in their control.

A business entity identifies with at least one industry. Among the variety of identifiable industries are manufacturing, construction, merchandising, insurance, banking, utilities, health care, and education. Each of these major categories can be subdivided; for instance, manufacturing can be subdivided into electronic products manufacturers, household goods manufacturers, and so on. The members of each subdivided industry category sell similar products or offer similar services, but they differ from entities in other industries in regard to their resource structures, operating conditions, and product mixes. For instance, entities in the automobile and steel manufacturing industries are typically capital-intensive and integrated, whereas those in the garment and insurance industries are labor-intensive and relatively unintegrated. Business entities in certain industries (e.g., microcomputers, jogging gear) face rapidly changing environments, whereas members of other industries (e.g., utilities, food processing) enjoy relatively stable environments.

Legal obligations and social responsibilities are becoming more important to business entities. Legal obligations include timely payments of taxes and payments to employee benefit programs. Often as onerous, however, are the heavy reporting requirements imposed on many entities. Reports may range from those concerning payroll taxes and workers' compensation to those involving pollution control and new issues of capital stock. Certain types of entities, such as public utilities, are also required to file reports with state commissions in support of requests for rate increases.

To satisfy their social responsibilities, business entities may contribute to community development projects and encourage their managers and employees to serve on public service boards, participate in charity drives, and support community activities and sports events in the communities where they reside and work.

Public-Sector Entities

Public-sector entities include government agencies at the federal, state, and local levels; churches; schools and universities; trusts and foundations; flood control and utility districts; transportation authorities; and social and fraternal organizations. Together these entities account for about one-half of all activity within the United States.

Public-sector entities undertake the same managerial activities as do business entities in the private sector. However, they differ in a number of respects from private business entities. Whereas private business entities engage in a competitive marketplace for sales and profits, public-sector entities do not have to compete in the traditional sense. Instead, they may provide services and receive support through funding authorities or voluntary gifts. For example, government agencies rely on taxing authority to obtain appropriations. Usually the appropriations are authorized by elected bodies, such as the U.S. Congress, state legislatures, or city councils. Appropriations are established within the framework of budgets, which define the amounts to be applied to various purposes. Actual expenditures are then made in accordance with the budgeted levels. (Certain public-sector entities, such as credit unions and cooperatives, do have earnings, but these entities are relatively few in number and generally small.) Public-sector entities measure their success in terms of the degree to which they comply with applicable laws or charters. However, the extent of their success is often difficult to determine clearly, since quantitative measures are seldom available. Thus, a public-sector entity may claim that it is successful as long as its expenditures do not exceed the budgeted amounts.

Public-sector entities do not normally employ the method of accounting that is typically used by business entities. Instead, they use a system known as fund accounting—a system in which funds are committed to specific purposes. Each fund's receipts, expenditures, assets, and equities are maintained separately. Thus, each fund has its own self-balancing set of accounts and its own financial statements.

Functional Areas within Entities

Most business and public-sector entities are organized according to functions. The following sections briefly describe the objectives, subfunctions, and activities of the most typical functional areas, especially those found in business entities. Consultants must deal with such activities and sub-functions in engagements involving the functions. Because of lack of space, this survey does not attempt to describe specific types of engagements involving the subfunctions and activities, nor does it indicate likely problems and possible solutions relating to them.

Finance and Accounting

The finance and accounting functions are closely related. In some firms, in fact, they are combined into a single function, perhaps headed by a vice president of finance. The objectives of the finance function are to obtain funds at the lowest feasible costs and to disburse the available funds in an effective manner. The objectives of the accounting function are to monitor the entity's fiscal operations, to report the entity's financial status and results of operations, and to provide documents that support daily operations.

To achieve these objectives, the finance and accounting function is subdivided into a number of subfunctions, including financial planning, credit and collections, and cash receipts and disbursements. Financial planning consists of determining the need for funds to undertake capital projects (i.e., for capital budgeting), determining working-capital requirements, determining the optimal methods of financing (e.g., issuing stock, selling bonds, borrowing from banks), and deciding how to invest excess cash. Credit and collections is the subfunction that controls bad-debt losses. Its responsibilities include establishing credit policies, investigating credit references, and collecting overdue payments. Cash receipts and disbursements are key elements of the revenue and expenditure cycles of an entity. The departments responsible for these subfunctions maintain custody of the entity's cash resources and protect them from loss or mishandling.

Other, related activities within the finance area may include securing and maintaining adequate financial protection through insurance coverage and managing the entity's tax liabilities.

Subfunctions within the accounting area include budgeting, general accounting, cost accounting, and internal control. Budgeting consists of projecting planned revenues and profit results by segments (e.g., products, sales territories, departments) and allocating costs for various operations and responsibility centers. General accounting includes the various activities involved in transaction processing and record keeping, such as accounts receivable, billing, accounts payable, general ledger, property, inventory control, and payroll. Cost accounting entails developing cost standards, recording costs pertaining to work performed, and producing related reports. Internal control involves ensuring the reliability of records and accounting information, safeguarding the entity's assets, promoting efficiency in the entity's operations, and encouraging adherence to management's policies. To achieve all these objectives, the entity employs a variety of controls, including internal auditors.

Logistics

The logistics function is concerned with the operations related to an entity's inventories. In a merchandising firm, the logistics function includes the physical activities of purchasing, receiving, and storing merchandise inventory, plus the distribution of merchandise to customers. In a manufacturing firm, the logistics function includes—in addition to the activities just listed—all the production activities. Production activities can most logically be discussed under two broad categories: production and physical distribution.

Production involves form utility; it consists of transforming certain inputs, such as raw materials, into desired outputs, such as finished goods. A number of subfunctions are often necessary to achieve this result. In a large and complex manufacturing firm, for instance, production activity might include the following subfunctions: production planning, manufacturing engineering, materials management, production operations, production control, and quality control. Production planning can in turn be subdivided into two major activities: (1) strategic planning, which consists of planning for facilities and labor and other needed resources for the long-range time horizon, and (2) production scheduling, which consists of establishing the monthly or weekly schedules (based either on specific orders or on sales forecasts) and arranging for the needed resources to meet these schedules.

Manufacturing engineering includes such activities as facilities design, plant layout, safety engineering, and product design. Materials management includes materials requirements planning (i.e., ensuring that adequate quantities of materials are available for scheduled orders or jobs), storing the materials until they are needed in production, requisitioning the materials according to bills of materials, and moving the materials to the production floor.

Production operations encompass all the actions and operations performed on scheduled orders as they move through the work centers or departments within the production process. Production control consists of dispatching the orders into production, monitoring the actual operations, and suggesting corrective actions when necessary. Quality control conducts inspections of work-in-process and completed goods, performs tests when necessary, and rejects or accepts units on the basis of evaluations of product quality.

Because the production function is so complex, it requires a number of supporting activities. Thus, extensive maintenance must be performed, both on a scheduled basis as preventive maintenance and on a nonscheduled basis when equipment or facilities break down. Also, elaborate cost accounting systems must be designed and installed to assign the materials, labor, and overhead costs to work-in-process and to completed goods.

Several important developments have taken place in recent years within the production function. Computer-integrated manufacturing systems have been devised to coordinate the production process and all the needed resources. Just-in-time inventory systems have been applied to eliminate or drastically reduce the levels of raw materials inventories.

Physical distribution often includes the following subfunctions: distribution planning, warehousing, transportation, and customer service. Distribution planning consists of identifying the markets to be served, analyzing alternative distribution systems, and translating broad plans into specific physical requirements and detailed implementation plans. Warehousing includes planning for needed warehouses, equipping warehouses with needed bins and handling equipment, and storing finished goods received from the production process until they are needed for shipment. Transportation consists of determining shipment requirements, identifying shipping routes and carriers, negotiating freight rates, maintaining the private fleet of trucks or other vehicles (if a private fleet is used), and monitoring the costs of shipment via common carriers versus private fleet vehicles. Customer service includes processing orders from customers (unless this activity is conducted by the marketing function), providing technical and repair services for products, and administering warranty policies.

Marketing

The marketing function encompasses the following subfunctions: market planning, sales operations, advertising, market research, and sales promotion. The purpose of market planning is to market the right products at the right times, places, and prices. This subfunction is also responsible for determining the entity's long-term marketing strategies and policies, forecasting sales and marketing costs, and establishing the prices and terms of sale. Often, market planning includes new-product development. Sales operations involve recruiting and training sales personnel, controlling the activities of sales personnel, supplying information in response to order inquiries, and selling products to and accepting orders from customers. Advertising includes developing advertising campaigns, selecting suitable advertising media, and preparing advertising copy. Market research consists of analyzing the likely markets for the entity's products or services, measuring customer attitudes and preferences, and analyzing actual sales data. Sales promotion includes developing catalogs, display materials, and dealer aids, as well as selecting and directing special promotions.

Business entities organize their marketing and distribution functions and logistics in different ways. For example, some entities may include sales order entry under logistics, whereas others may include it under marketing. The packaging activity may be included under any of the three functions, whereas the selection of distribution channels (e.g., dealing through wholesalers or bypassing wholesalers and dealing directly with retailers) may be placed under either marketing or physical distribution.

Human Resources (Personnel)

The human resources function is concerned with the acquisition of needed human resources, the administration of an entity's personnel (managers as well as other employees), the motivation of the human resources, and the provision of safe and reasonable work conditions. Among the subfunctions of the human resources function are planning, employment, training, benefits and safety, compensation, and industrial relations.

Human resources planning includes determining staffing requirements, developing personnel policies, developing performance standards and appraisal systems, and coordinating the formal organizational arrangements to which staff are to be assigned. The employment subfunction is concerned with establishing job specifications, recruiting prospective employees, screening and testing applicants, and coordinating the hiring of qualified applicants. Training includes developing training programs, conducting training programs, and evaluating training results. The benefits and safety subfunction is concerned with administering pension programs, devising suggestion plans, operating cafeterias and other employee-oriented facilities, providing medical facilities and treatments, and maintaining safety programs and other services. Compensation includes establishing and administering wage rates and salary levels, conducting wage and salary surveys, developing merit-rating programs, and completing actions on recommended individual merit ratings. Industrial relations consists of developing grievance procedures, establishing work and disciplinary rules, negotiating agreements with labor unions, and participating in labor dispute negotiations.

Research and Development

The research and development function has the purpose of applying basic research results to the creation and improvement of an entity's products, processes, and/or services. Its subfunctions include research, development, and product engineering. Research might include basic research (i.e., the exploration of natural processes and principles) and applied research (i.e., the use of the results of basic research to obtain specific knowledge or results that are beneficial to the entity). Development may be subdivided into advanced development, new-product development, product improvement, and new-process development. (Advanced development is the transition stage between applied research and product or process development, during which working models are devised to demonstrate the results of applied research.) Product engineering (which may alternatively be performed within the logistics function) consists of designing, specifying, prototyping, testing, interpreting, and modifying the features of new products.

External Affairs

The external affairs function is concerned with the various publics that have dealings with the entity as well as with the environment in which the entity resides. Its subfunctions include environmental scanning, stakeholder affairs, public relations, community affairs, and political relations. Environmental scanning consists of such activities as screening relevant publications, attending conventions, and communicating with executives and other secondary sources to acquire information that can enable the entity to gain competitive advantage and make full use of opportunities. Acquired information may concern new products, new consumer trends, new technology, and so on. Stakeholder affairs consists of maintaining communication with the entity's owners and prospective investors (e.g., by providing informative annual reports). Public relations involves maintaining effective relationships with the mass communication media, preparing information releases concerning news affecting the entity and speeches made by its top management, and so on. Community affairs involves coordination of the entity's participation in civic activities and projects, such as United Way drives and educational funds for worthy high school students. Political relations consists of coordinating policies and relations with government agencies and legislative bodies at the local, state, and federal levels.

Information Systems

The information systems function has the objectives of providing information to a variety of users and of facilitating the entity's daily operations, especially the processing of transactions. Among the subfunctions that might be included in an information systems function that employs computer-based processing are data processing, systems development, technical services, information systems administration, and user support services.

Data processing is the operational subfunction within the information systems function. Its activities include data preparation and entry, data control, file library operations, and computer operations. The systems development subfunction, which supports the systems development life cycle, includes systems analysis and design, application programming, and database administration. The technical service subfunction performs such activities as supporting telecommunications, developing systems software, and investigating the potential for applying new technologies to existing systems. Information systems administration includes strategic systems planning, budgeting for information systems resources, training systems personnel, and developing systems-related standards. User support services—which are often implemented through information centers—include providing consulting and support services to end users, training end users in the use of microcomputer hardware and software packages, and assisting users in employing application generators to develop new reporting applications.

Technical Disciplines

A variety of technical disciplines provides the tools and techniques that assist consultants in the definition and analysis of problems and the development of viable solutions. These disciplines are arbitrarily discussed under the categories of mathematics and statistics, quantitative and management science techniques, information technology, and communications techniques. Most of these disciplines have been enhanced in recent decades through significant findings and developments.[4]

Mathematics and Statistics

One foundation on which management consulting rests consists of the disciplines of mathematics and statistics. Although most topical areas within these technical disciplines are applicable to a degree, the topical areas of greatest interest are algebra, calculus, probability theory, sampling, statistical decision theory, queuing theory, mathematical programming and allocation theory, time series analysis, regression analysis, statistical inference, variance analysis, and other classical statistical theories. These theories and concepts are embodied in a host of applied quantitative and management science techniques.

Quantitative and Management Science Techniques

Quantitative techniques are used in engineering, management science, operations research, systems analysis, accounting, and other disciplines. Consultants who serve clients in each of these disciplines must be able to apply the techniques that are relevant to the problems faced by their clients. Obviously, all quantitative techniques cannot be discussed in this chapter; only those that are widely used are covered in the following paragraphs.

Forecasting Techniques. Forecasting techniques are used to estimate future sales levels, profit margins, market share percentages, and other key success factors of an entity. Among the proven techniques are those based on averages and statistical regression analyses. To forecast on the basis of averages, a consultant might simply compute the arithmetic average of past values. Alternatively, the consultant might employ a moving average, in which the older the past values are, the less weight they exert in the average. Perhaps the most valid type of moving average is exponential smoothing, which weights both the most recent values and the previous forecast by means of a constant of proportionality called ALPHA. The formula for estimating a future value by the exponential smoothing method is:

Forecasted value = previous forecasted value + ALPHA
(previous actual value − previous forecasted value)

Another method for using a moving average is regression analysis, in which the forecasted value is based on estimates of one or more other factors. For instance, the future sales of an entity's products may be forecasted by estimating the sales for the industry and the average income level, and then applying these estimates within the regression formula:

$$\text{Forecasted value} = a + bx + cy$$

where a, b, and c are regression coefficients
For long-term forecasts, perhaps the most useful technique is a time series in which the forecast values are extrapolations of the trend of past values.

Inventory Models. Two recurring decisions with respect to inventory are (1) how many units of an item to reorder and (2) when to reorder. The number of units to reorder is determined by an economic order quantity (EOQ) model, which is based on differential calculus. The EOQ model minimizes the total inventory costs, considering such factors as expected demand for the item, carrying costs, stock-out costs, and reorder costs. Determining when to reorder is based on the establishment of a reorder point for each inventory item. The key factors in establishing a reorder point are expected usage (demand) and lead time. Both the EOQ and reorder point models must be modified when inventory is to be manufactured by the entity or when other factors are relevant.

Scheduling Techniques. Two useful scheduling techniques are Gantt charts and network diagrams. A Gantt chart is a bar chart with a calendar scale. Each planned activity appears as a bar that marks the scheduled starting date, ending date, and duration. Below each planned activity appears a bar that represents actual progress to date. Although a Gantt chart is simple to maintain and read, it does not show the relationships among the various activities. A network diagram, based on the program evaluation and review technique (PERT) or critical path method (CPM), is able to show such relationships and allow the critical path through the activities to be determined. PERT diagrams can be used to schedule and control project costs as well as project times.

Simulation Models. Simulation involves the use of a model to duplicate the essential aspects of an activity or a system over a period of time. It is normally employed to forecast the actions and results of systems. Models used for purposes of simulation may represent physical systems (e.g., a traffic system) or financial information systems (e.g., a budgeting system). A model incorporates all the essential features of the system it represents, including inputs, processes, and outputs. Most models are symbolic, in that they combine a series of statements containing variables and operators and are capable of being manipulated. A variety of manipulative techniques may be employed, such as "what if" statements about the expected values of key variables, goal-seeking statements, and sensitivity analyses.

Risk Analysis. Forecasting involves risk, since the future is uncertain. Risk analysis is a technique for coping with the uncertainties that are inherent in forecasts; it is usually applied within the framework of simulation models. Instead of assigning single-point values as estimates of key factors, risk analysis uses probability distributions. The types of probability distributions typically chosen are normal, uniform, triangular, exponential, and Poisson. For instance, future sales may be forecast by means of a normal distribution having an expected value of 10,000 units and a standard deviation of 158 units. Models that contain probabilistic factors such as future sales and costs are simulated through a series of events or time periods, with values assigned to the factors by means of random tables. These simulations are repeated for a specified number of iterations. The model criteria (e.g., expected profits) are generated in the form of probability distributions. Thus, the expected profits obtained from 100 iterations of a financial model may be forecast as $5000 for the coming year and $7500 for the next year. This risk analysis procedure is commonly known as the Monte Carlo method.

Queuing Models. Problems that consultants are asked to solve often involve waiting lines, such as customers waiting to be checked out at groceries, trucks waiting to be filled at loading docks, raw materials waiting to be processed at machine centers, and automobiles waiting to enter car washes. These problems can be tackled with the aid of probability distributions incorporated in models that are based on queuing theory. Queuing models relate such factors as mean arrival times, mean service rates, and mean lengths of waiting lines to probabilities of new units entering the waiting lines and the times that each of the new units is served.

Capital Investment Models.   Investments in assets with expected service lives of longer than 1 year can be evaluated by means of capital investment models. These models generally employ criteria such as net present value and internal rate of return. Examples of capital investments are new plants, replacements of currently owed vehicles or machines, and new computer-based information systems. In addition to the expected service lives, capital investment models incorporate such factors as acquisition costs, expected annual operating costs, expected salvage values, depreciation rates, and marginal income tax rates.

Control Models.   Control can be defined as the process of monitoring operations in order to avoid or correct adverse conditions. The process generally involves comparing benchmark values against actual values and then feeding information on the comparisons to correcting agents (either humans or computer systems). Control models range from those based on arithmetic variations to those that employ classical statistics or Bayesian theory. The simplest models compute the arithmetic differences, or variances, between the benchmark values and actual values. Models based on classical statistics employ ranges rather than point values as benchmarks and compare actual values against the ranges, or control limits. Because probability analysis is used to determine the control limits, a statistical model can better indicate when actual values are "out of control." Models based on Bayesian theory can incorporate cost considerations, so that managers can determine not only when an operation is out of control but also whether it is worthwhile or cost-effective to take corrective actions.

Information Technology

Information technology provides consultants with tools that increase their productivity and improve the quality of their results. Perhaps the most obvious aids are computer hardware devices such as microcomputers, laptop and notebook computers, laser printers, and plotters. These devices can be enhanced by communications links—provided, for instance, by modems which allow consultants to "plug in" to larger computers or networks from their offices and remote locations. Computer software is as important as computer hardware to consultants in performing tasks related to client engagements as well as in managing a practice. Among the types of software packages that are particularly useful to consultants are:

- Word-processing packages (WordPerfect, Microsoft Word)
- Electronic spreadsheet packages (Lotus 1-2-3, Excel)

- Financial modeling packages (IFPS/Personal, Javelin Plus)
- Graphics packages (ChartMaster, Harvard Graphics)
- Electronic mail software
- Time management packages
- Application generators (RAMIS II, Application-by-Forms)
- Workbench software (Excelerator, AutoCAD, CASE)
- Groupware (Lotus Notes, Higgins)
- Project control software

Communications Techniques

As discussed in Chapter 5, management consultants must have the ability to communicate effectively, both verbally and in writing. Effective communications skills and techniques are based on the following key principles:

1. Analyze your audience.
2. Determine the purpose of the communication.
3. Organize your message.
4. Use an appropriate style.
5. Use visual aids such as computer-generated graphics.

Notes

1. Subcommittee on the Constituent Elements of Management, *Common Body of Knowledge for Management Consultants.* New York: Association of Consulting Management Engineers, 1957.
2. *A Body of Knowledge for the Accreditation of Management Consultants.* New York: Institute of Management Consultants, 1979.
3. AICPA MAS University Education Task Force, *University Education for Management Consulting.* New York: American Institute of Certified Public Accountants, 1978.
4. All the major textbook publishers (e.g., McGraw-Hill Book Company, John Wiley & Sons, and Prentice-Hall) have current editions that fully explain the variety of techniques introduced in the above sections. In addition, there are two classic reference works related to quantitative and management science theory and techniques: Russell L. Ackoff, *Scientific Method: Optimizing Applied Research Decisions.* New York: John Wiley & Sons, 1962. C. West Churchman, Russell L. Ackoff, and E. Leonard Arnoff, *Introduction to Operations Research.* New York: John Wiley & Sons, 1957.

4
Professional Attributes of Consultants

J. Owen Cherrington
School of Accountancy and Information Systems
Brigham Young University
Provo, Utah

The skills that a management consultant must possess can be classified into three broad areas: technical skills, interpersonal skills, and consulting process skills. *Technical skills* include both the understanding and the experience in a technical discipline—such as computer data processing, marketing, engineering, or organizational behavior—that qualify an individual to be considered an expert. *Interpersonal skills* include personal attributes that make an individual amiable to people and effective in accomplishing desirable objectives through people. The *consulting process* is the step-by-step approach used by a management consultant to (1) determine the cause of problems or inefficiencies, (2) identify alternative solutions, (3) select the most desirable alternative, and (4) implement the chosen solution. Understanding this process and using it to solve business problems constitute consulting process skills.

The objectives of this chapter are to identify the education generally required to obtain adequate technical skills and to examine the personal traits most commonly possessed by effective consultants. Professional ethics is one of the most important attributes of a consultant. Special attention will be given to the meaning of professional ethics, codes of ethics that relate to management consultants, and cases concerning the application of professional ethics.

Educational Requirements

The education required to obtain the necessary technical skills for management consulting depends on the area of specialization. Some generalizations can be made, however, concerning the amount of education required, the common core requirements, and the experience possessed by most consultants.

Technical Training

A consultant must bring something to the consulting process besides a likable personality and a willing pair of hands. That special something is gained through education and training, experience, or some combination of the two. Generally, the combination of education and experience is an important factor in consulting success.

The following examples of successful consultants' individual career paths illustrate some of the alternatives. They also demonstrate technical skills that are basic to any area of consulting.

Example 1. Patricia Straight completed, at reputable universities, an undergraduate degree in psychology, an MBA in management, and a DBA in organizational behavior. After working for 4 years as personnel director for the manufacturing division of an international organization, she accepted employment with an international consulting organization. Her primary areas of consulting are general management, leadership styles, wage and salary policies, hiring and promotion policies, and performance evaluations.

Example 2. Mark Round had earned only a BS degree in political science when he became a computer company salesman. After 18 months, Mark left that company to become sales manager for the direct-sales division of a cosmetics firm. His employment there continued for 22 years, during which Mark attended night school, completed most of the course requirements for a master's degree in marketing, and moved up the management ladder to vice president of sales.

Because he was tired of the job and the company, he accepted an offer from an old college friend to be vice president of sales and part owner in a new electronics firm. Mark's marketing experience and business knowledge helped the company grow so that it captured a major share of the market in the short space of 4 years. The company was then sold at a substantial profit, and Mark resigned his position. Mark turned his efforts to management consulting and established a solo practice. His major areas of consulting include product packaging and pricing, establishing distribution channels, managing the sales force, and creating sales incentive programs.

Example 3. John Modom completed his bachelor's and master's degrees in accounting with a minor in computer science. While attending school, John worked as a part-time programmer for a local software firm. Upon graduation, John joined an international CPA firm. His initial assignments were in auditing, small business practice, and systems analysis and design for retail organizations. This industry specialization continued to develop over a 7-year period. John is currently one of the firm's experts in the analysis and design of accounting and management information systems for retail enterprises.

Generalizations concerning the length and content of a management consultant's education can be drawn from these and similar career paths.

1. *Length of education:* A bachelor's degree is a prerequisite, and many, if not most, people going into management consulting today have one or two graduate degrees.

Education is important for many reasons. First, it is one measure of a person's intellectual ability, and intellectual ability is among the more important personal attributes in determining success as a consultant. Holding a university degree shows evidence of ability to think. Second, the competition involved in a sound educational program develops confidence, articulation, and literacy. Third, education helps an individual mature and gain understanding of human nature. Fourth, the university education provides technical training in the chosen area of specialization.

Top-flight management consultants have a great deal of technical training in one area of specialization. This training includes both theory and practice. In addition, the management consultant needs a broad knowledge of business, management, economics, government, and a variety of similar topics in order to evaluate decisions in the area of specialization and their impact on the larger business and the people who work in it. Neither the extensive training required to become technically qualified as an expert in one area of specialization nor a broad general education can be obtained in an undergraduate program.

Undergraduate programs generally teach the "how," rather than the "why." Students are trained to memorize and regurgitate, not to conceptualize and criticize. Most undergraduate programs can be criticized for their rote, cookbook approach to the business environment. Graduate programs help develop tolerance for the uncertainty and ambiguity inherent in business problems. They help increase an individual's ability to deal with frustration, to challenge the current, and to create the new.

Some of the academic subjects commonly used in management consulting engagements are taught only in graduate programs. These include many research skills, such as research design, research methodologies, and statistical analysis.

2. *Type of education:* Educational programs usually include a technical degree and a general degree.

Whether the technical degree comes first or second does not seem to make much difference. For example, one person might obtain a general business degree at the bachelor's level and specialize in computer data processing by earning a master's and a doctoral degree in computer science and information management. Another person might do the same type of consulting with a bachelor's degree in computer science and an MBA.

Common Core Requirements

A major portion of an educational program should be in the desired area of specialization. A person desiring to consult in marketing, for example, would expect to devote a substantial portion of his or her program to marketing-related courses. Another person who plans to consult in systems analysis and design would expect to concentrate on courses in accounting, computer information systems, and information management.

Regardless of the area of specialization, the would-be consultant should include certain common core courses in his or her educational program. At a minimum, these common core courses should provide exposure to communications, mathematics and statistics, and computer data processing.

Communications. A well-rounded education in communications is essential. Studies show that business graduates spend a fairly equal amount of time on each type of communications activity: listening, 29 percent; speaking, 26 percent; writing, 25 percent; and reading, 20 percent. The most common types of writing include memos, 32 percent; letters, 29 percent; short-form reports, 26 percent; and long-form reports, 13 percent.

A management consultant must be proficient in all forms of communication. Inability to master any form of communication will inhibit the consultant's effectiveness and efficiency.

Style, grammar, spelling, and mechanics are emphasized in most writing courses in business communications. However, an effective consultant must be able to go one step beyond these technical concerns and use communication to create changes in people and their organizations. The quality of the consultant's written communications ought to be equivalent to that of material published in professional journals and magazines.

Mathematics and Statistics. Mathematical models and statistical analysis are useful in analyzing a variety of problems. A consultant may choose not to analyze a particular problem with an available mathematical model or statistical tool. But the client is shortchanged if the consultant does not know about or use an available model or tool that will provide a better, cheaper, and faster result.

Computer Data Processing. A consultant needs to work efficiently in order to remain competitive. The availability of microcomputers in recent years has made computer data processing affordable to every consultant. Applications such as word processing, spreadsheets, and database management systems are the most popular productivity tools. Computer software provides the consultant with the capability to perform many consulting tasks more easily, more quickly, and more accurately.

Experience

Work experience, after completion of a formal educational program, is important for several reasons. First, it provides a track record that a consulting organization can review in evaluating the individual's potential as a consultant. Promotions achieved, interpersonal relations with others, and managerial style are all good indicators of potential success. Second, work experience that relates to an individual's area of expertise will provide added depth as well as breadth to the chosen area. Third, if the experience has been with an organization that is at the forefront of new knowledge and developments, the budding consultant will bring new skills and a fresh approach to the consulting organization. Finally, work experience helps ensure credibility with clients. Credibility is important in obtaining new clients and in obtaining buy-in to implement the consultant's recommendations.

In some consulting situations, experience can be combined with education. One such approach employs a relationship akin to that of a journeyman and an apprentice. The experienced consultant models his or her skills through on-the-job demonstrations, and the novice consultant learns from such modeling. This arrangement affords the novice consultant the opportunity to meld theory with practice. Programs of this type are typically offered only by large consulting firms that have well-developed practices in particular areas of specialization.

The length of experience required for entry into a consulting organization varies from almost no experience to 10 or 12 years of experience. As a general rule, people with more education require less experience. Very few people get by with fewer than 2 years of experience. Anyone who is hired without much experience typically must work under the close supervision of another consultant for an extended period of time. Five years of experience at a managerial level is the ideal for entry into the consulting profession.

Personal Traits of a Management Consultant

Many factors other than experience and education have a bearing on the success that an individual achieves in the field of management consulting. Several personal attributes are critical for success. Some of them can be learned by intelligent people through years of study and experience. Some are inherent at birth or are developed during early childhood. Unless an individual has the necessary personal attributes to meet the required high standards of competent conduct, he or she will surely fail.

A list of necessary personal attributes can be useful to those contemplating careers in management consulting and to recruiters in consulting organizations. Ideally, those who possess these attributes will be enticed to pursue management consulting, and those who do not possess them will save time, money, and personal frustration by selecting alternative employment. Recruiters assist in this weeding-out process by employing only those who have the necessary skills for success.

If you are new to the consulting profession and would like to evaluate your personal attributes, complete the exercise on pages 19 and 20 of this chapter. Completing the exercise before you continue reading will make you less biased in your response. Don't give up if your score is not as high as you think it ought to be. Not all the necessary attributes are inherent. Many can be acquired through diligent study and practice. History is replete with examples of people who have overcome seemingly impossible odds and imposing obstacles to become successful. This exercise is intended primarily to help you identify obstacles that you need to overcome.

Inherent Attributes

A few personal attributes *are* inherent. A person either has them by birth or does not have them at all. No amount of study, experience, or perseverance can create these qualities. They are intelligence, adequate physique, and empathy.

Intelligence. Intelligence may be defined as the capacity for reasoning, understanding, and performing other forms of mental activity. The limits of our capacity to learn are largely determined at birth. The best that each of us can do is to utilize our capacity to the fullest extent possible.

What level of intelligence is necessary to perform adequately as a management consultant? The most frequent answer is "enough to perform adequately in a graduate program." Various tests are used to measure intelligence, and different universities and programs use different tests and minimum test scores in their screening processes. Two commonly used tests are:

Exam	Minimum score	Percentile
IQ test	120	90th
GMAT	500	60th

Physique. Physique refers to physical body structure, organization, and development. The most significant part of physique that is determined by birth is the capacity to produce energy. This is largely determined by hormones and the nervous system. A high-energy level is required to support intellectual and emotional activity. It enables a person to withstand pressure, to avoid physical illnesses, and to maintain physiological equilibrium. Because of the time pressure, volume of work, problem-oriented environment, and a multitude of other frustrations, a consultant needs a high-energy level for survival.

Personal appearance, a neat look, and an attractive physique are extremely important in a consulting environment. However, only a very minor part of this is inherent. Very few people are born with physical handicaps that would impair their performance as consultants. Diet, physical activity, neatness in dress, and personal hygiene are all within our ability to control.

Empathy. Empathy is a personal trait that allows us to feel for other people. It is an intellectual identification with, or vicarious experiencing of, the feelings, thoughts, or attitudes of other people.

It is not clear whether empathy is inherent or whether it is acquired during early childhood. The exact point of its development is not really important for our purposes. Either way, it is fairly well developed by the time a person is old enough to consider management consulting as a profession.

Empathy, understanding, and sympathy for the feelings and desires of others make a consultant better able to identify problems and to develop appropriate solutions.

Developed Attributes

The most authoritative list of essential consulting attributes was developed by a subcommittee of the Association of Management Consulting Firms (ACME). The nine attributes and the definitions that follow were largely identified by this committee. The definitions are, in some cases, more restrictive than those found in general use, but they are relevant to the consulting profession.

Understanding of People. Critical to a consultant's success is human relations: the ability to anticipate human reactions to differing situations, to establish and maintain friendly relations and mutual confidence with people at all levels, and to recognize and respect the rights of others.

The desire and ability to understand people develop from empathy and the capacity for feeling discussed earlier. However, conscious study is required to understand how people act and react, both individually and in groups. It takes a high degree of intelligence to observe, sift, weigh, and finally evaluate the characteristics and attributes of different people.

Integrity. A cluster of attributes make up integrity, including moral and ethical soundness, fairness, equity, ability to distinguish between right and wrong, honesty, dependability, freedom from corrupting influence or practice, and strictness in the fulfillment of both the letter and the spirit of agreements made, regardless of personal considerations. This definition contains most of the basic philosophies underlying a code of ethics. The detailed contents of professional codes of ethics relating to management consultants are discussed in detail later in this chapter.

The main ingredients for maintaining integrity are self-confidence, intelligence, and conviction. People are apt to lose their integrity when they are anxious or unsure about their ability to face a given situation while maintaining their value system. They then shade or lose their integrity in spite of a well-developed set of ethical and moral standards. Intelligence is necessary to identify the relationship of existing situations to ideals of honesty and equity. Too often, people compromise their standards because they don't recognize a situation as unethical. Integrity is also contingent on the individual's convictions in a set of beliefs and principles that he or she is willing to support and from which he or she cannot be turned.

Courage. It is strength of mind that enables people to encounter disagreement, difficulties, and obstructions with firmness of spirit and determination, and to consider them as challenges rather than something to be avoided and feared. Courage also entails the ability to stand by one's convictions regardless of pressure.

Courage in management consulting refers to intellectual, moral, and emotional firmness. Courage causes the consultant to support convictions that have been arrived at through intellectual reasoning about the rightness of a situation or problem. Lack of courage is evidenced by feelings of inadequacy and dependency on others.

Objectivity. It is essential to grasp and to represent facts, unfettered by prejudice. The consultant's objectivity is threatened when personal considerations, biases, and anxieties about the engagement are present. Objectivity is questioned when there is a lack of independence. In order for a consultant to be completely independent and objective, there must be both an appearance of independence and an actual state of mental independence.

Several situations can jeopardize the appearance of independence. The consultant's independence is questioned any time there is a vested interest in the outcome as a result of ownership or management responsibility. Examples include activities as promoter, underwriter, voting trustee, director, officer, or any position equivalent to that of manager or employee of the company. Situations in which the consultant owns or has committed to buy an ownership interest, or has loaned money to the company, cause a loss of the appearance of independence.

Independence and objectivity, in fact, ultimately depend upon the consultant's mental attitude. Even though a consultant may have the appearance of independence, objectivity may be lost through personal involvement. True independence and objectivity are a state of mind or a mental attitude.

Consultants must avoid situations in which they appear to lack independence and objectivity; they must maintain independent and objective attitudes. Without this, their recommendations will usually be worth very little.

Ambition. Consultants must possess the motivation to earn and obtain full recognition for the attainment of professional status. A management consultant with too little ambition lacks the desire, drive, and commitment to achieve a professional status. A management consultant with too much ambition becomes self-centered, strives only for selfish ends, and regards the client as a pawn to be used to achieve those selfish ends.

The consultant with the right amount of ambition is one who needs to accomplish to be happy, who feels a strong urge to produce concrete results, and who regards work as an important aspect of life. Without ambition, the consultant is useless; with too much ambition, he or she is unbearable.

Problem-Solving Ability. It takes a significant degree of mental organization and development to absorb and relate facts in a logical and orderly fashion and to reason inductively and deductively.

Problem-solving ability is developed through the application of curiosity (the desire for knowledge) and imagination (the faculty that fosters creativity). It involves thorough analysis, original thinking, the synthesis of new ideas from elements experienced separately, and the development of practical solutions to complex problem situations.

Problem-solving ability is extremely important because the consultant's basic work is to analyze and solve problems. Because time is such a factor in this competitive environment, the consultant must be able to solve problems quickly.

Judgment.   Judgment is the ability and reasoning power to arrive at a wise decision, a course of action, or a conclusion, especially when only meager or confused facts are available.

Problem-solving ability, discussed above, brings the consultant to a decision point. Alternative solutions have been identified, and a recommendation with supporting justification must now be made as to the most desirable solution. The most successful consultants have the ability to forecast the outcomes of each alternative and to select the most desirable one.

Ease in selecting the most desirable alternative and the quality of the selection improve significantly with practice. This is one reason that experience is a prerequisite for new management consultants.

Communications Ability.   Consultants need an ability to use both written and spoken words to convey ideas. An accurate interchange of feelings, thoughts, opinions, and information between individuals is a critical consulting skill. Open and active listening and responding, coupled with candidness and respect for the client, are essential.

All transmitted communications, overt and covert as well as verbal and nonverbal, must be recognized. Failure results from the lack of ability to communicate effectively. For most people, however, the ability to communicate easily and effectively is not a natural gift. It must be learned through study, hard work, and practice.

Psychological Maturity.   People are considered mature when they are able to live life—with its frustrations, adversities, and inequities— and to act with poise and control in all situations, regardless of frustrations. They are able to refrain from any display of adverse reactions, to view situations in perspective, and to take needed action on a calm and controlled basis without being diverted from a sound, logical, and ethical course by outside pressure.

Maturity is judged more by reactions to people than to things. People are considered mature when they are capable of forgetting themselves for someone else. Psychologically mature people deal easily with others who would be considered equals, supervisors, or inferiors. They recognize that authority is necessary and accept it in all the limits of its power, realizing that the fragile human instrument chosen to exercise the authority does not automatically become invested with natural qualities not possessed before. Mature people see others as they are, judge situations as they are, and remain in contact with objective reality even when their emotions are aroused.

Psychologically mature people integrate their emotions into their personalities, keeping emotions firmly under the control of reason and in contact with objective values. They have a correct assessment of their own abilities and are not thrown into total confusion by failure or by recognition of some moral, physical, or psychological defect within themselves.

Compatible Lifestyle

The inherent attributes and the developed attributes discussed above are essential for achieving success as a consultant. In order to "make it" in consulting, however, you need to enjoy the work and lifestyle. Travel, job pressures, and concurrent projects are only a few constraints on a consultant's lifestyle. In order to stay with consulting, you need to enjoy these things.

Travel. The amount of travel varies extensively among consultants. Some spend as little as 10 percent of their time away from home; others, as much as 100 percent. The average is generally between 20 percent and 60 percent. The benefit of travel is that you have the opportunity to see much of this country and perhaps several foreign countries. A disadvantage is that you lose touch with family and friends by being away so much. The inside of one hotel, airplane, factory, or office building is about the same as any other.

Family relationships are subject to strain when the consultant spends little time at home. Strains are particularly likely when the married consultant cannot leave the problems of work at work and convert the few hours at home into times of contentment and enjoyment.

Irregular Living Conditions. Most consultants have some flexibility in determining their working hours. The typical consultant needs only to fit his or her schedule to the client's schedule and complete the required work on time. However, the days may be long. When a deadline for an engagement is approaching, a day of 12 to 16 hours is not uncommon. When an engagement is away from home, the consultant must, in addition, live out of a suitcase, sleep in a strange bed, and try to maintain a well-balanced diet while eating on the run.

Concurrent Projects.   Consulting work is frequently "feast" or "famine." When times are bad, few if any jobs are available. When times are good, the consultant may have several jobs in process concurrently and be forced to move from one job to the next in order to keep all under way and all clients satisfied. Many consultants prefer to complete one job before moving to the next and thus find this situation frustrating.

Job Pressures.   A client with a problem needs a solution now. The consultant who delivers the best product in the shortest period of time is the one who is most successful. Therefore, industry pressures to work efficiently—and client pressures to solve problems quickly—mean that the consultant constantly works under pressure. The amount of pressure may vary, but it is always there.

Staff Capacity.   From the client's point of view, a consultant's work is a staff function. Functioning in a staff capacity, the consultant does not make final decisions. He or she is limited to identifying problems, collecting and analyzing data, and recommending solutions. The decision-making function is a line function that rests with the client. The consultant must, therefore, enjoy functioning in a staff capacity if he or she is to have job satisfaction.

People.   Most of the work performed by a consultant is people-oriented. Interviews, observations, document collection, training, and other activities involve people. Because of the potential changes that may occur in their work environments, many of the people with whom a consultant interacts will feel hostile toward the consultant. Thus, the consultant should enjoy working with people, so that he or she is able to tolerate such negative or hostile situations.

Problem Solving.   Many people find problems depressing and frustrating; they avoid becoming involved at any cost. Consultants must be just the opposite. Their basic work is solving problems, and they must enjoy working with problems to be successful.

Negotiation.   Consulting situations are often reduced to either-or or win-lose strategies. Clients believe that in order to satisfy their wants (win), others must suffer (lose). This leads them to seek a stronger offense to overwhelm any resistance. A consultant must feel comfortable working in this environment. The consultant can frequently help the client by broadening the problem–solution perspective and by avoiding the win-lose mentality. This process requires negotiation away from win-lose toward win-win strategies. Knowing when to negotiate and being effective at it are important consulting skills.

Codes of Ethics for Management Consulting

Every profession has a standard of professional conduct and practice. Professional codes of ethics represent a unified effort to reduce to writing some of the more obvious, definable, practicable, and enforceable rules of conduct. Codes of conduct for management consultants represent the attitudes, principles, and approaches that have been found to contribute most to success and that make for equitable and satisfactory client relationships.

A professional code of ethics serves at least three useful functions. First, and perhaps most important, it has an educational effect by providing members of the profession with guides to the kind of ethical behavior that historical experience has found to attract and justify the confidence of the public. Second, it narrows the area in which a person has to struggle with doubts. Third, it serves as a visible, impersonal standard that professional men and women can use to support their decisions.

Both the client and the consultant benefit from a code of ethics. The client is generally untrained in the field for which consulting services are needed. Frequently, because of the nature of the problem, the client has no choice of whether or not to hire a consultant. Just as a person who is sick must employ a doctor, a firm that is "sick" must employ the services of a consultant. Needing consulting services, and being unable to evaluate those services independently, the client relies on the code of ethics to ensure fair business dealing.

Consultants also benefit from a code of ethics. In return for the faith that the public places in them, they accept certain obligations to behave in ways that are beneficial to the public. By following the code, the consultant remains relatively free from control, supervision, and evaluation by governing bodies. The self-discipline and voluntary assumption of the obligations specified in the code of ethics place consultants above and beyond the requirements of the law.

AICPA Code of Ethics

CPA firms are among the largest consulting organizations in the world, and for them the code of ethics of the American Institute of Certified Public Accountants (AICPA) is relevant. Within the AICPA there is a Management Advisory Services Executive Committee that publishes "Statements on Standards for Consulting Services." These standards must be followed by all AICPA members who represent themselves as CPAs and who provide consulting services.

The AICPA code of ethics has two parts: principles and rules. The principles contain six articles upon which the rules are based. These six principles are presented in Figure 4-1.

1. **Responsibility:** In carrying out their responsibilities as professionals, members should exercise sensitive professional and moral judgments in all their activities.
2. **Public Interest:** Members should accept the obligation to act in a way that will serve the public interest, honor the public trust, and demonstrate commitment to professionalism.
3. **Integrity:** To maintain and broaden public confidence, members should perform all professional responsibilities with the highest sense of integrity.
4. **Objectivity and Independence:** A member should maintain objectivity and be free of conflicts of interest in discharging professional responsibilities. A member in public practice should be independent in fact and appearance when providing auditing and other attestation services.
5. **Due Care:** A member should observe the profession's technical and ethical standards, strive continually to improve competence and the quality of services, and discharge professional responsibility to the best of the member's ability.
6. **Scope and Nature of Services:** A member in public practice should observe the principles of the Code of Professional Conduct in determining the scope and nature of services to be provided.

Figure 4-1 AICPA code of ethics principles.

Most of the AICPA code of ethics is rule-based, and there are many interpretations and case rulings for each rule. The rules that relate to management consulting are briefly summarized in Figure 4-2.

CCO, IMC, and ACME Code of Ethics

There are three other organizations that are important for consultants. Their memberships have worked together to develop one code of ethics acceptable to all three organizations.

- Institute of Management Consultants (IMC) is the primary organization responsible for certifying management consultants.
- Association of Management Consulting Firms (ACME) is the organization to which most major consulting organizations belong (except CPA firms, which are not admitted).
- Council of Consulting Organizations (CCO) is an umbrella organization for IMC and ACME.

Rule 101 *Independence:* A member in public practice shall be independent in the performance of professional services as required by standards promulgated by bodies designated by Council.

Rule 102 *Integrity and Objectivity:* In the performance of any professional engagement, a member shall maintain objectivity and integrity, shall be free of conflicts of interest, and shall not knowingly misrepresent facts or subordinate his or her judgment to others.

Rule 201 *General Standards:* A member shall comply with the following standards and with any interpretation thereof by bodies designated by Council:

Professional competence: Undertake only those professional services that the member or the member's firm can reasonably expect to be completed with professional competence.

Due professional care: Exercise due professional care in the performance of professional services.

Planning and supervision: Adequately plan and supervise the performance of professional services.

Sufficient relevant data: Obtain sufficient relevant data to afford a reasonable basis for conclusions or recommendations in relation to any professional services performed.

Three additional standards are required when performing consulting services.*

Client interest: Serve the client interest by seeking to accomplish the objectives established by the understanding with the client while maintaining integrity and objectivity.

Understanding with client: Establish with the client a written or oral understanding about the responsibilities of the parties and the nature, scope, and limitations of services to be performed, and modify the understanding if circumstances require a significant change during the engagement.

---

*AICPA Management Advisory Services Executive Committee, "Statement on Standards for Consulting Services No. 1," *Definitions and Standards for MAS Practice,* November 1991.

Figure 4-2 AICPA code of ethics rules for management consulting.

Communication with client: Inform the client of (a) conflicts of interest that may occur, (b) significant reservations concerning the scope or benefits of the engagement, and (c) significant engagement findings or events.

Rule 301 *Confidential Client Information:* A member in public practice shall not disclose any confidential client information without the specific consent of the client.

Rule 302 *Contingent Fees:* A member in public practice shall not:

1. Perform for a contingent fee any professional services for, or receive a fee from a client for whom the member or the member's firm performs: (a) an audit or review of a financial statement; or, (b) a compilation of a financial statement when the member expects, or reasonably might expect, that a third party will use the financial statement and the member's compilation report does not disclose a lack of independence; or, (c) an examination of prospective financial information; or,

2. Prepare an original or amended tax return or claim for a tax refund for a contingent fee for any client.

Rule 501 *Acts Discreditable:* A member shall not commit an act discreditable to the profession.

Rule 502 *Advertising and Other Forms of Solicitation:* A member in public practice shall not seek to obtain clients by advertising or other forms of solicitation in a manner that is false, misleading, or deceptive. Solicitation by use of coercion, overreaching, or harassing conduct is prohibited.

Rule 505 A member may practice public accounting only in a form of organization permitted by state law or regulation whose characteristics conform to resolutions of Council.

Figure 4-2 (*Continued*)

The code of ethics for these organizations has four sections dealing with clients, engagements, fees, and the profession. This code, presented in Figure 4-3, has a more positive tone than the AICPA statements and is not burdened with interpretations and case rulings.

Professionalism requires all individuals who represent themselves as management consultants to abide by the standards contained in these codes of ethics regardless of whether they belong to any of the above organizations.

Clients

1. We will serve our clients with integrity, competence, and objectivity.
2. We will keep client information and records of client engagements confidential and will use proprietary client information only with the client's permission.
3. We will not take advantage of confidential client information for ourselves or our firms.
4. We will not allow conflicts of interest which provide a competitive advantage to one client through our use of confidential information from another client who is a direct competitor without that competitor's permission.

Engagements

5. We will accept only engagements for which we are qualified by our experience and competence.
6. We will assign staff to client engagements in accordance with their experience, knowledge, and expertise.
7. We will immediately acknowledge any influence on our objectivity to our clients and will offer to withdraw from a consulting engagement when our objectivity or integrity may be impaired.

Fees

8. We will agree independently and in advance on the basis for our fees and expenses and will charge fees and expenses that are reasonable, legitimate, and commensurate with the services we deliver and the responsibility we accept.
9. We will disclose to our clients in advance any fees or commissions that we will receive for equipment, supplies, or services we recommend to our clients.

Profession

10. We will respect the intellectual property rights of our clients, other consulting firms, and sole practitioners and will not use proprietary information or methodologies without permission.
11. We will not advertise our services in a deceptive manner and will not misrepresent the consulting profession, consulting firms, or sole practitioners.
12. We will report violations of the Code of Ethics.

Figure 4-3   Code of Ethics—CCO, ACME, and IMC.

Independence, Integrity, and Objectivity

Independence, as defined by the AICPA, is relevant only in the performance of attestation services—namely, auditing and reviewing financial statements. However, integrity and objectivity standards apply to all services.

Integrity requires a consultant to be, among other things, honest and candid within the constraints of client confidentiality. Services and the public trust should not be subordinated to personal gain and advantage. Integrity can accommodate an inadvertent error and an honest difference of opinion; it cannot accommodate deceit or subordination of principle.

Objectivity is a state of mind, a quality that lends value to a consultant's services. It is a distinguishing feature of the profession. The principle of objectivity imposes the obligation to be impartial, intellectually honest, and free of conflicts of interest.

A conflict of interest may occur if a consultant performs a professional service for a client or employer and the consultant has a significant relationship with another person, entity, product, or service that could be viewed as impairing the consultant's objectivity. Any such relationship must be disclosed to, and consent must be obtained from, the client, employer, or other appropriate party before the service is performed.

To illustrate this conflict, consultants who own a financial interest in a service bureau cannot be considered objective enough to review a client's computer processing needs and recommend a service bureau to handle them. The vested interest in their own organization creates a conflict that prevents them from being impartial and intellectually honest. The same applies to computer software or other products in which the consultant may have a proprietary interest.

Fees and Profitability

Remuneration is a primary reason for entering the consulting profession. Many people are attracted to management consulting because of the perceived opportunities to earn substantial salaries or profits.

The profit motive and the ethics motive must be integrated in management consulting. An adequate profit is essential for good consulting. Consultants who have been poorly paid and are hungry for work may be tempted to accept jobs for which they are only marginally qualified. As a result, the work is not performed efficiently and the consultant gets a poor return on the time invested. Also, the result is generally less than optimal so that the client is poorly served. Only by having an adequate income can the consultant afford to spend the time necessary to remain current, and to develop new skills and new approaches to serve clients better. As a result of these activities, clients will be more profitable, services will be more valued, and higher fees will be appropriate. This cycle continues, benefiting both the client and the consultant.

Conclusion

Every management consultant benefits from the published codes of ethics. The solid reputation now enjoyed by the management consulting profession has developed over the years as a result of conformance to these concepts and principles. Each consultant has a responsibility to himself or herself, and to the profession, to live by these codes of ethics and to encourage others to do the same. Enforcement of the codes is everyone's responsibility.

Exercise and Cases

Exercise—Evaluation of Professional Attributes

The following exercise is intended to help you evaluate your personal attributes relative to those that are commonly possessed by successful consultants. For each statement, indicate how you feel on a scale of 1 to 5, where 1 represents "strongly disagree" and 5 represents "strongly agree." Instructions for scoring are given in the next paragraph.

Scoring. Add your responses to the even-numbered questions, subtract the sum from 60, and add the result to the total of your responses to the odd-numbered questions. Possible scores range from 20 to 100. Scores between 85 and 100 indicate high potential for success in the consulting profession. Scores between 60 and 85 are considered marginal; improvement or change needs to be made in some personal attributes in order to be a successful consultant. Scores below 60 indicate a poor fit with management consulting.

Ethics Cases

Several cases dealing with ethical issues are described below. A suggested solution to each case is provided at the end of this chapter.

Case 4.1. While working on an engagement for Forecast Inc. you copied three software packages onto the hard drive of your personal computer. Forecast Inc. had acquired one copy of each package for use on its computer and allowed you to copy it onto your computer to prevent the firm's computer from being tied up while you were working on the engagement. The software packages are Project Workbench for proj-

Strongly disagree		Neutral		Strongly agree		
1	2	3	4	5	**1.**	My home life as a child was full of love and affection from parents and brothers and sisters.
1	2	3	4	5	**2.**	Physically and mentally, I feel terrible on less than 7½ hours sleep per night.
1	2	3	4	5	**3.**	My IQ and GMAT scores (or similiar test scores) would easily qualify me for admittance to a graduate program at a quality university.
1	2	3	4	5	**4.**	I have a hard time understanding why other people feel the way they do.
1	2	3	4	5	**5.**	I work effectively under job-related pressure.
1	2	3	4	5	**6.**	Frequently, I have trouble explaining difficult concepts to other people.
1	2	3	4	5	**7.**	I would rather provide information and alternative courses of action to other people, and let them make the decisions, than make the decisions myself.
1	2	3	4	5	**8.**	It takes me longer than most people to establish my credibility and gain confidence and respect from others.
1	2	3	4	5	**9.**	I am totally honest and ethical in dealings with my fellow humans.
1	2	3	4	5	**10.**	I dislike and avoid conflict with other people, even when I am confident I am right.
1	2	3	4	5	**11.**	I enjoy solving a complex problem even if it requires me to dig through mounds of data.
1	2	3	4	5	**12.**	I dislike travel and an irregular work schedule.
1	2	3	4	5	**13.**	My career path to this point has always been well defined, with little time and energy wasted in abandoned objectives.
1	2	3	4	5	**14.**	I frequently have difficulty in interacting with my boss or supervisor.
1	2	3	4	5	**15.**	I enjoy writing, and my writing style is both clear and concise.
1	2	3	4	5	**16.**	It is difficult for me to distinguish between relevant and irrelevant facts when I am faced with a problem situation.
1	2	3	4	5	**17.**	I frequently think about becoming rich and famous and imagine myself accomplishing things that would make other people say I am a great person.
1	2	3	4	5	**18.**	I am opinionated and don't like to be bothered with other people's prejudices or views on a situation.
1	2	3	4	5	**19.**	I am the kind of person other people like to be around.
1	2	3	4	5	**20.**	My family life is disrupted when I am traveling in connection with work or when I come home from work late at night.

ect scheduling, SPSS for statistical analysis, and BACHMAN for data modeling. Your engagement lasted long enough for you to become proficient in using all three packages without the aid of documentation. Since completing the engagement, you have had the opportunity to use these software packages on other engagements. Was it ethical for you to copy the software onto your personal computer? Is it ethical to use the software on other client engagements?

Case 4.2. While working on the engagement for Forecast Inc., you met a Forecast employee who has some computer-processing skills that you need very badly within your consulting organization. In fact, they are skills that would be very helpful in completing the Forecast project and another project that you are running simultaneously. How do you approach the person about leaving Forecast and joining your firm?

Case 4.3. Your firm just completed a market survey for Wilco Research for $50,000. You obtained the project several months ago while attending your 30-year high school class reunion. As you were bringing an old classmate up to date on your activities over the intervening years, she expressed surprise about your management consulting practice but pleased that you specialized in marketing. She needed a market survey completed for her firm and already had bids for the project at $57,000 and $60,000. She added that you could have the Wilco contract for anything less than $55,000. Because you had just completed a similar survey for another company and had much of the data from that study available, you were able to complete the project in record time and at a cost (including your own time at normal billing rates) of only $20,000. What are the ethical issues involved in this situation? Is it right to use the data obtained from the other study? Is the $50,000 fee ethical?

Case 4.4. At the end of your annual performance evaluation of a female consultant who works for your firm, you ask, "Is there anything else about your job that you want to discuss?" After a long pause, she tells you about the following three situations that occurred during the past year:

1. A fellow consultant repeatedly asked her to date him and wrote sexually explicit love letters to her. However, none of this occurred at work.
2. While she was on a job with another consultant, he made demeaning comments about a client's pregnancy and her own imminent menstrual period.
3. Her supervisor (not you) frequently asked her to do his filing and to obtain coffee for him.

Are there ethical issues involved in filing her performance report?

Case 4.5.   You serve as both a director and a consultant for a medium-sized, publicly held company. In reviewing your plans for the next few months, you go through the following thought process:

> As a director I'm supposed to represent the stockholders, but I wouldn't be here unless our firm had been doing a lot of good consulting work for management. I know, too, that we've got a couple of darn good consultants coming off a long assignment next month, and so far there's no new assignment for them. The president has been thinking about applying some sophisticated planning techniques to replace the current, old-fashioned forecasts. Now might be the time to do it. Frankly, I don't think a company this size has to get so fancy, but if the president wants it, and considers keeping those two good staffers at full billing…I think I'd better have Charlie bring it up at the next director's meeting. I'll refrain from voting, so there should be no question….

Discuss the ethics of your position and thought process as consultant-director.

Case 4.6.   Your firm has been invited to perform a feasibility study on a new wing for the local hospital. Your firm has an outstanding reputation in this area, and the hospital feels that a positive recommendation from your firm would help it sell the bonds to provide the needed financing. As you discuss the engagement with the client, you become aware that the decision has already been made to construct the new wing and that your study is being pursued merely as an attempt to help sell the bonds. As you contemplate the study, you conclude there is only a 50 percent chance that the results will show the expansion to be economically desirable. However, a negative outcome would completely undermine any attempts to sell the bonds. The job is yours if you want it, and it would be a very profitable contract. What should you do?

Case 4.7.   A manufacturer engaged your firm to study top management. As the study neared completion, the president instructed you as to what she expected the recommendations and findings to be and directed you to come to this conclusion. What should your response be?

Case 4.8.   As an internal consultant, you were asked to evaluate and recommend reorganization of top management. From the beginning it was apparent that you were in "over your head," and you wished the job had been assigned to an external management consultant. Now you're on the brink of recommending some changes that literally involve the guy who signs your paycheck. He keeps telling you to pull no punches in your report, but it's hard to believe he could be that objective. What should you do?

Case 4.9. You are the sole owner of your own management consulting practice and have several consultants who work for you on a full-time basis. Your firm's specialty is marketing, and you have developed an outstanding reputation for your ability to develop successful marketing programs. One of the major tobacco manufacturers has recently offered you a very profitable consulting contract to develop a marketing program for the southeastern portion of the United States. You do not smoke, and you feel it is wrong for other people to smoke. Is it ethical for you to accept the engagement, feeling as you do?

Solutions to Ethics Cases

Case 4.1. Most software packages are acquired for use on only one computer. Site licenses may be purchased to allow multiple computers to use the same software package, but that does not seem to be the case for Forecast Inc. Therefore, it is wrong to copy the software onto your personal computer, and it is wrong to continue to use the software without acquiring your own copy.

Case 4.2. It is unethical for you to solicit a client's employee for employment with your firm. Even if you were approached by the employee for a job with your firm, you could not immediately hire him or her. Before you discuss employment possibilities, the employee needs to quit his or her current job and apply for a job with your firm, or to obtain permission from the current employer to apply for a position with your firm.

Case 4.3. There are at least three ethical issues here: (1) bidding on a project with information that other bidders do not have, (2) using data obtained for another client's project, and (3) accepting $50,000 for the engagement. Knowledge of your competitor's bids provided your firm with inside information not available to the others and thus gave you an unfair advantage. Using the data from the prior study may or may not be ethical, depending on the nature of the engagement, the type of data, and whether the prior study was for a competitor. People may not agree concerning the ethics of the $50,000 fee. The difference between the fee based on normal billing rates ($20,000) and the amount charged ($50,000) is so large that it seems unfair. If both Wilco and the prior client knew all the facts of the situation, they would probably not think that it was handled ethically.

Case 4.4. The ethical issue is one of sexual harassment, which is considered an act discreditable to the profession. The key in determining whether something constitutes sexual harassment is if it creates an offensive working environment. Clearly, comment 2 creates an offensive working environment for most women and would be considered sexual harassment. Even though comment 1 reports offensive activity off the job, some courts have held that it is still sexual harassment because of its carryover effect in the working environment. In comment 3, performing filing can be considered job-related; however, the coffee issue shows poor taste on the part of the supervisor.

Case 4.5. You are not in a good position from an ethical point of view. Your position as director provides you with a significant influence over the direction of the company. As such, you have a responsibility to do what is best for the company. Your responsibility to the consulting firm is to secure employment to keep your people busy. By being both director and consultant for the same company, you are in a position that creates a conflict of interest, which is in violation of the code of professional ethics.

Another problem is your planned conduct in the upcoming board meeting. It is not honest and ethical for you to remain silent when you have relevant information on a decision. You have a responsibility to express your feelings about the proposed engagement, even if it means losing the engagement.

The solution here is to resign from the board of directors and become an adviser to the president. You should point out how you feel about the installation of the sophisticated system at this time. An objective decision can then be made by the board on the basis of all the available facts.

Case 4.6. Professional ethics requires that you accept only those engagements which you feel will be beneficial to the client. Clearly, if the results of the study are favorable, the client will benefit. There is only a 50 percent chance, however, that a positive outcome will result. The question, therefore, is whether a 50 percent chance of benefit is sufficient to pursue the study. Many consultants would answer yes to this question and accept the engagement because of the potential profit.

The consultant who actually faced this situation declined the engagement and suggested that the client use the money set aside for the feasibility study to employ an advertising firm to help sell the bonds. This decision was justified by what the consultant thought was the client's best interest.

Case 4.7. Ethical conduct requires that you not misrepresent facts and never subordinate judgment to others. Further, you should not serve a client under terms or conditions that might impair objectivity, independence, or integrity, and you should reserve the right to withdraw if conditions develop that interfere with successful conduct of the assignment.

The consultant who actually faced this situation refused to follow the direction of the president, and the president refused to pay the consultant's fee. The president wanted to use the consultant's report as a means for firing a vice president. Ultimately, the fee was settled and no report was issued.

Case 4.8. Professional ethics require honesty, integrity, and placing the interests of the client or prospective client ahead of personal interests. The fact that you are an internal consultant, as opposed to an external consultant, makes no difference.

The internal consultant who actually faced this situation wrote the report on the basis of the available facts and was discharged.

Case 4.9. An ethical issue arises here because any solution involves the future of the consultant's personal doctrine and nonprofessional associations as well as the effectiveness and integrity of the consultation process in which the consultant is about to engage. The principles involved in this case are not uncommon.

Although accepting such engagements would not be in violation of the code of ethics, acceptance would be ethical only if the consultant's relationship with the client firm were completely divorced from the consultant's personal doctrine and the client was made aware of the consultant's values. These circumstances are not likely, and the consultant would be justified in declining such an engagement because of a conflict of norms.

5

Effective Communications Skills

Steven P. Golen

School of Accountancy
Arizona State University
Tempe, Arizona

An important attribute you must possess as a management consultant is the ability to communicate effectively. No matter how much technical expertise you possess, if you cannot communicate messages effectively, clients will have difficulty understanding, interpreting, and relating to those messages. Not only does misunderstanding frustrate the client, but the client will also begin to question your credibility as a consultant. To be an effective communicator, therefore, you must develop written and oral communications skills.

The purposes of this chapter are to discuss the principles behind effective communication of information, to identify and offer solutions to deal with or overcome barriers to effective communication, and to review some guidelines and problems of written communications. The chapter also will provide some suggestions for conducting interviews, leading problem-solving conferences, and making oral presentations.

Characteristics of the Communications Process

Regardless of the types of communications that a management consultant must undertake, each type follows a predetermined process. That is, each communication flows from one individual to one or more individuals and is thus a two-way process. This physical process takes place both when a message is sent and when one is received. More specifically, however, the communications process involves more than just sending and receiving. It contains certain characteristics that are common to any oral or written communications situation. These characteristics are (1) information source, (2) encoder, (3) transmitter, (4) channel, (5) receiver, (6) decoder, and (7) feedback.

The information source is a speaker or writer who develops an idea or observes some fact, object, or experience and wishes to convey this idea or experience to another individual. The idea or experience is encoded or translated into a message and transmitted or sent through a channel or medium, such as a spoken or written word. The message is received by the listener or reader and decoded or interpreted. On the basis of the interpretation, meaning is given to the message and the receiver takes action. The process is completed when the listener or reader provides feedback to the speaker or writer. A model of this communications process is presented in Figure 5-1.

This model can be applied to a consulting communications situation. For example, Joe Thompson, a management consultant, has been hired by a local bank to determine the parameters to be included in a request for proposal (RFP) for a new computer system. After reviewing the current system and talking to the bank officers involved with this project, he formulates in his mind the requirements that should be included in the RFP. Joe translates these requirements into a message that he places in a letter.

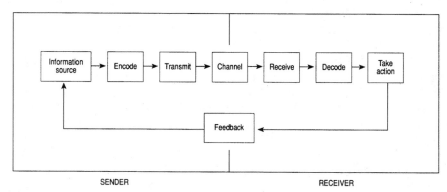

Figure 5-1   The communications process.

The letter is sent to Sandy Bell, the executive vice president of operations. Sandy receives the letter and interprets the message sent by Joe. She decides that the requirements Joe suggested for inclusion in the RFP are what the bank was seeking in a new system. Sandy instructs her assistant to prepare a formal RFP that includes Joe's requirements and to send it to the various vendors. Sandy calls Joe; she tells him that she agrees with his analysis and thanks him for the work he undertook for the bank.

Any communications situation will involve this process. Whether the communication consists of a letter, a report, or even a telephone conversation, the process is the same. The only difference is the time factor involved. A letter or report will take more time to travel through the channel and to complete the process than a telephone call or face-to-face conversation.

Barriers to the Communications Process

An assumption that may be drawn from the model in Figure 5-1 and the example above is that there has been a free flow of information from the sender to the receiver. This assumption is not always realistic, however, since problems occur that inhibit or impede the free flow of information from the sender to the receiver. When such problems occur, message formulation and transmission—as well as message understanding and interpretation—can be affected. These problems are often described as barriers to effective communication. Figure 5-2 shows the points at which barriers may occur in the communications process.

An important point to remember is that communications barriers may develop within the sender, within the receiver, between the sender and

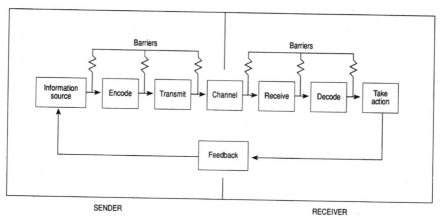

Figure 5-2   Barriers to the communications process.

receiver, or in situations external to both. In other words, these barriers can be classified as intrapersonal, interpersonal, or organizational.

- Intrapersonal barriers arise within the sender or receiver. For example, the user or receiver of a consultant's report may lack adequate knowledge of systems design to understand the report.

- Interpersonal barriers occur because of the interaction between sender and receiver. An example is the hostile attitude of a client's employee toward the consultant, arising from the possibility that the employee's job will be changed as a result of the consultant's recommendations.

- Organizational barriers develop as a result of the communications environment. For example, a barrier may occur when a relatively new consultant meets with a corporate president. The status or position differences between the two may have an impact on the communications exchange.

Barriers Common to Consultants

Before consultants can offer solutions to problems, they need to identify the specific problems. Problem identification also presents potential communications barriers. Consultants need to be aware of the specific types of barriers that may arise in their position before they can deal with or perhaps eliminate them. Diagnostic ability is extremely important, because it allows consultants to understand the circumstances surrounding the communications situation and the pitfalls that may affect it.

Figure 5-3 lists twenty-two barriers that may occur in a consulting situation. Each barrier is discussed below, with suggestions for improving the communications situation. Many of these barriers can arise collectively; in other words, two or three barriers may cluster together and occur at the same time. When one of the barriers is eliminated, however, the others are usually eliminated as well or dealt with more easily.

Know-It-All Attitude

In any business situation, you are likely to encounter an individual who is a know-it-all. Anything you say will probably be rejected by the know-it-all. This individual always perceives things in the light of his or her own interests; to reason with this individual is difficult, if not impossible, when the discussion goes contrary to his or her way of thinking. You must not try to change this individual's attitude, since it may be incapable of change. Instead, you should approach the know-it-all from his or her own perspective. Try to develop a cooperative and supportive climate. Build

1.	Know-it-all attitude	12.	Hostile attitude
2.	Inability to understand technical language	13.	Lack of feedback
3.	Inadequate background or knowledge	14.	Inappropriate physical appearance
4.	Poor organization of ideas	15.	Differences in status or position
5.	Differences in perception	16.	Information overload
6.	Prejudice or bias	17.	Lack of trust
7.	Personality conflicts	18.	Fear of distortion or omission of information
8.	Tendency not to listen	19.	Too many gatekeepers
9.	Resistance to change	20.	Poor timing of the message
10.	Lack of credibility	21.	Defensiveness
11.	Inability to understand nonverbal communication	22.	Overly competitive attitude

Figure 5-3 Potential barriers to effective communication in a management consulting environment.

on this individual's background and knowledge by reinforcing his or her role in a project. Use well-thought-out and logical reasoning that leads up to a particular action. By no means disagree overtly. Such action will likely dampen any future working relationship with the know-it-all.

Inability to Understand Technical Language

Among the most common barriers you may experience is a client's inability to understand technical language. This barrier does not occur when you deal with a client who is an expert in the field and is very familiar with the jargon. It may arise, however, when you interact with a nonexpert client or some of the client's employees. You should remember to use terms that are familiar to the receiver. Since various levels of understanding exist among receivers, you should exercise care when using words that may be misunderstood.

Learn as much as you can about the receiver. It takes careful audience analysis to determine the receiver's level of understanding. (More will be said about audience analysis in the written and oral communications sections of this chapter.) In addition, technical terms or words may not be the only language that is misunderstood; common words can cause problems as well. For example, the 500 most commonly used words in the English language have an average of 28 separate definitions each. You should remember, therefore, that meanings of words are not in the words themselves but in the minds of the sender and receiver of a message. Seek feedback whenever necessary in order to ensure that the meaning the receiver gives to a word or term is what was intended by the sender.

Inadequate Background or Knowledge

Closely related to the technical language barriers are background or knowledge differences. They deal with different levels of understanding. Audience analysis is essential, especially when you are dealing with clients or client employees who have varied backgrounds and expertise. Remember that no two people are the same. Each individual's background is made up of various experiences, interests, values, and viewpoints that are unique to the individual. The background determines how well an individual will understand or interpret a message. You cannot always expect clients or their employees to have similar backgrounds or the same degree of understanding. Be patient and have empathy for the receiver. Provide additional information for clarification and be prepared to explain things more thoroughly to individuals who need explanation for better understanding.

Poor Organization of Ideas

Poor organization of ideas is a barrier that stems from lack of planning and preparation. Nothing is more irritating to a receiver than a message that lacks coherence and logical reasoning. When a message is poorly organized, it reflects on the sender's ability to develop and structure an idea. The receiver may question this ability and may even lose interest in the intent of the message. Generally, poor organizational skills make the sender appear to ramble without a clear purpose. Thus, the purpose should be defined clearly at the outset. Once the purpose has been established, an outline should be prepared that identifies the main points in a logical arrangement that you wish to cover. This process should be followed whether you are writing a letter or a report or even preparing to make a telephone call.

Differences in Perception

Perceptual differences arise in a communications situation to which an individual brings his or her own frame of reference. Individual frames of reference consist of meanings that people assign to others or to situations. These meanings are based on past experiences and often are related to personal interests. For example, through experience you may favor a particular microcomputer system. This predisposition may become a problem if the client or receiver has a different preference. You must attempt to see the client's point of view and to exercise an empathetic attitude. Recognize that differences will occur and take the time to listen carefully to the client's reasoning before jumping to conclusions.

Prejudice or Bias

Prejudice or bias exists when individuals have a strong opinion about something and a tendency not to change this opinion regardless of what is said. Since such individuals often encounter information that does not support their feeling or position, they establish illogical defense mechanisms. Consequently, the use of logical reasoning with these individuals is counterproductive. You should remember not to denounce overtly the position of an individual with strong prejudices. Take the time to explain things clearly and logically and refrain from trying to influence the individual without first seeking to understand the situation from his or her perspective.

Personality Conflicts

No one will question the importance of having a pleasant personality. A good personality, coupled with the ability and aptitude to complete an engagement, is essential to a successful consultant. What happens when personalities differ or are in conflict? Problems can arise and communication can be affected. Conflict may be triggered because of a first impression or because of the role an individual is playing or the reputation of that individual. It is important to remember that personality differences cannot be changed. You should try to learn as much as possible about the client's personality and modify your behavior accordingly.

Tendency Not to Listen

Of all the communications activities—reading, writing, speaking, and listening—you will probably spend the majority of your communicating time listening. Research indicates that after hearing a speech, the typical individual will forget about 50 percent of the speech by the next day. A few weeks later, that same individual will have forgotten 25 percent more. Thus, ineffective listening can have a considerable impact upon retention. Determine whether you are listening effectively by answering some questions regarding your listening skills. Figure 5-4 contains a list of questions that will provide feedback on your ability to listen effectively.

To improve your listening ability, you should listen attentively, carefully, objectively, and empathetically to the speaker. Be patient and try not to jump to conclusions. Put your emotions aside and concentrate on the message, not on the speaker's mannerisms. Encourage the speaker through actions that show you believe that what the speaker has to say is important. Question the speaker or paraphrase a point for clarification. This action conveys interest on your part. A last point to remember is

QUESTION	YES	NO
1. Do you maintain eye contact while listening?		
2. Do you pay attention to the speaker's feelings as well as to what is being said?		
3. Do you lack interest in the speaker's subject?		
4. Do you often become impatient with the speaker?		
5. Do you overreact to certain language, such as slang or profanity?		
6. Do you often ask questions or paraphrase for clarification?		
7. Do you often daydream or become preoccupied with something else while listening?		
8. Do you concentrate on the speaker's mannerisms?		
9. Do you have tendency to disagree or argue with the speaker?		
10. Do you try to maintain a relaxing and agreeable environment?		
11. Do you often jump to conclusions before the speaker has finished?		
12. Do you often interrupt the speaker with your point of view?		
13. Do you put yourself in the speaker's shoes (i.e., do you empathize)?		
14. Do you often become distracted by noise from office equipment, telephones, or other conversations?		
15. Do you try to relate to and benefit from the speaker's ideas?		

Figure 5-4   Listening-effectiveness questions.

QUESTION	YES	NO
16. Do you have difficulty reading the speaker's nonverbal cues?	_____	_____
17. Do you often listen only for details?	_____	_____
18. Do you often think of another topic because of what the speaker has said?	_____	_____
19. Do you allow your biases and prejudices to hamper your thinking while listening?	_____	_____
20. Do you often become emotional because of what the speaker has said?	_____	_____
21. Do you listen even if the subject is complex or difficult?	_____	_____
22. Do you feel that listening takes too much time?	_____	_____

Figure 5-4 (Continued)

that you cannot listen effectively when you are talking. The role of a consultant is to gather information and seek clarification in identifying problems. What better way is there to accomplish this task than to practice effective listening skills?

Resistance to Change

To maintain a successful business firm, management must adapt continually to meet the varying needs of its customers and employees. However, generating change within individuals, including concerned managers, is generally a difficult task. People have a natural tendency to resist change when it is perceived as a threat to their work, and this tendency can be a barrier to communication. In a consulting situation, resistance to change can affect the client's managers and the employees. You should seek the support of the client and its employees and encourage their input regarding the proposed change. If change is recommended, explain it in a positive manner in order to reduce their anxieties. State clearly why the change is going to be made and how it is going to affect people individually. By being open and by encouraging participation, you will provide a better climate for implementing change.

Lack of Credibility

Credibility, or believability, is necessary to success in the consulting field. When a consultant lacks credibility, problems occur and communication can be affected. How do you establish credibility? The first way is by gaining expertise or competence in the field. Your confidence can be dampened when your ability is in doubt. Credibility can be influenced by reputation and personality. Reputation comes from experience and status, whereas personality can be developed. Effective consultants are likable; they get along well with people. The consultant's degree of credibility can affect the receiver's attitude or belief regarding the information conveyed in a message.

Inability to Understand
Nonverbal Communication

As a consultant, you need to remember that there are other means of message communication besides the written or spoken word. The old adage that actions speak louder than words is important in the consulting environment. If you say one thing and do something else, your words and actions are in conflict and communication can be misinterpreted. Individuals observe and pay attention to your actions, especially when such actions contradict what is said.

You should be aware of various nonverbal clues that, if read properly, will aid in message understanding and interpretation. Being aware of an individual's facial expressions, posture, gestures, tone of voice, eye contact, and even silence can help you read meaning into a message. For example, you explain a particular procedure to a client and then ask the client whether he or she understands. The client shakes his or her head yes, but at the same time looks puzzled. Does the client really understand the procedure? Upon sensing this confusion, you should probe with specific questions in order to determine if the procedure is really understood.

Hostile Attitude

Clients' employees often exhibit hostility toward consultants. Bad experience with a consultant in the past could have created these hostile feelings. Or an individual may have hostile feelings toward the consultant because he or she perceives a threat: You (as consultant) may suggest changes to the current work environment. Regardless of the reason, a hostile attitude is difficult to change. Try to approach the situation in a friendly and self-controlled manner. Do not get upset, because this reaction will only confirm the individual's suspicions and create even more hostile feelings. Convey an attitude of caring and support and encourage a cooperative environment.

Lack of Feedback

As illustrated earlier in this chapter, the feedback loop completes the communications process. Effective communication is a two-way street. Whether you are giving instructions, explaining a task, or training an employee, feedback is crucial to understanding a message. Encourage feedback by asking questions that require explanation. Also ask the receiver to repeat or paraphrase what was just presented so that you can determine the extent of understanding. By encouraging feedback, you will create an open and supportive climate.

Inappropriate Physical Appearance

Although sometimes taken for granted, one's physical appearance can affect communication. A well-groomed and well-dressed individual conveys an orderly and organized manner. Wearing the latest styles may not be the way to impress a client. Dress conservatively and wear clothes that convey a professional attitude.

Differences in Status or Position

Status or position differences can affect communication because the person in the inferior role usually becomes intimidated. He or she becomes nervous and reluctant to communicate. Individuals in the inferior role may fear that what they say will have a negative effect on the superior. The individual in the higher-status role should try to create an atmosphere of openness by encouraging others to talk about themselves and their interests freely. If you as consultant have the higher-status role, you should try to reduce the fear of those with lower status and secure their goodwill. Be friendly and cordial. This approach will open the lines of communication.

Information Overload

Any individual has a limit when dealing with information. Exceeding this limit can hamper further communication of information. You should be aware of the climate developed as a result of new job pressures and increased reporting requirements. Try to guide clients and employees by helping them manage their time, set priorities, and delegate work responsibilities to others. Do not approach anyone who for the moment appears to be overloaded with work. An idea may be rejected, no matter how ingenious it is, because it is perceived as requiring even more work for an overloaded individual. Exercise good judgment and timing when confronted with this situation.

Lack of Trust

People tend to develop trust in an individual when the behavior of that individual is predictable and has been reinforced through various experiences. For example, a client who lacks competence to evaluate the consultant's work may have a tendency not to trust the consultant. Or the client may simply distrust consultants in general. In order to avoid this barrier, you have to maintain open communications with your client and establish a rapport that is supportive and sincere in providing the client with beneficial advice at a level that is easy to comprehend.

Fear of Distortion or Omission of Information

If a client and his or her employees perceive the consulting situation as a possible threat to their security, competence, or authority, they may distort or totally omit valuable information necessary to complete the consulting work. They may view the distortion or omission as a way to enhance an understanding with the client's personnel that is nonthreatening and nonintimidating. Always keep the client informed of everything that you are doing and plan to do; at the same time, encourage feedback regarding the possible outcomes and ramifications of the work.

Too Many Gatekeepers

When multiple gatekeepers or transfer stations exist between the consultant and the client, the message is likely to become garbled and even distorted. It is much like the parlor game in which one individual starts with a message and whispers it into the ear of the next individual. The same procedure continues until the last individual in the room gets the message. The likelihood of this final message being exactly like the initial message is rather remote. The reason is that there are just too many variables that enter into the message channel: noise, commotion, lack of attention, and so on. The way to avoid this problem obviously is to remove the gatekeepers and talk directly to the client. This action may not always be possible; therefore, you need to follow up any oral messages with written messages in order to ensure that the content of each message is preserved throughout the transfer process.

Poor Timing of the Message

As a consultant, you need to be very sensitive to the timing of your messages. There are times when a message should not be sent. For example, when a client is in a perceived stressful job or family situation or he or she appears to be in a hurry or his or her mind seems to be elsewhere, it is best to avoid the communication at that point in time. In these types of situations, the client probably cannot comprehend any additional information, and any attempt on your part will be futile. Be aware of the communications climate and the demeanor of the client before you convey your message.

When your client becomes free of these stressful situations, your message will no longer contribute to an overload of information. The client will then be able to give you the proper attention so that your message can be understood and interpreted correctly. Always remember that your message is competing with other external or internal stimuli and that the timing of your message is critical to effective communication. Be succinct and concise and try to complete your message as quickly as you possibly can.

Defensiveness

A client and the client's employees may go on the defensive when they perceive that the consultant is trying to evaluate, judge, control, or manipulate them as individuals. When a consultant arrives at the organization, he or she is perceived as being the expert and is treated accordingly. As a consultant, you have to avoid using this perceived power and recognize the kind of behavior that may exist because of your position. Try not to use your position to intimidate the client or his or her employees. If you put these individuals on the defensive, you will find them not cooperating and possibly avoiding you entirely. Establish a rapport right at the outset and reassure people that you are there to help them with their problems. Be completely open and honest with them as you discuss their concerns, and encourage questions to eliminate any misunderstandings that they may have. Use language that employees understand, and keep them informed of your progress on the project.

Overly Competitive Attitude

Competition is healthy behavior in any organization. However, when competition becomes individualized within the organization and employees compete too much with one another, conflict can arise. This conflict can be detrimental to maintaining a cooperative and productive team orientation. As a consultant, you need to encourage and reinforce an open and cooperative work climate. Providing opportunities for the client's employees to participate and work together will go a long way to help foster an effective exchange of information.

Written Communications

The ability to write effectively is an important skill for a consultant to develop. When the written word is unclear, much time and even money may be wasted. Basic principles of effective writing can be learned; all it takes is discipline and practice. Regardless of whether you are writing a letter or a report, follow these principles:

1. Analyze the audience.
2. Determine the purpose.
3. Organize the message.
4. Use a proper style.

Analyze the Audience

Consultants face a diversity of information requirements from their clients. Consequently, they often deliver information that is not exactly what the clients seek. The reason for this problem is insufficient consideration of the needs and perceptions of the client. You should never lose sight of the receivers (i.e., audience) toward whom the communication should always be directed. One way of analyzing the audience is by answering several questions concerning the receivers' needs:

- Who are the receivers?
- What information do they need?
- When do they need the information?
- Where do they need the information?
- Why do they need the information?
- What are the receivers' educational levels?
- What kind of related experiences have they had?
- What are their attitudes toward the topic?

Gathering information about the audience will help in determining what content and how much detail will be needed. When you are writing to a layperson who may lack sufficient background in the subject, it is wise to include additional information to help clarify and explain some of the topics covered. In addition, define any words or terms that may be unfamiliar to this individual. The best place to define a term is upon first use in the narrative of the message.

Determine the Purpose

Every written communication should have a definite and clear purpose statement describing what the writer intends to accomplish. This purpose statement should be appropriately limited rather than broad. In report writing, one way of limiting a purpose statement is to answer the who, what, when, where, and why of a problem. For example, assume that you were hired to determine whether a new computer system would be feasible for an automotive parts store in Los Angeles. The answers to these questions, together with a statement that can be drawn from the answers, will provide guidance and direction:

Who: Top Quality Automotive Parts

What: A study of a new computer system

When: Within the next year

Where: Los Angeles

Why: To determine the feasibility of implementing a new computer system

Purpose statement: Is it feasible for Top Quality Automotive Parts of Los Angeles to implement a new computer within the next year?

When you are writing a letter or memorandum, you need to determine whether its purpose is to persuade or convince a client of the services a consultant offers, to request routine information, or to enumerate what was agreed to for an engagement. In other words, you need to establish what is (are) the main objective(s) of the message.

Organize the Message

Once the purpose has been identified, you need to structure the message in a logical sequence that will fulfill the purpose. One way to begin giving structure to a message is to identify certain factors, criteria, or characteristics. These factors are an extension of your purpose, and they provide the framework for an outline. This approach is particularly important in report writing.

To illustrate, assume that you are engaged in the review and evaluation of a computerized banking system. After the data collection and analysis phase, you need to prepare a report describing the results of the engagement. The following pattern could be followed in preparing this report:

I. Introduction

    A. Purpose of the project

    B. Scope of the project

    C. Methods of data collection

II. Findings

    A. User satisfaction

    B. Efficient use of computer and people resources

     C. Administrative procedures

III. Conclusions

IV. Recommendations

     A. Management controls

     B. Staff and equipment

     C. Business planning

This pattern or outline could be used first as a writing guide and eventually as paragraph headings in the final report. An important point to remember is that the findings should answer the question posed in the purpose statement for the project. The conclusion and/or recommendations are based on the findings. Organizing a report in this manner will allow readers to follow along logically from the introduction to the recommendations.

The pattern to follow when writing letters or memoranda depends again on the purpose or nature of the correspondence. Three plans—direct, indirect, and persuasive—can be used to cover most correspondence writing.

The *direct plan* is used when you want to communicate favorable news. Examples include a routine request, a favorable response to a request, an order for goods or services, an understanding or a confirmation of the requirements of an engagement, and a goodwill message. When the message is favorable, use the following direct plan:

1. Come right to the point with the main message.

2. Provide supporting facts that explain any details, concerns, or circumstances that deal with the message.

3. Close with a goodwill statement.

An extension of this approach, the justification report, allows you to select a particular course of action and then present your reasons. In other words, you make a recommendation and support it with facts. No alternative solutions are presented in this type of report because its purpose is to introduce the client to the recommendation. The organization of this report basically follows that of a direct plan. If the report is internal, you should format it as a memorandum. If it is external, use a letter format. The following parts could be included in the report:

- Recommendation (what you recommended)

- Primary justification (main reason you made the recommendation)

- Implementation (how to implement it)

- Conclusions (why it should be adopted)

- Justification of conclusions (why the conclusions are proper)

Figure 5-5 provides an example of this justification report.

When desiring to communicate unfavorable news, you use the *indirect plan*. Refusing a request for information or assistance and refusing a claim on goods or services are examples. The following plan should be used when sending an unfavorable message:

1. Open with a neutral or buffer statement that centers on something positive.
2. Give reasons for the refusal.
3. Refuse.
4. Suggest an alternative or substitute if possible.
5. Close with a goodwill statement.

If you need to persuade or convince someone about selling goods, services, or ideas, use a *persuasive plan*. The persuasive plan is as follows, and a letter example illustrating the plan is shown in Figure 5-6.

1. Open with an attention-getting statement.
2. Create interest in the subject.
3. Develop a desire in the subject.
4. Close with an action request.

The proposal, though usually placed in a letter format, is a persuasive report that essentially identifies problems that need to be solved and suggests ways to solve them. Here is a possible format that can be used:

- Problem definition
- Purpose of the project
- Scope of the project
- Role of the firm and client
- Benefits of the engagement
- Approach to carrying out the engagement
- Interim reporting requirements (status reports)
- Personnel
- Fees
- Time schedule

Because each engagement is unique, proposals will vary with respect to the number of items included and the order of their presentation. However, the above format should provide you with a guide for preparing proposals. The proposal process is described in detail in Chapter 14.

Bell Associates
1245 Lemon Street
Louisville, Kentucky 42905

July 17, 1995

Ms. Sandra Thompson, President
L&B International, Inc.
12 Stallcourt Drive
Louisville, Kentucky 42910
Dear Ms. Thompson:

Subject: Using Best Financial Planning Models to Develop Financial
Models

RECOMMENDATION

To improve the quality of your managers' decision making and alleviate
the workload of your Information Center, I recommend you purchase
Best Financial Planning Models (BFPM) computer software package.

PRIMARY JUSTIFICATION

Using the Best Financial Planning Models software package to develop financial models will significantly improve the quality and timeliness of planning decisions. Because the managers will develop their
own models with minimal help from the Information Center, the
Information Center personnel will have more time to devote to other
activities. In other words, using the package should increase your
overall competitiveness and profitability.

I estimate that the cost of the software package and the training cost of
your managers would be recovered within 1 year. There would be no

Figure 5-5   Example of a justification report.

additional cost for computer equipment because your current computer system has sufficient capabilities. I believe the benefits of the package will outweigh both its cost and training expenditures. Please note that if you are interested in this recommendation, Ms. Thompson, I will prepare a detailed estimate of both costs and savings.

IMPLEMENTATION

After acquiring the software package, your Information Center personnel can install the software in your computer system with the assistance of the software vendor. Furthermore, the vendor will provide training for your managers on how to use the package. Operational manuals and an interactive on-line help feature will be available to your managers whenever they need help in developing their financial models.

CONCLUSIONS

The following are specific advantages for using BFPM to develop financial models:

1. The model is expressed in natural language (i.e., English words and phrases).
2. Users can develop their own models even without any programming knowledge.
3. Time required for making decisions will be significantly reduced.
4. Managers can perform more in-depth analyses.

JUSTIFICATION OF CONCLUSIONS

The following reasons led me to recommend using BFPM to develop financial models:

1. Managers do not like programming because it requires learning a new language and using many special symbols that they are not familiar with. One distinctive feature of BFPM is its English-like modeling language. Managers will feel more comfortable using the package because of its language familiarity.

Figure 5-5   (Continued)

2. BFPM is very easy to learn even for managers who have absolutely no computer background. Unlike other programming languages such as Pascal and Basic, which require specifying the procedures in the programs, BFPM allows managers to describe the problems (i.e., what needs to be done) instead of specifying program procedures.

3. In the past, it usually took several days or even weeks for your programming specialists to develop a model for your managers because the managers had to communicate with the specialists regarding the details of the model that the managers needed. However, with the availability of BFPM, managers can develop their own models without programming specialists' assistance, except for occasional help.

4. To make good decisions, in-depth analysis is necessary. BFPM has built-in sophisticated data analysis techniques—what-if analysis, goal seeking, simulation, and more. By conducting different analyses, your managers can understand the relationships among the variables of the model and the impact of any change among the variables more thoroughly. Therefore, the managers can make more informed and better decisions.

As you can see from my report, I believe this package will be an effective resource for your company. Should you have any questions regarding any aspect of this recommendation, Ms. Thompson, please give me a call at 555-4391.

Sincerely,

Brad Williams, Manager
Management Consulting

Figure 5-5   *(Continued)*

Use a Proper Style

A suitable style for business writing employs short and simple words and sentences of varying lengths (with an average length of 20 words or less). The overall tone should be informal, though overused expressions should be avoided. In other words, you should write as you would converse, using the first- and second-person pronouns and easy-to-understand words. Most business situations do not require a style as formal as that employed in this handbook.

Thompson & Thompson
134 Main Street
Buffalo, NY 14207

March 15, 1995

Mr. Joe Williams
Williams and Smith, P.C.
65 Court Street
Buffalo, NY 14205

Dear Joe:

With the advent of the microcomputer, privately held businesses have access to computer capability unavailable a few years ago. Implementing a business computer can improve productivity and help a company address current challenges, such as competition, cash flow, government reporting requirements, and the information explosion. Companies have increasingly enhanced their effectiveness by implementing computerized accounting and operational business systems.

Small business computers today are referred to as "microcomputers," "minicomputers," "personal computers," and "small business systems." The distinction among them is very blurred and there are a host of vendors offering a vast array of hardware and software products. Some of these vendors offer a genuine contribution to the industry, and others simply come into existence only to disappear a few years later. For the potential computer system buyer, the end result can be confusion.

The process of acquiring and implementing an effective business computer system does not have to be a traumatic experience. By

Figure 5-6   Example of a persuasive letter.

employing a systematic and methodical approach to the evaluation, selection, and implementation of computer hardware and software, significant problems can be avoided. Thompson & Thompson has developed tools and techniques that can be of assistance when you implement a new or additional business system. I believe we are one of Buffalo's leaders in this area.

Currently, I am director of the management consulting department for Thompson & Thompson in Buffalo. I have extensive experience designing and implementing computer-based business systems. I was with Strategic Instruments, Inc., a computer services firm, prior to joining Thompson & Thompson. I have conducted workshops for the business community to provide participants with a basic and practical background for using computers in small and medium-sized companies.

I have recently completed projects for a number of Buffalo companies assisting in the evaluation, selection, and implementation of a business computer. The types of companies include manufacturing, distribution, services, construction, health care, and publishing. The approach to a project usually includes:

- Defining information requirements.
- Issuing a request for proposal (RFP) to selected vendors.
- Preparing a comparative analysis.
- Recommending the best alternative.

If you are considering acquiring a business computer or implementing a new or additional business system, I can provide professional advice. An independent, objective viewpoint combined with extensive experience can ensure that you select the right business computer. Please call me at 555-6617 so we can discuss your computer system requirements further.

Sincerely,

Peter Barber, Director
Management Consulting

Figure 5-6   (*Continued*)

One sign of a good writing style is the avoidance of imbalanced construction, wordiness, the passive voice, and nominalization. These problems and suggestions for correcting them are presented below.

Imbalanced Construction.   Thoughts and ideas appearing in consecutive phrases and not in balance with one another are poorly constructed. Ideas and thoughts, and the grammar used to express them, should be constructed in parallel (i.e., in balance with each other). Here are some examples of imbalanced and parallel construction.
Imbalanced construction:

Emphasis in the definition-of-requirements step will be on documentation procedures, looking for enhancements, and an assessment of where automation might be applicable.

Parallel construction:

Emphasis in the definition-of-requirements step will be on documenting procedures, looking for enhancements, and assessing where automation may be applicable.

Imbalanced headings in a report:

   I. System requirements
  II. Vendor proposal
 III. Presentation of final contract

Parallel headings in a report:

   I. System requirements
  II. Vendor proposal
 III. Final contract

Wordiness.   Do not use an abundance of words to express an idea when fewer words could be used without influencing the meaning. Some examples of wordiness and concise alternatives are shown in Table 5-1.

Passive Voice.   Use of passive voice dulls the verb in a sentence and usually relegates the doer of the action to a prepositional phase. For more lively writing use the active voice, in which the doer of the action is the subject of the sentence. Passive voice is not wrong, but its overuse can make your writing less forceful. Here are some examples:

Passive: The procedures were followed by the clients.
Active: The clients followed the procedures.

Table 5-1. Wordy versus Concise Constructions

Wordy	Concise
according to our records	we find
are of the opinion that	believe, think
at this point in time	now
despite the fact that	though
fully cognizant of	aware
in accordance with your request	as you requested
in the amount of	for
in view of the fact that	because, since
inquired as to	asked
pursuant to our agreement	as we agreed
with reference to	about
with respect to	about

Passive: The systems analysis was conducted by our firm.

Active: Our firm conducted the systems analysis.

Nominalization. Nominalization occurs when you change a verb into its noun form. The resulting sentences tend to be wordy and often require the passive voice. Here some examples of nominalization:

Weak: Cancellation of the engagement was effected by the client.

Strong: The client canceled the engagement.

Weak: An investigation of the new system was conducted by the controller.

Strong: The controller investigated the new system.

By avoiding nominalization, you use an active verb form and eliminate excess words. In addition, you might consider using personal pronouns when the doer of the action is not identified. For example:

Weak: Completion of the new system was accomplished.

Strong: They completed the new system.

Oral Communications

In addition to effective written communications skills, a consultant needs to develop skills in various forms of oral communications. You will be faced with many situations that require you to conduct interviews, lead problem-solving conferences, and make oral presentations.

Conducting Interviews

Consulting work encompasses two basic types of interviews. The first type involves meeting with a prospective client and determining his or her needs prior to the engagement. The second type entails gathering necessary information from the client and his or her employees once the engagement begins. No matter what type of interview is involved, you need to learn as much as possible about the interviewee. In other words, you need to analyze your audience prior to the interview. Analysis begins in the preparation phase. Answer the questions posed earlier in the audience analysis section of this chapter. Try to learn as much as possible about the interviewee before the interview. This preparation gives you a better perspective on the interviewee and serves as an excellent way to establish rapport at the beginning of the interview.

Another task to complete prior to the interview is determining the purpose for meeting with the client. Prepare a series of questions that relate to the purpose. Answers to these questions will provide the facts necessary for your analysis. The questions should serve as touchstones to keep the interview from lacking structure. Remember that they are guides only and should not restrict the use of other, related questions once the interview begins.

After learning about the interviewee, structuring questions, and arranging an interview place and time, you are ready to begin the interview. Schedule it for no more than an hour. If more time is needed, schedule a second interview. Remember to start with a friendly chat to establish a positive and cooperative atmosphere. The more comfortable the interviewee is, the more open and candid he or she will be during the interview. Be sure to explain the interview's purpose, method or structure, and perhaps even expected outcome. Be tactful and objective and expect some resistance, especially from the client's employees. Be mindful of the types of barriers discussed earlier in this chapter. Listen well and empathize with the interviewee. He or she may be nervous. When taking notes during the interview, try not to be obvious and do not write down everything the interviewee says. The interviewee can become cautious, suspicious, and defensive.

Once the interview is over, summarize the results. By reviewing your notes, you can clarify, check for accuracy, or even expand on some points. Remember, the interviewee will be concerned about what was written. Close on a positive note and always keep the lines of communication open; you may have to interview this individual again later in the engagement.

Leading Problem-Solving Conferences

Once all the data have been gathered and analyzed by each consultant participating in the engagement, it is likely that all the participants will meet to discuss the findings and arrive at possible solutions to the problems. To arrive at the desired end results in a conference, you need to plan and prepare carefully.

If you are serving as group leader, you need to identify the purpose(s) of the conference. Determine the points or topics that need to be covered and perhaps prepare an agenda. Forward this agenda to the participants so they too can prepare adequately for the conference. You must direct the meeting and maintain control. You need to create an atmosphere in which each participant feels free to express his or her ideas or opinions regarding the topic. Encourage involvement by asking open and leading questions. After an idea has been presented, give proper feedback. Recognize a good idea, but also expect to give and receive constructive criticism if an idea needs improvement. Remember, the success of a conference depends on giving all the participants an opportunity to express their ideas clearly.

Listen carefully and be sure to discuss one point or topic at a time. Try to arrive at a solution to one problem before going to the next item. Summarizing what has been said after each item is discussed is a good technique. It allows you to be sure that you understand the appropriate course of action, and it gives the participants a chance to check the correctness of solutions. Close on a positive note by thanking all participants for their contributions.

Making Oral Presentations

Perhaps one of the tasks consultants dread most is making an oral presentation. Whether you are presenting a formal proposal or conducting a training session, the task can be made easier if you spend enough time preparing and practicing for the presentation. Therefore, the following discussion will concentrate on preparing, practicing, and giving the presentation.

The first step you need to take in the preparation stage is determining the purpose of the presentation: to propose a new system, present findings, and so forth. Analysis of the audience is the next step. Review the audience analysis questions that were listed earlier in the chapter. Note the planned date of the presentation as well as how long it should take. Once you have completed this step, gather information or review the material previously gathered at the engagement. Be sure that the information is accurate, complete, and pertinent to the audience. Prepare an outline, from introduction to conclusions and/or recommendations. If a proposal or final report has been prepared, either item can provide the structure you will need.

Your opening should be more than "My presentation today is about....You should capture the audience's attention. Take a possible benefit and turn it into a question for the opening. Follow with related questions or comments. This approach will set the stage for the major points to be expanded in the body of the presentation. Organize all the main points in this section and discuss the most important items first. Include transition words and phrases (e.g., however, therefore, by contrast) to make the presentation flow smoothly from one point to another. The conclusion should summarize and reinforce the major points.

While preparing the outline, you should also write down possible questions that the audience may have about the material. Whether you decide to entertain questions during or after the presentation, having a list of likely topics ready beforehand will give you more confidence in handling this important part of the presentation. You might also note, on the outline, places where you may want to use a visual aid. Marking these spots clearly on the outline will remind you of when to show the visuals.

Perhaps the one technique that clearly separates a good speaker from an excellent speaker is practice. If you know the material well and if you practice, you can eliminate stage fright. When practicing, try to simulate the actual presentation. Stand up and speak aloud. Ask a colleague to listen to the presentation, and seek his or her feedback. Try to find out the type of room you will be using. If possible, go and see it. This information will help you visualize the actual presentation and reduce the anxiety of speaking in an unfamiliar location.

When the time has arrived to give the presentation, approach it with confidence. During the presentation, remember to define terms that might be unfamiliar to the audience. Keep audience feedback in mind. If people seem puzzled or confused, perhaps rephrase the points made previously. If they start to get restless, maybe it is time to take a break. Be sure that all visual aids help clarify and support your points. They should be easily read and understood and not contain too much detail. They should flow naturally during the presentation. Remember to speak toward the audience while referring to a visual. The projection of your voice will be affected if you face the visual rather than the audience.

When preparing visual aids, whether for oral or for written reports, you might consider using computer graphics. A number of good graphics packages run on large computer systems, but you might also consider one of the many microcomputer graphics packages. A list of popular microcomputer graphics software packages, along with their vendors, is presented in Table 5-2. Depending upon the package, you can create virtually any type of visual: everything from the basic bar, line, or pie graph to a time or flowchart. Not only can the microcomputer prepare prints for reports or handouts, it can also generate transparencies and 35-mm slides with appropriate attachments. In addition, color and hatching can be used to add more emphasis to the visual.

Table 5-2. Microcomputer graphics software packages

Software Package	Vendor
1-2-3	Lotus Development Corp.
Accuchart	Big Tree Software
BPS Business Graphics	Business and Professional Software
Business Graphics Systems	Peachtree Software
Chart-Master	Decision Resources
Chartstar	MicroPro
dGraph III	Fox & Geller, Inc.
DR Graph	Digital Research
Fast Graphs	Innovative Software, Inc.
Graph 'n' Calc	Desktop Computer Software, Inc.
Graph-in-the-Box	New England Software
Graphwriter	Graphic Communication
Harvard Graphics	Software Publishing
MicroChart	MicroSoft
SuperChart/SuperImage	Computer Associates

Although nothing helps a speaker more than practicing, consider the following when making an oral presentation:

- Relax.
- Be optimistic and enthusiastic.
- Speak loudly and slowly.
- Use an outline (don't read notes).
- Use a variety of sentences.
- Avoid fillers (ah, um, you know).
- Use a conversational tone.
- Use gestures for emphasis.
- Use proper body movement.
- Maintain eye contact.
- Have proper posture.
- Vary pace and volume.
- Use visual aids.
- Stop on time.

All these points are extremely important to becoming an effective speaker. There is one item that can be added to the list when applicable, and that is humor. Humor is effective when it is used in an appropriate and timely manner. A humorous anecdote or story that relates to the material can aid in establishing rapport, in easing tensions, and in giving the presentation a more informal tone. Humor should never be used at the expense of the audience. Never try to capitalize on something humorous that happened during the engagement if it could embarrass a member of the audience. Always remember to use good taste and common sense when considering humor in any presentation.

Part 2

Client-Consultant Relationships

6

Interpersonal Consulting Skills*

Charles J. Margerison
Institute of Team Management Studies
Toowong Brisbane, Queensland, Australia

In giving advice, seek to help, not please your friend. SOLON

In all consulting work many words are exchanged. It therefore requires considerable skills in managing conversations. I refer to such skill as conversational control. In this chapter I shall outline some of the issues of how to exercise conversation control and be effective in the interpersonal aspects of consulting.

What Is Conversation Control?

The essence of conversation control is your ability to manage your own conversation. It does not mean manipulating other people's conversation. The only way you can be effective is to understand what you say and how you say it and seek to influence others through your own example.

It is likely that if other people see you behaving in a reasonable fashion and exercising control over what you say, then they will respond in a positive way. There is no guarantee of this, but more often than not in a problem-solving situation people will respond well if they feel you are acting in an understanding manner. I shall deal here with some aspects of conversation control as they apply to consulting and advisory work. A full description of the elements is contained in my book, *Conversation Control Skills for Managers* (W. H. Allen, 1987).

The Cues and Clues

The vital aspect of any consultancy assignment is identifying the key points as quickly as possible. This is not always easy because, although clients may be willing to talk about the problems and the opportunities, they will not necessarily be prepared to trust you with particular details until they are confident about you and your approach.

They will judge this to a large measure on the cues that you give them (see Figure 6-1). If they feel comfortable they will then begin to give you some clues as to the main problems involved. You have to be patient and listen carefully for the important words.

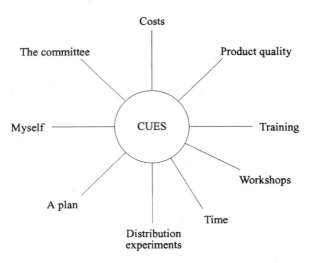

Figure 6-1

People are usually giving a vital message when they use the words "I," "me," or "my." This is particularly so when associated with adjectives which stress "concerns, worries, excitement, distress, interest, despair."

Sometimes the clues may not be so strong. People may just say, "I'm not sure," or they may indicate that there is much left unsaid, by a veiled reference such as, "I've been thinking a lot about that recently." When you hear doubts expressed or an indication that more could be said, show your interest and let them talk further. Don't make statements, or change the subject.

Clients will also give you clues as to the direction in which you should be asking questions. They may do this by emphasizing certain points or by prefacing what they are talking about with such words as "urgent," "important," "vital," "critical," and so on. These are the more obvious clues and it is more difficult to pick up the words that don't have such a strong connotation.

Selecting the Cues and Clues

I am surprised how often consultants miss the clues given to them. This may be in many cases because a mass of information is provided and it is possible to be misled. A client might for example say, "We have had a committee which has looked at ways of saving costs and how we can improve the quality of our products. They have met now for four or five meetings, but I'm disappointed we don't seem to be getting very far. The committee has talked about training people better and organizing some problem-solving workshops. We have also looked at the possibility of conducting some experiments in particular areas, particularly on distribution, which is one of our major costs. However, I am particularly concerned that we have not developed a plan which we can put into operation. Time is now running out."

The client stops at this point. Which of the cues do you pick up? The main theme is productivity, but various avenues have been opened from training through to conducting experiments, and a number of topic areas have been introduced from costs through to distribution. There are several ways that you could enter the conversation. Here are some possible responses that you might offer:

- "Tell me more about the costing system that you have been discussing."
- "What ideas emerged from the discussion on training?"
- "What sort of experiments have been tried?"
- "What are the main things blocking progress?"

Already you have a number of leads.

Follow the Personal Issues

A good rule in picking up important clues is always to follow what people say about themselves. In this case the client says that he was disappointed. The adviser could therefore say, "You mention that you were disappointed. In what way does this affect you personally?" At this point some vital information could appear, as the client would say, "Well, you see, I am chairman of the group that has been appointed to deal with this issue. The president of the company has made it clear that he wants a report within six weeks and so far we don't seem to be making much progress. I can't possibly go and see the president with the half-baked ideas that we have at the moment." Now by following this lead in what the client says about himself, the adviser has uncovered a whole new dimension to the issue. No longer is it just a committee working on a project. Your client has a personal commitment as the chairman of the committee, to the president of the company.

Identifying Listening Cues

Pick up the important clues, rather than get lost in the conversation. In particular listen for what people say about themselves. Listen for the adjectives they use. Listen for the words that they stress. Listen therefore to the emotional as well as the rational comments. Summarize the emotions. Seek to understand, recognize, and appreciate why people feel the way they do.

People rarely stop talking because they have nothing else to say. They usually stop talking to see whether you are still interested and whether you are able to assist by asking the right question or providing information. So listen carefully to what they say in the last paragraph and the last sentence. It will usually indicate where their center of attention is. They may not know what they should do next, but they usually know what is important.

The Signs and the Signals

Also, of course, watch the signals that they give you. The nonverbal clues can be just as important: maybe the wringing of the hands, the shaking of the head, the wagging of the finger, or the leaning forward or backward in the chair. They will all give you an idea of what the client thinks is important.

If clients, for example, begin to sit back and fold their arms, then you probably suspect that something has happened to make them defensive and perhaps withdraw somewhat. If this is so, then you might reflect on this behavior. Equally, if a person starts leaning forward and talking more quickly you can usually assume that he or she feels quite excited about the issues. Do not change the topic of conversation at this point. Stay with what they are interested in. Do not pursue your own intellectual interests at the expense of their thought processes. You are there primarily to help them think more clearly, not to gather information for your own personal satisfaction.

The cues and clues you give your client and the ones he or she will give you are vital to the development of a successful consulting relationship. Listen carefully to what they say and how they behave and then follow up, particularly on the personal aspects, and you won't go far wrong.

What Managerial Consultants Want to Develop

On a recent managerial consulting course for executives with a large oil company, I asked them what they personally wanted to gain. Most of their replies, as shown below, indicate the importance placed on interpersonal skills.

- More confidence in group situations.
- How to present ideas to others.
- Saving time and making life easier.
- Management of interviews.
- Communication skills.
- Improved skills in managing change.
- How to introduce new methods without upsetting people.
- Persuading others to take action.
- Listening to and understanding other parties' problems.
- Getting ideas across in a manner that wins acceptance.
- Saying no in nonthreatening manner.
- Getting people to work together.

Problem-Centered and Solution-Centered Behavior

In most consulting assignments people are naturally looking for solutions. They will often form the problem in such a way that they ask directly for a solution. However, I have found that if you give them one too quickly, even if it is correct, they will normally find some reason why it won't work. There are two elements therefore to any effective consultation. These are problem-centered action and solution-centered action (see Figure 6-2).

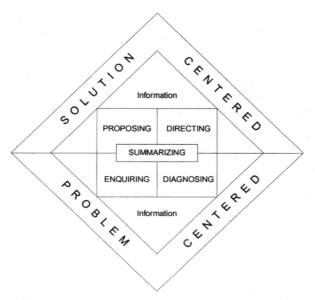

Figure 6-2

Identifying the Problems

In any situation, we have to assess how much time we should give to looking at the problem before we start coming up with solutions. In some professions the time element can be critical. For example, we normally expect our doctors to give a problem-centered diagnosis and move towards a solution within about five to ten minutes. If they cannot come up with an identification of the problem and provide some prescription within that time, we normally begin to worry. If we were not feeling particularly ill before the diagnosis, then we certainly start to sweat and our blood pressure will probably increase the longer the assessment goes on.

However, in looking at organizational problems we usually have more time. The clients may be rather impatient, or just be wanting to see how you respond when they ask for solutions. They may come up with a series of proposals like the following. "For a while now our managers have not been performing very effectively. What do you think we should do?"

You may suggest that it is important for you to gather some information before you can make a suggestion. However, the client may respond, "Well, I've been thinking for a long time that we should have a top class management course which they can all go on. What do you think of that suggestion?"

This is a classic situation where clients have not only done their own diagnosis but come up with their own prescription, and in medical terms would undertake their own surgery if they had the tools. In such situations they have called you in to be a technician to implement what they have already decided.

In such situations, however, you should resist the temptation to become solution-centered until you are convinced that you understand the problem and a correct diagnosis has been made.

Making an active commitment to being problem-centered is not only difficult but time-consuming. It requires considerable skill to gather data. In doing so, however, you should be helping clients think through all the issues and providing them with an opportunity to assess the judgments that they have made. Above all, develop the skill areas shown in the model.

When to Be Problem-Centered or Solution-Centered

It is important to look at these two approaches so that we know where we stand as advisers. For example, it is appropriate to use a *problem-centered* approach when:

- The problem is open-ended.

- The client must understand the process by which the solution is reached.

- The client is directly involved in managing the developing situation.

- Any solution depends for its success upon the acceptability of the details.

- The consultant is only a temporary member and there to act as a catalyst, rather than trying to solve the problem once and for all.

Techniques to solve problems, like any techniques, are valid if used in the appropriate way, at the right time, and with the acceptance and understanding of those who will use them. The "take it away *solution-centered approach*" is most appropriate when:

- The problem has been clearly diagnosed.

- The client has no interest in spending time working on the problem personally.

- The client is prepared to pay someone else to provide a solution without understanding how the solution is arrived at.

- The consultants have special expertise which enables them to do the job better and more quickly by themselves.

- The consultant believes that the solution arrived at will be accepted and implemented by the client, even though the client was not involved in the development of the solution.

How to Summarize

In your response to clients you need to make it clear that you are aware of what they are saying. You do not necessarily need to know every detail, but it is important that you pick up on a few words. You need to summarize regularly and accurately what is said so the client knows that you know what he or she knows.

Understand

Early in the conversation it is vital to understand rather than to judge. Do not imply by word or deed that you think that what the client has done is wrong or inadequate. It may well be so, but your job is not to pass judgment. Your job is to understand what they have done and indicate that.

By doing this you will show clients that you are following carefully the points that they are making. It is important for you actually to use words like, "I understand that the two key areas where you have been working which have caused problems so far...."

Appreciate

In addition you need to appreciate the way in which the client has been trying to solve the problem before you arrived. It is rare for clients to invite you in before they have made some efforts to resolve the problem. Therefore, summarize what they have done, not in the form of agreeing with it, but in the form of giving a clear indication that you appreciate that they have made such an effort.

Recognize

Everyone likes to be recognized in some way for doing the job. Therefore, show the clients that you recognize that there well may be difficulties, but also summarize accurately what you hear they have been doing.

If you can understand, appreciate, and recognize then the clients will give you good marks, not because you have agreed with them, but because you have taken the trouble to listen to what they say.

I had a long lunch with a client who talked a great deal. Much of the discussion was not particularly relevant to the main problem, I felt. However, during the lunch, I tried to understand, to recognize, and appreciate what the client was saying. At the end of the meal, the client said, "I know I talk a lot and have gone around in circles on this one, but it has helped me think it through enormously. What I have particularly valued is the way you have listened and tried to understand what I have been doing, which is more than I can say for the other people I have been talking to." As a result we secured a very substantial assignment with this company which lasted over a long period.

Avoid Seductive Detours

A common fault among consultants is that they pursue their own intellectual interests rather than tackle the problem. Beware of the temptation to ask for more and more information that is not directly related to the problem. This may be viewed as trying to seduce the client to discuss what is of importance to you rather than what is important to the client.

A good example of how a consultant can lead the client up an intellectual cul de sac is shown in the following excerpt from an assignment:

> CLIENT: The problem is that most of our managers are not using the new computers, despite being fully trained. (Diagnosis)
> CONSULTANT: What software do they have? (Inquiry)
> CLIENT: We have virtually nothing in our resource library. (Information)
> CONSULTANT: Have you got the new Superscan package? (Inquiry)
> CLIENT: I don't know. (Information)
> CONSULTANT: I was wondering, as I have heard it is very good. I was hoping you might be able to bring me up-to-date. (Inquiry for the benefit of the consultant)

Now this is an obvious detour, but it is not always so clear cut. Indeed the consultant's questions on scheduling, distribution, pricing, personalities, organization structure, pay rates, and a host of other items can often lead the client on a grand tour round the organization.

But are these relevant to an understanding of the problem, rather than satisfying the intellectual curiosity of the consultant?

Clients may assess consultants by how quickly they pick up the cues and whether they stick to the main points. Clients may ask "How does that relate to the understanding of the problem?" Or, be more direct and say, "I don't see how this information relates to the main problem." At this point the client may restate the issue and if the consultant can't pick up the cues, they may find another one who can.

Be aware that the client will judge you on how quickly you can get on the right wavelength. Don't take detours to satisfy your own intellectual interests. Stay with what the client says. Follow his or her leads. If, however, you feel this is not getting you to the point then say, "We have covered a number of points; which of these is most important in terms of the problem?" If the client says none of them are, then ask for permission to widen the diagnosis by saying "Well, I would like to broaden the area of discussion for a while if that is OK with you." At least you now have permission, but still use it with discretion.

On most occasions you won't go far wrong if you listen to what the client says about himself or herself. Remember clients are on a journey trying to reach a destination. You have to find out where it is and how they are getting there and what is in the way. That is the key. Once you know those things, you are on the right track.

Conversation Skills in Consulting

The following issues in conversation can be extremely important in consulting work.

Time Dynamics

You can talk in one or more of three levels (see Figure 6-3): If you are talking about the future (what will or should be) and the other person is talking about the past (what has been), then you will not succeed. Many grievance meetings fail because the problem is in the past and the manager will probably want to be discussing what will happen *next*. You need to be in the same dimension to make progress.

By recognizing the time dynamics in a conversation you can quickly move into the same time period before moving on by the use of conversational linking techniques. Your client may be fixated on talking about the past, and you will therefore need to ask him or her to consider future options. Alternatively you may find the client wants to move too quickly to the future-based solution before the past failure has been properly diagnosed.

Topic Dynamics

What you talk about will highlight differences or similarities in approach. The five main areas are:

- Myself
- You
- Us
- Them (who are not there)
- Things (e.g., the weather or cars)

Figure 6-3

Very often conversations fail because people cannot get on to the same topic wavelength. If you insist on talking about "things" when I want to talk about "myself," we shall have two opposed agendas going, and this is likely to result in talk without meaning. A sound rule is to get the clients to talk about themselves and their role.

Competition Dynamics

Very often in conversation you can have a situation where someone is trying to get the better of you. The conversation becomes a win/lose relationship. There are four possibilities.

- I win, you lose.

- You win, I lose.

- You lose, I lose.

- You win, I win.

The options can be seen as shown in Figure 6-4. Consulting should obviously be a cooperative exercise. Wherever possible, it is usually best to try for the win/win option. This is not always possible or desirable. There are occasions when you need to assert your views, even if it means others don't get what they want. Clients clearly want to gain a win out of the conversation, and there may be occasions, for example in negotiation, where there will be elements of win/lose about your relationship. However, a win/win is nearly always best because it will lead to more lasting success and commitment.

Movement Dynamics

The way clients and people in general react to you will depend largely on how you behave toward them. You can adopt one of three behaviors:

- You can encourage people.

- You can discourage people.

- You can ignore people.

		YOU	
		Win	Lose
ME	Win	Success	One up
	Lose	One down	Failure

Figure 6-4

As a result, people will move in one of three ways:

- Toward you
- Away from you
- Against you

It is not only what you say, but the way you say it, that counts. If people are moving away when you want them to move toward, look at what you are saying and how you say it. Their behavior is likely to relate to your approach. Likewise, you will find other people will "turn you on" or "turn you off" by their behavior. By observing behavior and knowing how to control your conversation, you can have better control of your relationships.

Direction Dynamics

Conversations need at times to open out and generate ideas and, at others, to become more specific. You have to decide when to

- Diverge
- Converge

If you converge too quickly you may not get all the information you need. Learn the skill of keeping judgment in suspense until you have the data and the time is right to converge on an option.

Facts and Feeling Dynamics

All conversations revolve round these issues. Make sure you discuss both. If you are given facts, ask for feelings. If you are given feelings, ask for facts. In this way you will cover both the rational and emotional aspects of the problem (see Figure 6-5).

Level of Conversation Dynamics

You will find conversations take place at one of two levels:

- Generalities
- Specifics

You can move conversation to either a general or a specific level. As a rule we start at a general level and then move to the specifics. However, you need to determine what the other person requires. It is no use you being general if someone wants you to be specific and vice versa (see Figure 6-5).

Gaining and giving information

In any consulting assignment it is important to know where the conversation is and where it should be. This particularly applies to the use of facts and feelings and moving the conversation from generalities to specifics. A useful way of mapping where you are is as follows.

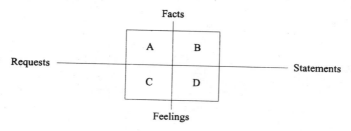

You may start out by requesting facts (A) but the client may give a statement of feelings and opinions (D). If that happens then accept that the client wishes to work in this area before you get to the facts. Likewise you may ask how the client feels about the issue (C) and get statements of fact (B). If so, this a strong cue you should follow. Another way of mapping conversation is to look at the level at which it is conducted.

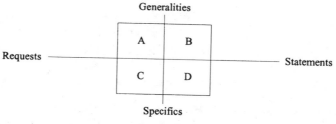

Initially in an assignment you will probably be presented with general statements (B). However, by understanding the principles of conversation control you can move the converstation into all four areas. You need to judge the atmosphere and not rush too quickly from area A to area C unless you have permission. People will only provide specific statements (D) when they begin to trust you. Keep your eyes and ears on the cues and clues.

Figure 6-5

Agreement Disagreement Dynamics

In all conversations people will move for or against what you say. Be prepared for it by recognizing the movements on a continuum (see Figure 6-6). This continuum will provide a good guide for your action. For example, don't regard disagreement as rejection. Find out what they disagree with and work positively on those points as you may get other

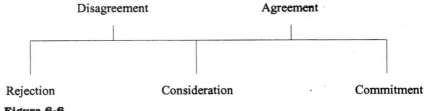

Figure 6-6

persons to consider, then agree with, what you are saying. Also, don't confuse agreement with commitment. The first only means people will verbally acknowledge what you say, but commitment means action. That is what you must go for and seek to get in writing when it really counts.

You can be master or victim of conversations. You have to decide what words to use and how to use them. You cannot control what others say, but you can control what you say. In doing so, you can influence the outcome of the matter being discussed. The techniques and methods listed here are just part of the skills an adviser needs to succeed, but a vitally important part.

My favorite quotation on conversation control skills comes from Lewis Carroll's *Through the Looking Glass,* when Humpty Dumpty says,

> "When I use a word, it means just what I choose it to mean—neither more nor less."
> "The question is," said Alice, "whether you *can* make words mean so many different things."
> "The question is," said Humpty Dumpty, "which is to be Master— that's all."

Guidelines

To be an effective consultant you need to manage your conversation effectively. This will require knowing

- When to be problem-centered or solution-centered
- When to converge or diverge
- When to emphasize facts or feelings
- When to speed up or slow down conversations
- How to identify cues and clues
- How to summarize and move conversation forward
- How to recognize, understand, and appreciate but assert your views

- How to move from the past to the present and future
- How to manage the win/lose aspect of conversations

In all of the various conversation dynamics the most important thing is to remember what the client says about himself or herself. That is the key to action.

Exercise

1. Consider how you manage your conversation in a consulting role. What do you do well?
2. What skills do you need to improve?

7

How to Gain Permission and Territory*

Charles J. Margerison
Institute of Team Management Studies
Toowong Brisbane, Queensland, Australia

If at first you don't succeed you are running
about average.   M. H. ANDERSON

As a consultant you are invariably working on someone else's problems or opportunities. You can only succeed in so far as they give you permission to operate on their territory.

The concepts of permission and territory are crucial to understanding the consulting process. When people are asking for advice they are not always prepared to tell you in the first instance many of the things you need to know. For example, clients may give you a little information just

---

to see how you respond. If you appear to be negative or critical or lacking in enthusiasm then they may not tell you any more. They will find a convenient way of changing the subject and cutting off discussion on the important matters.

How Far Can You Go?

If you show through both word and deed that you are genuinely interested in trying to understand what they are saying and are not prepared to jump to conclusions ahead of the evidence, then clients will open up a little further and tell you more of the details. In this way they will allow you to enter further into their territory.

It is something like knocking at doors which are half open and seeing them either close in your face, or open fully. It depends upon how you behave as a consultant adviser whether the doors open or close. For example, consider the exchanges in the two dialogues below, which briefly show two entirely different approaches and the results.

Case A

Understanding the Client

> CLIENT: I've been feeling under pressure for some time because things have not been going right. I made some changes to our distribution system about six months ago but there have been no improvements so far.
>
> CONSULTANT: You feel things could have gone better?
>
> CLIENT: I was looking for significant cost reductions and improvements in the speed of our deliveries. As it is our costs have gone up by 5 percent and we now have a larger number of items in stock awaiting distribution than we had six months ago.
>
> CONSULTANT: So overall you are worse off after the changes?
>
> CLIENT: Yes, in financial terms, and we continue to have resistance from the staff. On balance I probably did not sell it too well when we introduced the idea originally.

Now here the consultant through a series of reflective summaries has shown understanding of what the client is saying. As a result the client has opened up and provided more information. The case is now poised at a delicate point. What would you say next to encourage clients to open the door further and give you permission to look into what they have done?

The client has given a strong clue that he will be prepared to talk about his own approach in making the change. You are now at a vital point. The consultant who is on top of the job will follow this immediately and ask the clients to talk about what they have done, how they did it, and what they felt about the situation and this would be preparatory for discussing what they should do next.

Case B

Misguided Consultation

However, a consultant who was behaving in an ineffective way might respond in the following manner. The result is the doors would be shut and permission withdrawn so you could not go further.

CLIENT: We had some sound proposals but we could not implement them.

CONSULTANT: It looks to me that you made some mistakes in communication.

CLIENT: The changes were well researched before we put them into operation and everyone was formally notified.

CONSULTANT: But you failed to get the commitment of the people to the changes.

CLIENT: That's easy to say in hindsight, but at the time we were under a lot of pressure.

Already the client is becoming defensive and making excuses and explanations. The consultant has forced the client onto the defensive.

Instead of talking about how the problem can be resolved now and in the future, the discussion has reverted to the past. Already the client is starting to withdraw permission and will shortly move to cut down the territory where the consultant can operate.

It is therefore very important to be aware of the cues and clues that you get and know how to respond. If you can pick them up and work with the key words, phrases, and ideas, then you will find the clients will invariably move towards you rather than away.

They will start talking about themselves and their own role in proceedings. Instead of emphasizing the problems of the past they will talk about the concerns of the present and what needs to be done in the future.

Giving and Gaining Permissions

Who, What, When, and How

In order to make progress you need to find out who clients need to talk to, what they need to talk about, and how that should be structured (see Figure 7-1). In doing this you will be exploring the new territory on which they must move if they are to be successful. I take notice when one of my clients suggests that I should meet someone else in the organization.

What clients are saying at this point is that I have permission to go further. They are prepared to open up another door and allow me onto other territory. They are indicating that I am *persona grata* and have their

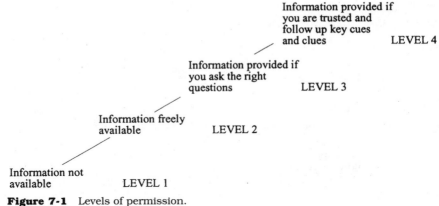

Figure 7-1   Levels of permission.

confidence and trust to meet with other actors in the real life work play in which they are engaged.

Gaining Permissions

To arrive at this point, however, you may need to ask questions which are related to permission and territory in order that the client can begin to think through what needs to be done. At the appropriate time you need to ask questions like:

- "Who else is involved with you in tackling this problem?"
- "To what extent is it useful if I talk with them?"
- "If you were to hold a meeting on the issue, who would you feel should attend?"

These may seem to be general questions, but they enable the client to think through the next steps and who they will involve. If clients are telling you things that they have not discussed with other people who they have indicated are important, then it is your job to enquire whether they should move on to that territory.

Giving Permissions

Clients may well have to give themselves permission. The whole notion of giving yourself permission is critical to action. However, it is not easy, particularly when problems are complex and difficult. Clients may not wish to talk to someone about the difficulty unless they are clear in their own mind what they are going to say. Much of my own consulting work involves getting managers to think through their own position and gather the confidence to raise matters which need to be discussed that have been so far avoided.

In a sense, it is not so much the client who gives me permission, but the other way around. In talking to me the client generates sufficient self-confidence to give himself or herself permission to open up discussions in difficult areas. Once this has been done, it is often a very great relief, and clients feel that a load has been taken off their mind before the discussions have taken place.

In essence what they have done is to give themselves permission to act rather than to worry. If you as a consultant enable them to do this through your questions and discussions, then you have made a significant contribution, even though you may not be directly involved in those subsequent discussions.

By understanding the nature of territories and permissions and picking up the cues and clues in such a way that people can talk more openly, you are facilitating the process where people can become more confident in taking action.

Identifying the Accessible Territory

Closing

Understanding permissions and access to territory is critical. You should listen for key words which will give you an instant clue that people are either opening or closing down territory. Here are some of the expressions that I have heard when people are closing down permissions and giving strong cues that certain territory is not open.

- "I don't think that's very important."
- "I can't see that working here."
- "We should tread carefully when dealing with such matters."

Opening Up

It is important to recognize when people will allow you to enter their territory or go further in a particular direction. Where people have been giving permissions they have been far more positive and come out with expressions such as:

- "I would like you to meet Jim, my boss, as he would be interested in talking this over with you."
- "Although not many people know, I can tell you confidentially…"

- "One or two things have happened recently which are important."
- "I'm not sure I should tell you but..."

These may seem obvious when they are written down, but when spoken they are not always picked up. The successful consultant, however, does not miss the clues which give permission and entry to territory. With practice you can begin to see more clearly the permissions that you get, which are in fact opportunities. As you respond in a positive and understanding way, you will find more and more doors open.

Why Are You There?

As the "doors" open up you may wonder what you are expected to contribute. There are a few rules that will help.

1. Listen carefully is the first rule. Perhaps that is all you are expected to do—at least initially.
2. The second rule is to ask the client what he wants. When you are on his or her territory it is not only good manners but good sense. Moreover you will quickly find out what permissions you have.
3. Third, provide advice and guidance, but ensure it is wanted before you give it, otherwise you will find the doors that opened up will close again and your permissions will be withdrawn. You will be on the outside looking in, instead of on the inside looking out.

How Others React to You

You can tell what reactions you are getting by observing people's responses. These can be summarized quickly based on the analysis made by Karen Horney when she noticed that people will move

- Toward you—problem solving
- Away from you—defensive, withdrawing
- Against you—aggressive, attacking

Now these responses depend to a large extent on your own behavior and how that is received by others. In every conversation you are sending out messages not just with your words but with your behavior which, as the model shows, will be encouraging, discouraging, or ignoring others (see Figure 7-2). If we encourage people, we are giving them permission to go in a particular direction. We do this in various ways. Some are to the point and indicate openly what we think such as, "I think that's a good idea," "You have my support if you do that."

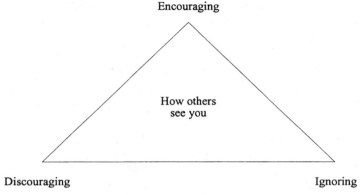

Figure 7-2　Consultant's message.

Encouragement

Other forms of encouragement are more subtle. Just listening to someone in a caring and empathetic way is a powerful form of encouragement. It enables people to say things that perhaps they would not otherwise say. Asking open-ended questions, reflecting on important words or phrases, nodding your head and smiling, are all ways of encouraging people and giving permission if they are done properly. Equally we can discourage people directly and indirectly. Again the words and behaviors either together or combined are powerful factors denying permission to proceed.

Discouragement

I recently asked for some advice about music. My music adviser said the issue I was raising was "irrelevant" and later said my concerns were "not important" and went on in that vein. I got the clear message he was trying to discourage me. He did it in a manner that I felt was unnecessarily critical. Instead of discouraging me, he made me more determined to find out what I wanted, but not from him. I ended his role as my adviser.

Other people discourage you in a more acceptable way by saying things like, "If I were you I wouldn't do that," "Given the advice I think what you are doing is risky." Most people don't object to being discouraged providing there is some evidence to back up your views and it is presented with their interests in mind, and allows them to make the final decision.

Ignoring

The third form of response is often the most difficult. If people ignore what you say it can be taken either of two ways. Either they have no interest in your views and are therefore opposed and will not give permission to enter any territory which they control, or ignoring you they may be saying you have permission to do what you want providing it does not involve them.

How Do You Get People's Permission?

People will not always say what they think and feel. They may be shy, or concerned that you will criticize their opinions. They may just not be sure they can trust you. There are countless reasons why you do not gain the right information. However, it can be vital in your job that you do know what other colleagues and team members are thinking, even if it is critical of you and your way of doing things.

A top manager with whom I was consulting said, "The higher I go in the organization, the less people are prepared to tell me what they really think of how I run things." We talked for a while and I asked him how he encouraged people to do this. He said it was difficult because most of the meetings were formal.

He agreed it would be useful to have a meeting on "neutral" territory away from the office where his team could talk about how they worked together. I interviewed the team members before the event and found that some members did have strong views which they had never let loose in front of the top manager. When I asked why, they said they were not sure he would listen particularly as a number of their points were critical.

I indicated to the top manager this general concern without naming the managers in question. His response was, "I might not like what they say about how I run things, but if I don't find out then neither I nor the team can improve." He therefore organized a weekend workshop at a country club and in so doing signaled that people had permission to talk about his style and the way the team worked.

As a result, team members "for the first time got down to fundamentals on what was helping and hindering their performance." By showing an example, the top manager had given permission for people to open up discussion on important territory. There was a feeling that this "cleared the air and produced a better working relationship."

Discussing Personal Territory Issues

So, if you want feedback from others you have to indicate they have permission to contribute. Often just telling people does not have the right effect. You have to set up the conditions, the time and the place and show both by word and deed that people have permission to do things. This is particularly so when you are introducing new and possibly risky ideas or, for example, reviewing someone's performance.

In most organizations there is some form of performance appraisal where a manager meets with members of staff to review what they have done, to counsel on improvements and set goals for the future. Most people agree that this is an excellent idea in theory, but very hard to do in practice.

The reason for this is that it involves discussing personal matters— such as what you have done, or not done, and why. Many people are reluctant to open up. Some managers therefore ignore this and insist on moving onto the other person's territory regardless of whether they have permission. This is usually resisted particularly if they adopt a judgmental and evaluative approach such as "I have noticed over the last couple of months your sales have been poor and your attitude to the job is lacking in enthusiasm. If you put more effort in, and take a more disciplined approach, you would be better."

Now this may be true, but the critical diagnosis followed by the quick-fire general solution is likely to lead to a defensive or aggressive response. It is unlikely the subordinate will give many permissions for the manager to find out what he really thinks, so how can you get people's permission to be open in sensitive areas (see Figure 7-3)?

The first rule is to give people an opportunity to assess themselves. The subordinates should be asked to write their own appraisals, which become the basis for discussion. In this way the manager can respond to the subordinate's points, preferably in a supportive and helpful way.

If the subordinate does not raise the important issues, then the second rule is to provide some evidence for opening up the conversation in the difficult area and then ask the other person how he or she feels about the situation.

If that doesn't work, then the third rule is to say that you are concerned about the situation and ask the other person what he or she will do to improve it. If the subordinate still refuses to give permission to discuss the matter, you may have to terminate the relationship.

How Doors Can Open with Permission

I met Frank initially at a conference. I was leading a workshop on consulting skills. Afterwards he asked me, "Have these ideas ever been used in tackling problems in a complex technical area?"

Frank described his own work situation and the problems he and his colleagues were facing. I asked what had been done so far and who had done it. As the discussion proceeded, it became clear there was far more behind the initial inquiry than was at first obvious.

Any consulting assignment will have a number of different perceptions and angles to it. Your job is to understand them and develop some agreed way of resolving any differences. There are five main perceptions in any assignment.

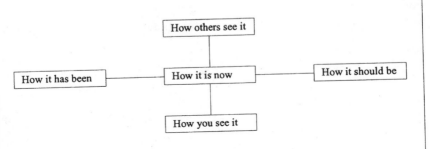

Your task is initially to understand the past and the present views. In this you should typically let others talk while you listen. A rule of thumb is that in the early stages you listen for 80 percent of the time. As you move towards 'how it should be', then more of your own views can come to the fore, providing you continue to listen to the views of your client and those who must implement the proposals.

Figure 7-3   Views on the consulting issue.

"You see, we have already had one rather expensive experiment in this area, and it failed. We have to get the next event right." I asked him what he meant by "we." He indicated that his boss was the key person, although he was the project manager with a group of technical people on a task force.

As a result of this conversation, he suggested I meet his boss. This meeting took place a month later and led to a meeting with the project team. I was asked to help design a new approach to their work and later joined in with the team as part of its development activity. I was then invited to meet with their international staff.

The assignment lasted on a part-time basis over ten years. It all stemmed from one short conversation, but as a result I received permission to enter an ever-widening territory. Each person I met opened another door to have me vetted by colleagues who then gave permission for me to enter deeper into their territory.

They made their judgments on various criteria, but most of all on whether I could pick up the cues and clues and relate to what they said. A crucial part of that was the questions I asked, rather than just giving answers, and that is why conversational control is important.

Process Consultation

Edgar Schein first put forward the concept of process consultation. This stands in comparison to the technical content expert aspect of consulting.

As Schein* writes, "The process consultant seeks to give the client 'insight' into what is going on around him, and between him, and other people."

He extends this later by saying, "as long as organizations are networks of people, there will be processes occurring between them. Therefore it is obvious that the better understood and the better diagnosed these processes are, the greater will be the chances of finding solutions to technical problems which will be accepted and used by the members of the organization."

His book on the subject, *Process Consultation,* is a landmark book and has stood the test of time. In it he described a number of assumptions underlying process- (rather than content-) based consulting. Some of these can be summarized as follows.

- Managers are keen to improve their organization but don't always know what is wrong and need help in diagnosing the situation. Managers must be involved in this so they see the problems and possibilities for themselves and learn how to respond.

- Process consultation therefore concentrates upon helping to establish the most effective means of diagnosis and effective helping relationships by getting people together in various ways to solve the issues.

It sounds simple and obvious, but like many things in life is more difficult in practice than in theory. For example, the basis of any success is knowing who should talk to whom, about what, when, and to what purpose to ensure some positive outcome. If you are good at this you are doing well as a process consultant. If not, then you may need one.

Working on the Clients' Territory

The organizational problems I am involved with are invariably a product of the relationships within the organization itself. If you really want to help the client with such problems you must work on his or her territory.

Territory is an important concept. If one is to explore territory one needs a map, but the consultant working on organization relationship

*Edgar H. Schein, *Process Consultation: Its Role in Organization,* Addison-Wesley, Reading, Mass., 1969.

issues does not have one. However, clients have one, even though they may never have talked about it or written it down. The consultant should therefore encourage clients to explain the important factors which they see as influencing behavior within their territory which relates to the problem.

Follow the Client

This means allowing the client to control the pace and direction of the conversation: try to pick up the essence of the message and inquire further. This often starts a historic review of the problem. It is tempting but dangerous to try and short-circuit this. Clients often give a discursive introduction to ascertain how far they can trust you. Do you show interest in what they have to say? If not, they are unlikely to let you know more of their world. Do they think you will respect confidences? Do they get the positive cues of encouragement from you to continue?

Follow Personal Issues

There is a pressure on consultant advisers to move away from the client's territory, particularly when the discussion becomes embarrassing or when personal disclosures are made. Consultants often fail to help clients explore such delicate aspects of their world. They push their concern to one side. If someone new to a job says, "I feel I am not up to this job," or "I find it really difficult to live up to what's expected of me," it is vital that you follow up the personal cues by inviting clients to say why they feel this way and exploring options they can take to deal with the issues.

Don't Avoid the Issues

The following are examples of avoidance:

- "This is a common problem. I wouldn't worry about it if I were you."
- "Let's get back to what we were saying earlier."
- "I've been interested in what you have said, but I would like to ask you a few questions about other matters now."

In each of these interventions the consultant seeks to change the direction. He may be well-intentioned but each of these interventions is destined to break the thread of a client's narrative.

The first plays down the client's concerns. The second pushes him back to some earlier topic. Lastly, the consultant seeks to control the meeting by proposing "a few questions."

Exploring the client's territory means concentrating on what he or she says. It means denying one's own personal interest. It means forgoing one's own experience on similar issues, unless that is requested. It means following the client's logic so that he or she begins to see his or her own logic more clearly.

How to Behave on Client's Territory

Remember you are always a guest. Never outstay your welcome. Never give cause for the client (host) to be embarrassed in front of others. If you have important things to say to the client, get agreement before launching forth, or do it in private.

You can be excluded from territory just as easily as you can be included. The phone will not ring, and letters don't get answered. The important thing is to respect the territory of others. Work with them, not against them, wherever possible, to make changes.

We all have organizational territory. We don't mind sharing it occasionally. Indeed most of us enjoy showing friends and acquaintances our territory if we take pride in it. However, we all object to our territory being taken over. Make sure your visit is exactly that, not a takeover. Ultimately the client has to do the job, not you. Your job is to help him or her manage the territory better.

Guidelines

Permissions are the key to successful consulting. You don't have to ask for them. If you behave appropriately they will be given to you. The points discussed in this section provide the basis for gaining entry, but be sure you do not take unfair advantage or outstay your welcome. Don't trespass for your own benefit. People will allow you onto their "territory" if they feel you understand and are willing to help. It is a trust relationship. Guard it with care.

Exercise

1. Consider situations where you have given people permission to discuss personal matters of importance to you. Why did you do it and in particular what did the people do?
2. Consider situations where you have been given permission by another person to go onto personal territory. What were the circumstances that led to such permission and what did you do?
3. What points do you need to concentrate upon if you are to gain permissions as a consultant?

8

Client-Consultant Compatibility: The Client Perspective*

Fredric H. Margolis
Potomac, Maryland

A critical part of the client-consultant relationship not often talked about is the personality mix. The consultant's personality may irritate the client or conflict with the organization's norms and expectations. On the other hand, the consultant may feel uncomfortable and distracted by the sponsor or the tone of the client organization as a whole.

There are other less easily measured personal characteristics that can have an even more profound effect on the success of the consultation. These include the consultant's belief system, source of motivation, personal ethics, objectivity, forthrightness, and capacity for loyalty. It is important these qualities be demonstrated early in the relationship.

The Consultant's Compatibility with the Organization

There are two legitimate reasons for seeking a client-consultant relationship with good "chemistry." The first is personal satisfaction. The sponsor is going to be spending time with the consultant so naturally will want the relationship to be enjoyable as well as productive. The second is the impact of personality on the success of a consultation. To some extent, the importance of this factor varies with the situation. When the client needs expert technical skills for a limited task, they clearly will want someone whose skill and knowledge is respected. The client may or may not like this person. A patient in need of open heart surgery, for instance, will find the *best* surgeon possible, rarely fussing if this surgeon happens to wear flashy clothes and espouse strange political views.

A comfortable personality fit, however, is essential if the consultant is to work closely with people in organization development activities. Participants must be able to talk as openly to the consultant as they would to a personal physician or other trusted adviser. Without this kind of confidence, clients will not be willing to disclose painful information or take risks often necessary to resolve a problem. A certain degree of personality fit is a prerequisite.

The judging of compatibility and integrity is more difficult. The client has to act intuitively on information often highly subjective; every situation is different. It's up to the client to decide the crucial ingredients for good chemistry in each unique situation. This chapter offers guidelines and raises questions for consideration in some of the important areas. The sponsor and the other people who will be working closely with the consultant must identify the criteria to use in making a decision.

Recognizing the Consultant's Belief System

The client is buying a system of beliefs when contracting with a consultant. It is important to find out what it is and estimate how well it will fit the situation and organization. One obvious way a client determines a consultant's belief is to ask some direct questions like: "What is your view of organization development?" "What do you think the role of the consultant should be?" "Can you describe how people best learn?" or "What are the crucial ingredients for organizational improvement?"

The trouble with direct questions is that the response may be the "official" belief system, not necessarily the *operating* belief system of the consultant. The consultant may say one thing in the interview and later do something entirely different. Operating belief systems can be inferred to some extent by listening carefully and drawing out the consultant about his or her approach to the problem. Reference checks also can help get an accurate picture. The client will never know for sure, however, until well into the consultation.

Clues can be provided by the consultant's emphasis and use of language. Some consultants may emphasize formal data collection and analysis methods and use the vocabulary of technical and business specialties. Another may talk about systems. Others may talk about analyzing the contingencies of reinforcement and setting up an effective positive reinforcement program. The focus may be on shaping the working environment. Still another consultant may emphasize development of individual people and groups and talk about growth, motivation, group process, trust levels, and team building. If clients hear unfamiliar terminology, they may ask where it comes from and ask for references to basic literature on the subject.

Other clues come from the way the prospective consultant relates to the client during the exploratory meeting. Does he or she appear to be outside or inside the consulting relationship? What kind of data does the consultant request and how does the consultant talk about the relationship with the client. When requesting data, some consultants will want "just the facts, Ma'am"—the hard data. Another may want to know the objective facts, but also will ask questions like, "What is your *impression* of the situation?" "What is your *hunch* about the causes of the problem?" and "How do you *feel* about what is going on?" This person will probably point out any inconsistencies between the objective and subjective data. For example, there may be lack of agreement about whether a problem really exists, or there may be a more fundamental problem under the one presented by the client.

After interviewing the consultant, clients may reflect on these questions: What are my and my organization's beliefs about change? What do we believe is the best way to motivate people? To learn new skills and knowledge? To manage the organization? Do people agree about these beliefs for the most part, or is there serious conflict? What are the beliefs of the people who will ultimately hire the consultant? Who will receive the consultant's help? What are the end user's beliefs? Is the consultant's belief system compatible with my organization's philosophy and practices?

The stability and climate of the client's organization should be taken into account when choosing a consultant. Clients should avoid hiring a consultant whose belief system contradicts the organization's philosophy, unless the client wants to consider *changing* the organization's beliefs.

Personality Fit

Personality elements that can have an impact on the consultation include dress and appearance, language, background and interests, interaction style, and character traits. Some of these, like appearance and background, are important only when they interfere seriously with the work the consultant was hired to do. The consultant's personality becomes a problem when people are offended to the extent that they cannot concentrate on a task or they reject an entire intervention effort. This doesn't mean, however, that in order to be effective the consultant's way of dressing, talking, and thinking *has* to conform to the organization's image. As an outsider, a consultant can say and do things not allowed normally. In fact, it can be an advantage to hire a consultant who isn't a carbon copy of people in the organization. A different perspective and viewpoint can help the sponsor understand the organization better—its unique qualities and strengths, and its hidden assumptions.

When sizing up the acceptability of dress, appearance, language, or any other personality variable, remember the consultant is not an extension of the organization's image or management style. As a group, consultants are staunchly independent. Their role is to provide new ideas and fresh perspective, not to endorse the status quo. The real issue is whether a consultant and a client organization can accommodate each other. Can the sponsor respect the consultant's difference? Is the consultant willing to compromise to some extent with the organization's ways? As a rule of thumb, *vive la difference*—until consultants step over the line from *doing* their thing to *flaunting* it. The sponsor has to judge where that line is by knowing the tolerance limits of the organization.

> A consultant was hired by a firm that had a dress code for men. They could wear a jacket of any color provided it was the same color as their pants! The consultant disliked business suits and preferred to dress in sport shirts and casual pants. He compromised by wearing a conservative sport jacket, tie, and contrasting pants. Had he shown up in an open shirt with no jacket, he would have been flaunting his difference.

Another case illustrates the stress that can result when organizations lack tolerance for differing standards of dress.

> An organization that makes sporting goods hired a consulting firm whose dress code called for vested suits. The client requested that representatives of the consulting firm dress in casual slacks and shirts when visiting company headquarters. The consultant was obliged to carry two outfits, one casual and the other formal, when shuttling back and forth from the consulting firms and client headquarters. He felt like Superman having to undergo a quick change in the men's washroom.

A consultant whose background and interests are very different from those of participants sometimes may be unable to get past this barrier to a productive working relationship.

> A consultant was hired to train first and second level supervisors in an Appalachian coal company. It was deer season and conversation

was dominated by hunting stories. The consultant had grown up in New York City and had no knowledge of hunting. Worse yet, the client's world of interests and values was so different that even to ask questions was to draw attention to his ignorance. He could neither share his experience nor understand theirs. For their part, the supervisors liked their "us versus the world" feelings and were not willing to let the consultant into their life. He was unable to work successfully with that client.

While such a contrast can inhibit the working relationship, it can sometimes help by fostering new perspectives, ideas, and views. The sponsor must judge if the gap becomes unproductive conflict instead of useful contrast.

Once appearance and other visible personality factors are accepted, other aspects of personality—sense of presence, interaction style, and character traits—become more important to the success of the consultation. Self-assurance is indicated if the consultant's manner is relaxed, confident, well-organized, and responsive to the here-and-now situation. Is the consultant speaking rehearsed lines or responding to what is happening right now? Personal *interaction style* is indicated by how the consultant treats people. A deferential manner probably means this style could be expected toward others with authority. An aggressive approach is an indication that participants or end users might receive the same treatment. Can the consultant state an opinion or viewpoint with confidence and still listen to the client's position without becoming defensive?

An interview helps form an impression of the consultant's character. The ideal consultant might sound like a cross between an Eagle Scout and Superman. But, there are only a few traits that are really critical—a stable personality, a mature sense of realism about what can and cannot be accomplished, a high frustration threshold, and a tolerance for ambiguous situations. Translated: Good consultants know themselves, know what they can do well, but don't have the illusion they can work wonders. Trust is also very important. The sponsor will have a better sense of whether to trust the prospective consultant when he/she knows something both about what motivates that person to work as well as his or her personal ethics.

The Consultant's Motivations

Everyone, including consultants, works for certain payoffs. These may include money, challenge, status in a consulting firm, recognition from professional colleagues, satisfaction in helping others, and advancement of professional beliefs or social causes. Any combination of payoffs is fine so long as it doesn't get in the way of the consultant's working for the client's best interests. The sponsor is not likely to find out directly what a person's motivations are. There are certain useful clues which help in drawing a tentative conclusion.

A consultant who is working solely for money or status is likely to be either a yes-man or a super salesman. In the first instance, the consultant may have an ingratiating manner calculated to flatter the client. In the second instance, the consultant will oversell his wares by painting a rosy picture of the proposed problem solution and assuring the client it will work in the situation. But there may be some reluctance to fully explain the rationale for the methods or to discuss the potential problems. The following scenario is an example.

> CLIENT: My managers are having trouble getting along with each other. They're always bickering and undermining each other's efforts. What should I do?
>
> CONSULTANT: What they need is a transactional analysis workshop. I have designed a training package that works in your kind of setting.
>
> CLIENT: What's transactional analysis?
>
> CONSULTANT: You haven't heard of TA? It's a proven way of analyzing structures of personality, interpersonal transactions, games, and scripts.
>
> CLIENT: (Looks puzzled.) Sounds like some kind of therapy.
>
> CONSULTANT: (Smiles.) You might say that.
>
> CLIENT: You want to run a TA workshop. What will happen if some of my managers don't want to be analyzed in that way?
>
> CONSULTANT: Believe me, that will never happen.

The consultant has not been willing to explain transactional analysis so the client can understand what it is about. Like a salesman, the consultant has also devalued the client's concern about manager acceptance of a TA workshop.

During an exploratory meeting, the client should insist on getting clear answers to questions about a consultant's principles or strategies. Does the consultant put down the client for asking questions or are concerns being ignored. If the client is saying "bull" to him- or herself very often, something is seriously wrong. It's time to terminate the conversation and seek another consultant.

Consultants should be cautious about championing a cause, whether it be affirmative action, ecology, participative management, or changing the corporate culture! Of course, every consultant has personal and professional biases. However, there is a difference between persuading others and badgering them into dealing with an issue. The best consultants do not seek out difficulties which are unresolvable for the sponsor, the staff, the customers, or the clients. They share their biases, but do not make issues of them. If a consultant is opposed in principle to the objectives or proposed methods of a consultation and the client organization is unwilling to change these, the consultant should decline to work with that client and explain the reason.

A consultant who values one particular cause above an organization's development will be impatient about using noncoercive ways of bringing about readiness to deal with that issue. In the 1960s, a number of organizations were injured by well-meaning consultants committed to civil rights. The same situation is happening in this decade over issues like affirmative action. Such a consultant doesn't hesitate to keep an axe close to the vest while being hired and to bring it out to grind on the job. Besides wasting people's money and creating unproductive conflict, the consultant with a cause can also drain material resources from an organization. To illustrate:

> A consultant was hired to head a task force charged with improving the working climate of an organization. This consultant was a radical feminist. At the first meeting, she challenged the membership of the task force because it did not have a balanced representation of men and women. She overlooked the fact that the task force has been appointed by management, had no say in its composition, but was genuinely interested in bringing about improvements. At the next meeting, the consultant used every opportunity to focus the discussion exclusively on women's issues and to criticize sexist attitudes of task force members. There were indeed a number of issues affecting women, but these were not the exclusive focus of the task force. Her tactics served to divide the task force prematurely into factions and to make productive work impossible. After the third meeting, this group was disbanded.

A consultant is more effective who is dedicated to the consulting profession, who believes in the work the client needs done, and who cares about what happens to the client and the participants or end-user group. Among the signs of genuine interest are:

- The consultant is willing to spend time and energy to learn about the organization and the need or problem.

- The consultant doesn't demand a long-term commitment at the beginning, but is willing to start with a limited task.

- The consultant is interested in how much involvement the sponsor wants in the project and shows willingness to include the sponsor at the appropriate points.

- During the exploratory discussion, concern is shown for the impact of a change effort on the organization. The consultant may express interest in (1) assessing readiness before starting the project, (2) field testing a product or system before instilling it systemwide, and (3) helping to alleviate anxiety about anticipated changes.

- The consultant doesn't try to make the client dependent on his or her expertise, but works to transfer it to the client organization.

Consultant's Ethics

Every consultant abides by a set of ethical do's and don'ts. These have evolved from professional beliefs, personal motivations, and experiences with the pitfalls of consulting. Certain ethical standards have become widely accepted in the consulting field. They include objectivity, honesty, loyalty, and confidentiality. However, consultants don't always interpret these in the same way or apply them consistently in specific situations. Clients should learn enough about a consultant's ethical views and track record to decide if that person is trustworthy in potential problem situations.

The sponsor can't very well ask a consultant direct questions like "Will you be loyal?" "Honest?" "Objective?" However, while discussing the consultant's past experiences and potential approach to problems, the sponsor can listen for the presence or absence of ethical sensitivity. The sponsor can ask "What if" questions about possible consulting situations that involve ethical dilemmas. The sponsor can also question previous clients about the consultant's ethical behavior.

Objectivity

A consultant with an investment in his initial conception of a problem and optimum solution is less effective. Someone who immediately says, "I have just the program you need," may be jumping the gun. A consultant must be willing to work with the client to understand the situation fully, so both can agree on what has to be done.

Effective consultants will listen carefully, absorb data, ask questions, and are open-minded all the way to the end. If the client wants an instant answer, the consultant will resist:

> CLIENT: We've been having problems here: sickness, absenteeism, lateness, longer coffee breaks, people disappearing at lunch. What should we do?
>
> CONSULTANT: I don't know what the problem is. What do you think it is?
>
> CLIENT: Some kind of morale problem.
>
> CONSULTANT: What do you think is causing the problem?
>
> CLIENT: Well, I'm not really sure. I thought you might have the answer.
>
> CONSULTANT: No, I don't, but maybe I can help you get it. You have mentioned some symptoms. There could be several causes: salary problems, supervisory problems. One way to find out is to...

When a tentative diagnosis is made, some reservations will be offered:

> CONSULTANT: I think your problem is that your selection system is inadequate. But there is a possibility that this and this and this is also true. We can try modifying the selection system, see what happens, and back up if we have to.

Effective consultants level with the client rather than try to please or to sell a particular solution. An ethical consultant who suspects a more serious problem or a different problem than the client is aware of will be candid about what he or she thinks, even if it's something the client doesn't want to hear. The consultant will also inform the client of any circumstances that might influence judgment or objectivity. An example is the consultant who is being paid a retainer or commission by a company whose products or services he is recommending.

Honesty about One's Capabilities

Some consultants may say they can do anything. Honest consultants accept only those assignments they are qualified to perform and which they believe will provide real benefit to the organization. They represent their skills and experience accurately. There are several signs of honesty. For example, the consultant can say "no" to a job not in his or her areas of competence.

> A consultant was asked to provide training to managers in communication skills and organizational planning. She replied that she had experience in the area of communication skills but not in planning. "To be very frank with you, that is not my area. I would have to go to the library and put something together. I could do a passable job. But you need somebody with knowledge and experience in planning. So I will not accept the offer."

When selecting a "full-service" management consulting firm, the client should check the extent to which the scope of available services matches specific needs. A firm may claim capability of staffing all phases of a consulting project but be unable to deliver the goods on one or more tasks. Some firms don't want to identify a problem they can't entirely solve and be obliged to refer the client to other resources. One way to check capability is to assess the track record of every individual who will be working on the project, just as if each is an independent consultant. The partner or prospective project director should be candid about staff capabilities as well as the weaknesses and strengths of the firm's consultants. To get maximum protection, the client should contract for a problem diagnosis separately from a problem solution. Once there is an accurate assessment of the problem, the client can decide whether the firm meets the needs or whether they should seek help elsewhere.

Another sign of honesty is willingness to disclose past failures as well as successes. Naturally, a consultant is selling knowledge and experience and will refer to successful projects. The consultant should discuss how previous clients would assess his or her strengths and weaknesses. The client may quote these statements when talking to these former clients and by comparing these statements help check the honesty and accuracy of both consultant and previous client. Sometimes a former client will not divulge negative information. Open-ended questions like "What are the consultant's strengths and weaknesses?" can draw out the former client and get a reaction.

Perhaps an even tougher test is for the consultant to describe a consultation that did not go well. What did the consultant learn from the experience? Did the consultation have minor problems or is a real disaster described? Has the consultant thought about past mistakes and learned from them?

Other signs of honesty are: clear communication during initial meetings about fees and the conditions under which the consultant is willing to work, willingness to have services evaluated, and corroboration from former clients about past consulting engagements.

Loyalty, Confidentiality, and Disclosure

Personal and organizational change involves taking risks to gain new advantages. People need a relatively safe environment in which to make mistakes, work out conflicts, and learn new skills. One of the consultant's functions is to create such a climate. For this reason, a consultant is obligated to use great care in withholding or disclosing inside information about a consultation. In general, the consultant has an obligation to enhance and not harm the client organization. Specifically, the consultant has an ethical obligation to the sponsor and to the end user.

The consultant's primary loyalty is to the sponsor. Occasionally the sponsor may be a top manager when the task involves systemwide issues and functions. Usually, however, the consultant reports to a lower echelon manager in charge of the unit where the problem or opportunity is located. A consultant should not betray the sponsor's confidence by leapfrogging to higher authorities. If the scope of consultation expands and communication with top management is needed, the lower echelon manager can still be kept informed and involved. The consultant should always get permission before repeating confidential information.

Not all consultants are scrupulous about maintaining confidential relationships with parties in conflict. When a consultant is hired to deal with interpersonal problems or conflicts, former clients should be contacted. "What if" questions about possible situations that could arise are helpful. Are there some points that seem threatening? The consultant should be responsible and supportive to the client. For example:

> MANAGER: This project could create some anxiety for me. I know some of my subordinates don't much like my ways of running the department. What if they start bad-mouthing me during team-building sessions? What will you do?
>
> CONSULTANT: I'll listen to what they say. I won't necessarily agree. But I will listen, and then I'll check out whether in my observation there's any validity to what they are saying. If there is, I will come to you and tell you what I'm seeing. You and I will decide together where to go from there.

An ethical consultant is also careful not to use inside information for personal benefit or help another client at the expense of the organization. Obviously, knowledge of a company's plans will not be used to tip off his relatives to good investment opportunities! When describing specific past consulting experiences, the identity of other clients will not be revealed. (Of course, references for previous work should be given.) The consultant who is doing an executive search for another organization won't steal your personnel. If invited to work for a competitor, the client should be asked if knowledge of the organization could directly benefit the other client. Consultants must be careful to use their knowledge to benefit and not harm clients.

9

Collaborative Client-Consultant Relationships

Sam Barcus

Barcus Britt Leiffer Consulting
Nashville, Tennessee

Introduction

The most critical component and intensely intangible element of consulting services is the client-consultant relationship. Consulting relationships, like all others, are vulnerable to personal idiosyncrasy, implication, and interpretation. These relationships require special care to ensure that they flourish. There is a mystique surrounding a client-consultant relationship that is unique. Often clients feel they are putting their fate in the consultant's hands.

The consulting process and a client-consultant relationship begin by diagnosing problems and the consultant's influencing the client to purchase a service. A successful relationship results when the client accepts the consultant's promise and then perceives that the consultant resolved a need. Success depends on the consultant's ability to develop a mutual-

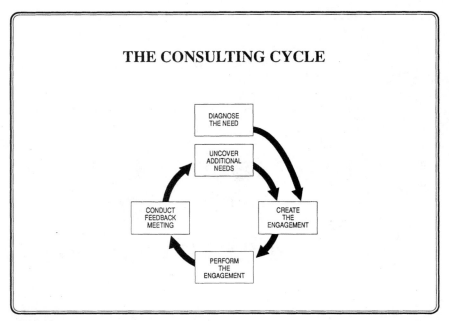

Figure 9-1

ly beneficial relationship that is based on need, understanding, credibility, and trust. Figure 9-1 shows the Consulting Cycle.

A fundamental part of influencing the client to purchase a service is understanding and appreciating the client's current business issues and perceptions. The consultant must demonstrate understanding by making a connection between the client's needs and the firm's abilities. Most consulting services have a large intangible component because results cannot be easily measured, seen, or touched. Dealing with the intangible nature of services and the client's perception of the services is a major challenge in the consulting process.

What the consultant is really asking the client to purchase is a "promise of satisfaction." The ambiguity of the promise depends on the features of the service, the degree to which it is intangible, the consultant's approach to marketing, professional fees, and the client's expectations. For management consulting services the promise of satisfaction can be even more ambiguous if the client is ambivalent about hiring a consultant. Many clients are uncertain why a consultant is needed and what the consultant is supposed to accomplish. The expectations of the client are influenced by the way the service is positioned, packaged, and delivered. The client is assessing the "present value" of the promise.

If the consultant demonstrates an understanding of the client's business environment, the consultant has the opportunity to link the firm's

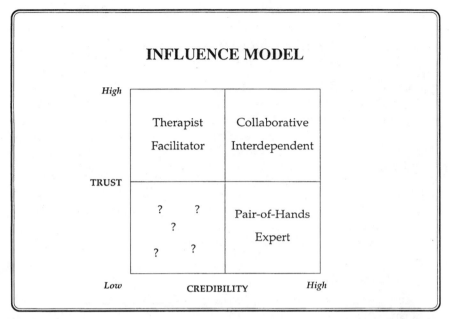

Figure 9-2

services to the client's success. Specific issue identification is the next step. Coming to grips with a substantive issue of interest and importance to the client generates both confidence and interest in developing the relationship. An accurate analysis and solution of the issue builds credibility and strengthens the client-consultant relationship. Each step along the way the consultant is establishing an "agreement in principle" with the client, which helps manage expectations and gets a commitment to proceed. Over time the consultant can build a collaborative relationship with the client (Figure 9-2) which allows the consultant to influence a variety of client decisions.

Understanding Issues

The consultant's services must come directly to grips with a fundamental issue in the client's business. The successful performance of the service depends on an in-depth understanding of the client's business. Confronting substantive business issues is one of the most difficult tasks of the consulting process. When the client-consultant relationship works perfectly the client says, "We have an issue. Here it is. How do we solve it?" Unfortunately this does not happen often because the client does not understand the role the consultant can play to help resolve the issue. The client may not participate in a quality diagnostic dialogue or the consultant may not be able to confront a concrete issue.

The consultant's ability to recognize and identify the true issue is critical to establishing and building a successful client-consultant relationship. The client may sense that an issue exists but may be uncertain as to the specific nature of the issue. The consultant is responsible for identifying and defining the client's issue in meaningful terms. The client may understand pieces of the issue but need help putting the pieces together in an integrated and comprehensive whole. The client may understand the symptoms of the issue but may need help working through the symptoms to see the real issue. The client may think that an issue exists but need help recognizing the substance of the issue. Uncovering real issues requires the ability to listen to the spoken words and the thoughts and emotions that are behind the words. Only by listening with interpersonal finesse can the consultant identify the true issue and communicate the ability to resolve the issue to the client's satisfaction.

Issue Diagnosis

The consultant's primary focus should be getting the client to accept the issue diagnosis. Gaining "agreement in principle" with the client along the way will help build the client's commitment to the diagnosis. Figure 9-3 is a diagnostic compass that will help guide the consultant through the diagnostic process. Political awareness helps the consultant navigate the people issues surrounding the issue diagnosis. Issues that have a heavy technical content are still managed by people working in politically minded organizations. Navigating through a client's management style and organizational politics and getting the client to understand the issue is a critical activity. The consultant has to address both the technical and organizational aspects of the issue to ensure success. Figure 9-4 shows an issue-mapping technique that will help the consultant identify the key stakeholders in the organization and their impact on the issue.

Effective diagnosis allows action on the issue leading to resolution and improvement in some aspect of organizational operations. Increasingly clients evaluate consultants' effectiveness by the impact of the recommendations, not the report on conclusions and findings. The emphasis on results and impact should influence and guide the diagnostic approach. Diagnostic work should simplify and narrow the issue, focusing on action steps to create a solution. The written diagnostic and the oral presentation should be straightforward, using visuals where possible and the client's language. Constant attention to the client-consultant relationship is important. Routine discussions about all aspects of the issue are important to build agreement in principle and deal with resistance to acknowledging the key issues. Organizational analysis is as

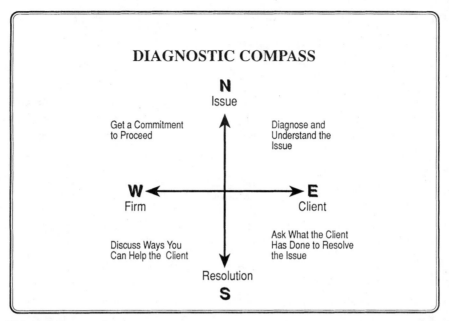

Figure 9-3

important as technical issue analysis, including understanding how the client is managing the issue. The consultant's ability to diagnose the issue has to be blended with the client's willingness to accept advice and act on the recommendations.

Issue Definition

Issue definition includes rectifying a deteriorating situation, improving a situation, or identifying and acting on new opportunities. All issues have a common characteristic: what is actually happening differs from what should be happening. There are five elements to issue definition:

1. Identification—description of the issue's substance and the basis of comparison
2. Scope—people affected by the issue and the nature of the issue (closed versus open-ended)
3. Location—organizational and physical units where the issue has been observed
4. Intensity—importance of the issue in absolute and relative terms, degree of impact on the organizational unit and the people affected
5. Timing—starting point, frequency of occurrence, and current stability

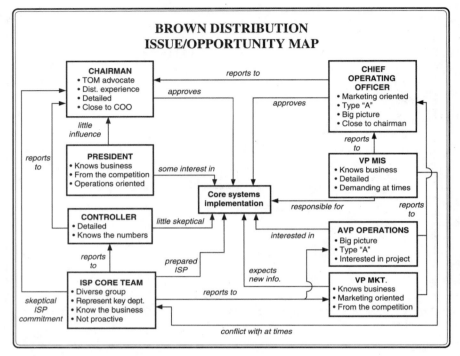

Figure 9-4

Issue definition also includes identifying the forces and factors which are causing the issue. Potential causes are identified by determining differences or changes in the issue area and assessing how these could cause the issue. Differences can help explain why the issue is happening in a particular situation and nowhere else. Change analysis is useful when there is an established history of success followed by the onset of an issue. Questions that help focus on differences and changes include:

- What is different or has changed relative to management style and the issue area?

- What is different or has changed relative to people and the issue area?

- What is different or has changed about the policies and/or procedures in the issue area?

- What is different or has changed about the business processes that are used in the issue area?

- Are there other differences or changes associated with the issue area that are a potential cause?

Figure 9-5 is a diagram of the issue definition model.

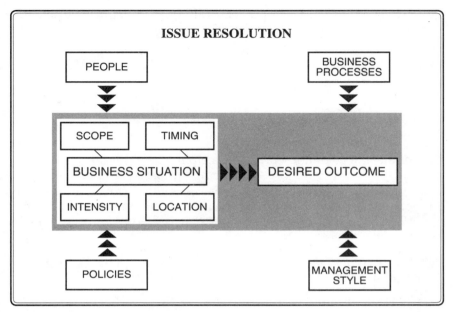

Figure 9-5

Issue Redefinition

When the client's explanation of what's causing the issue is accurate, the client usually solves the issue. When the client's attempts at solving the issue are unsuccessful or the client does not know how to solve the issue, the consultant has the opportunity to participate in the issue-solving process. Often the initial issue suggested by the client and the real or underlying issue are quite different. The consultant's contribution is to redefine the initial issue statement for the client.

Issue redefinition should focus on how the issue is being managed. The client's management style and organizational politics can help the consultant understand the management side of the issue. Personalities and relationships are an important part of organizational politics and provide clues and insight for effective issue definition. Technical and business issues inevitably have management and political components that should influence how the issue gets resolved. Addressing only part of the issue leads to partial resolution and recommendations that are ineffective.

The following activities guide and focus issue redefinition:

Determining the client's personal role in causing or maintaining the issue

Determining other members of the client organization that are contributing to the issue

Working with the client to collect and interpret data about potential causes, focusing on a few key issues

Describing the technical, business, management, and political aspects of the issue

Making and Keeping Promises

Part of the issue definition process is helping the client minimize uncertainty or increase the client's confidence and peace of mind. Successful issue resolution is holding out the promise of introducing more certainty in the area where the client feels uncertain. Even though the client may not specifically refer to the uncertainty, it is there. The client may be experiencing different types of uncertainty:

1. The uncertainty of knowing where to find the right consulting assistance—the consulting firm's distinctive capabilities

2. The uncertainty of knowing how much should be spent on consulting services—the soundness of the expenditure

3. The uncertainty of really understanding the issue—the specific nature of the issue being treated

These questions are always there and must be addressed by the consultant to the satisfaction of the prospective client. Also the consultant cannot assume that once the project is underway the client has full and continuing confidence. Often the client becomes apprehensive once the engagement starts and fees are being paid. Actually the selling has just begun when the proposal is accepted. The "sale" comes in delivering on the engagement's promise. The selling and delivering of a service cannot be separated.

Buying Promises

Clients purchase consulting services when the consultant is able to demonstrate understanding and appreciation of the client's business issues. The consultant should build on that understanding and make a connection between the client's needs and the firm's capabilities. Consulting services tend to be very intangible and difficult for the client to understand even when supported with promotional materials. The consultant's ability to address the intangible nature of services and the client's often unclear perception of services is the first hurdle to overcome in the consulting process.

As mentioned earlier, the consultant is asking the client to purchase "a promise of satisfaction"—a promise that the consultant will satisfy the client's needs. The fuzziness of the promise depends on the service features, intangibility, advertising and promotion techniques, and fee structure. The client's expectations also play a key role bounding and defining the promise. If the client has not used consulting services before, the promise of satisfaction will be even more ambiguous. Clients that are unclear about really needing and using consultants are difficult to work with and usually want very specific proposals, work plans, and fee estimates. The expectations of the client will be directly influenced by interactions with firm representatives, the definition of the issue, and how the promise is described and delivered. Remember the client is evaluating the "present value" of the promise.

Winning Over the Client's Mind

Potential clients weigh expectations, impressions, and perceptions when deciding whether to engage a consultant and buy a service. This decision-making process is neither simple nor necessarily rational. Winning over the client's mind is the central challenge of services marketing, and all types of things influence the client's mind. The consultant's ability to quickly perceive the client's mindset and then tailor the marketing approach is a major factor toward influencing the client's acceptance of the consultant's promise.

Attitudes toward a consultant, a firm, and services are developed over time through a collective series of events. First impressions will color many subsequent events, although clients may change their perception during a consulting engagement. Packaging is almost always used by the client to make judgments about the consultant, the firm, and the service. All three components are judged by the client to assess the promise of satisfaction. The promise of satisfaction is established, built, and affirmed based on a cluster of expectations, impressions, and perceptions formed through various encounters with the firm's people, literature, and services.

Building Client Relationships

Another element of making and keeping promises is establishing quality interpersonal relationships at the start of an engagement. The success of the engagement depends on the positive participation of the client and on the quality of the information provided by the client. A good basic rule in client-consultant relationships is to never surprise the client. Also clients expect the person who sold the project to actively participate and deliver the findings and recommendations. Successful client-consultant relationships endure beyond the first engagement. The relationship-building process occurs during the project and during implementation of the results. Part of this building process includes routine status meetings with the client followed up with brief status reports highlighting key items. Management involvement throughout the project is critical to keep things going smoothly.

Once a relationship is cemented, equity is created for the consultant. It is the responsibility of the consultant to enhance the equity lest it decline and become jeopardized by competitors. Maintaining relationships requires effort, but it is much easier keeping a client than attracting a new one. Also by maintaining a client relationship there are significant opportunities for adding on to current projects, expanding services, and generating referrals. If the consultant builds trust and credibility, the client will increasingly ask for advice. The quality of the relationship directly affects the consultant's opportunity to service the client. In a long-term client-consultant relationship, reliability and responsiveness become more important than the specific features of the service. An interdependence develops in long-term relationships that requires nurturing and reassurance. Without that attention the negative things accumulate. Developing a quality relationship with each client takes time but the investment in the relationship pays off in many ways.

Identifying the Provider

There are two possible approaches for the consultant to demonstrate an understanding of the client's issue. The extrinsic approach is used when the consultant focuses more on the firm's capabilities rather than on the client's issue. The extrinsic approach includes: describing a generalized method to issue resolution; describing the experience of key personnel in the firm; or describing projects conducted for other clients. The intrinsic approach is used when the consultant focuses on coming to grips with an issue that is important to the client. The intrinsic approach requires the ability to sufficiently grasp the issue so that the client begins to develop confidence in the consultant's skills. The consultant has to communicate enough knowledge about the issue to reinforce the initial confidence and create the issue of satisfaction that can later be fulfilled by actually conducting a project.

Persuasion by Method

This approach to helping the client understand how the firm can address the issue focuses on the characteristics of the services rather than the consequences of the services. For example if the firm is going to assist the client in an analysis and research project, the firm should emphasize the implications of the data gathered rather than the data-gathering process.

Techniques such as reviewing documents, forms, and reports and interviewing individuals and groups often get the emphasis. Too much emphasis on method can give the service the appearance of a commodity.

Successful consultants focus on the business issue first and the methods of solving the issue second. Unfortunately some consultants tend to approach the consultative sales process the other way around by defining the issue to fit the firm's methodology. If the consultant stresses the flexibility of the firm's methodology rather than strict adherence to methodology guidelines, a structured approach can help the consultant come to grips with a substantive issue. The consultant has to help the client understand that a methodical approach to issue resolution is important, and the method chosen to solve the issue depends on the scope and definition of the issue. A substantive client-consultant dialogue around the issue can help both parties understand and help the consultant be more responsive to the client's needs.

Persuasion by Key People

The background, experience, and reputation of a firm's key people is the major core competency of a consulting firm. A firm's marketing efforts should focus on this expertise when attempting to extend and/or expand client projects, build referral networks, and enhance community visibility. Well-written, tailored résumés should be included with firm marketing materials and proposals where appropriate. Prospective clients should be encouraged to investigate the firm's credentials and inquire about who will be working on a potential engagement.

Although the expertise of the firm's people is an important selling proposition, there are limitations if it is the only basis on which to communicate to the client understanding of the issue. The firm is asking the client to make the connection of people's skills to business issues and translate the connection into the benefits of hiring the firm. This is critical when the client cannot meet with and interview the individuals and has to rely on résumés. Résumés can indicate the firm's overall depth and experience, but the individual representing the firm has to demonstrate his or her own competence relative to the other members of the firm and particularly the client's issue.

Persuasion by Success Story

A firm's successful engagements are an effective method of communicating the firm's capabilities except when the success stories are overstated. Too much emphasis on particular projects, clients, industries, or results focus attention away from the prospective client's issues and needs. The success story is very effective when an analogy is drawn between the client's situation and the success story's objectives, approach, and results. The consultant needs to paint a picture of relevant issues resolved that relate to the prospective client's issues.

Success stories are most effective when the substantive nature of the issue solved is discussed rather than the successful aspects of the project. By emphasizing the key aspects of the issue, the consultant communicates to the client the firm's ability to recognize the unique elements of a particular situation. Also the client can elevate the consultant's ability to come to grips with the essence of the issue. For this process to work, the consultant has to describe a prior situation that the client both can identify with and can understand how the situation applies to the client's issue.

Intrinsic Issue Resolution

Effective consultants operate at two levels with clients—the substance issue-solving level, which tends to be rational and explicit, and the interpersonal level, which focuses on how the client and consultant feel about each other. Intrinsic issue resolution includes identifying the substance of the issue or project and the affective side of the client-consultant relationship. Both are important sources of data about the client's real issues and the possibilities for establishing a good relationship. Many consultants have a great deal of experience working at the substance level of issue resolution because of skills and experience. Equal attention should be given to the interpersonal side of issue resolution to ensure commitment and ownership on the client's part.

Intrinsic issue resolution requires certain assumptions and techniques to be successful. Valid data are necessary to eliminate confusion, uncertainty, and inefficiency. Valid data include objective, factual data about the issue and personal data about people's feelings. Most issue-resolution efforts cross functional and departmental boundaries involving many different people in the organization. To the degree these people participate in the issue-resolution process and have the opportunity to influence decisions that impact their work, they will be motivated to help make things work. Also people will more actively support projects they believe will further their interests and agendas.

Collaborative client-consultant relationships facilitate intrinsic issue resolution. Both consultant and client resources are used more effectively and the process becomes a model for the client to address and solve future challenges. Teaching the client issue-resolution skills ensures that the current issue stays solved and enables the client to institute an ongoing process for defining and resolving issues. Intrinsic issue resolution focuses both on the substance of the technical/business issue and the way people are interacting around the issue. In particular the consultant is able to address the people and political issues as an outsider with no vested interest in the people or process issues. A collaborative relationship allows the consultant to focus on people and process and get the client's attention.

Client commitment is the key to realizing the results of the issue-resolution process because consultants have no direct control over implementation. Clear and logical thinking, good communication skills, and strong convictions help the consultant move the client to action, but the client will always experience some doubts and concerns. Clients ultimately will decide whether to take action based on how internally committed they are to the consultant's ideas. The consultant must build internal commitment throughout the issue-resolution process. Building this commitment is partly a process of removing obstacles that block the client from acting on the consultant's advice and taking those steps and actions that build internal commitment.

Conclusion

Collaborative client-consultant relationships are based on the notion that business issues can be dealt with effectively by linking the consultant's specialized skills with the client's knowledge of the situation (Figure 9-6). An intrinsic issue-resolution approach is employed with equal attention

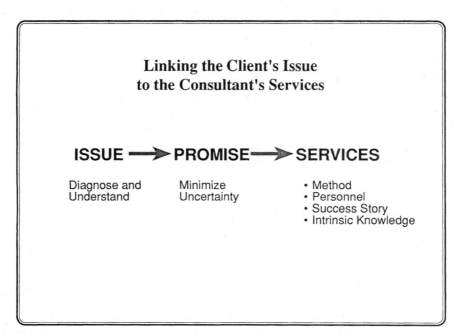

Figure 9-6

to the technical and business elements and the people elements surrounding the substantive issues. A collaborative approach emphasizes joint issue resolution where the consultant's specific skills are combined with the client's organizational knowledge. Both client and consultant are actively involved in goal setting, data gathering, analysis, and issue resolution, equally sharing the responsibility for success or failure.

The key elements of the collaborative approach to issue resolution and relationship building include:

- The client and the consultant work to become interdependent on all aspects of the issue-resolution process.

- Decision making is bilateral, acknowledging the responsibilities and expertise of both the client and the consultant.

- Data collection and analysis are performed by both the client and the consultant.

- Creative conflict is anticipated and seen as a source of new ideas.

- Collaboration is furthered by efforts to reach mutual understanding and agreement on expectations for the issue resolution process.

- Implementation responsibilities are defined through discussion about appropriate client-consultant roles and available resources.

- Skills transfer is a part of the issue-resolution process to increase the client's competence to solve future challenges.

Bibliography

Levitt, Theodore, *The Marketing Imagination*, The Free Press, New York, 1983.

Wilson, Aubrey, *The Marketing of Professional Services*, McGraw-Hill, New York, 1972.

Part 3
The Consulting Process

10
Problem Definition

Dennis F. Togo
Area of Accounting
The University of New Mexico
Albuquerque, New Mexico

Problem definition is the first phase of the problem-solving process. Its position in the problem-solving process is well established. The term *problem definition* assumes a variety of meanings, however, since it is used by numerous persons in reference to a wide variety of problem-solving situations. Each person has his or her particular view of the manner by which problems are approached, defined, and solved. Each problem-solving situation has its particular set of conditions and constraints. Because of such differing conceptual frameworks and circumstances, our initial concern is to establish standard definitions.

Definitions

How may a problem be defined? When a system or process behaves as expected, allowing for suitable tolerances, no problem exists. A problem arises only when behavior moves out of the range that an observer would normally view as being reasonable in the circumstances. Thus, a problem may be said to exist when the observed behavior of a system or process violates the bounds of reasonable expectations. This definition of a problem requires the presence of several factors: human awareness of the problem, predefinition of the allowable tolerances, and recognition of the established standards.

First, a problem requires that involved humans be aware of the implications of the existing situation. A system or process may be beyond the bounds of reasonable expectations; if no one recognizes this condition, however, no problem (and hence no correctable solution) is truly apparent.

Second, a problem requires that the tolerances be predefined, where tolerances are the allowed deviations or variances from the ideal situation. Unless the tolerances are predefined, no one can determine when the system or process is beyond the bounds of reasonable expectations.

The tolerances that determine the existence of a problem must be established by humans rather than by the system or process itself. For example, consider the allowable tolerances pertaining to a machined part. They are established by humans to accord with the ultimate use of the part. If they were to be established to accommodate the capabilities of the machine on which they are processed, the resulting part might not be fit for its intended purpose. To take another example, consider the tolerances related to processes in a service-oriented organization. These tolerances should be established in accordance with client or consumer expectations, rather than by the costs of the processes or the whims of the processors. Thus, the processing of any document received by a government agency from an applicant should reflect, in terms of time and service, the expectations of the applicant. If the applicant perceives the processing to be slow and the service to be poor, the agency can be said to have a problem.

The task of establishing suitable tolerances deserves the careful attention of judicious individuals. Sometimes tolerances can be established by clear guidelines such as contracts with customers, engineering blueprints, or procedures manuals. Often, however, tolerances must be established on the basis of unclear and inexact guidelines such as fuzzily written government regulations or vague oral statements from top management. Also, the range of allowable tolerances may vary considerably. For instance, the allowable tolerances of machined parts for toys may be much greater than those of machined parts for spaceships.

A third factor in a problem situation concerns the recognition by observers of the tolerances and hence the expectations or standards. Quantitative standards, such as sales quotas and budget levels, are easily recognized, as are variations of actual values from these standards. Qualitative standards are not so easily recognized, even though they are pervasive in the realms of human relationships and human-oriented processes. Qualitative standards appear as written and oral rules promulgated by official bodies, as unwritten traditions of work groups comprising informal organizations, and as observed regularities. Standards such as these, especially the observed regularities, are expressed as much by actions as by words.

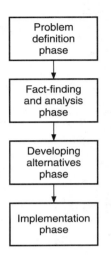

Figure 10-1 Problem-solving process.

Phases of a Problem-Solving Process

Most engagements undertaken by consultants will involve the solution of problems. Hence, a process that emphasizes the solution of problems is of great interest to a consultant. A sound problem-solving process consists of four phases: (1) the problem-definition phase, (2) the fact-finding and analysis phase, (3) the developing alternatives phase, and (4) the implementation phase. Each phase has one or more distinct purposes and occupies a separate period within the overall process. The set of phases demonstrates a sequential and hierarchical pattern, in that (1) each phase (except the first) follows a previous phase along a time dimension and (2) each phase builds upon the results of its predecessors. Figure 10-1 depicts the four phases of the problem-solving process.

Problem-Definition Phase

The problem-definition phase has the purpose of fully describing the underlying problem. It begins with the initial recognition of a symptom pointing to the problem and ends with the complete problem description. Thorough attention to this phase is vital to the success of the problem-solving process, since this phase requires the underlying causes of the problem to be identified. Its importance is found in a common saying of mathematicians: When a problem is fully understood, then the solution becomes obvious. Prematurely working on a solution to a problem that is not well understood will lead to wasted efforts. Another reason the problem-definition phase is important is that it detects those cases in which problems can be controlled only within certain limits, thereby influencing the feasibility of conducting the following phases.

Fact-Finding and Analysis Phase

The purposes of the fact-finding and analysis phase are to gather facts needed to solve the problem and to analyze these facts to clarify the requirements of feasible solutions. This second phase often overlaps with the problem definition phase in that it helps to sort the symptoms from the underlying causes of the problem. In addition, this phase may identify the resources capable of steering the defined problem situation in the direction of a desired solution. Furthermore, it should serve as a get-acquainted period, during which the consultant can gain the cooperation and commitment of persons who are affected by the problem situation and will be affected by its solution.

Developing-Alternatives Phase

The purpose of the developing-alternatives phase is to identify feasible solutions to the problem and to present a detailed plan of action for the recommended alternatives. This plan of action should include the rationale for an alternative's selection, expressed in terms of benefits and advantages, the schedule for its installation, and the needed resources.

Implementation Phase

The purpose of the implementation phase is to put the detailed plan into operation. If the previous phases have been conducted well, this phase should be the least difficult in logical terms. Nevertheless, this phase may exhibit a high degree of logistic complexity. Numerous activities may need to be meshed smoothly. Also, minor deviations to the plan are sure to be imposed, and circumstances in the environment are certain to change. In some situations, the deviations and changes could become so great that recycling to previous phases will be necessary.

The second, third, and fourth phases of the problem-solving process will be discussed at length in the three following chapters.

Facets of the Problem-Definition Phase

Now we are ready to focus on the facets of the problem-definition phase. It is the foundation upon which the following phases are built. A solid

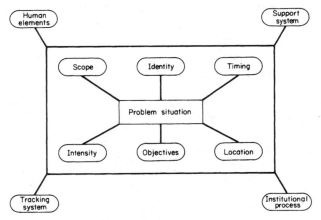

Figure 10-2 Problem definition.

foundation is especially important if the problem situation is complex and many factors are interrelated. All problems cannot be solved or corrected. In some cases the cost of the solution is larger than the benefits that might reasonably be expected. In other cases the solution may create another problem. For instance, correcting the problem of high production costs may cause a problem with respect to product quality. Problems in cases such as these can be controlled only within certain limits, which should be identified in the problem-definition phase.

Intrinsic and extrinsic facets of this phase are identified in Figure 10-2. The intrinsic facets focus on the unique aspects of the problem, whereas the extrinsic facets identify interactions between the environment or setting and the problem. By determining both the internal and external facets of a problem, you the consultant will have the information needed to fully describe the problem.

Identity of the Problem

What is the problem? This should be the first question you ask and the last question that you, as a consultant, answer during the problem-definition phase. An acceptable final answer can emerge only after two procedures are completed: problem finding and problem stating. A comprehensive answer will incorporate the several facets discussed in following sections. A valid answer will avoid the variety of pitfalls that await the unwary consultant.

Problem Finding The problem-finding procedure begins with identification of the (1) reasonable expectations pertaining to a system or process and (2) allowable tolerances from these reasonable expectations.

Problem finding continues with the comparison of actual conditions against these expectations. The last step is the flagging of conditions that exceed the allowable tolerances from reasonable expectations.

An example of the problem-finding procedure, especially familiar to accountants, is the operation of a standard cost accounting system. The first step is to establish (1) standards for unit direct materials and unit direct labor costs and (2) allowable variances from these standards. Periodically, the actual unit direct materials and direct labor costs are compared with these standards. Variances that exceed the allowable ranges are flagged for the attention of production management.

As described above, problem finding is often reactive in nature. That is, it addresses problems as they are detected. Problem finding can also be opportunistic. Opportunistic scanning consists of searching for beneficial opportunities to exploit. This aggressive approach seeks to improve the system or process, thereby reaping added dividends. For example, a consultant may note that installing a computer information system could improve customer service, thus increasing sales and profits. Opportunistic scanning, as well as reactive problem finding, can and should be ongoing activities.

Problem Stating   The consultant should prepare an initial written statement of the problem as early as possible in the phase. This initial statement may be relatively inexact and based on intuitive, "gut" hunches. Nevertheless, it represents a tangible starting point and should not be overlooked.

The final tangible result of the problem-definition phase will be a comprehensive and, it is hoped, valid statement of the problem. This final statement may represent an expanded and polished version of the initial statement. Alternatively, the final statement may bear scant resemblance to the initial statement, if the initial statement is found to be faulty or superficial.

Statement Content   The final statement of the problem should contain such facets as (1) the objectives to be achieved by the solution to the problem; (2) the problem's scope, intensity, time dimensions, and location; (3) the human elements involved in the problem; (4) the support system and tracking systems related to the problem solution; (5) and the institutional process for managing the problem. In addition, the statement may clearly separate the symptoms from the underlying causes of the problem, identify relevant constraints, and reveal key relationships among the factors involved in the problem situation.

Pitfalls in Identifying the Problem   Identifying the real problem will undoubtedly require patient and exacting investigation if the situation is complex. Possible pitfalls include the following:

1. *Mistaking symptoms for the underlying problem.* Symptoms are the effects, rather than the causes, of the problem. Although symptoms may point to the presence of the problem, they should not be viewed as the core of the problem itself. For example, scrap from milling machine operations is a symptom. The underlying problem may be a worn cutter, a bad bearing, or an alcoholic operator. Each of these problems may, in turn, be the symptom of deeper problems. Thus, a worn cutter or bad bearing may be the result of postponed preventive maintenance caused by budget cutbacks. You should continue searching and probing until you are satisfied that the causes of the problem have been uncovered.

2. *Accepting without question the opinions of others concerning the problem.* A consultant will necessarily talk with various managers and employees of the client organization to gather facts concerning the problem. Because these managers and employees are closely involved in the situation, you may give their opinions considerable weight. However, the managers and employees may be too close to the situation to see the real problem clearly. Sometimes their biases will color their views of the problem situation. You should, therefore, suspend early judgment with respect to such opinions. Do not be in a hurry to conclude the problem-finding procedure. Instead, ask probing questions such as: Why do you believe that? What experiences lead you to that opinion? When did the most recent incident (accident) occur? Furthermore, you should actively search for facts that either support or deny the opinions.

3. *Assuming that the problem is a person.* Problems can be due to the behavior or nonbehavior of people, but problems are not the people themselves. It can be dangerous to personalize problems. You, as consultant, may feel obliged to make personal attacks on the individuals involved in order to support your recommendations. Actions such as these are likely to create other, equally serious, problems.

4. *"Slaying the bearer of bad news."* Another way of personalizing problems is to confuse the messenger of news with the news itself. That is, you might view a manager who tells you of a problem to be the cause of that problem. If your questions or comments reveal this attitude, the manager is apt to "clam up." As a result, you could lose the source of vital information about the problem and perhaps its solution.

5. *Overlooking the multicausality of problems.* Multiple symptoms may point to a single problem. Likewise, a problem or problem situation may have multiple causes. For instance, declining net income is a problem that generally has more than a single cause. It might be due in part to weakening sales and in part to rising labor costs. Problems such as high employee turnover and poor customer service are also usually due to a combination of causal factors.

All the underlying causes of a problem should be isolated and clearly stated. A comprehensive statement of causes has two benefits. It provides more points of attack, so that a more effective solution is likely to be developed. Also, a comprehensive statement may help uncover key interrelationships among the causal factors.

Objectives of the Problem-Solving Process

The objective of the problem-solving process is the desired outcome. It should be prominently expressed in the problem-definition statement, generally in terms of clear-cut expectations or benefits. Preferably, the objective or objectives should be expressed quantitatively and with a specific time horizon. For instance, an objective might be stated as follows: "To increase the percentage of on-time deliveries, so that by the end of this year 99 percent of all deliveries are made on time." Objectives expressed in this fashion should enable interested parties to evaluate the effectiveness of the problem-solving process.

The nature of the objectives depends upon the type of problem, as well as the system or process involved. Typical objectives pertaining to systems and processes in business organizations are concerned with performance, efficiency, economy, control, security, or availability of information.

Scope of the Problem

The scope of the problem pertains to the extent of its effects. Thus, when defining the problem you should ask such questions as: How widespread are the effects of the problem at the present time? Are they confined to one area in a specific department? Have they spread to proximally or functionally related areas? Have they affected the markets of the firm?

A clear statement of problem scope should suggest the extent of the needed response or solution to the problem. It might also point to the need for repackaging the consulting engagement. For instance, if the scope is discovered to be immense and to extend to a variety of activities, it may be desirable to break the engagement into a series of smaller problem areas. Each partial problem can then be solved more easily, and the solutions can be combined to attack the overall problem.

The Intensity of the Problem

Another facet of the problem is its intensity—the degree of discomfort that its adverse effects cause to interested parties. For instance, the managers of a business firm may feel very intense discomfort when a new product does much more poorly than expected in the marketplace. The level of intensity may determine the relative urgency and importance of initiating a particular problem-solving process. Thus, if the president of a firm is informed of two problems, the one that exerts the greater intensity is likely to be assigned the higher priority for solution.

The Time Dimensions of the Problems

Relevant Questions   Three questions should be answered with respect to the time dimensions of a problem:

1. How long has the problem existed?
2. How much longer is the problem likely to continue if left unattended?
3. How frequently is the problem likely to occur in the future?

Answers to these questions should be included in the final statement of the problem, since the answers will probably have a bearing upon the development of a solution. Let us consider the effects of certain answers.

With respect to the first question, the answer may be a long time or a very short time. (Of course, either answer should state the exact length of time.) If the problem has been in existence a long time, its adverse effects probably have become quite clear. Thus, sufficient facts should be available on which to base a sound solution. If the problem has been in existence for only a very short time, a prompt solution should minimize its adverse effects. However, adequate data may not be available to provide a clear picture. The danger in prompt action is that an inappropriate solution may be developed and implemented. To avoid this danger, you may need to delay action until the adverse effects manifest themselves in several repetitions. Alternatively, you might try to replicate the effects of the problem in a laboratory setting, thus reducing the delay in development of a sound solution.

With respect to the second question, the answer may be a brief remaining life span or a lengthy remaining life span. If the expected life span is brief, the best choice may be to tolerate the problem during its short remaining tenure. If its life span will be long, it should be attended to as soon as feasible.

With respect to the expected future appearance of the problem, the answer may be very infrequent or very frequent. If the problem is expected to arise only once in one thousand occurrences of a recurring circumstance, an effort to solve it may not be cost-effective. If the problem is likely to arise during every other occurrence, however, an extensive effort to solve it will most likely be worthwhile.

Relationships between Frequency and Intensity   There are four ways in which the frequency and intensity of a problem may be related:

1. *Low intensity and low frequency.* A problem exhibiting these characteristics may be viewed as inconsequential.

2. *High intensity and high frequency.* A problem having these characteristics demands an immediate solution.

3. *High intensity and low frequency.* A problem having these characteristics requires continual monitoring. If a solution is not viewed as being urgent, a critical level of intensity should be established. As soon as this level is reached, an "all-out" effort should be made to develop and implement an immediate solution. A problem that exhibits high intensity and low frequency poses agonizing dilemmas. You cannot be certain when it will recur, or even that it will recur at all. Locating the causes of such a problem can be extremely difficult, since it cannot be observed with regularity. Selecting the proper course of action can be fraught with danger. On the one hand, lack of an attempt to solve the problem can result in a costly disaster if it suddenly arises in full intensity. On the other hand, an "all-out" effort to solve the problem can be very costly and politically disastrous.

4. *Low intensity and high frequency.* A problem having these characteristics tends to be annoying but not crippling. This type of problem is exemplified by the high rework situation. Many units of product emerging from a production operation must be reworked because key dimensions are not within the tolerance limits of the specifications. Although it may be tempting to allow the problem situation to continue, in the hope that it will correct itself, this "do-nothing" approach is generally not a wise choice. A better choice is to either correct the problem promptly or set a time limit and take corrective action if the problem has not rectified itself within the allotted time.

The Location of the Problem

The location of the problem is the geographic point or points where it occurs. For example, you may locate a problem in the Nashville plant, building 14, northwest corner, between pillars R and S. Alternatively, you may locate a problem in the accounts payable department at the Toronto home office. Although in most problem situations the location can be easily determined, the location may require laborious retracings of tangled paths in extreme situations. In every situation, however, it is necessary for you to pinpoint the location in order to provide a complete description of the problem.

The Human Elements of the Problem

A problem typically is associated with a host of human-related elements. Each of these elements should be identified and assessed in the statement of the problem. Examples of such elements include:

1. The training of involved employees and managers

2. The tenure of involved employees and managers

3. The attitude of involved employees and managers with respect to such matters as loyalty to the organization

4. The personal traits of involved employees and managers, including intelligence, motivation, leadership quality, dependability, trustworthiness, and interpersonal skills

Another human-related element that may often appear in the problem statement is the prevailing political climate. You should include not only an assessment of this climate but also an assessment of the priorities that have been established by the policymakers. This latter assessment should be based on the priorities that have been de facto applied rather than those that may be stated in speeches or policy statements.

The Support System Surrounding the Problem

A problem is also surrounded by elements that comprise a support system. These elements should be identified in the problem statement, together with an analysis of their functional or dysfunctional effects (if any) upon the problem. For instance, an inefficient mail room procedure may be identified as a dysfunctional element with respect to a problem involving claims-processing delays. A broken crane may be identified as a dysfunctional element with respect to a problem involving delays in parts shipments, and an aggressive overtime policy may be identified as a functional element that tends to minimize these delays. In some situations a support element may be found to be the sole cause of a problem, even though the support element may be located in a separate location from the problem itself.

The Tracking System Related to the Problem

A problem is often detected by a tracking system. The problem statement should reveal:

1. How the problem was brought to light

2. Whether the problem was detected by a tracking system so designed for the purpose or by another means (if not detected by the tracking system so designed for the purpose, why the tracking system failed)

3. Whether tracking systems other than the one designed for the purpose should have detected the problem

4. Whether tracking systems are available to monitor the situation reliably, as well as to measure the degree of improvement in the process or system due to an implemented solution

The Institutional Process for Managing the Problem

Problems in an organization are managed (i.e., defined, processed, delegated, solved) via an institutional process. The process may be informal in nature, with the management tasks being assigned quickly and with little written evidence. However, it may be quite formal, involving a chain of command and such written evidence as elaborate charts and graphs. The degree of informality or formality in the institutional process may extend outside the organization structure to encompass customers, lenders, suppliers, and consultants.

Validation of the Stated Problem Definition

As the above section amply displays, a statement of a problem may be lengthy and complex. It involves many facts and certain subjective evaluations, some of which may be contradictory. How can you, as a consultant, validate such a statement?

Perhaps the first step in the validation process is to reread the statement for internal consistency. If flagrant contradictions appear, recheck those sections of the statement. To do so, you might interview persons whom you have not previously seen. Or, you might review additional documents and records, observe further operations, and so on.

Another validation technique is to ask another consultant to review the statement and express his or her opinion. If another consultant is assigned to the same engagement, you could compare facts that you have gathered independently. Then you could jointly evaluate the facts and develop a common problem-definition statement.

Finally, the client should read and comment on the problem statement. This validation procedure may be enlightening to both the client and the consultant. The client may agree with the consultant's assessment of the problem and be ecstatic that someone else has formulated what she or he knew intuitively. On the other hand, the client may disagree strongly with the evaluation and challenge the problem statement. The latter reaction usually provides an opportunity for the consultant to gather additional information and obtain a better handle on the problem. For the most part, the purpose of having the client read the problem statement is to obtain agreement on the key factors causing the problem. Other reasons for the reading is to gain the client's participation and support for the project.

Client-Consultant Relationships during an Engagement

In a consulting engagement the consultant must maintain the two key relationships that are presented in Figure 10-3. One relationship is between the consultant and the problem-solving process. The other relationship is between the consultant and the client. The consultant also should be keenly aware of the client's relationship to the problem. As the figure suggests, the consultant's evaluation of the problem may be different from that of the client. Hence, a major task in the problem-definition phase is to have both the client and consultant agree on the problem and its causes. Without this agreement, subsequent phases in the consultant process may be fruitless and even counterproductive to the engagement. The formal agreement on the problem should be reflected in the problem statement.

Obtaining Support of the Client

The consultant must be assured of top-management support during the first phase of the engagement. Top management's full endorsement of the consultant's initial efforts will induce middle- and lower-level managers to become more supportive of the project. Furthermore, involving future users in the planning phase will increase their commitment to a successful implementation of the project. However, any hesitancy by some members of top management will be perceived by subordinates as resistance to change. Although this is a common behavioral problem encountered in most engagements, it can be minimized through the use of information releases. Announcements should explain (1) how the

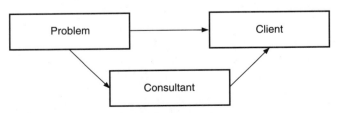

Figure 10-3 Key relationships.

problem adversely affected operations, (2) why changes are desirable, and (3) how affected employees and managers will benefit from the proposed changes. Job security during this time of change is usually the greatest concern to employees. Hence, early announcements related to job security, changes in job descriptions, or training available to employees will help them to support the upcoming engagement.

Definition of *Client*

Before discussing means of maintaining harmonious relationships, we need to define the term *client*. In the broadest sense of the term, the client is the organization that engages the services of the consultant. It might be a private business firm, a government agency, a hospital, or a university. In a more immediate and personal sense, however, the term *client* refers to the individual or individuals with whom the consultant has the initial and/or ongoing contacts. This person (or persons) discusses the engagement and its progress with the consultant and, at the conclusion of the engagement, accepts the final report from the consultant. In general, the client will be one or more of the higher-level managers or administrators of the organization. In engagements of limited scope, however, the client may consist of middle- or lower-level managers.

Of course, a consultant will need to establish relationships with other personnel of the client's organization. Among those that you, as consultant, should expect to see during a typical engagement are:

1. Managers and employees who have facts concerning the problem situation

2. Managers and employees who are likely to be affected by an implemented solution to the problem situation

3. Managers and employees who are assigned to perform tasks under your guidance

4. Managers and employees who are assigned to serve as liaison on a daily basis between you and higher-level managers or other organizational units within the support system

Guidelines for Harmonious Relationships

From the very beginning of an engagement you should aim to develop a sense of trust and openness. Since the presence of a consultant in an organization creates widespread anxiety and even fear, it is highly desirable to take specific measures to counteract this anxiety and fear and consequent hostility. These measures should have the dual effect of introducing you to the managers and employees and answering their urgent questions.

These measures may be accomplished through both written and oral means. A written announcement, prepared jointly by the client and the consultant, should be issued as soon as the terms of the engagement are settled. The announcement should be addressed to all employees and managers within the organization who are affected by the problem situation. Oral presentations should be made at meetings. Several presentations will probably be needed, since each presentation should involve a relatively small group of employees and managers from one of the affected areas, for example, a department. At these meetings the consultant should be introduced and should be willing to answer questions concerning the engagement. Such questions may pertain, for instance, to the likely impacts of the engagement upon the responsibilities and status of the affected employees. Although certain questions may need to be shunted to organization managers attending the meetings, polite and earnest responses from the consultant can establish incipient feelings of good will.

Harmonious relations can also be established through a round of get-acquainted interviews. You should make appointments to meet all the managers who are affected by the problem situation. During a typical interview you might chat about the responsibilities and difficulties of the manager's position. Your main goal during this initial interview should be to establish a friendly relationship. Although you may introduce the subject of the engagement, it is probably not wise to delve into its details at this time. Instead, you might mention that you would like to return later for a more in-depth discussion of the problem at a time convenient to the manager. (Of course, if the manager insists on discussing it fully at this first interview, you should be sufficiently flexible to accommodate his or her wish.)

During the engagement you might reflect an attitude of helpfulness. This attitude may be achieved in various ways. You can maintain an "open-door" policy, welcoming the questions and communications of anyone at any time. You can also arrange meetings to discuss the problem and provide written summaries of the meetings.

A final admonition concerns the solution to the problem. You should not directly tell the client what decision to make, that is, how to solve the problem. Instead, you might diplomatically guide the client toward the solution. For instance, you might provide copies of articles that discuss solutions by other organizations having similar problems. You might write memoranda summarizing the key factors and relationships in the problem situation, as well as possible alternative solutions. You might chair "brainstorming" sessions concerning the problem situation.

Example

An example should clarify the problem-definition phase. Let us consider a problem that is common to many business firms: Our consulting firm is engaged by the manufacturing vice president of the ABC Company, who is concerned about excessively high production costs. We begin the engagement by entering the main plant and observing the work force. We find within a short time that the employees are idle a considerable portion of the time. After random counts, we determine that certain employees are idle as much as 46 percent of their total work time.

Discussion with the manufacturing vice president reveals that the current level of idle time clearly exceeds reasonable expectations. Thus, we have established the presence of a serious problem. Although we need to explore the situation more deeply, we can begin to prepare the content of the problem statement.

Our first concern is the *identity* of the problem. Although idle time is the symptom or manifestation of a problem, it cannot be viewed as the underlying, root problem. To determine the underlying problem or problems, we undertake more observations. These observations point to such underlying causes as lack of orders, lack of needed raw materials, lack of proper tooling, lack of time-motion and methods studies, weak production controls, and (in some departments) poor supervisory practices.

We again discuss the excessive idle time percentage with the manufacturing vice president. He states that the *objective* that the company would like to achieve in this area is as follows: to reduce idle time to 10 percent or less of total work time by the end of this year. After noting this objective in the problem statement, we consider the scope, location, intensity, and time dimension of the problem.

The *scope* of the problem pertains to the extent of its effects. In which departments is idle time manifest? Is it worse in some departments than others? In which departments does it exceed 10 percent, 20 percent, 30 percent, 40 percent? We discover that the scope of the problem spans all production departments, except the quality control department; as we suspected, idle time is higher in some departments than others.

The *location*, or locus, of the problem seems to center on the fabrication department, which has the highest level of idle time. (Note that the location of the problem is closely related to its scope. In determining the scope we also determined the central location.)

The *intensity* of the problem first can be expressed in labor hours and then equated in dollars. We discover that 300 employees are idle part of each day. The average idle time per day is 20 percent, or 1.6 hours in an 8-hour day. If the average hourly wage (plus benefits) is $10, then an average of $16 is wasted each day by each of the above employees. The total loss per day due to idle time is therefore $4800.

The *time dimensions,* or timing aspects, of the problem can be stated as follows:

1 How long has the problem existed? The idle time has gradually grown to its present level from an unknown beginning date.

2. How long will it endure if left alone? There is a danger that the problem will become progressively worse and endure indefinitely.

3. How frequently does it occur? It is an everyday occurrence.

With respect to the frequency-intensity matrix, the idle time problem exhibits a high-frequency and high-intensity condition. Thus, it is sufficiently serious to warrant immediate attention.

Next we turn to the environmental facets of the problem: Its *human elements* are the idle workers, their supervisors, middle management, and possibly top management. The labor union represents an additional element. Furthermore, the human elements of supporting departments—such as production control and engineering—must be included, as well as vendors who are late in delivering raw materials.

With respect to the political situation, our observations and interviews reveal that most production supervisors, aided by a few middle managers, have been covering up the problem situation. On the other hand, a few middle managers have been advocating layoffs throughout the production function. It is expected that the union will stridently oppose any attempt to increase production quotas by reducing idle time.

The *support system* consists of the quality assurance, production control, engineering, and labor relations departments. Both the quality assurance and production control departments are impacted directly by the idleness and consequent lower productivity.

The *tracking system* includes production reports pertaining to departments and individual workers; reports concerning materials movements and work flows; and reports concerning materials replacements.

The *institutional process* consists of (1) the informal actions of suppressing information flows (i.e., the cover-up) on the part of supervisors and middle managers and (2) the sparse formal information flows via the reports listed above. The recommended process for correcting the problem is to present the data concerning idle time and its consequences directly to the production department supervisors.

11

Fact Finding and Analysis

Gary Grudnitski

School of Accounting
San Diego State University
San Diego, California

Mary V. Pilney
San Diego, California

Facts are the threads that run through the fabric of the consulting process. Facts aid the consultant in sorting out client symptoms from client problems, as well as in structuring and ordering the problems. Facts form the foundation for prospective solutions and direct the consultant to the solution ultimately rendered. Because facts serve such important functions, the consultant must be resourceful in fact gathering and skillful in fact analysis.

This chapter assists the consultant in developing fact-related skills. The first section deals with fact sources. It identifies places where the consultant can look to find facts associated with the operations of a client. The second section presents various techniques for gathering and analyzing facts.*

---

*J. G. Burch and G. Grudnitski, *Information Systems: Theory and Practice*, 5th ed., Wiley, New York, 1989, Chapter 16.

Fact Sources

A wealth of internal and external fact sources is available to help you, as consultant, zero in on a client's problems. Internal and external fact sources for a typical business firm are listed in Figure 11-1. For example, manufacturing produces data that describe the status of quantities of raw materials, work-in-process, and finished goods. Facts from these data, coupled with facts generated by marketing, can help you separate the symptom of many cancelled orders from the problem of inadequate customer back-order procedures.

Internal Sources

The single most important internal source of facts available to the consultant is people. This includes not only those in formal management but also clerical and production workers. Information requirements can best be specified by those who use the information. The consultant, however, can help users define their requirements by explaining to them what can be provided. It is important to note that most individuals are guided in formulating their needs by arbitrary and often antiquated notions of what they think can be provided. The consultant's function is to remove or expand these attitudes so that real information can be obtained.

A secondary source of facts for the consultant comes from existing paperwork within the organization. The paperwork in most organizations can be classified as that which describes (1) how the organization is structured, (2) what the organization is or has been doing, and (3) what the organization plans to do. Figure 11-2 provides a partial list of documents typically found in a client organization.

A word of caution is in order when you use an organization's documents as sources of facts. The documents identified as describing how an organization is structured and what it plans to do may not necessarily reflect reality. At best, these documents serve to give you an understanding of what management considers its structure and direction are at a particular time. It is common for organizations and plans to change while their documentation remains unchanged.

A third internal source of important facts to a consultant is relationships. Defining the relationships among people, departments, and functions can provide you with information and insights unknown or undocumented anywhere else within the organization.

Pitfalls

Throughout the process of internal fact gathering you must guard against overlooking the obvious. Frequently, an interview with a client employee uncovers excellent ideas unacted upon by management.

Internal Sources	Facts
Corporate planning	Corporate objectives
	Expansion plans
Marketing	Sales statistics
	Invoices and back orders
	Types of new products or services with market possibilities
	Customer response to existing products
	Planning and promotional campaigns
	Feedback from customers and sales force on product performance
Research and development	New-product development schedules
Engineering	Engineering schedule for products
Data processing	Systems for organizing files and reporting operating results
Manufacturing	Inventory status
Personnel	Background on employees
	Salary/performance review data
Accounting	Product pricing and costing
	Operating expenses
External Sources	
Industry reports	Corporate data and analysis
	Industry news
Competition	Products and product literature
Distributors	Market conditions
	Customer analysis
Customers	Profile facts
	Sales
State and federal statistical data and abstracts	Corporate statistical comparisons
	Economic/financial facts
	Securities and Exchange Commission facts
	Department of Commerce facts
	Bureau of Census facts
Database retrieval systems	Product, market, and industry news and analysis
	Economic forecasts

Figure 11-1 Internal and external fact sources.

Similarly, a brief analysis, based on something as simple as counting the number of times a particular event occurred, may help you discover an activity management does not realize or understand. Don't overlook the opportunity to present management, at a time when its attention is focused, with your discoveries as well as the suggestions of the client's employees and operating-level managers.

Documents describing how the client's organization is run	Documents describing what the client plans to do	Documents describing what the client organization does
Policy statements	Business plans	Annual reports
Methods and proce-	(long- and short-	Performance reports
dures manuals	range)	Internal staff studies
Organization charts	Budgets	Legal documents,
Job descriptions	Schedules and fore-	including copyrights,
Performance stan-	casts	patents, franchises,
dards	Minutes of board of	trademarks
Charts of accounts	directors	Reference documenta-
Delegations of	Statements of goals	tion about customers,
authority	and objectives	employees, products,
		vendors
		Transaction documen-
		tation, including pur-
		chase orders, time
		sheets, and expense
		records

Figure 11-2 Documents typically found in a client organization. (SOURCE: John G. Burch, Jr., and Gary Grudnitski, *Information Systems: Theory and Practice*, 5th ed. Copyright © 1989. Reprinted by permission of John Wiley & Sons, Inc., New York City.)

External Sources

You can also obtain many facts from external sources, that is, sources outside the client organization. These sources may be several times removed from the client's operations. For example, you may gather facts from customers concerning their perceptions of the client's products as compared to those of the major competitors. Or, during an engagement involving a long-range business plan, you may test the reasonableness of internally prepared sales forecasts by comparing them to projections obtained by an econometric model of the economy.

Fact-Gathering Techniques

One of your most important tasks, especially at the beginning of an engagement, is to separate the symptoms a client experiences from the real underlying problems. As noted in the previous chapter, it is the problems, rather than the symptoms, that deserve your close attention and treatment. The following techniques are available for gathering facts concerning the underlying problems.

Interviews

On many engagements the best way for you to zero in on problems is to conduct a series of interviews with client personnel. In essence, an interview is the face-to-face interchange of information. It can be conducted at all levels of the client organization—from the president down to the mail clerk. An effective consultant will be able to adjust to people who have differing commitments to the client's goals as well as to many environmental variables.

Getting Started   Before embarking on a set of interviews, you should ask your client contact to issue a memorandum to those you want to interview. This memorandum should explain the purpose of the interviews and to what use the facts you obtain will be put. Before going into each interview, you should become familiar with the duties and responsibilities of the interviewee, and you should also understand the working and personal relationships of the interviewee with others in the client's organization. Furthermore, you should be as aware as possible of the responses that the interviewee is apt to give.

Conducting the Interview   During the interview itself, remember to:

1. Confirm your understanding of the interviewee's job responsibilities and duties. You might use this approach: "As I understand it, your job is…(a brief job description). Is this correct?"

2. To the extent possible, ask specific questions that allow quantitative responses. A typical question of this type is: "How many telephones do you now have in this department?"

3. When questions are answered vaguely, pursue them (in a pleasant way) until they are fully answered.

4. Try to develop an awareness of the interviewee's feelings. You can best do this by listening well and reading the interviewee's body language.

5. Avoid stating your own opinions or acting like a know-it-all.

6. As the interview draws to a close, ask the interviewee if he or she has additional ideas, thoughts, or suggestions concerning the topics of discussion: "Do you have any other suggestions or recommendations about how the budget is calculated?"

7. Do not allow the interview to become too lengthy. One way to keep the answers brief is to ask questions in a manner that will obtain the needed facts in the least possible time.

8. At the end of the interview, summarize the main points you uncovered, thank the interviewee, and indicate that you will contact him or her again if further questions are necessary.

Questionnaires

The questionnaire is a restricted channel of communication. Hence, you should use it primarily to gather facts. Unlike the interview, the questionnaire does not provide you with an immediate opportunity to readdress comments that are vague or unclear. Moreover, you cannot follow up comments that might lead to additional facts or ideas.

Thus, use the questionnaire when the people from whom you desire information are physically removed and travel is prohibitive, when you must query many people (e.g., all the sales staff), or when the facts you gather are intended to verify similar facts you gathered from other sources.

When one or more of the above conditions exist, and you decide to use a questionnaire, you should clearly identify in your mind what you want to learn. Then you should structure your questions to elicit only the information you want, prepare the questionnaire form, and submit the questionnaire to the appropriate individuals.

Follow these guidelines:

1. Explain in an accompanying letter the purpose, use, security, and disposition of the responses your questionnaire generates.
2. Provide detailed instructions concerning how the questions are to be completed.
3. Set a deadline for the return of the questionnaire.
4. Ask pointed, concise, and clear questions.
5. Format questions so that responses can be precisely tabulated mechanically or manually.
6. Provide sufficient space for a complete response.
7. If a question cannot be answered objectively, provide the respondent an opportunity to add a clarifying comment.
8. Identify each questionnaire by the respondent's name, job title, department, and so forth.
9. Include a section in which respondents can state their opinions and criticisms.

Observation

Observation is a third technique available to a consultant. For instance, you can gather useful facts by watching your client's employees do their jobs. The purposes of observation are to help you determine (1) what is being done, (2) how it is being done, (3) who is doing it, (4) when it is being done, (5) how long it takes, (6) where it is being done, and (7) why it is being done.

Methods of Observation   One method of observing is to walk through an area and make notes about people, things, and activities. A second method is to observe secretly from a fixed location. A third method is to observe openly from a fixed point but without interacting with the person being observed. The final method is to observe and also interact with the person (or persons) being observed. The interaction may consist of asking questions about a specific task, requesting detailed explanations of tasks, and so forth.

The technique of observation is useful for gathering facts prior to an interview, for verifying statements made during an interview, and for ascertaining relationships between individuals.

Observation Guidelines   You can maximize the effectiveness of observations by following these guidelines:

1. Before beginning, identify and define what you need to observe. Then estimate how long it will take.

2. If persons are to be aware that you are observing them, explain to them what you will do and why.

3. Note the time periodically while making your observations.

4. Record what you observe as specifically as possible, avoiding generalities and vague descriptions.

5. Avoid expressing value judgments when you are interacting with people you are observing.

6. As soon as possible after the observation period, document all your observations and organize your notes.

7. Review the facts obtained and the conclusions drawn from observations with (a) the person being observed, (b) the person's supervisor, and (c) your own supervisor (when desirable).

Document Gathering

Another technique for gathering facts is to inspect all relevant documents (i.e., source documents, worksheets, and reports). From these documents you can understand what is being done and how it is organized, what is not available, and perhaps what the client considers to be important. You can often enhance efforts in gathering facts during interviews and observations if you have collected copies of documents and have them in hand. Moreover, if you have a working understanding of the client's documents, you increase the likelihood of maintaining smooth communications with the client personnel.

Fact Analysis Techniques

Most consulting engagements require you to use fact analysis as well as fact-gathering techniques. A variety of fact analysis techniques are available, including charts, input/output analysis, and structured diagrams. Although these techniques can aid you in gathering facts and can therefore be described as fact-gathering techniques, their main use is for organizing facts in order to perform logical analysis.

Charting

Charting is a term that represents the largest and most widely used group of fact analysis techniques. Charting techniques provide pictorial representations of one or more dimensions of a client's organization or its activities. This group of techniques facilitates synthesis, communication, and documentation as well as analysis. The organization chart, data flow diagram, system flowchart, detail flowchart, and decision table are typical examples of charting techniques.

Organization Chart   The organization chart provides facts about reporting relationships, quantities of resources, and levels of authority and responsibility within the client's organization. You may find it useful to prepare a brief narrative describing the functions and role of each manager shown on the organization chart.

Data Flow Diagram   This is a logical view of how data flow through a system. This diagram clearly portrays the workings of a complex system, such as a transaction processing system. Figure 11-3 illustrates four symbols that are used in data flow diagrams.

A square (or sometimes a rectangle) represents an external entity, a source, or destination of a transaction. People (such as customers, managers, and suppliers), things (such as warehouses and main offices), or

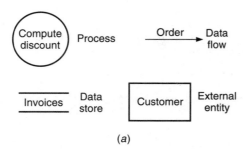

(a)

Figure 11-3   (a) Symbols used in data flow diagrams.

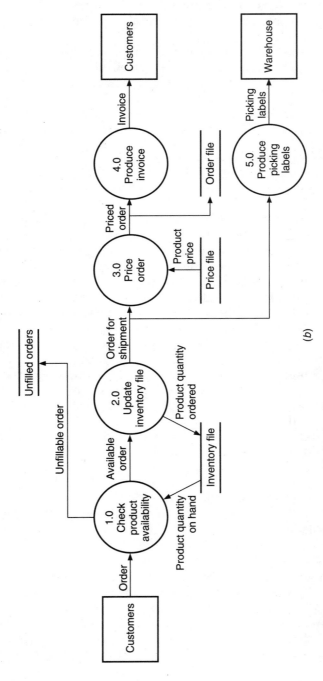

Figure 11-3 (*Continued*) (*b*) Example of a data flow diagram.

other systems (such as sales forecasting systems) are external entities. As such, they are outside the boundary of the system under consideration.

An arrow is the symbol for data flow. The arrowhead indicates the direction of the data flow. Each data flow arrow should be accompanied by a meaningful description of the nature of the data flow.

A circle is the symbol for a process (i.e., an activity or task). The symbol is used to indicate those places within the system at which incoming data flows are processed or transformed into incoming data flows. The name of the process is generally written within the circle.

An open-ended rectangle is the symbol for a data store (i.e., a place where data are stored between processes). Each data store symbol should contain a descriptive label (e.g., employee master file, canceled checks, purchase orders pending).

The lower part of Figure 11-3 shows a data flow diagram illustrating a sales order and invoicing system. Customers are the external entity that places orders and later receives invoices. In addition to the flows of orders and invoices just mentioned, data flows occur between the process labeled 1.0 Check product availability, 2.0 Update inventory file, 3.0 Price order, 4.0 Produce invoice, 5.0 Produce picking labels and the data stores labeled Unfilled orders, Inventory file, Price file, and Order file.

You should note two points about the data flow diagram in Figure 11-3. It illustrates the logical flows of the system; thus, it does not specify the physical resources used in the system, such as a computer with disk files, and so on. Also, the five processes portrayed in the figure can be enlarged to show additional details of the processing steps.

System Flowchart A system flowchart depicts an overall view of a system in terms of its major elements, such as processing programs or runs, files, inputs, and outputs. A system flowchart provides clear documentation of either a present system or a proposed system. Generally, a flowchart pertains to a computer-based information system. In contrast to a data flow diagram, therefore, a system flowchart specifies the physical nature of the data processing and data storage. Figure 11-4 shows a system flowchart of sales transactions.

Detail Flowchart A detail flowchart graphically represents the logic of a process. The most common form of detail flowchart, called a "program flowchart," describes the logic of a computer program or run. Program flowcharts may be developed at two levels of detail. A macro program flowchart shows the logic of a relatively broad programming process, and micro program flowcharts portray the details of each step within a macro program flowchart.

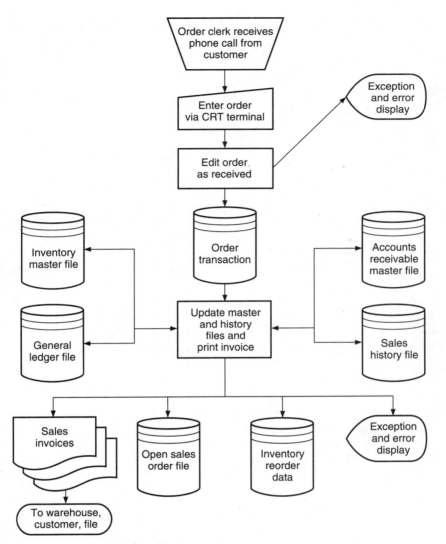

Figure 11-4 System flowchart.

Decision Table A decision table portrays, in a matrix or tabular form, a situation involving logic. The table particularly facilitates the understanding and communication of decision processes having complex logic (i.e., multiple conditions). The decision table lists conditions, actions, and rules without regard to sequence. The format of a decision table appears in Figure 11-5.

Decision table title	Rules						
	1	2	3	4	5	...	N
A							
B	Condition		Condition				
C	stub		entry				
D							
E							
F							
G							
I							
J							
K	Action		Action				
L	stub		entry				
M							
N							
O							

Figure 11-5 Decision table.

When you examine the decision table format closely, you see that the table is divided into two parts. Its upper half contains the conditions related to a decision. These conditions are expressed in the areas labeled as "Stub" and "Entry." In the stub area, the conditions are expressed as "if" phrases. In the entry area, the states of the conditions (usually either *Yes* or *No*) are entered.

The lower half of the table contains the actions that are to be taken when the conditions have been satisfied. Areas within this lower half are also denoted as "stub" and "entry." In the stub area the actions are expressed by "then" phrases. In the entry area, the particular actions are noted that pertain to each set of conditions.

Thus, a decision table portrays sets of conditions (rules) and actions. As Figure 11-5 shows, the rules are numbered horizontally across the top of the decision table. In effect, a decision basically table states: *If* this set of conditions (rule) occurs, *then* perform these marked actions. *If* that set of conditions (rule) occurs, *then* perform that set of marked actions. The number of rules that may exist for a particular decision situation depends on the number of conditions.

Each rule is reflected in a combination of *yes* and *no* entries in a column. Each *yes* (Y) means that a specified condition exists, and each *no*

Procedure Involving Unfilled Order File Reporting
Each record on the unfilled order file must be examined and classified as either a closed order, back order, in-process order, current order, or future order. Any record which has the order quantity equal to the shipped quantity is considered closed. Any record having a to-be-shipped date earlier than the report date is a back order. A record with the to-be-shipped date equal to the report date is treated as in-process. Any record with a to-be-shipped date more than seven days later than the report date is a future order. All other records are considered current except any record with net dollars less than zero (which are viewed as being closed).

If	1	2	3	4	5	6	Conditions	Actions
Net $<0	Y	N	N	N	N	N	The order quantity equal to the shipped quantity	Closed
Order qty = shipped qty		Y	N	N	N	N	A to-be-shipped date earlier than the report date	Backorder
TBS date = rep date			Y	N	N	N	The to-be-shipped date equal to the report date	In-process
TBS<rep date				Y	N	N	A to-be-shipped date more than seven days later than the report date	Future
TBS>rep date + 7					Y	N		
Then							Any record with net dollars less than zero	Closed
Closed order	1	1					All other records	Current
Backorder				1				
In-process			1					
Current						1		
Future					1			

Figure 11-6 An example involving the use of a decision table. (source: John C. Burch, Jr., Felix R. Strater, and Gary Grudnitski, *Information Systems: Theory and Practices*, 3d ed. Copyright © 1989. Reprinted by permission of John Wiley & Sons, Inc., New York.)

(N) means that it does not exist. (If neither is listed, then the condition does not apply.)

The example shown in Figure 11-6 should clarify the construction and use of a decision table. At the top of the figure appears a situation involving conditions and actions. Below, in the left half, is the decision table based on this situation. In the right half is a matching of possible conditions and resulting actions. Item 1 in the decision table shows that *if* the condition is "a record with net dollars less than zero," *then* the action to be taken by a decision maker is to classify the record as a closed order. Item 2 in the table shows that *if* the conditions are "a record with net dollars greater than or equal to zero" and "the shipped quantity equals the ordered quantity," *then* also classify the record as a closed order. Item 3 in the table shows that *if* the conditions are "a record with net dollars greater than zero" and "the shipped quantity does not equal the ordered quantity" but "the to-be-shipped date does equal the report date," *then* classify the record as an in-process order. The remaining rules require three other actions.

As this example shows, a decision table can be used to inform a "decision maker" (such as a processing clerk) about the appropriate action to take when confronted by a particular set of conditions. It may also be used to prepare a computer program, so that the computer can be instructed how to act when confronted by each set of conditions.

Input/Output Analysis

A problem situation may be analyzed in terms of its inputs and outputs. Figure 11-7 illustrates the input/output analysis technique applied to the inventory function. Note that although each input and output is described, nothing is included concerning the process (i.e., how the input is converted to output), the data requirements, the information flows, or the related decisions.

Structured Techniques

A set of structured analysis techniques have been developed and employed increasingly in recent years. The key assumption underlying structured techniques is that an organization is comprised of a number of well-defined functions, which in turn are made up of a series of activities. By focusing on these functions and activities, you can gain a clear understanding of the organization's essential inputs, processes, and outputs.

In performing structured analysis, the preferable procedure is to begin at the top or broadest level and then work down to the most detailed activity level. Broad functions can be repeatedly subdivided—through several levels of detail—until you reach the level with the narrowest scope and greatest degree of detail.

Several structured analysis techniques have been developed. Two such techniques are the data flow diagram and decision table discussed earlier. Other techniques include the structure diagram, the Warnier-Orr diagram, the decision tree, and the HIPO diagram.

The structure diagram has a structure like an upside-down tree. Thus, it looks very much like an organization chart. Also like an organization chart, it helps the consultant visualize relationships among the firm's activities. Figure 11-8 presents a structure diagram of the inventory control function. From the top level, labeled "maintain inventory control," the diagram is constructed by defining all the activities or subfunctions that support this function. The third level shows the detailed inputs, processing steps, and outputs related to "update inventory master file." The diagram could be expanded to show a fourth level of detail for each of the third-level activities (e.g., for "determining quantity to back order") and to show a third level of detail for the remaining second-level activities.

Input/Output Analysis: Inventory

Inputs:

1. *Production.* Production tickets show quality, product code, product number, batch numbers, operator numbers.
2. *Scrap.* A scrap ticket is prepared as necessary, containing the same facts as production tickets but coded as scrap.
3. *Receiving.* All receipts are noted with:
   Product number
   Receipt codes
   Receiver's number
   Product quantity
   Date received
   Purchase order
   Authorization number
4. *Shipments.* Invoices are from billing, sorted by product number, including date shipped, quantity shipped, customer order number.
5. *Transfers.* Intracompany transfers are recorded with transfer code.
6. *Inventory adjustments.* Inventory adjustments entered by auditors. The adjusted amount is entered with date of physical count.

Outputs:

1. *Input listing.* A listing of all inputs is prepared daily with errors in coding. This report is received by the supervisors of manufacturing, shipping, receiving, and accounting.
2. *Daily inventory status.* A daily report is prepared indicating the status of all products. Report includes opening inventory, production, shipments, transfers, adjustments, and closing inventory. Report is distributed to production scheduler, shipping supervisor, auditor, and inventory analyst.
3. *Monthly inventory status.* A monthly report is prepared with the same format as daily report, only reflecting that month's activity. This report is issued to plant manager and plant accountant, in addition to daily distribution.
4. *Monthly scrap report.* A monthly scrap report is issued showing all scrap reported lost. This report is issued to plant manager, plant accountant, supervisor of quality control, supervisor of operations.

Figure 11-7 An example of input/output analysis. (SOURCE: John G. Burch, Jr., and Gary Grudnitski, *Information Systems: Theory and Practice*, 5th ed. Copyright © 1989. Reprinted by permission of John Wiley & Sons, Inc., New York.)

Nonstructured Analysis

Fact analysis techniques such as those presented in preceding paragraphs have limitations. They are sometimes difficult to apply, since certain organizations consist of complex and fluid networks of people and

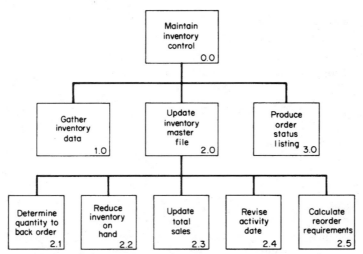

Figure 11-8   Structure diagram.

activities instead of clearly defined hierarchies of activities. Also, fact analysis techniques may tend to stifle creativity.

Therefore, you should consider relatively unstructured analytical approaches. These alternative approaches should take advantage of the combined wisdom of such parties as a client's managers. Various unstructured techniques, such as the Delphi and brainstorming approaches, are discussed in Chapter 12.

12

Solution Development

Lynn J. McKell

*School of Accountancy
and Information Systems
Brigham Young University
Provo, Utah*

Solution development is the third phase of the problem-solving process. As Figure 12-1 shows, the phase consists of several steps. These steps begin with the generation of potential solutions alternatives and end with the presentation of a recommended solution.

The solution-development phase links to the previous phases through the deliverables of those phases. Thus, solution development links to the problem-definition phase through the objectives and other facets revealed in the statement of the problem definition. Solution development links to the fact-finding and analysis phase through the specification of requirements and criteria. Each of the key deliverables—objectives, requirements, criteria—should therefore be established prior to the commencement of the solution-development phase. As reflectors of the desired outputs, the objectives and requirements drive the problem-solving process. As evaluation instruments, the criteria point to the preferable solution.

Nature of the Deliverable

Throughout the problem-solving process, you should keep in mind the nature of the deliverable, that is, the developed solution that is to be

12-1

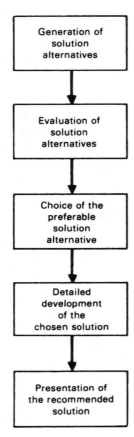

Figure 12-1   Solution development steps.

finally recommended. The following illustrate the range of deliverables that consultants may be expected to produce:

1. *Solution to specific problem.* Many consulting engagements consist of defining a specific problem, gathering and analyzing facts concerning the problem, and developing the preferable solution. Several examples of this type of consulting engagement appear in the discussion of the problem-definition phase in Chapter 10.

2. *Educational course or training program.* Another type of consulting engagement results in the development of an educational course or a training program as the solution. You may be expected to devise a course, for example, intended to enable employees and managers to understand the functions of computers. Alternatively, you may be expected to develop a training program that will teach employees to use a computerized transaction processing system. In some cases you

may be also expected to serve as instructor in the course or training program.

3. *Designed system component.* A third type of consulting engagement consists of developing a solution in the form of a system design. Your assignment would be to start at the point in the process indicated by the client and to conduct the systems project within prescribed constraints. For instance, you may be given the requirements for a desired database. Your assignment may then be to develop the design specifications, determine the feasibility of the database, and select the preferable hardware and software to implement the database.

4. *Implemented "turnkey" system.* A comprehensive consulting engagement consists of developing and implementing a fully operational "turnkey" system. This type of deliverable generally involves the entire system-development life cycle, from definition through implementation. In most consulting cases the implemented system is an information system. In some cases, however, it will be an operational system, e.g., a production system, or a management system (a management-by-objectives system, for example).

A danger posed by this type of engagement is that the ultimate users of the system, usually the manager and employees of the client firm, will not participate adequately in its development. Some authorities would contend that the consultant who performs this type of engagement has in effect become a vendor and hence has exceeded the legitimate bounds of consulting.

5. *Operational systems.* Specialized consulting teams are often engaged to examine an organization's operational systems. Typically this involves designing the physical layout, manual procedures, and material and physical flows to enhance the efficiency of the activities the organization performs. Most often this type of engagement involves the redesign of an existing operation, though occasionally the job may focus on a new operation. Decisions about plant and warehouse locations and related problems of distribution also fall into this category.

6. *Organizational development.* In recent years analysts have focused on the structure and culture of organizations as sources of success. Human resources are now recognized as one of the most important elements in most organizations. Team building, compensation and benefit structure, grievance handling, retirement planning, and hiring and firing procedures are now very significant management issues which can benefit greatly from consulting assistance.

7. *Advice or assistance.* In many consulting engagements a consultant is asked for advice concerning an area or methodology in which he or she has expertise. Or the consultant may be engaged to provide technical

assistance during the development of a system or the construction of a structure. For instance, audit consultants are often engaged to provide advice concerning internal accounting controls during the design of accounting information systems. Data-processing consultants are engaged to provide assistance during the initial selection and installation of new microcomputer-based information systems. Such advice and assistance, when provided during the various phases of the development of a system or process or structure, may be viewed as "interim" solutions to problems.

8. *Expert opinion.* A type of consulting engagement similar to the one just described involves the consultant as an expert witness. Your professional obligation, in such an engagement, is to deliver an expert opinion that is as unbiased and accurate as possible.

Generating Alternative Solutions

Need for Alternatives

The first step in the solution-development phase is to generate as many solution alternatives as feasible. This step is essential, even when time is short. Unless a consultant conducts a thorough search for alternatives, he or she cannot feel confident that the recommended solution to a problem is the best available. Also, a client should be given the opportunity to compare the recommended solution against the more reasonable of the alternatives. From the perspective of a client, a closely competing alternative might be more appealing than the one you recommend.

Search Approaches

Generating solution alternatives is like generating new ideas. Usually solutions and ideas grow from one's own experiences. As Sir Joshua Reynolds said in his *Discourses:* "Invention, strictly speaking, is little more than a new combination of those images which have been previously gathered and deposited in the memory. Nothing can be made of nothing; he who has laid up no materials can produce no combinations." Nevertheless, consultants must also employ creativity in order to devise innovative combinations. A variety of well-defined and controllable approaches that blend experience and the creative process can be identified.

Pattern Recognition and Matching Approach This approach emphasizes experience. To avoid "reinventing the wheel," the consultant can draw upon personal experiences or those of others. The experiences of others may be found in the files of professional organizations, at professional conferences, or in books and articles by consulting authorities. Successful consultants have long recognized that they can get useful ideas by belonging to a professional organization and attending relevant conferences.

Knowledge of experiences, especially those similar to a problem being investigated, can be the first step in developing a sound solution. By recognizing and matching features common to both the previous experiences and the problem at hand, you can judge the applicability of the previously employed solution.

Brainstorming Approach As Linus Pauling said: "The best way to have a good idea is to have lots of ideas." A widely used approach that begins with divergent thinking is described by the term *brainstorming*.

The first stage of brainstorming takes place in a group. Several people concerned with the problem situation meet and contribute ideas in a freewheeling and informal manner. Every conceivable idea is encouraged, even the wildest ones imaginable. During this stage participants are asked to suspend critical judgment.

The beneficial result of this first stage of brainstorming is to generate the maximum number of ideas in a short time. Focusing the attention of a group on one common problem creates a synergy that causes ideas to proliferate. Each person stimulates the others in the group, and in turn each person is stimulated by the group. Encouraging suspension of judgment creates an unguarded atmosphere in which the mental processes are freed from all constraints.

The flow of ideas during this process tends to follow a pattern. The most obvious and conventional ideas are suggested first. After a time, these ideas tend to be exhausted and an "idea wall" forms. With continued effort this idea wall is shattered, and less conventional ideas begin to emerge. Certain of these ideas seem to be ridiculous, even "wild and crazy." However, they generally have the positive effect of stimulating very good ideas. In other words, the best ideas tend to "piggyback" or pyramid on the foundations laid by the not-so-good ideas.

The second stage of brainstorming shifts from idea generation to idea selection and refinement. In this second stage each idea is judged in the light of the objectives and requirements established earlier in the problem-solving process. Most of the ideas generated in the divergent-thinking stage will be easily eliminated by this judgment process. Only a few really good ideas are likely to be identified. These good ideas should then be refined, if necessary, and preserved as likely solution alternatives.

The main drawback to brainstorming is the time it requires to weed out the large volume of unusable ideas generated. Thus, the primary focus during the second stage (known as the convergent-thinking process) is on narrowing the number of ideas or solution alternatives. The focus should not be so rigid, however, that additional new ideas are precluded from consideration. New ideas sometimes emerge, if participants are unstifled, from the process of identifying weaknesses in the ideas generated during the first stage.

SCAMPER Approach   An approach that is more deliberate in nature than brainstorming is known by the acronym *SCAMPER*, which stands for:

Substitute

Combine

Adjust (or adapt)

Magnify (or minimize or modify)

Put to other uses

Eliminate (or elaborate)

Reverse (or rearrange)

This approach emphasizes the use of a systematic process to generate ideas leading to solution alternatives. Each new idea represents an evolution of a presently stated idea. Thus, one new idea may emerge from asking the question: "What is a reasonable substitute for idea A?" Another new idea may develop from the combination of ideas A and B.

The SCAMPER approach, more deliberate and systematic than brainstorming, allows time for incubation. Ideas can develop and evolve in the consultant's subconscious. This incubation process can be especially fruitful if you apply the SCAMPER approach in several stages, with time lapses between. During the first stage you could list the more obvious solution alternatives. During the second stage you might allot a preset time to substituting, combining, rearranging, and so on. Then, after a time (during which you let the subconscious take over), you might allot another preset time to perform the SCAMPER functions again. You can repeat the process as often as you need to.

A drawback to the SCAMPER approach is that it tends to limit the range of likely ideas. Revolutionary ideas are not likely to emerge from this evolutionary approach. It is not a substitute for brainstorming.

Delphi Approach   This approach employs an idea-generation concept similar to brainstorming. Brainstorming involves the interaction of participants in a group, but the Delphi approach insulates the participants from one another. Experts are individually polled for ideas, and these ideas are then summarized and presented to each participant. After allowing time for each participant to review this feedback, the consultant again polls the experts. Presumably, each participant will adjust and revise his or her ideas in the light of the collective responses. This feedback and repolling cycle is repeated until the responses have stabilized. Then the stabilized results are summarized and presented as the refined ideas of the collective experts.

The Delphi approach should produce excellent ideas or solution alternatives, since they represent the refined views of experts. The approach is very time consuming, however, and it tends to be better suited to problems involving forecasts than to other types of problem situations.

Prototyping Approach In certain contexts (e.g., information systems) where a noninterfering working model is economically feasible, there are several advantages to constructing a prototype design:

1. It crystallizes various ideas and perceptions concerning a specific solution and thus helps detect undesired, poorly designed, or missing features.

2. It stimulates users and designers to work together.

3. It allows for the evolution of a preferred design.

4. It fosters convergence of opinion and agreement between conflicting parties.

A model or prototype provides a concrete basis by which to judge the effectiveness of the solution and therefore enables the organization to avoid the larger costs of a complete implementation if the recommended solution proves to be totally unsatisfactory.

If the protyping medium is the same as the medium for the operational system, only a small step may be required to go from a finalized prototype to the delivered solution. In less compatible mediums, the prototype provides a very graphic specification for the functional systems design. On rare occasions, prototyping may be used to develop alternative solutions, which must then be evaluated as part of the selection process.

The Alpha Site or Pilot Project Approach An important solution-development approach is the use of an Alpha site. In large organizations it is often advisable to use a cooperating host department as an environment in which to develop systems that are to be implemented later throughout the organization. This usually imposes an extra burden on the Alpha site, because it becomes a laboratory or pilot project for the new system development. Often such a pilot project requires additional effort to accommodate the planning, training, testing, evaluation, and feedback activities. By using a small organizational component in development, you can manage the problems that arise—problems that might be disastrous if they occurred organization wide. A problem with this approach is that the ideas and needs of nonhost departments may not be fully represented. To address this problem, Beta testing by other users can be incorporated into the evaluation and refinement before the recommended solution is released and implemented.

Evaluation of Solution Alternatives

After solution alternatives are sifted and refined, they must be evaluated to select the best one. This evaluation should be based upon a structured feasibility analysis that considers everything relevant. Whenever possible the analysis should employ a decision model that describes the relationships and behavior of the significant factors in the problem situation. A key evaluation step is comparing solution alternatives by means of established criteria, in which the criteria represent quantitative and/or qualitative factors chosen by the evaluators. An example of a familiar quantitative criterion is the return-on-assets ratio, and a qualitative criterion often employed is customer satisfaction.

Each solution alternative is evaluated, via the criteria, against all other solution alternatives. Note that each solution alternative is implicitly evaluated against the existing situation. Thus, a solution alternative that does not represent an improvement over the existing situation may be eliminated immediately.

Among the standards by which each solution alternative may be analyzed are economic feasibility, operational feasibility, technical feasibility, scheduling feasibility, and legal feasibility. Although certain of these standards may be irrelevant in particular problem situations, all are relevant to the domain of problems faced by modern organizations.

Economic Feasibility

Central to economic feasibility is a benefit/cost analysis. This type of analysis attempts (1) to identify and quantify all the benefits and costs associated with a particular solution alternative and (2) to weigh these benefits and costs by means of an economically oriented criterion.

Benefits generally consist of cost avoidance, cost reduction, revenue improvement, performance improvement, and/or product quality improvement. Certain of these benefits are relatively tangible or quantifiable, and others are not.

Costs can be categorized as development costs, implementation costs, and operating costs. Typical development and implementation costs incurred in a project to rectify a problem include those for hardware (i.e., computer equipment), software (i.e., programming), documentation, personnel, and supplies. The personnel costs in turn can be classified as those incurred for recruiting new employees, training new and existing employees, learning curves of employees having new jobs, and use of consultants.*

Typical operating costs include salaries for new employees, costs for equipment replacement and for new acquisitions and maintenance, and costs for supplies.

Since most of the factors are quantifiable, a variety of decision models are available for evaluating economic feasibility. Among the more commonly used models are the following.

Break-even Analysis Model Cumulative benefits are compared with cumulative fixed and variable costs to determine the level of activity at which each solution alternative reaches the break-even point (i.e., the point of zero net benefits). The solution alternative that has the lowest break-even activity is the best candidate for selection, other factors being equal.

Payback Model Cumulative benefits are compared with cumulative costs to determine the time at which each solution alternative reaches the point of zero net benefits (and thus fully recovers the cumulative cost outlays). The solution alternative that has the shortest payback period is the best candidate for selection, other factors being equal.

Net Present Value Model Cumulative benefits and costs are discounted by compound interest (discount) formulas that reflect the time value of money in order to obtain their imputed values at the present time (i.e., the time of the decision). The present value of all costs is then deducted from the present value of all benefits in order to obtain the net present value. The solution alternative that has the greatest net present value is the best candidate for selection, other factors being equal.

Internal Rate of Return Model Cumulative benefits and costs are discounted by compound interest (discount) formulas, as in the case of the net present value model. However, the internal rate-of-return process has the purpose of determining the internal rate of return—the interest rate that causes the net present value to be zero. The solution alternative that has the highest internal rate of return is the best candidate for selec-

---

*As new methods and procedures are incorporated into an organization, there is an initial drop in productivity. This drop is known as the "learning curve effect." It is generally attributed both to a temporary drop in morale because employees have uncertainties in adapting to changes in work patterns as well as to the slow-down that happens when employees are learning a new method or procedure and are acquiring an efficient work pattern.

tion, assuming that the internal rate of return exceeds the cost of capital interest rate and that other factors are equal.

Capital Budgeting Model   The present value model is combined with a constrained optimization procedure, using an integer programming algorithm. The result is the selection of a portfolio of investment alternatives (solutions) that maximize the total net present value. This rather complex model is needed when budget constraints exist on the overall level of capital expenditures.

Make or Buy Model   Total costs to make a component are compared with total costs to buy the component from an outside vendor. The solution alternative having the smaller total costs is the better candidate for selection, other factors being equal. This model attempts to answer the question: Should the organization obtain the components externally, or is the internal solution alternative preferable? In many cases this model is rather difficult to apply, since certain additional fixed overhead costs are hard to identify.

Operational Feasibility

Operational feasibility concerns the usability of each solution alternative in the environment and by the persons for whom it is intended. Some factors that may affect the operational feasibility of a solution alternative are:

1. The capability of management
2. The maturity of the organization and its planning process
3. The political environment, including the informal organization
4. The interruptions that the solution alternative may impose upon the organization
5. The requirements that the solution alternative imposes with respect to hiring and training, physical facilities, and intellectual understanding

Technical Feasibility

Technical feasibility concerns the adequacy of the existing state of technology to meet the requirements of each solution alternative. A solution alternative that imposes technical requirements near or beyond the existing state of technology carries an inherent risk. An organization must consider whether it has the ability to absorb the potential consequences of such a risk. Such consideration should include the following factors:

1. State of the art and availability of required hardware
2. State of the art of related software

3. Availability and capability of personnel who would be involved in the implemented system or process

4. Experience and aggressiveness of the organization.

Scheduling Feasibility

Scheduling feasibility concerns the realistic likelihood that each solution alternative can be put into operation by a specified time in order to achieve certain objectives or avoid certain consequences. An assessment of scheduling feasibility requires that the consultant carefully examine the timing of necessary activities, how one activity affects another, and the availability of necessary resources.

Legal Feasibility

Legal feasibility concerns the ability of each solution alternative to meet legal requirements imposed by outside authorities. Legal requirements include meeting government regulations promulgated by such agencies as SEC, EEO, OSHA, and ERISA. Legal issues also include not infringing the legal rights of other organizations with respect to patents, copyrights, and trademarks and voluntary observance of professional standards established by such associations as the American Institute of Certified Public Accountants. In ascertaining the legal feasibility of a solution alternative, you should consult attorneys or other authorities.

Other Evaluation Considerations

Other attributes besides the above feasibility dimensions should be factored into the evaluation procedure. Each solution alternative should be evaluated with respect to its simplicity, flexibility, adaptability, sensitivity, reliability, and robustness. It should also be viewed in terms of the degree to which it accommodates the mind set, traditions, and morals of the employees and managers and other parties (e.g., customers) who will be affected by its implementation. All these attributes can be important to the success or failure of a particular solution alternative.

Choice of the Preferable Solution

When using a decision process, follow this general rule: Choose the solution alternative that yields the best fit or value relative to the established criteria.

Difficulties in Making the Appropriate Choice

This rule can be easily applied when all factors can be quantified and related by an explicit decision model, when a single criterion is sufficient, and when values concerning the future situation are known with complete certainty. However, these conditions usually do not exist.

In most real-world problem situations, the following conditions prevail:

1. Certain important factors cannot be quantified and fit into a known decision model. For instance, a make-or-buy decision model does not anticipate or ensure the reliability of a vendor under consideration.

2. More than one criterion may be relevant to the decision process. Furthermore, one relevant criterion may conflict with another. For example, the criterion of high product quality conflicts with the criterion of low product price. In addition, such criteria are often not directly comparable. For instance, a financial criterion is not easily compared with a social or environmental criterion.

3. A degree of uncertainty usually pervades the problem situation and the respective solution alternatives. This uncertainty derives in part from unknown or dimly perceived actions of competitors, employees, vendors, customers, investors, and others. It leads to uncertainty concerning the future states of nature, such as the future cost of a unit of raw material or an hour of labor.

Degrees of Uncertainty

Let us focus on uncertainty, since we have explicit ways of accommodating uncertainty in the decision process. Three degrees of uncertainty may be identified:

1. Uncertainty, in which the available information is limited to knowledge as to the potential states of nature; insufficient information is available, however, for assignment of probabilities to the likelihood of each state of nature occurring

2. Risk, in which the future states of nature can be represented by a probability distribution

3. Complete certainty, or, simply, *certainty,* in which the particular future state of nature is known (i.e., in which the probability distribution reduces to a probability of one)

Separate explicit approaches are available for each of these degrees of uncertainty. Three sets of approaches are described in the following sections. In each approach an assumption is made that all payoffs or losses are known. (That is, we assume that we know the financial consequence of choosing each solution alternative, given a specified future state of nature. This assumption may not be realistic in some—or even most—situations.)

Approaches in an Environment of Uncertainty

Since an environment of uncertainty does not provide sufficient information to assign probabilities to the future states of nature, the decision approaches are necessarily crude. In essence they can only reflect personal attitudes concerning the willingness to accept risk. Four approaches are maximin, minimax, maximax, and rationality.

Maximin Approach This consists of (1) identifying the worst outcome (i.e., the minimum) that can occur for any state of nature under each of the solution alternatives and (2) choosing the solution alternative with the greatest (i.e., maximum) "worst outcome." Incorporated in the maximin approach is the cautious attitude of attaining "downside" protection to ensure survival.

Minimax Approach This consists of (1) computing the maximum opportunity loss (i.e., the regret) associated with each solution alternative for every state of nature and (2) choosing the solution alternative that minimizes the maximum summed-up opportunity cost. Reflected in this approach is an attitude of regret avoidance. If properly applied, the minimax approach provides the same decision choice as the maximin approach.

Maximax Approach This consists of (1) identifying the best outcome (i.e., the maximum) that can occur under any state of nature for each solution alternative and (2) choosing the solution alternative with the greatest (i.e., maximum) "best outcome." Incorporated in this approach is an optimistic attitude of accepting a high degree of risk in order to "hit it big."

Rationality Approach This begins with the assumption, in the absence of available information, that each state of nature has an equal probability of occurrence. It then consists of (1) applying these equal probabilities to the outcomes associated with the respective states of nature and (2) choosing the solution alternative having the highest expected payoff.

Approaches in a Risk Environment

In a risk environment we know the probability distributions associated with the potential states of nature. The additional information needed to develop the probability distributions is derived from historical reports, marketing studies, and other fact-finding investigations. Approaches for making decision choices in a risk environment include expected value calculations, Monte Carlo simulations, and decision tree analyses.

Expected Value Calculation   This consists of (1) weighting the outcomes for the states of nature by the probabilities of occurrence, (2) summing up the weighted outcomes to obtain the expected value of the payoff for each solution alternative, and (3) choosing the solution alternative having the maximum expected payoff. The drawback to this approach is that it does not consider the standard deviation associated with the expected value, thereby overlooking an important measure of risk.

Monte Carlo Simulation   This consists of simulating a model, usually in the form of a computer program, over one or more time periods during repeated trials or runs. The computer model incorporates one or more probability distributions to represent factors whose values are subject to variability. (These probability distributions may be based either on empirical evidence or on theoretical conjecture.) During each trial or run, values for the probabilistic factors are selected randomly from the distributions. The repeated trials or runs provide results expressed in probabilistic terms (i.e., expected values and standard deviations), thus yielding information concerning the likely ranges of the payoffs for the respective solution alternatives. The Monte Carlo approach is necessary in complex situations where analytical methods cannot be applied.

Decision Tree   Like the Monte Carlo approach, the decision tree provides probabilistic results. Instead of repeated simulation runs, however, the decision tree involves a series of computations that are based on branches representing probabilities. This approach is suitable to problem situations in which a series of sequential decisions must be made.

It should be noted that none of the probabilistic approaches is widely used today for choosing preferable solution alternatives. Instead, most managerial decision makers and consultants revert to the strategies associated with the environment of uncertainty and simply employ intuition. The probabilistic approaches are slowly gaining in acceptance, however, as decision makers recognize the usefulness of the added guidance they provide.

Approaches in an Environment of Certainty

In a certainty environment we know the values for all potential states of nature, but this environment is not completely problemfree. Most situations inhibit unrestricted decision choices because of resource shortages or other constraints. Choosing a preferable solution alternative in such situations can be a difficult evaluation task. Two approaches that have proved to be relatively useful are known as optimizing and satisficing.

Optimizing Optimizing is suitable when a search can feasibly and cost-effectively lead to one best solution alternative. Optimizing typically employs one of the techniques within the mathematical programming family (e.g., linear programming, integer programming, dynamic programming). Although the models incorporated in such techniques are quite elegant, the specific real-world situations in which this approach may be applied are severely limited. One reason for this limitation is the demanding nature of the information requirements: Detailed quantitative information is needed concerning both resource constraints and the objective functions. Another reason is that the simplifying assumptions imposed by most of the techniques (such as the assumption of linearity imposed by the linear programming technique) do not realistically conform to the actual complexities of real-world situations.

Satisficing Satisficing is often applied in situations for which solutions cannot be feasibly developed by the optimizing approach. It consists of a search among the solution alternatives for any solution that acceptably satisfies desired performance criteria. Once such a solution alternative is discovered, it is accepted as the choice—even though other available solution alternatives may be likely to provide higher payoffs. The satisficing approach is the most widely applied of all decision approaches because it appreciably reduces the required search time while usually providing a nearly optimal solution.

Responsibility for Making the Final Choice

Deciding upon the particular approach to apply can be quite difficult, since it forces the decision maker (e.g., a high-level manager) toward the step of choosing a particular solution alternative. While you can aid the decision maker in choosing and applying the approach that seems most appropriate in the prevailing circumstances, you cannot in your role as consultant accept responsibility for the final decision choice. The responsibility for that step must rest exclusively with the decision maker.

Detailed Development of the Selected Solution

Selecting a solution is not the final step, however. The selected solution must undergo detailed design and refinement. Furthermore, its implementation must be carefully planned in order to minimize required time and costly mistakes. An important concern during this phase is the makeup of the design team. Team members should be selected on the basis of their proficiency in technical design, skill in attaining management involvement, and understanding of the users' perspective.

Typical Design Tasks

The nature of the solution will dictate the specific tasks to be performed during this detailed design and refinement step. Nevertheless, the following tasks are often involved:

1. *Designing the outputs.* In designing the outputs you can provide the vital link to the objectives established earlier. You should be careful, therefore, to ensure that the outputs do in fact clearly reflect those objectives.

2. *Designing the inputs.* After designing the outputs, you are in a position to trace backward to specify the inputs that are necessary to produce those particular outputs. In addition to establishing the content of the inputs, you should specify the means by which the inputs can be acquired quickly and accurately.

3. *Designing the conversion processes.* Next you can design the methods by which the inputs are converted into outputs. Your design should incorporate the following attributes into the conversion processes: effectiveness, efficiency, simplicity, modularity, and reliability. These attributes should produce conversion processes that are useful, acceptable to users, and relatively easy to operate and maintain. They are as relevant to industrial processes involving mechanical or chemical operations as they are to financial information system processes involving paperwork or electronic processes.

4. *Designing the resource repositories.* The next task is to design the repositories for the valuable resources. These repositories both insulate the respective processes and provide interfaces among the processes. If the overall design pertains to an information system, the repositories consist of databases, and the valued resources are data. If the overall design pertains to a physical system, the repositories consist of storerooms and warehouses, and the valued resources are inventories.

5. *Designing the organization.* Finally, you should design the organizational aspects that are affected by the solution, to ensure that the person-

nel will be clearly guided concerning their activities. One organizational aspect includes job descriptions—assigned responsibilities and standards. In many situations you may find it necessary to develop revised management structures and organization charts.

Management of Design Activities

During activities involved in the above design tasks you should employ sound design and project management techniques. These management techniques should ensure that the various design components are consistent with each other and with the desired objectives. The design components should also conform with the evaluation criteria, as well as with time and cost budgets.

Specific project management techniques are discussed in Chapters 15 and 16. A specific design management technique that may be noted, however, is *stewardship structuring*. Stewardship structuring consists of assigning clear authority for making decisions and clear responsibility for paying allocated design-related costs to the entity (e.g., function, department) that is to benefit from the developed solution. Prototyping is also sometimes used as a project management technique, although its primary role is really to serve as a vehicle for solution development as discussed previously.

Presentation of the Recommended Solution

The last step in the solution development phase is to present the recommended solution to the client organization's management. You must present the recommended solution in a persuasive manner if you expect to obtain the client's acceptance. Gaining acceptance can best be achieved by fully justifying the recommendation. If you do not sincerely believe that a recommended solution is justifiable, you should not present it.

Although the justifiable nature of a solution is of primary importance, you should not overlook the style of the presentation. Justifiable solutions are sometimes not accepted because the consultant's presentation style has been weak. Let us therefore consider desirable aspects of presentation.

Normally, the presentation should be made orally and should be accompanied by audiovisual aids and a written report. The facts and arguments should be presented in a clear, concise, and nontechnical manner. It would be counterproductive to overwhelm the client with numerous details and arcane discussions of data analysis techniques. However, do not attempt to hide facts or techniques. If the client asks, you should be ready to describe briefly the significance of any gathered fact and the purpose of any technique you used. Furthermore, you should volunteer information concerning the tasks that a recommended solution entails and the difficulties that are expected in implementing the solution.

An important principle to remember is that the client should *never* be surprised. Interim presentations and written reports should be made throughout the solution-development phase. As a minimum these presentations and reports should be offered at the completion of each step or milestone. If the client management and users have been properly involved and informed at these milestones, they should easily understand the final presentation and be open to the findings.

Tools That Facilitate Solution Development

Whereas many traditional tools—such as flowcharting, decision tables, and mathematical programming—are still potentially important in the process of solution development, the past decade has seen an influx of new tools—marked by the rapid assimilation of personal computer technology. The following paragraphs briefly describe several of the more widely used and useful tools.

Spreadsheet Software

Spreadsheet software can be useful in several of the solution-development steps. In generating alternative solutions for an information system, spreadsheets can be used effectively to model (in some cases, even prototype) components and functions of the information system. Second, spreadsheet software has become the standard medium for structuring economic feasibility analyses. The familiar tabular format with copyable formulas makes it easy to rapidly generate pro forma forecasts, budgets, income statements, balance sheets, and other financial analyses. These analyses can provide the basis for sound economic decisions. In fact, certain spreadsheet software packages include an optimizing algorithm which searches for the best solution. Third, most spreadsheets include a powerful macro language which can be used to prototype or even to implement small systems. (However, it should be recognized that the interpretive nature of this software generally does not result in very efficient systems.) Spreadsheets are particularly popular with end users, who can obtain powerful results without the need for advanced systems training.

Fourth-Generation Languages (4GLs)

A fourth-generation language is in effect an advanced language layer, often added to a database system and query language. The additional commands enable a 4GL to develop very quickly a working prototype of an information system. The convenience of an interface with a powerful database and query language caused 4GLs to become very popular with professionals as well as inexperienced end users. Fourth-generation languages are being used with increasing frequency as implementation platforms, though they tend to be operationally too inefficient for medium- and large-scale applications. (This is changing as software improves and hardware becomes more powerful.)

Computer-Assisted Systems Engineering (CASE)

CASE software packages vary significantly in features and capability. Integrated CASE packages typically include charting support for procedure and flow control specifications, data dictionaries, formats for specifying database schemata and file designs, graphics for specifying input and output design, decision tables for logic specification, and so forth. Although the use of CASE software packages has been limited in certain situations because of the long learning curve, this drawback appears to be lessening. CASE systems are primarily employed as specification and design tools. However, the most advanced systems include interpreters/compilers for a specification language, thereby allowing a computer code to be generated that implements certain portions of a designed system.

Groupware

Groupware is a development based on research performed at the University of Arizona. In essence, it consists of using computer terminals as a neutral communications medium in a meeting, thus permitting participants to anonymously "discuss" a matter of common interest. A typical example involving the use of groupware is a meeting that discusses an organizational problem and potential solutions. Groupware systems typically allow anonymous votes to be tabulated, such as those concerning the potential solutions to an organizational problem. They often maintain a record of the inputs of participants, so that the group can recall earlier contributions as desired. In many respects groupware systems reflect an automation of the brainstorming and Delphi techniques discussed earlier. Organizations using such systems have found that the participants are able to examine more openly all ideas (without the domination of a few "power centers") and therefore to converge on better decisions than might be achieved in a traditional setting. Furthermore, participants seem to achieve convergence more quickly. The groupware concept has spawned several companies and products, including Ventana Corp. of Tucson, TeamFocus (marketed by IBM), and Vision Quest (marketed by Collaborative Technologies). LOTUS NOTES (marketed by the Lotus Development Corporation) is a popular variation which integrates aspects of groupware, E-mail, and database. It also relaxes certain constraints, such as the need for participants to be assembled simultaneously. Groupware appears to have a bright future, since it facilitates the generation of solution ideas, the decision-making process, and the dissemination of information. Several large consulting firms have made a major commitment to this technology.

Guidelines for Solution Development

Throughout the solution-development phase, you should follow several guidelines. Certain of these guidelines have already been noted; others warrant attention as this phase concludes:

1. Be sure that the selected solution relates directly to objectives that the client desires to achieve.

2. Maintain a comprehensive view of the problem and how it relates to the overall organization. At the same time, however, focus on the key issues or concerns.

3. As an aspect of the above, search for all the important relationships involved in the situation.

4. Employ systematic procedures and methodologies while maintaining an openness to creative insights.

13
Implementation

Scott Cosman
Andersen Consulting
Phoenix, Arizona

Implementation is the important and lengthy phase that follows the solution-development phase (also called the "preliminary design" phase) during a problem-solving process. A number of activities are usually involved in the implementation phase. These activities are likely to include developing a work plan, establishing controls over the implementation activities, selecting and training needed personnel, installing needed physical facilities, developing standards and documentation, testing the solution being implemented, and following up and evaluating the implemented solution. Although their sequence will vary somewhat from engagement to engagement, the activities are typically performed in the order listed above. Many implementation activities may be completed concurrently with the design phase, however.

Each of the above activities is discussed in this chapter. In order to provide concreteness to the discussion, we assume that a newly redesigned information system is the "solution" being implemented. Implementation projects involving the installation of information systems are among the most frequently encountered.

To be successful, implementation must be accompanied by changes on the part of those who will use the implemented solution. Therefore, the chapter contains a concluding section that discusses strategies for the management of change.

Work Plan Development

The development of a sound work plan is critical to a successful implementation phase. The work plan defines which tasks are to be performed, when the tasks are to be performed, and who will perform them. Without this information, the consultant and client management would have no means of measuring how well a project is progressing.

The key steps in the development of a sound work plan are:

1. Define the scope of the implementation project.

2. Define the work units to be performed.

3. Identify the skill levels required to complete the work units.

4. Estimate the times required to complete the work units.

5. Establish milestone dates within the life of the project.

6. Develop the details of the work plan.

7. Review and approve the work plan.

A format of a work plan (also called a "work program") appears in Figure 13-1. You may want to refer to these examples during the following discussions.

Define the Scope of the Implementation Project

One or more problem areas were identified during the problem-definition phase. At this point the scope of the implementation project must be more sharply defined. That is, you must clearly define those areas that are to be included within the implementation and those that are not. If the scope is not well defined, the project can become open-ended and it can "last forever." Furthermore, you must define the scope *before* the implementation commences. If the scope definition is delayed, the project boundaries will probably shift and thus cause confusion for the participants. A well-defined project scope will help the implementation project and prevent "scope creep."

Define the Work Units to Be Performed

The next step is to identify and define the work units (i.e., tasks) to be performed. For instance, the following tasks should be included in the implementation of an information systems project:

1. Organization of the project

2. Completion of the detailed system design

MANAGEMENT SERVICES
WORK PROGRAM

CLIENT NAME

Community Services Corp.

PRELIMINARY SURVEY ☐   IMPLEMENTATION ☑   ENGAGEMENT ☐   FOLLOW-UP ☐

INFORMATION TO OBTAIN AND REVIEW PRIOR TO ACTUAL SURVEY:

ORGANIZATION CHART ☐   POSITION DESCRIPTIONS ☐   FLOW CHARTS ☐   SYSTEMS QUESTIONAIRE ☐

POLICY STATEMENTS ☐   PROCEDURES MANUAL ☐   OTHER (LIST ON REVERSE SIDE) ☐

AREAS TO BE REVIEWED (IN ORDER OF PRIORITY)

1. *Implement feasibility study*
2. *conducted as prior engagement*
3.
4.
5.
6.
7.
8.

PERSONNEL TO BE INTERVIEWED

NAME	REGARDING	WHEN
See prior engagement		

PLAN OF ACTION

ACTION STEP	TECHNIQUES TO BE USED	ASSIGNED TO ✱	TARGET DATES START	TARGET DATES FINISH	EST. TIME
1. PLANNING ENGAGEMENT					
2. PRELIMINARY SURVEY					
Design input-output forms		T.S.	7/27	9/18	120
Prepare detailed specs.		T.S./R.B.	7/27	10/23	560
Programming		Various	7/27	1/5	630
Write use manual		T.S.	11/13	12/18	44
System conversion		R.B.	11/13	12/18	280
Post implement support		R.B.	1/15	2/12	80
Supervision		C.S.	7/27	2/12	120
Clerical support		TOTAL			80
DAILY TOTALS					

✱ *Includes firm personnel only. See engagement letter for client and manufacturer's responsibilities.*

(a)

Figure 13-1

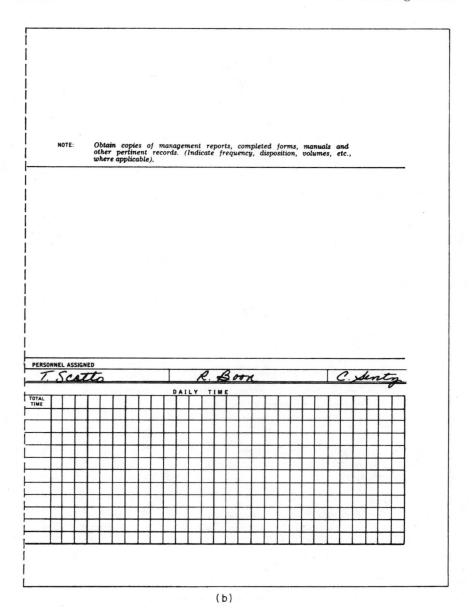

(b)

Figure 13-1   (Continued)

3. Coding of the programs

4. Testing of the programs and the overall system

5. Conversion to the new system

Several other tasks often included in a systems implementation project are:

1. Selection and installation of hardware and system software

2. Development of the systems documentation for users, for management, and for the computer operations personnel

3. Development of the appropriate testing environment

4. Establishment of the conversion plan and procedures

5. Training of system users

The type and size of the implementation project are likely to have a significant impact on the particular tasks that need to be performed and on their relative importance. For example, a project involving the implementation of application software would probably place *more* emphasis on the conversion of the package to the available hardware and *less* emphasis on the coding and testing of programs. A large project may dictate the use of separate teams assigned to logically related tasks, with added time allowed for project administration and communication. A small project will require less time for administration and communication, because it will probably use only one project team; however, it will have less flexibility in sequencing the various tasks.

Identify the Skill Levels Required to Complete the Work Units

An appropriate skill level or experience level must be identified for each defined work unit or task. For example, relatively experienced personnel are needed for the scope definition and system design tasks. Less experienced staff may be assigned to programming and documentation tasks. After identifying the appropriate skill level for each task, you can assign specific individuals to each task.

Estimate the Times Required to Complete the Work Units

The next step is to estimate how long each work unit or task will take to complete. It may be possible to use estimating guidelines, such as programming estimates based on a judgment of the complexity of the program. If guidelines are not available, you can draw on your past experience, the past experience of the client, or estimates provided by others (e.g., vendors in the case of application software). Regardless of the estimates' source, they should be consistent and should be viewed cautiously; the source should be clearly documented.

Establish Milestone Dates within the Life of the Project

In order to establish milestone dates, you should first determine the project completion date. For certain projects this date is specified by an external event. In the case of an accounting system, the completion date is typically at the end of an accounting period. If the completion date cannot be tied to an external event, perhaps the beginning date can be. For instance, the beginning date may be determined by the availability of key consulting or client personnel. Then the completion date can be determined as the beginning date plus the overall project time.

Once a key date (either for beginning or completion) has been identified, the other milestone dates can be established. As the name implies, these dates should represent the completion of major work activities such as detailed testing of all programs, system test, or acceptance test of selected application software packages.

Milestone dates should be determined with the concept of *critical path* taken into account. The critical path for a project is represented by the progression of key tasks that need to be completed before work on other tasks can begin. In most cases, the overall length of a project will be a result of the time required to complete all tasks on the critical path. Numerous automated tools, such as application software packages, are available to help you to determine and diagram the critical path.

Milestone dates provide you and the client management with the means to ascertain if the project is on schedule. They also represent logical points in time at which to review the quality and scope of the project.

Develop the Details of the Work Plan

After completing the previous steps, you are ready to develop the details pertaining to the work plan or program. First, you should determine all the smaller work units (i.e., subtasks) that comprise each major work unit or task. Then prepare a network chart, such as a PERT or CPM chart. This chart should show all the milestones as well as the final completion date. Take care to sequence the tasks so that they are in proper relation to each other. When you are satisfied that the tasks are complete and properly related, sequence the smaller work units within each task.

Figure 13-2 shows a CPM chart for a system implementation project, with all the major tasks and subtasks sequenced relative to each other. The critical path begins at Task I, continues through nodes 1.1, 1.3, 1.4,

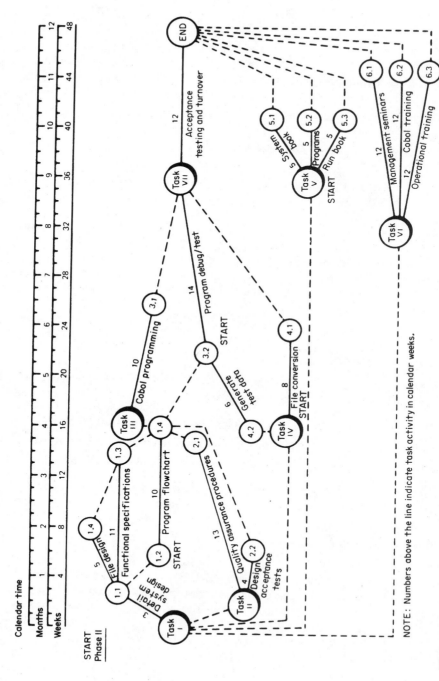

Calendar time

NOTE: Numbers above the line indicate task activity in calendar weeks.

Figure 13-2

3.2, and concludes with Task VII. The estimated overall project time, as shown on the time scale, is 48 weeks. (Normally, you would also fill in the calendar scale shown at the top of the chart.)

It should be emphasized that the detailed work plan, including the CPM chart, would typically be prepared with the aid of such automated tools as electronic spreadsheets (e.g., Lotus, Excel), project control software packages, and other scheduling tools (e.g., Andersen Consulting's Manage/1).

Review and Approve the Work Plan

The final step in the development of a work plan is to review the plan with client management. At this point, the client may indicate changes in the milestones or the number of client personnel who are available to be assigned to the project. If this happens, the plan should be adjusted and reviewed again. Once the plan is accepted by client management, it should be formally approved in writing. This ensures that both parties have a clear understanding of the beginning and completion dates, as well as the quantities of resources to be devoted to the implementation project.

Project Controls

Project controls provide the means to successfully administer the work plan. Specific objectives of project control are:

1. To ensure that the project is on schedule and within budget

2. To communicate the exact project status of all concerned personnel

3. To provide assurance that a quality product will be implemented

Project controls include administrative controls, time-reporting procedures, and independent quality assurance reviews.

Administrative Controls

Project controls should begin in the organizational stage of a project. In this stage, the administrative framework is formed to provide overall guidance and control to the implementation process. It should consist of individuals who have direct interest in the quality of the final product (e.g., an installed information system).

The administrative framework should be established in accordance with the size of the project and the client. The framework for a simple project and small client firm should be simple, perhaps involving only a single top-level manager. For a complex project and large client firm, the framework may be quite involved. Our description assumes the latter case. It also assumes, as stated earlier, that the project pertains to the implementation of an information system. Thus, the description given below should be scaled down to suit simpler projects and smaller firms; it should also be modified as necessary to fit other types of implementation projects.

The administrative framework should consist of one or more client management committees, with representatives from the user areas, the top (executive) management, and the information processing services department. (See Figure 13-3.) It is important that users be represented on the management committees, since their participation helps ensure that users will accept the new system. In larger firms that have several levels of management, it may be desirable to have more than one committee. For instance, a firm might establish both a project steering committee and a management advisory committee. While each committee formed should share responsibility for controlling the project, each would have distinctive purposes: The project steering committee would maintain direct control over the project, while the management advisory committee would coordinate the activities of the information processing services department.

Since the project steering committee is most closely involved with projects, it deserves additional attention. The committee should be comprised of senior management from each area of the client organization that is impacted by the system project. The leader of the project, as well as the manager of the information processing services department, should also be on the committee. This committee provides direct guidance over the project; thus, it has control over and is responsible for all costs and benefits pertaining to the development and operation of systems spanned by the project. In addition, the committee monitors project activities to ensure that all changes to the system design are made only with proper approval.

The committees hold regularly scheduled status meetings to carry out the monitoring responsibilities. In addition, ad hoc meetings are held when specific problems of significance arise.

Time-Reporting Procedures

Time-reporting and analysis procedures are necessary to keep the project within its time schedule and dollar budget. Specific objectives of these procedures are:

1. To provide project management with information necessary for planning, administering, and controlling the project
2. To prepare and control the project work plan (program) updates
3. To assist the project leader in preparing management status reports

JOB TIME REPORT

PRO. NO.	ACT. NO.	TASK NO.	DESCRIPTION		Actual to Date	MON	TUE	WED	THU	FRI	SAT	SUN	End Actual to Date	Earned Hours	TOTAL PLAN	Remaining to do	Check Complete
02	002	001	Interview Dept. Mgmt.	P		8									16		
				A	8	10	2						20				✓
02	002	002	Define Needs of Users	P			8	4	8	8					44		
				A	8		8	4	8	8	2		38			6	
01	003	001	Design Cash Flow Stmt.	P			4								8		
				A	4		4						8				✓
				P													
				A													
				Total Planned P		8	8	8	8	8					68		
				Total Actual A	20	10	10	8	8	8	2		66			6	
				Attendance Variance V		2	2				2						

Herman Corporation | 4 | Design Financial & Responsibility Reports | T. Scotto

ORGANIZATION: X.00/HC — T. Scotto — JOB NO. 4 — JOB NAME — RATE — NAME OF PERSON — FROM 5/25/06 TO 5/31/06 — PREPARED BY J.F. Pallar — APPROVED BY

SUMMARY

PROJ. NO.	TOTAL HOURS	TIME CHRGS	EXP	TOTAL CHRGS
01	4	X.00	X.00	XX.00
02	42	X.00	X.00	XX.00

NOTE TO PERSONNEL

The hours and expenses which appear in the summary section of this report must equal those which appear on the semi-monthly time report. Therefore, this information will be entered only on the engagement report for the week in which a semi-monthly time report is submitted.

A - ACTUAL   P - PLANNED   V - VARIANCE

Activity Manning Sheet

Date 5/30/06
Job No. 04
Project No. 02
Activity No. 002
Page 1
Activity Name: Define Resp. Report Requirements
Organization: Herman Corporation
Prepared by T. Scotto
Approved by J.F. Pallar

Week/Month Ending

Name		5/23	TD	5/30	TD	TD	TD	TD	TD	TD	TD	TD	TD	Total
Scotto	P	16	16	36	52									52
	A	16	16	42	58									58
	O	-	-	6	6									6
Yalton	P	8	8	4	12									12
	A	8	8	5	13									13
	O			1	1									1
	P													
	A													
	O													
	P													
	A													
	O													
Totals	P	24	24	40	64									64
	A	24	24	47	71									71
	V	-	-	7	7									7
	O													

P - Planned   A - Actual Against Plan   V - Variance
O - Actual Nonplan Other

Figure 13-3

4. To account for all time incurred on the project by team members

Several procedures relative to time reporting should be observed. Actual time incurred on a project should be reported at the same level of detail as the budgeting of time on the work plan. Both project hours and nonproject hours should be reported by each team member. The estimated time to complete each task currently in progress should be included in the report. The upper portion of Figure 13-3 shows a time report for a job.

The time reports of all team members should be reviewed for accuracy, with actual time and estimated time to complete being compared to the work plan. If the client has an automated time-reporting system, it should be employed by the project team when appropriate. If the client does not have an automated time-reporting system, the feasibility of obtaining one for use by the project team should be studied. Numerous automated time-reporting systems (i.e., software packages) are available at reasonable prices.

Time reports should be summarized at a team level, activity level, or project level, depending upon the structure and size of the project. All variances between actual and budgeted time should be recorded and their causes determined. The lower portion of Figure 13-3 shows a summarized report for job no. 04, an activity in project no. 02.

Common causes of time variances include:

1. Improperly applied estimating guidelines

2. Improperly communicated task scopes and objectives

3. Inappropriately assigned personnel (people who are either overqualified or underqualified for the assigned tasks)

4. Unexpected changes to task scopes and objectives

5. Unexpected difficulties with respect to the availability or functioning of project resources

When changes make is necessary, the project leader should revise the budgeted hours in the work plan.

Independent Quality Assurance Reviews

Quality assurance programs represent another means of control over projects. The objectives of quality assurance are:

1. To ensure that the system satisfies all user requirements and is operable on a day-to-day basis without assistance

2. To ensure that the system is being developed within the time frame and cost estimates originally agreed upon

3. To ensure that the system is simple and efficient to operate, maintain, and control by client personnel

4. To ensure that the system employs satisfactory methods and techniques that are within the sphere of competence of the majority of client personnel

5. To ensure that the presentation and format of all procedures, documentation, and coding are neat, well organized, and in conformance with established client standards

6. To ensure that risks are identified, communicated, and managed

7. To benefit from the quality assurance reviewer's expertise and experience

Components of a quality assurance program include:

1. *Independent reviews.* These reviews should be conducted prior to reaching implementation project milestones. They should be performed by a person who (1) is not associated with the project and (2) has a skill level at least as high as the project leader's. (On very small projects some of the review may be performed by the project leader.)

2. *Quality assurance checklists.* These checklists contain a series of questions concerning the quality of work performed and should be (1) prepared by the project supervisor responsible for the work and (2) reviewed by both the project leader and the independent reviewer. (On very small projects, in which supervisors are not used, checklists would be prepared by the project leader.)

The independent reviewer should prepare written comments concerning the findings of reviews and checklists. Problems should be resolved by the project leader, if possible. Unresolvable problems should be presented to the project steering committee. Quality assurance reviews should be scheduled at regular intervals appropriate to the size and complexity of the project.

Selection and Training of Needed Personnel

Selection of Project Personnel

Skilled and experienced personnel are critical to the success of an implementation project. Thus, the selection and training of needed personnel for the project are important.

Selecting the needed personnel for a specific implementation project is often difficult. The following aspects must be considered:

1. Staffing levels needed
2. Skills and experience required for project tasks
3. Budget levels
4. Past performances of available personnel
5. Availability of resources and skills
6. Availability of client personnel

The first three requirements are determined during preparation of the work plan, and the fourth is ascertained (at least in part) by the time variances that appear on project control reports. The last two aspects are discussed below.

Availability of Resources and Skills

Determining who is available for assignment is a fairly informal task in a small consulting firm. In larger consulting firms, however, tracking the availability of personnel requires formal procedures. On a short-term basis, a daily staffing sheet may be used. This sheet alphabetically lists each consultant's name and the project to which he or she is assigned on a particular day. On a longer-term basis, a staff availability schedule is often used. Figure 13-4 lists information that should appear on such a schedule.

Availability of Client Personnel

Client responsibilities must also be established. The consultant may not "exercise absolute administrative control of client personnel since he is not a member of their organization." You can, however, advise client

---

1. Time frame for which the information is provided
2. Name of consultant
3. Employee identification number
4. Staffing level of the consultant (e.g., partner, manager, senior)
5. Skills
6. Availability status information
   a. Project to which individual is currently assigned
   b. Type of project (e.g., installation)
   c. Project scheduled starting date
   d. Project schedule completion date
7. Date the staff person becomes available for other projects

Figure 13-4   A staff availability schedule.

management on the selection of qualified personnel to perform the project tasks. If a client lacks personnel who are capable of assuming responsibilities with respect to project tasks, you may recommend that the client employ additional personnel who are so qualified. "The right mixture of consultant and client personnel is a critical consideration" when planning project assignments.*

Criteria similar to those used to select consultants may be utilized to choose appropriate client members. Development of such criteria, however, must be based on client policies and standards.

Types of Training Methods

Although personnel may be selected on the basis of skills and experience, they nevertheless need training at various times during their employment. Staff development and training are as essential to the continued well-being of the consulting firm and the projects undertaken as they are to the careers of the consultants. Chapter 20 discusses staff development and training in depth. Here, several types of training methods are considered briefly, since they bear upon the needs of implementation projects.

Formal training Depending on the complexity of the proposed project, consulting (and perhaps client) personnel may need to attend formal training classes. For instance, if a software package is to be purchased from an outside vendor, the personnel assigned to the project may be asked to attend a vendor-sponsored school. This formal instruction will enable the project members to acquire a working knowledge of the functional and technical aspects of the package.

Another situation warranting formal training for the staff consultant is a project involving an unfamiliar technical environment. In this situation, the client might offer the outside consultants the same training program that is attended by the client's personnel. Such training could involve reading technical manuals and attending client-instructed classes.

Ongoing training Every consulting firm should provide ongoing training that employs a variety of educational methods and covers various subjects. This ongoing training might involve a combination of in-house and outside training programs. Outside training programs that could be considered are those offered by the American Institute of

---

*American Institute of Certified Public Accountants, *Management Advisory Services. Guideline Series Number 1*, AICPA, New York, 1968.

Certified Public Accountants, Association of Systems Management, and American Management Association.

Informal training Every consulting firm should maintain an assortment of periodicals, research materials, reference manuals, and past project documentation within its library and files. Each firm should encourage its personnel to use such materials to prepare for engagements such as implementation projects. College and university libraries are also excellent sources of training materials. In addition, informal discussions with other consulting personnel having experience on similar projects can provide relevant information.

Installation of Physical Facilities

The implementation of new information systems may involve the installation of physical facilities. Although this task occurs mainly during the implementation phase, it nevertheless should also be considered in the context of the entire system development life cycle. Figure 13-5 shows the four phases of an information system development life cycle. In each phase certain tasks are performed and decisions are made concerning the

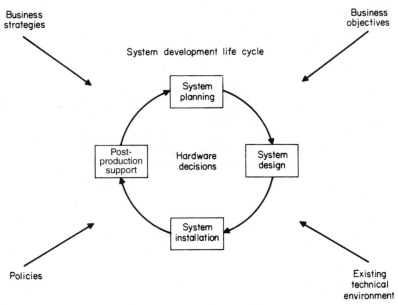

Figure 13-5 Diagram of the system development life cycle.

installation of physical facilities such as computer hardware. Many of these tasks are closely related. All are influenced by existing business objectives, strategies, and policies, including those pertaining to computer hardware and software.

Let us review the impact of each phase shown in Figure 13-5 on the installation of the particular physical facilities known as computer hardware.

System Planning

If a computer hardware strategy does not already exist, it should be developed during the system planning phase. If one does exist, it should be updated as the new systems are developed. It should span several years into the future, taking into account all expected future development projects as well as the changing operating and information needs of the organization. This strategy should be revised and updated often.

System Design

Specific computer hardware recommendations must be made during the system design phase. Hardware selection is very important, since it has a critical impact on the overall performance of the information system. The preliminary selection should occur prior to technical design of the system, and the final selection should be completed before the implementation phase begins.

System Installation

When the implementation project schedule is prepared, it should include tasks labeled "Preparation of Physical Site" and "Installation of New Hardware." Although the vendor of the hardware may actually perform the installation, the project leader or consultant must coordinate the activity to minimize disruption to the client firm. Numerous details may be involved, such as the installation of a special power supply and air-conditioning, plus the layout of space requirements for the equipment.

Postproduction Support (System Operations)

During the operation of the installed system, a major concern is the effective utilization of the computer system and the identification of potential bottlenecks. Overutilization may indicate the need for additional hardware. Increasing maintenance costs and other problems may indicate the need for new equipment.

Development of Standards and Documentation

Objectives Achieved by Standards

Standards are needed with respect to the solution (e.g., an improved information system) being implemented. Thus, the development of standards, followed by the preparation of standardized documentation, is a task to be performed during the implementation project. Normally, standards should be developed by the most experienced and qualified members of the implementation project team so that the standards will be as sound as possible. Establishing sound standards should help achieve the following objectives:

1. To provide a basis for effective communication within the areas served by the implementation project
2. To improve the efficiency of installing and operating the solution (e.g., an improved information system)
3. To serve as an aid in training all personnel affected by the implementation project

Well-documented, easily understandable, and strictly adhered-to standards establish an effective framework for communication. They help illustrate both concepts and specific details to all those involved with the implementation project, including client management, user personnel, technical experts, and staff consultants. By referring to the standards, any authorized person should gain a faster and more complete comprehension of the system being implemented.

Sound standards also improve productivity and efficiency, both during the implementation project and later during the operational phase. Standards tend to reduce the possibilities of duplicated efforts and conflicting procedures and encourage the performance of similar activities using similar techniques aimed at standardized results. Since standards help to define the procedures to be used, they make easier the activity of estimating requirements pertaining to project work units. In addition, standards ensure that the maintenance of the system during the postproduction support phase (i.e., operational phase) will be simple and straightforward.

The third objective relates to training. Standards should provide a common framework for familiarizing all affected persons with the environment in which they will be working. Standards provide guidance in training the members of the implementation project team or teams. Standards also facilitate the training of user personnel, such as newly hired or transferred employees who are assigned to the information systems department. By making training easier, standards reduce training costs.

Factors that should be considered when developing standards include the following:

1. Standards and other guidelines presently in existence

2. Relative size of the project

3. Relative complexity of the project

4. Standards, if any, that have been prepared by the vendors of the physical facilities being implemented

Standardized Documentation

Documentation of the implemented project should be developed in accordance with established standards. The purposes of standardized documentation are to:

1. Record decisions

2. Communicate ideas

3. Specify procedures

4. Assign responsibilities for tasks

5. Provide a means of reviewing the quality and completeness of work performed and indicating approval or disapproval of the work performed

6. Provide historical support and backup

The documentation process is necessary to the implementation phase (see Figure 13-6), providing the following benefits:

1. A means of communicating to the client management

2. A memory aid for the designer of the project being implemented (e.g., an improved information system)

3. A reference for use during the postproduction support (operational) phase.

4. A vehicle for resolving misunderstandings concerning the functioning of the implemented facilities (e.g., an information system)

Figure 13-6 lists several implementation activities and the documentation that should be produced by each during the implementation of an information system.

Activity	Document	Description
1. Develop implementation plan	a. Program description b. File definition c. Personnel assignments d. Implementation schedule e. Hardware installation schedule f. Cost/benefit analysis—operations g. Estimate of installation costs	Abstract of logical program function, flow of control File structure diagram, data contents Chart of people and their tasks and time estimates to complete Chart of tasks and milestones List of hardware to be installed and dates
2. Develop detailed design (if not completed during design phase)	a. Manual procedures b. Program specifications c. Test conditions d. Test data e. Expected results	Step-by-step instructions for doing tasks Program logic in narrative or diagram format or both Conditions to be tested for layout of test records Expected results of program execution
3. Estimate needs and establish controls	a. Estimates of staff requirements b. Approach memorandum c. Conversion schedule	Length of the conversion and who will do it Conversion files and cycle approach definitions Time when conversion tasks will take place
4. Develop security standards	a. Security memorandum	Restriction of personnel, data security, recovery from system failure, password IDs
5. Develop operating standards	a. User manual	Statement of exactly when and how each task is performed, brief and concise
6. Train user personnel	a. General computer concepts b. Equipment overview	User orientation to computers, if new to them User orientation to equipment and operating instructions
7. Test implemented system	a. Test data b. Actual results c. System modifications d. Resolution of system problems	Comparison of actual test results against expected results What system should do according to design request for system change, with differences well documented

Figure 13-6   List of implementation activities and related documentation.

A variety of standardized systems development methodologies exist to aid the documentation process, including:

1. STRADIS (STRuctured Analysis, Design and Implementation of Systems), marketed by McAuto Systems

2. PRIDE (PRofitable Information by DEsign), marketed by M. Bruce and Associates

3. 50M/70, marketed by Atlantic Software

4. FOUNDATION, marketed by Andersen Consulting

Testing of Solution Being Implemented

Testing is an indispensable activity within the implementation phase. Thorough testing of the implemented solution ensures that the system works as designed and meets the users' needs.

The testing activity can be subdivided into three steps: unit test, string test, and system test. Each step requires considerable planning and preparation prior to actual execution of the tests.

Unit Test

This consists of testing the smallest unit of the solution being implemented. In the case of a computer-based information system, the unit is often viewed as being a computer program. The purpose of conducting a unit test is to ensure that each separate unit functions properly. The steps of a unit test consist of:

1. Identifying the test conditions (from the design documentation)
2. Preparing the test data
3. Computing the expected results
4. Performing the actual tests
5. Comparing the actual results obtained with the expected results
6. Correcting program logic errors
7. Retesting as necessary

String Test

After unit testing has been successfully completed, string testing should begin. A string test is a test of closely related units. Its purpose is to determine that the units (e.g., computer programs) work together or interface properly. Test conditions may be created during a string test that could not be performed during a unit test. Such extra test conditions should test the design features that link the constituent programs as well as the overall design of the programs operating in combination.

System Test

A system test consists of testing the entire solution being implemented. In the case of an information system, the system test extends from the preparation of source documents to the distribution of outputs. A system test has the purposes of ensuring that

1. Documentation is adequate to operate the implemented system successfully.

2. User departments affected by the implementation can properly and easily prepare the necessary inputs and can use the outputs successfully.

3. Overall flows through the system are in accordance with the developed solution.

A system test can be subdivided into two component tests: an integration test and a user test. The integration test is performed to verify that all units in the new system communicate properly with each other. Integration testing also verifies that the new system interfaces properly with all external systems. The user test is performed to verify that the system can operate within the new environment to satisfactorily meet the needs of the users. This test should simulate as exactly as possible the actual working conditions to be faced, and in the case of a new information system this test should employ live production data.

The length of a system test should be a function of the benefits derived from detecting each and every system problem. If system tests find no problems, too much effort was likely expended during the unit and string testing.

Follow-Up Evaluation of the Implemented Solution

Objectives of a Postimplementation Evaluation

A thorough postimplementation evaluation should be conducted shortly after the solution has been fully implemented. Reports should be prepared as written documentation of the evaluation and presented to management. The objectives of the evaluation, in the case of an information system, are to

1. Compare the actual performance of the implemented system with the expected performance

2. Compare the details of the implemented system with the documented design

3. Determine potential improvements to the new system

4. Determine means of improving the systems development methodology employed by the client firm

An early question that must be resolved concerns who is to conduct the evaluation. While the implementation team is most familiar with the implemented system, it may be viewed as biased. Therefore, it is probably better to choose qualified personnel other than members of the implementation team. Three suitable choices are

1. A special audit team selected from among the managers of the client organization

2. An internal audit team that performs operational reviews as a part of its customary duties

3. An external team of consultants

The follow-up evaluation is not a one-time process. Additional evaluations should be performed at regular intervals during the operational life of the implemented system. User needs change over time, and these changes will lead in time to the need for further improvements via future system development cycles.

Each review and evaluation should focus on three specific areas:

1. Economics

2. Operations

3. Future performance

Economic Review

The economic review should involve the comparison of (1) the actual benefits and costs of the new system with (2) the expected benefits and costs that were developed during the system design phase. Typical questions that may be asked during an economic review include:

Were the development cost estimates on target?

Did the expected benefits materialize?

Were the operational costs in line with estimates?

Have significant variances occurred?

As the last question suggests, all variances should be calculated. Large variances, over or under, should be thoroughly investigated, and the reasons for their occurrences should be carefully documented. Figure 13-7

Benefits versus Cost Analysis			
Cost/benefit	Estimate	Actual	Variance
Initial cost of new system			
Site preparation cost			
System design and analysis			
cost			
Programming costs			
Training, conversion, and other			
implementation costs			
Total one-time development costs	_____	_____	_____
Annual operating costs			
Computer hardware and related			
equipment rental or purchase			
Software rental or purchase			
Analysis and programming			
maintenance costs			
Operating personnel costs			
Space charges, supplies, etc.	_____	_____	_____
Total annual operating costs	_____	_____	_____
Annual operating costs			
Reduced personnel savings			
Personnel efficiency savings	_____	_____	_____
Total annual savings	_____	_____	_____
Rate of return			
(Rate at which present value of			
savings equals present value of			
one-time costs)			
Payback period			
(Length of time required to			
recover one-time costs)			
Other intangible benefits			
(List)			

Figure 13-7   Format of an economic review analysis.

presents an analysis format that may be employed to document the benefit and cost variances. Note that it also provides space for displaying the rate of return and payback period, which can be useful to client management when making key decisions.

This analysis of benefit and cost variances often yields satisfying results. For instance, operational costs may be found to be too high or operational benefits to be missing. Upon investigation, the unsatisfactory results are attributed to improper use of the system. A relatively simple and low-cost adjustment may be the only corrective action needed to produce a significant saving in costs or an increase in benefits.

The analysis is useful even when immediate results are not likely. For example, development costs are historical in nature and thus cannot be recovered. By learning the reasons for variances in development costs, however, client management can modify the system development and thus reduce development costs in future implementations.

Operational Review

An operational review focuses on the actual use of the implemented system by the intended users. Typical questions that might be asked during an operational review include:

Is the system being used currently?

Is system response time as satisfactory as planned?

Does the system operate successfully?

Has the system solved the organizational problems that it is intended to address?

Is the system being used or is it being resisted?

Are the automated and manual processes as efficient as intended?

An evaluation of operations after implementation should consider how well they function, with particular emphasis (in the case of an information system) on inputs, error rates, timeliness of outputs, and utilization of outputs. Various elevation techniques may be employed. For instance, a report can be terminated for a period of time in order to determine if it is actually being used. If no one complains, the report is probably not being used. A performance monitor can be applied, in the case of an online information system, to determine the use of frequency of a particular CRT screen.

Future Performance Review

A future performance review identifies potential improvements to the implemented system and estimates the effort required to implement these improvements. Both benefits and costs should be considered in this review, just as they were during the planning of the currently implemented system.

Possible improvements, to be conducted by means of systems maintenance projects, can be subdivided into short-term attributes and long-term attributes. Client management can then prioritize the tasks, determining which efforts should be undertaken immediately and which should be delayed.

Effecting Change

Implementation leads to change. Both the client management and the direct users of an implemented solution must undergo change. Adjusting to change is never easy for humans. Thus, you should be aware of three steps in a change process and the strategies by which you as a consultant can successfully effect needed change in client personnel.

Change Model

According to the change model, three steps are involved:

1. Unfreezing established behavior patterns
2. Changing by moving to a new behavior pattern
3. Refreezing by firmly establishing the new behavior pattern

Strategies for Managing Change

Each of the three steps can be achieved by positive actions on the part of the consultant. To effect the unfreezing step, you need to create the desire for change. For instance, you might shock client management by revealing an undesirable current state of affairs (e.g., a very high unit cost of production) or current dissatisfaction (e.g., a very low level of employee morale). Once management's attention has been captured by this negative news, you can paint a positive view of improvement through specific changes. In order to create the desire for change in the client's employees, you could show that the proposed change has the support of management. Alternatively, you might show specific benefits to the employees (e.g., an easier way to get a job done).

The essential point is that people accept change when they are involved in making the change. Thus, it is necessary to involve users in the process. Satisfying involvement leads to a commitment to action and change. Effective strategies for gaining involvement include the following:

1. Use of brainstorming sessions or other means of soliciting ideas
2. Use of "what-if" sessions or other means of projecting views of a future that contains the change
3. Use of pilot programs in which small organizational units serve as "pioneers"

4. Use of committees to investigate the desirability of the change
5. Use of training programs in which the change is taught

To refreeze the change, you can employ such strategies as:

1. Positive individual encouragement (e.g., "You are really catching on!")
2. Well-designed training sequence, in which the change is subdivided into parts and taught in a building-up fashion and in which achievement targets are clearly established
3. Repetitive practice (i.e., many repetitions involving the change, each followed by a rest period)
4. Group meetings in which achievements are displayed and the benefits of the change are repeated
5. Records of achievement in which written records are maintained to reflect performance improvements

The preparation for such activities should be undertaken as early in the planning phase as possible. In fact, as suggested above, the seeds of change are planted at the initial meeting with client management. By careful cultivation, you can reap the satisfaction of fully effected changes within the client's organization.

Part 4

Engagement Management

14

The Proposal Process

Ira Kasdan, President
Business Writers & Trainers, Inc. (BWTI)
Minneapolis, Minnesota

A proposal is a sales tool that presents an offer to provide assistance or service to a potential client. The overriding objective of the proposal is to present the offer in the most persuasive and professional manner.

Proposals are an important component of the sales and marketing efforts of most management consultants. Because a proposal reflects the consultant's thinking and organizing abilities, a poorly written document can create a negative perception that is very difficult to overcome.

Although a poorly written proposal is a common cause of losing business, few engagements are won *solely* on the basis of the written proposal. A client often uses a proposal to reinforce a decision already made on the basis of experiences with the consultant during information gathering, elsewhere in the sales process, or through prior engagements.

Not surprisingly, many of the same elements that make other sales and marketing activities successful also apply to proposals. The most effective proposals demonstrate the following:

- A client-oriented or client-focused perspective
- An accurate understanding of the client's problem and/or need

- A realistic plan of action or service to address the problem
- A thorough understanding of the client's decision makers and their decision-making process
- An awareness of the business, financial, political, and technical considerations likely to affect the buying decision
- A knowledge of the seriousness of the problem and the level of urgency needed to address it
- An established credibility or reputation for providing the types of products or services being offered
- An interpersonal rapport and trust with the client's decision makers
- A fee arrangement that reasonably reflects the value that the offer will provide for the client

This chapter presents guidelines for preparing effective proposals and examples illustrating how these guidelines apply.

Organization and Content of the Proposal

Consulting engagements are extremely diverse in size, complexity, and fees generated. A formal written proposal is necessary and desirable for most significant engagements. The main elements of a formal written proposal typically include:

- Description of the problem
- Approach or work plan
- Results/Benefits
- Schedule
- Consultant's pertinent experience
- Staffing
- Assumptions
- Fee arrangements

Description of the Problem

The problem description clearly identifies the reason for the engagement: the problem the consultant will attempt to solve. No other element of the proposal is more important. When the consultant shows in simple and precise language that he or she understands the client's problem thoroughly and accurately, the client is more likely to have confidence in the solution that the consultant proposes.

A concise but complete review of the key elements of the client's problem or situation also helps to ensure that the consultant and client fully agree on the project's scope. The consultant should use the client's own language or terminology throughout the proposal. Use of the client's terminology immediately captures the client's attention. It also establishes credibility by showing that the consultant truly understands and is in tune with the client organization.

Approach or Work Plan

The approach or work plan provides a high-level overview of how the consultant proposes to address the problem. Properly prepared, this section of a proposal serves two purposes: It tells the client what to expect and it structures the project, thereby guiding the consultant's activities.

For example, a work plan for a study might list and briefly describe these five tasks:

Task 1   Analysis within the problem area

Task 2   Interviews with employees and staff

Task 3   Time and motion study

Task 4   Evaluation of equipment

Task 5   Selection of the best option

The approach or work plan also explains how work will be performed both at the client's premises and at the consultant's office. If techniques such as time and motion studies will be used, this section should describe them. Likewise, if the plan includes the study of various procedures, this section should explain how such a study will be conducted.

When writing the work plan, always show sensitivity to the client's situation and likely concerns. For instance, if the plan requires in-depth interviews with the client's staff as part of a fact-finding effort, emphasize how interviews will be scheduled and conducted to minimize disruption of the client's business.

Results/Benefits

The results and benefits that the client can expect to derive from the engagement must appear prominently in the proposal. It is not enough just to explain how the project will be completed. The positive outcome, bottom-line results, or other payoffs that the engagement will produce for the client must also be stressed. For example, do not state merely that the engagement will provide an improved inventory system. Add that the inventory system improvements resulting from the engagement will generate greater cash flow, raise service quality, and increase profits.

You should also identify how and why the benefits of the proposed approach, schedule, experience, and/or staffing are unique or superior to those that other consultants or competitors might offer. Without this information, the client may be convinced of the need to solve the problem but may not be convinced that you are the one to solve it.

Schedule

The schedule section should:

- Specify when the project will begin (this is often expressed as a number of days or weeks following notification of the proposal's acceptance)
- Identify the sequence in which the consultant will complete each phase or step of the work
- Estimate the completion time required for each phase or step
- Identify the date or time frame by which all work will be completed

The schedule provided in the proposal does not have to be overly detailed. The consultant can provide the client with a more detailed schedule, including specific completion dates for each step, when the engagement begins.

Consultant's Pertinent Experience

In the pertinent experience section, the consultant should include any statements or references that add to the prestige or strength of the proposal. Common inclusions are:

- A brief history of the consultant's firm
- Number and locations of firm offices
- Other clients and industries that the firm has served
- Examples of how the firm has provided similar services or solved similar problems for other clients

When describing pertinent experience, always focus on those experiences or credentials that relate most directly to the client, its industry, and its problem or situation.

Staffing

Many formal proposals also include a description of planned staffing for the engagement. The staffing section identifies who is responsible for the project and who represents the firm on key issues. It may also list project team members with a brief description of the team's experience and how that experience relates to the engagement.

Consultants who include information on team members' backgrounds when such information is not specifically requested by the client hope to build the credibility of the proposal. There are, however, at least two key risks in providing this information:

1. Descriptions of team members' backgrounds may give the client a reason to *reject* rather than accept the proposal if, for instance, the descriptions fail to indicate that team members possess specific experience or skills which the client desires.

2. If the engagement start-up is delayed (a common occurrence), project team members identified in the proposal may be committed to other engagements or may be otherwise unavailable by the time the engagement begins. If the backgrounds of the project team members were a key factor in the client's acceptance of the proposal, the resulting difficulties are obvious.

Assumptions

A distinct assumptions section is optional, but is often important to include in a proposal, for two reasons:

- Clients frequently expect "instant wonders."
- Consultants often allow clients to develop unrealistic expectations about likely engagement results.

Although it is desirable to avoid understating an engagement's potential benefits, it is risky to overpromise or imply overly optimistic outcomes. To avoid these pitfalls, include qualifying statements which identify possible occurrences that could preclude "instant" success or limit the positive results of the engagement. Two examples of qualifying statements follow:

"The extent to which the potential cost reductions this project identifies actually result in hard dollar savings will depend heavily on how closely company management monitors results on an ongoing basis."

"The corporate mission statement that we assist you in developing during your annual business conference will not immediately change your company's culture. However, it is a necessary first step in establishing the focus on quality and customer satisfaction as a way of life in your organization."

Fee Arrangements

The proposal should clearly specify fee arrangements for the engagement. Since there are many kinds of fee arrangements, the specific content and language of this section will vary.

A professional fee can be based on a fixed dollar amount, a not-to-exceed amount, or time plus out-of-pocket expenses. At a minimum, the fee arrangements section should clarify which of these will apply for the proposed engagement; it might also provide a payment schedule. For example: A partial fee is due at the onset of the engagement with the balance to be paid in equal installments at each of several project milestones.

Types of Proposals

Responses to Requests for Proposals

Consulting firms often receive requests for proposals (RFPs) from potential clients. An RFP usually outlines a specific format in which the proposal should be prepared. This ensures that all responses will be sufficiently similar to allow easier and more accurate comparisons of competing proposals. Deviating from the specified format is often grounds for disqualifying a proposal from consideration. Even in situations where it is not an absolute disqualifier, failing to respond in the recommended format may significantly reduce the proposal's likelihood of acceptance. Following the response guidelines flatters the prospect and demonstrates the consultant's willingness to cooperate.

A consultant is generally well advised to resist the urge to respond to every RFP submitted. According to many consultants, responding to RFPs is one of the *least* desirable ways to pursue business. There are several reasons:

1. The consultant may have no information regarding the prospective client beyond what is provided in the RFP itself and/or at the bidders' conference (discussed later in this chapter).

2. The consultant may have little, if any, opportunity to build relationships with key decision makers and to learn their preferences, biases, and buying motives.

3. Once a client decides to bid out an opportunity, the client is more likely to view the requested products or services as "commodities" and to make buying decisions based heavily on price rather than on other factors (like value).

Therefore, evaluate each RFP carefully before deciding to respond. Consider whether the size of the engagement and the likelihood of winning the business merit the level of effort a response will require.

When responding to an RFP, use imagination and creativity. Responding in the format requested seldom means there is no place for fresh ideas or innovative approaches. Avoid letting format or organizational boundaries drive the proposal development process to the exclusion of your best thinking.

Consider submitting an alternative proposal. In some cases, a consultant may feel that the RFP fails to get at the heart of what the client really needs. In this situation, the consultant will submit two proposals: one responding to the RFP guidelines and requirements and the other offering a "creative submission" or "alternative proposal" that presents a different way of looking at and responding to the client's need. This dual approach has numerous benefits.

1. It demonstrates the consultant's insight, creativity, and concern for providing the client with the best solution.

2. It shows the client that, at the same time, the consultant has not simply ignored the RFP and its stated requirements.

3. It presents a viable proposal that follows the RFP requirements, *if* the client will not consider the creative submission.

Unsolicited Proposals

Unsolicited proposals represent good initiative marketing. Current engagements, often provide opportunities to suggest some type of consulting service. There is almost always some operational problem with which the consultant can provide assistance. Alertness in this area can develop considerable consulting business. Even though the consultant is not an expert in every field, opportunities should not be overlooked. Applicable expertise can always be brought in to conduct the engagement.

Because unsolicited proposals avoid many of the difficulties and limitations involved in responding to RFPs, many consultants consider them to be the best way to win business. With unsolicited proposals:

- The consultant generally has access to more information about the client's situation

- The consultant has greater opportunity to build relationships with key decision makers (if these relationships are not already established)
- The consultant has greater opportunity to learn the decision makers' preferences, biases, and buying motives (and even to "pretest" their reactions to possible solutions)
- The client is less likely to view the proposed solution as a commodity
- The consultant may be able to win the engagement *without* the client's considering competitive bids

Letters of Understanding

A letter of understanding specifies what an engagement will involve. Its purpose is to prevent misunderstandings and ill will that can result from differing expectations on the part of either party.

A letter of understanding is neither lengthy nor overly formal. It should:

- Summarize the problem(s) the consultant will address
- Explain what the client can expect the consultant to do about the problem(s)
- Define the limits of the consultant's accountability or the scope of the consulting engagement to protect the consultant and set realistic expectations for the client
- Provide a schedule or time frame for services
- Clarify the type and amount of cooperation, if any, expected from the client's staff
- Include a statement concerning the compensation or professional fees

Proposal Writing Guidelines

Client Involvement

Creating an effective proposal and winning the engagement become significantly easier if the consultant involves the client throughout the entire proposal development effort. By forging a relationship with the client and building consensus around the proposed solution during the proposal process, the consultant gains insight into the client's perspective, ensures that the proposal answers the client's questions, and fosters shared ownership of the proposal with the client. In short, the consultant makes it easier for the client to say yes to the final proposal.

Focus

The consultant must keep the client and the client's perspective in mind throughout the proposal writing and editing process. When evaluating the proposal's content, organization, and appearance, the consultant must strive to see the document through the eyes of the client.

Length

Proposal documents can range from short, formal letters itemizing key points to longer, more complex documents. Regardless of length, most proposals cover much the same ground. Longer documents simply provide greater detail or more explanation, because of the technical complexity of the subject matter or because of the client's expectations or requirements.

The proposal should provide sufficient detail to stand on its own or to make a strong case even if there is *no* opportunity to explain the proposal orally or present it in person. However, avoid providing so much detail as to overwhelm or intimidate the client.

Style

The best proposals begin with an outline and take shape through a series of "drafts" or multiple iterations. It's important to maintain a consistent style throughout the document. Use uniform tenses and follow the rules for good grammar. Refer to style and grammar books and current microcomputer tools. Inconsistent style or tenses and grammatical errors make it more difficult for clients to grasp your message.

Few clients expect a consulting proposal to read as if it had been prepared by a staff of prizewinning journalists. Clients *do* expect pertinent information, well-thought-out plans, and appropriate recommendations that are presented clearly and logically. If no one in your firm is a proficient writer, consider contracting a free-lance business writer or a local university journalism professor or graduate student to assist in your proposal development efforts.

Graphics

The old adage "A picture is worth a thousand words" also applies in developing proposals. One way to set a proposal apart from the competition is by dressing it up pictorially. Consider adding graphs, flowcharts, diagrams, illustrations, or other visual aids to make the proposal more interesting and understandable. But avoid overdoing it. Graphics must be simple, neat, and easily comprehensible to be helpful.

Many consultants have sophisticated graphics programs that work with their microcomputers. These relatively inexpensive tools produce excellent and accurate graphics that demand attention and bring otherwise dry and dull information to life. Color is not essential, but it can be a plus if used properly.

The Proposal Cycle

Initial Opportunity

The opportunity to prepare a proposal usually results from several sales or marketing contacts between the client and the consulting firm. Ideas for new proposals often arise during engagements with current clients when the consultant identifies a business problem or need of the client that requires attention, or when the client mentions an area that needs study or review. If such an opportunity arises, the consultant should be prepared to do the necessary research to begin the proposal process.

Bidders' Conferences

For a particularly large prospective engagement, a client may invite a number of qualified consulting firms to make proposals and offer solutions at a bidders' conference. A bidders' conference is a meeting that allows the client to present a brief description of the services being sought and/or the problem being addressed to a number of prospective bidders at one time. Questions from bidders are answered at the conference or in writing at a later date.

Prior to attending a bidders' conference, review the RFP and any other available information about the bid carefully. Prepare a thorough list of the questions to ask at the conference. Consider both questions to clarify requirements stated in the RFP or the bid specifications and questions to discover unstated buying motives and decision-making processes and time frames. In some cases, the organization sponsoring the bidders' conference may not entertain any additional questions after the conference.

During the conference, pay close attention to others in attendance. Doing so will give you valuable insight into the degree of competition for the engagement as well as the caliber of the competition.

Background Research

Background research is generally necessary to prepare a top-quality proposal. Proper emphasis at this stage is important and should not be treated lightly. The consultant should know as much as possible about the problem to be solved and the possible approaches to addressing it.

Also, the consultant should not overlook the personalities of the people who will be involved in the project; human relations skills are as important as technical skills. A consultant who does not understand what makes the client tick may lose the job to a competitor with better people skills.

On-Site Fact Finding

As part of the research necessary in preparing a proposal, the consultant may need to perform on-site interviews to glean additional facts or perspectives. On-site fact finding may include:

- Interviewing the client's executives, employees, suppliers, and/or customers
- "Job shadowing," or observing work in the area in which the problem appears to reside or in which the project will be conducted
- Reviewing pertinent written policies and procedures
- Auditing related employee or management training sessions
- Identifying and reviewing other pertinent client records, such as employee job descriptions, complaint records, customer satisfaction data, and department mission statements

When fact finding involves interviewing employees, the consultant should raise all pertinent questions that will assist in accurately assessing the situation and recommending appropriate solutions. For example:

- What tasks or activities do employees' job responsibilities include?
- What barriers or obstacles do employees encounter in performing their jobs?
- What do employees feel could be done differently to help them overcome these obstacles and/or better accomplish their key responsibilities?

When interviewing employees, the consultant should make it clear that the objective is to help them, not to replace or hurt them.

Proposal Preparation

Common courtesy and good sense dictate that the client's expectations come first in the drafting of a written proposal. The consultant must know what the client expects and target the proposal to address these expectations. It is also important to spend the proper amount of time preparing the proposal. Large proposals may take more than a week of effort to yield a high-quality product.

Submission or Presentation and Evaluation

Once the proposal is written, it must be submitted or presented to the client. If at all possible, deliver and present the final proposal in person. The proposal is intended to develop a clear understanding between the parties, and a face-to-face meeting will help to surface and resolve any questions.

One person from the consulting organization will generally present the proposal to the client. Most often, this person will be the one who has had primary contact with the client throughout the proposal process. In some cases, additional people who have particular technical or presentation abilities may participate in the presentation.

Preparation prior to the presentation is critical! Those making the presentation should rehearse their roles, with other staff members playing the role of the client. All probable objections and questions should be raised so the consulting team can practice responding in a direct, concise, and positive manner.

When presenting a proposal, the consultant will usually "talk through" the high points with the client, using overheads, slides, or flipcharts as supporting visual aids. The consultant will then provide the written proposal to the client at the conclusion of the presentation as a "leave behind," which the client can study in depth later.

How elaborate or formal the presentation should be depends on numerous factors. These include the consultant's relationship with the client, the culture or norms in the client's organization, and the expected level of formality and sophistication of any competitive presentations. As in any other sales presentation, it is important for the consultant to conclude by stressing that his or her firm wants the opportunity to completely assist the client and will provide a solution that truly satisfies the client's need(s).

At this point, it is appropriate for the consultant to ask the client when a decision regarding the proposal will be made. Most likely, the client will want a period of days or weeks to review and consider the proposal. Immediate acceptance or rejection is rare, even in situations where there are no competing proposals or offers.

Follow-up

The consultant should follow up with the client after a reasonable time to check on the proposal's status and determine if there are any questions that need answering. Follow-up is often the key to capitalizing on the time and expense that the consultant has invested in the proposal process.

15

Engagement Management Planning

Lamar Bordelon

Pound International, Inc.
Dallas, Texas

Consultants provide their specialized knowledge, skills, and experience to their clients through engagements. These engagements vary widely in scope and complexity—from providing interim hourly rate services (even a billed telephone conversation) to managing lengthy, complex projects—and despite similarities in their appearance, no two engagements are identical. Thus the techniques of managing engagements also must vary widely to meet individual circumstances. The purpose of this chapter is to help you understand the nature of engagements and to provide you with ideas and suggestions on how best to manage your own engagements.

Nature of an Engagement

Deliverables

The purpose of an engagement is to provide your client with one or more predetermined items of value. These products are called *deliver-*

ables. Although a deliverable can be as simple as a verbally presented idea, most deliverables take the form of written reports, often accompanied by formal presentations. For a complex engagement, such as a long-term project, you may be required to provide numerous deliverables. These deliverables might include entire working systems of hardware and software, and they may be supplied to the client at various stages of the project, rather than just at the end.

Simple Engagements

In the simplest engagement, you provide your services to the client at an hourly rate, usually for a very short time. You could be providing these services on retainer or under a contract, but the only deliverables in this case would be your unique knowledge, skills, and experience. As an example, you might supplement a client's staff to help employees through a seasonal overload.

The techniques you use to manage simple engagements are the same as those for managing engagements of any size. These techniques include:

- A thorough understanding of the client's requirements
- Frequent and fully open communication with the client
- Accurate accounting and billing of your time

The underlying assumption is that you will exercise due diligence in the providing of your services, as defined in previous chapters of this handbook.

Average-Complexity Engagements

When engagements require a written report, your participation becomes more involved. The greater the requirement for written material, the more complex the engagement. The primary deliverables of average-complexity engagements are one or more written documents summarizing the results of the engagement. Examples of these written reports, described in other chapters of this handbook, are findings, analyses, recommendations, plans, and proposals.

Managing an engagement that involves a written report adds one more technique to the list:

- Accurate and appropriate reporting of the engagement results

In this context, "appropriate" may seem open-ended. But its meaning is usually resolved by a review of the engagement requirements and the client's political environment.

Projects

Projects are the most complex types of engagements. A project is an activity that stands alone and apart, with a definite beginning and conclusion. It differs from a process, which is continuous. When a project is undertaken, it should be organized as separate from the client's regular business activities. If not, the project will probably not be successful. However, the results of the project will affect the client's regular business activity.

Let's take the example of a semiconductor manufacturer that decides to build a new plant to increase production capacity. (This goal might have been the result of a market survey conducted by a consultant.) The manufacturer's regular business is producing semiconductors. It is not building new semiconductor plants.

The manufacturer considers producing semiconductors a *process*. But the building of the plant in which to manufacture semiconductors is, for the manufacturer, a *project*. As a *project*, it begins with the initial project preparation and concludes when the plant is completed. The activities surrounding the *project* are separate from the manufacturer's regular business *process* activities; and the results of the *project* affect the manufacturer's *process* by providing the additional production capacity.

Once this distinction is made, you need to follow a structured process if you expect to manage a project to a successful conclusion. More precisely, there are several processes which experience has shown are effective for various projects. Your challenge is to select processes appropriate to your project and then to organize and apply them in a calculated and structured way. As stated earlier, this type of engagement is the most complex one that a consultant can undertake. The remaining sections of this chapter are devoted to helping you succeed in that effort.

Project Characteristics.   Projects exhibit the following three characteristics:

- Specific expectations to be fulfilled
- A set period of time in which to fulfill the specific expectations
- Finite resources (including money) to help fulfill the specific expectations

Whenever you are in an activity that has these characteristics, you are in a project. Many consultants have found themselves faced with a firm deadline for meeting a client's requirement, and then realize that they have neither enough time nor sufficient resources left to produce the deliverable. They were in a project and didn't even know it!

Project Stages Successful projects typically go through a specific set of stages. By contrast, unsuccessful projects are ones in which one or more stages are given little regard or omitted entirely. The stages are interrelated and may be repeated, at least in part. This repetition happens particularly when the project's original expectations must be changed. Each project stage can be divided into multiple phases, as shown in Table 15-1.

Project phases don't follow one another in orderly sequence, as Table 15-1 might indicate. The phases within each stage interact, and they may be repeated as often as necessary to complete the stage satisfactorily. The length of each phase depends on the complexity and size of the project. Sometimes a single phase is a complete project in itself. Further, previously completed stages may be repeated because of the results of subsequent stages. The most common example of this phenomenon is when a requested and authorized change results in revisions to the specific expectations, the risk assessment, and/or the budget.

Let us now briefly review the activities in each phase of the project stages. Along with the activities, we will examine the documentation typically produced by the phase.

Preliminary Stage

Business Need Determination

Someone in the client's organization with sufficient authority and adequate budget must sponsor a project if it is to happen. This individual must understand the goals of the project well enough to be convinced of its value to the organization. Such an understanding may come about by your own efforts or by the efforts of those in the client organization. However it comes about, you should document the intended purpose of the project and its expected benefits to the business in as much detail as possible. To be complete, the documentation should also list all the assumptions made at the outset of the project.

A *project needs statement* is valuable as a focus for the numerous parties involved in the preliminary stage of the project. It can avert duplication of effort and misunderstandings and reduce the tail chasing and blind alleys that often plague the start of a project. Because it sets clear directions and specific limitations, the project needs statement keeps those involved in the formation of the project on track.

Justification Development

A client enters into a project for reasons as varied as the client's interests themselves. For instance, a client may wish to expand into new markets,

Table 15-1. Project Stages and Phases

Project stage	Project phase
Preliminary	Business need determination Justification development Feasibility determination Initial risk assessment/contingency planning Initial budget development
Preparatory	Specific expectation detail development (i.e., requirements specifications) Bid request* Secondary feasibility determination Secondary risk assessment/contingency planning Secondary budget development Vendor selection and contracting* Initial project team assembly Test/acceptance plan development
Planning	Task identification and estimating Resource determination Scheduling and balancing Plan completion and documentation Final budget development Baseline establishment Final risk assessment/contingency planning Final project team assembly and organization
Implementation	Plan execution Progress monitoring Result evaluation Management reporting Plan adjustment Risk management Preliminary incremental testing Initial user training Deliverable presentations and preliminary acceptance
Change control	Change request evaluation and authorization Change implementation and communication
Conclusion	Final overall testing Final user training Parallel operation Cutover to new system Final deliverable presentation and acceptance
Postproject	Project audit

*Applies only to projects performed by outside contractors.

improve efficiencies, broaden a product line, or streamline the organization. Whatever the motive for considering a project, the decision should be financially justifiable on its own. Much to their eventual regret, and the regret of others, project sponsors often try to use their enthusiasm, influence, or authority to push a project along without properly justifying it. One outstanding contemporary example is Donald Trump's sponsorship of Trump Air and Trump Casino.

Because so little can be known about the actual costs and results of a project in the preliminary stage, most of the effort in the justification phase consists of generating realistic assumptions and then developing reasonable financial predictions on the basis of those assumptions. Your ability as a consultant to bring experience, impartiality, and balance to the process is highly beneficial to your client's deliberations. Be certain that any assumptions accepted as part of the winning financial scenario are well documented and added to the list of assumptions on the project needs statement. These will service as further guidelines for the phases that follow.

Feasibility Determination

Even a project that is economically feasible must be technically and practically feasible as well in order to be successful. A financial justification can show why a project would be economically desirable to perform, but if a project is justified on a financial basis alone, the client (or the consultant) may well ignore the technical or practical obstacles which can prevent the project from ever having a favorable outcome.

Technical Feasibility Determination.   A financial justification is usually derived from a "top down" view of the project. The financial considerations used are typically broad-based and general, with the phrase "in the ballpark" frequently used to describe the financial parameters.

Technical feasibility, on the other hand, should be considered as much as possible from a "bottom up" view of the project. This means that you must have a grasp of the feasibility of most, if not all, of the detailed tasks that must be performed. If similar work has been completed successfully in previous instances—and there are no obstacles apparent which would prevent completion this time—then that particular effort should be feasible.

Technological-Breakthrough Projects.   The real difficulty comes when the project tasks include work which has never been done before. This is typical of research projects or projects such as those of NASA, which involve technological breakthroughs. Many high-technology companies, such as semiconductor or genetic engineering firms, also have projects which fall into this category.

The first step in determining the feasibility of a technological-breakthrough project is to identify the parts of the effort which have been performed successfully before. These can be rapidly validated for feasibility, and the process should well delimit the more tenuous activities. Even more contrast becomes apparent when the kinds of activities that *are* anticipated and the kinds that *are not* are identified as part of the exploratory effort.

You are now ready to look at the unprecedented activities in more detail. The intent is to develop a statistical probability curve predicting the feasibility of this part of the project. It may be necessary to consult specialists in specific disciplines, either within or outside the client organization, to assess the reasonableness of your predictions. Keep in mind, however, that even experts do not always prophesy accurately. In the last quarter of this century, a large high-technology company began a project to construct a facility to manufacture high-capacity flexible storage devices. The feasibility of the project was based on expert predictions that a technological breakthrough was imminent for manufacturing these devices. Unfortunately, the company needed several technological breakthroughs, not just one. It abandoned the project, but only after spending tens of millions of dollars.

The amount of predicted breakthrough effort is factored against the amount of known effort to determine the probable feasibility of the overall project. The standard deviation of the probability curves developed during this phase of the project become valuable input to the risk analysis phase, which follows.

Practical Feasibility Determination. Determining practical feasibility is not as straightforward as determining technical feasibility, but it is equally important. Experience and common sense are the primary assets a consultant can bring to this endeavor. However, not only are these tools rarely employed, so are the recommendations resulting from a consultant's analysis—especially if they conflict with the political climate, current common practices, or the perceptions of the project sponsor.

Nonetheless, you would be remiss not to alert your client to potential problems with the project results. The scope of practical feasibility determination is not confined to the success of the project alone. It should also include consideration of the effects of the project when the results are applied. If a business process is affected by the project, then you should assess the overall effects that the project brings to that process, the other processes tangential to the affected process, and the people involved in both areas. Assessment becomes even more critical when the project affects the general public or organizations outside the client organization.

An excellent example of a practical feasibility determination that failed (or was never performed) occurred in the first half of this century. Under political pressure to expand Soviet industrial production, the central planners in Moscow decided to build a huge power plant near the Ural Mountains. The construction phase was successful, but the plant had to be shut down as soon as it was started up because there was insufficient water in the area to cool the turbine exhaust steam. So another project was started—this one to dig a 600-mile canal to bring water to the plant. Once again the power plant was started, and once again it had to be shut down. This time, a practical reason for failure besides lack of water emerged: There was a scarcity of users in the immediate area of the plant for the huge amount of power it generated. Further, all the power that was generated dissipated when it was transmitted the long distances to the population centers where it was needed.

Although that project was unsuccessful, it did have a beneficial effect in the long run. Research began immediately on ways to overcome the high power losses in transmission lines, and this led to new transmission techniques based on cryogenically cooled lines. It would seem that Moscow's central planners should have learned their lesson from that one project. Unfortunately, many of the same types of mistakes were repeated on similar projects such as the Kama River Truck Plant. The United States is not immune from practical feasibility failures, of course. A classic example is the Edsel.

Initial Risk Assessment/ Contingency Planning

Risk is the likelihood of something going wrong—or, as it often applies to projects, of something not going according to plan. Blinkered by their initial enthusiasm, project participants often assume there will be no problems, or at least no significant problems which can't be overcome. Conversely, problems are all that critics of a project will predict. Reality is somewhere in between.

No projects are totally riskfree. The prudent consultant helps the client predict and contain or, if possible, avoid potential risks. Understand that not all possible risks will be identified in this phase—or, for that matter, in subsequent phases. Managing unforeseen risks is often the true test of a project manager's capabilities.

Identifying Risk.   Risk assessment consists first of identifying all possible problems (within reason) that could affect the project. The second step is to assign each identified potential problem a rating to indicate the possibility that it will occur. The third step is to categorize the most probable risks as avoidable or unavoidable.

Since risk deals with the realm of probabilities, statistical techniques are often recommended for this assessment. However, these techniques do not appear to offer any particular advantage. In fact, statistical probabilities can sometimes work against you. The most effective risk assessments seem to be derived from a combination of experience, foresight, good judgment, and practical common sense.

Risk Assessment and Contingency Planning. The status of the project determines what you do with the completed risk assessment and when the contingency plan is developed. Table 15-2 shows the more common applications of risk assessment and contingency planning at various project stages. Each application is predicated on the assumption that the risks were first assessed and the contingency plan first completed during the project stage shown for that application.

Risk assessment and contingency planning permeate our everyday existence. Dams to control specific flooding; fire departments to handle emergencies; air bags, seat belts, and spare tires in our cars; flashlights, candles, and fire extinguishers in our homes—all are examples of successful risk assessment and contingency planning. Consulting projects, too, depend on good risk assessment and contingency planning. You cannot take for granted that critical elements or strategic operations will go on working no matter what the circumstances. Success happens only

Table 15-2. Risk Assessment/Contingency Plan Applications

Project stage	Risk assessment/contingency plan application
Preliminary	Modify the project needs statement to avoid the risks identified as avoidable.
	Increase the budget to accommodate the most probable unavoidable risks.
Preparatory	Include provisions to avoid the risks identified as avoidable, and compensate for the most probable unavoidable risks.
	Increase the bid by the amount presumed necessary to compensate for the most probable unavoidable risks (outside contractor).
Planning	Develop a contingency plan to avoid the risks identified as avoidable or contain (limit) the most probable unavoidable risks.
Implementation	Follow the contingency plan (if devised above) to handle unavoidable risks should they occur.
	Try not to panic when an unforeseen risk occurs.
Summary	Review the initial risk assessment/contingency plan against actual occurrences to improve future risk prediction/risk avoidance techniques.

when the risks of their *not* working have been identified and plans have been implemented to compensate for those risks.

Risk Assessment Methodology. The data processing industry provides excellent examples of this kind of planning. Since the critical information that constitutes a company's "lifeblood" is contained within the various elements of a data processing system, organizations take significant steps to keep their systems functional and available to their users. Over the years, these systems have become extremely complex, and an equally intricate methodology has evolved to cope with the exponentially increasing risks. A number of consultants have specialized in this arena, often called *disaster recovery planning* or *business continuation planning.*

This distinct methodology is not unique to the data processing industry. It is applied with equal effectiveness to the design and functioning of many other complex systems, such as power grids, war planes, and critical projects. One example of the techniques used to assess risk probabilities in such complex systems is *component failure impact analysis* (CFIA).

CFIA assesses the effect on the system of the failure of each of its components and may be extended to include the effects of failure of each of the major subsystems. The effects are prioritized by severity of impact to the functioning of the system. A contingency plan is then devised which contrasts the cost of duplicating each component against the effect of the failure of that component. Then a determination is made as to which components would be economically feasible to make redundant. The former Soviet Union's space program incorporated triple redundancy in its systems. Yet, despite many successes, these precautions often proved to be insufficient.

Other risk assessment and avoidance techniques used in this methodology include *survivability assessment* and *change control.* Change control is addressed as a separate phase later in this chapter.

Examples of Risk Assessment and Contingency Planning. Sometimes risk preparations can seem excessive. One company located its computing center three stories below ground level, between the two office towers which contained the user community. The reason was that the computer center was located close to the flight path of bomber and fighter planes at a USAF airfield. The risk assessment indicated a sufficiently high probability that a mishap caused by the falling of one stray airplane could put a ground-level computing center out of business. (The company went out of business for economic reasons before the risk became a reality!)

As a contrasting example, the NASA Manned Spacecraft Center in Clear Lake, Texas, has three full-capacity power generator systems, plus as many as four redundant computing systems, all operational whenever a manned space shuttle or capsule is aloft. During one problem-plagued mission, all but one of the power generators and computer systems stopped functioning for a time. Thus far, the NASA center has been a superb example of precise risk assessment and contingency planning.

Risk Factors. As you consider the various risks facing your project, you will see that the most significant factor is time. Time brings change. Thus, time affects every project. And the longer the project, the greater the opportunity for change. From a risk standpoint, the ideal project is one for which you can instantly produce results (provided the requirements are understood), leaving no time for change to occur. So the project with the least risk is the shortest project. This is why you should always plan to complete a project in as short a time as possible.

Other risk factors vary with the characteristics of the particular project. You must identify these individually by answering questions designed to illuminate the nature of the risks specific to that type of project. Table 15-3 lists examples of general questions which you might ask in a risk assessment survey. It also shows the risk factor ratings that are typically applied to the answers given.

The risk factors in the table could be rated on scales of 1 to 5 or 1 to 10, or by any similar ranking scheme. The purpose of ranking the risks is to determine, first, how risky the project is overall and, second, where the greatest risk exposures lie. The results should give you some indication of what should (or can) be done about the various risks. You also benefit by understanding which risks you do *not* need to be concerned about. At some point, you will realize that it is impossible to identify all the potential risks and that you must proceed with the project anyway.

In 1972, shipyards around the world were busy with projects to build larger and larger supertankers. Each of these projects was a 2- to 3-year effort and involved massive outlays of money and other resources. Then, without warning, the Arab OPEC partners turned off the oil tap. The unfinished supertankers sat rusting in their ways for months. When oil flow was resumed, it never again reached earlier volumes, so most of the supertankers were obsolete before they were ever completed. Today, those vessels that were brought to completion are rusting as well—in mothballed storage in Norwegian fjords. Your project, too, will always be subject to unexpected risk factors.

Initial Budget Development

Budgets are necessary if an organization is to keep project expenditures within some reasonable bounds. At this juncture, you have expended considerable effort to try to generate the project parameters. But you don't yet have sufficient prescience to establish a firm, fixed budget. The best you

Table 15-3. Sample Risk Assessment Questions and Risk Factor Ratings

Risk assessment questions	Risk factor ratings		
	High	Medium	Low
How long is the project?	Long (>1 year)	Medium (0.5–1 year)	Short (<0.5 year)
Is the project complex, or are significant parts of the project complex?	Yes	Less than half	No
Have we or those implementing this project ever done a project like this before?	No	Similar project	Often
Will this project create or modify a critical business operation?	Yes	Somewhat	No
Does the project have executive-level support and involvement?	No	Partial	Yes
Does the project have adequate budgeting and financial support?	Very tight constraints	Some flexibility	Yes
Can the requirements be well understood and well defined?	No	Somewhat	Yes
Is the project breaking new technological ground?	Pushing the limits	Almost	No
Are the requirements subject to change?	Very much so	Somewhat	No
How firm is the deadline for completion of the project?	Rock solid	Flexible	Mushy
Is the time allotted adequate for the completion of the project?	No way	Close	Plenty enough
What types of results are expected from the project?	Turnkey working system	Gradual implementation	Study results or report
If this is a complex system project, will the project be broken into multiple phases?	Only one phase for the entire project	Only two phases: requirements and implementation	Multiple phases as required
How many parties must be satisfied before the project results are accepted?	Multiple	Two or at most three	One—the end user
How many parties will have management or veto authority over project implementation?	Several	Two at most	One only
Does the project enjoy the support of all parties involved?	Some may resent the project	Wishy-washy support	All are warmly enthusiastic

can do, as you develop the initial budget for the project, is to establish an economic weather vane—a gross indicator of the probable costs.

Budgeting Mistakes. Many projects have foundered and then failed because of the way the initial budget was defined. In some instances, the budget authors were too timid to present the entire cost picture at once. Their concerns may have been based on the political or economic climate of the organization at the time. A common presumption here is that the additional funding will come once the project is under way and begins to prove its worth. After all, what executive sponsor or user wants to see his or her pet project go under for lack of additional funds?

What budget authors often fail to realize is that a responsible executive will sit still for only so many order-of-magnitude increases in a project's original budget. And when the original sums are woefully inadequate, most executives will cut their losses rather than continue pouring more money into what appears to be a "black hole." Establishing the initial budget is quite similar to preparing to jump a chasm. You had better be prepared to go the whole distance, for it may be difficult to find additional support for a second jump when you are part way across.

In other instances, the budget authors consider the initial budget infallible and unalterable once it is established. This usually happens when those involved are used to working with budgets for business processes and are not experienced with project estimating procedures. When you work day in and day out with budget numbers which assume a maximum deviation of, say, ±10 percent, you can see how difficult it is to deal with numbers in orders of magnitude.

Budget Estimating Precision and Flexibility. An order of magnitude is as close as you can hope to get with the initial budget. You must always remember that an estimate is *only* an estimate and that it is only as accurate as the details available at the time it is made. But details simply are not available at the preliminary phase of a project. So whatever estimate you make now must allow for change—usually growth.

You should allow for some growth in the overall initial budget rather than in specific areas. Do not add a certain percentage to each and every element of your initial estimate to allow for all possible contingencies. The compound effect of all those percentage add-ons can drive the total cost of the project out of reach. So the best initial estimate is one which (1) aims to determine the most practicable numbers available under the circumstances, (2) includes the minimum additional percentage appropriate to the estimated risks, and (3) allows a percentage for expansion as a buffer for unforeseen growth. The growth percentage must be closely managed and generally should not be disclosed as part of the budget document. It should be known only by the top members of the project team and the sponsor.

Common Omissions. The project team functions best when all its members are assembled in one location and isolated from their normal organizational duties. Establishing a project location resembles establishing a small business. The main difference is that a project has a fixed, predetermined life expectancy, whereas a small business is usually started to perpetuate and grow. (Some projects, misguidedly, are placed within this small business paradigm.)

Location costs are a common omission in preliminary budgets. The project team must have office space and facilities and administrative support, just the same as the small business. The amount to which these may be shared with the organization sponsoring and/or funding the project depends on the degree to which the project is independent of the organization. Whatever the requirement, the necessary office facilities and administrative functions must be included in the initial estimate.

Another item often omitted from a budget estimate is an allowance for the time necessary for the project team to perform project-related duties, primarily paperwork. A well-run project can generate a surprising amount of paperwork, and handling all this paperwork usually takes 95 percent of the project manager's time. It can also consume as much as 20 percent of the time of the project team members. These numbers are multiplied when the project involves a large number of subcontractors, takes place in a rapidly changing environment, or operates in a highly sensitive or political climate (such as a government project). Time must be added to the estimate for these factors, as well as for project team meetings, report completion, and presentation preparation and delivery.

Preliminary Stage Conclusion

The objective of the preliminary stage is to determine if the original concept can be transformed into a successful project. If correctly carried out, this phase should also give the decision makers within an organization the time and opportunity to take a hard look at the effect the proposed project will have on their operation. The amount of money spent at this stage is miniscule compared with the cost of committing to a full-blown effort on just a hunch. In other words, the preliminary stage can make the difference between management and gambling.

Preparatory Stage

The preparatory stage begins when the client considers the preliminary deliberations to be complete and decides to formally initiate a project. At this point you may expect the client to display an ever-increasing impatience to see the project actually get under way. "After all," the client might say, "the decision was made days (or weeks or months) ago! I need to see some results!"

As a consultant, your task here is to mollify the client long enough to allow adequate groundwork for the project to be laid. Help the client to understand that he or she will be living with the results of this stage for the remainder of the project. Any changes made after the completion of the preparatory stage will incur additional cost. Further, the refinements and adjustments made during this stage will have enormous effects on the project in later stages. Thus it is both highly cost-effective and time-conserving to perform the preparatory work with as much diligence as can be afforded.

Preparation: The Difference Between Successful and Unsuccessful Projects

When today's project management methodology was in its formative stages, just after World War II, one contractor, IBM, was involved in numerous large government projects. Some of these projects proved to be highly successful, completed both on time and within budget, while others were just as unsuccessful and incurred extensive overruns. IBM set about to determine the difference, using extensive data gathering and statistical techniques.

IBM discovered three major differences between successful and unsuccessful projects. One category of unsuccessful projects involved those which were bid and/or begun before the requirements (specifications) were completed and agreed upon by all parties concerned. In any number of instances, the contractor bid the development of the requirements together with the project implementation in one fixed price. The losses and overruns on these projects were exorbitant.

The second category of unsuccessful projects involved those which lacked formal procedures for managing change. No change that sounded reasonable was rejected, and anyone could suggest a change. As the contractors attempted to please everyone and adjust to all the requested changes, the projects were brought to a standstill.

The third class of unsuccessful projects involved those with inadequate or inappropriate staffing. Further refinement of the data showed that staffing for successful projects followed a specific curve, as shown in Figure 15-1. This curve, for obvious reasons, was affectionately known as the "dead dinosaur curve." At IBM, it became the basis for courses on project management offered both within and without the company.

Several points about the project staffing curve should be emphasized:

1. The end users of the results of the project must be heavily involved in the initial phases—at least until the beginning of the implementation

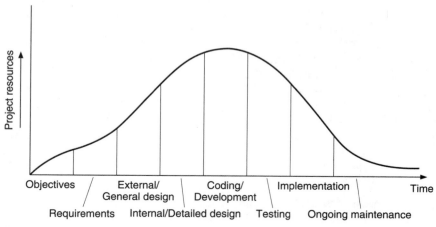

Figure 15-1   Project phases: initial implementation.

stage. In the case of information processing projects, their involvement must remain heavy until the conclusion of the external design segment of the implementation stage.

2. The end users of the results of the project do not "disappear" once the implementation stage begins. They maintain their involvement in order to keep the ultimate project results relevant to their needs; but they serve a lesser role to the project staff during this stage.

3. The project staff assembled to complete the preparatory stage (particularly the requirements and specifications) will probably be different, both in number and in skills, from the project team implementing the project. Some of the initial project staff—the project manager and other key personnel—will remain to provide the consistency needed for continuation of the project. Other skills will be added as the project moves into the implementation stage. This is especially the case when an outside contractor is involved in implementation.

4. The number of project staff required to implement the project is approximately twice the number used to complete the preparatory stage. Many projects have faltered, their results delayed beyond usefulness, because project sponsors or administrative managers limited the project implementation stage team to the number of personnel required to perform the preparatory stage.

In recent years, the emphasis on quality has shifted project management thinking toward a greater role for the preparatory stage. The Japanese, in particular, have altered their version of the project staffing curve to that shown in Figure 15-2—nicknamed, again for obvious reasons, the "dead whale curve." The philosophy behind this staffing curve

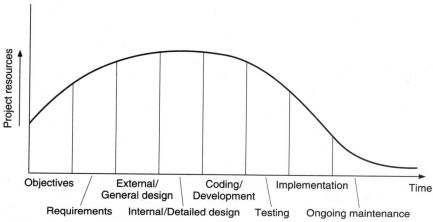

Figure 15-2 Project phases: recent implementation.

is that the more attention is paid to the initial requirements of the users, the faster and better the implementation can be accomplished. In addition, there is a lesser need for residual maintenance. Looking once more to the information processing industry, we see that reducing residual maintenance is crucial, since this element alone can represent as much as 75 to 80 percent of the original project implementation staffing level.

Specific Expectation Detail Development

In the expectation development phase, the relatively nebulous needs expressed in the project needs statement are transformed into the specifics of the project requirements or project specifications. If the needs statement can be likened to "where the rubber meets the sky," the project requirements may be called "where the rubber meets the road."

Producing a document which accurately, clearly, and thoroughly specifies the expectations of a project is a daunting task—one which often becomes a project in itself. Clients regularly rely on a consultant to translate their intentions into written descriptions that are adequate to serve as contractual statements.

However, precision is an elusive goal. Don't be discouraged if, after an exhaustive effort, you still feel your results are incomplete. If the voluminous laws that result from the best attempts by our lawmakers are any guide, there aren't enough words to concisely define the project expectations, plus cover every situation, nuance, or condition which may arise during implementation. The role of the project manager is to use good judgment, delegated authority, and the appropriate tools at hand, such as negotiation and change control, to resolve any deficiencies in the project requirements. The challenge to the consultant developing the project requirements is to ensure that those deficiencies are not obvious, injurious, or extensive.

Client Interviews.   The documents produced by the preliminary stage are not sufficient in themselves to allow complete development of the project requirements. Still remaining are innumerable questions and interpretations which can be resolved only by interviews with the client executives, sponsors, or potential users of the project results. The different perspectives obtained by interviewing these groups contribute to the detailed picture presented in the project requirements. This is the picture that the project implementers will attempt to "bring to life," so the details must reflect the client's thinking as closely and as completely as possible.

You need to structure these interviews properly if you want to get all the information you need and keep the irrelevancies to a minimum. Unbounded, open-ended questions easily lend themselves to interminable interviews, which result more in "wish lists" than usable requirements. The best way to limit your interview is to devise a questionnaire or similar outline which keeps the responses confined to the appropriate areas. You should also script your questions to keep both yourself and the interviewee from wandering too far afield.

Consultant/Client Team.   The best project requirements are produced when the consultant works hand in hand with a client team established to assist in creating the requirements. Ideally, members of the team will continue on to implement the requirements they produced. To keep the results relevant, the client members of the team should be led by, or at least include, the potential users of the project deliverables. As an alternative, the users may have veto authority over the requirements that emerge from the team efforts.

Client Project Manager.   The key member of the consultant/client team is the person who has authority to make decisions on behalf of the client on all aspects of the project. If the client has not yet appointed anyone with such full project responsibility, now is the ideal time to do so. The appointee can represent either the sponsor or the eventual user of the expected project deliverables. In either case, he or she should have the authority to make whatever decisions are required within the scope of the project without fear of reversal by higher management. With this authority, of course, usually comes the responsibility for producing a successful project, brought in on time and within budget.

Whether the title for this position is project manager, project coordinator, project administrator, or something similar, the level of the position must be commensurate with the management responsibility. In one instance, a contracting firm had a very large, highly technical, 18-month project to which it assigned the responsibility of project manager to a very experienced technical specialist (nonmanager). When the project became immobilized, because the project manager dabbled with resolving all the technical details, the contractor brought in another technical specialist as a replacement. Predictably, this had the same result.

The project didn't get moving again until the contractor appointed a third-level manager. By then, the engagement was 6 months behind. The new project manager exercised the authority commensurate with his level, took command of all the project personnel (both contractor and client), doubled the staff, and completed the project within the original deadline (but not within budget, of course).

Project Requirements Content. No matter how the project requirements are structured, the consultant must always keep in mind their two primary objectives:

1. They must describe the project and its deliverables thoroughly and clearly enough for potential contractors to respond adequately with a reasonably accurate proposal for implementation. (Accuracy and precision also apply to the consultant, who may be making a bid for the implementation. Too often consultants write cleverly worded specifications, only to find themselves having to try to live up to them.)

2. They must describe adequately the full deliverables that the client wishes to receive as a result of the project. And these deliverables must be functional.

Project Requirements Review. The first of the two major project reviews takes place at the completion of the project requirements, or project specifications. (The other major review involves the completed deliverables.) Completed project requirements must be presented to the client sponsors, or to others whom the sponsors designate. Since the requirements precisely define the deliverables to be produced by the project, they must be reviewed in detail and *approved* by the responsible organization executive(s). Completed requirements are usually voluminous, and you will be able to cover only the "high spots" in a face-to-face presentation. You will need to leave the bulk of the reading to the executive(s). Unfortunately, few executives have the time or inclination to pore over page after page of detailed specifications, looking for inconsistencies, errors, or omissions. Most often, executives will pass the completed requirements on to staff members (who may or may not be familiar with executive priorities).

Communications Skills and Project Reviews. Communications skills are the most important ones the consultant can bring to bear on project activities. Key to successful project reviews are well-written documents and well-organized and succinct presentations, professionally delivered. Project requirements have a much better chance of being thoroughly reviewed if they are clear and concise, with graphs, tables, and illustrations used in place of verbiage whenever possible. Paragraphs should be relatively short, with limited use of technological jargon. Titles and subtitles should be used to break long sections into multiple, logical segments. Long explanations and reference notes should be relegated to exhibits at the end of the document.

One of the purposes of project requirements is to provide contractors with the majority of the information they need to bid on the implementation of the project. If the project is to be divided into multiple phases or segments, or if bids are requested for several options, the documents must be clearly divided into sections that reflect the various phases, segments, and options.

Project Requirements Transmittal. Completed project requirements may be formally transmitted to a designated individual or to a review committee appointed by the client sponsor or executive. When transmitted to an individual, the requirements are usually physically delivered to that individual, accompanied by only a cover letter. Quite often, transmission of the completed requirements takes place as part of a stand-up presentation. This presentation should summarize the significant features included in the requirements as well as highlight the correlations between the specified project deliverables and the major items of concern expressed previously in the needs statement. Known customer priorities addressed in the requirements should also be underscored when appropriate.

The objective of the stand-up presentation is to "sell" the client on the project requirements. In making such a presentation, you must employ every possible "staging" skill. Charts, graphs, and similar visual aids can provide valuable support to the effort, and may be copied from the requirements themselves as needed. However, written comments should be limited to "bullet" points or summaries. Avoid lengthy quotations or wordy excerpts from the documentation. Presentations for extensive project requirements may need handouts for clarification. All of this takes considerable preparation, which may even include rehearsal if the presentation is complex. Be sure to allot enough time for these activities when submitting your estimates.

Change and the Requirements Review Process. After the completed project specifications have been transmitted to the interested parties, you must allow the client sufficient time to study the documentation thoroughly. During this period, you must be available to answer questions, clarify wording, and correct mistakes and omissions. In well-written project requirements, the client sees the project laid out in its entirety, with the expected results spelled out in detail in the form of deliverables.

Time will have passed since the original needs statement was produced, and the client's perspective and priorities regarding the project's objectives may well have changed. Changing economic circumstances can certainly have an effect on the original justification of the project, as can technological advances or political climate shifts or judicial decisions or personnel changes—the list is endless.

For whatever reasons, as the completed project requirements are reviewed, you can expect the client to make changes. This can be a burden if you are working under a fixed-price contract and have not allowed for anticipated changes. However, even if you have to negotiate an addition to your contract, it will be far cheaper for the client to make changes now, rather than after the project is under way.

"Freezing" and "Melting" the Completed Project Requirements.
The project requirements define the project deliverables and, through inference, if not directly, the work required to produce those deliverables. They form the technical "road map" to be followed as the project progresses toward completion. The steps remaining in the preparatory stage do not materially alter the project requirements. Once the project requirements have been completed, the project feasibility studies revalidated, the risks assessed, the budget needs established, and the team members put in place, the project is ready to move on to the planning and implementation stages. In other words, the project is ready to set about satisfying the project requirements by producing the specified deliverables. If this effort is to have any hope for success, the project requirements must be firmly established. They must become the stable platform—the reference document from which all project activities spring.

If the project requirements are allowed to continually evolve, they become a "moving target" and they cannot serve as a stable platform. This doesn't mean they must be "cast in bronze" and can't be changed. But, until the project begins and a structured change control program has been implemented, changes to the requirements must be "frozen" at certain times so all parties involved can work with a "fixed target." The project requirements must be frozen at least three times during the preparatory stage: at the completion of the initial requirements development phase, at the completion of the secondary budget development phase, and at the completion of the preparatory stage, just prior to the start of the planning stage. So, during this preparatory stage, the project requirements become a series of fixed targets with changes allowed only during the periods they can be "unfrozen."

Project Requirements—Mandatory Approval Sign-off. Since changes to the project requirements can be made at any time during the review period, and the project requirements are the only source for defining the project deliverables, *no* work on the project should begin before the requirements are finalized—modified until they accurately and completely reflect the client's requirements. Any work performed while the project requirements are still in flux has a high probability of simply being wasted effort. So the changes must be stopped and the requirements frozen in order for the project to proceed.

The authority to proceed comes in the form of signed approval of the project requirements by the client. This sign-off is the formal validation by the client of the project requirements and serves as the consultant's major protection against unacceptable deliverables and future faulty memories. The sign-off opens the way for the bid request phase, since it gives the bidding parties an even start by allowing them all to bid to the same, set specifications.

A Project That Committed All the Cardinal Sins. One large corporation with a considerable consulting contingent aggressively marketed its project capabilities to a comparably large public utility. The consulting company executive quoted a price of $9.5 million for the completed project on the basis of requirements which were informally expressed by a few of the utility company's executives. The project requirements were to be developed as the first step in the project, since significant technological breakthroughs were necessary for the project to succeed. The probability of achieving these breakthroughs was not assessed, nor was the risk of not achieving them. No structured change control program was implemented, so changes occurred freely at the whim of any executive who felt the urge.

The first real indication of trouble came after the consulting company had billed $11.5 million, and the client refused to pay anything because the requirements appeared to be no closer to completion, and there was no sign of any progress on the new technology. The project floundered along until the costs reached $17.5 million, with predictions that they could reach almost $40 million before completion. However, the completion itself was questionable, since there was no indication that the technological breakthrough would ever occur. At this point, the consulting firm decided to bite the bullet and pull the plug on the project, offering to deliver to the client the documentation produced to that point for whatever compensation the client thought fair. (The executive responsible was reassigned out of the country.)

Rare Exceptions Can Be Successful   Under a rare set of conditions a project may be started without approved project requirements. This situation usually arises when the time to implement the project is too short for normal project procedures to be followed. For such a project to have any chance of success, several conditions must exist:

- Both the client and the consultant must be willing to be very flexible in their relations.
- Both the client and the consultant should have a satisfactory history of cooperative dealings.
- Both the client and the consultant must be willing to work with each other openly in a spirit of mutual trust and mutual cooperation.
- The project teams for both the client and the consultant must be compatible and amicable.

In one example, the bureaucratic machinations of one government's defense agency delayed the timely completion of the project requirements for a critical, complex project until the deadline for completion was too close to allow the normal project bid and implementation processes to be followed. Worse yet, when the project requirements were finally published for bid, they were found to be incomplete. Under ever-increasing pressure, the agency's project team selected the contractor that seemed to ask the greatest number of astute questions about the project, and set about trying to have the majority of the project completed by the deadline.

The contractor's and client's project teams worked together virtually side by side for the first 90 days to fill the gaps in the project requirements. Technological differences were hammered out, compromises quickly struck, and changes approved on the spot, bypassing or short-circuiting long, involved procedures. The original seven volumes describing the project requirements, which had taken 18 months to produce, were doubled during the 90-day period in an effort so intense that serious consideration was given to the installation of water-cooled keyboards. The resulting project requirements, though still not complete, were formally presented to the agency's review board with the understanding that the unfinished or unresolved issues remaining could and would be worked out.

The revised project requirements were hastily approved, and the contractor paid for that portion of the work. The contractor then immediately bid for and was awarded implementation of the project. Most of the project was completed within the 9 months remaining under the original deadline, with the rest of the project—the lower-priority items and finishing touches (including the documentation)—finished over the next year, in comparative leisure. The most remarkable aspect of the project—despite the incredible stresses generated by the immense pressures on both project teams, and despite strongly held differences of opinions on both sides—was that neither team resorted to the acrimony and bickering which often divide client and consultant. The credit for this goes to the respective project managers, who were able to maintain a calm, cooperative demeanor and long-range perspective throughout. Unfortunately, the stresses took their toll: Both project managers left the business and changed careers after the project was concluded. Yet their efforts showed that, under just the right circumstances, with project teams on both sides compatible and amicable, an exception to the normal rules can be made and the project can be reasonably successful.

Bid Request

If the sponsoring organization has sufficient in-house resources, it may choose to implement the project itself. Most often, an organization will look outside for help with a project. (This particularly applies to today's leaner organizational structures.) Assistance can range from simple guidance and advice from a consultant to a turnkey completion contract with a contracting or consulting organization. If you worked with the client in the development of the project requirements, you may be the most qualified to continue with the project through completion.

Although some consultants slant the wording of the project requirements to favor their expertise or specialty, many government and some private organizations consider this practice to be a breach of ethics. However, these same organizations just as often will employ the consultant to monitor and/or audit the project implementation team or to act in some similar tracking capacity which takes advantage of the consultant's intimate working knowledge of the project requirements.

There are three major categories of contracts used for project implementation: (1) time and material, (2) time and material, not to exceed (or budget limited), and (3) fixed price (or turnkey completion). Other types of contracts are typically variations of these three.

Time and Material Contracts. The time and material contract poses the least risk to the consultant, and the greatest risk to the client. Here the consultant applies whatever resources are needed for whatever length of time is needed to produce the contract deliverables. The client may not go through the bidding process, depending on factors such as the client's confidence with its budget estimates, or the contractor's capabilities. The client usually tries to limit its risk by keeping a very close watch on the "pulse" of the project and, if possible, a tight rein on the approval of resource usage. Nonetheless, under this arrangement the client bears all the burden of cost overruns and estimating errors.

The time and material contract is most often used for projects with one or more of these characteristics:

- High-priority projects with short time frames or urgent deadlines
- Projects which only one contractor can implement—single-vendor contracts

- Projects in which the consultant or contractor enjoys a favored relationship with the client.
- Extensions to an existing contract.
- Projects involving complex arrangements or logistics in which certain contractors are favored because of prior satisfactory results, preparations, or status (i.e., security clearances)

Contracts for Time and Material, Not to Exceed. The second contract category, "time and material, not to exceed" (or budget limited), is intended to put an upper limit to the client's risk exposure by imposing constraints on project expenditures. The practice works so long as the client keeps pressing the contractor toward completion and doesn't allow the contractor to delay or stretch out the work in hopes of obtaining a contract extension when the original budget is exhausted.

As before, the client may or may not go through the bidding process. The client may not have a good way to estimate the cost of a project, and may look to the consultant or contractor who was involved in the development of project requirements to provide the upper bound for the costs. The consultant or contractor would then be in a good position to be awarded the implementation contract because of the consultant's inside knowledge.

This category of contract is most often used under the following circumstances:

- The deliverables of the project are not well defined or will be defined as the project progresses.
- The potential deliverables have limited value and, if they cost more than the specified amount to produce, would not be worth the effort.
- Similar reasons to those used for the previous category of contracts, with the added requirement to stringently limit total project expenditures.

Fixed-Price Contracts. The fixed-price contract is the most popular because it transfers the risks associated with the project to the contractor. Under this contract arrangement, the completed project requirements are the primary source documents used to obtain bids from qualified contractors. The contractors study the project requirements, then use their experience to estimate the total time and resources required to implement the project and produce the deliverables. The contractors are also responsible for assessing all the risks associated with the project implementation. The contractors then submit their proposals to the client in the form of bids, each with one, total fixed price—the price for which each contractor is willing to implement the project.

A client may issue requests for bid to one or more of its own internal departments if the organization's staff is sufficiently large and experienced in project implementation. Some companies even have a policy that departments charged with the responsibility to implement internal projects bid against one another or against outside contractors for implementation contracts.

Fixed-Price Contract Opportunities. The fixed-price contract offers a wealth of consulting opportunities. Here are a few examples of the ways a consultant can be involved in addition to project management:

- *Project requirements validation.* The consultant reviews the project requirements for contradictions, for errors and omissions, or for other purposes specified by the client.

- *Subcontractor recommendations.* The consultant uses his or her experience, industry knowledge, and/or contracts to help the client compile a list of qualified subcontractor candidates.

- *Bid evaluation criteria development.* The consultant helps the client prepare the criteria used to evaluate the bids from the various potential subcontractors. (See below for additional information.)

- *Subcontractor selection.* The consultant assists the client in selecting the most qualified subcontractor from the bid respondents.

- *Subcontract development.* The consultant helps the client prepare the subcontract used to employ a subcontractor. (See below for additional information.)

- *Subcontract management.* The consultant manages the subcontractor for the project under contract to the client.

- *Sourcing and logistical assistance.* The consultant helps the client source specialized items or identify and obtain sources for custom items and services required for the project, plus the sources for the parts and follow-on services required to continue the project operations.

The consultant can provide services for subcontractors as well, if the client has not employed the consultant to provide the same or similar services—in other words, if there is no conflict of interest:

- *Proposal management and development.* The consultant assists the subcontractor in responding to the request for proposal, and/or manages and coordinates the subcontractor's effort to develop the response.

- *Subcontract implementation management.* The consultant manages the subcontracted part of the project for the subcontractor, or performs part of the subcontract for the subcontractor.

- *Sourcing and logistical assistance.* The consultant helps the client as described above.

Although the consultant normally concentrates on the technical aspects of the project, a request for bid also involves the terms and conditions for the contract to be issued. The legal terms of the contract should be left to the client's legal staff, unless the consultant has the specialized training and experience required. But the consultant can provide guidance in other areas, such as reporting frequencies, formats, and project management software standards and requirements.

Contractor/Subcontractor Relations. Whether you are assisting a client in the bid request or you are the contractor issuing a request for bid to potential subcontractors, several points should be kept in mind regarding subcontractor relations and involvement.

The reasons for using subcontractors are the same as those for employing consultants. In fact, you may be a contractor hiring a subcontractor in one instance, then a subcontractor to the former subcontractor (now the contractor) in another.

Subcontractors need much the same information as does the general contractor. Many contractor/subcontractor relations have foundered because the contractor, being overly protective of its position, held back critical information the subcontractor needed. If necessary, a nondisclosure/noncompetitive agreement and/or a confidentiality agreement should be entered into to allow a free flow of information between the parties.

If you are preparing a response to a request for bid and plan to employ one or more subcontractors, the subcontractors should be involved as early as practical. You must issue your own request for bid to each subcontractor. This means that the project requirements must be translated or divided into individual contracts which are subsets representing the part(s) of the project to be bid on by each subcontractor. The contracts used to obtain bids from the subcontractor(s) must reflect the same terms and conditions of the request for bid that you are responding to, particularly when it comes to penalties and acceptance criteria. You must set a deadline for the submission of subcontractor proposals so that you have sufficient time to incorporate these proposals in your own response to the client's request for bid.

If you are issuing a request for bid to more than one subcontractor, you must treat all subcontractors equally. Each subcontractor must have access to the same information, and each must have the same access and response time for questions. No subcontractor can be given preferential treatment. Otherwise, you will earn the reputation of playing favorites, and those who believe they are on the outside will stop responding to your requests for bids. This guideline particularly applies to the enforcement of the deadline for proposals. If you allow one subcontractor additional time to respond, you should allow all other subcontractors the same amount of additional time.

Between the time you issue a request for bid and the specified bid response due date, the subcontractors will be studying their copies of the specifications and raising questions. Should the questions raise major issues or point out omissions, errors, or contradictions in your specifications, you not only must respond to the inquiring party but must also advise all other bidders of your corrections or changes to the specifications. Further, should one subcontractor devise an innovative or otherwise unique approach to the specifications, or ask questions which indicate that such an approach will be forthcoming, you must hold the information in strict confidence, and not communicate any hints of the approach to the other bidders. This guideline also applies to information which the subcontractor has identified as confidential or proprietary. Of course, the pricing, costing, estimating techniques, or rules of thumb of any one subcontractor must not be communicated to the other subcontractors.

Often the questions generated by the subcontractors in its review of the specifications are questions which you, in turn, must ask of the client. There may be other instances as well in which the subcontractor needs to communicate with the client. You must control all communications between subcontractor and client, or between two or more subcontractors or suppliers. Otherwise, you may find yourself bypassed.

You need to stay on good terms with all bidders, whether they are the successful or not. In these uncertain times, subcontractors that seem stable and secure one day may disappear the next. Subcontractors that repeatedly submit the lowest bids often bid themselves into bankruptcy. You may need to rely on an alternate subcontractor to complete a contract which a failed subcontractor abandoned. Also, you will need the subcontractor on other contracts, so good relations with all your potential subcontractors are essential.

The Role of Price in Bid Evaluation.   The most critical aspect of the bid request phase is the evaluation of the bids submitted by aspiring bidders. It is widely believed that bids are decided only on the basis of low price. Even astronauts have expressed trepidation that their space capsules are built and furnished by "the lowest bidders." However, the worst reason to award a contract is on the basis of price alone. Such a policy attracts the "contract lawyer" type of bidder who purposely enters a cutthroat price, clings to the strictest interpretation of the project requirements even when it doesn't make sense, and spends more energy trying to find loopholes in the terms and conditions than in trying to implement the project appropriately.

This is not to say that price is not important. Price is probably the most important factor in most bids. However, there are factors other than price which can influence the probability of success of a project. These should also be taken into account when evaluating the bids from potential contractors.

The Decision Matrix. One technique which allows appropriate consideration of all the success factors in a project is the decision matrix. A *decision matrix* is a grid custom-designed for each project which lists and weights all the criteria that the client considers significant to the project, then weighs these criteria against each contractor's bid.

To develop a decision matrix, first list all the criteria that the client considers significant in the evaluation of the bids. Initially, generate these criteria in any order that comes to mind, to avoid missing or forgetting any. Then, next to each criterion, list the percentage weight that the client feels the particular item contributes to the overall project. Following is an example of such a weighted list:

Criterion	Weight (% of Project)
A Bid price	60
B Contractor with previous successful history	10
C Contractor with experience in similar projects	12
D No exceptions taken in bid	6
E Financial strength of contractor	8
F Bid indicates flexibility or special capabilities of contractor	4
Total	100

With the exception of the bid price, the criteria are typically subjective. Also, all the weighting numbers are definitely subjective, so it is important that they faithfully reflect the opinions of the client. There is no rule that states the bid price must command more than 50 percent of the total. In some instances, it might be desirable to have a combination of the percentages for other criteria total more than the percentage for the bid price. Equally important is the requirement that the weighting numbers add up to 100 percent. Otherwise, they may have so farfetched a basis as to render the matrix unusable. Similarly, the number of criteria should be held to ten or fewer to keep the matrix from becoming unwieldy.

One good way to avoid falling into the "price is the only criterion" trap is to publish the decision criteria for the contractors to use as they prepare their bids. They will then understand that they must address all the client's concerns in their proposals, not just price.

These criteria with their associated weights become the columns of the decision matrix. Each contractor is placed in an individual row of the matrix. The decision matrix ready for value assessment now looks like Table 15-4.

After the proposal deadline has passed and all bids have been submitted, each proposal is opened and studied. The decision matrix is then completed by assigning a value to each box corresponding to the degree

Table 15-4. Decision Matrix Ready for Assessed Values

Criterion	A (60%)	B (10%)	C (12%)	D (6%)	E (8%)	F (4%)
Contractor 1						
Contractor 2						
Contractor 3						
Contractor 4						

Table 15-5. Decision Matrix with Assessed Bid Values Assigned

Criterion	A (60%)	B (10%)	C (12%)	D (6%)	E (8%)	F (4%)
Contractor 1	7	8	10	10	7	6
Contractor 2	9	10	5	7	10	8
Contractor 3	10	5	5	5	9	7
Contractor 4	8	7	9	6	9	10

Table 15-6. Decision Matrix with Calculated Bid Values

Criterion	A (60%)	B (10%)	C (12%)	D (6%)	E (8%)	F (4%)
Contractor 1	7 (4.2)	8 (8.0)	10 (12.0)	10 (6.0)	7 (5.6)	6 (2.4)
Contractor 2	9 (5.4)	10 (10.0)	5 (6.0)	7 (7.0)	10 (8.0)	8 (3.2)
Contractor 3	10 (6.0)	5 (5.0)	5 (6.0)	5 (5.0)	9 (7.2)	7 (2.8)
Contractor 4	8 (4.8)	7 (7.0)	9 (10.8)	6 (6.0)	9 (7.2)	10 (4.0)

to which a contractor's proposal meets each of the criteria. This value can be on a scale of 1 to 5 or 1 to 10, for example, but the range must be identical for all entries in the matrix. Again, the values are subjectively determined and must faithfully reflect the client's assessment. At this point, the decision matrix might look similar to Table 15-5. The criteria percentages are then multiplied by each of the assigned bid values to derive the calculated bid values. The results are shown in Table 15-6.

All that remains is to sum up the calculated bid values for each contractor. Admittedly, the results are highly subjective. But if the criteria are carefully chosen, and the percentages and assessed values truly reflect the client's priorities, the contractor with the highest total (in this case, Contractor 4—which was not the lowest bidder) has the highest probability of implementing the project to the greatest satisfaction of the client.

Secondary Feasibility Determination

Contractor proposals are usually the products of detailed studies of the project requirements combined with considerable experience in imple-

menting similar projects. As such, they can provide invaluable information useful in this and the next two phases of the project process. The
proposals serve first to validate the feasibility of a particular approach to
the project. After considering the deliverables and the methods to
achieve those deliverables as defined by the project requirements, the
contractors respond in one of several ways:

1. Proposing to implement the project as specified, with no changes to
   the project requirements

2. Proposing to implement the project with minor changes to the project requirements

3. Proposing to implement the project with major exception taken to
   parts of the project requirements, offering alternative approaches to
   the implementation

4. Submitting a "no bid" response to the implementation of the project
   as specified in the project requirements; proposing instead a completely different alternative to achieve the desired results

5. Proposing some combination of item 4 and one of the other options

In your role as consultant, you and the client can evaluate the various
responses proposed, comparing them against your original project
requirements and deciding whether or not the requirements should be
changed to incorporate any of the suggestions submitted. If no changes
or only minor changes are contemplated, you can proceed with the contractor selection process described earlier. If one contractor's proposal is
obviously head and shoulders above the rest, and there are no mitigating
factors, the choice should be easy.

On the other hand, you and the client may decide that the contractor
responses suggest that major changes to the project requirements are in
order. If so, you should definitely not plan on proceeding according to
your original timetable. Major revisions to the requirements at this point
require that you and the client revisit almost all the preceding steps,
making adjustments to the documentation and reviewing your previous
decisions. The overall feasibility of the project is placed in question, but
of equal concern is the time required for revising the requirements and
repeating the bid process.

This is a time when it would be easy to panic. You and the client have
gone through all this work and raised many expectations (those of the
client's executives, in particular), and you appear to have little to show
for it. Nonetheless, it is still less costly at this juncture to change the project to one which is truly feasible than to try to plow ahead with a project
that has, at best, a questionable possibility of working as hoped. You are
going to have to keep giving this message to the client, calmly and

repeatedly. The client may still decide to cancel the project for reasons which may or may not have anything to do with the newly imposed time constraints, but your solid, well-thought-out advice in this phase should put you in a good position for the next project or the restart of this one.

Secondary Risk Assessment/Contingency Planning

The contractor proposals also include information which can be used to update the risk assessment and corresponding contingency planning that was previously documented. A contractor indicates the risks associated with a project or parts of a project in several ways.

- *Explicit description.* The contractor may explicitly describe the risks and their effects on the proposal. If the risks are considered to be too high, the contractor may take exception to the parts of the project requirements considered most risky.

- *Pricing.* The overall price of a contractor's proposal includes the costs that the contractor anticipates with the risks and contingencies the contractor sees in the project. If the request for bid allows incremental or segmental pricing, the contractor will adjust the price for each increment or segment according to the corresponding risks and required contingencies. The adjustments to the pricing may not be spelled out as being directly related to risks and contingencies. Instead, they may be incorporated in the estimating guidelines, standards, or rules of thumb. In this case, you may need to ask the contractor approximately what percentage of the bid represents the risk or contingency amount, and if there are any changes that can be expected to reduce that factor.

- *Alternatives.* A contractor may or may not price a project (or part of a project) if the contractor feels the risks are too high to allow a reasonable estimate. Instead, the contractor will describe less risky alternatives and the prices for those alternatives.

The information gleaned from this phase can be used to fine-tune the risk assessment and contingency plans developed earlier, or it may be used as the basis for changing the project requirements. Just remember, any changes must be handled as described in the previous phase.

Secondary Budget Development

The prices in the contractor proposals provide excellent reference points for adjusting the estimates resulting from the initial budget development phase. The proposals represent the actual firm amounts for which the contractors will implement the project as specified in the project require-ments. The proposals also give you or the client a good opportunity to validate your budget development techniques. This is particularly true if the project is broken into increments or segments, with each part sepa-rately priced. Occasionally contractors will share some of their estimating techniques, and this information can aid you in the budgeting activity.

If the bids are equal to or less than the original budget estimates, no problems are presented—that is, unless the bids come in drastically below the original budget estimates. If this occurs, either the budgeting process or the description given in the project requirements is way out of line. You and the client will need to confer on the causes for the low bids, and make certain they were not the result of something you omitted or something a contractor felt could be omitted from the project requirements. Conversely, you should scrutinize the proposals to determine if any of the contractors has intentionally "low-balled" its bid in the hopes of making up the difference with elevated charges for anticipated changes.

Typically, contractor bids are higher than the budget estimates. The normal range is between 10 and 20 percent higher. This often happens when you develop estimates on the basis of client labor costs or client overhead and facilities. If you included an excess bid allowance in the initial budget development phase, again there should be little or no prob-lem with the client.

A significant problem arises when the bids go more than 20 percent over the original budget estimates, or when the original budget estimates do not allow for any increases as a result of the proposals. In these instances, the client's executives must agree (1) to increase the budget by the required amount, (2) to cut back the scope of the project to meet the budget amount actually available, or (3) to cancel the project entirely.

Vendor Selection and Contracting

If the project is to be implemented fully or partially by contractors, rather than by client personnel, it must be done under appropriate contract. A typical contract has three major parts:

- The project requirements, which comprise the technical aspects of the project
- The terms and conditions of the contract, which comprise the business working relationship
- The legal terms, which define the legal rights and obligations of both parties

Vendors that propose to implement a project must come to agreement with the client on all three parts. Often, the business and legal terms will be negotiated, sometimes at great length. The clauses that present the most difficulties are those concerning contingent liabilities and acceptance criteria. Consultants often serve as arbiters in these negotiations, assuming the role of a neutral third party even when they are engaged by one of the negotiators.

Vendor selection and contracting is the last step in the overall bid process, described earlier in the bid request phase. If the vendor is to have a major involvement in the planning stage of the project, then vendor selection and contracting should take place at least by this point in the preparatory stage. On the other hand, if the vendor is only a minor player in the planning stage, or is a minor subcontractor, vendor selection and contracting can probably wait until early in the planning stage. However, it should not be put off too long, since the vendor will need sufficient time to prepare and contribute its part to the project plan.

Initial Project Team Assembly

The composition of the project team is the most critical factor affecting the outcome of the project. So selecting a team which matches the nature and needs of the project is crucial. The selection process must not only address the technical aspects of the project. It must also consider the people interactions and the organization and management structure—both formal and informal—appropriate to the project. This process is too important to leave to selection by default. The consultant can contribute to every aspect of the selection process, as well as serve as the leader or a member of the project team itself.

Project Manager Selection.   One of the first steps in the preparatory phase calls for the client to designate a project manager. Whether this is the person to carry the project forward may be apparent by now. The project environment makes complex demands on a project manager, and each project's demand mix is different.

Projects have certain innate characteristics. Projects are political—often intensely so. They bring together representatives of various client departments plus the representatives of any number of outside organizations. Projects have high-level visibility to executives with expanded egos. The effects of project activities and results are felt in numerous departments throughout an organization. Thus the project manager is burdened with trying to satisfy multiple constituencies, which usually have varying agendas. The manager must be highly sensitive to this type of political environment.

Projects are bureaucratic by necessity. Procedures must be established and faithfully followed. Standards must be set and followed as well. And both must be monitored for compliance. Every step and decision must be thoroughly and accurately documented. Numerous periodic status and progress reports and reviews must be presented in forms that are acceptable to the reviewees—even if the presentation brings unwelcome news. A project manager must have the discipline to fulfill the bureaucratic requirements of the project in a timely manner.

A project requires extensive accounting. The activities of every resource involved in the project must be reported at least daily and sometimes hourly. Statistics must be compiled and communicated. Budgets must be established and compared against actual numbers. The project manager must be able to specify and implement appropriate accounting methods, including the software to be used, and monitor their compliance.

A project must be staffed. Very few projects can be implemented by only one person, and those that can do not need a formal project manager. Small- and medium-size projects often require the whole project team, including the project manager, to wear several hats. The least expensive way to staff a project is to use as many client personnel as possible. But most client organizations are already so lean that few if any personnel are available for reassignment to a project. Rarer yet are the highly skilled individuals available to make the project implementation most efficient and timely. (They may have been promised to the project earlier, but unless the promise is "guaranteed in writing," it all too often evaporates.)

The most expensive way to staff a project is to ignore the skills requirements and staff the project with "whomever is available." If a project is shortchanged in talent, it follows that the results will be less than expected. Compounding the problem is the "reverse synergy" that arises when a project team is comprised of lower-level performers. The most qualified people will avoid assignment to that project like the plague, or, if made to join the project, they will give only a half-hearted effort.

One alternative is to staff the project with people from the client organization who may be available for only part of the engagement or who can be made available on a part-time basis. Today, more and more projects are staffed by qualified outside consultant or contracting personnel. A project manager must be able to negotiate the availability of key organizational personnel as well as contract for qualified outside personnel when required.

The project participants must be managed. All the usual people management skills are needed. For smaller projects, the project manager must be able to influence the activities of personnel assigned to the project who do not directly report to the manager. As the project size grows, so grows the size of the staff reporting directly to the project manager. However, no matter how large the project, there will still be subcontractors or other personnel who do not report to the project manager. So the need to influence "outside" others remains.

With larger projects, the project manager will be more involved in people management activities and less involved in the technical "nuts and bolts." Team building and managing skills also rise in importance, as do performance counseling and evaluation skills. A project manager must be a leader and an excellent communicator, motivator, negotiator, and people manager.

. A project presents a high stress environment. This is particularly true when the project nears completion of a major deliverable or when the inevitable schedule slippage occurs. The project manager must be the calm voice of reason and demonstrate the controlled leadership necessary to pull the project through its crises. A project manager must be able to function rationally in highly stressful situations.

A project must be kept focused. It must not be allowed to wander into unplanned activities or drift into unscheduled ones. Its resources must not be allowed to trickle away or be watered down with unqualified substitutions. The attention of both the client management and team members must be concentrated on the deliverables, the schedule, and the budget. A project manager must be able to see both the details and the "big picture" concurrently.

Other Project Team Members.   When a project is designated to be performed by a consultant, the role will probably go to the consultant who has been working with the client during the preliminary project stages. This role could include serving as project manager over all the project activities and personnel, including the client project manager and personnel, personnel provided by the consultant's organization, and personnel supplied to the project by any other contractor or subcontractor.

Others who have been involved in the project thus far may be candidates for the project team, but previous involvement alone does not mean that a person is suitable to work on the project beyond the planning stage. The skills necessary for implementation of a project can vary significantly from those used to bring the project up from the concept through the planning.

The number and makeup of the project team are customized to the project needs, but all projects share some elements. If the project is small, the project manager can also serve as the technical "guru" for the team. As the project size grows, the project manager must spend more time reporting and reviewing, and devote less attention to technical direction. At this point, the organizational structure should be adjusted to include a technical "manager."

Subcontractor management consumes a significant amount of time. The load can quickly grow as additional subcontractors are used or the amount of work performed by existing subcontractors increases. The point is reached where the subcontractor management load takes up so much time that a separate project function must be established to handle it and relieve the project manager. This position is second in importance to the project manager's position, and the title is usually designated as assistant project manager. Each instance is unique, so there is no one number of subcontractors that must be reached before the assistant position is established. A good rule of thumb is that when the project consists of six or more active team members plus six or more subcontractors, an assistant project manager's position should definitely be considered.

Project Organization Example.   Software development projects are so commonplace today that the project organization has become almost standardized. Smaller software development projects are typically divided into five functions:

- Systems architect
- Application programming
- Hardware installation
- System software
- Testing and implementation

One person can perform multiple functions, or the team can have one person per function, as the project needs demand. For larger software development projects, the same functional divisions are used. Only this time, each function, with the exception of the systems architect, is represented by a manager who has a staff size commensurate with the scope of the project.

Project Team Compatibility.   Finding the most qualified person to fill each of the various functions is only one of the challenges facing the project manager assembling the project team. An additional challenge is finding people qualified for the function who are also able to work compatibly and cooperatively in a team environment. The people who best perform technically oriented tasks are generally introspective. Interpersonal skills are usually secondary to their technical objectives. They tend to be X's in McGregor's Theory X and Theory Y model. Information gives them their edge—knowledge is the power base in the technical world—so they are reluctant to share it. Yet the project team environment requires information to be exchanged as openly and freely as possible. So the project manager cannot rely on technical credentials alone in making the decision on the best team members. Conversely, interpersonal skills alone cannot be the criterion for team selection. A team composed only of Y's in McGregor's model will be unable to perform the technical tasks adequately. Besides, Y's would just want to sit around and talk to one another.

The project manager needs a better guide to personnel selection than just "gut feeling." Time does not normally permit the luxury of assessing potential team members with instruments such as the Myers-Briggs scale. Nor is there any real indication that this or any other currently popular model (such as Carl Jung's 4 Quadrants) provides real help in assessing potential project-related performance. Such models seem to concentrate mainly on behavior, which is superficial and which rapidly changes.

Priority Assessment.   A more stable predictor of performance over the longer term can be found in an assessment of a candidate's priorities. People will do what they are paid for, but how well they will do it depends on how much they *want* to do the job—whether or not *they* consider it worthwhile. What is rewarding to someone is what he or she considers valuable, not what a manager considers valuable. What people consider valuable to do becomes their high priority, and drives them to excel at any assigned task. And people will gravitate to this type of task or style of effort no matter how much they may try to conform to others' expected or requested behavior.

So the project manager's task is twofold—to define in the job descriptions the priorities required by each of the project functions, and to recruit candidates whose priorities match those defined as closely as possible. Again, no time is available for formal assessment. However, there is one model which lends itself to an adequate initial assessment during the interview process—the values model developed by the late Clare W. Graves, professor emeritus at Union College in New York. If appropriate, this initial assessment may be followed by a more thorough evaluation, or the model can be used simply to confirm the conclusions drawn from an initial assessment.

Brief examples of assessed priorities and appropriate assignments follow. These examples are intended to illustrate a single category of priorities represented in the Graves model. As such, they are not intended to be representative of any particular individual. People's actual priorities and values are unique blends of these and other categories from the model.

Bureaucratic Focus.   People with a bureaucratic priority place a high value on procedures, forms, standards, and organization. They tend to the traditional and adhere strictly to the rules and regulations, even when it hurts. They follow the chain of command described in the organization charts, and fiercely protect and defend their defined group. Such people perform well-defined tasks with diligence and will produce results that meet or exceed the task specifications, provided that the specifications are detailed and the procedures for accomplishing the task are well understood. They would serve well in applications/programming, in which the modules have been precisely described, or in any function that requires accurate record keeping or following complicated instructions to the letter. Engineers in the various disciplines are good examples of people with these primary priorities.

Production and Achievement. Priorities to produce and achieve are hallmarks of managers in general and managers associated with projects in particular. These candidates tend to take the initiative and move their tasks along toward completion, even if it means jumping across the normal organization chart lines. They are tuned in to the politics of the project and can effectively represent the project to organizational executives. They tend to avoid the nitty-gritty details whenever possible, focusing instead on the larger picture. They work hard at trying to bring the project in on schedule, and within budget—particularly if there is a bonus or other reward associated with this accomplishment. These candidates perform best in any management position associated with a project. They are particularly motivated by competitively measured performance and rewards. They are usually excellent spokespeople for the project in reviews and presentations. They also work well as assistant project managers for subcontractor management or in similar assignments involving liaison work or outside relationships.

Attention to Detail. Not everyone places a high priority on handling repetitive, detailed tasks. But those who do are usually dedicated, reliable workers. They also put a high priority on relationships with co-workers and close, personal relationships with their managers. They consider their project teammates as family, and hold a fierce loyalty to that family. But they place a high priority on stability, which limits their ability to change rapidly as the situation requires. These candidates do extremely well with the administrative work and details that normally cascade out of a project. They also excel at synchronizing the project test plan with the changes that occur to the project requirements during implementation.

Technical Focus. A number of people place a high priority on intellectually grasping the working principles of highly complex systems. They also thoroughly enjoy developing and implementing such systems. They maintain both a broad perspective of the overall project and an in-depth understanding of the technicalities of the tasks. They are self-starters who demand little of management, but have a low priority on detailed record keeping. Organizational boundaries are transparent to these people, as are titles or positions. They are immune to the project's political environment. These candidates are well suited to be the technical "gurus" or system architects for a project. They can also work well with the interfaces between the project and outside technical operations, such as software houses or equipment suppliers.

Ego Gratification. A very few in the business world today are self-possessed to the point of holding their highest priority on instantaneous ego gratification. Their short-term perspective drives them to bursts of high energy to accomplish quick results. They then expect equally rapid reward for their efforts. Though often difficult to manage, uncooperative, and sometimes abrasive, these candidates can easily establish rapport with labor union organizations used on a project. They also have a large following in the ranks of those who handle the detailed, repetitive tasks described above, and can manage such people quite successfully.

Consensus Building.   Making decisions by consensus may seem inefficient and time-consuming, but teams whose majority hold this as a high priority work together very harmoniously with a high degree of cooperation at all levels. Teams of this nature are quite successful on government projects or projects which affect the working assignments or conditions of large numbers of client personnel.

These examples show the variety of priorities described in the Graves model and found in real life. Further, the differences defined by the model can aid in making assignments which take advantage of the strengths of the various priorities.

Test/Acceptance Plan Development

The first order of business for a newly organized project team is to learn the details of the project to be implemented. One of the best ways to accomplish this is to have the team develop the test/acceptance plan. This is the plan which confirms that the deliverable(s) meet the project requirements, and outlines the procedures to be followed to demonstrate this to the users and/or sponsors and obtain their acceptance and sign-off that the project is completed.

The best time to develop such a plan is after the project requirements have been completed and accepted, but before project implementation begins. Otherwise, it may be difficult to keep up with the effects of changes to the project once the implementation is under way.

A test/acceptance plan is a description of the step-by-step activities that must take place to verify that each deliverable item specified in the project requirements is reviewed and functionally demonstrated to meet the specifications. In the case of complex systems, the plan is broken into stages which allow testing of each major component on its own, then testing combinations of components for functional compatibility. Finally, all components are combined for an overall test of the complete, functioning system.

The acceptance segment of the test/acceptance plan can be performed concurrent with the testing, but is more likely to follow completion of the test segment, because the testing may uncover problems that must be overcome before the system will pass acceptance. A complete test/acceptance plan includes the actions to be taken to retest the system or faulty portion of the system contingent on the failure of each portion of the test.

The acceptance segment includes all activities that must take place to adequately demonstrate to the user and/or sponsor the functional capabilities of the completed project deliverable(s). The acceptance segment is normally performed following a successful completion of the testing segment. To be certain that the deliverable(s) are accepted on completion of a successful demonstration, the test/acceptance plan must be signed off, just as the project requirements are.

The test/acceptance plan is not a static document. It reflects the deliverable(s) being produced by the implementation of the project requirements. For this reason, procedures must be as established to ensure that, as changes are made to the project requirements, corresponding changes are made to the test/acceptance plan. This procedure is best followed if it is incorporated in the project change control plan.

Preparatory Stage Summary

The preparatory stage confirms the validity of the project and organizes the systems, processes, and personnel required to implement it. The next step begins the formal project planning process, which sets the implementation in motion.

If it has not been already done, now is the time to adopt the computer software to be used to support the project. Some software development projects now employ a combination of compatible software programs assembled to support the project from inception through implementation. This software compilation is called computer-aided systems engineering (CASE). The CASE package in its full implementation is extremely large and complex, and correspondingly difficult to implement.

More conventional project management software is readily available in widely varying capabilities and costs. However the costs do not always reflect relative capabilities, so careful comparisons must be made before selecting the one most suitable for your project. There are several functions that should be included in a first-rate project software program.

1. The program should be easy to learn and easy to use. The documentation should be easy to understand and well cross-referenced. There should be on-line tutorials on its use, as well as exercises and example projects. There should be extensive, on-line help and prompting functions. The program should be menu-driven and should afford error recovery without trauma.

2. Implementation of the features should be able to be staged. The program should allow beginners to operate at one level, then allow advancement to more complex levels as the user grows in familiarity and knowledge. The expansion into advanced capabilities should take place

with no loss of data or any requirements to reenter data. There should be no need to learn all the documentation, features, and operations before being able to use the program productively.

3. The screens should be multicolored and use a variety of symbols to illustrate the different data. The displays should allow graphical representation of data and the PERT network with the task block movable for clarity, their last position remembered. The critical path should be clearly identifiable and dynamic.

4. The program should not arbitrarily restrict data entry and manipulation. It should be possible to enter data from any screen, and the changes made to the data should instantly reflect throughout the system.

5. The project information should be transportable on diskette and flexible in its systems requirements. The software should be usable on DOS, Unix, and OS2 systems, and should also have a compatible mainframe version. The various systems versions should allow compatible upload/download capability. The software should also provide for the project to be divided into logical subsets so the various functions can be worked on separately, then combined for overall operation. Similarly, the software should run on almost any machine configuration plus include drivers for output to all the popular printers and plotters. The import/export functions should match industry standard formats, and the program should have the ability to generate macros.

6. The program should have considerable flexibility in displaying and reporting data. It should allow for display of combinations of graphics and text. Reports should be available in both numerous standard formats and customizable formats with customized report formats remembered. There should be a choice of work breakdown display formats. The task and resource scheduling and balancing and similar functions should be fully flexible, including multiple relationship/dependency definitions, hammock (span) task capabilities, and multilevel hierarchical headings, along with the ability to selectively expand and contract functions without loss of data. The data should be displayable in various ways, such as by task, by resource, by time, by date, or by segment.

7. A full range of details should be available for project resources. There should be individual resource calendars in addition to the projectwide calendar. The program should allow the assignment split and balancing of resources across several projects at once, and resource utilization should be able to be prioritized.

8. The program should support automatic time and resource cost recording. The costing function should include the ability to enter a base or start-up costing and fixed costs. It should also perform automatic independent cost recording of time-dependent variables. The program

should have the ability to create a baseline cost and perform comparisons between the baseline and actual costs. Similarly, it should be able to compare the budget versus the planned versus the actual costs.

9. The PC version of the program should be able to handle approximately 2500 tasks without overwhelming the PC's compute capacity.

Many project management software programs on the market offer the above listed capabilities at reasonable cost. A knowledgeable consultant wanting to assist a client in a project will have researched the available software and be able to make recommendations on what to use, as well as be able to use it.

You should now be ready to begin the planning stage of the project. If you hurry, you may not be too far behind schedule.

16

Engagement Documentation and Control

Charlotte A. Jenkins
Price Waterhouse
Los Angeles

Most successful projects are the result of well-executed and controlled project plans. The purpose of the project plan is to define the specific tasks necessary to achieve the project objectives and to identify the resources needed to accomplish these objectives. The project plan becomes the road map for all phases of project execution, while answering such critical questions as these:

1. How can the objectives be accomplished?
2. What are the interrelationships among the identified tasks?
3. When should the work be completed?
4. Who is responsible for completing specific tasks?
5. Where is the work to be performed?

The documented project plan provides a basis for fee estimates and project direction and thereby becomes the schedule and key control mechanism for the engagement. All documentation, progress reports, and project revisions are based on the original project plan.

This chapter describes the documentation and control techniques that support the development use of the project plan as a basis for conducting a successful engagement. Figure 16-1 provides an overview of various documentation and control components needed to support engagements.

The chapter is divided into three sections, following the presentation in Figure 16-1. The first section focuses on project management. Once an engagement has been obtained, the consultant's first priority must be to implement control mechanisms that ensure delivery of the results expected by the client.

The second section addresses documentation policies and guidelines—the various what, how, when, who, and where questions that relate to engagement documentation. Topics discussed include:

1. What documentation guidelines should be established internally?

2. How should documentation be prepared, obtained, and organized?

3. What type of documentation is needed?

4. How long and where should documentation be retained?

The third section describes work paper preparation: documenting the work performed and the data collected throughout each engagement. Work papers serve as support and reference for all engagements.

Overall, the chapter focuses on fundamental engagement documentation and control techniques. By mastering an understanding of the concepts and tools described, you can learn to plan, execute, and control any consulting engagement.

Project Management

Project management means planning, scheduling, and controlling activities to provide solutions to problems. In your capacity as a consultant, you may solve problems, improve systems and procedures, define organizational structures, or engage in any number of projects to satisfy a client's needs. Because fully understanding and satisfying your client's expectations is your primary business objective, you must use proven methods and techniques to ensure that your projects are successful.

The project management tools outlined in this section are critical to continued successful consulting projects. Consistent use of these project management tools provides current information for responding to frequently asked client questions, such as "What is the project status?" and "When will the tasks be completed?"

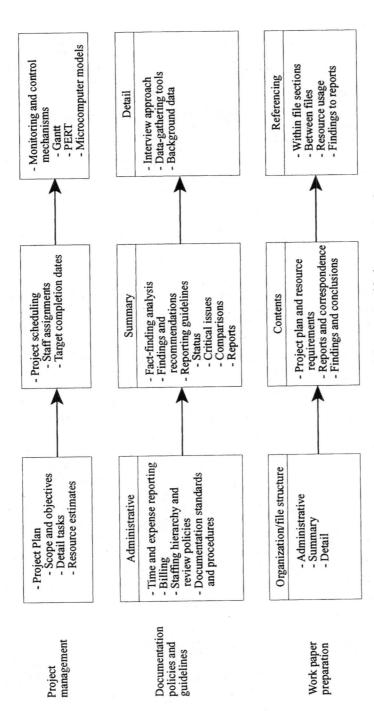

Figure 16-1 Engagement documentation and control overview. (*The overview block diagram of project management and delivery requirements in this chart were adapted from the Price Waterhouse Effective Engagement Management Continuing Education Course.*)

The Project Plan

The first step in embarking on a consulting project is to prepare the project plan. Project plans are divided into specific sections to categorize and analyze problems prior to providing a total solution. The major components of a good project plan include a list of tasks, estimated time to complete each task, target completion dates, and estimated resource requirements by task. Upon completion of the plan, actual resources used to accomplish tasks should be reviewed. The estimates and tasks are communicated to the client and serve as the road map for accomplishing project objectives.

The project plan is the nucleus of a consulting engagement. It serves as a guide for staff assignments and completion dates, providing the consultant with an updated status at any point during the project. In order to maintain a current status, the project plan should be updated at least weekly, providing an ongoing comparison of planned and actual resources and results.

The project plan is usually prepared using some kind of spreadsheet. Because of the frequency and importance of updates to the project plan and the need for evaluation of actual resources used at any project point, some consultants have developed microcomputer models for project planning and control.

A microcomputer-based spreadsheet software package provides a means for developing a tailored model to plan, estimate, and track projects. An example of a basic project plan developed with spreadsheet software is provided in Figure 16-2. The objective of the model is to provide complete project information for the consultant's use; however, this level of detail should be summarized for presentation to a client. Most spreadsheet software packages will allow the user to pass summarized hours and fees into another model, as illustrated in Figure 16-3. The summary model can be updated with other data such as outputs and timetables, or it can simply outline specific tasks and hours estimated to complete each task. The summary model is most appropriate for presentation to the client.

Schedules

Once the overall project plan has been developed, schedules and target completion dates should be prepared for each person assigned to the project. The schedules should be based on specific tasks, time estimated to complete tasks, and critical completion dates. Figure 16-4 provides an example of a daily schedule for a consultant, outlining tasks for a specific project. The schedule should also outline tasks that can be done independently and tasks that have prerequisites for most efficiently utilizing slack time.

ENGAGEMENT PLANNING PROJECT CONTROL SAMPLE CLIENT

Staff: Billing value:	STI $ Bud	STI $ Act	MGR $ Bud	MGR $ Act	SMR $ Bud	SMR $ Act	Total hours budgeted	Total hours actual	Hours variance	Total dollars budgeted	Total dollars actual	Dollars variance
Phase I - Project Control												
A. Accumulate documentation and review	XX		XX		XX		XX			$$$$		
B. Define project control documentation			XX		XX		XX			$$$$		
C. Assign staff and target completion dates			XX				XX			$$$$		
D. Prepare final report outline			XX		XX		XX			$$$$		
E. Tailor analysis and review techniques			XX		XX		XX			$$$$		
F. Identify interviewees and schedule	XX		XX		XX		XX			$$$$		
G. Prepare interview questions	XX		XX				XX			$$$$		
H. Prepare work paper and billing guidelines			XX				XX			$$$$		
I. Conduct client meeting - start project	XX	XX	XX		XX		XX			$$$$		
Phase I totals	XX	—	XX	—	XX	—	XX			$$$$		

Figure 16-2 Basic project plan.

ORGANIZATION REVIEW WORK PLAN

Task description	Resource estimate			Outputs	Target completion date
	CRD	PW hours	Fees		
PHASE III - RECOMMENDATIONS AND ACTION PLANS					
A. Prepare organization chart from director level to president		4 - 4		Organization chart	7/24
B. Prepare recommendations of functional responsibilities for subsidiary positions		38 - 40		Recommendations/job descriptions	7/25
C. Prepare suggestions for personnel qualifications for recommended positions		18 - 20		Qualifications by position	7/26
D. Review draft recommendations, organization chart, and position qualification suggestions	4	12 - 16			7/29
E. Finalize recommendations and discuss action steps for implementing recommendations	4	10 - 10			7/31
Total - Phase III	8	82 - 90	$$$$$		

Figure 16-3 Summary project plan.

SAMPLE CLIENT

PROJECT CONTROL PHASE							
Staff assigned _____ Date last updated _____							
Task description	December dates						
	22	23	27	28	29	30	31
1. Accumulate client documentation and review	X		X				
2. Define project control documentation	X						
3. Assign staff and target completion dates		X					
4. Prepare final report outline			X				
5. Tailor analysis and review techniques				X			
6. Identify interviewees and schedule				X	X		
7. Prepare interview questions						X	
8. Prepare work paper and billing guidelines						X	
9. Conduct staff meeting to review project							X

Figure 16-4 Daily work schedule.

Project Control

The project plan can be represented graphically using a Gantt chart, as illustrated in Figure 16-5. The horizontal axis shows the elapsed time required to complete the activities and tasks that are listed vertically. This simple graphic representation does not show interrelationships and prerequisite tasks. It is easily understood and direct, and is thus a good choice for client presentations.

Another effective project management tool is the performance evaluation and review technique (PERT) diagram, which graphically outlines activities and time estimates for completing activities. The PERT method allows the consultant to chart activities using earliest and latest start and completion dates to predict the overall project completion date. Activities whose completion is critical, or prerequisite, to other activities can be identified, and these activities become the primary focus in charting completion dates. The set of connected lines with the greatest start-to-finish combination is known as the *critical path*. Other activities not on the critical path are addressed during slack time; they are secondary to critical path activities. The PERT method provides an accurate depiction of the importance of time and the interdependency of activities and prerequisites in accomplishing project objectives.

A basic PERT diagram uses circles for events; lines extending between the circles connect associated events. PERT information is very useful in rescheduling work when additional tasks are needed or target comple-

SAMPLE CLIENT

Phase/task	Hours	Week	Elapsed time in weeks (1 2 3 4 5 6 7 8 9 10)
1. Initiate project and collect preliminary data	XX		————————
2. Review background data	XX		————————
3. Determine the effectiveness of each major software application system	XX		————————
4. Determine the adequacy and effectiveness of the Computer Center staff in satisfying user needs in each functional area	XX		———
5. Determine adequacy of physical facilities	XX		———
6. Determine adequacy of service to users	XX		———
7. Review provisions for acquisition, allocation, and control of computing resources	XX		———
8. Evaluate the effectiveness of Computer Center staff in training users	XX		———
9. Evaluate Computer Center personnel relative to the latest technological developments and methods	XX		—
10. Prepare a report of recommendations, plans, and policy guidelines	XX		————————————————
	XX		

Figure 16-5 Gantt chart.

tion dates are missed. Note that in a PERT diagram, circles signify activities taken from tasks outlined in the project plan. The arrows signify the time required to complete each task (also taken from the project plan). When read from left to right, the diagram outlines the sequence of tasks to be performed. An example of a PERT diagram is provided in Figure 16-6. Note that PERT diagrams also help managers control their activities on multiple-client assignments.

Microcomputer Applications

Several project management microcomputer programs are available to assist with planning, scheduling, and controlling project tasks and resources. Common features of project management software include:

- Project plan and resource requirements model
- Project calendar
- Critical path reports
- Project summary reports
- Estimated versus actual resource usage reports

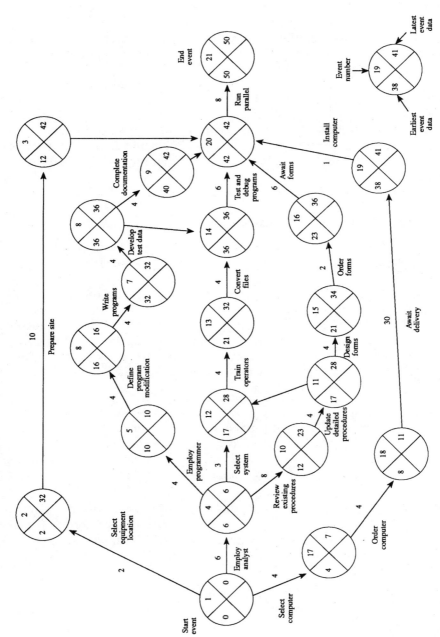

Figure 16-6 PERT diagram.

Many articles have been written comparing various project management packages. Consultants interested in project management software should research computer magazine articles or check with local computer stores for demonstrations. Microcomputer word processing packages are also invaluable tools for preparing status documentation for work papers and drafts of client reports.

For the consultant, the primary advantages of using microcomputer resources are that time is saved and control is improved. A computer can perform the calculations and repetitive tasks, leaving the consultant more time to work on specific project activities. "Work smarter and more efficiently" is the kind of recommendation that consultants like to make to their clients. In this case, they can follow their own advice by utilizing microcomputers.

Documentation Policies and Guidelines

Formalized documentation policies and guidelines ensure that events and agreements affecting the project findings and conclusions are properly documented and filed. A comprehensive approach to documentation collection should include some variation of the file categories and source documents described in the work paper section below. This section focuses on some key questions that a consultant should address when establishing documentation policies and guidelines. The section also provides sample formats and guidelines for document preparation and control.

1. *What documentation policies and guidelines should be established for internal use?* Documentation policies and guidelines should address (1) a defined structure for all documentation with sample formats; (2) timing for preparing, updating, and completing documentation; (3) procedures outlining instructions for documenting and complying with documentation policies; and (4) responsibilities for documentation and review at various project stages.

Certain documentation should have formal policies and procedures established to provide direction, communication, and control. Types of documentation that should be required and formalized include:

Documentation	Illustration
Project plan	Figure 16-2
Time and expense reporting	Figure 16-7
Internal status reports	Figure 16-8
Client accounting and billing	Figure 16-9

DAILY LOG

Client _____
Client code _____
Consultant _____

Date	W/P x-ref.	Hours	Brief description of work performed	Additional activity required problem to be resolved	Task status	Expenses

Figure 16-7 Daily time and expense log.

PROJECT STATUS REPORT

Client _____

Project/task _____

Prepared by _____

Beginning date ___ / ___ / ___ / thru

Ending date ___ / ___ / ___

Project plan task reference	Significant activities this period	Budget hours	Actual hours this period	Total actual hours	Percent complete	Estimated completed date	Comments

Figure 16-8 Project status report.

FEE ANALYSIS / BILLING SUMMARY

Billing period _____

Client name _____   Prepared by _____

Client no. _____   Approved by _____

Activity	Actual hours	Hours billed	Amounts billed			(Over) under budget/comments
			Net fee	Expenses	Total	
TOTALS						

Description and amounts to be shown on bill

_____

_____

_____

Mailing Instructions: ( ) Mail   ( ) Mail and Send One Copy   ( ) Give Bill to Me

Name, title   _____
and address   _____

_____

Summary Information

	Hours	Fees	Expenses
Original budget as of _____			
Revised budget as of _____			
Total billed as of _____			
Remainder to bill as of _____			
Variance as of _____			
Comments _____			

Figure 16-9 Client accounting and billing analysis.

Procedures or guidelines for other documentation described in the work paper section should also be considered; however, less formal guidelines are acceptable in many organizations.

2. *How should documentation be prepared and reviewed to ensure quality control and responsibility for the documentation?* Specific procedures, providing instruction to consultants using the suggested formats, should be defined for each type of documentation. Procedures should explain the format, give a complete example, and suggest situations and stages within each project in which the format can best be used. The procedures should also identify responsibilities for completing documentation. At the beginning of each project, the project manager should decide what

documentation formats are most appropriate and should communicate responsibilities to other consultants working on the project.

The project manager should also establish quality-control review points at the beginning of each project. Some organizations request that managers not involved in a specific project perform periodic reviews of completed project documentation. This approach offers an objective review and ensures that all project documentation is in compliance with documentation policies to provide complete support of recommendations presented to the client.

Finally, the project manager may institute documentation checklists to promote quality-control reviews. The checklists provide a means of specifying the documentation required for the project and the staff responsible for completing the documentation. Most checklists also include columns for indicating manager reviews and the corresponding review dates.

3. *What documentation is needed to support conclusions?*   All background data, interview results, research data, and client-prepared documents should be filed and reviewed prior to preparing conclusions. These results should be analyzed, consolidated, and cross-referenced to a summary of findings and conclusions. Cross-referencing provides the linkage of findings to conclusions in support of recommendations. The consultant should also document (1) a statement of assumptions and alternative solutions and (2) factors influencing conclusions and recommendations. This documentation should be cross-referenced to detailed work papers and later to the draft report. These analyses and narratives help the consultant organize ideas and develop alternative solutions.

4. *How long and where should client work papers be retained?*   Each client engagement should have an established retention period for work papers. The retention period should be based on internal requirements, client requirements, or legal requirements. For example, engagements involving changes to accounting policies and procedures would require a work paper retention of 7 to 10 years. This retention period is determined by the number of years for which a client's accounting data require support for audit work. Other engagements, such as hardware and software selection, may have a work paper retention of 3 to 5 years, since technological advancements significantly affect prior analyses. A statement outlining the project description, number of files, and retention period should be included in the administrative file for each project.

Client work papers should be retained by the consulting firm, since papers are the support for client recommendations. Many firms use a central file room in which files are organized either in sequence (by assigned client number) or by client name. The central file room should contain the most recent engagements—those within the last 3 years. Work paper source documents with retention periods longer than 3 years may be archived at a location outside the central file area. If a consultant has space limitations, he or she may prefer to microfilm the source documents and discard the mass volume of paper, using this economical alternative for storing work paper files with longer retention periods.

Work Papers

Purpose

As noted above, the primary purpose of work papers is historical substantiation of work performed, providing the basis for developing conclusions. Work papers are a consultant's source of reference during an engagement. They also serve as support for recommendations once an engagement has been completed. Since work papers may ultimately be subpoenaed, good documentation practices—combined with explicit organization—are imperative. Good documentation records a consultant's activities and provides references to data used for decision making and recommendations. Work papers may be supplied by the client or prepared by the consultant.

Contents

A consultant gathers background data at the beginning of each project, providing an overview of the client environment. Background data usually consist of documents provided by the client, such as financial statements and existing procedures. The consultant gathers additional data while conducting steps outlined in the project plan. The most common tools for collecting additional information important to a client project are questionnaires and interviews.

The purpose of collecting information is to research, study, and analyze client problems relating to past, present, and future events that may affect recommendations. A consultant must assess various options and alternatives for satisfying client objectives and must test the possible impact of recommendations prior to issuing the client report. All alternatives, assumptions, and comparisons that play a role in developing the recommended solution should be documented in the work papers.

Typically, work papers are categorized into three major sections: administrative, summary, and detail information. Further subdivision of these sections provides specific reference by data location. An example of a detailed subdivision by section is provided in Table 16-1. The documented outlined within the administrative category of the table are usually standard forms defined by a consulting firm's documentation and quality-control policies and guidelines.

Table 16-1. Suggested Work Paper Content by Section and File Category

File category	Section	Source documents
Administrative	Index	Cover page, with references to other work paper volumes and staff references Table of contents
	Checklists	Work paper contents checklist
	Controls	Project work plan revisions, with explanations Time analysis by work plan task Engagement status reports Billing memoranda Work paper retention instructions
Summary	Proposal documentation	Record of inquiry Listing of key client personnel Competitive bidding approach Competition summary Proposal
	Report documentation	Summary and findings analysis Statement of assumptions and alternative solutions Factors influencing conclusions and recommendations Client report (draft and final)
	Correspondence	Client letters Client progress reports Memoranda documenting key events
Detail	Detailed client data	Questionnaire data Interview results Client-prepared documents
	Background data	Report on client's present financial condition Annual report Long-range plan Overview of client operations
	Research data	Documentation gathered from similar client projects Industry background and recent industry updates

The documents outlined in the summary and detail categories of Table 16-1 may vary in format for different types of client engagements. Many of the source documents are narrative descriptions in which a standard format is not necessary. These documents include:

- Record of inquiry
- Listing of key client personnel
- Competitive bidding approach
- Competition summary (if known)
- Statement of assumptions
- Alternative solutions and factors influencing conclusions and recommendations

The consultant should create these documents, describing key points by listing names and sources of information, purpose of documentation, basic facts, and opinions regarding the source and impact of the documented information.

Format

The client proposal, the summary of findings analysis, and the client report are normally a combination of a defined format and a project-related narrative. A defined format provides the framework for developing a narrative to support conclusions and recommendations resulting from the project. By defining a basic client report format, for example, the consultant can enhance the consistency and quality of all reports. The report format should include all or part of the following sections:

- Statement of engagement objectives
- Background information and activities conducted to analyze the client's business
- Findings and conclusions
- Recommendations
- Benefits of implementing recommendations

Organization

Work papers should be combined in a way that secures individual documents while providing ease of reference. Cover pages, indexes, and sectional dividers should be used to make specific document sections more identifiable. Figure 16-10 illustrates the basic data and format for printed work paper cover pages.

Cross-Referencing

Cross-referencing connects data gathered during one part of an engagement with that gathered during another part. It eliminates the need for

WORK PAPER COVER PAGE

Client Name: Sample Client

Client Number: 999-99

Engagement Dates: July 1, 19 _ _ – December 1, 19 _ _

File Name/Number: Administrative—File A

Index to other files for this engagement:	Staff Responsibility/ Workpaper Completion Dates
Summary Report—File SR	James Doe 12/15/19 _ _
Detail Background Data—File B	Shirley Brown 11/30/19 _ _
	Teresa Stevens 11/30/19 _ _

Figure 16-10   Work paper cover page.

duplicating facts in several documentation sections. Cross-referencing also provides a means of tracking pertinent information from the detail section to the final report. In addition, page numbers used in cross-referencing should link key documents within each work paper section to the table of contents.

Cross-referencing involves placing a reference number in a common location on each document filed in the work papers. The reference number is usually assigned to each page; if further subdivision into paragraphs or specific sections of a page is desired, a unique reference number should be placed beside each subdivision. Cross-referencing within specific sections, and between the detail and administrative files, should be an ongoing activity throughout the project. Cross-referencing to report documentation within the summary file is usually addressed after the project is completed and all documents have been filed.

An example of cross-referencing is provided in Figure 16-11. The example cross-references two different documents from the same project that are located in separate work paper files and sections. Thus, a consultant could locate the associated summary of conclusion by reviewing the interview notes on page D-21 and then referring to the report file on page SR-9. Likewise, a consultant could locate the detail support for the report conclusion by referring back to the interview notes.

Cross-referencing should also be used to compare the consultant's actual time expended for each project activity against the project plan resource budget. Actual time can be documented on daily time logs and summarized on the actual project plan.

DETAIL FILE	SUMMARY AND REPORT FILE
Detail Client Data Section	Report Documentation Section
Interview notes Page D-21 General ledger is the client's most important system. The account structure is XXX-XXX, which allows account classification by cost center within the organization. This structure is important for sample client to remain consistent with other entities within the organization. SR-9.	Report Page SR-9 Sample client requires a six-digit chart of account structure to maintain consistency with other entities within the organization. D-21

Figure 16-11   Cross-referencing.

Conclusion

Good project management means never surprising the client with changes to the project plan projections after the changes have already occurred. The tools and guidelines outlined in this chapter provide the who, what, when, where, how, and why to keep clients informed and to guide you through even the most difficult assignments.

17

Client Presentations

Martha A. Nord

Associate Professor
Owen Graduate School at Vanderbilt
Nashville, Tennessee

When asked about client presentations, experienced consultants invariably cite two realities: Strong presentations are crucial for successful consulting, and delivering top-quality service to clients depends on the ability to organize and express ideas orally. But delivering presentations typically receives less attention than the technical and analytical processes.

Why do otherwise well-organized, disciplined technical professionals skimp on a key success factor? The question suggests an answer. Consultants *are* technical professionals. Most consultants are more comfortable analyzing systems and designing solutions than making presentations. Many feel uncomfortable *performing* and some are even terrified speaking before a group!

The pressures of consulting reinforce the fears. Given the mountains of data to analyze, the demanding travel schedule, and limited staff support, it is difficult to find time to plan presentations, develop graphic aids, and rehearse delivery. Fears of presenting are reinforced because the steps that ensure successful presentations are often overlooked. As a result, the presenter feels only marginally comfortable rather than truly confident and envies the skills of the experienced presenter who appears well rehearsed, relaxed, and energetic—whose ideas seem to sell themselves and whose strong rapport with the client audience helps weather critical moments, win buy-in, and renew contracts.

This chapter describes *best-practice* techniques for client presentations. Experienced presenters use these techniques to reduce preparation time, select the right information for the audience, package the information so that it is easy to comprehend and remember, choreograph a seamless group presentation, and always speak with confidence. The techniques will help you become your own communications specialist or work effectively with communications specialists on the team. The chapter takes two approaches:

1. It focuses on current trends and the role of presentations in the consulting engagement life cycle.

2. It explains key success factors—the plan, package, practice, and performance—taken from interviews with experienced practitioners and from training approaches used in presentations coaching.

What Is a Client Presentation?

One reason that business professionals develop *presentation phobia* is that they equate presentations with giving a speech. But presentations are not speeches. A speech is usually a one-way transmission. The speaker's association with the audience is limited to the time of the performance. Presentations are intended as two-way exchanges, usually as part of an ongoing relationship. They model a conversation or dialogue. Sometimes the dialogue develops during the planned presentation. Sometimes it follows the presentation. Sometimes it is only implied in the structure of the presentation. But the objective of a presentation is to create an exchange of ideas between the presenter and the audience that builds shared understanding, agreement, and action.

A presentation falls somewhere between a formal speech and a free-wheeling brainstorming session and discussion. Like a speech, it is planned. It has a structured message with a main point and a framework of ideas to deliver that point. But this structure is only the foundation, not the presentation itself. The presentation is what happens in the actual moment of performance. The outcome depends on the chemistry of the message, the presenter, and the audience. The key is that the presenter has a structured message that drives and anchors the performance. The presenter can adjust to the dynamics of the moment but use the structure to stay on track. The goal is not to impress but to involve the client. As one consultant put it, "We are problem solvers, not after-dinner speakers."

Presentations are not afterthoughts to the real substance of consulting. They are part of the job. They serve the engagement life cycle in two ways: as a tool to support the consulting process and as a deliverable to the client. Presentations that occur upstream in the engagement are likely to spark more discussion and debate. By the final report, the consultant would like to get nods of approval and few surprises. The techniques covered in this chapter apply to presentations at all stages in the engagement—no matter how formal or informal the discussion, how elaborate the media, or how many people in the audience.

Benefits of a Client Presentation

Whenever possible, *ask* to make a presentation. The reluctant presenter misses exchanges that can separate the adequate from the winning engagement. The real-time exchange has substantial benefits.

1. *It allows time to adjust findings and analysis.* Presentations offer the best chance to test the accuracy of your work. It is much easier to make course corrections when you're not far off course. Making a presentation gives you a chance to watch reactions, answer concerns, and try out ideas. You get immediate feedback. The dialogue that emerges from presentations leads to accurate analysis and effective solutions.

2. *It builds credibility.* No matter what your credentials are when you go into an engagement, the real test is *keeping* that credibility high in the client's mind. Credibility is the foundation for long-term relationships and the bond that maintains rapport, even when purposes get crossed. Presenting to the client gives you opportunities to manage three dimensions of credibility:

- *Expertise:* You can demonstrate your technical ability to reassure clients that they have bought the right service. Equally important is that you can confirm your ability to organize and express ideas. Technical expertise carries little weight without the ability to convey the thinking that comes from applying that expertise.

- *Trustworthiness:* The exchange of ideas during a presentation lets you show sincerity, objectivity, and other qualities that build trust.

- *Dynamism:* All the technical expertise and fair-mindedness you can muster will have no impact unless you convey a real emotional commitment. Experienced consultants say that clients are often won for no logical reason other than that the chemistry is just right. They like you. A lackluster presentation can destroy good chemistry developed in one-on-one sessions. Presenting with personal energy helps maintain an emotional bond needed to sell even the best solutions.

Current Trends in Client Presentations

Presentations and simple written documentation have replaced the weighty written report. The increased significance of presentations in the engagement life cycle is influenced by the changing nature of the client–consultant relationship and the impact of technology. These two factors contribute to five trends related to the way presentations are organized and delivered.

1. *Presentations are more collaborative.* Today's consulting relationships focus on process consulting, a shared effort between client and consultant to create change in an organization. More collaborative engagements lead to more collaborative presentations. Team presentations typically follow three formats:

- Facilitated meetings
- Team presentations with the client taking the lead
- Team presentations with the consultant taking the lead

Collaborative meetings serve as a research vehicle for defining problems and gathering information. They create an opportunity to develop solutions in real time. Getting the client team members to present solutions helps build consensus and buy-in.

2. *More presentations are made during an engagement.* The collaborative structure leads to *more* presentations embedded in the engagement life cycle. In fact, presentations become a major tool for doing the work. A consultant might, for example, present a tentative problem definition, working hypotheses, or a systems analysis to check the accuracy of the consultant's interpretation of the client's situation. The idea is to present work in small increments to get commitment early in the process and to involve as many stakeholders as possible.

3. *Presentations are shorter.* The day-long meeting is rare today, except for training and demonstrations of prototypes for large-scale projects. Clients expect all issues to be covered in less than half a day. The most common length of a presentation is 1 to 2 hours. The exception is for senior management presentations. Those high-level overviews tend to be shorter, often just 30 minutes. Shorter means less detail, more summary, and more visual support, as described below.

4. *Presentations use more visual support.* The lengthy written report—the one that gathers dust rather than solving problems—is being replaced by bound copies of slides or transparencies used in presentations. This is a natural outcome, given the shift of emphasis from the written report as an end in itself to processes as a means to create change in the organization. Visual support appears in two forms: (1) as a problem-solving tool to facilitate processes and (2) as a presentation tool to facilitate understanding and memory. Throughout the engagement, consultants use a variety of diagrammatic tools to gather and analyze facts,

propose hypotheses, and discover solutions. These diagrams frequently form the basis for the final presentation. Visual reinforcement can include charts, graphs, photographs, maps, diagrams, and even cartoons.

5. *Presentations use high-tech multimedia tools.* A number of larger consulting firms and consultants with technical specialties stress the importance of using varied media and high-tech presentation tools to add excitement. As one consultant phrased it, they provide the "snazz." *Multimedia* refers to a combination of techniques and tools, such as animation and sound in slide shows or computer demonstrations. The technology is especially useful when it aids in managing change, such as in demonstrating and teaching new information technologies. In this case, the presentation technology becomes part of the solution. Multimedia works best when it naturally punctuates the engagement or is part of the deliverable, rather than just a sound-and-light show at the end.

Types of Client Presentations

A consultant has multiple opportunities to use presentations to build credibility during the engagement. The course of least resistance may be to submit a written report. But a consultant looking to apply *best practice* in customer service will put in the extra effort to present in front of the client in order to build the relationship and keep the project on course.

The Sale. The first step is to sell your services. In the preliminary phase you meet with the client to determine needs, explain previous work, and suggest an approach to the issues. These early presentations range from full-scale slide or multimedia shows that present consulting services and credentials to informal meetings. But even the informal meeting offers an opportunity to apply techniques for effective presentations.

The Proposal. The proposal presents your qualifications and background on the issues as well as your approach to the specific problem. The objective is to show the client that you understand the problem and the environment (culture and politics), and that your approach will best attack the problem. An oral presentation accompanying the written proposal increases the likelihood of buy-in from the client and others who will work on the project.

The Kickoff Presentation. No written report can substitute for a presentation to launch the project. The kickoff creates the opportunity to get everyone on board by introducing client and consultant members of the project team. The presentation can include a high-level overview of the project, a chart to identify all the players and their roles, a calendar of events and meeting schedule, and a communications plan. The main goals are to build credibility and get the project off on a positive note.

Interim Status Reports.   The number of progress and other interim reports required depends on the client. The purpose of interim reports is to keep the client informed of progress and to keep the project on track. Progress reports typically relay the status of the project—where you are relative to objectives, schedule, and budget, and any problems and changes. A consultant can take advantage of any number of other reasons to make interim reports, like reporting a revised problem definition, findings, tentative conclusions, possible solutions, and proposed action plans.

The Final Report.   Depending on the type of consulting engagement, the final report may consist of a study or a process. The report may support a written deliverable, such as a market study, an acquisition study, an engineering study, a strategy analysis, or a systems design. Such a report typically begins with a summary of the problem and recommendations and then develops an argument based on findings and conclusions. When the deliverable is the implementation of a process, the final report will likely take the form of demonstrations and training as well as a formal presentation. Many of the techniques in this chapter apply to training sessions as well as formal presentations.

Four Key Success Factors

The success of a presentation depends on staying focused on the *client*. Keeping that focus depends on four factors: (1) a clear plan for the production and the message, (2) an effective package of visual support, (3) enough practice to build confidence, and (4) a dynamic performance. The remainder of this chapter is organized around best-practice techniques to master these four success factors: the *plan, package, practice,* and *performance.*

The Plan: Production and Message

Presentations must be planned as carefully as the engagement itself. The plan applies to both production and message. The purpose of planning is to reduce rework and presentation development time, and to increase client focus. This approach is not difficult if you view a presentation as part of the engagement cycle, not as an afterthought or off-the-cuff commentary at a meeting. Messages in presentations become an extension of the analytical work. Planning processes (often using visual tools) facilitate structured thinking and collaborative work.

The Production Plan

The purpose of the production plan is to schedule the tasks for designing the presentation and visual support. The last-minute rush can be reduced if you build in time for preparing visuals and practicing. A production plan can be covered quickly at a kickoff meeting. The plan keeps all team members carrying their own weight and controls bottlenecks, since everyone knows what to do and when to do it. If the presentation is to be done by the entire team, it is helpful to have a coordinator—someone willing to take responsibility for pulling together all the tasks related to creating the presentation. The coordinator does not need to be a presentation expert, just careful with details.

One way to schedule presentation planning tasks is to incorporate the tasks into your overall planning chart. A Gantt chart or any other matrix of responsibilities can identify the people responsible and the time frame for each task. The tasks might be set out as follows:

- Plan a strategy for the message.
- Outline or diagram the presentation.
- Prepare a script and storyboards.
- Review, revise, and approve the presentation.
- Produce visuals.
- Design and produce handouts.
- Rehearse the presentation.
- Reserve and check equipment to be used in the presentation.

The Message Plan

Generating the message is not a task separate from the engagement. *It is a by-product of the analytical work.* All the care that goes into solving the client's problem must be reflected in the organization and expression of presentations. Two techniques can help ensure that the presentation message gets attention. You can expand project management to incorporate tasks needed to plan the message, as well as produce it, or you can think about main messages to communicate to the client while doing the analytical work.

This section introduces questions and techniques for capturing the information while actually doing the work for the client. The goal is to develop a client-focused communications strategy. If you adopt these techniques, when the time comes to design the presentation message, you will (1) know your objectives, (2) understand what the audience cares about and needs to know, (3) have a core message, and (4) have a story with main points and convincing evidence to support your case.

You will be ready to add a presentation framework and capture the story in visual aids.

Increased emphasis on planning delivers a host of benefits:

- It focuses attention on what the audience cares about to ensure that the presentation does not become a *core dump* of all information gathered. Rather, the presentation tells a story with information necessary and sufficient to make your case.

- It makes it easier to remember the points when the time comes to present, because attention has been focused on the message from the time the work began.

- It enables the presenter to get emphasis and timing down to avoid using more time than allotted for the presentation.

- It ensures appropriate choices of media and presentation style by paying attention to audience preferences.

- It creates a mechanism for bringing in a communications specialist early in the cycle to help shape the message and begin preparing graphic aids.

You should approach message design as a separate problem-solving exercise. The message plan has two steps that reflect familiar patterns of problem-solving: (1) analysis of the presentation situation (fact-finding and analysis phase) and (2) design of the message (solution phase). The same visual tools used for problem solving, such as issue trees and flow charts, can be used in planning and delivering the presentation.

Analysis of the Presentation Situation.   In the fact-finding and analysis phase, the presenter determines presentation objectives and analyzes the audience. This information will influence the design of the message. The design objective is to select only the information that fulfills the presenter's purpose and meets what the audience needs. No other phase is more important, because *client focus* begins here.

1. *Define the business and communications objectives.*   Given that the presentation is a tool to support the consulting process, it needs to focus on the *business objective.* What are you trying to accomplish with your client? Design a new information system to increase productivity? Develop a process to improve delivery time to customers? Develop a strategy to improve profitability? Whether the presentation is a 5-minute status report or a 30-minute strategy presentation to the board of directors, one message should drive the design: How will these ideas accomplish the business objective? The *communication objectives* focus on how you want the audience to react in order to accomplish the business objective. You can anticipate two kinds of reactions: a direct *action* response and an indirect *feeling* response.

Action Response. The action outcome can take any number of forms. You want the client to buy your services, accept your analysis, approve your plan, and implement your program. The presentation will have to *ask* for this outcome. Too often, presenters do not ask for the response and wonder why action is slow to come or does not come at all.

Feeling Response. The feeling generated during a presentation helps build the relationship with the client. A consultant's success can depend solely on chemistry with the client. Sustaining good chemistry requires building goodwill during presentations. Goodwill may be an elusive concept, but you can build it by paying attention to more specific communications objectives, such as getting new players to feel a part of the team, calming fears, reducing hostility, and creating consensus. You cannot always ask for these responses. Nor can you depend on logic, although not using clear logic could generate a negative response.

Techniques for building credibility generate feeling responses. One approach is to build *themes* or *minimessages* into the presentation to underscore your expertise, trustworthiness, and commitment. To reinforce expertise, you might play up your knowledge of the client's industry, refer to a successful track record, or show your knowledge of computer systems. To build trust, you might stress the pros and cons of multiple alternatives to prove that you consider all angles. You might stress shared values, such as teamwork or attention to detail. Your demeanor as much as the message counts here.

You can also build goodwill by keeping a positive attitude and showing you care about people and personal relationships. Client audiences value energy, enthusiasm, and active listening. They appreciate having the *real you* as a presenter.

2. *Analyze the audience.* The client audience will often be mixed, with different people having different interests. To the degree possible, the presenter will want to control who attends to reduce the problems of dealing with varied interests. One strategy is to ask to make presentations and suggest a guest list *before* the client plans a difficult mixed gathering of senior managers and technical staff. But even if you have little control over who attends, you can produce a client-focused presentation by answering the following questions.

Who are the key players? Determine who the key client representatives or decision makers are, what roles they play, who influences the key decision makers, and who else participates in the process. You will need names, titles, and responsibilities to know where to direct comments during the presentation.

What are the key questions and concerns of the players? Determine what the key players care about the most, what questions they want answered, and what criteria they use to measure success. Ask whether they are more concerned about cost, efficiency, compatibility, or job changes, and what they consider to be the risks or drawbacks and benefits of your ideas. Will they agree with your cost-benefit analysis? Do some see your proposal as disruptive, while others see it as the only way to turn a profit?

How much do the key players know?   Find out what these people already know about the engagement. Determine whether they have been working in the trenches or observing from headquarters. Do they want a high-level overview or details about technical processes?

What are the key players' attitudes?   Learn whether the key players hold attitudes (friendly, hostile, neutral) that might influence their response to the presentation. Consider their attitudes toward the situation (whether they agree with your interpretation of the problem), the players (including co-workers, you and members of your consulting team, and senior management), and the products or services (including software or hardware and training programs).

How mixed is the audience?   Determine the mix of the audience members you will face. Will they be high-level executives who have some distance from daily operations, or will they be technical experts? What functional areas do they represent (marketing, legal, finance, human resources)? What detail will they need as evidence? One of the greatest challenges is selecting the appropriate level of detail, especially for mixed audiences. The best scenario is to present for the decision makers, unless the goal is to build consensus. Then all stakeholder groups are equally important. You may want to address each group separately, focusing on the details of interest to that group. Best practice is to acknowledge the different points of view in the audience at the beginning of the presentation.

How might the corporate culture influence your presentation?   Find out what approach the client expects from you. Many clients expect informal interactive brainstorming early in the engagement and more formal presentations with well-developed visual support toward the end. More and more companies have meeting rooms with projection equipment for computer software. Determine whether the client expects you to forgo the standard transparencies and use the computer. Will client representatives participate as presenters? Do clients expect an interactive session or a more formal, lecture format—that is, in shirtsleeves or with coats on?

A thorough analysis of the audience forces your attention on how the proposal, recommendations, or other information presented will meet the client's wants and needs or answer the client's questions. In short, a client-focused presentation will achieve the following:

- Show a clear understanding of the client's needs and concerns.

- Show the importance of acting on those concerns.

- State the solution.

- Show how the solution meets the needs or concerns.

- Stress the benefits to the client.

- Show evidence of success in similar situations.

- Answer concerns about risks and trade-offs.

Design of the Message.   A well-designed message separates the adequate presentation from the exceptional presentation. The design of the message directly reflects the quality of the thinking and determines how easy it will be to understand. Consultants too often design presentations around the information rather than the message. That is, they start with standard topics borrowed from written reports, such as objectives, scope, benefits, findings, and recommendations. They simply discuss a list of bullet points under each standard topic. Although standard topics should not be ignored, a more client-focused message will tell a logical story, using a framework to make it easy to comprehend and remember.

A good message design not only helps the listener listen; it also aids the presenter. When you are thoroughly familiar with the structure, you can easily fast-forward or present the "bare bones" when time runs short or when a client asks for a nutshell summary. You will also be able to get back on track when the discussion wanders.

The well-structured presentation story has four characteristics: (1) a core message, (2) an argument structured in levels or hierarchies, (3) groupings, or "chunks," of information to support the argument, and (4) a presentation framework, or "map," to guide the listeners.

1. *Core message:*   If you can make only one point, what do you want the client to remember? The core message is your answer to the client's main question. It should be stated up front and woven in like a theme through the presentation. For example, a proposal would state your plan and how it will create opportunity or solve the client's problems. A strategy report would stress key strategy recommendations and reasons for each. An acquisition study would emphasize what to acquire and why. The core message usually answers "What should we do and why?"

2. *Argument structured in levels or hierarchies:*   The key to an effective story is an argument that displays the evidence to make your case. The goal is to build a fact-based platform to support hypotheses and select details that reflect what you learned in the project work and audience analysis. This part of presentation planning can be transferred directly from the project plan and analytical work.

Training in large consulting firms frequently stresses logical thinking. Some companies use proprietary models of logic to drive analyses and structure presentations. You can design your own, since the tools are based on fundamentals of logical thinking. The model in Figure 17-1 shows a main proposition supported by other propositions and evidence.

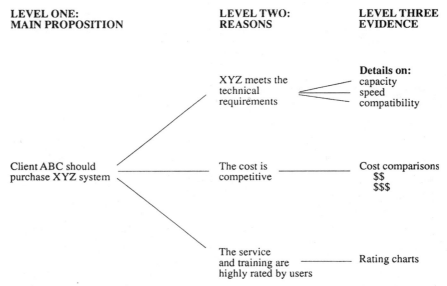

Figure 17-1 Proposition-and-evidence model to structure the middle of a presentation.

You may have more than one diagram to put into the final presentation or you may create one diagram that incorporates the entire presentation.

Devising a logic diagram has quality-control and efficiency ramifications. It improves the final product by forcing attention to logical structure and making obvious what information is missing. It simplifies the design task by using one tool to link analysis and presentation. It automatically groups information and creates a presentation framework. Figure 17-2 illustrates three visual structures to diagram thinking: a pyramid, a logic tree, and a mind map. The only difference between the pyramid and logic tree is that one moves from the top down and the other moves from left to right. The mind map gives a more flexible alternative. You draw the picture as you go, and the branches take shape in no particular location or order. This technique may appeal to you if you are a nonlinear type of thinker who feels constricted by ordered outlines.

3. *Groupings, or "chunks," of information:* Creating "chunks" means putting similar ideas together. Grouping ideas increases the quality of thinking and how the thinking is communicated by showing how ideas relate and by reducing the number of "information bits" to remember.

The mind can hold no more than 7 items, plus or minus 2, in short-term memory. When presentations are filled with long lists of bulleted points, the listener has to work harder to comprehend and remember information—and often the listener will not make the effort. In the words

Pyramid Structure

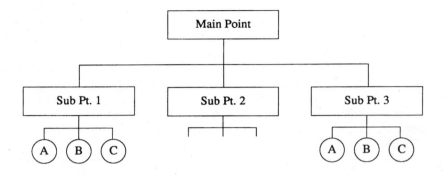

Tree Structure

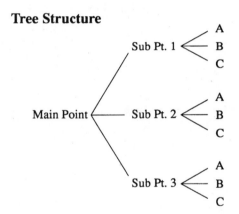

Mind Map

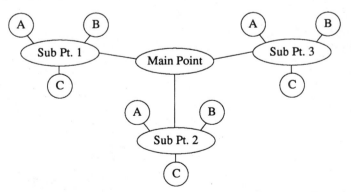

Figure 17-2   Sample diagrams to structure the middle of a presentation.

of one experienced consultant, "There's a fine line between dots and boxes and something that means something."

You can apply this technique in any number of situations. Rather than listing 15 steps in project management, 20 findings, or 12 recommendations, try grouping the items or categories. One approach is to use topics that reflect what the client cares about. Your 15 steps in project management can become objectives for the functional groups involved in the project: manufacturing, marketing, and so on. Rather than listing 20 findings about the competition, you can categorize findings to address the client's concerns: the competition's manufacturing process, the competition's customer service standards, the competition's expansion plans. Rather than listing 12 actions to improve customer service, you can group actions according to staff responsibilities: new ordering processes, techniques for responding to customer requests, quality standards to measure response.

Compare the two examples below. Example 1, which lists topics from a proposal, pushes the listener to remember 11 items. Example 2 gives the listener (and the presenter) only 3 "chunks" of information to remember.

Example 1	**Example 2**
Current situation	*The Client's Situation*
Desired outcome	
Client's questions or problems	Current situation
Other questions	Desired outcome
Constraints	
Scope	*Client Objectives*
Methods	
Deliverables	Client's questions or problems
Expected outcomes	Other questions
Impact on the client's operation	Constraints
Cost justification	
	The Project Approach
	Scope
	Methods
	Deliverables
	Benefits
	Expected outcomes
	Impact on the client's operation
	Cost justification

Hurriedly constructed messages often use neither hierarchies nor groups. The result can fog the message for even the most resolute listener. Contrast the two examples below, which list a computer company's core products.

Example 1	**Example 2**
Hardware	*Computer Systems*
Software	Hardware
Computer systems	Software
Computer services	
Consulting	*Computer Services*
Applications development	Consulting
Scientific and engineering applications	Applications development
Peripherals	Scientific and engineering applications
	Peripherals

Three techniques may be used to create "chunks," as in the second of each pair of examples presented above. First, the information is given through visual cues, such as capitalization, bold or italic type, bullets, and indents. Other types of visual techniques include summary matrixes, simplified tables, and side-by-side lists of pros and cons. Second, the language is parallel. All the words are in the same grammatical form, such as all nouns or all phrases beginning with a verb. Third, each grouping is at the same conceptual level and no items overlap. For example, *hardware* and *software* are not on the same conceptual level as *computer systems*; they are subsets of that larger category. These simple visual and verbal techniques for creating "chunks" can boost comprehension and memory significantly.

4. *Framework, or "map," for the listeners:*   All good stories have an organizational structure—a framework of beginning, middle, and end. The hierarchies and groupings structure the story in the middle. The last step is to add a beginning, transitions, and ending.

Beginning.   The beginning serves a number of purposes: to give the listener a reason to listen, to increase the presenter's confidence, and to provide a "map" to follow during the presentation. One way to set the stage effectively is to include four elements—the ABCDs.

A = Attention   Handbooks often recommend opening with a startling statistic, vivid story, or rhetorical question. Attention getters can fall flat unless they really relate to the point and do not sound contrived. Jokes rarely work and dictionary definitions sound like speech class. You can focus attention simply by referring to your relationship with the audience in a way that acknowledges the audience's concerns. The point is to tell the audience members what they want to know: What is this presentation about and why are we here? One of the most effective ways to focus attention is to list benefits.

B = Benefits   All listeners want to hear the presenter state what is important to them. The opening must go beyond identifying a topic such as customer information systems. Audiences need a message with a benefit (your core message): *"Adding a customer information system will give you the tracking capabilities needed to double sales in the next year."* You may be concerned that some members of the audience will be naysayers. If that is the case, you can embed the message with an open-ended question, without giving the answer right away: *"To decide whether to add a customer information system, we will look at the value of tracking customer responses relative to the expense of the system."*

C = Credibility   Your rapport with the audience will depend on your credibility. Establishing credibility presents little challenge if you have worked with everyone during the consulting engagement. Others may not automatically accept you as knowledgeable and trustworthy. You can fill the gap by mentioning your role in the consulting engagement and your association with people in the audience. Alternatively, someone else from the client's organization or your consulting group can do the work for you in an introduction. Avoid apologies for nervousness or hastily prepared visual aids. Audiences will be more irritated or uncomfortable than sympathetic.

D = Direction   Listeners want to know what the presentation will cover. This is the "map" or blueprint, of the presentation. It falls at the end of the opening to serve as a bridge to the main body. This is where you follow the often repeated advice: "Tell 'em what you'll tell 'em." A typical structure could be: (1) a review of objectives, (2) what we found, (3) what we recommend and why, and (4) the next steps.

Transitions.   Transition statements keep the audience on track by summarizing and forecasting. They repeat points to increase the likelihood that clients will remember the message. For example, you can summarize findings or benefits before moving to the next section. Transitions also reinforce the logic of your story by showing how ideas relate. You can remind the listener where you are in the design of hierarchies and groupings of ideas with transitions like *therefore, in conclusion, as a result,* and *the final step.* Well-structured visual aids help you reinforce transitions.

Endings. The ending gives you one more chance to sell your core message and reach agreement. One or more components comprise an effective ending. A summary of recommendations and restatement of benefits will ensure that the core message stands out from other detail. You can add a visual picture of successful outcomes, especially if you need to build commitment. Finally, you can conclude with "next steps" to clarify the action needed from the group. The stronger the buy-in, the shorter you can make the ending.

The Package

Clients expect ideas to be presented visually. The trend toward more visual information packages makes good sense. Visual language quickly captures complex concepts and summarizes information to ensure shared understanding and increase memory. A picture really is worth 1000 words.

Computer graphics software has simplified the visual-aid process to the point where the level of expectations is high. with so many media and tools available, consultants often hire specially trained technical staff to produce visual support. The guidelines presented in this chapter are intended to help you work more efficiently with media experts or to get the most from your own work.

Choosing the Best Visual Media

The spectrum of media choices and audience preferences ranges widely. The minimalist approach argues for simple, black-and-white transparencies and flipcharts. Consultants in this camp have clients who say, "Tell me, don't wow me." Clients may equate sound-and-light shows with added dollars and less substance. At the other end of the spectrum, the extravaganza advocates use color, sound, and animation. These techniques appeal to the MTV generation and are standard tools in some industries. The trend is growing toward more computer applications, with less censure for state-of-the-art technical shows. Cost is decreasing, expertise is developing, and business applications are growing. Once labeled "only show," interactive video and other multimedia tools have earned a respectable role in making company and product presentations and in developing prototypes. The choice is justified when the presentation will be used repeatedly, when clients expect it, or when the presentation is part of the deliverable. The various media choices and their typical uses are described below.

Flipcharts. Flipcharts are used to record and present ideas during working meetings. They are coming back into favor for interactive, collaborative meetings when everyone benefits from seeing ideas as they grow. They can be saved as a record of the meeting. An electronic board with a copy facility serves the same purpose, but such tools are not widely available. Some presenters adapt the flipchart concept by simply changing the type of paper used. Some anchor long rolls of butcher paper or posterboard around the walls as a surface for recording ideas and images. Others pin note cards to corkboard or use Post-it notes.

Overhead Transparencies or Foils.   Transparencies or foils are used frequently for client presentations because they are easy to prepare and flexible to present. The lights can stay on and the order of the transparencies can be easily changed. Experienced presenters mount transparencies in cardboard frames to keep the visuals from sticking together and slipping around on the projector. And they often use the frames to write notes to themselves.

Lap Visuals as Takeaways.   Copies (often bound) of transparencies or slides used during the presentation are often prepared for audience members as takeaways. A growing trend is to make these detailed enough to substitute for a written report. The format is typically $8\frac{1}{2}'' \times 11''$ with a horizontal or landscape layout. One practice is to reproduce the slide on one page and add text on the facing page; another is to use half the page for the slide and the other half for the text. Although presenters often prefer not to distribute handouts ahead of time, the client may insist on having the handouts to follow during the presentation. In this case, lap visuals are the medium of choice.

Viewbooks.   A viewbook is a notebook, often with laminated pages, used to show a portfolio of past work, key benefits of processes, product features, and the like. This medium is more a sales tool than a tool for presenting the outcome of work.

Posters and Boards.   Posters and boards are used to show blueprints, sketches of buildings, engineering drawings, or flowcharts. Engineers and architects favor this technique to focus attention on a few or just one visual and to reproduce accurate detail with high visual appeal.

Slides.   Often, 35 mm slides are used for frequently repeated marketing-type presentations, such as an overview of a company, product, or service. They are also used for presentations with high visibility for large audiences, such as conference, seminar, and recruiting presentations. Consultants often avoid using slides for project presentations because the client may find the medium too slick or consider the cost excessive.

Another drawback is the need to darken the room, which reduces the presenter's ability to interact with the audience.

Videotape. Videotape, which is frequently selected for training, also works well for marketing presentations on consulting services. Videotape is playing an increasing role in research for consulting work, such as clips from focus group interviews to get the customer in front of senior management; views of building sites and manufacturing processes to get an accurate picture of findings; and testimony from experts to support arguments.

Computer Graphics and Software Demonstrations. Computer-generated slides with sound and animation can be used to show rotating diagrams, buildups of ideas and processes, and other moving images. Prototypes of computer screens demonstrate applications of new systems, such as loan processing and customer information systems. When the engagement deals with PC solutions, the presentation must demonstrate the consultant's mastery of the technology. Large-screen projection systems are appearing in more and more meeting rooms, especially in companies with technical products and services and with global operations that depend on high-tech communications tools.

Interactive Video. Laser disk technology, part of the growing trend toward multimedia, is used for presentations combining text and video, with growing applications for training and introducing new products and services. One benefit is high flexibility, because the user chooses the order of presentation to answer questions as they arise. The presenter plays a secondary role as technician, with the media display itself dominating the show.

Applying Design Principles

The advice to "keep it simple" applies to the argument or story line of the presentation, but often it is misapplied in designing visuals. Visuals should not look cluttered or appear dense with text. At the same time, too few words can be as ineffective as too many. If all word charts have only two or three bullet points using two or three words each, the audience will not have enough information to understand how ideas are related or how a system works. One way to avoid oversimplification and make the logic of your thinking clear is to apply three design principles.

1. *State the main message as a headline.* The use of action statements as headlines outlines your argument so that it tells the story. Even the best presenters do not expect to hold the audience's attention 100 percent of

the time. One way to keep listeners on track is to state full thoughts, not topic words, on each visual. The audience can always read what was missed. Try presenting the main message at the top of the visual using an action phrase or a full sentence. For example, rather than labeling a chart "Third-Quarter Sales," use a title that explains an outcome, such as "Widget Sales Increased 15 Percent in the Third Quarter" or "Region III Leads Third-Quarter Sales." A topic such as "Focus Group Results" can become "Customer Response Varies Widely According to Age" or "Customers Prefer the More Flexible 'Pod' Design." This technique will reduce the possibility that data will be misread or misinterpreted. Stating messages in headlines is particularly valuable when you are using copies of the visuals as takeaways and want to be sure that the message is clear when you are not around to interpret.

2. *Set design standards.* Setting a standard or consistent design for all visual aids conveys a professionalism that client audiences have come to expect from presenters. The design elements include layout and type choices. Creating a unified layout, including logos and borders, and using an easy-to-read typeface sends the message that you take your material and presentation seriously. Standards also can improve comprehension and memory. Design features create embedded cues to help listeners keep track of the organization, especially the hierarchical structure of main points and groupings of evidence. Design standards save production time. Once a layout and type style are set, each visual can be created quickly following those standards. Computer graphics packages have templates to make the task easy. Numerous handbooks on presentation graphics explain and illustrate design guidelines.

Here are some key points:

- Use horizontal rather than vertical format.
- Use uppercase and lowercase letters, not all capitals.
- Vary the size of type to indicate levels of information.
- Use color for emphasis, contrast, and highlighting ideas, not just for variety.
- Consider symbolic uses of color, such as green for profits and red for losses.

3. *Use visual reinforcement.* The trend to more visual support means relying less on word charts and more on visual images. Television and computers have accustomed us to more sophisticated visual designs and messages. Visual reinforcement certainly adds interest, but more important it clarifies thinking and aids memory. Consider choosing visuals from three categories: charts and graphs, diagrams and maps, and pictures.

Table 17-1. How to Choose Charts and Graphs

Chart type	Function	Relationship words
Pie chart	Shows relationships between parts and the whole	*percentage, share*
Bar chart	Shows rankings; compares and groups items	*compares, ranks, equals, exceeds, deviates*
Column chart	Shows changes over time; best for up to six or seven points; emphasizes levels or magnitudes	*increases, grows, fluctuates, decreases, varies*
Line graph	Shows changes over time; best for long time periods; emphasizes movement	*increases, grows, rises, decreases, falls, fluctuates*
Scatter diagram	Shows relationships among two or more variables; uses dots or bubbles	*varies with, does not vary, correlates*

Charts and Graphs. Charts and graphs are the most common visuals used in presentations. One caveat, however. If you use charts and graphs to gather and analyze data, you will have mountains of them by the time you make your presentation. This availability leads to a practice sharply criticized by clients: dumping the data. Just because a chart was made is no reason to present it to the client. Summarize only the most important findings and conclusions. Table 17-1 lists charts and graphs that demonstrate relationships.

Diagrams and Maps. Diagrams form a natural presentation tool when the analytical work includes process analyses. Familiar diagrams include flowcharts, organization charts, blueprints, and equipment assembly instructions. You can create your own original diagrams to show how processes and ideas relate. Figure 17-3 illustrates a technique favored by many consultants: a diagram of the argument or main ideas covered in the presentation. You can transport ideas directly from your logic trees into the presentation.

Diagrams are easy to construct with an array of boxes, circles, and arrows, sometimes using the draw capabilities in graphics packages. Clip art, also available in graphics packages, includes a variety of maps for showing regional divisions, office locations, proposed expansions, distribution channels, and the like.

The Issue

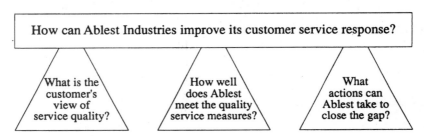

Figure 17-4   Diagram of main points for a client presentation.

Pictures.   Photographs, videotapes, or conceptual drawings offer creative alternatives. You might photograph buildings or equipment, or videotape a customer focus group. You might use icons and other clip art to represent both abstract concepts (e.g., a light bulb for an idea or a rain cloud for a problem) and specific products and services (e.g., computers linked in a network). You might draw a pipeline to depict business processes. A growing trend is to organize an entire slide presentation around a visual metaphor. For example, you might sketch a bridge to show the client "bridging the gap" between the current situation and the desired outcome. Each bridge support could represent an action item in your recommendations. Water under the bridge could hold "obstacles to be overcome."

The Practice

The best presenters practice for two reasons. Practice lets you find the "bugs" in order to refine the presentation. Practice also ensures that you are completely familiar with the content so that during the performance, you will be able to concentrate on the audience. Practice is the best way to control nerves and stay focused during the presentation. Practice can help the most if it starts early in the planning cycle.

Making a Dry Run

Make a dry run early in the presentation development cycle, before content is too solidified to change. The dry run provides feedback for both individual and team presentations. If you are the sole presenter, you might schedule a review session with peers or with a superior. Peers who know the project but have some distance from the information can help evaluate whether the message answers the client's questions and whether the level of detail is appropriate. A senior consultant can use the review process to coach associates. A team dry run not only ensures the best presentation design but also simplifies coordination. Without early practice, the final presentation can look like a series of individual efforts rather than a seamless piece woven around one core message.

The most efficient technique is to plan a dry run *before* the visual aids are so far along that they cannot be changed easily. Rough copies of visuals can be used in a dry run to check timing, add transitions, and eliminate redundancies. During the dry run, spread out all the sketches of visuals on a large conference table so that everyone can review the entire presentation. This technique makes it easy to spot visuals that are out of place or repetitive, that contain questionable logic, or that are missing information.

To gain the most from a dry run, try videotaping the practice presentation. Think of the videotape as a rough draft that you can review for revisions.

Planning the Performance

Once you are satisfied with the message and the visual support, you are ready to orchestrate the actual performance. Details make a difference.

1. *Organize your notes and materials.* Put notes, visual aids, and handout materials in order. Decide whether you need notes as a backup. You might try notes on photocopies of visuals, on cardboard frames for transparencies, or on note cards. To project a professional image, avoid speaking with a handful of note cards or outlines on legal pads (page flipping or note card shuffling is distracting). Be sure that someone with a good memory or a "to do" list is in charge of bringing handouts. Pack your briefcase with a good supply of blank transparencies, extra markers, masking tape, extension cords, and adapters, and any other emergency supplies you can think of. Preparation translates into confidence.

2. *Check out the location and equipment.* If you know the layout of the room and the equipment you will be using, your confidence will increase. If at all possible, schedule a practice session in the room (and with the equipment) that you will actually use. Even knowing the layout of the room helps; you can practice on the same kind of equipment with a picture of the room arrangement in mind.

3. *Coordinate with other presenters.* One person can coordinate a team presentation by communicating the date, time, room arrangement, equipment, and the like to all members. This step is particularly important when you are presenting with client representatives. Remember to plan for different expectations in other cultures, such as tea breaks in Britain, long lunches in France, and interest in details in Japan.

Rehearsing to create "Memory Paths"

Practice is not simply running main points through your head while driving to work or on a plane to the client's office. Even so, consultants do not have to become amateur actors or practice for weeks. Actors know that the performance does not have a life until it is spoken. Speaking the actual words out loud gives you something to remember, and playback of a videotaped practice session reinforces memory even more.

The idea is *not* to memorize. The more you try to hold in memory, the greater your chance of forgetting. The best practice is to create memory hooks to help recall the material. You should expect each performance to be slightly different as you interact with the different audiences. The tools introduced in the sections on message design and visual reinforcement serve as memory aids. Levels and "chunks" of information and visual cues organize the message around natural thought processes.

Consultants often protest that they do not have time for practice. One consultant told the story of accidentally learning the value of practice thanks to Hurricane Hugo. When the client site was destroyed by the hurricane, the consulting team was forced to condense a 2-day meeting into 1 day. The good news was that the team had the extra day to condense and to rehearse. All the parties were impressed by the consultants' execution. Don't wait for a natural disaster to add time for practice to your schedule. Just 2 hours spent in front of a mirror can mean the difference between an adequate and an excellent performance.

Practicing Demonstrations

More and more client presentations include demonstrations. You may have to present a new computer system to the client or train staff on its application. Preparation has three elements:

1. *Master the system well in advance.* Once you know the system, you can concentrate on the client, not the machines. Better yet, bring along another technical expert who can do the demo while you answer questions.

2. *Choreograph the demonstration.* The best demos organize the steps in a logical order for the user, demonstrate elements that answer the client's questions (not just show off technology), and stay within the expected time limits. You may be tempted to plan only the high points and wait to see what the client asks. You will certainly want to be flexible enough to change your plans for the client. But the danger of too little planning is getting off the track into descriptions of small features and extraneous detail that dilute the impact of the whole. Detailed information on how to set up a computer screen may interest the users but will tax the patience of other listeners.

3. *Use your own checklist.* Make sure of the following points:

- The equipment is in working order.
- You have all the components—including the demo disk or videotape.
- You have spare parts, extension cords, electrical tape, and other emergency aids.
- The client is providing needed support (people and equipment).
- All the team members are informed about the presentation plan.

The Performance

Controlling the Butterflies

Audiences may not agree with your ideas, but they want you to succeed as a presenter. Empathy is strong. A presenter's nervousness makes the audience uncomfortable and undercuts credibility.

Butterflies can attack even the most experienced presenter when he or she is challenged by a new situation or an antagonistic audience. But experienced presenters have techniques to counter the attack. The goal is to get the adrenaline pumping to produce positive energy, to get the butterflies flying in formation. These tips apply to any performance.

1. *Know it cold.* Nothing substitutes for knowing what you are talking about. The better the planning, the higher the confidence. Memorize your opening and closing lines. A well-prepared opening helps you through the first few minutes while your body and mind get in gear. Knowing the ending gives you confidence that you can close on track and leave the audience with the core message. Don't memorize anything else. Know the map, or diagram, of the middle. If you incorporate the diagram into your notes or visual aids, the visual cues will trigger your memory.

2. *Keep a positive attitude.* Next to lack of practice, the greatest cause of nervousness is a negative attitude. Don't let negative thoughts about your ability undermine your confidence. You are the expert consultant and no one is better qualified to talk about your project. If you have trouble countering negative thoughts, work with a presentation coach to improve your confidence.

3. *Warm-up.* Presenters forget that a presentation is a demanding physical and mental performance. Just as an athlete or singer warms up body and voice, a presenter needs to move gradually into the performance. Warm-up can include physical exercise, such as a trip to the gym or a game of tennis. You can add relaxation techniques, like deep breath-

ing and stretching. A few slow neck rolls and a good yawn work wonders to relax the shoulders and jaw, the source of greatest tension for presenters. Also try visiting with the client audience right before you begin. The presentation then becomes an extension of your conversation—and conversation is what a presentation should be.

Dressing for the Audience

How you dress will depend on the image you want to project and what the audience expects. Sometimes you may want to appear conservative; at other times you may want to look casual. Senior executives at corporate headquarters expect conservative business dress for a formal presentation. But the same audience may expect business casual dress for a weekend retreat. Casual dress is often encouraged for planning meetings, presentations in a plant or operations facility, and hands-on demonstrations. Matching your dress to the client's suggests that you are a member of the client's team. If you are not certain about appropriate dress, a rule of thumb is to dress up rather than down for the audience. Both men and women can choose a conservative version of the business suit.

Setting the Stage

Controlling the environment builds confidence. The idea is to prevent unexpected interruptions and arrange the room to encourage participation and limit distractions.

1. *Arrange the chairs and tables.*   Many presentations occur in a conference room with participants seated around a long table. If you have a choice, arrange chairs so that participants can see one another and not be facing you in lecture format.

2. *Check the lighting.*   Rooms often have rheostats and multiple switches to control the level of light on the audience, presenter, and screen. Try to keep the lights as bright as possible without jeopardizing the clarity of the image on the screen.

3. *Remove physical barriers.*   Avoid using a lectern. Just because a room has a lectern does not mean that you must use it. Standing behind even a portable lectern conveys the image of speech giver rather than information provider and facilitator. Remember to move extraneous equipment to the back of the room.

4. *Arrange equipment for best use.*   Move an overhead projector far enough back to project a large image on the screen. If the screen is portable, place it to the side of the room so that you will have more "stage space" in which to move without blocking the screen.

5. *Test all equipment.* Always have a backup plan in case your best-laid plans go awry. A seemingly small item, such as an upside-down slide or no markers for the flipchart, can create an impression of disorganization.

6. *Have handouts ready.* Experienced presenters recommend not giving handouts until after a presentation. But that will not work in every instance. You can ask an audience to listen to a general overview, as in a marketing presentation. However, when you report actual work, clients will want to follow along. If the visual aids are well designed with the core message clearly stated up front and the arguments clearly diagramed, an audience is likely to stay with the presenter. But there is always the danger of having one person interested in detail who will drill down into an appendix in search of a specific number. The best practice is to limit handouts up front to copies of visuals and to hold back detailed material until the presentation is over. Another approach is to hand out charts or diagrams only when you are ready to use them in the presentation.

Building Delivery Skills

No matter how skillful the analysis or cogent the argument, success depends on engaging the audience. Presenters too often distance themselves from the audience by performing like robots. Then after the presentation, they return to their own engaging personalities. Delivery skills help you use your real personality to connect with the audience. The skills are reflected in the following qualities.

Visual Image

Expression. A presenter's genuine smile and spontaneous facial expressions naturally warm up an audience. Frowns, squints, and grimaces signal that you are not happy to be there. A smile can be a strong offense against naysayers and critics. It is hard to attack through a smile.

Eye Contact. Presenters and listeners alike get energy when they really look at each other. Think of a presentation as a conversation and hold eye contact for a few seconds with different people. You may be tempted to favor decision makers in the client audience, but include everyone. It is best not to scan the room, looking at foreheads and noses.

Gestures. Presenters often explain that they deliberately control gestures because they talk too much with their hands, but few people really gesture too much. A more frequent negative is a repetitive gesture that becomes a mannerism (such as waving a pointer, playing with markers, or adjusting glasses). The key to effective gestures is not to think about them. Let the arms relax and they will move naturally to emphasize points and reach out to the audience.

Posture.   A confident posture means shoulders back, chin up, weight balanced on both feet, and body leaning slightly toward the audience. This stance makes you appear energetic and gives your body room to breathe. Presenters limit their oxygen supply and sabotage themselves by hunching over and letting the diaphragm press against the rib cage.

Verbal Impact

Range of Notes and Inflection.   You do not have to be a singer to work with a range of notes, from high to low. Voice variety creates interest that holds attention. A monotone simply puts people to sleep, a sing-song tone can sound childish, and ending on a high note or a questioning note sounds uncertain. Identify your natural conversational range of notes and give yourself permission to use them all in a presentation.

Emphasis.   One way to overcome a monotone is to emphasize or "punch" important words and phrases. Not only will this technique keep the audience alert it will also make your main points stand out.

Pace and Pauses.   Pacing and pausing, like emphasis, will help you match your voice to your meaning. Pauses, for example, signal that something important or new is coming. Fast pace works for storytelling and easy-to-understand information. Deliberate pace keeps the audience from missing the point when you want to stress an important theme or explain complex data. These techniques also help presenters control the *er's* and *um's* that fill dead air—and annoy listeners.

Bringing in the Audience

The difference between a speech and a presentation is the activity that fosters the dialogue between you and your audience. The point is to engage and involve the client while delivering the planned presentation. Here are methods to bring the audience in and manage the time.

1. *Personalize on the spot.*   One way to engage an audience is to mention individual audience members by name and refer to situations you have shared with them. These references especially help to establish rapport at the beginning of the presentation. Another approach is to re-create a conversation you had with someone in the audience or with someone known to the audience. For example: *"Just yesterday, John and I were discussing the positive impact we can anticipate from installing the new system."* Quoting clients shows that they support your ideas and emphasizes teamwork. Personalizing can be planned or spontaneous.

2. *Question the audience.*   The audience will be more likely to experience the presentation as a conversation if you ask questions related to their concerns. You can start a dialogue by asking specific questions, such as *"What do you see as our next step?"* You can encourage involve-

ment without discussion by asking for a show of hands: *"How many of you participated in the focus group?"* If you do not want to start a discussion, you can simulate an exchange. For example, you can structure the presentation around questions that the audience would ask, such as *"What are the key success factors?"* and *"What impact will the new system have on employees?"*

3. *Manage the time.* A presentation must begin and end on time. One way to manage time is to match timing to visuals and include visuals that can easily be cut if time runs short. A rule of thumb is 1 minute per slide or other visual. But the more complex the information, the longer an explanation will take. Another technique is to know the framework, or map, so well (particularly the ending) that you can fast-forward when the discussion of details gets the planned presentation off track.

Managing a Team Presentation

The best practice is to have one presenter lead, usually a senior member of the consulting team. But if someone else directed the engagement and has been closely involved with the client, that person may be a better presenter. The key is to choose someone who is intimately familiar with the client and the work. No matter how strong a person's platform skills, it is difficult to speak with commitment and knowledge about work someone else has done. Another useful practice is to bring along junior members—assistants who have done analysis and research—to answer questions. Some team leaders invite junior members to present their own work as a way of giving them practice presenting. Sometimes members of the client team will make the presentation, particularly when they need to persuade their colleagues to get buy-in to the plan. Having a technical or operations expert—someone who really knows the inner workings—can add credibility.

Presentation specialists debate the merits of having one or multiple presenters. Several rules of thumb can guide your decision:

- Have the most knowledgeable person take the lead.
- Let junior members do small parts to build confidence.
- Let the length of the presentation dictate the number of presenters (the shorter the presentation, the fewer the presenters). If a presentation takes over an hour, having more than one presenter can add variety and reinforce the impression that the work has been done by a team.

For a team presentation to really click, each person should have his or her own visual aids and handouts organized ahead of time. Everyone should also be aware of body language. A blank stare, a bouncing foot, or a glance at your watch can detract from your colleague's time in the spotlight.

Controlling the Question-and-Answer Session

A Q&A session is typically led by the senior consultant, especially if the audience includes senior representatives from a client firm. But it is important to include the consultants who actually performed the work as well as the technical experts who are most knowledgeable about the details of the engagement. The goal is to give clients plenty of airtime to keep the conversation going. But the more open the exchange and the more diverse the audience, the greater the risk of losing control of the Q&A session. To keep the exchange productive, the presenting team must be prepared to manage disruptive responses from the audience.

The Naysayer. The best defense against the person who will never be convinced is a good offense. Identify these individuals early in the game. Concentrate on getting buy-in before a presentation. If you are not successful, look for peers (or a primary decision maker) to squelch the negative attitude.

The Long-Winded Team Member. Presenters frequently get carried away with their own answers. If you see that the client has the answer, it is wise to interrupt a team member and redirect the discussion. The best plan is to agree ahead of time to monitor one another and invite interruptions from teammates.

The Complicated Questioner. If an audience member raises a long or complicated question, break the question into parts by writing the parts on a flipchart; then handle one part at a time. If the question seems off base, restate it with your own twist. Some questions do bear repeating. But do not routinely repeat if it is clear that everyone has heard a question; that risks annoying the audience. (Of course, always repeat a question if the room is large and you are the only person with a microphone.)

The Out-of-Sync Questioner. If a question truly disrupts the flow and you plan to cover it later, ask the questioner to hold it. But if the client wants an answer on the spot, you need to respond. A good forecast at the beginning of the presentation can reduce out-of-sync questions by letting listeners know what you will cover and in what order.

The Challenger. When someone challenges your data or analysis, the temptation is to become defensive. To avoid that negative response, try asking the challenger to fill in his or her version. The dispute may simply arise from a misunderstanding—or you may learn something new that will contribute to the project.

Conclusion: Tips from Practitioners

Experienced practitioners stress the importance of allowing plenty of time to prepare client presentations and developing the ability to deliver with confidence. Consultants with successful track records offer the following advice:

- Assess yourself—get expert help through videotaping and coaching.
- Model the masters.
- Build in reviews for feedback on presentations.
- Get up to bat.
- Create opportunities to present.
- Start small.
- Practice, practice, practice.

Effective presentations cannot take the place of top-quality work or guarantee success. But ineffective presentations can lose clients. Consultants who can describe their work, explain its impact, and show how to use it increase the likelihood of getting commitment and results—the real measure of success.

Part 5
Practice Management

18
Practice Business Plan

Larry E. Kuhlken
Kuhlken Associates, Inc.
Dallas, Texas

Leaders of professional services firms are entrepreneurs. The principals in a small firm and the local executives of large firms are empowered to make all decisions that affect the success or failure of their practices. These leaders of practices control demand, supply, and price. As is pointed out throughout this book, the successful consulting firms are those that are led by individuals that combine the management, marketing, and technical skills to meet this entrepreneurial challenge.

Long-range planning is a discipline that often eludes entrepreneurs. They want the freedom to take opportunity as it comes. Some view annual planning as useless in light of the uncertainty of our business prospects in the next 12 to 18 months. This is often ironic, since they are often experts in convincing their client executives that business planning beyond 30 to 60 day horizons is essential to successful management of a complex enterprise.

A plan puts a stake in the ground that lets you judge whether you are in the vicinity of your objectives. Whether you take action to keep the business on the original path is irrelevant. With a plan, you avoid spending precious energy worrying about how successful you are. The manager with a business plan can make an educated choice as to whether or how to deviate from the path. Paraphrasing the Cheshire Cat: If you know not where you are going, it matters not which path you take.

Business planning is performed in two complementary exercises. One is *strategic planning,* which plots a path for the business enterprise beyond one year. Three years is usually enough challenge for most professional services firms, though some define objectives for 5 and more years. The second planning exercise is *tactical planning* and is typically a one-year plan.

This chapter addresses both types of planning for a consulting services practice. Later chapters expand the planning process to address marketing and staff acquisition. This chapter also includes a practical example of strategic and tactical business planning for a six-person firm, including staff size and utilization assumptions, revenue segmentation strategy, cost, and expense. The chapter ends with a discussion of planning in a firm that uses contractors and planning when a practice is small.

Strategic Planning for Consulting Services

The market for professional services is very broad, as are the skills of its professional people. Each successful management consulting practice has established a position in this broad marketplace. A practice cannot take on any assignment with any client. Each practice has its strengths, and a firm protects its market share with a long-range strategic plan.

Growing the Practice

Most firms intend to grow and must make conscious decisions about where to focus growth. Chapter 19 provides some excellent examples of directions a management consulting firm can take to expand its market. In developing a strategic plan, a firm needs to select the paths it will take to grow: more offices; same services to a wider market; and/or new services with the same staff.

Expanding by Adding Offices.   A firm that performs a few services very well can grow by acquiring and training staff in new locations to serve comparable clients in that geography. The strength of such a firm is the consulting methods it employs and its ability to instill the disciplines of these methods in new staff. When the methods are applicable to clients nationally (or internationally), adding offices can be a significant strategic growth opportunity.

Choosing growth by locations means availability of capital, which often must be funded by strong earnings. Price competition can substantially slow this type of growth. The firm that best implements growth by location is one that has exclusive methods that command high margin and has in place strong quality control to ensure satisfaction with each new client.

Extending a Service to a Wider Market. Sometimes a firm that specializes in a narrow client industry can create demand for similar services outside that client set. Accounting firms learned that analysis techniques for data flow in purchasing and accounts payable were applicable across many businesses and many business processes. Personnel firms that specialized in labor relations in smokestack industries found their expertise in great demand as governments became more unionized. Expansion by this strategy requires an identification of the proven methods, skills, and intellectual capability within one's staff that are transportable beyond their current application.

Extending services requires minimal investment. Some time must be taken from billing to think through the packaging and marketing needed for transportation of the techniques, causing a limited period of lost revenue. Typically, an extended services strategy need not be financed through high margins. References from a solid list of satisfied clients will usually win against stiff price competition.

Extending services requires a change to marketing. Past clients are good references but may not be the source of leads to new clients. The firm may need to actively develop alliances with other firms. These alliances are beneficial to both firms, when the clients of one are in need of the techniques and methods of the other. The practice might choose to make its presence known through a wider set of trade and industry organizations.

Expanding the Services Performed by Current Staff. Most firms have learned that good professionals are multifaceted and have used this intellectual capital to become providers of multiple services. Consultants who analyze can also teach. Analysts who define requirements can design and implement. Many firms now offer education and custom development in addition to traditional management consulting. Many firms that migrated to custom development have now extended their market to systems integration. Although the size of their staffs has increased dramatically, the cross section of experience and skills in the practice has remained much the same. Senior people are still management consultants and project leaders, and junior people are analysts and technicians.

Firms that have implemented this strategy have seen substantial growth. They have also taken on significant risk, and many have fallen by the wayside. The business management of a multiservice business is very different compared to one that offers a single service, even in multiple locations. Major changes in business control and administration are essential for success.*

Maintaining Status Quo

Obviously, one strategy is to not grow and to maintain one's current business. This requires no less thought than the growth strategies. Do you need to increase profits, and where can you increase price or lower cost? How will you meet increased competition and a threat of lower margins? How will you keep your people challenged?

Very often a status quo strategy contains elements of a growth strategy, in order to provide contingency against the unknown. Improving services, expanding the credentials of the staff, finding new clients, and increasing quality are all strategic actions that will influence tactical plans. These need the same level of commitment and should be addressed with the same level of discipline.

Documenting a Strategy

Choosing a particular strategy among the choices above is fairly simple. Deciding on the tactical plans that follow is the hard part. The process will be iterative, since the tactical planning process may discourage an aggressive strategy (and just as likely encourage a conservative strategy). The strategic plan document should be brief and concise. It rarely is more than 2 or 3 pages and often is in the form of a briefing that communicates its contents to others. The following is a suggested outline for a strategy document:

- A description of the current practice, including a list of its services, an assessment of its professionals, a characterization of its clients, and a statement of its strengths and weaknesses

- A list of the needs and factors that will cause change over the strategic period

- A list of the changes that should be made to the business and when these changes should occur

- A forecast of the revenue and profit to be expected from the business in each year of the strategic period—separate forecasts should be made for each location and each separate line of service

- A list of the risks anticipated and the tactical steps to manage each.

*Larry E. Kuhlken, *Expanding Professional Services, a Manager's Guide to a Diversified Business,* Business One Irwin, Homewood, Ill., 1992, pp. 11–12.

The strategic plan addresses simple, overall questions about the direction of the business. Does it grow? Does it become more profitable? Does it expand? Can it meet the challenges of its changing personnel, client, competitive, and economic environment? The strategic plan is a starting point for each tactical plan that follows. It provides the means to integrate those further plans that define how to implement its overall objectives.

Tactical Planning for Professional Services

A professional services practice needs three tactical plans: business plan, marketing plan, and a staff selection and development plan. The remainder of this chapter focuses on a process to prepare an annual business plan; marketing and staff development plans are addressed in later chapters. Each describes the immediate implementation of the business strategy. Specifically, the business plan establishes the assumptions for staff utilization, effective billing rates, income segmentation, costs, and expenses to meet strategic revenue and profit targets.

An aggressive strategy of new locations, extended services, and expanded service offerings requires disciplined tactical planning. An action to expand services is a major project, similar in character to a client engagement. In this engagement, though, the firm is the end user. Not surprising, the plans for these projects require the same skill and discipline as those described in the project management sections of this handbook.

Practice business planning is an iterative process. A business plan for maintaining status quo requires at least two iterations. A tactical plan that satisfies an aggressive strategic plan will require at least three iterations and likely many more before all trade-offs between expansion and profitability have been reconciled. The minimum set of plans are described as follows.

1. *Business-as-usual plan.* The business-as-usual plan is a base business plan that continues current staffing, traditional utilization, and the current trends in cost and expense structure. The purpose is to establish the revenue and profit that can be generated by maintaining the current business assumptions. Typically the business-as-usual plan anticipates attrition and compensates with the acquisition of new staff. The business-as-usual plan accommodates expected or desired shifts in client demand and distributes revenue accordingly. This base plan should include the replacement of staff who are not meeting performance objectives or will not meet the challenges of shifting client needs.

The primary utility of the business-as-usual plan is to lay a base for further plan iterations. The plan allows the overall effect of shifts in the underlying cost and expense structure to be analyzed without the distortions that are introduced by changes in staff levels, rate assumptions, and more optimistic utilization. This first plan iteration provides a view of the profits to be expected from maintaining the status quo. The business-as-usual plan is a fallback, if early-year performance against more aggressive plans does not materialize.

2. *Profit-optimized plan.*   The next iteration beyond a base plan is to make those adjustments in rate and utilization assumptions that compensate for the expected cost and expense structural differences in the new year. The resulting revenue and profit volumes may not meet the strategic objectives, but the profit-optimized plan shows the best that can be done with current resources. However, this iteration demonstrates the most profitable shift toward the objectives of the strategic plan and is a fallback plan if the resources needed to implement the strategy are not available. Often, this is the final plan iteration, where the status quo is to be maintained, but corrections for cost and expense problems are to be made to maximize profits.

3. *Strategy-optimized plan.*   The last iteration is a plan that balances growth, market direction, and financial strategies. It accommodates significant revenue and people growth. Strategy-optimized planning models different alternatives to supply labor and nonlabor resources against changing demand in order to make the best financial choice. The number of alternatives to achieving growth can be mind-boggling for firms that are product installers or systems integrators or use contractors to supplement their staff. The choices for a management consulting practice that makes all of its revenue from people are much fewer, and a third plan iteration is usually sufficient.

The tactical planning process for professional services has three distinct steps. There is a *staffing plan* that defines staff mix, expected billing, and utilization rates and that computes hours and labor-generated revenue. There is a *revenue segmentation plan* that defines how to assign the hours billed and computes the distribution of labor revenue by each strategic market. Finally, there is a *profit plan* that combines labor- and nonlabor-generated revenue into an income summary, defines the cost and expense structure of the supporting business, and computes profit.

The three parts of the tactical plan are most easily developed on a series of linked spreadsheets. Once the business-as-usual plan sections are in place on their separate spreadsheets, a change to rate and utilization assumptions for the staffing part of a profit optimization plan would propagate directly through to the revenue segmentation step and on to the profit computation step. This greatly simplifies and shortens the overall time needed to generate profit- and strategy-optimized plans.

Business-as-Usual: The Starting Point

The plan example that follows describes a firm that practices in a single location. It offers a mature management consulting service to enterprises that manage warehouses. It has been offering education services to retailers and wholesalers in warehouse management and expects to expand these offerings to manufacturers and government agencies that have similar facilities. The firm has begun to offer its expertise in distribution logistics as additional consulting to the general management of their existing clients. Consultancy at the general management level is allowing the partners to charge higher effective rates for their time.

Demand for warehouse process consulting is very steady, and the backlog of hours yet to be billed is healthy. Planning for the coming year should consider higher utilization for these consultants. The education business represents an opportunity to raise prices and to increase the resulting effective billing rates for the senior people who teach these classes.

The strategy plan calls for maintaining status quo in warehouse process consulting, growing education services by 10 percent, and a specific revenue target of $305,000 for the new general consulting services (a growth of 22 percent). In addition, the partners want to increase their variable compensation above what they were able to pay themselves in the previous year.

Implementing a strategic plan that designates specific revenue targets for warehouse process consulting, general management consulting, and education services means tactically separating their contributions to revenue. The tactical planning process should first examine how next year's cost and expense structure changes will affect profitability, then determine how much more revenue and profit (and corresponding variable compensation) can be generated by higher utilization and higher rates, and lastly look at alternatives to increase the staff, if the profit-optimized plan iteration falls short of strategic targets.

Staffing Plan: Defining Rates and Utilization

The consulting firm is made up of two partners and a staff of five. One partner is strong in marketing, and the other is strong in warehouse management and engagement coordination. The latter partner bills more hours, but the marketing partner brings in more new clients. For planning purposes, one half of the marketing partner is charged to expense, and the remainder of the two achieve 50 percent utilization at an average of $204 per hour against their corresponding cost.

The current staff contains two very senior people, who bill at an average $170 per hour and 70 percent utilization, two experienced consultants, who bill at an average $125 per hour and 75 percent utilization, and a junior person, who bills at an average $110 per hour and 88 percent utilization. Utilization is the hours billed on hourly engagements plus the hours assigned on fixed-price engagements out of a 2080-hour year. Average rates are computed as a combination of two amounts: revenue billed per hour by the hours that were billable and the revenue distribution for each person on fixed-priced engagements divided by the hours they were assigned to those engagements. Methods for distributing revenue in fixed-price engagements can be found in *Expanding Professional Services.**

Figure 18-1 is a business-as-usual staffing plan for this office of seven. The plan is a month-by-month estimate of direct personnel, expected utilization, and expected average revenue per hour. (The figure shows detail for the first 3 months and summary for the next 3 quarters and for the year.) The plan spreadsheet computes the billable hours and billed labor revenue for each of the personnel groups, for all nonmanagers, and for all employees (managers and nonmanagers). Four of the months contain 5 weeks, and the number of hours is higher accordingly.

The overall utilization is 69 percent with 75 percent for the nonmanaging consultants. Notice that the two managing partners are counted as $1\frac{1}{2}$ head count. The remaining $\frac{1}{2}$ head count is later carried as a marketing expense. Such planning options are an optional refinement for small firms. Notice that the shift to general management consulting has increased and continues to increase the effective billing rate for the partners. As a result, their revenue contribution has increased, even in the business-as-usual plan.

The overall revenue rate for the firm is $146 per hour ($134 per hour for consultants), leading to a business-as-usual labor revenue outlook of $1,424,000. Later in the planning process, nonlabor revenue such as travel expense recovery is added to labor-generated revenue to make up total income. The previous year was a status quo period as evidenced by the year-to-year production of hours remaining constant at 9721.

---

*Larry E. Kuhlken, *Expanding Professional Services, a Manager's Guide to a Diversified Business*, Business One Irwin, Homewood, Ill., 1992, pp. 255–260.

Clearly, this plan does not achieve the growth as prescribed by the strategy. It does, however, provide an excellent planning base. It establishes the seasonal variations that can be expected in utilization:

Quarter 1. Nominal utilization with kickoff and planning activities in January, followed by growing utilization in the next 2 months.

Quarter 2. Higher utilization through mid-June, with some interference from early-year education.

Quarter 3. Significantly lower utilization due to vacations, with a rapid improvement in September.

Quarter 4. Very high utilization through the third week of December.

Another element of the base plan is the estimated loss of one junior consultant and the replacement of that individual with a college hire. This is a conservative plan assumption based on this firm's history. The plan shows the rate dilution to be expected by the addition of the new hire in June. The average rate decreases $3 per hour in the second quarter, $10 per hour in the third quarter, and $5 per hour in the fourth quarter over its high in the first quarter.

Even though this business-as-usual plan contains an increase in revenue from an equivalent staff against that of the previous year, it may not produce the same profit. The underlying cost and expense base for the new year must yet be examined, particularly in terms of a strategic objective to improve variable compensation payout. The next step in the planning process is to distribute the revenue forecast into market categories, in preparation for computing profit.

Revenue Distribution Plan: Segment Labor Revenue Estimates

Revenue segmentation planning distributes the labor revenue generated by each group of direct personnel into three service lines. The step first assesses whether strategic market objectives can be achieved. Later, the differing travel expenses and corresponding recovery can be forecasted for each type of service.

Figure 18-2 is a labor distribution spreadsheet for the business-as-usual plan. Each month and quarter corresponds to the months and quarters of the staffing plan (including a summary for each of the previous and coming years). The three lines of service are shown with the amount of billable time to be devoted by each group of personnel to each line. You can see that our practice used three-fourths of its staff time last year in its mainstream business of warehouse process consulting, 21 percent on education and only 2 percent on the new general management

Month / Weeks	Prev Year	Jan 1-4	Feb 5-8	Mar 9-13	Qtr 1 1-13	Qtr 2 14-26	Qtr 3 27-39	Qtr 4 40-52	Year 1-52
Trainee									
End Hcount	0	0	0	0	0	1	1	0	0
Added Hcount	0	0	0	0	0	1	0	-1	0
Ave Hcount	0.4	0.0	0.0	0.0	0.0	0.3	1.0	0.3	0.4
Ave Util	62.7%	65.0%	65.0%	65.0%	0.0%	41.5%	68.1%	73.8%	63.9%
Ave Rate	65	65	65	65	65	65	65	65	65
Hours	554.0	0.0	0.0	0.0	0.0	72.0	354.0	128.0	554.0
Revenue($000)	36	0	0	0	0	5	23	8	36
Associate									
End Hcount	1	1	1	1	1	1	0	1	1
Added Hcount	0	0	0	0	0	0	-1	1	0
Ave Hcount	0.8	1.0	1.0	1.0	1.0	1.0	0.7	0.7	0.8
Ave Util	87.5%	80.0%	90.0%	90.0%	86.9%	95.0%	72.7%	91.7%	87.5%
Ave Rate	110	110	110	110	110	110	110	110	110
Hours	1,516.0	128.0	144.0	180.0	452.0	494.0	252.0	318.0	1,516.0
Revenue($000)	167	14	16	20	50	54	28	35	167
Consultant									
End Hcount	2	2	2	2	2	2	2	2	2
Added Hcount	1	0	0	0	0	0	2	0	0
Ave Hcount	2.0	2.0	2.0	2.0	2.0	2.0	2.0	2.0	2.0
Ave Util	75.6%	70.0%	75.0%	75.0%	73.5%	80.4%	68.1%	80.4%	75.6%
Ave Rate	125	125	125	125	125	125	125	125	125
Hours	3,144.0	224.0	240.0	300.0	764.0	836.0	708.0	836.0	3,144.0
Revenue($000)	393	28	30	38	96	105	89	105	393
Senior									
End Hcount	2	2	2	2	2	2	2	2	2
Added Hcount	0	0	0	0	0	0	0	0	0
Ave Hcount	2.0	2.0	2.0	2.0	2.0	2.0	2.0	2.0	2.0
Ave Util	70.5%	65.0%	70.0%	70.0%	68.5%	71.9%	64.6%	76.9%	70.5%
Ave Rate	170	170	170	170	170	170	170	170	170
Hours	2,932.0	208.0	224.0	280.0	712.0	748.0	672.0	800.0	2,932.0
Revenue($000)	498	35	38	48	121	127	114	136	498

CONSULTANTS

End Hcount	5	5	5	5	5	6	5	5	5
Added Hcount	1	0	0	0	0	1	-1	0	0
Ave Hcount	5	5	5	5	5	5	6	5	5
Ave Util	74.5%	70.0%	76.0%	76.0%	74.2%	77.5%	67.4%	80.1%	74.6%
Ave Rate	134	138	138	138	138	135	128	136	134
Hours	8,146.0	560.0	608.0	760.0	1,928.0	2,150.0	1,986.0	2,082.0	8,146.0
Revenue($000)	1094	77	84	105	266	291	253	284	1094

MANAGEMENT

End Hcount	1.5	1.5	1.5	1.5	1.5	1.5	1.5	1.5	1.5
Added Hcount	0	0	0	0	0	0	0	0	0
Ave Hcount	1.5	1.5	1.5	1.5	1.5	1.5	1.5	1.5	1.5
Ave Util	50.5%	45.0%	50.0%	50.0%	48.5%	51.9%	44.6%	56.9%	50.5%
Ave Rate	204	205	207	209	207	210	210	210	209
Hours	1,575.0	108.0	120.0	150.0	378.0	405.0	348.0	444.0	1,575.0
Revenue($000)	321	22	25	31	78	85	73	93	330

EMPLOYEE TOTALS

End Hcount	7	7	7	7	7	8	7	7	7
Added Hcount	1	0	0	0	0	1	-1	0	0
Ave Hcount	6.8	6.5	6.5	6.5	6.5	6.8	7.2	6.5	6.8
Ave Util	69.2%	64.2%	70.0%	70.0%	68.2%	71.9%	62.6%	74.7%	69.2%
Ave Rate	146	149	149	150	149	147	140	149	146
Hours	9,721	668	728	910	2,306	2,555	2,334	2,526	9,721
Revenue($000)	1,415	100	109	136	345	376	327	377	1,424

Figure 18-1 Business-as-usual staffing plan.

Month	Prev Year	Jan 1-4	Feb 5-8	Mar 9-13	Qtr 1 1-13	Qtr 2 14-26	Qtr 3 27-39	Oct 40-43	Nov 44-48	Dec 49-52	Qtr 4 40-52	Year 1-52
Warehouse Process Consulting												
Trainee	36.0	0.0	0.0	0.0	0.0	4.7	23.0	8.3	0.0	0.0	8.3	36.0
%	100.00%	100.00%	100.00%	100.00%				100.00%	100.00%	100.00%		
Associate	167.0	14.1	15.8	19.8	49.7	54.3	27.7	0.0	20.9	14.1	35.0	166.8
%	100.00%	100.00%	100.00%	100.00%				100.00%	100.00%	100.00%		
Consultant	314.4	22.4	24.0	30.0	76.4	67.9	57.5	22.1	27.6	18.2	67.9	269.8
%	80.00%	80.00%	80.00%	80.00%				65.00%	65.00%	65.00%		
Senior	333.7	14.9	16.0	20.0	50.8	39.0	34.3	12.6	15.2	10.7	38.5	162.6
%	67.00%	42.00%	42.00%	42.00%				29.00%	28.00%	28.00%		
CONSULTANTS	851.1	51.3	55.8	69.8	177.0	165.9	142.5	43.0	63.8	42.9	149.7	635.1
%	77.79%	66.29%	66.53%	66.53%				50.14%	54.12%	53.57%		
MANAGEMENT	240.8	15.6	16.1	18.7	50.4	38.2	32.9	13.6	17.0	11.3	42.0	163.5
%	75.00%	70.00%	65.00%	60.00%				45.00%	45.00%	45.00%		
TOTAL	1,091.8	66.9	72.0	88.5	227.4	204.1	175.4	56.6	80.8	54.3	191.7	798.6
Education												
Trainee	0.0	0.0	0.0	0.0	0.0	0.0	0.0	0.0	0.0	0.0	0.0	0.0
%	0.00%	0.00%	0.00%	0.00%				0.00%	0.00%	0.00%		
Associate	0.0	0.0	0.0	0.0	0.0	0.0	0.0	0.0	0.0	0.0	0.0	0.0
%	0.00%	0.00%	0.00%	0.00%				0.00%	0.00%	0.00%		
Consultant	78.6	5.6	6.0	7.5	19.1	26.1	22.1	8.5	10.6	7.0	26.1	93.5
%	20.00%	20.00%	20.00%	20.00%				25.00%	25.00%	25.00%		
Senior	164.3	11.7	12.6	15.7	39.9	45.0	41.1	16.1	20.7	14.5	51.2	177.3
%	33.00%	33.00%	33.00%	33.00%				37.00%	38.00%	38.00%		
CONSULTANTS	242.9	17.3	18.6	23.2	59.0	71.1	63.3	24.6	31.3	21.5	77.4	270.8
%	22.21%	22.30%	22.12%	22.12%				28.66%	26.57%	26.78%		
MANAGEMENT	48.2	3.3	3.7	4.7	11.7	12.7	11.0	4.5	5.7	3.8	14.0	49.4
%	15.00%	15.00%	15.00%	15.00%				15.00%	15.00%	15.00%		
TOTAL	291.1	20.6	22.3	27.9	70.8	83.8	74.2	29.1	37.0	25.3	91.4	320.2

General Management Consulting

Trainee	0.0	0.0	0.0	0.0	0.0	0.0	0.0	0.0	0.0	0.0	0.0	0.0
%	0.00%	0.00%	0.00%	0.00%				0.00%	0.00%	0.00%		
Associate	0.0	0.0	0.0	0.0	0.0	0.0	0.0	0.0	0.0	0.0	0.0	0.0
%	0.00%	0.00%	0.00%	0.00%				0.00%	0.00%	0.00%		
Consultant	0.0	0.0	0.0	0.0	10.5	10.5	8.9	3.4	4.3	2.8	10.5	29.8
%	0.00%	0.00%	0.00%	0.00%				10.00%	10.00%	10.00%		
Senior	0.0	8.8	9.5	11.9	30.3	43.2	38.8	14.8	18.5	12.9	46.2	158.6
%	0.00%	25.00%	25.00%	25.00%				34.00%	34.00%	34.00%		
CONSULTANTS	0.0	8.8	9.5	11.9	30.3	53.7	47.7	18.2	22.7	15.7	56.7	188.3
%	0.00%	11.42%	11.34%	11.34%				21.20%	19.31%	19.64%		
MANAGEMENT	32.1	3.3	5.0	7.8	16.1	34.0	29.2	12.1	15.1	10.1	37.3	116.6
%	10.00%	15.00%	20.00%	25.00%				40.00%	40.00%	40.00%		
TOTAL	32.1	12.2	14.5	19.7	46.4	87.7	76.9	30.3	37.9	25.8	94.0	304.9
Total	1,415.0	99.7	108.8	136.1	344.5	375.6	326.6	116.1	155.6	105.4	377.0	1,423.7

Figure 18-2 Business-as-usual labor distribution.

consulting. Notice that 10 percent of last year's management time was on the new business.

The revenue distribution plan is shown with detail for both the first and last quarters. This illustrates an implementation of the strategy to shift resources to the new line of service and to grow education services. The base plan has been constructed to generate $305,000 in general management consulting revenue and to grow education by 10 percent. This is accomplished by shifting senior people away from warehouse process consulting. As a result, our mainline revenue from warehouse process consulting drops from $1,092,000 to $799,000. This is very undesirable and needs to be corrected in subsequent iterations of the plan. The final step in business-as-usual planning, though, is to test the profitability of the base plan.

Profit Plan: Testing Income against Cost and Expense

The first step in building the income and expense plan that corresponds to base staffing and revenue segmentation plans is to add nonlabor revenue to the income assumptions. Nonlabor revenue comes from three generic sources:

1. *Travel expenses recovered from clients.* Much of the travel expense incurred by the practice will be billed to clients. The expense may be billed separately, with or without its own markup, or it may be a portion of the hourly rate or fixed price for labor charges. In any event, the expense represents a separate income stream with its own costs and profitability considerations. Each line of service has its own travel characteristics. Figure 18-3 is an income plan for this practice. Travel is moderate for warehouse process consulting ($0.25 for every dollar of labor revenue), heavy for education (more than twice the ratio for warehouse consulting), and minor for general consulting, since the practice intends to concentrate on local clients during the first full year of offering this service. The shift to education has increased travel recovery revenue from $454,000 to $475,000.

2. *Product revenue.* A practice may receive income for products and materials that it or another unit in the firm develops. These are ancillary to the professional services business and usually are documents and software that complement the value of the people. The firm may recover their entire development, as well as implementation cost each year, or it may capitalize a portion of the development. In any event, the firm uses an internal transfer cost as a charge against revenue for these products credited to the labor services business. The example practice sells education materials ancillary to performing education services. The plan pro-

	Month Weeks	Prev Year	Jan 1-4	Feb 5-8	Mar 9-13	Qtr 1 1-13	Qtr 2 14-26	Qtr 3 27-39	Qtr 4 40-52	Year 1-52
Warehouse Proc Cons	Consultants	851.1	51.3	55.8	69.8	177.0	165.9	142.5	149.7	635
	Management	240.8	15.6	16.1	18.7	50.4	38.2	32.9	42.0	163
	Travel(Nonlabor)	273.0	16.7	18.0	22.1	56.8	51.0	43.9	47.9	200
	Product(Nonlabor)	0.0	0.0	0.0	0.0	0.0	0.0	0.0	0.0	0
	TOTAL	1,364.8	83.6	90.0	110.6	284.2	255.2	219.3	239.6	998
Education	Consultants	242.9	17.3	18.6	23.2	59.0	71.1	63.3	77.4	271
	Management	48.2	3.3	3.7	4.7	11.7	12.7	11.0	14.0	49
	Travel(Nonlabor)	174.7	12.4	13.4	16.7	42.5	50.3	44.5	54.8	192
	Product(Nonlabor)	120.0	10.0	10.0	11.0	31.0	33.0	33.0	35.0	132
	TOTAL	585.7	43.0	45.7	55.6	144.3	167.1	151.7	181.2	644
Gen'l Mgmt Consulting	Consultants	0.0	8.8	9.5	11.9	30.3	53.7	47.7	56.7	188
	Management	32.1	3.3	5.0	7.8	16.1	34.0	29.2	37.3	117
	Travel(Nonlabor)	6.4	2.4	2.9	3.9	9.3	17.5	25.4	31.0	83
	Product(Nonlabor)	0.0	0.0	0.0	0.0	0.0	0.0	0.0	0.0	0
	TOTAL	38.5	14.6	17.4	23.6	55.6	105.2	102.3	125.0	388
TOTAL INCOME	Labor	1,415.0	99.7	108.8	136.1	344.5	375.6	326.6	377.0	1,424
	Nonlabor	574.0	41.5	44.3	53.8	139.6	151.9	146.8	168.8	607
	TOTAL	1,989.0	141.2	153.0	189.9	484.1	527.5	473.3	545.8	2,031
REVENUE RATES										
Per month & year	CONSULTANTS	208.1	15.5	16.8	21.0	53.3	54.5	44.7	56.8	208.4
	ALL EMPLOYEES	209.4	15.3	16.7	20.9	53.0	55.0	45.6	58.0	211
Per hour (average)	CONSULTANTS	134.30	138.29	138.03	138.03	138.10	135.20	127.63	136.31	134.32
	ALL EMPLOYEES	145.56	149.23	149.40	149.56	149.41	147.01	139.91	149.26	146.46

Figure 18-3 Business-as-usual profit plan.

jects a 10 percent growth in the materials business, commensurate with the growth in labor revenues from education.

3. *Vendor product and services revenue.* Many firms buy services and OEM products that are integrated into their overall service offerings. These may be products that require implementation services or other vendor activities that make up a systems integration service. The example practice does not engage with other firms for this purpose.

Nonlabor revenue will add $30,000 to income for an overall revenue growth of 2 percent. Revenue productivity has improved slightly, as evidenced by the annual and hourly revenue rates. If the previous year had been one of staffing changes, revenue productivity computations in the business-as-usual plan would show whether the current staff could achieve a revenue productivity improvement next year over prior years.

Proceeding to Figure 18-4, the next step is to build the cost structure for the base plan. The major benefit from a business-as-usual plan is the platform it provides to analyze the effect of fundamental shifts in the cost and expense structure, before these are obscured by changes in staffing levels, utilization assumptions, or pricing.

Costs are first separated between labor and nonlabor, in order to measure the relative gross profit of each. Within labor cost are the two components of compensation and other direct costs. Within nonlabor cost are the costs of each nonlabor revenue component before its markup and an additional cost for any special allocations of indirect expense that are necessary for the direct distribution of nonlabor components.

Direct labor cost is expected to increase during the coming year. Its components are as follows:

Salaries. Salaries will increase only slightly. Attrition of one person and the hiring of a replacement almost compensates for planned merit and promotional increases. Annual salaries will average in a range of $45,000 to $90,000 for nonmanagers and $120,000 for partners.

Benefits. Benefits and payroll taxes will increase by $900 per employee for the year to $15,000. (All employees in the firm receive the same benefit package.)

Commissions/bonuses. The major increase in cost comes from increasing the variable compensation for the partners. This accounts for a 6.5 percent increase in variable compensation cost. Consultants are paid variable compensation of 10 percent to 25 percent of their salary. The new variable compensation for partners will be 50 percent of salary. For planning purposes, the compensation is averaged over the entire year, whereas, in fact, actual payment is quarterly and skewed toward the final quarters of the year.

	Month Weeks	Prev Year	Jan 1-4	Feb 5-8	Mar 9-13	Qtr 1 1-13	Qtr 2 14-26	Qtr 3 27-39	Qtr 4 40-52	Year 1-52
DIRECT COMP	Salaries	575.0	47.5	47.5	47.5	142.5	146.3	149.2	141.4	579
	Benefits	93.0	8.1	8.1	8.1	24.4	25.6	26.9	24.4	101
	Commissions	153.5	13.6	13.6	13.6	40.9	40.9	40.4	40.4	163
	Other Comp	20.0	0.0	0.0	5.0	5.0	5.0	5.0	5.0	20
DIRECT COMP	TOTAL	841.5	69.3	69.3	74.3	212.8	217.8	221.5	211.2	863
OTHER DIRECT COST:	Travel/Commute	15.0	0.7	1.3	1.3	3.3	5.0	2.8	5.2	16
	Education/Fees	68.0	6.0	6.0	6.0	17.9	18.8	19.7	17.9	74
	Recruiting	15.0	0.0	0.0	0.0	0.0	0.0	15.0	0.0	15
	Facilities	36.0	2.5	2.5	3.2	8.2	8.4	9.2	10.2	36
OTHER DIRECT COST:TOTAL		134.0	9.2	9.8	10.4	29.4	32.2	46.7	33.2	142
DIRECT LABOR	TOTAL	975.5	78.4	79.1	84.7	242.1	250.0	268.2	244.4	1,005
DIRECT TRAVEL	TOTAL	454.0	30.9	33.6	42.0	106.5	116.5	111.5	131.1	466
TRANSFER COST	TOTAL	91.2	7.6	7.6	8.4	23.6	25.1	25.1	26.6	100
NON-LABOR APPORTI	TOTAL	47.7	3.9	3.9	4.0	11.9	11.9	13.1	12.6	50
DIRECT NON-LABOR	TOTAL	593.0	42.4	45.1	54.3	141.9	153.5	149.7	170.3	615
TOTAL DIRECT COST		1,568.5	120.8	124.2	139.0	384.0	403.5	417.9	414.7	1,620
GROSS PROFIT	Margin	420.6	20.4	28.8	50.9	100.1	124.0	55.4	131.1	411
	Labor Gross	21%	14%	19%	27%	21%	24%	12%	24%	20%
	Labor Margin	439.5	21.3	29.7	51.4	102.4	125.6	58.4	132.7	419
	Nonlabor Gross	31%	21%	27%	38%	30%	33%	18%	35%	29%
	Nonlabor Gross	-18.9	-0.9	-0.9	-0.5	-2.3	-1.7	-2.9	-1.6	-8
	Nonlabor Margin	-3%	-2%	-2%	-1%	-2%	-1%	-2%	-1%	-1%
COST RATES										
Per month & year	CONSULTANTS	126.3	10.4	10.5	11.6	32.4	31.8	32.7	32.7	130
	ALL EMPLOYEES	144.3	12.1	12.2	13.0	37.2	36.6	37.4	37.6	149
Per hour (average)	CONSULTANTS	81.53	92.70	86.21	76.17	84.14	78.96	93.30	78.57	83.56
	ALL EMPLOYEES	100.35	117.37	108.59	93.04	105.00	97.83	114.91	96.75	103.35

Figure 18-4 Business-as-usual cost structure.

Other compensation.   Other compensation includes perks for the senior staff and surprise recognition to the younger staff. It will remain at the same amount.

Travel and commute.   Nonrecoverable travel and commutation costs (exclusive of those for education, relocation, and marketing) were an average of $205 per month per employee in the previous year and are expected to increase only slightly in the new year.

Education and conferences.   Cost of educational materials, classes, conference fees, and associated travel will increase from $10,100 to $11,000 per employee.

Recruiting.   The cost of hiring one person is $15,000 and is primarily the cost of that person's relocation.

Facilities.   In order to compare gross profit for labor and nonlabor revenue components and to more accurately assess changes in cost productivity for people resources, the plan allocates a portion of the cost of facilities and administration services to the cost of labor. This is a variable cost and includes those expenses that realistically will increase or decrease as staffing levels change. It assumes that office space can be added or subtracted from overall rental area and the administrative resources are not fixed. For those firms that are small, reside in fixed-space facilities, or do not have income from products or systems integration, the allocation of facilities cost is likely more trouble than it is worth. As seen later, no changes in administrative levels or rents are expected.

Other direct costs are:

Direct travel cost.   Actual direct travel expense is marked up by 2 percent. It, of course, grows at the same rate as its corresponding revenue.

Transfer cost of products sold.   The cost of products may include any number of development, distribution, and investment expenses. In this example, the cost is that of reproduction and packaging, which is increased by 32 percent when sold.

Nonlabor-apportioned cost.   This includes administrative support, facilities, and distribution costs that are specific to education material–generated revenue. The apportionment is for administrative support, shipping charges, and a library for the materials. Notice that the cost of this support is causing nonlabor income to generate a negative gross profit (the increase in nonlabor component revenue has improved profitability by 2 percent).

Overall gross margin is 20 percent, with labor contributing 29 percent. This is more than a 2 percent decrease against the previous year and is reflected in the corresponding decrease in annual and hourly cost productivity rates. The two major cost components contributing to gross profit dilution are increases in benefits and variable compensation. The increase in nonlabor gross margin almost, but not quite, compensates for decreased labor margin.

Figure 18-5 contains the indirect expense plan and expected net profit. The indirect expense is divided into selling, administration, and other indirect expenses. The main components of selling are:

Marketing compensation (salary, benefits, commissions and bonuses, other compensation, recruiting, education, and facilities/support).   These are equivalent to those described under direct compensation, but for any individuals dedicated to marketing. Marketing resource is drawn from the professional resources of the practice and are planned and tracked separately when gross profit analysis between lines of service and revenue generation components is useful or when month-to-month cost productivity analysis of direct people resources is important. In the example, one-half of a partner is expensed to marketing expense (the other half was direct cost). The marketing compensation contains comparable increases in benefit and variable compensation expense.

Marketing travel expense.   The nonrecoverable travel and commutation expense for any of the people in the practice is separated from the travel costs described earlier. Marketing is a variable activity, and its expenses are discretionary. The expenses incurred by consultants for marketing support activities are proportional to their time spent in selling, but their other travel expenses are related to the locations of their homes and the clients they serve. In the example, the average monthly expense for consultants and managers while participating in marketing in the previous year was $20 and $200, respectively. These are used as planning assumptions for the new year.

Marketing materials and promotion.   These are materials and advertising expense to support the marketing program. They are expected to remain the same for the new year.

Lead source compensation.   Firms may have alliance agreements that compensate other firms and product vendors for referrals. The compensation can be a variety of fee computations, paid in a plethora of computations at engagement initiation and/or during performance. In this example, the firm expects to pay finders fees to lead sources amounting to approximately 1 percent of revenue billed.

Revenue will increase by 2 percent in the business-as-usual plan. Selling expense will increase by 2 percent. Again, the primary difference is in benefits and variable compensation.

Month Weeks		Prev Year	Jan 1-4	Feb 5-8	Mar 9-13	Qtr 1 1-13	Qtr 2 14-26	Qtr 3 27-39	Qtr 4 40-52	Year 1-52
MARKETING COMP	Salary	60.0	5.0	5.0	5.0	15.0	15.0	15.0	15.0	60
	Benefits	6.9	0.6	0.6	0.6	1.9	1.9	1.9	1.9	8
	Commissions	27.0	2.5	2.5	2.5	7.5	7.5	7.5	7.5	30
	Other Comp	0.0	0.0	0.0	0.0	0.0	0.0	0.0	0.0	0
	Recruiting	0.0	0.0	0.0	0.0	0.0	0.0	0.0	0.0	0
	Education	1.3	0.1	0.1	0.1	0.3	0.3	0.3	0.3	1
	Facilities/Support	6.0	0.4	0.4	0.5	1.3	1.3	1.4	1.6	6
MARKETING COMP	TOTAL	101.1	8.6	8.6	8.7	26.0	26.0	26.1	26.2	104
MARKETING EXPENSE	Travel	6.0	0.5	0.5	0.5	1.5	1.5	1.5	1.5	6
	Materials	12.0	1.0	1.0	1.0	3.0	3.0	3.0	3.0	12
	Lead Sources	2.0	0.1	0.2	0.2	0.5	0.5	0.5	0.5	2
	Promo/Advert	20.0	0.0	0.0	0.0	0.0	10.0	10.0	0.0	20
MARKETING EXPENSE	TOTAL	40.0	1.6	1.7	1.7	5.0	15.0	15.0	5.0	40
SELLING	TOTAL	141.1	10.3	10.3	10.4	31.0	41.0	41.1	31.3	144
ADMIN COMP	Salary	54.0	4.5	4.5	4.5	13.5	13.5	14.4	14.4	56
	Benefits	20.6	1.9	1.9	1.9	5.6	5.6	5.6	5.6	23
	Commissions	0.0	0.0	0.0	0.0	0.0	0.0	0.0	0.0	0
	Other Comp	1.0	0.0	0.0	0.0	0.0	0.0	1.0	0.0	1
	Supplemental	4.5	0.0	0.0	0.0	0.0	1.5	3.0	0.0	4
	Recruiting	0.0	0.0	0.0	0.0	0.0	0.0	0.0	0.0	0
	Education	1.6	0.0	0.0	0.4	0.4	0.4	0.4	0.4	2
	Travel	1.2	0.1	0.1	0.1	0.3	0.3	0.3	0.3	1
ADMIN COMP	TOTAL	82.9	6.5	6.5	6.9	19.8	21.3	24.7	20.7	87
OFFICE SERVICES	Vendor Personnel	6.0	0.0	0.0	0.0	0.0	0.0	1.4	4.2	6
	Vendor Services	4.8	0.4	0.4	0.4	1.2	1.2	1.2	1.2	5
	Supplies	1.2	0.1	0.1	0.1	0.3	0.3	0.3	0.3	1
	Nonlabor Apportion	-0.6	-0.1	-0.1	-0.1	-0.2	-0.2	-0.2	-0.3	-1
OFFICE SERVICES	TOTAL	11.4	0.5	0.5	0.5	1.4	1.4	2.7	5.4	11

FACILITIES									
Rental/Occupancy	99.0	8.3	8.3	8.3	24.8	25.0	25.2	24.8	100
Services	14.0	1.2	1.2	1.2	3.6	3.6	3.6	3.6	14
Telecomm	4.5	0.4	0.4	0.4	1.1	1.2	1.3	1.1	5
Equipment/Furn	6.0	0.0	0.0	1.4	1.4	1.3	1.4	1.5	6
Direct Apportion	-36.0	-2.5	-2.5	-3.2	-8.2	-8.4	-9.2	-10.2	-36
Non-labor Apport	-21.0	-1.7	-1.7	-1.8	-5.1	-5.1	-5.2	-5.4	-21
Marketing Apport	-6.0	-0.4	-0.4	-0.5	-1.3	-1.3	-1.4	-1.6	-6
FACILITIES TOTAL	60.5	5.2	5.2	5.8	16.2	16.2	15.6	14.0	62
BUSINESS COMP SERV TOTAL	68.0	5.6	6.1	7.6	19.4	21.1	18.9	21.8	81
ADMINISTRATION TOTAL	222.8	17.8	18.2	20.7	56.8	60.0	62.0	62.0	241
OTHER INDIRECT									
Meetings	7.5	2.5	0.0	0.0	2.5	1.0	2.5	1.5	8
Regional Apportion	0.0	0.0	0.0	0.0	0.0	0.0	0.0	0.0	0
Miscellaneous	3.5	0.3	0.3	0.3	0.9	0.9	0.9	0.9	4
OTHER INDIRECT TOTAL	11.0	2.8	0.3	0.3	3.4	1.9	3.4	2.4	11
INDIRECT EXPENSE TOTAL	375.0	30.9	28.8	31.4	91.1	103.0	106.5	95.7	396
NET EARNINGS (NEBA)	45.6	-10.5	0.0	19.4	9.0	21.0	-51.0	35.4	14
Margin	2.3%	-7.4%	0.0%	10.2%	1.9%	4.0%	-10.8%	6.5%	0.7%
ALLOCATED EXPENSE TOTAL	45.6	3.8	3.8	3.8	11.4	11.4	11.4	11.4	46
NET EARNINGS (NEBT)	0.0	-14.3	-3.8	15.6	-2.4	9.6	-62.4	24.0	-31.3
Margin	0.0%	-10.1%	-2.5%	8.2%	-0.5%	1.8%	-13.2%	4.4%	-1.5%
EXPENSE RATES (NEBA)									
Per month & year	183.8	15.4	15.3	16.5	47.2	47.3	47.7	47.8	190
Per hour (average)	127.79	149.97	136.74	117.80	133.12	126.53	146.38	122.92	131.93

Figure 18-5 Business-as-usual indirect expenses and net earnings.

Administration expenses are the compensation to administrative people, supplies, services needed to run the office, facilities, furniture, equipment, and charges for computer services. The administrative staff for our practice is two permanent people, supplemented by a student supplemental in the summer and a part-time office temporary in the fall. The facility contains 200-square-foot offices for the two partners, 50-square-foot cubicles for consultants with an average of two per desk, an administrative area, the library, and a conference room. The firm is also charged for a share of building common area. Each desk has a computer workstation and the administrative area contains common equipment, including a printer, a copier, a fax machine, and filing space. Equipment and furniture expenses are depreciated capital expenditures.

Specific indirect administration expenses include:

Administration compensation (salaries, benefits, bonuses, other compensation, supplemental salaries, recruiting, education, and travel).   Compensation for administrative people is primarily salary, benefits, other compensation for overtime and awards, and some education. The average annual administrative salary is $27,000 growing to $28,000. Again benefits are growing, but other compensation, education, and travel are remaining constant. No recruiting is anticipated, and administrative personnel are not paid variable compensation.

Office services (temporary vendor personnel, vendor services for reproduction, etc., and supplies).   These are office expenses that are separate from people and the facility. These expenses are remaining constant in our example. Subtracted from office service expense is the apportioned cost to nonlabor revenue for the library operation, as discussed earlier.

Facilities (office space, building services for security, etc., telecommunication charges, and equipment and furniture depreciation).   These are the expenses to house the people of the office. Occupancy charges of $36 per foot plus $1200 per month for landlord services (security, cleaning, etc.) are expected to increase only slightly and no new additional facilities are needed for the base plan. Telephone was $470 per person in the previous year and is expected to increase to $480 in the coming year. Subtracted from facilities expense are the apportioned costs and expense to house direct people, the library, and marketing.

Business computer services.   These are the charges for billing and accounting services purchased from a vendor, supplied by another part of the firm or those expenses for people, facilities, and equipment needed to run one's own computer shop. In the example practice, the firm leases transaction services from a computer servicer. These averaged 3.5 percent of revenue for the previous year and are expected to increase by .5 percent of revenue in the coming year.

Total administration expenses for the firm are expected to increase 8 percent against a revenue increase of only 2 percent. As you can now see, a business-as-usual plan will not maintain profit levels of the previous year and certainly does not support raising variable compensation for the partners.

The last set of expenses (other indirect) are for discretionary meetings, miscellaneous charges that do not fall elsewhere, and an allocation for regional management support and services to offices of large firms. The example practice is an independent firm with no regional allocation. Its meeting and miscellaneous expenses are nominal and should remain the same in the new year.

Total indirect expense is $395,000 compared to $375,000 last year. This 5 percent increase coupled with a 3 percent increase in cost is well below the 2 percent increase in revenue and leads to lower earnings of nearly $40,000. This gives a NEBA (net earnings before allocation) margin of 0.3 percent. (NEBA is the net of service-generated revenue after subtraction of service operation expenses.) Allocated expenses on top of this are for debt service and other nonrevenue-related charges. These were $46,000 in the previous year and are expected to be the same. The business-as-usual plan leads to a 1.5 percent earnings loss. According to expense productivity rates at the bottom of Figure 18-5, the practice is seeing an increase of over $4 per hour in the overall cost and expense of people against a revenue per-hour increase of only $0.90.

This profit plan illustrates a very important phenomenon of the people services business. Profitability varies greatly through the year. Notice that the first quarter is slightly below breakeven, the second quarter is slightly profitable, the third quarter has a major loss, and the fourth quarter sees a nominal gain. This pattern is inherent to people services businesses, and the annual planning provides data needed to manage cash flow in order to avoid being short in August and September (or at least to not be surprised by it).

Profit Optimization Plan: Another Iteration

Once you have determined how your business will perform with current staffing and the previous year's utilization and rate assumptions, you are ready to interject changes that will derive the best profit. The purpose is to fine-tune such variables as utilization, pricing, costs, and discretionary expenses. You may choose to change your people mix to get higher overall revenue productivity or reduced cost against revenue. You should defer additions to staff intended to achieve greater revenue growth until another plan iteration, in order to avoid obscuring the knowledge you gain from the fine tuning.

Our example practice needs to improve the profitability of its plan and to increase projected revenue from warehouse process consulting. Most important, though, the practice needs to determine how to make money with the staff it has. Actions taken to increase profitability can also increase revenue. Fine-tuning determines whether addressing the cost and expense structure problems that have been highlighted in the business-as-usual plan will both improve profit and meet strategic market objectives. If not, the plan process proceeds to a third iteration that adds people.

Fine-tuning a business-as-usual plan involves making judgments about your current market for people and translating those judgments into actions. Each action is intended to improve revenue and/or reduce cost and expense. The options include:

1. *Increase utilization.* You should examine whether your people can work more hours or whether you can get more of the hours they worked billed to your clients. Do you have client work that is billable but not staffed? Could your engagements be performed more quickly without compromising client satisfaction? Could you perform more concurrent engagements? A yes to any of these questions means you could bill more hours per week than your people inventory has been delivering.

Assuming you track all hours for your staff (not just those devoted to clients), you should look for inhibitors to billing. Can you decrease time spent in internal activities, such as administration and marketing? Are there investment activities that can be stretched out in time to reduce the hours per week currently consumed? If demand is higher, can you reduce pro bono work? Should you reduce the current investment in education? Somewhere in the information you have about how your people are spending their time are some hours you could be billing but are not.

Asking people to work more hours is an employee relations decision faced by all people managers. It is particularly relevant to a business that gets revenue per hour for the time people devote to their work life. Young, single people often see this opportunity for more work time as a means to prove their worth and increase their credentials. Most loyal employees will work more hours, when they see it as a way to preserve the firm and their own personal opportunities with the firm (particularly, if they believe it is for a specific period with rewards at the end).

2. *Increase effective rates per hour charged.* You need to decide whether you can charge more for all or some of your people. This can be made possible by greater demand for the skills and methods of your people or by shifting to work that inherently commands higher rates. This can also

be accomplished by a shift to fixed price and the confidence that the resulting engagements will be performed to manage the risk and deliver the higher profit. The primary question: Will your clients pay more for the same results?

3. *Reduce costs and expenses.* You need to reexamine your cost and expense structure and plan actions that will reduce the cost and expense per hour. Can you operate with less administrative support? Should you look for lower-cost alternatives to your benefit package? Can you reduce the amount of space you occupy? Should you raise prices on your ancillary products, such as the education materials in the example firm, or should you drop such ancillary businesses? As in the example, can you defer increases in variable compensation?

4. *Change staffing mix.* You can experiment with a different mix of personnel. Do you have staff who are not generating revenue commensurate to their cost? Can you dismiss some staff and hire others who will perform with a better revenue per hour to cost per hour, taking into account the cost of recruiting? As in the example, would replacing attrition with an experienced professional that commands higher revenue be better than continuing to hire college students as trainees? Staff mix iterations can be extended to various trials of personnel mix within reasonable limits of reducing the current staff and acquiring others. As you will see later, this is a very important option in those offices that have contract personnel in addition to permanent employees.

The assumptions for a profit optimization plan for the example practice are revised as follows:

1. There is strong demand for education. On-site classes are steadily growing in students per session, putting greater demands on instructors. Education prices should be increased. This will have the effect of increasing the average rate billed for senior level consultants, who are the bulk of the teaching staff.

2. Work can be accelerated in the warehouse business. The practice can get the additional hours from higher utilization. A monthly seminar by consultant-level people for junior people on methods can be changed to a bimonthly schedule, with the expectation that the employees will study more material on their own time and get more on-the-job training. This will be one source for a higher level of utilization from both associate- and consultant-level people.

In Figure 18-6, utilization has been increased for associate level from an annual average of 87.5 percent to 90 percent, and for consultant level utilization from 75.6 percent to 80.2 percent. By year end, the practice is charging an additional $10 per hour on average for senior level consul-

	Month	Prev	Qtr 1	Qtr 2	Qtr 3	Qtr 4	Year
	Weeks	Year	1-13	14-26	27-39	40-52	1-52
Trainee	End Hcount	0	0	1	1	0	0
	Added Hcount	1	0	1	0	-1	0
	Ave Hcount	0.4	0.0	0.3	1.0	0.3	0.4
	Ave Util	62.7%	0.0%	41.5%	68.1%	73.8%	63.9%
	Ave Rate	65	65	65	65	65	65
	Hours	554.0	0.0	72.0	354.0	128.0	554.0
	Revenue($000)	36	0	5	23	8	36
Associate	End Hcount	1	1	1	0	1	1
	Added Hcount	0	0	0	-1	1	0
	Ave Hcount	0.8	1.0	1.0	0.7	0.7	0.8
	Ave Util	87.5%	89.0%	97.0%	76.8%	94.4%	90.0%
	Ave Rate	110	110	110	110	110	110
	Hours	1,516.0	462.8	504.4	266.4	327.2	1,560.8
	Revenue($000)	167	51	55	29	36	172
Consultant	End Hcount	2	2	2	2	2	2
	Added Hcount	1	0	0	0	0	0
	Ave Hcount	2.0	2.0	2.0	2.0	2.0	2.0
	Ave Util	75.6%	77.5%	83.3%	74.1%	88.2%	80.8%
	Ave Rate	125	125	125	125	125	125
	Hours	3,144.0	806.4	866.4	770.4	916.8	3,360.0
	Revenue($000)	393	101	108	96	115	420
Senior	End Hcount	2	2	2	2	2	2
	Added Hcount	0	0	0	0	0	0
	Ave Hcount	2.0	2.0	2.0	2.0	2.0	2.0
	Ave Util	70.5%	68.5%	71.9%	64.6%	76.9%	70.5%
	Ave Rate	170	172	178	180	180	178
	Hours	2,932.0	712.0	748.0	672.0	800.0	2,932.0
	Revenue($000)	498	123	133	121	144	521

Figure 18-6 Profit optimization staffing.

tants for an overall increase of $8 per hour on average for the year. These changes have resulted in an increase in hours delivered by 161 and additional labor revenue of $54,000.

When these adjustments are distributed as illustrated in Figure 18-2 (base plan), warehouse process consulting revenue increases to $853,000. This is still $239,000 below last year's performance of $1,092,000.

Figure 18-7 demonstrates that these changes will achieve profit improvement objectives:

- Total revenue is at $2,099,000, which is up over $100,000 over the previous year, a 5.5 percent growth.

- Revenue per person has also grown, with a $2.51 per hour improvement in average revenue rate for the entire staff.

- Gross profit is $465,000, which is a 1 percent margin improvement over last year and a 2 percent improvement over the base plan. Labor gross margin improved by 3 percent over the base plan.

Month Weeks	Prev Year	Qtr 1 1-13	Qtr 2 14-26	Qtr 3 27-39	Qtr 4 40-52	Year 1-52
CONSULTANTS End Hcount	5	5	6	5	5	5
Added Hcount	2	0	1	-1	0	0
Ave Hcount	5	5	5	6	5	5
Ave Util	74.5%	76.2%	79.0%	70.0%	83.5%	77.0%
Ave Rate	134	138	138	131	139	137
Hours	8,146.0	1,981.2	2,190.8	2,062.8	2,172.0	8,406.8
Revenue($000)	1094	274	302	270	303	1148
MANAGEMENT End Hcount	1.5	1.5	1.5	1.5	1.5	1.5
Added Hcount	0	0	0	0	0	0
Ave Hcount	1.5	1.5	1.5	1.5	1.5	1.5
Ave Util	50.5%	48.5%	51.9%	44.6%	56.9%	50.5%
Ave Rate	204	207	210	210	210	209
Hours	1,575.0	378.0	405.0	348.0	444.0	1,575.0
Revenue($000)	321	78	85	73	93	330
EMPLOYEE TOTALS End Hcount	7	7	8	7	7	7
Added Hcount	2	0	1	-1	0	0
Ave Hcount	6.8	6.5	6.8	7.2	6.5	6.8
Ave Util	69.2%	69.8%	73.1%	64.7%	77.4%	71.1%
Ave Rate	146	149	149	142	151	148
Hours	9,721	2,359	2,596	2,411	2,616	9,982
Revenue($000)	1,415	353	387	343	396	1,478

Figure 18-6 (Continued) Profit optimization staffing.

- Cost per hour is now only $0.30 higher than last year. Most of the increases in salaries, benefits, and variable compensation have been absorbed into more hours delivered.

- Indirect expense has grown only slightly for those expenses such as lead source compensation and business computer services that are estimated as a function of revenue volumes.

- Net earnings before tax (NEBT) is now $20,000 after all allocations and variable compensation are paid.

- Total expense per employee per hour is up only $1.01 over last year, which is well covered by the effective revenue rate improvement of $2.51.

Obviously several variations can be made on the options above. Each will have slightly different income and profit results. The objective is fine tuning that is most practical in light of client demand and which produces the most profit at the least risk. The two assumption changes in the example are minor and together produce a profit-optimized plan. If this plan were adopted and either change is later judged to compromise client satisfaction, the firm can easily back off to the utilization expectation and rates of the previous year.

	Month Weeks	Prev Year	Qtr 1 1-13	Qtr 2 14-26	Qtr 3 27-39	Qtr 4 40-52	Year 1-52
INCOME							
Warehouse Proc Consult	TOTAL	1,364.8	291.9	273.8	240.3	260.4	1,066
Education	TOTAL	585.7	146.8	163.4	150.2	183.9	644
Gen'l Mgmt Consulting	TOTAL	38.5	56.1	103.3	102.7	126.1	388
TOTAL INCOME							
	Labor	1,415.0	352.6	386.6	342.7	396.2	1,478
	Nonlabor	574.0	142.1	153.9	150.5	174.2	621
	TOTAL	1,989.0	494.7	540.5	493.1	570.3	2,099
REVENUE RATES							
Per month & year	CONSULTANTS	208.1	54.9	56.5	47.6	60.6	219
	ALL EMPLOYEES	209.4	54.2	56.6	47.8	60.9	219
Per hour (average)	CONSULTANTS	134.30	138.46	137.64	130.68	139.46	136.60
	ALL EMPLOYEES	145.56	149.46	148.93	142.13	151.43	148.07
DIRECT COST							
DIRECT LABOR	TOTAL	975.5	242.1	250.0	268.2	244.4	1,005
DIRECT NON-LABOR	TOTAL	593.0	144.4	155.5	153.3	175.7	629
TOTAL DIRECT COST		1,568.5	386.5	405.4	421.5	420.0	1,634
GROSS PROFIT		420.6	108.2	135.0	71.6	150.3	465
	Margin	21%	22%	25%	15%	26%	22%
	Labor Gross	439.5	110.5	136.6	74.5	151.8	473
	Labor Margin	31%	31%	35%	22%	38%	32%
	Nonlabor Gross	-18.9	-2.3	-1.6	-2.9	-1.5	-8
	Nonlabor Margin	-3%	-2%	-1%	-2%	-1%	-1%
COST RATES							
Per month & year	CONSULTANTS	126.3	32.4	31.8	32.7	32.7	130
	ALL EMPLOYEES	144.3	37.2	36.6	37.4	37.6	149
Per hour (average)	CONSULTANTS	81.53	81.88	77.49	89.82	75.32	80.97
	ALL EMPLOYEES	100.35	102.63	96.29	111.25	93.42	100.65
INDIRECT EXPENSE							
SELLING	TOTAL	141.1	31.0	41.1	41.1	31.3	144
ADMINISTRATION	TOTAL	222.8	57.2	60.5	62.8	63.0	243
OTHER INDIRECT	TOTAL	11.0	3.4	1.9	3.4	2.4	11
INDIRECT EXPENSE	TOTAL	375.0	91.6	103.5	107.3	96.7	399
NET EARNINGS (NEBA)		45.6	16.6	31.5	-35.7	53.6	66
	Margin	2.3%	3.4%	5.8%	-7.2%	9.4%	3.1%
	% of Revenue	2.3%					2.2%
NET EARNINGS (NEBT)		0.0	5.8	19.6	-46.5	41.0	20
	Margin	0.0%	1.2%	3.6%	-9.4%	7.2%	0.9%
EXPENSE RATES (NEBA)							
Per month & year		183.8	47.3	47.4	47.8	47.9	190
Per hour (average)		127.79	130.29	124.81	142.17	119.10	128.80

Figure 18-7 Profit optimization results.

The profit-optimized plan did not increase the warehouse process consulting revenue forecast enough to maintain last year's achievement. The firm can choose to reduce its general management consulting expectation, reduce the corresponding expected improvement in partner effective rate, and see if resulting profit still supports raising partner variable compensation. Otherwise, the planning process should move to testing alternatives for increasing staff.

Growth Plan: The Final Iteration

To generate another $240,000 in revenue from additional people, the revenue productivity statistics in the example practice indicate a need for more than one person and less than two people fully productive for an entire year. Two consultant-level people are added in the first four months, and consultant-level utilization assumptions are adjusted to compensate for a period of internship for each. The additional staff are acquired early enough in the year to get the full benefit of billing volumes in the fall. Using linked spreadsheets is useful for this exercise. Various combinations of staff mix, acquisition timing, effects of learning curve, and costs of recruiting can be tried to find the least-risk solution that accomplishes the objective (in this case, $240,000 in increased revenue).

The plan iteration in Figure 18-8 shows that the two professionals at the consultant level are hired in February and April, respectively. Each will be qualified in warehouse process consulting but will need 6 weeks to learn and credibly perform the unique methods of this practice, during which time each will achieve only 50 percent billable utilization.

Since the trainee-, associate-, and manager-level people are the same as that in the profit optimized iteration, no detail is provided for them in the illustration. Both the first two quarters are detailed by month to show the effect on utilization for the new consultants and the corresponding effect on overall consultant staff and total staff utilization. Utilization for consultants and for the overall staff is lower in every quarter against that illustrated in Figure 18-6:

Quarter 1. Consultants down 4 percent; all staff down 2.6 percent

Quarter 2. Consultants down 7.6 percent; all staff down 5 percent

Quarter 3. Consultants down 2.5 percent; all staff down 1 percent

Quarter 4. Consultants down 4.3 percent, all staff down 1.7 percent

The new people are not expected to achieve levels of utilization comparable to the rest of the staff even before the end of the year. On the other hand,

		Prev Year	Jan 1-4	Feb 5-8	Mar 9-13	Qtr 1 1-13	Apr 14-17	May 18-22	Jun 23-26	Qtr 2 14-26	Qtr 3 27-39	Qtr 4 40-52	Year 1-52
Trainee	End Hcount	0	0	0	0	0	0	0	1	1	1	0	0
	Hours	554.0	0.0	0.0	0.0	0.0	0.0	0.0	72.0	72.0	354.0	128.0	554.0
	Revenue($000)	36	0	0	0	0	0	0	5	5	23	8	36
Associate	End Hcount	1	1	1	1	0	1	0	1	1	1	1	1
	Hours	1,516.4	129.6	147.2	186.0	462.8	155.2	194.0	155.2	504.4	266.4	327.2	1,560.8
	Revenue($000)	167	14	16	20	51	17	21	17	55	29	36	172
Consultant	End Hcount	2	2	3	3	3	4	4	4	4	4	4	4
	Added Hcount	1	0	1	0	1	0	0	0	0	0	0	2
	Ave Hcount	2.0	2.0	3.0	3.0	2.7	4.0	4.0	4.0	4.0	4.0	4.0	3.7
	Ave Util	75.6%	73.0%	66.0%	67.0%	68.7%	64.0%	71.0%	66.0%	67.3%	67.2%	79.2%	70.8%
	Ave Rate	125	125	125	125	125	125	125	125	125	125	125	125
	Hours	3,144.0	233.6	316.8	402.0	952.4	409.6	568.0	422.4	1,400.0	1,396.8	1,648.0	5,397.2
	Revenue($000)	393	29	40	50	119	51	71	53	175	175	206	675
Senior	End Hcount	2	2	2	2	2	2	2	2	2	2	2	2
	Hours	2,932.0	208.0	224.0	280.0	712.0	240.0	300.0	208.0	748.0	672.0	800.0	2,932.0
	Revenue($000)	498	35	39	49	123	42	53	37	133	121	144	521
CONSULTANTS	End Hcount	5	5	6	6	6	7	7	8	8	7	7	7
	Added Hcount	1	0	1	0	1	1	0	1	2	-1	0	2
	Ave Hcount	5	5	6	6	6	7	7	8	8	8	7	7
	Ave Util	74.5%	71.4%	71.7%	72.3%	72.2%	71.9%	75.9%	67.0%	71.4%	67.5%	79.8%	72.6%
	Ave Rate	134	138	137	138	138	137	137	131	135	129	136	134
	Hours	8,146.0	571.2	688.0	868.0	2,127.2	804.8	####	857.6	2,724.4	2,689.2	2,903.2	####
	Revenue($000)	1094	79	94	119	293	111	146	112	368	348	394	1403
MANAGEMENT	End Hcount	1.5	1.5	1.5	1.5	1.5	1.5	1.5	1.5	1.5	1.5	1.5	1.5
	Hours	1,575.0	108.0	120.0	150.0	378.0	132.0	165.0	108.0	405.0	348.0	444.0	1,575.0
	Revenue($000)	321	22	25	31	78	28	35	23	85	73	93	330
EMPLOYEE TOTALS	End Hcount	7	7	8	8	8	9	9	10	10	9	9	9
	Added Hcount	1	0	1	0	1	1	0	1	2	-1	0	2
	Ave Hcount	6.8	6.5	7.5	7.5	7.2	8.5	8.5	9.5	8.8	9.2	8.5	8.4
	Ave Util	69.2%	65.3%	67.3%	67.9%	67.2%	68.9%	72.2%	63.5%	68.1%	63.7%	75.7%	68.7%
	Ave Rate	146	146	147	148	148	148	139	139	145	139	146	144
	Hours	9,721	679	808	1,018	2,505	937	1,227	966	3,129	3,037	3,347	12,019
	Revenue($000)	1,415	101	119	151	371	138	180	135	453	421	488	1,733

Figure 18-8 Growth plan staffing.

the practice expects no deterioration in average rate billed for the staff. It has chosen a combination of cautious and less cautious assumptions.

This solution generates $255,000 in additional revenue and 2,037 hours over the profit optimization plan. This allows the practice to maintain its market in warehouse process consulting (actually improve it by 1 percent), grow the education business, and aggressively enter general management consulting. Labor generated revenue will grow by $318,000 (22 percent) over the previous year, with a corresponding growth of 33 percent in staff. The question, of course, is whether this plan is profitable and will support payment of higher variable compensation.

Figures 18-9 to 18-11 show the new profit plan. Total income forecast is now $2,417,000, also an increase of 22 percent over the previous year. In Figure 18-9, the revenue productivity rates reflect the dilution of addition of lower-level people that require start-up before reaching full capacity. Annual average revenue per person is down $3000 over the previous year, and the effective revenue rate will decrease by $1.40.

In Figure 18-10, the average salary for consultant-level people has increased, anticipating that the two professional hires may cost more than paid currently. This prompts further increases to the current consultant-level people to keep pay equitable. Other direct cost increases reflect additional training for the new people, additional recruiting costs, and slightly higher facility and equipment needs. All these have increased direct labor cost to $1,269,000, an increase of 30 percent over the previous year (including the additional cost of variable compensation objective for the partners).

Gross profit is higher than last year, but margin is down 2 percent. This is mainly due to a decrease in labor margin from 31 percent to 27 percent. This is also reflected in cost productivity. Cost per person is up $7000, and revenue is down $3000 for a productivity decrease per person of $10,000. Effective cost rate is up $5.22 per hour, which, when combined with the revenue rate drop, gives a productivity loss of $6.62 per hour.

Finally, Figure 18-11 shows the effect of growth on net profit. More temporary administrative support is needed, along with a slight increase in facilities and equipment expense projections. Most expenses, though, are unaffected by the increase in people, although lead source compensation and business computer services are again affected by the increase in revenue. The net before expensing allocations for the practice has decreased to 1.4 percent, which will not cover all of the $46,000 in nonoperational expense incurred in the previous year. Growth in permanent staff has caused an $11,100 net loss before taxes. By keeping indirect expenses down relative to the increase in direct cost, though, the total expense per employee increase is now $4000 for a $7000 loss in annual productivity and a $4.27 loss in overall per-hour productivity.

It is useful to note here that gross profit analysis overemphasized the effect of the growth on profits. The complete analysis through net profit

	Month Weeks	Prev Year	Jan 1-4	Feb 5-8	Mar 9-13	Qtr 1 1-13	Qtr 2 14-26	Qtr 3 27-39	Qtr 4 40-52	Year 1-52
Warehouse Proc Cons	Consultants	851.1	52.5	64.1	81.1	197.6	253.1	238.3	254.6	944
	Management	240.8	15.6	16.1	18.7	50.4	38.3	32.9	42.0	164
	Travel(Nonlabor)	273.0	17.0	20.0	25.0	62.0	72.9	67.8	74.1	277
	Product(Nonlabor)	0.0	0.0	0.0	0.0	0.0	0.0	0.0	0.0	0
	TOTAL	1,364.8	85.1	100.2	124.8	310.1	364.3	339.0	370.7	1,384
Education	Consultants	242.9	17.5	20.6	26.1	64.3	64.6	60.7	81.3	271
	Management	48.2	3.3	3.7	4.7	11.7	12.8	11.0	14.0	49
	Travel(Nonlabor)	174.7	12.5	14.6	18.5	45.6	46.4	43.0	57.2	192
	Product(Nonlabor)	120.0	10.0	10.0	11.0	31.0	33.0	33.0	35.0	132
	TOTAL	585.7	43.4	49.0	60.3	152.6	156.7	147.7	187.5	644
Gen'l Mgmt Consulting	Consultants	0.0	8.8	9.6	12.2	30.7	50.5	48.8	58.4	188
	Management	32.1	3.3	5.0	7.8	16.1	34.0	29.2	37.3	117
	Travel(Nonlabor)	6.4	2.4	2.9	4.0	9.4	16.9	25.8	31.6	84
	Product(Nonlabor)	0.0	0.0	0.0	0.0	0.0	0.0	0.0	0.0	0
	TOTAL	38.5	14.6	17.5	24.0	56.1	101.5	103.8	127.3	389
TOTAL INCOME	Labor	1,415.0	101.1	119.2	150.6	370.9	453.3	421.0	487.6	1,733
	Nonlabor	574.0	42.0	47.6	58.4	148.0	169.2	169.6	197.9	685
	TOTAL	1,989.0	143.0	166.7	209.1	518.8	622.5	590.5	685.4	2,417
REVENUE RATES										
Per month & year	CONSULTANTS	208.1	15.8	15.7	19.9	51.6	50.2	45.4	56.3	203
	ALL EMPLOYEES	209.4	15.5	15.9	20.1	51.7	51.3	45.9	57.4	206
Per hour (average)	CONSULTANTS	134.30	137.98	137.09	137.59	137.54	135.17	129.36	135.82	134.34
	ALL EMPLOYEES	145.56	148.80	147.48	147.97	148.03	144.85	138.60	145.66	144.16

Figure 18-9 Growth profit plan.

Month Weeks		Prev Year	Jan 1-4	Feb 5-8	Mar 9-13	Qtr 1 1-13	Qtr 2 14-26	Qtr 3 27-39	Qtr 4 40-52	Year 1-52
DIRECT COMP	Salaries	575.0	47.5	54.2	53.8	155.5	186.8	190.5	183.1	716
	Benefits	93.0	8.1	9.4	9.4	26.9	33.1	34.4	31.9	126
	Commissions	153.5	13.6	14.6	14.6	42.8	47.0	46.6	46.6	183
	Other Comp	20.0	0.0	0.0	5.0	5.0	5.0	5.0	5.0	20
DIRECT COMP	TOTAL	841.5	69.3	78.2	82.7	230.1	271.8	276.4	266.6	1,045
OTHER DIRECT COST	Travel/Commute	15.0	0.7	1.5	1.5	3.7	6.5	3.6	6.8	21
	Education/Fees	68.0	6.7	7.7	7.7	22.0	27.2	28.2	26.1	104
	Recruiting	15.0	0.0	0.0	20.0	20.0	20.0	15.0	0.0	55
	Facilities	36.0	2.5	2.7	3.7	8.9	10.0	12.7	13.1	45
OTHER DIRECT COST	TOTAL	134.0	9.9	11.9	32.9	54.6	63.7	59.5	46.1	224
DIRECT LABOR	TOTAL	975.5	79.1	90.1	115.6	284.8	335.5	335.9	312.7	1,269
DIRECT TRAVEL	TOTAL	454.0	31.3	36.8	46.5	114.7	133.5	133.9	159.7	542
TRANSFER COST	TOTAL	91.2	7.6	7.6	8.4	23.6	25.1	25.1	26.6	100
NON-LABOR APPORTI	TOTAL	47.7	3.9	3.9	4.1	11.9	12.1	13.9	13.1	51
DIRECT NON-LABOR	TOTAL	593.0	42.9	48.4	58.9	150.2	170.7	172.9	199.4	693
TOTAL DIRECT COST		1,568.5	122.0	138.5	174.5	435.0	506.2	508.8	512.0	1,962
GROSS PROFIT		420.6	21.0	28.3	34.6	83.9	116.2	81.8	173.4	455
	Margin	21%	15%	17%	17%	16%	19%	14%	25%	19%
	Labor Gross	439.5	22.0	29.1	35.1	86.1	117.8	85.1	174.9	464
	Labor Margin	31%	22%	24%	23%	23%	26%	20%	36%	27%
	Nonlabor Gross	-18.9	-0.9	-0.8	-0.5	-2.2	-1.5	-3.3	-1.5	-9
	Nonlabor Margin	-3%	-2%	-2%	-1%	-1%	-1%	-2%	-1%	-1%
COST RATES										
Per month & year	CONSULTANTS	126.3	10.5	10.6	14.1	35.3	34.3	33.0	33.1	135
	ALL EMPLOYEES	144.3	12.2	12.0	15.4	39.7	38.0	36.6	36.8	151
Per hour (average)	CONSULTANTS	81.53	91.84	92.08	97.48	94.12	92.34	94.10	79.71	89.66
	ALL EMPLOYEES	100.35	116.47	111.51	113.51	113.67	107.21	110.60	93.41	105.57

Figure 18-10 Growth plan cost structure.

Month Weeks		Prev Year	Jan 1-4	Feb 5-8	Mar 9-13	Qtr 1 1-13	Qtr 2 14-26	Qtr 3 27-39	Qtr 4 40-52	Year 1-52
MARKETING COMP	Salary	60.0	5.0	5.0	5.0	15.0	15.0	15.0	15.0	60
	Benefits	6.9	0.6	0.6	0.6	1.9	1.9	1.9	1.9	8
	Commissions	27.0	2.5	2.5	2.5	7.5	7.5	7.5	7.5	30
	Other Comp	0.0	0.0	0.0	0.0	0.0	0.0	0.0	0.0	0
	Recruiting	0.0	0.0	0.0	0.0	0.0	0.0	0.0	0.0	0
	Education	1.3	0.2	0.2	0.2	0.6	0.6	0.6	0.6	3
	Facilities/Support	6.0	0.4	0.4	0.5	1.4	1.4	1.7	1.8	6
MARKETING COMP TOTAL		101.1	8.7	8.7	8.9	26.4	26.4	26.7	26.8	106
MARKETING EXPENSE	Travel	6.0	0.5	0.5	0.5	1.5	1.6	1.7	1.6	6
	Materials	12.0	1.0	1.0	1.0	3.0	3.0	3.0	3.0	12
	Lead Sources	2.0	0.1	0.2	0.2	0.5	0.6	0.6	0.7	2
	Promo/Advert	20.0	0.0	0.0	0.0	0.0	10.0	10.0	0.0	20
MARKETING EXPENSE TOTAL		40.0	1.6	1.7	1.7	5.1	15.3	15.3	5.3	41
SELLING	TOTAL	141.1	10.4	10.4	10.6	31.4	41.7	42.0	32.1	147
ADMIN COMP	Salary	54.0	4.5	4.5	4.5	13.5	13.5	14.4	14.4	56
	Benefits	20.6	1.9	1.9	1.9	5.6	5.6	5.6	5.6	23
	Commissions	0.0	0.0	0.0	0.0	0.0	0.0	0.0	0.0	0
	Other Comp	1.0	0.0	0.0	0.0	0.0	0.0	1.0	0.0	1
	Supplemental	4.5	0.0	0.0	0.0	0.0	1.5	3.0	0.0	4
	Recruiting	0.0	0.0	0.0	0.0	0.0	0.0	0.0	0.0	0
	Education	1.6	0.1	0.1	0.4	0.4	0.4	0.4	0.4	2
	Travel	1.2	0.1	0.1	0.1	0.3	0.3	0.3	0.3	1
ADMIN COMP TOTAL		82.9	6.5	6.5	6.9	19.8	21.3	24.7	20.7	87
OFFICE SERVICES	Vendor Personnel	6.0	0.0	0.0	0.0	0.0	1.4	7.0	8.4	17
	Vendor Services	4.8	0.4	0.4	0.4	1.2	1.2	1.2	1.2	5
	Supplies	1.2	0.1	0.1	0.1	0.3	0.3	0.3	0.3	1
	Nonlabor Apportion	-0.6	-0.1	-0.1	-0.1	-0.2	-0.3	-0.7	-0.5	-2
OFFICE SERVICES TOTAL		11.4	0.5	0.5	0.5	1.4	2.6	7.9	9.5	21

FACILITIES Rental/Occupancy	99.0	8.3	8.5	8.5	25.2	26.1	26.3	25.9	104
Services	14.0	1.2	1.2	1.2	3.6	3.6	3.6	3.6	14
Tel Factor	470.8	40.0	40.0	40.0	40.0				480
Equipment/Furn	6.0	0.0	0.0	2.2	2.2	1.4	1.6	1.9	7
Share		0.4							
Share		0.1							
Marketing Apport	-6.0	-0.4	-0.4	-0.5	-1.4	-1.4	-1.7	-1.8	-6
FACILITIES TOTAL	60.5	5.2	5.2	6.2	16.7	15.9	13.2	12.3	58
% of Revenue	3%	4%							
ADMINISTRATION TOTAL	222.8	17.9	18.9	21.9	58.6	64.7	69.4	69.3	262
OTHER INDIRECT Meetings	7.5	2.5	0.0	0.0	2.5	1.0	2.5	1.5	8
Apportion Factor	25%	25%	25%	25%					
Miscellaneous	3.5	0.3	0.3	0.3	0.9	0.9	0.9	0.9	4
OTHER INDIRECT TOTAL	11.0	2.8	0.3	0.3	3.4	1.9	3.4	2.4	11
INDIRECT EXPENSE TOTAL	375.0	31.0	29.6	32.8	93.4	108.3	114.7	104.4	421
NET EARNINGS (NEBA)	45.6	-10.0	-1.3	1.8	-9.5	8.0	-33.0	69.0	35
Margin	2.3%	-7.0%	-0.8%	0.8%	-1.8%	1.3%	-5.6%	10.1%	1.4%
% of Revenue	2.2%	2.0%	2.0%	2.0%	2.0%	2.0%	2.0%	2.0%	2.0%
NET EARNINGS (NEBT)	0.0	-13.8	-5.1	-2.0	-20.9	-3.4	-44.4	57.6	-11.1
Margin	0.0%	-9.6%	-3.1%	-1.0%	-4.0%	-0.6%	-7.5%	8.4%	-0.5%
EXPENSE RATES (NEBA) Per month & year	183.8	15.5	14.8	18.6	49.1	46.9	45.6	45.5	187
Per hour (average)	127.79	148.76	137.67	136.73	140.32	132.41	137.52	115.59	130.66

Figure 18-11 Growth plan indirect costs and net earnings.

shows that there is a problem, but not nearly as bad as gross profit analysis would predict. Again, the purpose of gross profit is to segment profitability between labor and nonlabor components. In a pure people service business, net profit analysis serves as the only arbiter of financial decisions.

Growing the business base, growing the staff, and growing profit and its distribution through partner compensation are very difficult to do all together, as these plan iterations illustrate. To get 22 percent growth in the coming year, the partners may not be able to increase their own incomes; in fact, they may have to give up compensation to find the growth.

The assumptions in the final plan iteration were conservative. Higher utilization from the new people could fix the problem. Getting the new people at lower-than-expected salaries could be possible. An entrepreneur would accept this last plan as the final plan, with the knowledge that partner compensation payout must be delayed until after midyear to see how much the new people actually cost and how quickly they begin to bill at full utilization and optimum rates. In the meantime, a marketing plan must now be developed that focuses on increasing the education and general management consulting business opportunities, and our staff development plan needs to be changed to reflect new people and changes to methods training.

Planning for Subcontractors

One of the tactical choices that might be available to the partners in the example firm above is to acquire subcontractors to supplement their consultants on warehouse process engagements, rather than new permanent employees. This assumes much about the willingness of their clients to accept people who are not direct employees of the firm. Firms that successfully intermix subcontractors with their staff are those that demonstrate value in leadership and methods rather than simply through the skill of their people. The client in an engagement involving subcontractors is looking to the firm to guide the effort and ensure the quality of the outcome, regardless of the source of the individuals assigned to the task. Clients will defer to the firm on the choice of staff, even on per-hour engagements, when they believe that the firm's value is knowing how best to get to a satisfactory conclusion to the effort and that the firm will make right any unsatisfactory results.

The annual business planning process does not change when a firm incorporates contractors as part of its available and billable staff. The assumptions for these people are very different, though, than for staff on the payroll. Contractors are of two types:

1. *Outside contractors.* Outside contractors are those people hired by the hour from another firm. Management is not obligated to treat them as employees and can terminate their services at will (unless restricted by agreements with the vendor that supplies these people). Outside contractors do not attend employee meetings and are expected to work on all days except holidays. Only on rare occasions are outside contractors allowed to take their vacations while assigned to the firm.

2. *Inside contractors.* Many firms have multiple offices, and many of these are part of a larger business that has related operations staffed with people with skills that are useful to the consulting offices. A major strength of these firms is their ability to loan skilled employees to their consulting offices to meet specific client and engagement requirements. The local management must treat them as employees but is usually only obligated to pay for an agreed-to portion of the overall time they devote to their job. Typically, the firm office is billed at an internal salary transfer rate per hour for all time that the individual devotes to engagements, for time spent on administrative and marketing tasks in behalf of the office, and for time spent in employee meetings held locally. The employee may be allowed to take vacations while assigned, but usually the local office is not obligated to pay for hours devoted to personal time.

Contractors should have higher utilization than members of the permanent staff, simply because they expend less personal time while assigned. Contractors also tend to bill more hours per week than comparable employee staff, because the typical assignment is shorter term, very specific to a portion of the engagement and its schedule, and not interrupted by marketing or other local office support activities. The contractor may be personally compensated for high billing volumes and will likely look for opportunities to work overtime.

Outside and inside contractors need to be kept separate when developing the staffing plan. Their utilization assumptions are different. Their cost rates are usually vastly different. The corresponding effective revenue rates may be very different, and they will almost certainly have different assumptions for both the cost of travel and the revenue compensation that the firm may receive from the client for travel and commute.

To illustrate how contractors can affect the planning process, another iteration of the strategy-optimized plan for the example practice will be performed. This time, however, the additional $240,000 in revenue will be attained through the use of resources other than local firm employees. This will illustrate that planning for the use of subcontractors also means reevaluating some fundamental assumptions about management time and administrative expense.

Staff Planning with Mixed Resources

To introduce subcontractors into the staff mix, the partners need time to assure warehouse process consulting clients that their interests and needs will continue to be well satisfied. An outside contractor is added to the staff in February. As a planning assumption, all subcontractor assignments are to be less than 1 month throughout the remainder of the year, and 6 days of turnover is expected each month. While under contract, outside resources should bill as many hours per week as the work allows, with time off only for holidays (for which the firm also does not pay the subcontractor).

In April, the expected monthly turnaround loss for contractors is reduced to 4 days per month. This is still a conservative assumption. Tasks might be assigned to a fully qualified subcontractor for weeks at a time. The risk is high, though, that the individual does not work out and must be replaced, or the person chooses to leave the job for their own reasons. Prudent planning means being cautious.

Using subcontractors changes assumption regarding distribution of management time. Ten hours per month of management will now be needed specific to the subcontractor. This reduces management utilization by 4 percent. The resulting loss of billable time to the new general consulting business needs to be replaced by another resource.

The practice can shift more senior consultant time and increase the level of subcontractors on warehouse process consulting. The practice can hire as described earlier. For the purposes of this example, though, the practice is assumed to be part of a larger professional services enterprise and can borrow (rent) a management consulting specialist from another location. This person is needed in the fall as demand builds in the new service, and the borrowed person is expected to defer all personal time off, except holidays, until after the assignment. To compensate for employee meetings and minor interferences in billing, the utilization from this person is planned at 91 percent.

Figure 18-12 shows a summary of a staffing plan that utilizes both outside and inside consultants. Subcontractors are billed at the associate consultant rate of $117 per hour, while the borrowed specialist is worth senior consultant effective rates. This approach adds $242,000 to the labor revenue forecast, generated by 1985 of contractor hours.

Overall staff utilization in this approach is much higher (73.6 percent) as would be expected. This is higher than all three previous plan iterations. The average revenue rate is lower with this mix of people than both last year and with the profit-optimized plan, but it is higher than with the growth plan. This is the effect of getting new people billable faster.

Revenue distribution changes with this plan. Management would have provided 40 percent of their billed time to warehouse process consulting in the growth plan. This is now 57 percent. Obviously, the borrowed person makes up the difference in general management consulting. Total revenue is also slightly less than the growth plan.

Profitability of Mixed Resources

To accommodate contractors, the administrative support resources in the office are increased, but permanent facilities are not. Generally, if gross profit remains the same or improves when contractors are added, the nearly constant indirect expense will create improved net profit from the increased revenue stream. For this reason, firms use cost-per-person computations to test choices among resources for large projects.*

Figure 18-13 is a summary income and expense plan for mixed resources. Direct labor cost has been broken out to show the cost of outside and inside contractors. Outside contractors are expecting to cost an average of $62 per hour, with a minor cost of $50 per month for unusual commutation expenses.

The person borrowed from inside the firm is going to cost a lot more. The practice expects to pay $122 per hour for salary recovery and $2800 per month in temporary assignment expenses (which are not expected to be recovered from clients). The good news is that gross profit is just as good as in the profit optimization plan, even though the gross profit for the inside contracted person is only 13 percent. This is more than covered by a gross profit of 46 percent for the outside contractor.

This profitability is carried on to a net earnings before tax of $59,000 or 2.5 percent of revenue. With contractors, rather than new permanent employees, the practice is able to meet its strategic market objectives, increase partner variable compensation share, cover at least as much allocated expense as the previous year, and have some earnings left over. Productivity has improved for the permanent resources over last year, and the practice expects a healthy $19.45 net return from every dollar billed for the entire mixed staff (effective revenue rate minus effective expense rate).

The mixed resource plan is fraught with risk, just as the growth plan has its inherent risks. The delicate relationship between the firm and its clients can easily be frayed by the introduction of subcontractors. Contractor work products may lack quality, and resources from the office may be diverted away from the growth opportunities in education and general management consulting to bring warehouse process consulting results up to client satisfaction. Worse, the subcontractors might require substantially more management time, and all areas of the business may suffer utilization and quality deficiencies.

*Larry E. Kuhlken, *Expanding Professional Services, a Manager's Guide to a Diversified Business,* Business One Irwin, Homewood, Ill., 1992, pp. 253–254.

Month	Prev Year	Jan 1-4	Feb 5-8	Mar 9-13	Qtr 1 1-13	Qtr 2 14-26	Qtr 3 27-39	Oct 40-43	Nov 44-48	Dec 49-52	Qtr 4 40-52	Year 1-52
CONSULTANTS End Hcount	5	5	5	5	5	6	5	5	5	5	5	5
Added Hcount	1	0	0	0	0	1	-1	0	0	0	0	0
Ave Hcount	5	5	5	5	5	5	6	5	5	5	5	5
Ave Util	74.5%	71.4%	78.0%	78.6%	76.2%	79.0%	70.0%	83.2%	89.2%	76.8%	83.5%	77.0%
Ave Rate	134	138	138	139	138	138	131	135	141	142	139	137
Hours	8,146.0	571.2	624.0	786.0	1,981.2	2,190.8	2,062.8	665.6	892.0	614.4	2,172.0	8,406.8
Revenue($000)	1094	79	86	109	274	302	270	90	126	87	303	1148
MANAGEMENT End Hcount	1.5	1.5	1.5	1.5	1.5	1.5	1.5	1.5	1.5	1.5	1.5	1.5
Added Hcount	0	0	0	0	0	0	0	0	0	0	0	0
Ave Hcount	1.5	1.5	1.5	1.5	1.5	1.5	1.5	1.5	1.5	1.5	1.5	1.5
Ave Util	50.5%	45.0%	46.0%	46.0%	45.7%	47.9%	40.6%	56.0%	56.0%	46.0%	52.9%	46.8%
Ave Rate	204	206	207	208	207	210	210	210	210	210	210	209
Hours	1,575.0	108.0	110.4	138.0	356.4	373.8	316.8	134.4	168.0	110.4	412.8	1,459.8
Revenue($000)	321	22	23	29	74	78	67	28	35	23	87	306
EMPLOYEE TOTALS End Hcount	7	7	7	7	7	8	7	7	7	7	7	7
Added Hcount	1	0	0	0	0	1	-1	0	0	0	0	0
Ave Hcount	6.8	6.5	6.5	6.5	6.5	6.8	7.2	6.5	6.5	6.5	6.5	6.8
Ave Util	69.2%	65.3%	70.6%	71.1%	69.2%	72.2%	63.9%	76.9%	81.5%	69.7%	76.5%	70.3%
Ave Rate	146	149	149	149	149	148	141	147	152	151	151	147
Hours	9,721	679	734	924	2,338	2,565	2,380	800	1,060	725	2,585	9,867
Revenue($000)	1,415	101	109	138	348	380	336	118	161	110	390	1,454

OUTSIDE

Metric												
End Hcount	0	1	1	1	1	1	1	1	1	1	1	1
Added Hcount	0	1	0	0	0	1	0	0	0	0	0	1
Ave Hcount	0	1	0	0	1	1	1	1	1	1	1	1
Ave Util	0.0%	98.0%	98.0%	98.0%	101.8%	98.0%	98.0%	98.0%	98.0%	98.0%	98.7%	98.8%
Ave Rate	0.0	117	117	117	117	117	117	117	117	117	117	117
Hours	0.0	109.8	137.2	247.0	407.7	407.7	125.4	156.8	94.1	376.3		1,438.6
Revenue($000)	0	13	16	29	48	48	15	18	11	44		168

INSIDE

Metric												
End Hcount	0	1	1	0	0	1	1	1	1	1	1	1
Added Hcount	0	0	0	0	0	1	0	0	0	-1	0	1
Ave Hcount	0	0	0	0	0	1	0	1	1	1	1	1
Ave Util	0.0%	91.0%	91.0%	0.0%	0.0%	84.0%	91.0%	91.0%	91.0%	91.0%	92.4%	90.0%
Ave Rate	0.0	170	172	174	172	178	180	180	180	180	180	178
Hours	0.0	0.0	0.0	0.0	0.0	145.6	145.6	182.0	72.8	400.4		546.0
Revenue($000)	0	0	0	0	0	26	26	33	13	72		98

NON-EMPLOYEE TOTALS

End Hcount	0	1	1	1	1	2	2	2	2	2	2	2
Added Hcount	0	1	1	0	0	1	0	0	-1	-1	0	1
Ave Hcount	0	1	1	0	1	2	2	2	2	2	2	1
Ave Util	0.0%	98.0%	98.0%	101.8%	98.0%	93.9%	94.1%	94.1%	94.8%	95.3%	96.2%	
Ave Rate	0	117	117	117	117	134	151	151	144	149	134	
Hours	0.0	109.8	137.2	247.0	407.7	553.3	271.0	338.8	166.9	776.7	1,984.6	
Revenue($000)	0	13	16	29	48	74	41	51	24	116	267	

STAFF TOTALS

Metric												
End Hcount	7	7	7	7	7	8	8	8	8	8	8	2
Added Hcount	1	0	1	0	1	0	1	0	0	-1	0	1
Ave Hcount	7	7	7	7	7	8	8	8	8	8	8	8
Ave Util	69.2%	65.3%	73.3%	73.7%	71.3%	74.9%	68.0%	80.7%	84.3%	73.3%	80.1%	73.6%
Ave Rate	146	149	145	145	146	144	140	148	152	151	150	145
Hours	9,721.0	679.2	844.2	1,061.2	2,584.6	2,972.3	2,932.9	1,071.0	1,398.8	891.7	3,361.5	11,851.2
Revenue($000)	1415	101	122	154	377	428	410	159	213	134	506	1720

Figure 18-12   Staffing plan using inside and outside consultants.

	Month Weeks	Prev Year	Jan 1-4	Feb 5-8	Mar 9-13	Qtr 1 1-13	Qtr 2 14-26	Qtr 3 27-39	Oct 40-43	Nov 44-48	Dec 49-52	Qtr 4 40-52	Year 1-52
INCOME	Labor	1,415.0	101.1	122.0	153.9	377.0	427.7	410.0	158.7	212.5	134.4	505.7	1,720
	Nonlabor	574.0	42.2	48.1	58.9	149.3	165.4	167.4	64.8	83.1	57.2	205.0	687
	TOTAL	1,989.0	143.3	170.1	212.9	526.3	593.1	577.4	223.5	295.6	191.6	710.7	2,408
REVENUE RATES													
Per month & year	CONSULTANTS	208.1	15.8	17.3	21.8	54.9	56.5	47.6	17.9	25.2	17.4	60.6	219
	EMPLOYEES	209.4	15.5	16.8	21.2	53.6	55.6	46.9	18.1	24.8	17.0	59.9	215
	ALL STAFF	209.38	15.55	16.95	21.38	54.12	56.04	49.40	19.12	25.61	17.69	62.69	222.23
Per hour (average)	CONSULTANTS	134.30	137.98	138.33	138.91	148.46	137.64	130.68	134.62	141.43	141.85	139.46	136.60
	EMPLOYEES	145.56	148.80	148.66	149.23	148.92	148.19	141.24	147.28	152.30	152.23	150.73	147.35
	ALL STAFF	145.56	148.80	144.54	145.06	145.87	143.91	139.80	148.18	151.95	139.40	147.25	144.29
DIRECT COST													
DIRECT COMP	TOTAL	841.5	69.3	69.3	74.3	212.8	217.8	221.5	67.7	69.3	74.3	211.2	863
OTHER DIRECT COSTS	TOTAL	134.0	9.2	10.0	11.2	30.3	34.7	49.2	12.2	12.2	11.5	36.0	150
OUTSIDE LABOR COST	Fees	0.0	0.0	6.8	8.5	15.3	25.3	25.3	7.8	9.7	5.8	23.3	89
	Travel Reimburse	0.0	0.0	0.0	0.0	0.1	0.2	0.1	0.1	0.1	0.0	0.2	0
	Facilities/Support	0.0	0.0	0.0	0.0	0.0	0.0	0.0	0.0	0.0	0.0	0.0	0
OUTSIDE LABOR COST	TOTAL	0.0	0.0	6.8	8.5	15.4	25.4	25.4	7.8	9.8	5.9	23.5	90
INSIDE LABOR COST	Transfer	0.0	0.0	0.0	0.0	0.0	0.0	17.8	17.8	22.2	17.8	57.7	75
	Unbilled Travel	0.0	0.0	0.0	0.0	0.0	0.0	2.0	3.0	3.0	1.0	7.0	9
	Facilities/Support	0.0	0.0	0.0	0.0	0.0	0.0	0.2	0.2	0.2	0.1	0.4	1
INSIDE LABOR COST	TOTAL	0.0	0.0	0.0	0.0	0.0	0.0	19.9	20.9	25.4	18.8	65.1	85
DIRECT LABOR	TOTAL	975.5	78.4	86.0	94.0	258.5	277.8	315.9	108.6	116.6	110.4	335.7	1,188
DIRECT NON-LABOR	TOTAL	592.9	43.1	48.9	59.6	151.6	167.4	170.6	65.4	83.1	57.7	206.2	696
TOTAL DIRECT COST		1,568.4	121.5	135.0	153.6	410.1	445.3	486.5	174.0	199.7	168.2	541.9	1,884

	1	2	3	4	5	6	7	8	9	10	11	12
GROSS PROFIT	420.6	21.8	35.2	59.2	116.2	147.8	91.0	49.4	95.9	23.5	168.8	524
Margin	21%	15%	21%	28%	22%	25%	16%	22%	32%	12%	24%	22%
Labor Gross	439.5	22.7	36.0	59.9	118.5	149.9	94.1	50.1	95.9	24.0	170.0	533
Labor Margin	31%	22%	29%	39%	31%	35%	23%	32%	45%	18%	34%	31%
COST RATES												
Per month & year CONSULTANTS	126.3	10.4	10.5	11.7	32.6	32.2	33.0	10.5	10.9	11.7	33.1	131
EMPLOYEES	144.3	12.1	12.2	13.2	37.4	36.9	37.8	12.3	12.5	13.2	38.0	150
ALL STAFF	144.35	12.06	11.95	13.06	37.10	36.40	38.06	13.09	14.05	14.53	41.62	153.45
Per hour (average) CONSULTANTS	81.53	90.89	84.19	74.45	82.25	78.37	90.77	79.16	60.86	95.56	76.29	82.11
EMPLOYEES	100.35	115.43	107.85	92.51	103.99	98.43	113.74	79.86	76.88	118.29	95.60	102.70
ALL STAFF	100.35	115.43	101.93	88.60	100.00	93.48	107.72	101.44	83.38	114.50	97.75	99.63
INDIRECT EXPENSE												
SELLING TOTAL	141.1	10.3	10.3	10.5	31.1	41.3	41.4	10.5	10.6	10.5	31.6	146
ADMINISTRATION TOTAL	222.8	17.9	18.9	22.3	59.1	64.5	68.1	22.6	25.5	22.0	70.1	262
OTHER INDIRECT TOTAL	11.0	2.8	0.3	0.3	3.4	1.9	3.4	0.3	0.3	1.8	2.4	11
INDIRECT EXPENSE TOTAL	375.0	30.9	29.6	33.1	93.6	107.7	112.9	33.5	36.4	34.3	104.2	418
NET EARNINGS (NEBA)	45.6	-9.2	5.6	26.1	22.6	40.1	-22.0	16.0	59.4	-10.8	64.6	105
Margin	2.3%	-6.4%	3.3%	12.3%	4.3%	6.8%	-3.8%	7.2%	20.1%	-5.6%	9.1%	4.4%
ALLOCATED EXPENSE TOTAL	45.6	3.1	3.4	4.3	10.8	12.0	10.8	3.8	5.1	3.6	12.5	46
NET EARNINGS (NEBT)	0.0	-12.3	2.2	21.8	11.8	28.1	-32.8	12.2	54.3	-14.4	52.1	59
Margin	0.0%	-8.6%	1.3%	10.2%	2.2%	4.7%	-5.7%	5.5%	18.4%	-7.5%	7.3%	2.5%
EXPENSE RATES (NEBA)												
Per month & year EMPLOYEES	183.8	15.4	15.1	16.5	46.9	47.0	46.9	15.0	15.6	16.2	46.8	188
ALL STAFF	183.82	15.42	14.89	16.39	46.73	46.58	47.73	15.95	17.21	17.70	50.80	192.08
Per hour (average) EMPLOYEES	127.79	147.562	133.671	115.745	130.485	125.344	141.368	121.917	95.6435	145.52	117.695	128.311
ALL STAFF	127.79	147.562	127.036	111.185	125.958	119.621	135.063	123.623	102.098	139.44	119.331	124.706

Figure 18-13 Summary income and expense plan for mixed resources.

The point of the exercise, though, was to achieve both growth and improved profits. Each of the plan iterations focused on adding risk to achieve strategic and tactical objectives. You as a planner of a practice start with a very low-risk business-as-usual approach that achieved only a portion of the growth and profit objectives to a very high risk plan that achieves all the objectives. The learning process that parallels the planning process has shown you options. Regardless of which level of risk you choose, you have fall-back options already in your pockets, ready to pull out when your plan is challenged by reality.

Planning in the Very Small Firm

Every firm, even the smallest one-person firm, needs to prepare a forecast of income and expenses. This may be no more elaborate than marking up the previous year's tax statement to see what will change. No plan exists until it is written down.

The simplest income and expense plan need not be month by month. In order to understand cash needs, though, income and expense ought to be broken out by quarter. The profit plan should have key assumptions written on each line or attached as a separate list. The important assumptions are: expected hours to be spent in behalf of clients, the portion of those hours that will produce billable results, the portion of those hours that will be actually billed, and the effective rate to be charged.

In the very small firm it is difficult and not very satisfying to break time that is not directly billed into components of marketing time, pro bono time to get business, and rework time to achieve satisfaction. It is important, though, to know the aggregate time spent directly with clients in order to know the effective rate one receives for the time spent. This will help determine whether that time can continue to generate enough income to be profitable.

For example, if you plan to devote half your life to your consulting practice and you typically devote 55 hours per week to your work time (including travel), you will make 1430 hours available to the practice. If this last year you actually spent 1015 hours directly with or traveling to and from clients, you were utilized 71 percent of the time. If you price yourself at $150 per hour, but you typically only bill for two-thirds of the time you actually spend directly on a client, you realized 680 hours at full rate out of the 1430 hours you were prepared to spend. For planning purposes, you received $100.50 per hour for the time you actually spent on clients (1015 hours) and $71.30 for the time you think you devoted to your business (1430 hours). Your challenge is to decide whether the new year will be different and which of these factors will change.

Obviously, the staffing plan for a single-person firm illustrated above can be written on a napkin. (Be sure to attach the napkin to your written income and expense plan!) This becomes much more difficult and error-prone when the firm moves to even two people. A prudent practice leader and entrepreneur will develop a month-by-month staffing and revenue forecast plan as described in this chapter. The number of possible combinations of utilization and average rate for two people is exponential to that of one person. A spreadsheet of these assumptions and the resulting hours and revenue will pay dividends in the number of times it will be slightly revised during the planning process and the benefit it will serve in shortening decision time when actual time and revenue do not track to the plan.

A small firm rarely needs a revenue segmentation plan. Usually, each member of the firm has a specialty, and the staffing plan itself provides enough distribution to show where demand for the service is increasing or decreasing. Only when the individuals (three or more) in a firm are splitting their time between lines of service is a revenue segmentation plan useful.

Obviously, the accounting structures of professional services firms vary widely. The examples used in this chapter are simply that: a helpful list of the kinds of expenses that might be expected. A very small firm will have fewer line items, because it rarely has the complexity of large rented facilities, multiple sets of furniture and equipment, and a permanent, multiperson administrative staff. However, the small firm may have home office and other intricate expense sharing that is charged off to the business. Again, the best approach is to annually list all expected expense by quarter to ensure that income and expense will be synchronized and that the business will see the financial results that your time and energy deserve.

All Good Business People Plan

The purpose of this chapter was to provide you practical examples for planning professional services and, particularly, management consulting. No business is too small or too uncertain for a plan of how it will achieve its basic objectives in the coming year. The existence of a plan enhances the entrepreneurial practice leader's ability to assess alternatives when things go wrong and how to grab the brass ring when the business produces beyond one's wildest dreams.

Key points to keep in mind regarding a practice business plan:

Every firm, regardless of size needs an income and expense plan. A prudent person does not risk time and money without some guess as to the financial consequences. The most important aspect of a simple income and expense plan are the written assumptions that go with it. These assumptions always include:

1. People time to be devoted to clients
2. The effective rate to be realized for that time
3. The amount of money each person needs to get in salary and benefits
4. The basic nonpeople expenses of the business

Business management becomes the process of testing these assumptions and making decisions that protect the profitability of your business.

Every firm should have a strategy. Too many consultants get into a groove supplying the same services to the same clients and miss the opportunity to change their offerings to meet changes in the market. Once a year, you need to step back from today's engagements and think more than a year into the future. The larger the practice, the more necessary this becomes, since the future of many depend on sustaining or growing the income of the practice. Once strategic goals are established, they should provide tantalizing options to the annual tactical planning for a firm.

Annual tactical planning should be an iterative process. The annual planning process should have at least three iterations: business-as-usual to see the effect of maintaining current staffing and current utilization and effective billing rates; profit optimization to see what changes in current assumptions will produce profits against next year's cost and expense assumptions; and a final plan that balances what the current market is bearing, profit needs, and strategic objectives.

Planning is a learning process. Each plan iteration teaches you how the elements of your business interact to create revenue and expense. Each plan iteration better prepares you with alternatives when you are faced with reality. The plan's sole purpose is to tell you when you are off the path. A thorough planning process gives you clues as to where to start the new path while in midjourney.

19
Marketing Consulting Services

Sam Barcus
Barcus Britt Leiffer Consulting
Nashville, Tennessee

Introduction

For most professional service organizations, new business opportunities are created through activities in four major areas. Whether an organization has a formalized marketing plan or pursues opportunities on a less structured basis, research has shown that most new business flows, as indicated in Figure 19-1, through present client activities, referral relationships, community visibility activities, and potential client activities. Specific marketing efforts in each of these areas may be undertaken by individuals, by a firm as a whole, or by any segment within the firm such as an office or industry group.

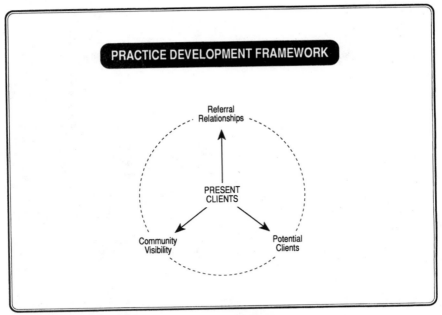

Figure 19-1 Practice development framework.

Present Client Activities

Present clients form the core of most new business activities for all firms except those in a completely new, start-up situation. In the professional environment, a start-up situation usually means initially working with a single client or small group of clients and almost always precedes a decision to "start" a consulting, accounting, or law practice. The three primary purposes of business development activities directed toward present clients are (1) retention, (2) expansion of services, and (3) generation of referrals for new business. Figure 19-2 provides a work plan and worksheet to assess current clients.

Retention

Most professional service firms subscribe to the maxim that it is easier to keep a current client than to attract a new one. Firms that aggressively pursue new clients while taking client retention for granted have often experienced unexpected losses and decreasing profitability that are not offset by gains from new clients. Perhaps of greatest importance, emphasis on new client acquisition over client retention overlooks the way most professional firms have grown—through referrals from satisfied clients and by meeting a full range of present client needs.

Current Clients Workplan

1.0 Audit Present Client Base for the Previous Twelve Months:

    1.1 Rank clients by amount of revenue received and determine percent of total fees

    1.2 Determine nature and quality of relationship(s)

    1.3 Determine industry and geographic concentrations

    1.4 Rate short-term and long-term fee potential

    1.5 Rate referral potential

    1.6 Rate displacement potential

    1.7 Identify sources of new clients

    1.8 Determine causes of lost clients

2.0 Classify Present Clients as:

    2.1 Key client

    2.2 Strong potential client

    2.3 Limited potential client

    2.4 Marginal client

3.0 Develop Client Service Priorities:

    3.1 Develop client-centered information database on priority clients

    3.2 Establish general goals for improved/expanded relationship(s)/service with client service team

    3.3 Set and assign tasks necessary to accomplish goal

    3.4 Monitor and evaluate progress

Figure 19-2 Current clients work plan and client assessment worksheet.

Many professional service firms espouse quality service to current clients and active, ongoing monitoring of client satisfaction. Few firms, however, have established a systematic approach for ensuring that these goals are met. Specific activities such as those listed below have been effective:

Current Client
Assessment Worksheet

Client Name _____

Client Account Team

    Partner: _____

    Manager: _____

    Consultant: _____

Client Financial History

Year	Sales	No. of Employees
19____	$_____	_____
19____	$_____	_____
19____	$_____	_____

Client Financial History with Firm

Year	Category 1	Category 2	Category 3
19____	$_____	$_____	$_____
19____	$_____	$_____	$_____
19____	$_____	$_____	$_____

Nature of Client's Operations

_____

_____

_____

_____

_____

_____

_____

_____

_____

Figure 19-2 (*Continued*) Current client assessment worksheet.

- Client satisfaction letters, surveys, or meetings in which evaluations of personnel and performance can be gathered
- Partner/colleague programs which ensure that more than one key professional maintains regular contact with significant clients

Client's Major Business Goals

_____
_____
_____
_____
_____
_____
_____
_____

Client's Major Problems

1. _____
_____
_____
_____

2. _____
_____
_____
_____

Client Relationship with the Firm

_____
_____
_____
_____
_____
_____
_____
_____

Figure 19-2 (*Continued*)   Current client assessment worksheet.

- Client service planning in which detailed plans for providing additional services to key clients are developed

Client satisfaction and retention can often be a priority marketing goal for younger members of a professional service firm who want to meet

Background of Client Personnel

Board: _____

_____

_____

CEO: _____

_____

Marketing Executive: _____

_____

Sales Manager: _____

_____

Production Manager: _____

_____

_____

CFO: _____

_____

Controller: _____

_____

Information System Officer: _____

_____

Information System Manager: _____

_____

Figure 19-2 (*Continued*) Current client assessment worksheet.

management's expectations regarding business development. Many younger, ambitious professionals tend to equate marketing with bringing new clients in the door, which sometimes results in less-than-ideal situations. While attracting new desirable clients is a key goal of any firm's business development efforts, a somewhat wider definition of marketing needs to be promulgated so there is full understanding of all

Client Organization Chart

Example:

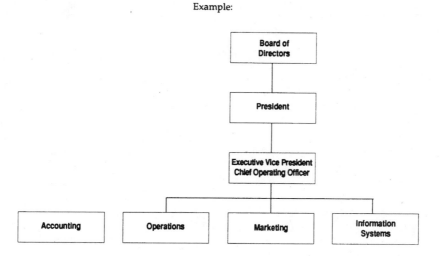

General Goal for Improved/Expanded Service

_____

_____

_____

_____

_____

_____

_____

Figure 19-2 (*Continued*)   Current client assessment worksheet.

aspects of the firm's program. Most important, young professionals will learn how to sell to new prospects when they learn how to keep a present client satisfied.

Specific Tasks for the Client Service Team

	Planned Action	Responsibility	Target Date	Actual Completion Date
1.	_____	_____	_____	_____
	_____			
	_____			
	_____			
	_____			
	_____			
2.	_____	_____	_____	_____
	_____			
	_____			
	_____			
	_____			
	_____			
3.	_____	_____	_____	_____
	_____			
	_____			
	_____			
	_____			
	_____			
4.	_____	_____	_____	_____
	_____			
	_____			
	_____			
	_____			
	_____			
5.	_____	_____	_____	_____
	_____			
	_____			
	_____			
	_____			
	_____			

Figure 19-2 (*Continued*)   Current client assessment worksheet.

Expansion of Services

The second purpose of present client marketing is the "cross-marketing" of services to current clients. Many firms have realized the substantial

Planned Action	Responsibility	Target Date	Actual Completion Date
6.			
7.			
8.			
9.			
10.			

Figure 19-2 (*Continued*) Current client assessment worksheet.

potential in providing further services beyond those originally proposed to the client. Most firms find that the $20,000 client of today can become the $300,000 client of 3 years from now. For example, accounting firms of all sizes learned early on that clients using accounting and auditing services also needed tax planning expertise. The full range of consulting services being provided by accounting firms to clients is a further example of the development of new business within the current client base. Law firms have only begun to tap the potential of cross-selling. Professional firms will find growth easier if they build on their present clients. Personnel recruiting firms, for example, may find that adding a training function would add more profits.

There are three important reasons that effective cross-selling should be a marketing goal for all professional service firms. First, the profit margin on additional services is usually greater because they are more specialized (tax research is less a "commodity" than an audit) and require less start-up time to know the client.

Second, increased attention to cross-selling more services to current clients reduces vulnerability to client loss. A client who has an unmet need and is aware that the needed expertise is available from his or her current firm will probably ask for the assistance. A client who is not fully aware of the additional expertise will go outside seeking assistance, and a firm may find itself competing to retain the client. Worse yet, if the client is simply not aware of a need (e.g., compliance with a tax regulation) and the professional service firm doesn't raise the issue, the unmet need may result in a problem that could endanger the firm-client relationship.

Several studies have shown that the decision-making process regarding the selection of outside professional service assistance is greatly influenced by direct experience. The trust and confidence that develops because of a satisfactory service relationship is often cited as the key criterion in the selection of a professional service firm. Thus, the current provider of a service tends to be in a much stronger position to provide additional services than another firm with which the buyer has had little or no experience. For this reason, effective cross-marketing to develop more business is usually an easier "sell."

To be able to take full advantage of cross-marketing opportunities, a professional service firm needs to be sure there is proper internal communication. Specialists in one area should be aware of the services available from their own colleagues down the hall. Too often one professional shies away from a client question in an unknown area rather than encouraging and facilitating a meeting with a fellow partner-specialist who could address the client need. Until such barriers can be removed, a firm is really marketing individuals and not the firm as a whole.

Generation of Referrals

Almost without exception, professional service firms will categorically state that present clients are their best single source of referrals for additional clients. Firms tracking the sources of new business report that 50 to 75 percent of new clients come from the direct or indirect referral of a current client. Regardless of statistics, it would appear safe to assume that current clients provide the best single source for referral of new clients.

It is important for a professional service firm to develop and cultivate service and personal relationships with clients that will encourage referrals when an opportunity arises. Clearly, satisfaction of the client is critical to his or her willingness to serve as a sponsor with business colleagues. Beyond ensuring clients' satisfaction, many firms have developed specific programs to take the fullest possible advantage of current clients' referral potential. For example, a CPA firm cosponsoring a seminar with a restaurant wholesaler was found to be effective both in strengthening the relationship with the client and in establishing new contacts. Making sure clients are aware of the firm's full range of services is an important dimension of such programs; brochures, newsletters, and seminars have been used effectively in this regard. Attending trade association meetings with current clients can also provide opportunities for formal or informal referrals to business colleagues.

A professional service firm has to be conscious of the image it creates in the community regarding its interest in new business. Rarely is a professional considered "too aggressive" or too interested in new work. Usually, a more neutral or even "not interested" image is conveyed. A large number of current clients, when surveyed, have indicated that they don't know if their professional service firm is interested in new business. This perception often results from the professional's failure to indicate interest forthrightly by asking for the additional work or for the referral. Less direct indicators include failure to return phone calls promptly or frequent comments about how busy the firm is. To a great extent, marketing and business development represent a frame of mind—a recognition that business development is an integral part of one's professional life. Opportunities to convey an impression of sincere interest in providing service must be lost.

Overall, marketing to current clients to retain them, expand services, and generate new business should be the foundation of a professional service firm's efforts to develop new business opportunities. Without a strong commitment to present client marketing and equally strong programs to carry out the commitment, other marketing activities will be less fruitful in the long run.

In addition, as shown in Figure 19-1, present clients provide a key link to the other three marketing activity areas. For example, an effective way to develop relationships with referral sources is to meet with the other professionals (attorneys, bankers, insurance people) who serve current clients. Opportunities for speeches, articles, and other community visibility activities are often generated by professionals via current clients' membership in trade associations or civic groups. Finally, the link between present and potential clients has typically been the most lucrative source of new business for professional service firms.

Referral Relationship Activities

The Importance of Relationships

A second important activity to facilitate building a consulting practice is the development of relationships with significant third-party referral sources. Most often, these referral sources are fellow professionals who serve mutual clients; however, third parties are by no means restricted to other professionals. For example, any consultant building a computer software development practice would do well to maintain a strong liaison with computer brokers, dealers, and sales representatives. Attorneys, accountants, investment personnel, insurance brokers, bankers, and financial planners are frequently cited as significant third-party referral sources. Clearly, the relative importance of any particular group of referral sources will depend on the nature of a firm's practice as well as its goals for the future. Other referral sources of potential influence include firm alumni and client alumni (i.e., former client personnel). Although it is often very difficult to maintain contact with the two alumni groups, those who have had direct experience with a firm's services and personnel are in the best position to serve as a source of referrals. Former clients are a particularly good source for new business if you are just starting a practice. Such contacts take time to develop—plan on a year or more—but need to be cultivated from the start.

The primary purpose of developing relationships with significant third-party referral sources is to build a communications network that provides significant information about clients and potential clients. Many professionals put too much emphasis on the second agenda—generation of referrals—without recognizing the importance and long-range value of the primary objective—building the communications network. For example, the sharing of information and the discussion of common problems between accountants and attorneys working in the tax area can create the foundation for a long-lasting relationship between individual professionals and their firms. This dialogue is not only a valuable source of knowledge but a necessary prerequisite to mutual referrals. Often, referrals are made solely on the basis of a personal relationship rather than a rigorous search for the "right" firm. Studies have reportedly shown that referral sources rarely know what various professionals actually *do* for their clients. Bank loan officers may know what an audit is, but they rarely understand how management information systems or cash management programs work. Unfortunately, loan officers rarely know when their clients need such assistance and would appreciate referrals. Finally, most professionals indicate that they refer more to a specific individual with whom they have a relationship than to a firm as an institution.

Strategies for Building Relationships

Specific strategies for developing relationships with third-party referral sources can be implemented by a firm as a whole, by individual officers, and by individual professionals. For example, some accounting firms have developed specialized brochures or newsletters for bank loan officers outlining their expertise in conducting cash flow studies and management reviews. These brochures are used to make it clear that the firms can do more than audit historical financial data. At the local office level, organized programs for periodic mailings, social events, or round-table luncheons have become standardized parts of many contact development programs. However, since the foundation for strong relationships among professionals is personal contact, successful programs use publications and group meetings as a tool to get the ball rolling. The primary focus of the program is follow-up by key individuals to build the types of relationships that will be mutually beneficial to the individuals and the firm.

Several studies have suggested that professionals prefer personal contact and direct experience as the media for learning about another professional service firm's expertise. Traditional activities such as seminars and brochures/newsletters are also cited as being important and valuable but still do not have the same impact as direct and indirect personal communication. Advertising, as such, is not typically perceived by professionals to be an effective medium for communicating about specific expertise. Even though the emphasis is on the personal dimension of third-party referral relationships, there should be coordination between the firm's efforts and those of individual professionals to ensure a meaningful program. To ensure that all significant third-party groups are exposed to consulting or other services being offered, an organized, coordinated plan is important. However, research shows far too often that individual professionals do not consciously work on relationship development because they think a firm program such as educational seminars for bank loan officers will do the job. Follow-up is important in formally monitoring as closely as possible which third-party referral groups and individuals have been important sources of new business. It is equally important to investigate and evaluate which groups may be most helpful in referring the types of clients a firm may be targeting for the future. The increased competition among professional service firms of all types has given added significance to the term *reciprocal referrals* as firms and individuals have become less reticent about directly asking each other for referrals. In fact, many professionals will define the ideal professionals as one "who services my clients well and refers work to me."

Building the Target List

One of the most common misconceptions in building a consulting practice is that developing a mailing list focusing on third-party relationships is unnecessary until the practice is started. Developing a list of third-party contacts may often be a good way to determine if marketing a particular service will be effective. If few third-party relationships exist, starting a consulting practice should probably be postponed until these contacts can be developed. In today's world of computers, any consultant can build a segmented contact list with minimal investment that will help throughout her or his career. The development of relationships with fellow professionals is typically seen as an activity area in which both senior and junior members of a firm can become effectively involved. In general, specific relationships will be based on mutuality of interest or area of expertise among peer groups of similar age, experience, and position. For example, the founder of a computer software consulting practice will typically be familiar with owners/managers of hardware dealers. However, because it is important to establish and maintain a contact base with fellow professionals over time, younger consultants ought to be encouraged to develop their own relationships with sales representatives and others who work for the owner/manager. Such relationships may not provide short-term immediate referrals of potential clients, but these relationships will contribute to developing a communications base and building individual involvement in an overall firm program.

Finally, professionals must remember that the quality of relationships is more important than the quantity. Although relationships need to be built continually, a natural "weeding out" process will also occur. Out of every ten contacts a professional makes, perhaps only one or two will be important referral sources over the long term. When building a consulting practice, the key is to make sure the "pipeline" of third-party relationships is continuously being expanded. This ensures that the very best contacts are identified and cultivated over the years. Figure 19-3 is a work plan for building a referral network.

Referral Relationships Work Plan

1.0 Establish an Inventory of Your Relationships:

    1.1 Alumni

    1.2 Association executives

    1.3 Attorneys

    1.4 Bankers

    1.5 Former customer executives

    1.6 Influentials

    1.7 Reciprocals

    1.8 Referrals

    1.9 Stockbrokers

2.0 Determine Your Key Relationships:

    2.1 Assess the nature and quality of these relationships

    2.2 Set priorities

    2.3 Build multiple relationships as required

3.0 Enhance Your Key Relationships:

    3.1 Plan a contact program

    3.2 Follow through

    3.3 Add/delete relationships on a periodic basis

Figure 19-3 Referral relationships work plan.

Community Visibility Activities

Scope of Public Relations

Marketing professional services through greater visibility involves promotional and public relations activities and includes a wide range of traditional as well as innovative strategies. Historically, professional services firms have used public relations activities such as membership in a country club or making a speech as their major effort in business development. In today's world, focusing on such activities is too general and can cause frustration for a firm which believes that public relations or promotional activities will lead directly to new business. Because professional services are highly personal, most authorities agree that promotional activities should be viewed primarily as vehicles for creating and enhancing awareness of the firm. This awareness can be leveraged so that it builds a contact base to be cultivated on a personal basis through follow-up.

Special activities that would fall under the heading of public relations and promotion range from advertising to the sponsorship of golf tournaments to giving a speech at an appropriate trade organization. An all-inclusive list of standard promotional activities would be impossible to create, but the following might be considered representative:

- Institutional advertising
- Product and service-oriented advertising
- Newsletters
- Seminars and workshops
- Speeches
- Articles in professional or industry publications
- Press relations
- Trade shows
- Participation in community trade and professional organizations
- Symposia and panels

Effective Promotional Activity

The effectiveness of public relations and promotion depends in large part on targeting. Although the development of strong name recognition is an important overall goal, establishing contacts with key influences or decision makers at selected businesses is more likely to produce new business in the long run. It is more important, for example, for a law firm with a strong labor practice to be recognized by construction companies, which have frequent need of legal assistance in labor-related matters, than it is for the general business community to recognize the firm's name. Similarly, a consulting firm that wishes to market software development assistance to small retailers should probably become active in downtown and regional business associations. As a result, many professional service organizations are now producing specialized brochures, newsletters, and seminars targeted at specific audiences among which the firm hopes to expand its business.

Perhaps most important, all public relations and promotional activities should be designed to establish contacts that can be enhanced on a personal basis as a follow-up to the activity. If a seminar is conducted, an attendance list should be maintained so follow-up mailings and telephone calls can be made to establish and enhance personal relationships. A professional on a fund-raising committee for a community activity should make a point of getting to know other committee members. Far too often, professionals see the public relations activities as the goal rather than pursuing the opportunities the activity creates. In fact, the follow-up yields the real benefits in marketing a professional service.

Seminars

Seminars remain a popular tool for many professionals primarily because they offer an opportunity to meet a large number of people and to demonstrate indirectly the quality of the firm's people and expertise. Both business executives and other professionals acknowledge seminars to be an effective medium for the communication of expertise. Seminars that are designed for a specific audience on a topic of interest, that are short (2 or 3 hours), and that provide the participants with practical suggestions are typically the most successful. Seminars or symposia cosponsored by two groups of professionals offer the opportunity for enhancing relationships between the cosponsors as well as between participants. A CPA firm and a bank might cosponsor a seminar on cash flow planning aimed at the clients of both organizations.

Community Involvement

Community involvement in civic or charitable organizations continues to be an important dimension of many professional service firms' promotional programs. From an idealistic standpoint, such activities offer professionals the opportunity to "repay" their communities; more pragmatically, these opportunities allow professionals also to meet fellow professionals and future business contacts. Participation in such activities should be based primarily on the individual professional's interests and desire to contribute to the community. Enhancing the firm's image and generating contacts, although secondary, will be a fairly natural occurrence if those who participate really like what they are doing. The involvement of a firm's professionals needs to be planned, coordinated, and monitored, however, for maximum benefits to be derived. If a firm is developing a practice in executive search, for example, it would be a serious omission not to become actively involved in local trade groups made up of personnel managers. In all cases, leadership in such activities—or at least maintenance of a very high profile—is highly recommended if good results are to be achieved.

Because reputation is among the most important criteria in the evaluation and selection of a professional service firm, all public relations or promotional activities should be evaluated for their impact on the firm's reputation. Although name recognition and reputation are not synonymous, a long-term objective of promotional activities should be to make the firm's name synonymous with quality people providing quality expertise and service. Figure 19-4 provides a work plan for developing a high community profile.

Potential Client Activities

The ultimate objective of all business development activities is to attract new clients. Because of the combined long-term and short-term nature of professional services marketing, a wide variety of strategies involving present clients, referral sources, and community visibility activities is required for aggressive pursuit of specific prospects. The fourth general activity, which focuses on "real" potential clients, is perhaps the most critical but complex component of an effective overall program. Even the most sophisticated professional service firms have difficulty targeting and acquiring specific clients. Figure 19-5 provides a work plan to target potential clients and a potential client questionnaire.

Potential Client Profiles

In general, the purpose of potential client activities is to identify potential clients, to position the firm or individual for an opportunity, and to ultimately acquire the clients. In some instances this process occurs quickly and without a great deal of overt effort on the part of the service firm. In most instances, however, the process is longer term and requires ongoing monitoring and evaluation.

It is important for the firm to define its potential client profile. To accept any client who will pay a fee is not necessarily in the firm's long-term best interest. Although the acceptance criteria will vary widely from firm to firm, two factors deserve special consideration:

Community Profile Work Plan

1.0 Define Primary Purpose(s) of Participation:

    1.1 Self-development

    1.2 Contribute to the community

    1.3 Make new contacts

    1.4 Enhance image of firm

2.0 Evaluate Match Between Present Participation and Purposes

3.0 Set Definite Plan with Short- and Long-Term Goals to Improve Value of Participation:

    3.1 Reduce/eliminate participation in less useful groups

    3.2 Identify potential groups to meet purposes

    3.3 Choose appropriate organization

    3.4 Set career plan

4.0 Evaluate Improvement in Six – Twelve Months

5.0 Plan Involvement to Obtain Maximum Benefits

    5.1 Customer involvement

    5.2 Colleague involvement

    5.3 Multipliers

Figure 19-4 Community profile work plan.

1. Be sure that the potential client has needs that are related to the firm's expertise and service capabilities.
2. Be sure that the potential client is able to enhance the firm's practice.

Potential Clients Work Plan

1.0 Define Your Potential Client Profile. They Should:

    1.1 Meet acceptance criteria

    1.2 Have needs related to your service capabilities

    1.3 Be able to enhance your service opportunites

2.0 Analyze the Market to Identify Specific Potential Clients Meeting Your Criteria

3.0 Match Existing Relationships with Potential Client List

    3.1 Build on your strengths

    3.2 Work as a team

    3.3 Classify in terms of potential

4.0 Consider Existing Relationships with Other Nonclients

5.0 Establish Priorities:

    5.1 Start with limited number of potential clients

    5.2 Assign responsibilities for tracking potential clients

6.0 Undertake Plan:

    6.1 Use team approach to position the firm with the potential clients

    6.2 Establish continuing contact

    6.3 Monitor progress

    6.4 Add/delete potential clients as appropriate

Figure 19-5   Potential clients work plan and questionnaire.

By pursuing any and all projects, some firms have mistakenly sold to a prospective client services that the firm cannot really deliver. This can create substantial problems and the decreased profitability that comes with learning a new service area. For example, the computer consulting

Potential Clients Questionnaire

Client Name ──

1. Who is the decision-making group in the client organization?

   _____

   _____

2. In what order should members of this group be approached?

   _____

   _____

3. How can proposed project be broken down into phases, and what are the probable phases and total costs? Is there a better project approach? If yes, describe.

   _____

   _____

   _____

   _____

4. Who from the Firm should head the project?

   _____

   _____

5. What are the reasons the client should act now?

   _____

   _____

   _____

6. What are the reasons the client should have the work done by an outsider?

   _____ a. Expertise (specialized/technical knowledge) not available within the client organization

   _____ b. Gain experience from outsider solving similar problems for others

   _____ c. Need is temporary (project-oriented)

   _____ d. Project, if done by insiders, would interfere with efficient management of current guidelines

   _____ e. Independence/objectivity

   _____ f. Confidentiality

Figure 19-5 (*Continued*)   Potential clients work plan and questionnaire.

firm that always does work for banks may find trying to provide the same services for retailers less profitable and frustrating. Selling a service the firm does not normally deliver can create problems beyond the

7. Who from the firm should participate in the client meeting?

   _____

   _____

8. Are the client decision-makers:

   ——— a. Sophisticated or naive?

   ——— b. Brisk and businesslike or casual and friendly?

   ——— c. Detail-oriented or big-picture-oriented?

   ——— d. Directive or expectant of leadership?

   ——— e. Open-minded about services?

9. Who should lead the marketing team?

   _____

   _____

10. What horror stories are relevant to this client's situation?

    _____

    _____

11. What references shall we offer?

    _____

    _____

    _____

12. Who is our competition? What are their strengths and weaknesses?

    _____

    _____

    _____

13. Why should the client use us for this project?

    _____

    _____

14. What has our firm done for this client before, and how did it work out?

    _____

    _____

Figure 19-5 (*Continued*) Potential clients work plan and questionnaire.

immediate project with the individual client. However, a new client who provides opportunities for expanding expertise, developing the firm's reputation, and increasing its base can have a beneficial effect that transcends the specific project. In either case, the issue is making an intelligent choice based on overall goals rather than simply pursuing new clients without any predetermined criteria for acceptance.

Targeting Potential Clients

Once a potential client profile has been established, the firm should analyze the overall marketplace in order to identify specific potential clients who meet the criteria. Such an analysis would include examining the market in terms of industry groups, size of companies, geographical areas of growth, and the fee of potential of desirable companies. Analysis of competition must also be considered in establishing the realistic potential for attracting specific new clients. To the extent possible, such an analysis might also include examining the types of services currently being received and needed by potential new clients. Relationships among potential clients and their current providers of the other professional services should also be considered.

An effective bridge between identification and positioning can be built by determining existing relationships with potential clients through the firm's own professionals, current clients, and referral sources. Knowing a potential client's attorney and banker may enhance opportunities, especially if other mutual client relationships already exist. Because businesses in similar industries develop their own relationships and thus share information about providers of professional services, leveraging off the current client base can be very effective. In addition, matching on the basis of current relationships helps a firm to build on its strengths and work as a team in the positioning effort. Most important, firms must classify prospects realistically in terms of their potential so they pursue realistic opportunities and use their resources wisely.

Establishing a Monitoring System

Establishing a system for monitoring progress on target prospects is perhaps the most critical factor in successful programs. Goals should be realistic and based on a limited number of potential prospects. Responsibilities for establishing and maintaining contacts should be assigned to individuals or teams so that effective ongoing monitoring of progress can take place. Internal communication regarding progress helps to motivate those who are responsible for implementing the contact program and to ensure that significant opportunities don't "slip through the cracks." Part of the monitoring process should be periodically adding or deleting prospects from the list.

To help monitor their activities and progress with potential clients, many firms have created marketing databases with information about clients, prospects, referral sources, services, fees, current relationships, and status. Such an information system helps track progress, assists the internal communication process, and provides an external stimulus for active participation by members of the firm.

Conclusion

The checklists included in the chapter should provide some assistance in helping a firm building a consulting practice determine which of the four types of activities discussed in the chapter requires the most attention.

20

Consultant Development

Bruce A. Esposito, Ph.D.
Senior Faculty
IBM, Advanced Business Institute
Executive Consulting Institute

Edward J. Koplos
Group Leader
IBM, Advanced Business Institute
Executive Consulting Institute

Introduction

One of the most critical processes at work in any consulting firm is the growth and development of its people. Each member of the firm must grow in knowledge and capability, just as the firm itself must grow to keep pace with competition and the needs of its clients. To succeed, a management consulting firm must have sufficient skills and knowledge at each level of its hierarchy. The firm puts a development program in place to ensure the vitality and consistency of knowledge and the culture and growth of its members. This allows the group of practitioners to leverage its existing professionals to deliver successful engagement results. At the same time each member of the team must be able to develop along the way. A firm that serves its clients well but ignores its people will soon find its quality slipping and its most important assets, the people, leaving for more self-fulfilling positions.

The "development process" is the integrated collection of education, the use of mentors, and experience (often called on-the-job training or "OJT"). "Education" in this context is the transfer of knowledge and skill through a variety of approaches. Knowledge is typically transferred through lecture, reading, or other more passive techniques. Skill is typically grown through the combination of some of these knowledge transfer techniques used in conjunction with experiential approaches, such as the use of case study or interactive self-directed approaches.

To get a better perspective on the best way to develop consultants, each firm should ask some basic questions. If consultant development is such an important process, then why do many firms leave it to chance? How do the requirements of a firm differ when it is starting up, growing, or in a steady state? What are the key skills and qualities that make consultants successful, and can any of them be improved with traditional education? If so, what obstacles must be faced when trying to develop consultants? How do age and experience affect the consultant development process? Finally, what approach should be taken to develop consultants, and how can that approach be kept consistent with the marketplace?

Development Needs

To discuss the topic of consultant development, it should be put in context with the development of the firm. Our research tells us that there are many ways to grow a viable consulting firm. However, posing a conceptual model of the stages of a firm's growth can be very helpful in discussing the development needs of its members. This model has three stages (see Figure 20-1), with characteristics that are quite distinct. The stages are described in terms of growth characteristics, but the stages also track fairly closely with size of the firm and its impact on the firm's consultant development approach. In other words, the consultant development processes, as described below, of a small firm of one to three practitioners will be similar to those of a start-up firm, independent of its growth profile. Although the focus will be on the differences between these stages, these distinctions will blur depending on the firm's desired start-up timetable, preferred size, available capital, and personnel turnover profile. The three stages are start-up (small firm of 1 to 3 practitioners), growth (medium-size firm of 4 to 25 practitioners), and steady state (large firm of greater than 26 practitioners).

Characteristics	Stages		
	Start-up (Genesis)	Growth (Adolescence)	Steady State (Maturity)
Clients	Initial Backers	Client Set Growing	Current Clients (>70% of revenue) Plus Growth
Practitioners	Experienced Entrepreneur(s)	Additional Experienced Consultants	Full Range of Experience-Expert through the "Apprentice"
Methodology	Initial Thinking Enhanced and Tested with Initial Client	Strengthened by Practice and Ideas from New Members	On-Going Process to Grow It and Communicate to Firm
Hiring	Very Limited	Experience through Sponsorship and Subcontracting	New PLBA's through Experience Professionals at All Levels
Consultant Development	Very Limited ■ OJT ■ Outside Trainers ■ Multifirm Seminars	■ Induction Sessions ■ Methodology Reviews ■ Mentor as Needed ■ Prior Steps Continue ■ Classroom Training May Start	Full Development Process Coordinated: ■ Mix of OJT, Classroom Mentors, Self-Directed ■ Induction Sessions ■ New Consultant Training ■ Experienced Consultant Development ■ Evaluation Feedback
Size	Small 1–3	Medium 4–24	Large 25 and Up

Figure 20-1 The consulting firm conceptual stages of growth. (© *IBM Corporation, 1994.*)

Start-Up

In the start-up stage, one or more experienced consultants, or individuals with unique skills and knowledge, get together in an entrepreneurial spirit to strike out on their own. They have gained their experience and training working in established firms and feel that they have knowledge, skills, and a unique approach that justifies the new venture. The consultants also have a client who believes in their ability to bring value on a first job. In this chapter, the term *job* (synonymous with assignment or engagement) means a piece of consulting work commissioned by a client, for a fee, to meet an expressed need. In the start-up stage the firm invests heavily in its clients and itself at the same time. In human terms, this first stage resembles the first 10 years of life, where all the body's systems get started, and the learning and early growth is supported, sponsored, and shaped by the parent (client). It is here that the child solidifies its personality and sets its foundation from both a learning and an ethical standpoint.

The firm will work with this first client or set of initial clients for a period of a year or two solidifying the concept of the firm and its ideas, standard consulting frameworks (e.g., analysis techniques, tools, problem-solving approaches), and ethical approach to the market. This collection of intellectual concepts and tools can be called the firm's *methodology*. The primary focus at this stage is to present quality and value in everything that is done. More than at any other time in the firm's life, highly qualified resources must be assigned to each engagement to ensure outstanding references and follow-up business. To do anything less would jeopardize the reputation of the emerging firm before it has had a chance to establish itself. At this stage, firms will develop, enhance, and test their methodology by charging less for their early engagements, overstaffing, or overextending their jobs, but pricing them at the proper value to the client. This reduces profitability for the firm but maintains high client satisfaction and sets an important value/price relationship in the client's mind.

In such a start-up environment with limited capital, the consultant development process will be very limited. If additional resources are needed, the firm would more likely be apt to acquire highly qualified individuals, through an alliance or subcontract arrangement. If skills are needed to enhance the already mature firm members, the firm would turn to professional training organizations, or multifirm seminars sponsored by a professional consulting organization to enhance core skills. It is very unlikely that the firm would develop its own course offerings at this stage, because of the single-minded focus on establishing the firm in the marketplace and on the investment of time and resources required.

This profile is also similar to that of the firm that chooses to stay small, with one to three consultants at a given time. A 1992 *Consulting News* study of 1533 consulting firms in North America[1] found that 48.5 percent of the firms studied fell into this size category (see Figure 20-2). The same study[2] indicated that over 76 percent of all firms in the study were established between 1970 and 1989 (see Figure 20-3), making those

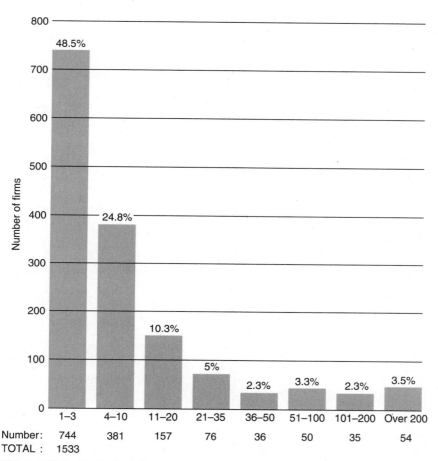

Figure 20-2   North American consulting firms. (*Kennedy Publications*, "An *Analysis of Management Consulting*," 1992, © *Kennedy Publications*.)

two decades a watershed period for management consulting. These small firms will also consistently lack the infrastructure and resources to do their own consultant education, depending instead on outside training firms to fill in skill voids. The use of mentors and OJT are the major firm-based development approaches for a start-up or small firm.

Growth

At the growth stage, the firm begins to attract new business driven by prior successes. The firm must then decide whether it wants to handle this new activity in its current form and size or respond to the demand

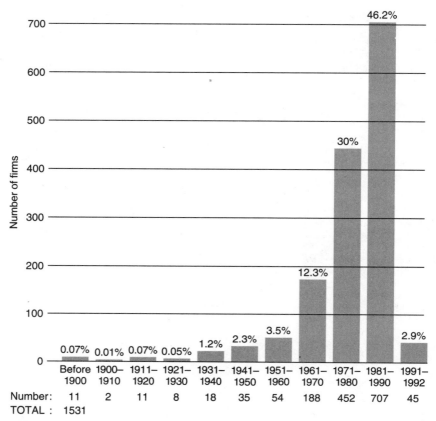

Figure 20-3 North American consulting firms. When were the firms founded? (*Kennedy Publications, "An Analysis of Management Consulting," 1992,* © *Kennedy Publications.*)

opportunity through growth. The human counterpart of the growth stage is adolescence. Here the body shoots up in odd proportions responding to the haphazard growth of the maturing systems of the body. Foot size often leads height, and great height is gained with very little muscle and flesh to fill out the frame.

The most common approach for growth from 2 to 3 members to 20 or fewer is through hiring or subcontracting. The new members are often chosen through a sponsorship approach, brought in and recommended by a firm member. It is not unusual for the firm to use such individuals as subcontractors to test their skill and their chemistry with the other members before making an offer. Because each consultant needs to work closely with the other consultants in the practice, the interview process is often long and thorough. Once hired new members must go through an orientation or induction process; it is here that they are shown the firm's concept, ethical framework, and methodology. As these skilled individuals come on board, they bring knowledge and methodology of their own that is tested against that of the firm. If those new members bring stronger skills, techniques, and approaches, the methodology is strengthened; if they do not, they are asked to get in step with the firm's approach and work to contribute to the growth of the methodology.

As the number of consultants joining the firm grows, the firm's mixture of skills can get lopsided. Responding to client needs, the firm may develop strengths in some areas and weaknesses in others. Firm members will learn more than 60 percent of their skills through on-the-job training and mentors. Mentors give "real-time" advice on the use of the firm's methodology, ensure consistent application, act as coaches to improve performance, and monitor quality in all aspects of the job.

Where skill gaps are perceived by the firm, or consistent knowledge and information needs to be shared, training is considered to fill the voids. Most growing firms consider classroom education to be a luxury in terms of both time and money. New members of medium-sized firms may take two or three courses offered by the firm, courses usually devoted to induction processes and updates of the firm's methodology. Professional training firms are most often used for improving skills or fostering skill consistency among current members, although some firms develop grass roots training programs taught by their best practitioners. Firms in the growth stage rarely are able to make a substantial investment in formal training programs, but such programs can pay off in the long run, in terms of both productivity and quality of work.

Steady State

Steady state is the last stage of the development model; it corresponds to the period of maturity. At this stage, the firm reaches an equilibrium between marketplace demand and its human resource plan. Steady state parallels adulthood, where basic education is complete, the profession is developed, clients are at hand, and there is a need to set the ongoing processes in motion. The firm has developed a lean support structure for teams of consultants to work in a very flexible manner. It has the system, methodology, and personnel development responsibilities to field multiple consulting teams in a variety of client jobs. It must continue to change and develop new ideas and people to ensure the viability of these teams in the competitive environment in which it competes.

At this stage, a staff pyramid (see Figure 20-4) with multiple tiers is formalized. In this structure, the most experienced firm members are at the top (e.g., partners, principals, and directors), those managing the

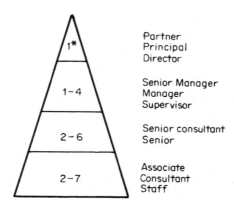

*Each pyramid is built around a signal partner, principal, or director. In large practices, there will be multiple pyramids. The numbers in the pyramid refer to the typical number of personnel at each level (per pyramid).

Figure 20-4   Staffing pyramid.

business and engagements on a week-to-week basis are on the next tier (e.g., senior managers, job managers, and supervisors); the third tier has the "bread and butter" consultants experienced at performing all consulting tasks and supervising the daily work of new employees (e.g., senior consultants, consultants); the last tier, if it is formalized, has the newly hired firm members learning the trade (e.g., associate consultants and staff). The staffing pyramid should be relatively stable in size if not content, with a comfortable turnover rate that allows the strong performers to rise to the top and disenchanted, weaker, or miscast players to move on to other opportunities. Turnover rates of 10 to 25 percent a year are not unusual in this environment. Often, the firm members who leave to go to work for valued clients, take with them strong positive ties back to the firm. This not only enables the firm to develop a strong loyalty among its client base but it also allows for a continuous stream of new entrants into all levels of the staff pyramid, particularly at the lower-paid levels, which improves the firm's profitability.

At this stage, a systematic approach to consultant development, preferably begun during the start-up or growth stages, should be enhanced with the necessary feedback mechanisms. If the firm had invested in training efforts in the past, such efforts can be resurrected in a number of forms. Where quality courses and materials have been developed, they should be updated and offered on a regular basis to employees new to their positions to assure a consistent level of culture, orientation, knowledge, skill, and methodology proficiency. Self-directed modules can be created to prepare students for more intense classroom-based learning. For new employees at least a core of these classroom-based modules should be packaged in a contiguous block of time, to form a strong learning experience and to develop firm spirit and comradeship. Where applicable, such materials can be considered for client consumption, if they are high in quality and can be tailored quickly to meet the client's needs. If this can be done, proper attention should be given to ensure that the firm's intellectual assets are protected.

For experienced firm members alternative delivery mechanisms must be considered to allow them to respond to billing, utilization, and travel requirements. The full spectrum of development options (e.g., classroom and self-directed education, on-the-job training, and mentoring), discussed later in this chapter, should be utilized to balance effectiveness versus cost. For example, there is still significant value in bringing these groups together regularly to share knowledge and experiences and to build needed skills. The format should be less structured, however, allowing the practitioners to attend main tent sessions of interest and pursue specific knowledge and skill needs in elective sessions. Self-directed learning lends itself well to knowledge sharing, methodology updates, and foundation skill development in preparation for more intense learning experiences. The feedback mechanisms that are put in place (e.g., client satisfaction results, end of engagement evaluations, yearly partner evaluations) should be used to guide the practitioner in forming a road map to build knowledge and skills using the appropriate development options.

If the firm is pursuing an international business plan, it must consider the impact that this will have on the consultant development process. Careful consideration should be given to the applicability of the consulting approach and to the education offered to all practitioners in light of cultural differences that may exist between the different countries in which the firm plans to practice. Efforts to educate firm members together on core elements can promote strong networking ties and help each of the players to gain insights into the overall vision of the firm and the marketplace that it serves.

The most important goals of consultant development during steady state is to deliver value within an affordable budget and to speed the progress of the workers of today and the leaders of tomorrow. The development approach should allow the firm the flexibility both to maintain currency and enter into a growth stage once again depending on the market forces in place.

The Effective Consulting Mind

A successful consultant development process produces effective consultants, whose assets are a combination of what they brought to the firm (determined during the selection process) and what they gained from the firm's development program. This combined selection and development program should be formulated to produce a group of individuals with a common subset of characteristics and skills. This section focuses on the core characteristics. The section outlining the development approach identifies the core skills.

Among the many characteristics that are highly valued in a consultant candidate, two are critical to becoming an effective consultant: efficient and unique thinking capability, and the ability to perform effective pattern recognition, which fuels the consultant's thinking process. These two characteristics set good consultants apart from the rest.

Thinking

The ability to think clearly is obviously an asset in any profession, but in fact it is especially so for consultants. A consultant is sometimes called a "mind for rent," or a "time-share brain." A consultant must be able to assess the client's needs, restate them in a clear, concise, impartial, and complete manner, and put forth a plan to address them; the thinking process needs to be flexible, open, analytical, and creative. At the same time, the consultant must convey to the client that the conclusions and recommendations are the right ones. The ability to perform at a consistently high level across this spectrum of mental activities is found in an individual with strong intellect, strong stamina, and unique personal traits.

To get a better sense of the challenge of such a consultant see Figure 20-5, in which the thinking characteristics of a 5 year old and a 45 year old are compared. Five year olds view the world as a new experience, continually exploring and trying to determine how things work. They are spontaneous, creative, eager to explore new areas, willing to try anything, seeking fun along the way. They take risks because they are innocent of the dangers brought on by their actions. And they are very critical because they are still attempting to make order out of the reality around them.

The world of the 45 year old has been put into perspective by 2 score years of additional experience. The outlook is mature, and newly gained information is placed into frameworks built over time, which can become inflexible. The 45 year olds are often blocked from viewing things from different perspectives. They weigh risks based on the knowledge of the benefits as well as the costs associated with the actions. They have learned to think about consequences before they act, realizing that they will be held accountable for their actions. Experience allows them to make routine decisions quickly, building on a history of success and failure. They also have a set of core ethical, legal, and social values that guides their actions. Finally, the plans that they formulate tend to resolve the combined inputs from many diverse variables.

FIVE-YEAR-OLD	FORTY-FIVE-YEAR-OLD
Continually exploring	Accepting of fixed paradigms
Spontaneous	Predictable
Magically creative	Expressive but conservative
Eager	Paced
Energetic	Energy varying with health and habits
Ultimate risk taker	Risk taking tempered with caution
Innocent	Mature and experienced
Critical	Forgiving
Ever questioning	Knows answers
Weak analytically	Strong analytically
Lacking in frameworks	Set with ethical, legal, social frameworks

Figure 20-5   Mental profile over time. (© *IBM Corporation, 1994.*)

A major challenge in consultant development is how to help the consultant recapture the best aspects of thinking at age 5, without losing the experience and insight of a 45 year old. Both these profiles have positive characteristics and inherent weaknesses. Outstanding consultants engage the best of both profiles at the proper time during each engagement, just as they utilize different tools and play different roles as the situation unfolds. Consulting development programs need to encourage the behaviors seen in both of these profiles. The ability of students to perform in this way will be a function of their inherent nature and their willingness to change.

Pattern Recognition

Mature individuals often have difficulty making order out of what they see because they have formed their view of reality based on past experiences. As they grow older and more experienced they often form a consistent view of the things that they see. Once these views are formed, it is difficult to change them. This may be one of the reasons that so many large companies are having difficulty adjusting to the realities of doing business in the twenty-first century.

Parikh[3] points out that two broad types of learning must be exercised to gain knowledge. He calls them additive and subtractive learning. In additive learning, information is received sequentially, over time the information turns into knowledge, and, through education the knowledge can mature into wisdom. In subtractive learning there is the realization that over time a certain body of knowledge, attitudes, or beliefs has been accumulated and that parts of the accumulation either are obsolete or are forming barriers or blocks to growth and must be removed. There is a continuous need for both types of learning in consulting, and subtractive learning (which is often overlooked) is critical to opening the mind to new ideas and concepts. This allows the consultant to recognize patterns that others miss.

The patterns of our life and our view of our surroundings can also become too comfortable for us to question. Adams[4] points out that discontent is prerequisite to problem solving because it allows us to question the status quo. An ability to view the world and recognize new and emerging patterns is one of the most important characteristics of a consultant. This is particularly true at the beginning of engagements when consultants are forming their initial views of clients and the issues that are being thrust upon them. In some ways, good consultants never fully grow up; they are always trying to make order out of the things around them.

Therefore, a key element in the training of consultants is to help the individuals break down their preferred patterns and to look at the world with fresh eyes. Consultants must recognize that there are other answers to the obvious, that having only one answer is dangerous, and that growth and success come from seeing things differently. For this reason, many firms prefer to hire recent college or graduate school graduates who are at a "teachable moment" of their lives.

However, the key factor of success in this area is mental flexibility and energy, not age.

Summary

In summary, management consultants have two key capabilities that determine their success or failure: the ability to create new ideas—intellectual capital—and the ability to spot patterns. The new ideas are necessary to remain vital and to provide a competitive edge. Clients hire individuals who have insights, and these insights come from forming new ideas and taking new positions. Positions are formed from the collective experiences that the consultant or the practice has gained from dealing with a wide variety of clients. This is really the identification and interpretation of patterns.

Challenges of Consultant Development

Once the firm understands its growth needs and its target consultant profile, then it must come to grips with the development process itself. What are the realities of the profession that any new consultant must face? Who will be selected for development, and what challenges do these different choices give the firm? What are the development options, and what are their strengths and weaknesses?

The Realities of the Profession

Consulting must be viewed as an ongoing learning experience. To stay competitive, consultants must have a passion for the work, and a thirst for knowledge, new patterns, challenging issues, conclusions, and recommendations. These principles, therefore, must be put into practice. But, even with a strong development program and on-going guidance from a mentor or coach, there is no guarantee of success, since many people lack the innate abilities to be a consultant. Candidates must be honest with themselves about why they are getting into consulting. They must decide whether they are really willing to put the requisite energy into this new profession. Consulting should not be viewed as an interesting place to spend some time before something better comes along but, rather, as an exciting and stimulating profession. The combination of prior life experience and the consultant development offered by the firm is only of value if it helps in the day-to-day practice of the craft. An environment must be established during and following an engagement that reinforces the learning that has taken place to ensure a consistent approach across all practitioners.

Sources of Potential Consultants

Firms that choose to train new consultants usually recruit them from colleges and universities, most commonly from graduate MBA programs. Other firms only hire consultants that have had several years of business experience. Both of these starting points have an upside and a downside.

The Recent Graduate. On the up side, a new entrant, recently out of college or graduate school, will come to the firm at a salary that can optimize the financial leverage the firm can apply to an engagement. In addition, recent graduates will be familiar with the latest business trends, flexible in their thinking, and unencumbered by patterns that form during business careers. This may give them an advantage in the early idea formulation, creativity, and pattern recognition stages of an engagement. They are also less likely to be encumbered by family ties and health problems so that the aggressive work and travel schedules will be easier to tolerate.

On the downside, a recent graduate's knowledge and expertise is limited, and his or her leadership skills are relatively untested. As an engagement proceeds to the recommendation and implementation stages, recent graduates will not have the experience to draw on when weighing the value of options. Here, a rigorous problem-solving framework will be important to their success. These individuals are generally best suited for larger, more established firms.

The Professional Hire. When hiring a seasoned business expert, with limited or no consulting experience, the issues are quite the reverse. Their pay scales, and therefore billing rates, will be higher to reflect their prior experience. The very expertise that gives them value may also make their thinking less flexible with prejudgments and set patterns formed through years of business practice. There is a higher probability that family commitments and health problems will keep them from extended travel. Considerations of physical and mental fitness come into play. Lastly, the management system in which seasoned professionals have worked has seen very little change in the century but is under serious scrutiny today. Unless these professionals are well versed in new management thought and are open to new thinking, they may have difficulty breaking out of their molds.

On the upside, seasoned business experts have very compelling advantages. Their proven expertise and experience offer dividends not only in engagement performance but in recruiting new clients. Professional hires often relate better to their executive clients as peers. During the later stages of an engagement, when conclusions must be sorted out and recommendations formulated, a seasoned professional has the potential for strong, analytical, business, and often personnel experience to rely on. This is of particular value in formulating and evaluating implementation strategies. These individuals tend to be better suited to smaller firms, often in the start-up or growth phase of development.

Development Options

There are three methods of development that should be considered when putting together a development program: education, on-the-job training (OJT), and the use of mentors. Each approach has its strengths and weaknesses and finds its place and applicability in the firm's plan depending on the student population's size and mix of experience, the required timetable, and the availability of qualified resources to implement the plan.

Education. Education can take a variety of passive and active forms, regardless of whether it takes place in a classroom or in a self-directed manner. To transfer consulting skills, there must be an active or experiential component to any educational program through which a student can practice the learned skills in a "safe" environment rather than in the client's office. Generic consulting skills and practice-specific methodology skills, discussed in the next section, are tools that a consultant must first understand before they can be put to use.

A classroom delivery method, with carefully constructed lectures reinforced by experiential learning, can be very effective in transferring skills. Both generic and practice-specific skills can be taught efficiently enabling large groups of consultants to become engagement-ready sooner and more consistently than with OJT and mentoring alone. This, however, does not mean that OJT and mentors are not needed. Rather, a classroom method allows the trained individuals to be productive sooner and in a position to respond more favorably to both of these other approaches. This can form a very effective way to bring along an experienced set of business learners in a telescoped time frame.

A significant advantage of classroom training is the cross-pollination from and the exposure to colleagues and ideas from other geographic and organizational arenas, which is particularly important to more established firms. A consistent eye on the needs of the firm as it passes through its various stages of growth will govern how much or how little this approach is used. In an environment of steady state a firm may fulfill 10 percent or less of its need with this approach; it can be increased to 20 percent or more if sufficient development funds are allocated and if the firm has an aggressive timetable for growth or puts a high value on professional vitality.

A limitation of classroom education is that the lectures and the cases are often construed as theoretical, less practical, and more structured than in the real world of consulting. Time spent in the classroom is time spent away from the client, combining cost of delivery with the loss of billing opportunity. Well-structured classroom delivery requires strong development, monitoring, and fine-tuning processes, which in turn require infrastructure and funding to ensure success. In addition, the student-teacher ratio should never be more than 20–24:1 and in some cases 12:1. This requires a significant commitment of resources to the instructor pool. A firm can use in-house staff as instructors or contract outside consulting firms to assist in developing and initially delivering the program until the firm can become self-sufficient. Our experience indicates that the use of outside consultants works only if you have someone from in-house on hand to answer firm-specific questions. Furthermore, it is difficult to establish a unique culture within the firm if an outsider is in control of the development process.

Another aspect of education is self-directed learning, the use of work-books and self-tests combined with attendance at conferences and semi-nars. Computer-based techniques with multimedia technology are increasingly being used to improve the learning process and maintain the student's interest. Students can learn at their own pace in between or during engagements as dictated by their individual needs. New technol-ogy is constantly being developed in the areas of training and interactive learning that will greatly affect the teaching of generic and practice-spe-cific skills.

Mentors.   The role of the mentor has many facets. The dictionary defin-ition of this role is that of a trusted counselor or guide. The mentor as a coach is a secondary definition. More traditionally mentors are several levels more senior than protégés, helping to guide them through their careers by giving advice built on their knowledge, position, and experi-ence. In practice, mentors perform this role but are also more heavily focused on improving the performance or skill growth of their protégé through coaching and are often one level above the protégé or at the same level in the consulting firm hierarchy. In consulting, mentors can be assigned to individuals, engagement teams, or to practices to perform these roles. Another critical role is that of model for complex consulting skills (e.g., client handling, selling, critical thinking). In addition, the mentor monitors the quality of the new consultant's or new practice's work to ensure that clients receive the value they expect. This could involve direct or indirect supervision of key engagement tasks. Finally, the mentor can play an important role in assessing the progress of the consultants who they assist, giving input into their evaluation and rec-ommending development activities or engagement assignments that could speed their progress.

In many cases the mentor program is an informal one, with unclear goals and duration. More recently, facilitated mentoring processes are being used in many firms to ensure the success of this important tech-nique. In this model, skills can be built or enhanced by the proper pair-ing of mentor and protégé with mutual interests and strengths in mind. In one relationship, a consultant may serve as a mentor for a colleague and in another that same consultant may be a protégé of a different con-sultant. Contracts are formalized by the teams to clearly define the expectations of all parties and the duration of the relationship. Simple skill growth may only require a relationship of several months in length, whereas a more traditional career guidance need may have a multiyear duration. Here a coordinator function is often built into a process for pairing the mentor-protégé teams, to track the current contracts against their objectives, and to ensure the vitality of the mentor pool.

Whether formal or informal in nature, the mentor's role must be one that is valued and rewarded by the firm for it to succeed. Quality must be tracked and credit given to both parties for succeeding in their relationship. A mentor's inherent experience and expertise can be significantly enhanced by building both nondirective as well as directive coaching skills. Lastly, the mentor should be familiar with the firm's development program to be able to reinforce prior learning through other development approaches and to avoid contradicting best practices set by the firm.

The use of mentors is an invaluable element of consultant training. By assigning a mentor to an individual or group, teaching and learning can occur in the client environment, during a normal or overstaffed engagement. The client's value is preserved, and the student can gain valuable work experience. If the consultant has been involved in solid experiential learning prior to the mentor experience, he or she will be in a much stronger position to appreciate advice and criticism. In a classic development plan, with limited classroom instruction (10 percent or less), the mentor's role might rise to 40 percent or more of the development work, which can become problematic if the firm is in a start-up situation with an aggressive growth plan and limited mentors. In this case, classroom instruction can make better use of the available mentors.

Although the use of mentors can be an expensive training technique because it draws on the time of the most experienced practitioners, substituting subcontracted outsiders for this task is not advisable, because of the loss of quality control.

On-the-Job Training (OJT).   OJT has always been the workhorse development approach of consulting firms. In some ways OJT is the least efficient method but the one that allows the consultant to grow at the pace of assignments tailored to his or her needs. It is the ultimate experiential learning approach in a client "billable" environment, allowing the learning plan and the business plan to work in unison. Without the advantages gained from classroom experiential learning, however, OJT lengthens the learning process and may not result in a set of consistently trained individuals.

In OJT, the consultant learns many of the clear lessons of the profession without the benefit of relief from time or client pressure. But new consultants can recognize their real needs from an educational and mentor-assisted environment so that when the development opportunity is then offered at a later time, they will be able to take advantage of it in a more efficient way. Many firms rely too heavily on this type of learning, feeling that it is the more natural way for consultants to learn the trade. In most firms about 50 percent of the learning will be done through OJT. OJT is fundamental to the profession and is clearly the most cost-effective approach of consultant development.

The Development Approach

This chapter has discussed the development needs of the firm as it grows, some of the essential characteristics of a successful consultant, and the obstacles to the consultant development process. This section will identify some of the essential tools and skills that should be imparted in a strong consultant development plan. It will then give some guidelines on how to develop a plan that focuses on the needs of the firm as it changes and enable the consultant to find value in the development process throughout his or her career.

Generic Consulting Skills

There is a debate in the consulting community as to the advantages of training new candidates in generic consulting skills as opposed to letting those skills evolve over time. Most firms have decided not to conduct training in generic consulting skills. New consultants arrive at the firm and are given assignments; engagement managers or partners regularly monitor the new consultants' work to see if they have acquired the right skills; if they have acquired the right skills, they are encouraged to stay on and develop, but if they haven't they are eventually encouraged to leave. In this construct, the firm believes that self-discovery and mastery of core skills is a sign of a real consultant.

A core set of tools is fundamental to the success of the consulting process. Although use of a mentor system or OJT can develop these tools, development can be accelerated by using a formal training system. These tools, or skills, are listed below in the order of their use during an engagement:

- Marketing and selling
- Organizational and change analysis
- Creativity
- Problem solving
- Data gathering
- Communication

- Team building

- Influencing and negotiating

Marketing and Selling. Fundamental to the growth of any consultant is the approach that is taken in marketing his or her, and by extension the firm's, available expertise and service capabilities. On the average, 80 percent of the revenues of consulting firms worldwide are generated from a client-driven "pull" rather than a product-oriented "push" strategy. In an extensive study of U.S. consulting firms, Alpha Publications[5] found that the areas of personal relationships, hearsay, and seminar participation alone make up that number.

Marketing is the sum of all activities that are designed to establish the image and reputation of the consultant or firm to make the target audience aware of the availability and quality of services offered. The opportunity to sell an engagement results from successful marketing. This type of activity is often foreign to even seasoned sales individuals. Therefore, a program of initial and ongoing initiatives to familiarize new consultants with the process and its goal can bring positive results.

The key to the marketing process is to create a series of regular events that will drive a spectrum of activities that can be performed during the most hectic of consulting calendars. The marketing process must be in steps to allow for interruptions, and it must be alert to new opportunities. This is one of the biggest challenges facing relatively new and smaller firms, which succumb to a vicious cycle of work interrupted by pauses to sell the next job (see Figure 20-6). The firm must keep both the marketing and selling processes and the implementation processes at work concurrently, so that consulting teams can be proposing or starting one engagement, performing a second, and finishing a third, at the same time. This is the type of leverage that can significantly improve profitability.

To market successfully, a plan must be developed to set and execute short-term tactical actions, work toward medium-range targets, and drive toward long-term goals. Short-term actions could include: (1) updating and maintaining a client list; (2) calling a preset number of prior clients each week with relevant ideas; (3) sending clients helpful information or focused articles; (4) taking key clients to lunch; or (5) developing and updating your consulting biography. Medium-term actions could include: (1) writing and publishing articles; (2) preparing and delivering speeches; (3) pursuing a leadership position in an industry or civic organization; or (4) developing and sending to a list of potential clients a direct mail piece outlining the firm's services. Long-term actions could include: (1) writing a book in your area of expertise; (2) seeking certification from a consulting or industry organization; (3) pursuing an educational degree respected by your client set; or (4) develop-

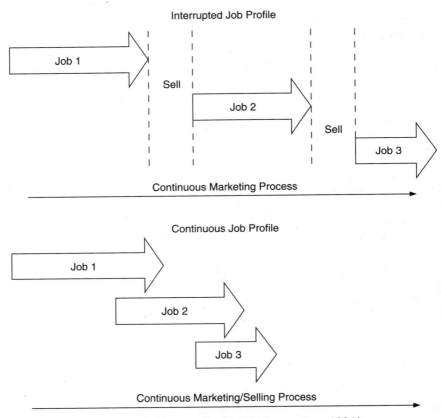

Figure 20-6   Marketing/selling profile. (© *IBM Corporation, 1994.*)

ing a multiple-day seminar to draw new or existing clients into some new area of thinking.

In all cases, the ability to continue along each of these paths in a parallel fashion and in an efficient manner is critical to future success. These activities must be organized to fill the time between and during engagements, dead time on the road, in planes, airports, train stations, or hotel rooms to maximum effect. In addition, the activities involved should be those that are essential to the marketing of the firm, such as research projects and the development of brochures and public relations activities that focus attention on the firm.

The marketing development program can focus on several key skill-building areas that teach and encourage the most efficient and effective methods of approaching the tasks. For example, it is important to convey the firm's fundamental, consistent standard for writing a consulting biography and how to maintain it. A biography is typically used as a client selling tool that highlights the skill and expertise of the consultant or firm rather than a sequence of experiences like a résumé.

Another skill to focus on is the writing and placement of articles on pertinent topics. A workshop led by a skilled communications specialist or a member of the firm who has done a lot of writing can be held. If a first-time author has access to assistance from an experienced author, the new author will have a much higher degree of success in writing and placing articles in the future.

In a classroom, the firm-defined elements of marketing and selling can be taught. The mentor's role is to model these skills for the consultant, encourage their use in practice, and ensure that they are used properly. One of the most difficult things to learn, especially for seasoned business people, is how to sell intangibles. There is no physical product to show to the client. Selling intangibles can, however, be learned and practiced in the classroom. The ability of the firm to develop and teach a consistent approach to selling, down to the look and feel of the required deliverables, will allow the firm to present a consistent and professional face to clients and improve its ability to close business. With such standards in place, lectures supported by role-playing sessions can establish the key processes in a safe, nonclient environment.

The ultimate goal is to gain experience by putting to use the techniques learned in the development process on an actual client engagement, using a mentor to solidify the skill on the job, so that these skills can be mastered.

Organization and Change Analysis. One of the most important measures of success for any consulting firm is the extent to which clients implement its recommendations. In almost every case, this means that the client firm must understand, accept, and undergo some significant change. Hans Becherer, president and CEO of Deere & Co., once said, "How we educate our people to respond to change and keep pace with the future is critical."

With a better understanding of the organization in place, the firm's readiness, willingness, and ability to change must be evaluated. Change typically either happens as a result of vision, or a clear and well-communicated sense of direction, or occurs when an organization reaches a state of terminal inefficiency, with no clear sense of direction and impending demise. In this regard, the two primary areas to work on to instill change are the people and the organization (see Figure 20-7). If neither is addressed, change will be reactive, unfocused, and unplanned. Often the organization is changed without addressing the training of, communication to, and roles and systems for the people. This usually results in temporary change and frustration at all levels. If the people are retrained and prepared for change, but have to work in their old unchanged orga-

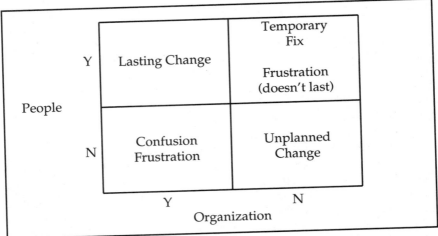

Figure 20-7   What do you work on in change? (© *IBM Corporation, 1994.*)

nizational structure, confusion reigns, and frustration rather than change occurs once again. When both the needs and preparation of the people are matched with the corresponding changes in the organization, a real and lasting change can occur. Consultants must be prepared to address these issues and be given the training and tools to foster change to ensure success in implementing their recommendations.

The firm's development process should focus on a common framework that can be used by all consultants of the firm. The framework should be rich in function and applicability and relatively easy to use. Experiential education through the use of case studies either in the classroom or self-directed can be applied to enable students to test their knowledge before trying it out on the client. Cases should continually be reviewed and updated to reflect the current business environment of the clients. The best cases are ones which are actual situations which the firm's consultants have worked on, and discussion will be even better if the actual consultant can be available for the debriefing of the case. Once the student is familiar with and feels confident using the new skills, the skills can be brought to work on a client engagement. At this stage a mentor can add significant value by positioning the need for organizational analysis and how to integrate it into the job.

Problem Solving   Any consultant development program should support the common problem-solving needs of the firm. This section discusses four of the many available problem-solving frameworks currently used in consulting. Each framework takes a different view of its target spectrum of problems or issues. In choosing a framework several factors should be weighed: Does it address the most common set of problems faced by your consultants? Will it be robust enough to apply to the most difficult client challenges and yield creative solutions? Can the tools within the framework be used both efficiently and effectively to complement the client's strengths?

The development process must achieve two goals: It should teach the consultant to know when to apply the tools, and it should enable the consultant to develop skills in using the tools. The student should be prepared to use the simplest, most direct tool called for by the problem, which in turn allows for rapid and effective resolution for the client. Experiential learning through the use of sample cases is effective in both of these areas. First, exercises should be devised that test the thinking used to define a problem and to select the proper tool. Then challenging cases should be built to explore the many facets of the framework chosen in the program. Training firms can be very helpful in this process either to devise the initial training or to offer the training itself. There are several helpful books and pocket guides with lengthy lists of problem-solving tools that are simple and effective in specific circumstances. One such guide is the "Memory Jogger" by Goal/QPC, containing over 30 techniques and examples of how to apply them. Learning is then completed through the guidance of mentors on actual client jobs to validate how these techniques are used and when to use them.

The remainder of this section focuses on four approaches to problem solving described by VanGundy, Brightman, Kepner and Tregoe, and Reeder. In describing each approach we first focus on how problems are classified and where the inherent strengths of the approach lie. Second we will describe the stages of each process and how they differ.

The first approach to problem solving is that of A. B. VanGundy,[6] who classifies problems across a dimension of structure, dividing them into three major categories: well-structured, semistructured, and ill-structured. To understand the techniques to solve a given problem, the problem must first be classified. VanGundy then offers techniques for addressing each, through a five-stage process (see Figure 20-8): (1) The pre-problem-solving phase, (2) the refining and analyzing phase, (3) the idea generation phase, (4) the evaluating and idea-selecting phase, and (5) the implementation phase. The size and complexity of these stages depend on the category of problem that is being addressed.

VanGundy defines a well-structured problem as one in which all the information needed to solve the problem is available and where the problem-solver knows either the current or desired state. Such problems tend to be routine and often repeated and thus lend themselves to solutions using standard operating procedures or algorithms.

Semistructured problems fall between well- and ill-structured problems. The amount of information available is usually enough to define

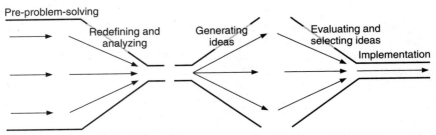

Figure 20-8 VanGundy identifies five phases involved in resolving any type of problem. (© *IBM Corporation, 1994.*)

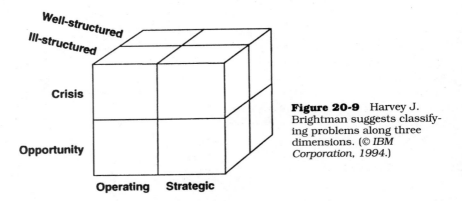

Figure 20-9 Harvey J. Brightman suggests classifying problems along three dimensions. (© *IBM Corporation, 1994.*)

the problem only partially. Uncertainty surrounds either the current or desired state or both. Routine procedures alone will not solve such problems; they require a combination of standard operating procedures and creative responses. Guidelines will be needed to increase the odds of finding a satisfactory solution.

With an ill-structured problem, little or no information is available. Significant effort must be spent analyzing and determining the proper scope of the problem and generating many alternative solutions. VanGundy offers a process flow that can be applied to each of these problem categories with varying degrees of detail and rigor.

Harvey Brightman[7] suggests that problems should be classified along three dimensions (see Figure 20-9): well-structured versus ill-structured, operating level versus strategic level, and crisis versus opportunity. The first dimension is similar to VanGundy's and represents a problem's degree of structure. Well-structured problems again lend themselves to standardized or automated solution techniques, whereas ill-structured problems require the use of intuition, creativity, judgment, and general problem-solving techniques. The second dimension ranges on a continuum from operating level to strategic level and focuses on the organizational level at which the problem occurs. Operating-level problems, although common, do not affect the long-term survival of the firm. In resolving strategic-level problems, actions are taken, resources are committed, and precedents are set that may very well decide the ultimate success of the client. The crisis-versus-opportunity spectrum represents how the organization first became aware of the problem. Problems arising out of crises must be dealt with immediately. On the opportunities side of the spectrum are things which can be exploited to strengthen the underlying firm but usually do not have a sense of urgency unless they are precipitated by other factors such as a competitive threat. In each of these dimensions, problems can get worse if ignored (e.g., turning from operating to strategic or from opportunity to crisis). Brightman focuses his efforts on a seven-step process to address ill-structured operating and strategic-level problems. This process consists of three phases: diagnosis, analysis, and solution. Diagnosis identifies and studies the "deviation" that is occurring; analysis is the hypothesis-identifying phase, and solution is the hypothesis-testing and verification phase.

Kepner and Tregoe[8] use problems and decisions as their primary classification categories. Figure 20-10 shows several examples of these categories. By their definition, a "problem" is an observed difference between what should be and what is, where the cause of the difference is unknown. A "decision" does not represent a difference between expected and actual performance, but rather a choice or set of choices that must be made. To some degree, their problem-versus-decision spectrum has the

Problem Analysis	Decision Analysis
Problems	Decisions
■ From the day we introduced the computer we've had nothing but trouble in getting our inventories to balance. ■ Our number 11 paper machine never produces more than 80% of its design capacity.	■ There is no way we can meet our deadline on the project with our present staff and no way we can get authorization to bring on anyone new. This is a serious problem.

Figure 20-10 Kepner and Tregoe present a different classification scheme. (© *IBM Corporation, 1994.*)

flavor of the structured-versus-ill-structured dimensions of VanGundy and Brightman. They view problem analysis as the pursuit of answers to questions—questions about why differences exist between what should be and what is, especially when the cause of the difference is unknown. Kepner and Tregoe offer two separate processes for problem and decision analysis.

Kepner and Tregoe's problem-solving approach has five stages (or steps) and seeks to find the cause of the deviation and identify means to remove it, thus resolving the problem. The first step is to define the problem, and here they give specific guidelines for developing concise "deviation statements." The second step is to describe the problem in four dimensions: identity, location, timing, and magnitude. In this step, data are collected on the deviations and placed in a four-dimensional grid for later analysis. The third step seeks to develop possible cause strategies by extracting information from the four-dimension analysis. In the fourth step, testing is done to determine the most probable causes of the deviations. In this step, analysis is also done to see if all dimensions of the problem can be explained by these causes. The fifth and last step involves testing the most probable cause of the deviation in the actual situation to verify that it is the "true cause."

Kepner and Tregoe's decision analysis process also has five steps. The first step is to develop a decision statement. The second step is to develop a set of "objectives" or criteria by which the possible alternatives can be judged and compared. The third step is the alternative generation step. Here, an ideal alternative may also be developed against which the more realistic alternatives can be compared. The fourth step involves the analysis of the alternatives, weighing each in its ability to meet the objectives identified in the second step. The last step assesses the potential risks associated with the implementation of each alternative. With these two approaches, Kepner and Tregoe offer strategies to understand and explain deviations from the norm and to formulate a course of action to respond to the problems.

Another recommended approach is described by Tim Reeder from P. D. N Ltd. (The Professional Development Network). Reeder codified best practice in general management consulting and developed effective processes for learning the approach. Reeder's approach is designed to develop effective and interesting solutions to unstructured business problems, offering a complete foundation to integrate many of the consulting processes. It is an issue-based, hypothesis-driven approach that is particularly strong in handling medium to complex situations. It leads to the development of effective, focused data-gathering efforts and is well suited to teams of varying sizes. The approach has nine steps, divided into four phases: planning, fact gathering, analysis, and communication. Reeder's approach seeks to define the client issues and then, through the use of hypotheses and questions, to plan the thinking process. Attention is given throughout the process to creativity and analysis, and the development of client deliverables is integrated from the outset.

It is important to choose a problem-solving approach that results in the best solution with the least overhead. Standard problem-solving approaches can offer the firm a way to form a coherent consulting team that has limited experience working together by giving team members a common language with which to solve the client's problems. A standard approach is also important in that it allows the firm to move consultants on and off jobs with minimal learning and disruption. The consultant development process should focus primarily on those techniques that will benefit the entire firm. Experiential learning is the most effective method of developing and exercising skills in this area.

Creativity. Since one of the most important objectives of a consulting firm is to build value for the clients, it is critical to ensure that creativity is given careful consideration in the area of consultant development. Although there is no single approach to engendering creativity, some suggestions may be helpful. First, it is very important to create an environment that places a high value on ideas. Do not allow the firm or its members to become closed to new ways of thinking and trapped by past experiences and solutions. Without a proper focus on creativity, there is always a danger of applying old reasoning and solutions to new problems. An effective way to teach creativity techniques is to integrate the tools of divergence (idea generation) and convergence (idea selection and filtering) with the firm's chosen problem-solving framework. As shown in Figure 20-8, problem-solving frameworks all have divergent and convergent stages. When both types of tools are used together to find, select, and refine ideas to solve relevant problems, the learning experience becomes more relevant to the consulting experience.

Facilitated divergent techniques such as "brainstorming," should be an integral part of the development program. Groups should get together to generate as many ideas as possible in a nonjudgmental environment. The training is enhanced if these sessions are led by the consultants. In a brainstorming session, ideas should be described and captured quickly so that the participants build on them or can create new ones. At the end of the session, the participants can step back and judge their output with convergent tools from a new perspective. One such tool is the nominal group vote technique (discussed in more detail in the Team Building section of this chapter) which allows a group to filter the output without fostering defensiveness or ownership of individual ideas. Individuals with a sense of ownership of ideas lose objectivity and are less able to accept constructive criticism, suggestions, or modifications. VanGundy identifies[9] nine different idea-generation techniques for individuals and another nineteen for groups, including classic brainstorming. He also classifies techniques by training importance and implementation difficulty, which is particularly useful in developing a training program.

At times, a consultant's thinking process may become blocked in some way from achieving effective or creative thinking. In his book *Conceptual Blockbusting*, Adams[10] identifies six different types of blocks: perceptual, emotional, cultural, environmental, intellectual, and expressive. His belief is that "the process of identifying conceptual blocks takes one quite a distance toward overpowering them," and he offers specific techniques to identify and overcome blocks.

Contrary to popular belief, creativity techniques can be taught, especially to receptive students. However, although these creative techniques can be effectively taught in the classroom, they must be put to use or they will be lost.

Data Gathering.   Every consultant must possess basic data-gathering skills. All problem solving first involves gathering facts that must be sorted and refined to form the basis of the problem solving. The amount and type of data needed should be dictated by the assignment's type, scope, and budget. This is where time spent in planning the desired outcome pays off. Reeder points to the "rule of thirds," which says that any consulting assignment is roughly divided into three equal pieces: planning and analysis; data gathering; and communications. The data-gathering stage is the most difficult to hold in check. Sloppiness can result in mountains of data that are not properly targeted and that result in wasted time. The idea is to do the proper up-front research and planning before diving in to data collecting to get maximum benefit from minimum time spent.

A proper balance must be struck when collecting data. The aim is to solve the client's problems, not expand one's own knowledge. In this regard, it is important to know when the point of "optimal ignorance," as defined by Barry Stein of Goodmeasure, Inc., has been reached. This is the point past which additional data will not change the conclusions or recommendations but will make them more defensible.

There are three main types of data gathering: (1) interviewing one or more individuals either in person, by phone, or through some other form of survey; (2) reviewing available public or private documents; and (3) observing. In-person interviews can be conducted in several ways: one-on-one, several-on-one, one-on-many, or several-on-many. The last method is often called a "focus group" or "round table." Careful planning is critical to the success of all the interview techniques.

A one-on-one interview allows for flexibility and thinking that is uncolored by the input of others. In a one-on-several interview, the interviewer's flexibility is retained, but interaction among the interviewees starts to color opinions. When using a survey, flexibility is limited by a prearranged set of questions and the inability to ask follow-up questions, but this is offset by the opportunity to gain the uncolored insights of a great number of individuals with little additional effort or cost.

Gathering information from documents requires less planning but must be done in a thorough and rigorous manner. Preengagement research of standard information sources can be pivotal to the selling process and is often done by associates new to the firm; in this way the new associates learn the consulting process as well as the value and accessibility of such information. In addition, they learn the importance that good data can have on latter stages of the process. This type of information is usually gathered to enhance the chances of closing an engagement and to demonstrate the firm's knowledge of the client's business. During an engagement, focused document searches and analysis are common. Many firms use only in-house associates to do this type of research, rather than hiring outside research professionals. Their reasoning is that staff members have several incentives to produce high-quality work, the most obvious being a desire to advance by demonstrating their abilities. With the availability of both public and private computerized information-gathering techniques, this area clearly lends itself to basic classroom- or mentor-based training.

Observation is fundamental to developing a well-rounded view of the client issues and environment. Obtaining information through observation is the responsibility of every member of the consulting team in all aspects of the engagement. Observation should be used both to obtain new information and to validate the information already gathered. For example, a client's company may have very well-defined behavioral or business practice rules, but if in practice the rules are observed to be largely ignored, the opportunity arises to learn what the real process is, to put the old rules in a new light, and to gain understanding as to why the old rules are being ignored. Observations should be integrated into the data gathering. It is particularly important to see if clients' actions match their words in this area. Observation can contain key indicators about the client organization's ability to accept change. One company complained that they had poor communications within their ranks, regardless of prior attempts to address the issue. When their environment was observed, it was found that their only form of consistent communication was on paper. A lot of paper was being generated, but very little understanding and communication was taking place.

Communication.   As mentioned earlier, about one-third of the time on any assignment is spent communicating. This includes initial discussions, where the consultants are working to understand the client and the job objectives. The consultant must then describe both orally and in writing how the client's needs will be met. Throughout the assignment, all members of the team interact with one another and with the client to discuss existing ideas or introduce new ideas and to persuade one another to understand the various positions. Finally, a successful consultant must be able to get the client to act on the consultant's recommendations. In the marketing and selling section of this chapter, a systematic process to sell was discussed. This selling process obviously contains some of the most important points for communication on the job.

This section discusses the most common consulting deliverables: the proposal; the "kick-off package"; the progress report; and the final report. Each of these deliverables is typically accompanied by an informal or formal team presentation.

The proposal is a document that is instrumental in selling and determining the scope of the engagement and in setting the client's expectations. It is the place in which the consultant's understanding of the client's objectives and the approach that will be taken will be stated clearly and succinctly. During the proposal stages there is also a need to discuss expected results and benefits to the client as well as to convey the strengths that the consulting firm will bring to the assignment.

The "kick-off package" is a document and presentation often delivered at the first meeting between the client and consulting team at the beginning of the engagement. The major objectives of this deliverable is to manage the expectations of both teams, to communicate the details of the engagement plan, and to ensure that key responsibilities are assigned and accepted on both sides. Among these responsibilities is the delivery of the necessary client data that the consultants have identified and the client has agreed to furnish.

The progress report updates all parties involved on the status of the job at that point. It is an opportunity to compare the progress against the plan, share valuable insights, test options for implementation, and reaffirm the client's expectations.

In the final report, the consulting team delivers recommendations based on conclusions that the team must be prepared to defend. The final report should present a clear argument that persuades the client to accept the recommended implementation plan.

Of all the above documents and associated meetings, the initial proposal document is the starting point for agreement on issues, objectives, and scope. It is the one most consistent communications vehicle of the job. Thereafter, the consultant should attempt to add value with each communication with the client.

The consultant development process should foster strong, consistent capabilities in each consultant and in the consulting team as a group, to communicate clearly and effectively. The ability to link the thinking and problem-solving processes with the communication process is of significant benefit in ensuring the delivery of well-thought-out and constructed deliverables. The firm should consider developing format standards for their key deliverables and giving instruction on how to write and deliver these products. This training may be as simple as a required review process or as elaborate as a workshop in quality consulting communication.

Several techniques can help a consultant to map out logical thinking processes. Hierarchies of ideas and supporting data should be delivered in a logical flow. Clients can then follow the highest level story line of ideas that gives them the understanding and desired detail that satisfies their needs. A "story board" can be used to map the development of these deliverables in a "sketch" or "mock-up" format. This allows the consultant to create the overall message, filling in necessary supporting details as they become available. The entire consulting team should be involved in producing the document, which can be broken down into pieces and assigned to different team members for more effective use of time. High-level report outlines or story boards should be built very early in the assignment and enhanced as the thinking progresses. Many consultants feel that the work on the final report begins with the delivery of the proposal; each step along the way is then just a refinement. If the team waits until the major work is done on the job before it starts on the final deliverable, this important document will be of no use in shaping the team's thinking, and the risk is greater that the team will either miss their deadline or deliver a poor-quality product.

In the current consulting environment, it is essential to consider all the ways of enhancing the deliverables, including tabular, graphic, and pictorial images. There is a wide range of inexpensive graphics programs available, but care should be taken to ensure any graphic or special effect used really does improve communications without adversely affecting the productivity of your valued consultants. Consistency in approach and look can be fostered by using a set of standards and by regularly sharing and reviewing each other's work. When developing a set of standards, avoid a "fill in the blanks" approach; each assignment must be tailored to the client, and misuse of such an expedient could end up limiting the thinking to fit the template.

The basic principles of creating deliverables, including format and style evaluation, can be taught effectively in the classroom. As a result, many firms invest a lot of effort in educating their consultants in effective writing skills. However, to ensure effective learning and critiquing of exercises, classes of 24 or less should be used to allow for individual attention.

Team Building.   As consulting engagements have gotten more complex, larger, and more ambiguous, the consulting team has become central to the success of the management consulting firm. In many firms, virtually all assignments involve teams. Furthermore, the client is typically represented by a team, so it is important that these two groups are able to work together both smoothly and effectively throughout the assignment. Unlike management teams, sports teams, and many other business teams, the consulting team has some very particular challenges. First, the team often is comprised of individuals who have never met before and who may never work together again. The team must get up to speed very quickly and perform at a high level for a relatively short time, usually about 3 to 6 months.

Each member of the team is a highly skilled and empowered individual who will respond to leadership much more positively than to management. The team is very much a peer group in intellectual terms, and its members have come together to work on a very complex set of issues with a fixed time frame to accomplish the tasks. In this environment team players are valued very highly by both the consulting firm and the client. The behavior of each member must be team-centered, rather than self-centered, to ensure success. Individuals seeking personal fame and glory from the effort will not last long. Since most good consultants have sizable egos, they must have good reasons to subjugate these egos for the good of the team. To accomplish this, the job manager must work with each player at the outset of the assignment to ensure that each team member understands his or her role in relation to the group. The danger is that the team will flounder, not work in unison, and develop mediocre results.

If team building is a priority for the firm, then an approach, like the one described below, should be blended into the experiential classroom or client engagement environment where other skills are developed concurrently. To start with, students who have not come to grips with the value of consulting teams must be taught the concept that solutions to complex problems developed by many strong minds working in unison are better and more comprehensive than those developed by single individuals faced with similar dilemmas. As an age-old consulting axiom says, "None of us is as good as all of us." A variety of engagement simulations or survival scenarios are available to make this point nicely.

The next step is for each consultant to better understand how his or her own behavior impacts team performance. Each member must learn her or his own "team playing" strengths and weaknesses as well as those of the other team members. Many firms use self- and peer-assessment tools to accomplish this. Meredith Belbin[11] developed assessment techniques with a particularly strong focus on team dynamics. He discovered that teams that didn't seem to work very well together didn't have a representative mix of role preferences within the given group. He categorized these roles and constructed a "Self-Perception Inventory" that could be given to team members to determine their two strongest and the two weakest preferences. According to Belbin, successful teams have a full complement of all these roles being played within the team. If teams are chosen to ensure such a balance, it will greatly improve the performance of the team. If, as is often the case in the consulting world, the players are defined by their expertise, then a shortfall of these Belbin traits often results. Belbin contends in this case that the team would not function optimally, because he believed that it is very difficult for individuals to overcome their natural preferences. However, our experience shows that once the team recognizes that they lack certain strengths, the team members can indeed improve their performance in these areas and enhance the team's results. This approach to team work can be taught effectively in a classroom environment as well as on the job.

A successful team must understand which characteristics are most valuable in the given circumstance. There are mechanisms designed to draw out this information at the beginning of an engagement. Two such approaches involve the use of nominal-group techniques or team-mapping tools.

In the first approach, a large group is encouraged to think as individuals to formulate the three most important characteristics of high-performing teams. These are recorded individually on index cards, collected, shuffled, and divided among subteams of the larger group. The subteams are asked to prioritize these characteristics and come to consensus as to what their top three choices are. A facilitator then polls each team for their choices, avoiding repeats, until all choices are depleted. Then every member of the group is given three stick-on dots and asked to vote again, as individuals, for the characteristics garnered from this final list that they feel are most important to high-performing teams. They can choose to add the three dots on one characteristic, on two, or on three. This "nominal voting" approach can bring a group as large as fifty people to a consensus as to their top choices for high-performing-team values in fewer than 30 minutes.

In a "team-mapping" approach, the team is given the client's objective and must develop a team vision for the job and map the needs of the job to the many skills of the team members. This exploration of mission and team value at the start of an assignment engenders a fast start as well as a successful result.

The next step is to test team behavior in progressively more challenging and complex team situations, receiving and tracking peer feedback in the process. This can be accomplished both in an experiential classroom setting and in a real client environment. Once the strengths and weaknesses of the team members and the group as a whole are identified, it is up to the individuals to correct the weaknesses. This may sound simple, but some students struggle and even give up in this regard, particularly if they have had prior successes as "lone wolf" types in the past. In the end, each firm must understand its own need for teams and devise a development and ongoing monitoring process to ensure the strength and vitality of this important consulting tool. Team building can be taught and should be embedded in appropriate team activities, both in the classroom and on the job. Both approaches are necessary for success. Combined they have been found to provide a significant increase in the understanding and awareness of the team's needs and in improved team behavior in a very short period.

Influencing and Negotiating.   The life blood of the consultant's business is the relationship built up with the client. Understanding the fundamental elements of negotiation are crucial to meeting the challenges of consulting. From the initial inquiry to the final report, the consultant is faced with a seemingly neverending string of options, alternatives, and decisions. Negotiations are conducted with teammates, client workers, client executives, and third parties such as suppliers. To succeed in the assignment and get follow-up business from the client, it is best to seek negotiated solutions that benefit all parties, so-called win-win solutions. A solid agreement will result from careful listening to understand and address the needs of the interested parties. A consultant development program should include education on some basic tools and techniques in this area of negotiation. Consideration should be made as to what types of outcomes are desirable, how to prepare for negotiations, and how to carry out negotiations in single-party and multiparty environments. A very important skill is knowing when to walk away from a negotiation and how doing so will affect the relationship with the potential client. Role-playing workshops are very helpful here. A number of consulting firms specialize in this area, offering workshops for general skills building and direct assistance for specific negotiations. In such cases they are usually paid equally by all sides of the negotiation to ensure fairness in the final outcome.

Summary.   The generic skills identified above are basic to the success of the standard practitioner. As the consultant rises in the ranks of the consulting pyramid, these skills need to be enhanced with a set of secondary skills that accompany the management and leadership role expected at these levels. For example, job management can be learned on the job, through the help of a mentor, or jump-started with classroom education. The ability to manage the writing of others should be added to the normal consulting writing skills. Teamwork skills should be enhanced with methods of bringing a team together quickly, developing a common vision, performing thought leadership, and resolving issues that arise in high-pressure situations. Lastly, the ability to coach others productively is critical to becoming a successful mentor. Although many of these more advanced skills are left to chance in most firms, the skills are relatively easy to support with education and can lead to significant benefits to the firm.

Practice-Specific Knowledge

Successful consulting firms develop a common body of knowledge, tools, frameworks, techniques, and engagement approaches that will be referred to as methodology. A firm's methodology is a common thread that ties its members in such a way that they can quickly and efficiently work together to produce high-quality consulting for their clients. Whether the methodology is formally written down or is shared by word of mouth, it represents the combined learning of the firm over the total of the firm's engagements to date. Firms should continually upgrade these methodologies and keep them moving into the forefront of thinking in their areas of expertise in order to attract new clients and to provide continuing value to existing clients. Key ideas can be published and introduced during speaking engagements to foster interest in the firm. Firms must ensure that new members learn these methodologies quickly and apply them correctly in combination with their own generic consulting skills.

The danger of teaching strict adherence to these methodologies is that they might be relied upon too heavily, they might never be updated, and they might encourage too rigid an approach to consulting. Parts of assignments can be greatly expedited by well-documented prior thinking, targeted question lists, exhibits, etc., but where complex, unstructured problems are the order of the day, nothing can replace strong generic consulting skills, familiarity with the firm's methodology, a strong team, and creativity. What should be taught in methodology training programs is the way to think about the relevant problems of the firm's specialty rather than the solutions themselves.

Training and Work Balance

Each firm must choose the training and work balance that fits it best, giving it the flexibility and affordability to thrive as a profitable enterprise. Very small firms may never have sufficient infrastructure to warrant a formal development team. This does not mean that they shouldn't focus on the development of their employees. They can utilize multicompany seminars, university offerings, and published materials. Organizations of consulting or industry professionals offer seminars that can be helpful in honing both generic and firm-specific skills and knowledge.

For medium- to large-sized firms the balance of work-driven learning versus scheduled training activities will depend on the time constraints and experience level of new employees.

Needs of the Experienced Consultant

Firms composed largely of experienced consultants have to keep several things in mind. First, due to the continuous need to maximize "billable" hours, it is difficult to get such individuals to commit to skills development or enhancement. It is up to the practice leaders and principals to create an environment that values this mission. One way of achieving this goal is to schedule a fixed number of mandatory education days each year in which in-house personnel and outside consultants conduct classes on various subjects. At these sessions, practice-specific knowledge is updated, generic skills are polished, and productivity tools are introduced. Firms must also carefully choose the reading materials available in the firm library and circulate key periodicals and books.

Evaluation and Career Planning

The unifying element of a consultant's growth is the feedback received from the environment in which he or she works. Feedback should begin at the engagement level, from the engagement leader and possibly from other team members. The consultants should also be given the opportunity to offer feedback to the engagement manager. The evaluation should include the identification of strengths and weaknesses in the key generic and practice-specific skills discussed as well as in the areas of personal effectiveness (e.g., interpersonal skills, initiative and drive, tenacity). Reviews of all consultants should be conducted regularly at the end of each engagement and on an annual basis. Annual reviews should be conducted by a firm partner or practice leader and should include the feedback summaries of each engagement, supplemented by interviews of firm members who worked with the consultant during the year. Every review should also contain recommendations for future development. In some firms, reviews are conducted by a different partner each year; this benefits all parties involved by giving the consultant a broader view of consulting and the firm a broader view of the consultant. The reviews also can be used cumulatively to assess the firm's development process as a whole. Common weaknesses identified across the board may point to problems in the existing development strategy or a need for a new strategy. Timing is also critical. Thought should be given to the importance of "just-in-time education." Few firms ask anyone to do everything on the first day in their job. It is therefore important to remember that a skill once learned but not used may be lost.

Summary

The evolution of a consulting firm and the associated development of its consultants is an integrated process that can take many forms. The industry is divided in its opinion of the value of formal education versus evolution in the development process. We believe that a well-thought-out and coordinated experiential education program, supported by the use of mentors and OJT, can significantly aid in the growth of consulting skills. If all these considerations are properly balanced, this process for the development of the firm's most important assets can revitalize itself and become self-regenerating.

Notes

1. David A. Lord and James H. Kennedy, eds., *An Analysis of Management Consulting in North America* (Fitzwilliam, N.H., 1993), pp. 8–9.
2. Ibid., pp. 14–15.
3. Jagdish Parikh, *Managing Your Self* (William Kaufman Inc., Cambridge, Mass.: Basil Blackwell, 1991), p. 18.
4. James L. Adams, *Conceptual Blockbusting: A Guide to Better Ideas* (Reading, Mass., Addison-Wesley Publishing, Inc., 1986), p. 105.
5. *The Market for Management Consultancy Services in the U.S.A.* (Beaconsfield, U.K., Alpha Publications, 1990), p. 86.
6. A. B. VanGundy, *Techniques of Structured Problem Solving* (New York: Van Nostrand Reinhold, 1988), pp. 4–15.
7. Harvey J. Brightman, *Problem Solving: A Logical and Creative Approach* (Atlanta: Georgia State University, 1980).
8. C. Kepner and B. Tregoe, *The New Rational Manager* (Princeton: Princeton Research Press, 1981), pp. 33–54, 83–102.
9. VanGundy, *Techniques*, pp. 31, 33, 79.
10. J. L. Adams, op. cit., p. 103.
11. R. Meredith Belbin, *Management Teams* (Oxford, U.K.: Butterworth-Heinnemann, 1981), pp. 153–159.

Bibliography

Adams, L., *Conceptual Blockbusting: A Guide to Better Ideas,* Reading, Mass.: Addison Wesley, 1986.

Belbin, R. Meredith, *Management Teams.* Butterworth-Heinnemann Professional Publishing, Oxford, U.K., 1981.

Brightman, Harvey J., *Problem Solving: A Logical and Creative Approach.* Atlanta: Business Publishing Division College of Business Administration, Georgia State University, 1980.

Kepner, C., and Tregoe, B., *The New Rational Manager.* Princeton: Princeton Research Press, 1981.

Lord, David A., and Kennedy, James H., *An Analysis of Management Consulting in North America.* Fitzwilliam: Kennedy Publications, Fitzwilliam, N.H., 1992.

Parikh, Jagdish, *Managing Your Self.* Cambridge: Basil Blackwell, Inc., 1991.

Tanner, Richard Pascale, and Athos, Anthony G., *The Art of Japanese Management.* New York: Simon & Schuster, 1981.

VanGundy, A. B., *Techniques of Structured Problem Solving.* New York: Van Nostrand Reinhold, 1988.

The Market for Management Consultancy Services in the USA, Beaconsfield, U.K.: Alpha Publications, 1990.

21

Communications

Dreams with Deadlines

Patricia M. McCracken

Director, Olympics Communication
International Business Machines
Corporation, Armonk, New York

Introduction

You may think of communications consulting as inextricably linked with consulting in general and, you're right, it is. But there's also a formal type of communications consulting in which a consultant analyzes the effectiveness of communications within an organization and determines ways to build or improve performance. It's an exciting and challenging consulting practice for communications is an integral building block to organizational effectiveness.

Because people often think of themselves as good communicators who know how to speak, write, and listen well, communications consulting can be a delicate balancing act. Performing in that complex spotlight, practitioners must persistently practice what they preach to be effective.

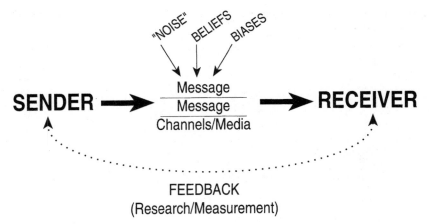

Figure 21-1   Interpersonal communication.

Although there are many types of specialized communications consulting, this chapter focuses on core principles that apply to all. Basically, the purpose of communications consulting is to help a client manage relationships with important constituencies using the fundamentals of scientific interpersonal communication (see Figure 21-1), with the goal of influencing attitudes and behaviors toward some organizational cause or need. It's a strategic approach to planning methods of communication for specific results.

Communications consulting is very much like the process of helping elect a political candidate and then maintaining his or her popularity and ability to get things done in office. First there's the "sell" challenge—getting people to understand, believe in, and vote for your candidate. Then there's the more difficult and enduring challenge of sustaining support over a longer term during which reality comes face-to-face with campaign rhetoric. Whether it's the selling of the president or the selling of ideas, it's a business that starts and ends with people.

The Four "C" Critical Success Factors

To deliver a winning communications consulting engagement, you've got to sell your client on the four "C" critical success factors: credibility, candor, consistency, and commitment.

First, the client's goals and objectives must be credible and realistic. Too often, issues considered to be caused by ineffective communications are business strategy problems.

For example, an advertising campaign won't fix a pricing error. If a product is overpriced for its market, advertising is a waste of money. Glossy publications won't improve employee morale, especially if executive actions belie what's written about. Sponsoring a documentary on public television won't distract attention from a business crisis. If you sense that the situation or the client is not credible, graciously decline the engagement.

Next, your client must be willing to be completely open, honest, and candid in all communications efforts. Anything less is a formula for failure, because the truth will emerge sooner or later and credibility will be destroyed. Once that happens, it takes a long time to rebuild.

Third, you'll need to convince clients that consistency, though often tedious for them, is the backbone of success. Everything related to the communications effort must link in a cohesive, complementary way so momentum is maintained. Inconsistencies create setbacks, confusion, and discounting or rejection of information.

Finally, you must be certain your client and all appropriate participants are committed to taking personal, active roles in executing the communications plan. Talk, even along with the money for your fees, is cheap. The actions your client takes are the currency that counts—for the success of both the plan, in particular, and your consulting engagement, in general.

Getting Involved

There are professional associations for both general and specialized communications disciplines. This list will get you started:

IABC (International Association of Business Communicators)
One Hallide Plaza, Suite 600, San Francisco, CA 94102, 415-433-3400.

Worldwide network of communications professionals across disciplines; affiliates in 40 countries. Offers workshops; local, regional and international meetings; case studies and other reference materials, and a monthly publication, *Communication World*.

PRSA (Public Relations Society of America)
33 Irving Place, New York, NY 10003, 212-995-2230.

Organization of public relations practitioners with over 100 chapters across the United States. Emphasizes professional development; publishes Code of Professional Standards for the Practice of Public Relations.

PRSSA (Public Relations Student Society of America)
33 Irving Place, New York, NY 10003, 212-995-2230.

PRSA student affiliate with over 160 chapters on college campuses throughout the United States. Offers internship programs to qualified members.

Women in Communications
P.O. Box 17460, Arlington, VA 22216, 703-528-4200.
  Network of professionals in diverse communications fields. Call or write
for a local chapter contact. Despite the name, it's NOT for women only.

Specialized Communications Consulting

Before focusing on communications consulting fundamentals, here's a
brief description of some specialized areas of communications practice.

Internal Communications

Internal or employee communications focuses on an organization's relationship with its workforce, which often includes suppliers, business
partners, and nonregular or contract workers as well as full-time
employees. The importance of this practice becomes more relevant as
organizations understand, either through intuitive leadership or painful
experience, that the days of paternalistic governance are gone. To accomplish goals and objectives, leaders need the understanding and involvement of their workforce. People are the lifeblood of all organizations and,
to some extent, without winning their hearts and minds, success is elusive, short-lived, or bloody. (See *Handbook of Organizational
Communication*, Ablex Publishing, Norwood, N.J., February 1988, G. M.
Goldhaber and G. A. Barnett, Editors; and *Communicating Change* by T.
Larkin, McGraw-Hill, New York, 1993.)

Integrated Marketing Communications

Integrated marketing communications consulting studies the efficiencies
and effectiveness of an organization's advertising (print and broadcast,
product and image), sales promotion and direct response marketing. (See
Integrated Marketing Communications by Don E. Schultz, Stanley L.
Tannenbaum, and Robert E. Lauterborn, NTC Business Books,
Lincolnwood, Ill., 1992; *How to Advertise* by Kenneth Roman and Jane
Maas, St. Martin's Press, New York, 1992; and *Marketing Warfare* by Al
Ries and Jack Trout, New York, McGraw-Hill, 1986.)

Media Relations

Often when an organization calls in a consultant, it's because they're getting bad press. Negative media coverage influences everything: stock
price, opinions of the organization as a place to work or to do business
with, employee morale and productivity, and customer confidence.

Media relations consulting focuses on working relationships with the media, analysts, consultants, and other opinion leaders whose voices carry news, speculation, and misinformation in print or broadcast media, whether in general major media or vertically targeted media in a specific field of interest. (See *Good-Bye to the Low Profile* by Herb Schmertz with William Novak, Little Brown, Boston, 1986.)

Crisis Communications

Crisis communications consulting helps an organization prepare for, deal with, or analyze methods of communicating in crisis situations. Crises can include accidents, product quality problems, environmental hazards, product tampering, or scandal associated with the organization. The secret to successful crisis communication is planning and the ability and courage to act fast. (See *PR Crises,* a collection of ten case studies, published by Public Relations News, 127 E. 80th Street, New York, NY 10021, 212-879-7090.)

Common Ground

All these unique but interrelated disciplines share common principles of practice as well as one overriding rule for success. They must be conducted in harmony as a kind of orchestra where each instrument has unique strengths and weaknesses—but where one instrument playing out of tune creates a distraction and several out of tune create cacophony. (See Figure 21-2.)

To avoid cacophony, all aspects of organizational communications must be linked on a routine basis and treated as part of a holistic strategy. In today's wired world where technology blurs borders and barriers, neither messages nor groups of people can be isolated. Internal decisions or problems can be, and often are, leaked to the media and the information is carried worldwide by wire service, radio, and television within minutes. That means employees, customers, business partners, suppliers, analysts, consultants, and other influencers will read, hear, or see this information in a matter of hours.

The power of effective communications strategy lies in getting there first, in having a solid base of credibility that ensures messages will be received in context, and in establishing good working relationships that ensure appropriate involvement and decision making happen quickly.

To be effective, communications consultants need a closed-loop methodology that includes a set of transferable tools and techniques. Once you have a portfolio developed, you can selectively create solutions for any client and continue to add to the portfolio through experience and continuous learning.

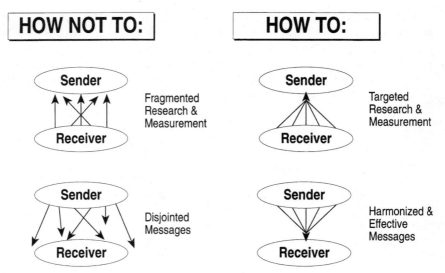

Figure 21-2 Harmonize communication.

The Heart of the Matter

In his book *The Seven Habits of Highly Effective People* (Simon & Schuster, New York, 1989), Stephen Covey writes: "If I were to summarize in one sentence the single most important principle I have learned in the field of interpersonal relations, it would be this: 'Seek first to understand, then to be understood.' This principle is the key to effective interpersonal communication."

This is also a simple but powerful formula for success in communications consulting. As it implies, you must first get beyond symptoms to the heart of your client's concerns and needs before you can hit a home run.

How to Begin

An effective approach to Covey's "seek first to understand, then to be understood" principle is to follow the parameters outlined by change consultant Victor Bond (see Chapter 28): content, context, and contact.

Content—Background and Information-Gathering Stage

Before the consulting engagement begins, you've got homework to do. Read annual reports and other stockholder information, do a media search and read related press coverage, study advertising and promotion deliverables, call and request employee communications materials—make it your business to seek out and review anything you think appropriate to help you begin selling yourself and engaging the client at the initial meeting.

This does not mean walking in with the attitude ascribed to Henry Kissinger in his handling of White House press conferences: "Do you have any questions for my answers." Your main goal at the meeting is to listen. However, being informed will help you listen more strategically and will allow you to ask questions or make comments that immediately identify you as part of the team.

Once engaged, your first step is to determine the client's specific needs by conducting a communications audit. In the first phase of this audit you'll interview key players in the client's organization to determine the scope of the problem. This first step ensures you can set realistic expectations and then develop a solution that responds on your client's terms and fulfills those expectations.

Questions in this phase include:

What are you trying to accomplish?

What specific messages are you trying to get across?

What results (attitudes, behaviors, actions) are you trying to achieve?

What has been done so far?

What has or has not worked and why?

What do you perceive as barriers or weaknesses?

What do you perceive as opportunities or strengths?

Whom do you most want to influence?

How do you define success?

Interviews should be one-on-one and allow plenty of time to answer these and any other related questions that come up during the session. This is the foundation of your work, and also an important opportunity to build trust and credibility for yourself.

Next you'll need to analyze the responses to get beyond symptoms and clearly define the problem, so you can move on to the *context phase* of solution building.

Context—Understanding the Environment

In this stage, you'll define and develop an understanding of the audience(s) you'll want to target, as well as the environment that influences those audiences—the context for your communications plan. This is a vital underpinning for your proposal because, without understanding the barriers, inhibitors, existing mindsets and environmental conditioning surrounding target audiences, there is little hope of getting through with relevant messages.

This phase of implementation requires research, some of which may already exist, some you'll need to conduct or commission. The right mix will depend on your client's schedule, budget, and the nature and scope of the assignment. Options include demographics, psychographics, values research, opinion surveys, and behavioral patterns (e.g., media viewing or buying habits). You'll want expert help with this, whether from inside the client's organization or from an outside expert.

To deliver the right solution, you must be able to answer the following questions for each segment you want to reach:

Who is the audience?

What do we know about them?

Are there specific subsets we should target (high flyers, early adoptors, key influencers)?

What have they heard so far?

What are their concerns?

How do they get information?

What are their values?

What do they want to hear?

Once you have a composite picture of each audience and the channels they prefer, you can determine how best to connect, or *make contact* with them.

Contact—Reaching and Influencing Audiences by Design

The contact stage is the time for crafting messages and selecting media channels that strategically match your client's goals to the various audiences' values and needs.

Questions pertinent to developing a powerful communications channel strategy include:

What channel(s) works best for each audience?

What is the timing (long term, short term)?

What are the lead times and deadlines for each channel?

What research or measurement is available on each channel?

Who is the appropriate spokesperson?

Is that person (or persons) an effective communicator?

How will the key messages be reinforced?

Mind the Gap

The power of communications as a competitive weapon lies in its ability to influence attitudes and behaviors. Because these are human- and emotion-based results, the communications plan you propose must take into consideration what motivates each audience segment so you can open not only their eyes and ears but their hearts and minds to your messages.

An effective way to develop such a plan is to use a gap strategy matrix. This matrix maps objectives by target audience and determines for each what gaps exist—for example, information gaps, channel gaps, credibility gaps, leadership gaps, or technology gaps, among others.

Once you're identified specific gaps, you can build a plan to close them. The plan should prescribe media, messages, and goals along with a time line and measurement process to track progress and results (see Figure 21-3).

There are two important lessons to keep in mind here. One is to be aware of communications overload. Creating communications tonnage is not the idea. People today suffer from information and sensory overload—"noise" and "clutter" intrude from everywhere. Effective communications must break through those inhibitors, appeal enough to the receiver to get attention, and then deliver meaningful information in a way that packs a punch.

To be remembered, however, any communication must be repeated and reinforced. The scientific rule of thumb is that a message doesn't get through until it is heard, seen, or read three times. That doesn't mean

Audience	GAP	Desired Result	Media/ Channels	Message	Time	Measurement

Figure 21-3 Gap strategy matrix.

simply delivering it three times, because it's naïve to think every communications delivered is received. It means developing a channel strategy that plays to each medium's unique strengths, and playing the message(s) over and over again.

For clarity and consistency, both message and medium must be appropriate to the situation. You don't want to recommend a glossy, four-color brochure to advise employees their benefits are being cut. And you wouldn't want to suggest an advertising campaign if your client doesn't have the budget or the time to do it right, and perhaps a direct mail campaign would work just as well.

The best strategy is to use a variety of channels that have the best track record with the target audience. The bottom line is: a message must be repeated until results show it's gotten through.

Once "through," of course, results can be positive or negative. The important thing is to have a way of determining that, then finding out why. That's where measurement comes in. Your plan needs a monitoring mechanism that provides early and ongoing feedback so refinements can be made and progress tracked.

If the area is internal or employee communications, collaboration with the human resource department makes sense since they often track employee opinions and attitudes. If you're advising on marketing communications, fulfillment devices such as mail-in coupons or toll-free telephone numbers can provide tracking data.

You don't want to count clips for media relations effectiveness, but you do want to count how often and how accurately desired messages are reported. In crisis communications you'll want minute-by-minute feedback which you'll have no problem getting from the media, but you'll also want to set up a crisis hotline and "war room" where information can be analyzed constantly.

Research and Measurement

For every discipline, various types of research and measurement are available. Based on the scope of the assignment, your job is to help determine what technique or combination of techniques is best. The important thing is to tie the two together. Research should shape the what, how, and to whom elements of the communications plan; measurement should track results and shape enhancements to the plan. Harmonized research and measurement yield communications plans that work (see Figure 21-2).

Following are some general descriptions and guidelines:

One-on-one interviews are exactly what they sound like—individual meetings where an interviewer personally asks an interviewee a series of questions. One-on-ones are best when the questions are complex, when the issues are emotional, and when a personal perspective rather than a group viewpoint is desired. A two-hour session is usually best, to allow for thoughtful probing and to accommodate any tangential but relevant discussion that may emerge.

Focus groups consist of an interviewer working with a group of people representing target audiences. Focus groups can be as small as 6 but should not exceed 10. This method is effective when the goal is to test concepts against group versus individual norms, and when feedback is needed quickly.

Surveys are written instruments that can be conducted as a stand-alone or used as part of an interview or focus group. Questions can ask for a scaled rating response (1 = totally agree/approve through 5 = totally disagree/disapprove), for yes/no or true/false answers, or for personal commentary. Surveys work best when there is confidence in the questions that need asking, when quantitative measures are preferable to qualitative, when a larger sample is desired, and when the goal is establishing initial measures for ongoing assessment.

Here again, the scope and needs of the engagement and the client's schedule and budget will help you determine the best solution.

Summary

Communications consulting is an emerging practice with plenty of opportunity for talented practitioners. It takes a creative mind, persuasive personality and an ability to ask the right questions and design the right solutions. It takes a strategic thinker who knows how to use research and measurement to the client's advantage. It takes a person who knows how to put deadlines to dreams by turning vision into action.

Part 6

Business Consulting Services

22

Business Planning

Gordon Hornbaker
Grand Designs, Inc.
Phoenix, Arizona

Paula L. Dawson
Midrange Systems Solutions
Phoenix, Arizona

When a business is successful, praises are sung for the daring entrepreneur, or for the timely product introduction, or for the unfaltering dedication to customer service. Few areas of the company look bad when the money is rolling in. If an ongoing concern fails, it seemingly takes everyone by surprise: How could such a thing happen? Yet most reasons for business failure fall into one of just two categories:

- Undercapitalization
- Poor management

The first category is undeniable and fairly straightforward: Either a company has sufficient capital reserves for ongoing operations or it does not. The second category, which is more closely related to the first than most realize, might not be as easily explained. Bad management usually involves inadequate knowledge about the business or situation with which the manager is involved; lack of capital is often related directly to the bad manager or indirectly to the party who gave it to the manager in the first place.

Both deficiencies can be better described as bad planning, a malady that affects more businesses than merely those that fail. The ability to anticipate the future, through planning, is often an overlooked skill in today's management profile. Yet there are few matters as important to the future survival and growth of the company as effective business planning.

Why Business Planning?

Depending on where an executive is sitting, planning may be approached with different perspectives. A CEO may be particularly concerned with broader issues—how the entire organization will react to the economy and future competition, for instance. A marketing manager may be concerned with how a specific product will perform in a chosen marketplace. A financial officer may choose to concentrate solely on cash flow planning for a particular division.

These individual planning efforts result in careful, well-thought-out analyses. All too often, however, strategies developed for different functional areas by different managers lack consistent focus, an essential ingredient. There are simply too many unrelated strategies, in too many areas, in too many directions, with each strategy competing for scarce available resources. The planning process gives company managers a structured method of pulling all these divergent strategies into one consistent philosophical structure. The strategies can then be focused upon those specific areas critical to the success of the enterprise.

In itself, business planning allows an organization to play an active role in creating its future, rather than simply letting the future happen. By involving individuals with different perspectives in the planning process, an organization encourages the setting of more achievable goals and gains commitment from all corners of the organization. Managers collaborate to develop a shared vision of the future they want and then establish the goals and action plans needed to achieve that vision.

Planning is the ongoing process or action that a company takes now for the future it desires. It is a continual, dynamic process. As an organization grows and survives, its detailed business plan provides a road map for those goals. The business plan reviews today's situation but does not respond to today's problems. An effective plan calls for solutions to tomorrow's problems and actions that respond to tomorrow's opportunities.

Planning can be especially critical for the small business, in which smaller numbers of staff and entrepreneurs are generally responsible for many more functional duties. Indeed, planning can assist the small business to identify and allocate scarce resources, including capital and personnel, that can guide the company in the desired direction. Without an explicit plan, these resources might be committed to immediate needs that may compromise longer-term objectives.

Smaller businesses generally do not have the ability of larger firms to cushion the impact of mistakes; therefore, problems and risks must be continually identified. Sound business planning helps to identify these potential pitfalls earlier and to develop contingency plans. Furthermore, the flexibility common to smaller businesses can often enable its managers to implement a plan more easily and quickly. Since small firms can make major changes in direction, they can more readily capitalize on economic opportunities or market shifts if sound plans are in place.

What time frame should the business plan cover? Timing usually can be determined by considering management's objectives in putting the plan together. For a start-up company, an in-depth analysis of at least the first 3 years of the company's operations will be required, although many financial investors recommend 5 years. Established companies should develop long-term strategic plans (involving major resource commitments) over a 3- to 5-year time frame and operational detail plans for the coming year.

In summary, all managers engaged in business planning must ask:

- "Where are we now?"
- "Where do we want to go?"
- "How will we get there?"

Answering these simple questions is the essence of business planning.

Business Planners and Consultants

Most business managers realize the value of planning; they just never do anything about it. Virtually every successful business owner and corporate executive agrees that a properly constructed and well-thought-out business plan will contribute positively to the overall success of the company. Time spent assembling a thorough business plan should play a significant role in the growth and profitability of the company.

Many larger companies have an internal planning department that is responsible for assembling departmental input, monitoring the environmental and competitive pulses, and updating the company plan on an ongoing basis. Internal planners may function in these roles year round, or they may act only as plan facilitators as the annual plan is updated. In either case, outside consultants might be brought in to provide a "fresh approach" or to assist in the revision of certain critical portions of the planning process.

Assume that a company wants to initiate a strategic planning process but does not have the time to do so. It must decide whether to engage an outside consultant or assign someone inside the organization to perform the task. Several of the advantages of using an outside planning consultant may be compelling.

Prior Experience in Planning

Most planning consultants are versed in strategic planning, well able to lead the client through the mechanics of defining goals, gathering managerial input, discussing alternatives, and so on. Managers with little or no experience in planning will benefit from the consultant's instruction. Planning consultants usually understand the sensitive ground they are treading upon and should be skilled in handling the personal dynamics of the planning process.

As important as this concept is, it can lead to open conflict and wasted effort if it is ignored. Most consultants will owe their planning experience to one or several industry-specific clients or employers—a background that will help the current client expedite its environmental assessment. A background in marketing research and pertinent data-gathering techniques will also provide assistance to a client that lacks its own internal research department. Finally, there may be a specific expertise or informational void within the company that the consultant will be asked to fill.

Dedication to the Planning Process

Busy company executives never seem to have adequate time to spend on planning, even when the overall commitment is there. Even worse, company plans always seem to interfere with another important project of some kind. A planning consultant can usually provide a schedule within which all the necessary pieces of data and input can be collected, analyzed, and collated. With the consultant acting as project leader, the planning function is not subordinated to other pressing responsibilities or conflicting job functions.

Economies of Scale

When calculated on the basis of executive time per hour—of having, say, eight or ten highly compensated managers spin their wheels for days or weeks on their own noncohesive plans—the expense of a skilled planning consultant seems more than justified. Having the consultant set the initial guidelines according to top management's goals and then systematically blend the input from all departments into a working company plan will usually provide a demonstrable economy of scale.

Knowledge of Planning Technique

Planning consultants should also be familiar with various systems techniques—including financial reporting systems, financial projection systems, and "what if" scenario systems—that few company executives will know. Input and participation from the systems managers can greatly assist not only in planning but also in providing the monitoring and feedback that will play a crucial role in effective implementation of the business plan.

Interaction with Information Systems

Although most organizations have computerized their bread-and-butter transaction systems for accounting, finance, manufacturing, and marketing, they sometimes overlook the potential contribution that the information systems (IS) department can make toward achieving the overall business plan. In order to support the needed response to the organization's ever-changing environment, IS professionals within the organization must be aware of top management's objectives and the strategic direction of the firm. In addition, because advances in technology increase the opportunities and competitive threats to the organization, it becomes increasingly important for management to collaborate with the IS department to identify new opportunities and determine how best to use technology. By encouraging a planning partnership between management and IS technologists, the consultant facilitates the development of information technology to support the company's strategic goals and organizational objectives.

Objectivity

Almost without exception, the greatest asset a consultant can bring to the planning process is objectivity. Playing the devil's advocate throughout the planning process will force management to reexamine the company's goals and objectives and also continually challenge the strategies and tactics formulated in the action portion of the business plan.

Preliminary Steps in Business Planning

Once the planning engagement has been accepted, it is time to perform one of the most critical portions of the job: preplanning. A planning mission must be developed, taking into account all the key participants. Risks and constraints must be acknowledged, responsibilities assigned, and time lines set for each part of the plan. If a consultant is involved, his or her role must be established. For instance, the consultant may be responsible for recommending implementation strategies, devising plans for future changes, monitoring progress of the project, and proposing future improvements to the process. If the consultant serves as the planning facilitator, he or she will be in charge of the overall direction of the project and will be held responsible not only for the finished plan but also for the quality of the process. It is imperative that the client not expect the consultant to do all the work involved in implementing the plan; otherwise, the client may become too dependent.

When planning is performed as part of an engagement, whether for a fixed or an hourly fee, the consultant must also develop a time budget before commencing any substantive activities. Other key preliminary steps that should be taken before any work is actually undertaken on the plan include the following:

- Secure top management commitment.
- Determine management objectives.
- Plan the planning.
- Commit to a schedule.
- Assemble resources.
- Undertake departmental interviews.

Secure Top Management Commitment

Securing the commitment of top officers may seem obvious, but without it the consultant will be unable to smoothly perform the tasks involved throughout the planning process. Also, a final delivered plan may be politely accepted but stubbornly ignored. Middle managers will quickly determine that the planning effort has not been fully endorsed by top management and will work through the planning process only halfheartedly (if at all).

If company executives view the planning process as an overly formal, uninspired ritual, full of redundant meetings with endless opportunities to criticize and be criticized, the consultant's support will be as thin as his or her patience. The planning activities must be viewed as creative exercise, requiring imagination and a give-and-take attitude. Learning must be emphasized as the key element of the planning process.

If the consultant has been hired by anyone else but the top officer, an appointment with that top manager should be scheduled immediately—before any meetings with staff. Participation of the top officials should be requested not only for the initial commitment but for follow-through as well. (Other managers will see this involvement and redouble their efforts.)

Determine Management Objectives

When the consultant meets with the top managers, the purpose of the engagement must be reiterated. There should also be a consensus among the managers involved in the process. Is the consultant to act as a guide through the planning process, explaining each manager's responsibility as the plan is assembled for the president? Or is he or she to act as facilitator, gathering each department's input and assembling the components into a workable plan? The client's expectations must be determined; it is essential that the consultant's version and that of the client be identical.

Plan the Planning

"Planning to plan" is a critical step that is often overlooked. Many planners plunge headlong into the tasks involved, failing to properly review all the steps necessary to produce the finished planning document. A small investment of time here will pay huge dividends to a consultant's sanity and to the client's deliverables.

The following questions should be asked as the key areas are reviewed:

Time schedule. When? Where?

Responsibilities. Who makes arrangements for meeting rooms, supplies, refreshments? Who directs the process? Who sets the agenda? Who leads the sessions? Who assembles the plan?

Information. What information is required for the sessions? Who supplies market surveys? Financials? Past years' plans? What do the managers receive to review before the sessions? When?

Commit to a Schedule

Assign as specific a time frame as possible to action steps. Allow enough time to perform each one, or the end result will suffer.

Assemble Resources

One of the main responsibilities of planners is to ensure the participation of key executives and managers. These are the people who know the most about the issues involved, and they will also play the most critical roles in successful implementation. If they will not be working directly on the plan, a method for their input and in-progress reviews must be in place.

One of the best ways to achieve involvement is the "blue sky" planning session. Top managers are assembled away from the normal business routine and interruptions (off-site is ideal) for an unqualified review and discussion of the key issues. Functional managers can provide basic background leading up to the discussions. Then a free-for-all, no-assumptions-made skull session can provide an enlightened review of the company's current practices and policies. It will at the least provide invaluable background for the upcoming strategy formulation, and at best lead the planning team toward opportunities and alternatives not previously considered.

Undertake Departmental Interviews

If interfunctional planning sessions are impractical, the consultant must meet with the department heads individually. These managers should be informed of the purpose of planning and of top management's objectives. The sooner everyone is on the same wavelength, the closer the plan will be to completion. If each manager submits a portion of the plan, the content and the corresponding time frame must be reviewed. If the consultant will be responsible for assembling all the data, the individual managers should be invited to contribute to the process by submitting a departmental summary that includes the following (at a minimum):

- Departmental reviews of personnel and salaries
- Budgets (current and expected)
- Key departmental objectives
- Specialized data for the department (marketing, manufacturing, human resources, information systems, and so on)

Figure 22-1 is a checklist to guide you in obtaining needed information from the various managers during these preliminary steps.

Format of the Business Plan

Managers and consultants who have been through several planning cycles likely have their own favorite format for a business plan. Each planning engagement must allow for the individual company's needs and objectives as the planning process proceeds. Sound business planning will include a thorough discussion of the three basic questions described above. These in turn can be analyzed in terms of the following planning guidelines:

- *Situation analysis*—where we are
- *Goals and objectives*—where we want to go
- *Strategy formulation*—how we can get there

Business Planning

1. Has the company articulated a clear mission statement?
2. Has the company developed clear and formal objectives for the business?
3. Are the objectives quantified in terms of rate of return, growth, market share, product or service development, and so on? Have measurements been identified for these objectives?
4. Are there clear and nonconflicting objectives for each function in the company?
5. Is the company planning expansion into new products or markets?
6. Has management identified the critical success factors for the business?
7. Does the company have a formal business plan, including
    a. description of the business?
    b. market definition?
    c. competitive analysis?
    d. management overview?
    e. key personnel plan?
    f. key financial data, including projections, cash flow analysis, and breakeven analysis?
8. Does the company have a systems plan to assist in the planning process and to monitor and evaluate product progress and environmental events throughout the year?

Financial Planning and Control

1. Are annual operating budgets prepared?
2. Are the budgets consistent with the objectives of the company?
3. Are individual functional managers responsible for preparing their own sections of the budget?
4. Are budgets prepared on detailed assumptions that are reevaluated each year?
5. Do assumptions consider
    a. changes that may affect revenues or costs?
    b. capacity?
    c. staffing requirements?
    d. market trends?
    e. sales mix?
    f. contribution by product or service?

Figure 22-1 A planning checklist. (Market Driven Management, *B. Charles Adams.*)

6. Are budgets sufficiently detailed to provide a measure of control by
   a. time period?
   b. area of responsibility?
   c. line item?
7. Are budgets well documented to provide capability for variance analysis?
8. Does financial reporting provide
   a. comparisons of plan to actual?
   b. basic reports, including balance sheets, income statements, and sources or uses of funds?
   c. exceptions?
   d. percentages of revenue for major items?
   e. statistics and ratios that focus attention on critical success factors?
   f. measures of profitability by product group, customer group, geographic area and sales region?
9. Are the reports produced on a regular basis and in a timely manner?
10. Are variances documented and plans adjusted accordingly?
11. Is cash flow monitored on a routine basis?
12. Is there a linkage between budgets and cash flow analysis?
13. Does the company have an adequate credit line?
14. Has the company made adequate use of leverage?
15. Are financial monitoring systems in place to assist functional managers?

Management

1. Does the company have sufficient numbers of qualified personnel at the right levels to function in
   a. marketing and sales?
   b. finance?
   c. production?
   d. research and development?
   e. human resources?
2. Do managers have the appropriate background and skills to oversee these functions?
3. Are the organizational structure and reporting lines defined?
4. Are job descriptions and responsibilities defined?

Figure 22-1 (*Continued*) A planning checklist. (*Market Driven Management*, B. *Charles Adams*.)

5. Does the company use procedures manuals?
6. Are managers given authority for decisions and accountability for results?
7. Are individuals aware of their duties and responsibilities?
8. Is there a well understood mechanism for employee-manager feedback and communication?

Figure 22-1 (*Continued*) A planning checklist. (Market Driven Management, *B. Charles Adams.*)

The results of applying these guidelines should be expressed in a formal business plan. Figure 22-2 lists the contents of a business plan that is based on a thorough analysis of the situation, a statement of the goals and objectives, and a formulation of the strategy. It also includes additional sections that can aid in the presentation of the plan.

Implementation of the Business Plan

It is common for the management team to heave a collective sigh of relief once the formal company plan has been committed to paper and issued for circulation. The most difficult aspect of planning is not in the planning per se. It is in the doing. A great plan not implemented means wasted expense for the client and wasted credibility for the consultant. Many managers, including chief executive officers, state that their major disappointment in the planning process is their inability to see any sustained result from those strategies so carefully constructed the previous year. Although the planning process may be threatened by several uncontrollable events, disaster can often be circumvented if the consultant understands the causes of planning failure. Figure 22-3 lists several common causes.

One of the most critical steps in implementing a business plan is monitoring the plan's progress. A carefully integrated set of monitoring measures must be established for all functional departments within the operations environment. These should measure accomplishment against the stated goal—for the company as a whole and for individual strategies within the company plan. This type of monitoring, if connected to an efficient methodology for review and discussion of actions taken in the plan, should greatly boost the chances of implementing the plan successfully. Quarterly or semiannual review sessions with departmental managers will not only assist the plan's implementation but also enhance the anticipated success of future planning cycles. Such regular opportunity for input will also increase the likelihood of lower-level manager buy-in and support.

Situation Analysis.   What are the factors, both inside and outside the company, that will influence the company's ability to achieve its stated goals? Does the company understand the market in which it is competing, its customer's needs and the competition's position?

1. *Internal analysis:* All company strengths and weaknesses are examined through a critical assessment of internal mechanisms, including management (leadership, planning abilities, and personnel development), functional areas (sales and marketing, production, human resources, and so on), and resources (financial, personnel, facilities, and informational).
2. *External analysis:* All external threats to the success of the company, and all opportunities that might be exploited for additional success, are examined.
   a. A macroenvironmental assessment includes a review of relevant government, political, regulatory, demographic, socioeconomic, and technological factors affecting the overall business industry.
   b. A microenvironmental assessment includes a more carefully focused examination of factors affecting the client's market and market segment, including customers, suppliers, labor, competitors, and barriers to entry.
   c. A market and competition survey focuses on the specific market that the client is competing in, including market trends, growth rates, market shares, and potentials. Each significant competitor within that marketplace is examined individually for strengths, weaknesses, and other factors.

Goals and Objectives.   What objectives does the client have for the future? Where and what does the company wish to be?

1. *Mission statement:* The purpose of the business is defined, including why the company is in business and who the customer is. This statement provides a foundation for the company's existence and linkage to its customers. (Nebulous nonspecifics, such as efforts to work together for the greater good, are ignored.)
2. *Assumptions:* Future events that have the greatest potential to affect the company's ability to achieve its stated goals are identified, and assumptions are made about their likelihood of occurrence.
3. *Objectives:* Financial and nonfinancial goals (including specific objectives such as those relating to marketing, products, operations, and human resources) are stated. These goals are results-oriented, measurable, nonconflicting, and attainable.

Figure 22-2   Format of a business plan.

4. *Critical success factors:* Identification is made of the two or three conditions or variables that "must go right" for the client to succeed. These critical success factors, which will have significant impact on the company's operations, are assigned a high priority.

Strategy Formulation.   What specific plans will be placed into action to answer the threats and opportunities discussed in the situation analysis? How will the client reach its objectives?

1. *Marketing strategy:* Plans for product positioning, segmentation or niche strategy, packaging, pricing and promotions, and distribution are discussed, with appropriate time frames or schedules assigned to each.
2. *Operational plans:* A description is made of the allocation of resources that will support the product or service sales—including supply and production, research and development, and information systems.
3. *Personnel planning:* The human resources plan to support operations for the appropriate time frame is specified.
4. *Critical risks:* The most important events and risks that can derail the proposed plan of action are identified, and an anticipated solution is suggested for each.
5. *Contingency plans:* Alternative strategies are developed for the most likely alternative events, with accompanying probabilities. Since it is often the unexpected events that torpedo a company's long-term success, this section is critically important. Yet it is most often overlooked in the planning process.
6. *Financial projections:* Estimates are provided of the financial resources that will support the business plan, including sales and costs forecasts, departmental budgets, cash flows, and balance sheets. Breakeven analysis and "best case" and "worst case" scenarios can be added as further measures of contingency planning.

Additional Data.   Several other items can be added to the business plan.

1. *Executive summary:* A summarized version (two or three pages) of the entire plan, prepared for a "quick read," is often used by financiers to determine if the business is worthy of investment or expansion capital.

Figure 22-2   (*Continued*)   Format of a business plan.

2. *Appendices:* Useful reference information can be documented, including industry or background articles, charted references mentioned in the body of the plan, detailed expenditure lists, critical time charts, and key financial ratios.
3. *Résumés and management data:* Required additions in start-up plans, and optional in others, are résumés of the top officers or principals and a detailed organization chart of the company managers and staff responsibilities. The history of the company, and its form, may also be included. ,

Figure 22-2   (*Continued*)   Format of a business plan.

1. Management underestimates or ignores the resources necessary to execute the business plan. Planning is a process of change, and generally companywide change is going to result in additional expenses related to organization, personnel, processes, and informational systems.
2. The business plan lacks enough specific detail describing the work needed to achieve the plan's objectives. Every manager and employee involved should understand his or her part in the plan's supporting tactics.
3. Management does not realign existing resources to effect the changes allowed for in the new plan. This failure is easy to understand, since the people, procedures, controls, systems, and products that preceded the intended changes probably have been in place for years. The type of fundamental change often required by a business plan does not occur easily, but lack of change can sink the planned strategies before they have a chance to work.
4. Functional managers charged with implementation of the plan do not have the ability to make revisions quickly and conveniently. If needed revisions become too cumbersome, managers will often fail to make them, thereby destroying the planning process. Competent and easy-to-use support systems are a critical element of planning implementation.

Figure 22-3   Reasons for failures in business planning.

Relationship to Systems Planning

The business plan for an organization has a clear relationship to the plan for the organization's information system. Therefore, the objectives of the information system must coordinate with the objectives for the organization. The business plan should identify the information needed by the organization that the information system is to provide. Thus, the IS department must understand the organization's plan in order to establish and maintain IS priorities that are consistent with it. The IS department must also address new opportunities for the organization's information resource, as well as provide appropriate feedback for monitoring and controlling to support all top management decision-making activities. To accomplish these goals, the information system should be viewed as a strategic resource of the organization.

Information systems planning can be enhanced by means of development methodologies. One planning technique that combines several proven systems development methodologies, a technique known as *information engineering,* is summarized in Figure 22-4.

Benefits of Planning

Because most of the normal business day is conducted in a task orientation—answering telephones, conducting meetings, supervising staff, and meeting deadlines—precious little time is devoted to searching for opportunities. A conscious planning process prompts the management of an organization to focus on its long-term development, including needed resources, personnel, and expertise. It also provides several other significant benefits, both to the individuals involved and to the organization.

Facilitating Organizational Coordination

Planning can lead to a well-defined organizational structure. In fact, a sound business plan goes beyond organization charts and job descriptions; it also allows the management team to strategically decide what needs to be done, who is the best to do it, and how the staff can work together most effectively. The often intimidating challenge of managerial delegation is eased when the planning process allows assignments to be made on a logical basis, after careful consideration of task, timing, budget, skills, and results required.

Overview

Traditionally, separate information systems were built independently of one another. As a result, nonintegrated systems generally failed to provide the information needed for overall management control. Systems were unnecessarily redundant and expensive to maintain. Some painful manifestations of this failure to align IS priorities with the overall organization needs are unused systems, premature scrapping of systems, the need for extensive maintenance, and high IS staff turnover.

Once management accepts the challenge to its IS planning in relation to its overall business plan, new approaches to systems development make the task easier. Through an ongoing search for better development methodologies, many new examples have emerged, including data-centered design, end-user computing, design automation, productivity tools, reusable design and code, expert systems, and prototyping. Although any one of these approaches could achieve noticeable results, *information engineering* offers a planning technique that integrates these various methodologies.

Information engineering (IE) has been defined as an interlocking set of formal, automated techniques for the planning, analysis, design, and construction of information systems on an enterprise-wide basis or across a major section of the enterprise. Rather than representing a single, rigid methodology, IE encompasses a variety of structured techniques.

In contrast to traditional systems development, IE aims to build applications that work together rather than on a project-by-project basis. It analyzes the needs and strategic opportunities of top management and then integrates top-level business planning with the analysis, design, and generation of systems. Because they participate in building the high-level organizational plans and models, IS professionals are able to use the high-level plans as a framework for developing a computerized organization.

In conjunction with the business planning process, IE builds a steadily evolving repository (sometimes referred to as an *encyclopedia*) of knowledge about the organization. By compiling information about the organization's data models, process models, and systems designs, IE can prioritize and coordinate systems to best aid the strategic goals of the company.

Figure 22-4 Information systems planning by the information engineering technique.

IE encompasses the following four stages:

Strategy planning
Business area analysis
Systems design
Construction

Strategy Planning

If an organization effectively conducts its business planning as a collaborative effort among various representatives from top management, including the IS department, much of the information gathered from the planning effort will serve as input to information strategy planning. This first phase of IE uses the same critical elements of the planning process that would interest top management:

Analysis of goals and problems
Identification of critical success factors
Analysis of technology impact
Development of a strategic systems vision

An information strategy plan that works hand in hand with the organization's business plan logically flows from the overview model of the organization and the resulting analysis of these critical elements.

Business Area Analysis

The second stage of IE, business area analysis, identifies the processes needed to operate the enterprise, how they integrate, and what data they need. By understanding this information, IS planners can better prioritize systems development efforts. As in the first phase of IE, planners conduct their analysis without regard to existing information systems and technology. Their findings may actually lead to a rethinking of systems and procedures and may identify areas for new systems design.

As part of this phase, planners must define an overall information architecture. This architecture provides a high-level map of the current and projected information requirements of the organization to support decision making and operations management. It examines information independently of the personnel using it or of the organizational area and technology involved in acquiring and presenting it. Essentially, it serves as the fundamental building block for the development of information systems. The analysis provides a proactive rather than reactive basis for IS development.

Figure 22-4 (*Continued*) Information systems planning by the information engineering technique.

Systems Design and Construction

Under the IE approach, only the IS resource opportunities with the greatest potential benefits to the organization as a whole will be implemented. This contrasts with the necessity of many IS departments today to produce short-term results by designing and building a large number of small systems. Instead, IE recommends an implementation procedure that ensures that systems are compatible and consistent with the organization's overall goals in the first place. In this manner, businesses can avoid the high cost of redesigning systems for integration purposes.

Using various modeling and productivity tools, organizations can design, build, implement, and refine their systems relatively quickly and then link them in a manner that benefits the organization. A wealth of computer-aided software engineering (CASE) tools (including analysis and diagraming tools), data dictionaries, and features like prototyping and rapid application design (RAD) facilitate achievement of the desired results.

While organizations will continue to face gaps in what is desired, what is feasible, and what is actually implemented, implementation of a methodology like IE can greatly reduce the risks associated with unplanned systems implementation. As the IS department develops its business skills in conjunction with its technical specialization, staff members will be better equipped to respond to their organization with systems solutions that enhance the way the company does business.

Figure 22-4 (*Continued*) Information systems planning by the information engineering technique.

An effective company plan can also provide a consensus. If the process has involved managers from all functional areas, the end result will reflect a common goal, without competing objectives. People can channel their efforts in one direction, thereby increasing the overall efficiency of the organization.

Integrating with Systems Planning

The organization's information resource and the latest systems technology are key strategic success factors in today's complex, data-sensitive business environment. The information systems managers who focus on business problems, rather than solely on technical concerns, can adapt quickly and work in conjunction with corporate management to find solutions to business problems that make sense in the overall organizational context. By better aligning information systems priorities with the goals of the business plan, the organization can more effectively achieve business-targeted systems that readily adapt as the company changes.

Motivating Employees and Managers

Planning provides motivation for individuals throughout the organization. By involving managers across the company, the company strategies reflect wider ownership and increased involvement in securing the company's objectives. By announcing the company goals, the plan allows employees to align their individual objectives more closely with those of the organization. Employees know the exact nature of their long-term objectives, the measures of their performance, and the rewards associated with effective goal accomplishment.

Enhancing Management Growth

The most important benefit of planning is within the process itself. The historical review, critical analysis of the current environment, and formulation of strategic alternatives yield the true value of planning. The constant emphasis on asking why creates a continual learning process for the management team.

23
Marketing and Distribution

Michael P. Kipp

Kipp & Associates
Nashville, Tennessee

The events of the last few years have created a truly Olympic playing field for competitors in virtually all businesses. People conducting business in the 1990s no longer do so within "a league of their own." Moreover, the excesses of the 1980s and their attendant business failures have strengthened the survivors. Against this backdrop are the following emerging facts of competitive life:

Investment levels and hurdle rates will be more demanding for sustained participation in any sector.

Competitors will have deeper pockets.

Windows of opportunity will be smaller, product life cycles shorter, and success more uncertain.

A dynamic response to market shifts will be critical for all enterprises well into the next century and, therefore, a fertile field for consultants.

Although it is easy to acknowledge that people see what they look for, the bulk of "presenting problems" in business today are marketing problems at their root. Of the many contributing factors, five seem especially relevant to the consulting field:

1. Many markets are mature, highly consolidated, and intensely competitive. The rewards for participation are meager and the cost of misfire can be mortal.

2. Slow population growth makes it increasingly important to target with precision and to retain hard-won customers.

3. Although competition is growing, most markets are not. New household formation, for example, will be less than 2 percent for the foreseeable future.

4. Small businesses are being created at record levels—the incubation period often financed with severance money—bringing more local competition with leaner participation costs.

5. Virtually all companies in all countries face growing global competition for the domestic markets they once owned outright.

Consultants who can add value to the marketing dimension of their clients' businesses will always be held in high regard.

A Practice Theory

Any statement on the practice of consulting should begin with the point of view of the author-as-consultant. My own positioning is that of a process rather than a content expert. *Process consultation,* best explicated by Edgar Schein,[1] proceeds from the affirming philosophy that most companies know—or can develop—their own solutions, given the right line of inquiry and some tools for pursuing it. In other words, "the answer is in the group." So, first, I typically address marketing issues in cross-functional teams. Opportunities occur "on the horizon," and will hence require horizontal integration to be successfully addressed.

Second, I always couple a diagnosis of the client's problem with a prognosis regarding the most likely favorable outcome of our work together. This forces me to begin with a fact-based picture of what *is* rather than my favorite advice or intervention, and to end with a working hypothesis of how those facts are likely to change *regardless* of what we do. This serves as the best antidote to the rescue fantasy that sets in when the opposite of "problem" is inadvertently framed as "all better." In my experience, consultants must constantly guard against becoming more invested in the change process than the client.

Finally, I follow the injunction in the Hippocratic Oath against "cutting for stone"—consulting for the billable hours alone. To do so is corrosive of self-respect and mitigates against building a sustainable practice base.

An Intervention Model

In the following four-step protocol, the elements are circular rather than linear. These elements are contracting, assessing, planning, and executing. This protocol applies regardless of the scope of the project, lending itself to a summative evaluation and recontracting, as appropriate for a new initiative.

Contracting

Contracting begins during the initial exploratory conversations between consultant and prospect. All too often, this stage is regarded as a form of courting or relationship building, the aim of which is to secure the engagement. On a deeper level, these conversations establish subtle agreements regarding how the parties might work together, what the boundaries might be, and what constitutes "success" in the eyes of the client. This stage offers important opportunities to elicit perceptions of the presenting problem and gain sanction for proceeding along a particular path.

Assess

Our assessment is driven by a marketing audit, selected or designed to give perspective to the issues that surfaced during the contracting stage. Such a perspective is critical, since initial descriptions of presenting problems or aspirations tend to be simplistic. Problems often have a probable culprit lurking just behind the words. Typical among these are such symptoms as sales management difficulties, quarrels with representative organizations, fumbles in product commercialization, and conflicts between channels of distribution. Aspirations are often stated as targets without an appreciation for their implications. "To generate 35 percent of our revenues internationally," for example, begs the question of whether the company is positioned to carry out an export or an investment strategy—or neither. With margins declining and selling costs on the rise, there's usually an unspoken hypothesis that the blame or salvation lies with a specific person, group, or function. A solid audit, conducted and shared broadly, helps frame these matters as systems issues and builds a constituency for their ultimate resolution. To be truly useful, an audit needs to be tailored to the company and industry under scrutiny. There are, though, some very solid general models that give the consultant a point of departure.

Ames and Hlavacek[2] provide an extremely useful format for such an audit, presented in Figure 23-1. Much of the utility of this format stems from their distillation of market-driven management into a comprehensive framework easily recalled or taught, if need be, as the "five Cs":

Liabilities	-5	0	+5	Advantages
1. *Market Facts* nonexistent, unverified, or underutilized in planning and decision making	I I I I I II I I I I I			1. Value of market intelligence is widely recognized as the foundation for all planning and decisions
2. *Market Definitions* too broad or based on products or manufacturing technology	I I I I I II I I I I I			2. Priority market niches defined by applications or user needs and profit potential in each country
3. *Competitive Comparisons* result in a laundry list of generalized strengths, weaknesses, threats, and opportunities	I I I I I II I I I I I			3. Competitor analysis used to define a demonstrable competitive advantage that can be used to protect or build each product/market business
4. Accounting Systems driven by GAAP rather than management information needs	I I I I I II I I I I I			4. Net profitability regularly reported for each key product line, channel, and customer group
5. Low Cost Claims unsupported and competitor results imply otherwise	I I I I I II I I I I I			5. Documented comparisons show costs are in line with or better than global competitors
6. Quality Goals are nonexistent or talked about without the dedication and programs essential for improvement	I I I I I II I I I I I			6. Superior quality is constantly demonstrated through global comparisons or product, costs, yield rates, and life-cycle performance
7. Machine Efficiency and Capacity considerations disproportionately influence management decisions	I I I I I II I I I I I			7. Manufacturing management committed to continuous productivity gains that measurably lower costs and/or enhance customer value
8. Response and Cycle Times are lagging and targeted improvement programs do not exist	I I I I I II I I I I I			8. Response and cycle times are equal or superior to leading competitors and the organization urgently searches for more improvements
9. Existing Products and Technology suppress thinking about changing market needs and opportunities	I I I I I II I I I I I			9. Willing to think beyond existing product and technology to serve present and new customer groups
10. New Products too costly, too late, or not demonstrably better to target customer groups	I I I I I II I I I I I			10. New products are a major source of profits guided by cross-functional teams focused on customer problems
11. Sales Training and Promotion programs mostly product driven and often at odds with market customer groups	I I I I I II I I I I I			11. All sales activities highly focused to communicate to and serve the needs of target markets
12. Organization highly structured around functions or large families of products	I I I I I II I I I I I			12. Organization hierarchy streamlined and profit responsibility assigned for each discrete product/market business
13. Planning done sequentially by individuals, functions, and staff without necessary market focus, cross-functional integration, or commitment	I I I I I II I I I I I			13. Cross-functional teams develop and implement business plans for each product/market business
14. Incentive Systems not designed to encourage changes in direction or longer term performance	I I I I I II I I I I I			14. Reward systems and recognition programs designed to reward both shorter and longer term results that are consistent with market priorities.

Figure 23-1   Market-driven factors and rating scale.

A *Cross-functional* process beginning with specific *Customer* needs, *Competitive* offerings, fundamental *Capabilities*, and the aggressive management of *Costs*.

The Ames and Hlavacek audit exposes the underbelly of each of these areas and provides an agenda for meaningful continuous improvement *throughout* the organization—not just within the marketing department or function. In any business hoping to retain its vitality, for example, inflation-adjusted costs must inexorably trend downward over time. Fully grasped, this insight puts the question of, say, price points in a different light and invites the attention of the entire management team to opportunities to achieve cost advantages all along the value chain. Their comprehensive assessment based on this framework puts narrowly defined marketing problems in the broader contexts of strategy and business system.

Companies often know far less about their competitors than they should. Organizing and improving upon a competitive intelligence system goes a long way toward creating a sense of urgency. Lorna Daniells of the Harvard Business School has an excellent compilation of some of the more readily accessible sources of competitive intelligence.[3] A partial list is given in Figure 23-2.

Fundamental capabilities, or what Prahalad and Hamel refer to as *core competencies*,[4] go well beyond a superficial listing of strengths like "unused debt capacity" or "stable work force." Core competencies are the wellsprings of competitiveness, facilitated by technology but deeply embedded in the social fabric of the company. The product commercialization record of 3M, positioning the firm as a seemingly endless incubator, and Wal-Mart's cross-docking system, which enables the company to retail efficiently in any niche it chooses to enter, are solid illustrations.

And, naturally, there's no substitute for asking the customer directly about the important aspects of the seller's offering as compared with available alternatives. Customer needs and preferences as defined from within can often be skewed by the dominant paradigm in the industry or the complexity of the distributor–buyer–user equation. Utilities may think, then, in terms of new service installations within 24 hours rather than by customer convenience; newspapers might optimize editorial content rather than focus on the print remaining on the hands; and medical equipment vendors might overemphasize rep organization commissions or physician preferences at the expense of lab tech practice. Companies usually have more information of this variety than they use—often in the form of "fugitive data" collected by a single person or department. If not, it is relatively easy to construct an importance/performance scale, as shown in Figure 23-3. Such a scale solicits the relative value of a range of product or service attributes to a particular segment, then plots those against that segment's assessment of

1. **Fortune Company Profiles**   1-800-989-INFO
   Approximately 15-page report on a company's financial statements, executives, current news. Includes a listing of related articles compiled from 300 periodicals.

2. **DIALOG Information Services**   1-800-3-DIALOG
   Electronic library of full-text industry reports, financial tables,
   worldwide company data, market data, patents and trademarks,
   technical articles, current news.

3. **DRI/McGraw-Hill**   1-617-863-5100
   Electronic library of World Markets, U.S. Economics, Regional
   U.S., Canada, Europe, Energy & Chemical, Cost Information, plus
   customized Research Team.

4. **Lexis®/Nexis®**   1-800-227-4908
   Electronic library of Trade/Technology, News/Business,
   International, Company/Industry, Legislative/Regulatory,
   Advertising/Marketing/Public Relations/Financial Information.

5. **Dow Jones News/Retrieval®**   1-609-520-4629
   Electronic library of Business and World Newswires, Dow Jones
   Text Library (*The Wall Street Journal, Business Week*, etc.),
   Company/Industry Information (D&B, SEC filings, analysts'
   reports, S&P profiles & earnings), Worldscope (International
   companies), Quotes/Statistics/Commentary, General Service.

6. **Public Library**

a.	STANDARD & POOR'S	Corporation Descriptions
		Register of Corps. Dirs, Exec's
b.	DUN'S MARKETING SVCS	Million Dollar Directory
		America's Corporate Families
c.	MOODY'S	Industrial Manual
		Public Utilities Manual
		Bank & Finance Manual
		International Manual
d.	THOMAS REGISTER	Vols. 1–16 Products & Services
		Vols. 17–18 Company Profiles
		Vols. 19–25 Catalog File
e.	VALUE LINE	Good single-page source of info

7. **Your Own Sales Reps**   Call Reports/Sales Meetings

Figure 23-2 Sources of competitive intelligence.

8. **Company Sources**	Annual Report/10K and 10Q Product Literature/Advertising Recently retired employees
9. **Trade Publications**	
10. **Trade Shows**	
11. **Trade Associations**	
12. **Market Research Specialists**	
13. **Industry Consultants**	
14. **D&B Reports**	
15. **Society of Competitive Intelligence Professionals** 818 18th St. NW Suite 225 Washington DC 20006 202-223-5885	
Trade group of specialists who research, evaluate, catalog, and disseminate competitive information.	

Figure 23-2 (*Continued*) Sources of competitive intelligence.

how well the seller performs on that attribute against alternative offerings. Profiles of various segments can be compared, as can internal versus external perceptions of such attributes as "on-time delivery," "credit terms," and "ease of handling." Such precision goes well beyond global assessments of satisfaction. Moreover, it points out priority problems and prevents an overcommitment of resources on relatively unimportant attributes.

The three "legs," then, of an assessment are the initial characterizations of the presenting problem, an audit putting those problems in the context of strategy and organizational system, and a review or solicitation of customer-specific preferences by segment.

A great deal of mileage can be gained from processing the results of an assessment broadly among senior managers, working toward a common language and a shared view of the issues. This processing creates valuable learning opportunities for consultant and client alike. For example, most companies can gain considerable insight by revisiting familiar issues within a structured framework of fundamentals that forces dialogue across horizontal lines. One widely used approach is called "Marketing 101," consisting of five lines of inquiry:

1. Markets are made up of users or user applications. (How do we define ours?)

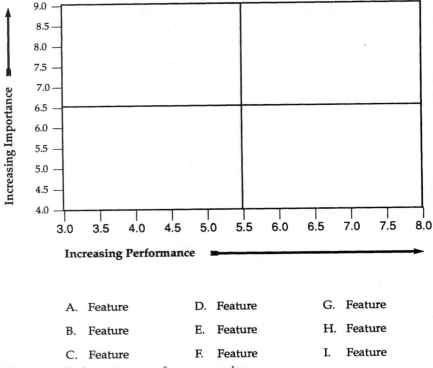

A. Feature	D. Feature	G. Feature
B. Feature	E. Feature	H. Feature
C. Feature	F. Feature	I. Feature

Figure 23-3 Importance performance scales.

2. Markets grow or shrink. (Which way, how much, how fast?)

3. Businesses gain, hold, or lose share of market. (Who is taking share? How and why?)

4. Market share battles depend upon the customer's perception of value. (Who *is* our customer? What does he or she value?)

5. Value encompasses all factors that affect quality, access, service and functionality in exchange for price. (What might the customer value more *if...?*)

Most managements can spend many useful hours debating who the customers truly are, what they really want, and whether others are more successful at getting their attention. Under the best of circumstances, of course, this dialogue links the core competencies *behind* current offerings with the needs and uses *behind* alternatives in a search to define new competitive space.

In this stage, diligent efforts are also made to discover "market-hostile assumptions." These often unspoken, self-limiting beliefs stand in the way of critical breakthroughs. They fall into five broad classes:

- *Corporate purpose*—"But it absorbs a lot of overhead."
- *Customers*—"They don't notice the difference anyway."
- *Competitors*—"Those folks are on borrowed time."
- *People*—"Floor help is a dime a dozen."
- *Improvement*—"Ten-day delivery is the industry standard."

These beliefs can be exposed through interview, observable behavior, psychodrama, candid group discussion, or structured experiences. The more a group is conscious of its underlying beliefs—not just the ones in the newsletter or on the wallet card—the better equipped it is to change them in its own best interests. So the assessment process is really both a discovery process and a "situation analysis" in the service of a plan.

Planning

The outcome of the planning phase is an activity-rich, goal-driven profile of what might be done to bring about a desired future state. As with all good planning, this phase needs to address where the organization is now (and how it got here), where it wants to go, and how it is going to get there. Much of the answer to the first question will have been covered in the assessment phase. The rest is a decision-making process, again involving cross-functional, multilevel teams or even the whole system—customers, suppliers, distributors, and so on.

There are a number of menu-driven approaches to documentation that help to ensure clarity. Documentation is critical to facilitating midcourse corrections, providing for managerial control, and preventing the "erosion of intent." The "recipe" for a strategic business unit's marketing plan is provided in Figure 23-4. Other plans can be very useful for remapping a distribution system, accelerating new product development, and other matters. Components of these "master menus" can also be prestructured, as in a Gantt chart covering several months of promotional activity supporting a business unit's foray into a new geographic environment. Although it is important not to advance off-the-shelf solutions to poorly defined problems, such templates serve to organize data produced in the pursuit of predictable discussions. Planning consultants often tell their clients, "We don't know where you're going, but we have some idea of how to get you there." The most productive planning sessions always begin with questions—not answers—from both parties. Consultants tend

---

Perspective

Industry Definition

What are the boundaries of your market?

What are the major segments served?

What are the industry assessment and projections?

Demand

Who are the customers in the buyer/end-user chain?

What are the drivers of customer demand?

What do customers want?

How is that likely to change?

What growth (or contraction) in market size is expected?

What potential substitutes are occurring or anticipated? What are the most important sources of new demand?

Supply

What is total industry capacity versus demand?

Is capacity growing slower or faster than demand?

What is expected to happen to industrywide costs in raw materials, technology, labor, productivity, and distribution?

Industry Buying/Paying Behavior

Industry Price Levels

What is current practice?

What is anticipated?

Why?

General Environment

What are the major factors likely to affect the industry in the coming years—political, economic, social, technological?

Figure 23-4 Business unit strategic marketing plan.

Competitive Environment

Who are the key competitors?

What are their apparent objectives and strategies?

What are their vulnerabilities?

What new entrants to the market are possible?

Game Plan

Company-Specific Position

What is your current positioning?

What differentiates your offering from your competitors'?

What are the alternative positions available in the industry?

What is your current share of the market?

Company Strategy

How might your company strategy need to change in the future?

What are the key success factors associated with this strategy—management style, custom manufacturing capabilities, captive distribution, ownership of raw materials, and so on?

What might your enduring competitive position be?

Action Items

Product Program

Current lines

New product development

Distribution Program

Channel mix

Channel support requirements

(Continued)

Figure 23-4 *(Continued)* Business unit strategic marketing plan.

Pricing Philosophy/Credit Policy

Service After Sale

Promotional Program

Execution Requirements

Required Changes in Organizational Infrastructure

Resources

    Sources and uses of funds; internal rates of return
    Predictable "draw" on other business units or functions

Control Mechanisms

    Where does accountability lie?
    What are the critical benchmarks, go/no-go points?

Figure 23-4   (*Continued*)   Business unit strategic marketing plan.

to look first, though, at questions which, if answered creatively, would have the effect of creating new competitive space. For example:

    "Can we reduce assets significantly?"

    "Have we segmented our market enough?"

    "Can we engage in stronger market concentration?"

    "Can we redefine product or buying behavior entirely?"

Executing

Regardless of the brilliance of its planning, any business comes down to a "game of inches." Difficulties in plan execution—or, indeed, in the fundamentals of a marketing function or in the business itself—will render the most clever strategy irrelevant. Companies with great ideas often get into trouble because they do a less-than-adequate job of handling objections or managing their true "pocket price"—the yield that remains after co-op advertising, volume discounts, and special shipping terms. It is critical to determine the execution skills required to optimize the value to the customer *and* the value to the company. Sales departments will often claim that "you can't sell from an empty wagon," but the judicious management of inventory is just as important a value driver as the availability of untitled stock in regional warehouses. Optimizing one at the expense of the other will lead to eventual failure in the market. The consultant must pay careful attention to defining these issues and their attendant skills— and to encouraging training or systems change where appropriate.

Beyond the skill level, execution difficulties in marketing and distribution occur for three generic reasons:

- Vague goals or objectives
- Inadequate horizontal involvement
- Failure to tie plans to controls

The most successful plans are those that can be translated into specific, measurable objectives expressed as both results (penetration, coverage, segment margin) and critical processes (stock-outs, delivery time, invoicing errors). Vague goals that speak of becoming "a trusted commercial leader" or "a leader in nonmetallic conduit," for example, give little guidance to operations and fail to provide for control.

Execution often falters if initiatives were developed with insufficient attention to the internal demands and linkages required to be successful. Pumps to be marketed to the agricultural sector might call for filtration systems with different specifications than a company's traditionally successful formula. Important variations that make the difference between building a new presence and recovering from a fiasco can be anticipated only with thorough horizontal involvement from the supply side through to the end user.

Finally, control systems play a big part in execution. The three areas that bear closest examination are management information, incentive compensation, and budgeting. Information systems that don't provide timely data on such matters as profitability by product or selling costs by customer make it difficult to carry out fact-based adjustments. Years after the introduction of managed care, many hospitals still have an imperfect grasp of revenues and profitability by insurance carrier in their respective markets. Incentive systems that reward volume or production quantity rather than margin provide unintentional incentives for concentrating on the wrong things. And budget systems that don't adequately reflect market realities doom marketing to a functional rather than an organization-wide issue. Each of these areas lends itself to surveillance both before and after the fact.

Like any system, the four-stage protocol presented here is no panacea. It must often be adjusted or abandoned to meet the needs of the project.

Most consultants find, though, that approaching a client systematically inspires confidence, promotes efficiency, and precludes promotion of a favorite solution. Successful consultants conduct their "problem seeking" systematically, co-creating solutions that their system surfaces. Time spent developing your own system is a sound investment in your future as well as in your prospective clients.

Notes

1. Edgar Schein, *Process Consultation*. Boston: Addison Wesley, 1976.
2. Ames and Hlavacek, *Market Driven Management*. Homewood, Ill.: Dow Jones/Irwin, 1989.
3. Lorna Daniells, *Sources of External Marketing Data*. Cambridge, Mass.: Harvard Business School, 1993.
4. Prahalad, C. K., and Gary Hamel, "The Core Competence of the Corporation," *Harvard Business Review*, 68, no. 3, 1990, 79–91.

24

Financial Planning and Control

Joseph W. Wilkinson
School of Accountancy
Arizona State University
Tempe, Arizona

Planning and control are essential to the success of any entity. As discussed in Chapter 22, overall planning for a business organization as a whole is important for two reasons: (1) it forces management to look to the future and to anticipate problems, challenges, and opportunities, and (2) it encourages management to mold an organization, to assemble the resources, and to conduct the activities needed to achieve desirable goals. Control is necessary in order to evaluate how well the plans are being met through actual events and to encourage corrective actions when deviations from the plans are detected.

Within this broad framework, various specialized planning activities—ranging from market planning to inventory planning—are conducted and managed. Perhaps the most important specialized planning activity is conducted under the auspices of financial management. Since control is the opposite side of the planning function, financial management also includes the control of financial activities. This chapter begins by surveying financial management and reviewing business planning. Then it discusses three types of budgeting and introduces such decision-oriented systems as decision support systems, executive support systems, and expert systems.

Overview of Financial Management

To set the stage for financial planning and control, we need to identify the purposes of financial management and the activities and organizational units that it encompasses.

Purposes

Financial management is concerned with the inflows and outflows of funds, both in the short run and the long run. Suitable financial management policies and procedures enable a business organization to acquire funds as needed, to process efficiently the funds received from customers and other sources, to conserve invested and earned capital, to avoid cash shortages and excessive surpluses, to optimize the capital structure, to minimize doubtful accounts, to make sound investments and appropriate expenditures, to safeguard assets, to provide financial information for decision making and operations, and to disseminate financial reports to the appropriate users.

Activities

To fulfill the purposes of financial management a business organization generally establishes a finance function, which often encompasses both financial and accounting activities. The function may be headed by a vice president of finance, with a treasurer and controller as the two key subordinate officers. Within this finance function may be subfunctions or activities relating to capital budgeting, operational budgeting, cash budgeting, cash receipts and disbursements, credit management, investments management, financial reporting, and internal auditing. (Operational accounting activities such as inventory control, billing, accounts receivable, accounts payable, and payroll may also be included for organizational convenience, although they do not relate directly to financial management.)

Most of the policies and key procedures should be established by a high-level finance committee, which may be headed by the vice president of finance and consist of his or her key subordinates and members from the other major functions of the organization. The resulting policies and procedures should be codified in a financial manual and review by competent independent financial consultants. Figure 24-1 is a selective list of policies and procedures pertaining to working capital management (i.e., the management of short-term cash receipts, cash disbursements, receivables, and payables). Separate sections in this chapter discuss desirable policies and procedures relating to the various types of budgets and to financial reporting.

Cash forecasts and budgets are to be prepared on a regular basis.

An open line of credit is to be maintained at one or more banks.

All bank accounts are to be analyzed regularly for activity and balances.

Balances in non-interest-bearing bank accounts are to be maintained at a minimum level needed for effective daily operations.

Cash funds above the minimum needed for effective daily operations are to be invested in marketable securities.

All cash received is to be deposited intact the same day in a bank account.

Petty cash is to be controlled by an imprest system.

Short-term financing is to be arranged in advance when the cash balance is expected to be short.

Credit limits, discounts, and due dates are to be established by explicit policies and enforced consistently.

Collections of past-due accounts are to be facilitated by periodic reviews of aged accounts receivable, past-due collection notices, follow-up telephone calls to delinquent customers, and so forth.

Adequate credit insurance is to be carried.

All purchase discounts are to be taken.

Cash disbursements to vendors are to be delayed to take advantage of the full discount periods.

Key ratios—such as the current ratio, quick ratio, dividend payment ratio, and receivables turnover ratio—are to be computed frequently and analyzed.

Figure 24-1 Policies and procedures concerning working-capital management.

Review of Business Planning and Control

Planning is a continuous process that attempts to provide answers to several major questions: (1) What business are we in? (2) Where are we at the present time? (3) What and where do we want to be in the future? (4) How do we get to be what and where we want to be? Forward-looking business organizations adopt a three-cycle planning process to help in answering these questions. These three cycles are long-range planning, medium-range planning, and short-range planning. Business organizations also employ management and operational control to ensure that the plans stay "on track."

Long-Range Planning

Long-range planning, often called strategic planning, consists of six integrated steps:

1. Defining the mission and boundaries of the business organization
2. Reviewing the environment that is external to the business organization (the industry of which the organization is a part, the competitors, the economy, the political scene, the state of technology, and so on)
3. Assessing the situation currently facing the organization, in terms of both the problems facing the organization and the opportunities that are presented
4. Setting goals and objectives, with the objectives being stated both quantitatively and in time periods (e.g., to increase return on investment to 20 percent within 2 years)
5. Developing the strategies (i.e., policies that are based on the goals and objectives)
6. Devising the long-range business plan, including such projected financial statements as 10-year income statements and balance sheets

Medium-Range Planning

Medium-range planning is the process whereby the long-range plan is carried out. Whereas long-range planning may span 5 to 20 years or even longer, medium-range planning (also called tactical planning) normally spans 2 to 5 years. Medium-range plans provide certain details that are only implied by the long-range plans. Also, medium-range plans focus more on the divisions and functions within an organization, rather than on the organization as a whole.

Short-Range Planning

Short-range planning is to medium-range planning as medium-range planning is to long-range planning. Thus, short-range plans, which range from daily plans to 1-year plans, provide the operational details to fulfill medium-range plans. Short-range plans also are focused at the level of operational departments and other responsibility centers, rather than at the functional or divisional level. For instance, short-range plans are developed with respect to sales order departments, shipping departments, inventory operations, and production operations. Both management and operational control processes are integrated with the short-range plans, in order to signal when corrective actions are needed.

Management Control

Management control is the process by which an organization ensures that its resources are used effectively and efficiently according to established plans. As suggested in the discussion of short-range planning, it is often focused around cost, profit, or investment responsibility centers. However, management control can be centered around programs—product lines, projects, or other activities. Generally, the process depends on two types of data: planned values and actual values. Differences between these values provide the signal that deviations from the plans are occurring. Often the management control process is built around a financial structure, with resource flows and status being expressed in monetary terms. It also tends to be periodic in nature, with monthly or yearly cycles.

Operational Control

Operational control is the process of assuring that specific tasks and activities are performed effectively and efficiently. This type of control is usually based on rules that are established through quantitative calculations. Examples of operational control are inventory control, production control, credit control, sales order control, and cash control. For instance, inventory control involves the determination of economic order quantities and reorder points based on such factors as expected demands, carrying costs, reorder costs, lead times, and safety stock levels. As this example shows, operational data are often nonmonetary.

Budgeting Fundamentals

An effective overall technique that supports and implements financial planning and control is a set of interrelated budgets. A budget is a plan expressed in financial terms that covers a specified period of time. Budgets are based on forecasts, which in turn are developed in conjunction with long-range, medium-range, and short-range plans. Sound budgets incorporate relevant performance measures, are built by sound budget processes, and provide an integrated group of performance-oriented reports and financial statements. They often are constructed with the aid of such approaches and tools as zero-based budgeting, present-value analysis, and financial modeling.

As instruments of financial planning and control, budgets should be tied to an organization's goals and objectives as well as to its management structure. Profitability is generally viewed as being the primary goal of an organization; hence, budgets are sometimes described as profit plans. However, such goals as return on investment and rate of growth can also be reflected through budgets. To provide more precision, the budgets are often subdivided according to organizational units or segments. Thus, budgets may be prepared for a business organization's divisions, functions, and departments; separate budgets may also be prepared for the product lines that the organization provides and the markets that it serves. An example is a budget for the Brass Products Division of Selmon Corporation, in which the goals stated by the budget are in terms of annual profit for the division and the return on investment.

Three major types of budgets are capital budgets, operational budgets, and cash budgets. As suggested earlier, budgets such as these are based on forecasts in long-range, medium-range, and short-range plans. Financial reports, especially those that reflect performance, are prepared by reference to these three budgets and provide the basis for control. Following sections will explore these types of budgets and reports.

Capital Budgeting

Among the key concerns to be faced in the long-range future are the investments in capital resources needed by a business organization. Thus, strategic planning incorporates multiyear budgets composed of approved capital expenditure projects and developed by a process called capital budgeting.

Purposes and Benefits

Capital budgeting is the process of planning and controlling the strategic and tactical expenditures for capital resources. Capital expenditures are uses of funds for resources that are intended either (1) to enhance future revenues for the organization or (2) to reduce future costs of the organization. They range from investments that replace current equipment to investments that expand the productive capacity. Capital expenditures include plant assets (e.g., machinery, plants, computer systems, and property), product-research projects, and executive development programs. Capital budgeting leads to capital expenditure budgets that span a number of years into the future. In addition, the process may provide a short-term capital expenditure budget that links with the operational budget.

Capital budgeting provides several benefits to the management of the organization. A capital expenditure budget accumulates the planned investments that are intended to enable the organization to meet competition, satisfy customer demands, and ensure growth. Thus, it provides a convenient overall means of review by top management. Furthermore, the preparation of a capital expenditure budget forces management to make careful decisions within a limited supply of available funds for investment. It encourages the use of a careful procedure for allocating the available funds and focuses attention on the need for adequate cash flows. Finally, a capital expenditure budget increases coordination among the various responsibility centers because many capital investments affect the entire organization.

Budget Planning Process

Since capital investments involve long-range commitments of large amounts of resources, planning and capital budgeting are of paramount importance to an organization. Poor decisions concerning investments could significantly affect the health of the organization. Thus, two critical planning steps are (1) to identify all projects that are needed to meet challenges and opportunities and (2) to evaluate competing projects within the limits of available capital funds and time horizons.

Suitable projects can best be identified if appropriate organizational arrangements are made. A planning department may be established, for instance, that scans for potential investments. This department might review current periodicals and visit other organizations, in order to spot capital additions that could usefully be applied within the organization. A capital projects committee, composed of several higher-level managers, could be assigned to review proposals from managers within the organization. Middle-level and departmental managers might be encouraged to submit proposals to this committee. A proposal, in writing, should consist of (1) a description of the proposal, (2) reasons for the recommended capital expenditure, (3) benefits and possible drawbacks, expressed to the extent possible in terms of tangible dollar benefits and costs, and (4) expected time period to install the capital item.

Clear-cut procedures should be established for processing and evaluating capital expenditure proposals. Each written proposal would be evaluated on the basis of certain specified criteria. One criterion might be size of the expected expenditure or investment. For instance, investments below a certain dollar amount could be approved with less formality than investments of larger amounts. Thus, a proposed investment of $2000 for repairing a currently owned machine might be approved by the production manager, while a proposed investment of $100,000 for a new computer might require the approval of the president on the recommendation of the capital projects committee.

The most important criterion involves economic feasibility—the comparison of economic benefits and costs. Several methods of determining economic feasibility are available; they are discussed in the next section.

If a proposal is found to be economically feasible, then the project must be incorporated into the capital budget. Not all feasible projects can be undertaken immediately, since an organization has a limited amount of funds available for capital projects. However, projects that are of an urgent nature, such as a replacement for a broken machine that cannot be repaired, and projects that promise a high payoff, such as a new "hot" product, can be scheduled for early start dates. Projects that extend over several years would appear in the long-range capital budget. Projects that will be completed within a few months, as well as the current year portions of long-range projects, would be detailed in short-range capital expenditure budget.

Capital Investment Analysis Methods

The four methods used to determine economic feasibility are the accounting rate of return, payback period, internal rate of return, and net present value. Since the first two do not take into account the time value of money, they are of limited value and thus will not be discussed. The internal rate of return method and the net present value method—both called discounted cash flow methods—explicitly recognize the effects of the time value of money. Because the net present value method is easier to apply, it is more often employed.

Capital investment analysis, using the net present value method, requires that a number of factors be measured or estimated. Management must ascertain what rate of return it desires with respect to the investment. Although this desired rate of return may be equal to the opportunity cost of capital, normally the riskiness of an investment leads management to add a premium. For instance, if a proposed investment is an addition to the production facilities and the opportunity cost of capital is 10 percent, management might add 2 percent to reflect the nature of the risk, so that the desired rate of return becomes 12 percent.

Relevant factors in addition to the desired rate of return include the following:

1. Expected economic life of the investment

2. Acquisition value of the investment (i.e., the invoice price plus all costs required to put the investment into effective operation)

3. Salvage value of the asset (if any) that is to be replaced by the investment

4. Expected salvage value of the new investment at the end of its expected economic life

5. Investment tax credit, if any

6. Marginal income tax rate of the organization

7. Expected rate of obsolescence of the investment, as measured by its yearly decline in salvage value

8. Expected rate of increase in replacement value of the investment, as measured by the yearly increment in invoice price

9. Method by which the investment is to be depreciated

10. Cost savings and/or revenue enhancements that are expected from the investment, relative to the present situation and existing set of capital assets

These factors can best be understood through an example. Assume that an organization currently owns a machine that has a salvage value of $3000 and an expected physical life of 10 more years. The book value of the machine is expected to remain equal to the salvage value through the remainder of its physical life. Each year the machine requires an outlay of $10,000 to maintain and operate. A new machine that performs the same functions has just become available and will cost $19,000 to buy and install; however, it is so efficient that it will cost only $4000 to maintain and operate each year. It has an expected economic life of ten years, with a salvage value of $3000 at the end of its life. If the marginal income tax rate is 50 percent and the desired rate of return is 18 percent, is the new machine economically feasible at this time? (Assume for the sake of simplicity that the investment tax credit is zero at this time and the machine will be depreciated on the straight-line basis.) Computations in accordance with the net present value method are as follows:

Total investment	($19,000)
Less: Salvage value, current machine	3000
Net investment	($16,000)

Before-tax annual cost savings on new machine:

$$\$10,000 - 4000 = \$6000$$

After-tax annual cost savings on new machine:

$$\$6000 \times (1 - .50) = \$3000$$

Present value of after-tax cost savings:

$$4.494 \times \$3000 = \$13{,}482$$

Depreciation tax shield of new machine:

$$(\$19{,}000 - \$3000)/10 \times (1 - .50) \times 4.494 = \$3595$$

Present value of salvage value of new machine:

$$0.191 \times \$3000 = \$573$$

Present value of returns from new machine:

$$\$13{,}482 + \$3000 + \$573 = \$17{,}650$$

Net present value of returns from new machine:

$$\$17{,}650 - 16{,}000 = \$1650$$

Since the net present value is positive, the project appears to be economically feasible. Management, however, cannot prudently approve a project only on the basis of this type of quantitative analysis. It must take into account the following:

1. Nonquantitative factors, such as the ease of use of a new machine
2. Errors in estimated factors, such as the estimates of cost savings
3. Alternative uses of limited capital funds

Thus, management must apply considerable judgment in its evaluation of the present proposals. It must also assign priorities to those projects that appear to be economically feasible. In determining such priorities, management may apply additional criteria. For instance, it might rank competing proposals by computing cost-benefit ratios (i.e., the net present values divided by the investment amounts of the respective projects).

Control of Capital Expenditures

As soon as a capital expenditure project is approved, a project control number is assigned and project control records are established. A capital expenditure project is generally approved for the overall dollar amount which has been specified on a request for capital expenditure form. This investment amount is one basis on which the project is to be controlled, since it represents the key budget figure. For more precise control, the overall amount is broken down on the request form according to object categories (e.g., materials, labor, supplies). In addition, the project is scheduled, showing the start date and completion date.

Periodic capital expenditure reports are prepared to show the status of each active project. These reports are, in effect, budgetary control mechanisms, since they show the actual amounts expended to date and the amounts remaining to be expended.

Capital expenditure reports can be used to reflect both time and cost performance. On each report date they can show the percentage completion of the projects, based on the time schedule previously established. If the actual percentage completion of a particular project is less than the scheduled completion, the project is seen to be behind schedule. Gantt charts and PERT diagrams can help show such time performance. If actual expenditures are tied to percentage completion of the projects, the performance reports can also show cost overruns or underruns to date.

Operational Budgeting

A short-range financial plan concerns the allocation and use of resources—personnel, materials, equipment, facilities, and money—over the coming year. An operational budget reflects the allocation of such resources, expressed in terms of funds. Establishing an operational budget is an important and time-consuming process that involves managers at all levels of an organization. It can be aided by techniques such as zero-based budgeting and financial modeling. Budgetary control is effected principally through performance reporting.

Benefits

An operational budget provides several benefits to an organization. First, it forces management to review its goals and objectives carefully in order to allocate the available resources in the most effective manner. Management must consider its medium-range and long-range plans as well as its short-range plans and objectives, so that all plans are integrated and reflected in the budgetary values. Top management can thereby express its priorities and constraints in a tangible manner. Second, an operational budget shows managers at all levels what performances are expected during the coming year. Each manager has specific targets toward which to strive, so that he or she will likely be motivated to perform efficiently. Third, budgetary values provide the bases of comparison with actual results, so that managers can be evaluated on their performances and corrective actions can be taken when necessary.

Process

Preparing an operational budget involves a sequence of events or steps, usually referred to as the budget process. Various approaches to the budget process are employed. Thus, the goals on which the budget is developed may be determined by a top-down or bottom-up approach. In the top-down approach, the overall goals are articulated by top-management and then broken down into component goals or objectives at each lower management level. In the bottom-up approach the goals are set at the lowest management level and progressively aggregated at higher levels until they are formulated as overall goals. Most organizations have adopted the top-down approach; however, they temper it with a participative approach in which all managers provide inputs concerning their areas of responsibility during the budget formulation period. The following description is based on this generally accepted hybrid approach.

The budget process begins with the strategic and tactical planning sessions undertaken by top management. As a result of this planning, management generates forecasts of business conditions as well as target values for key factors, such as sales revenue and share of the market. These target values, or quantitative goals, are distributed to the organization's major functions and divisions, together with budget formulation instructions. In turn, the major functions and divisions distribute more detailed goals to the departments and other subordinate units. The divisions, departments, and other units then develop detailed budget schedules pertaining to their areas of responsibility. The subordinate units are often aided in this formulation by a budget officer or some financial manager such as the controller. Assistance may take the form of schedule formats, computerized budget models, and budget work sessions.

The budget schedules prepared by the subordinate units are then compiled by the budget officer or financial manager. These budget schedules are closely related to the organizational structure and major functional activities. They represent components of the overall budget, reflecting the resources needed by the various responsibility areas and activities to achieve the detailed goals assigned to them. For a manufacturing organization these component budgets may include the following:

- Sales budget
- Purchases budget
- Sales expense budget
- Inventory budget
- Production budget
- Administrative expense budget

- Distribution expense budget
- Appropriate short-range budgets for capital budgets

These budgets are compiled and integrated in order to produce pro forma income statements, balance sheets, and cash flow statements. Figure 24-2 illustrates the budget process, which culminates in these pro forma financial statements.

The final step in budget formulation is management review and budget approval. Each manager is usually given the opportunity to present a justification for the portion of the budget for which he or she has responsibility. If the reviewing management does not accept the amounts requested, then the budget schedules must be revised and resubmitted. When all revisions have been completed at all levels and top management agrees that all the budget schedules and pro forma statements reflect the organization's goals for the coming year, the president then issues the approved budget as the official short-range operational plan.

Since this budget review step is so critical to the success of the entire budget process, an increasing number of organizations employ the zero-budget approach. With this approach, each manager is expected to justify his or her entire budget request in detail, with particular attention to any increases over the previous budget year. Each activity under a manager must be explained in terms of purpose, measures of performance, costs and benefits, plus the costs and benefits of alternative courses of action.

Throughout the year during which the budget is in effect, the accounting and finance function will issue periodic performance reports. Usually these reports are prepared monthly and provide the means of effective management control. The contents of performance reports are discussed in a later section.

Financial Modeling

Budget preparation can be greatly aided by a technique known as *financial modeling*. A financial model expresses the financial relationships of an organization in terms of its activities. In the case of a financial model that is to be used in the budget process, the expressions comprising the model typically reflect the detailed financial and operational relationships. Outputs of a financial model can be (and usually are) pro forma financial statements. In the case of operational budget models, a key output may be the projected income statements for the 12 months of the coming year.

Financial modeling offers several benefits during the process of developing budget estimates. First, a detailed financial budget model

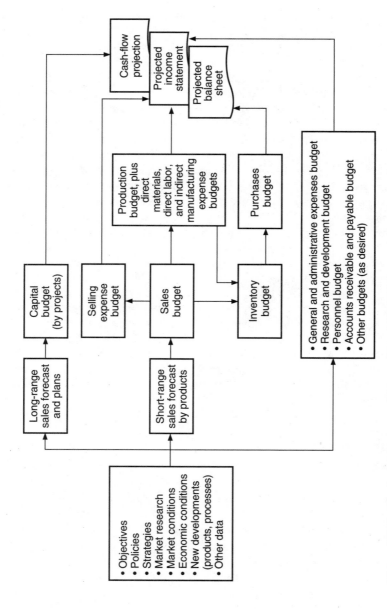

Figure 24-2 The budget process. (*Source: Joseph W. Wilkinson, Accounting and Information Systems*, 3rd ed. Copyright © 1991. Reprinted by permission of John Wiley & Sons, Inc., New York.)

provides better understanding of the key factors affecting the financial and operational aspects of the organization being modeled, of the relationships among the factors, and of their sensitivities to changes in budget values. Second, a budget model enables managers at each of the levels to evaluate the effects of various alternatives, such as the effects of alternative volumes of production on inventory costs. Third, a financial model allows the time required for the budget process to be reduced.

Much of the power of a financial budget model derives from the ability to manipulate the factors within the model and thus to experiment with alternative possibilities. This manipulative ability is due to the fact that models are comprised of collections of programming statements. Many of these statements reflect aspects of the accounting equation (i.e., assets equal equities). Financial models, therefore, are constructed by such programming languages as Interactive Financial Planning System, CUFFS, and Express.

Four manipulation techniques used with financial models are what-if analysis, goal seeking, sensitivity analysis, and Monte Carlo analysis. These techniques may be applied after an initial set of factor values is entered to generate base-case outputs. Thus, in the case of a budget model, initial values for sales volume, prices, resource costs, and other factors may be entered to produce a base case income statement.

In a what-if analysis, the assumed value for one of the factors is varied from its base value. For instance, the sales volume might be increased by 10 percent above its base value, thereby generating an income statement having a higher value for the sales amount (and also for net income). In order to employ the goal-seeking technique, a desired value is set for a criterion or other factor and the needed change in a key factor is computed. In the example, a desired value of net income may be set and then the necessary sales volume is determined. As may be apparent, the goal-seeking technique is the reverse of the what-if analysis.

In a sensitivity analysis, the sensitivity of a criterion or other factor to changes in a specified factor is determined. Thus, the sales volume may be changed by increments of 5, 10, and 15 percent from the base-case value, with the changes in the sales amount and net income values being observed. In the Monte Carlo technique, the values of certain key factors are expressed as probability distributions rather than as point values. Through repeated simulation runs, randomly selected values for these factors are manipulated by the model to generate probability distributions for the criterion and other factors. For instance, probabilistic distributions of the sales volume and unit price may be employed, with the resulting net income value being expressed as a probability distribution such as a normal curve.

Performance Reporting

A variety of performance reports should be provided during the period of time spanned by the operational budget. Prompt reports are essential for effective control. Hence, daily, weekly, and monthly reports should be prepared. Effective control also requires that actual results be compared against benchmarks. Comparing actual revenues and expenses for this period against like values for previous periods is useful. Even more useful, however, are comparisons of actual values against standard values. Thus, most performance reports compare actual revenues and costs against budgeted revenues and costs, reflecting the differences in terms of revenue and cost variances. If the budgeted values are to be most effective for control purposes, they should be based on realistic plans and policies and reflect achievable goals and objectives. Finally, performance reports should focus on centers or areas of responsibility, so that the managers in charge can be held accountable for taking corrective actions. Responsibility centers include cost centers, profit centers, and investment centers. They range from departments and divisions to entire functions and organizations. Areas of responsibility may also include projects and activities.

Examples of performance reports include:

- Shipping department cost performance report
- Brass products division profit contribution report
- Eastern sales division revenue performance report
- Marketing function performance report
- Capital projects investment performance report
- Income statement performance report

Expenses, which are very important to most organizations, can be controlled more precisely by means of flexible expense budgets. These budgets, also known as variable or sliding-scale budgets, can be incorporated into the broader operational budgets. They enable budget amounts to be adjusted according to the levels of activity, such as volumes of production.

Underlying a flexible budget are formulas for the various expenses for the respective responsibility centers. Each formula expresses the relationship of an expense to the levels of activity in a center. The formula contains a fixed component and a variable component, which may be shown as:

Expense = fixed amount + (variable rate × level of activity)

For example, monthly budgeted indirect labor expense within a production department might be expressed by the following formula:

$1000 + ($.50 × direct labor hours)

In the case of fixed expenses, the variable component would be zero; the case of purely variable expenses, the fixed component would be zero. Monthly performance reports for the production department would compare the actual costs incurred during the month against the budgeted values computed on the basis of the number of direct labor hours expended.

Cash Budgeting

Cash flows are critical to all organizations. Thus, the planning and control of cash inflows and outflows, via cash budgeting, deserve separate consideration.

Purposes

The major purposes of a cash budget are to:

1. Plan short-term cash requirements, normally a quarter or year
2. Anticipate possible cash shortages or excesses during each budget period
3. Coordinate cash planning with planning for working capital and the various components of the operational budget (i.e., sales revenue, expenses, and short-range capital investments)
4. Provide a vehicle for monitoring and controlling the cash position from budget period to budget period

If these purposes are achieved, an organization will maintain adequate liquidity for all planned needs. It will not encounter unexpected cash shortages that require borrowings at unfavorable rates; likewise, it will not carry excess cash that incurs opportunity costs of lost interest or dividend income.

Process

A cash budget is largely based on the operational budget and the short-range portion of the capital budget. Thus, the cash-budgeting process must proceed in close collaboration with the other financial budget processes. Timing of cash inflows and outflows is as important as their amounts.

Two alternative approaches may be employed in preparing a cash budget for the coming year. (Cash budgets for shorter or longer periods will not be discussed.) The financial accounting approach begins with the planned, or budgeted, net income computed in the operational budget. This net income amount is then converted from the accrual basis to a cash basis, with adjustments made for changes in the noncash working-capital accounts. Finally, other cash sources and requirements are identified, and the expected cash position is determined. In contrast, the cash receipts and disbursements approach involves a detailed analysis of the increases and decreases in the budgeted cash accounts. All plans reflected in the operational budget that lead to cash inflows or outflows are carefully reviewed and translated from the accrual basis to cash basis. Both approaches should provide the same cash flow amounts. Since the latter approach is employed more often, it will be used in the following discussion and illustrations.

Cash inflows arise from transactions involving cash sales, collections of accounts based on credit sales, collections of notes receivable, interest on and dividends from investments, and miscellaneous receipts such as sales of bonds and fixed assets. Most of these sources generate immediate cash and thus cause the least problem in estimating cash inflows. However, credit sales transactions create a lag between the times of sales and the times when cash is realized. This lag between sales and collections must be estimated in addition to the amounts of sales. For instance, on the basis of past experience an organization may estimate that 80 percent of the sales amounts will be collected in the same month when the sales are made, that 12 percent will be collected in the first month following the sales, that 6 percent will be collected in the second month following the sales, and that 2 percent will not be collected (i.e., will be bad debts).

Cash outflows arise from payments made for costs of goods sold, expenses, capital additions and replacements, dividends paid to owners, plus interest on and retirement of short-term and long-term debt. As in the case with credit sales, most purchases give rise to a time lag. This lag, which also must be estimated, is the time between the incurrence of the accounts payable obligation and the cash disbursement to discharge the obligation. Its estimation is complicated because of the varying payment terms offered by vendors. Since most organizations prefer to take purchase cash discounts when offered, the lag will typically range from 10 days (the usual period of discounts) to a month or more. In addition, prepayments for such items as supplies, rent, and insurance must also be factored into the picture. The resulting estimation formula for purchases time lags may be similar to the following: Of the purchases made in a given month, 70 percent are to be paid in the same month and 30 percent are to be paid in the following month.

Other types of cash expenditures may present difficulties of estimation. Cash dividends and tax payments may be closely related to net income, which in turn is subject to numerous variables. Purchases of merchandise for resale can be affected by buildups or reductions of inventory as well as by expected sales. In the case of manufacturers, purchases of raw materials and direct labor will be affected by production schedules and changes in finished-goods inventories. When estimated levels of expense are based on expense budgets in the operational budget, the noncash items (such as depreciation expense) must be identified and removed.

After cash inflows and cash outflows are summarized, their totals must be compared—month by month—in order to assess the expected cash position throughout the budget period. The formula for determining the ending monthly cash balance is:

Beginning cash balance + cash receipts during the month
− cash disbursements during the month = ending cash balance

If a deficit in the cash balance is computed for the end of a particular month, a need for financing is indicated. The financial officer, such as the treasurer, can make prior arrangements for a short-term bank loan in most of such cases. If an excessive positive balance is expected in the cash account, the financial officer can be prepared to invest the excess amount in short-term instruments such as money market funds.

Financial Reporting

Financial reports can aid in both planning and controlling cash. Planning reports consist essentially of those that separately detail the cash inflows and the cash outflows, whereas control reports summarize both inflows and outflows within reasonably short time spans.

Cash inflow planning reports include (1) a report that shows the expected collections from credit sales for the months and quarters of the budget year, (2) a report that shows planned cash inflows from other sources, and (3) a report that summarizes cash inflows from all sources. Cash outflow or requirements reports include (1) a report that details the expected purchases and related payments for the months and quarters of the budget year, (2) a report that shows the cash requirements for various operations, administrative, sales, and other expenses for the months and quarters of the budget year, (3) a report that shows the cash requirements for deferred and accrued items (e.g., unexpired insurance, accrued property taxes, accrued interest expense, dividends, supplies used, and contingent liabilities), plus income taxes, for the months and quarters of the budget year, and (4) a report that summarizes cash outflows for all purposes.

Cash control reports focus on the anticipated cash balance, means of financing cash imbalances, and summarized cash flows. A cash budget for control purposes may show the following line items:

Cash balance, beginning

Add:

Cash receipts

Collections

Other sources

   Total cash available

Less:

  Cash payments

  Accounts payables

  Administrative expenses

  Selling expenses

  Operational expenses

  Dividends

  Other payments

   Total payments

Indicated cash balance, ending

Financing:

  Borrowings

  Repayments

  Interest

  Total financing

Cash balance after financing

Columns across the top of this report may list the remaining months and/or quarters of the budget year. For more timely control they may alternatively list the weeks of the current month or the days of the current week.

Decision-Oriented Systems

Computer-based decision-oriented systems are increasingly being employed to aid in financial planning and control. These systems are commonly known as decision support systems, executive information systems, and expert systems, although such terms as strategic support systems are sometimes seen in the literature. Although detailed discussion of these decision support systems is beyond the scope of this handbook, each will be briefly characterized below.

Decision Support Systems

A decision support system (DSS) aids higher-level and middle-level managers of an organization in making strategic and certain tactical decisions. These decisions are characterized by involving semistructured problem situations, such as those pertaining to capital investments and operational budgeting. A distinctive aspect of decisions involving a DSS is that they always require active managerial participation. Three major components of a DSS are a model base, database, and user interface. The model base contains the computer-based financial models (i.e., computer programs) needed for analyzing the problem situation. A budget model, such as the one described earlier, is an important type of model incorporated in a model base. It is usually supplemented by sales-forecasting models. The database contains the data needed in the models, such as the input factors for a budget model. The user interface includes the computer terminal by which the manager-user accesses the model and data, and the facilitating software, such as a query language.

Executive Information Systems

An executive information system (EIS) is a customized information support system. It is designed for the chief executive officer of an organization or for one of the other top managers. The purposes of an EIS are to provide the information that its user needs to meet his or her responsibilities, including information for making strategic and tactical planning decisions and for controlling key operations. An EIS is similar to a DSS in that it serves managers at the higher levels of an organization and helps them to make decisions. However, it differs in that it is concerned as much with control as with planning. The essence of an EIS is a database that contains up-to-date and relevant data and information. In addition to providing data about the organization, the database usually includes data drawn from on-line commercial data banks such as the Dow-Jones Retrieval Service.

Expert Systems

An expert system (ES) is a knowledge-based computer system that imitates the reasoning of human experts in recommending solutions to specific but difficult problems. In a sense an ES is a variation of a DSS in that both employ computer processing of models or programs. However, an expert system can be designed for a problem that arises at any managerial level. For instance, an ES can be employed to help select the best type of financing to employ (bank loan, stocks, bonds, and the like) when undertaking a new capital project. Not only will an ES provide a good decision choice based on the knowledge of experts; it will also provide the choice very quickly.

An ES is built by "knowledge engineers" with the inputs of people who have expert knowledge in the problem area for which the ES is intended. As in the case of a DSS and an EIS, an ES will be most successful if it is built with the active participation of the ultimate users.

An ES has several components: a knowledge base, an inference engine, a user interface, and a task-specific database. The knowledge base incorporates the knowledge of the experts to the domain of the problem situation. In most cases the knowledge is expressed as a collection of production if-then rules. For instance, *if* (1) a patient was caught unprepared in a sudden rainstorm and (2) the patient has developed a fever, *then* the patient likely has a cold. The inference engine contains the heuristic reasoning procedures that simulate the decision-making processes of human experts. It "drives" the ES; that is, it determines the sequence in which to apply the production rules. The user interface, as in a DSS, is the means by which the user communicates with the system. The task-specific database contains the facts relevant to a specific application of an ES. For a financing decision, it might contain the amount of financing, the time horizon or life of the project being developed, the current interest rates, and so on. Data are typically entered into the task-specific database by the user, who answers questions posed by the user interface software.

Conclusion

Financial planning and control have gained powerful tools in recent years. Improved planning and control methods have been promulgated through numerous textbooks and reference books. Computer-based systems—such as DSS, EIS, and ES—have been developed and enhanced. These tools can be effective, however, only if the managerial climate is favorable. Top managements of organizations should become familiar with the purposes and basic workings of such methods and systems, and they should employ the expertise needed to incorporate these elements into the planning and control processes of their organizations.

25

Human Resources

Elaine Dickson

Corporate Transitions, Inc.,
and
Center for Nonprofit Management
Nashville, Tennessee

The human resource function is broad. It can include anything that concerns the human side of an enterprise and it takes different shapes in specific organizational settings. Business organizations depend on the human resource function "to ensure that the culture, values and structure of the organization and the quality, motivation and commitment of its employees contribute fully to the achievement of its objectives."[1]

If, as has often been suggested, managers have to manage three things—ideas, things, and people—people undoubtedly are the biggest challenge. Human beings not only are complex in their needs, wants, aspirations, commitments, and motivations; they also are the greatest resource and asset of an enterprise. People are the producers; results are in their hands. They control the use of all other resources—effectively or ineffectively, efficiently or inefficiently.

The purpose of this chapter is to help human resource consultants understand the relationship between business strategy and human resource strategy, the scope of the human resource function, the issues in positioning consulting services, the newer needs for services, and the packaging of services.

Business Strategy and
Human Resource Strategy

In recent attempts to benchmark human resource practices, considerable attention has been paid to human resource competencies and to the relationship between business strategy and human resource strategy. One view of competencies identifies three: knowledge of the business, world-class delivery of human resource practices, and management of change processes. Management of change processes, as a competency, links knowledge of the business with human resource practices, since human resource strategy ultimately is justified by business strategy.

Business strategy is illustrated by the following questions: What business are we in? What are our strengths, weaknesses, opportunities, and threats? What are the main strategic issues facing the business? What are the critical success factors that determine how well we achieve our mission?

As these questions are being answered, human resource strategists are asking: What sort of people do we need in the business? What are the strengths and weaknesses of our human resource capabilities? What opportunities do we have to develop and motivate our staff? What are the threats of skill shortages and the retention of key personnel? How far will business success be helped or hindered by the quality, motivation, commitment, and attitudes of our employees?

It is important for consultants to remember that successful human resource practices are carried out in relationship to the business strategy of a specific organization.

Scope of the Human
Resource Function

Work activities identified with the human resource function are many. The list below describes work activities that have at times been assigned wholly or partially to the human resource or personnel function. An asterisk (*) indicates the activities that are more mainline to the human resource function. The list was compiled by the American Society for Personnel Administration and Bureau of National Affairs.

Personnel records/reports*	Complaint/disciplinary procedures*
Personnel research*	Relocation services administration
Insurance benefits administration*	Supervisory training*
Unemployment compensation*	Employee publications/communications

EEO compliance/affirmative action*

Wage/salary administration*

Worker's compensation administration*

Tuition aid/scholarships

Job evaluation*

Health/medical services*

Retirement preparation programs*

Pre-employment testing*

Vacation/leave processing*

Induction/orientation*

Promotion/transfer/separation processing*

Counseling/employee assistance*

Pension/profit sharing plan administration*

College recruiting*

Recreation/social/recognition programs*

Recruiting/interviewing/hiring*

Union/labor relations*

Payroll processing

Executive compensation administration*

Human resource planning*

Safety programs/OSHA compliance*

Management development*

Food services

Performance evaluation, nonmanagement

Community relations/fund drives

Suggestion systems

Thrift/savings plan administration*

Security

Organizational development*

Management appraisal*

Stock plan administration

Skill training, nonmanagement

Public relations

Administrative services

Travel/transportation services

Library

Maintenance/janitorial services

In very small start-up companies, the human resource function is usually handled by the chief executive or shared by managers. Estimates vary, but the function is usually not established as a formal, separate entity until a business reaches 70 to 100 employees. As the business grows, the human resource function grows at a rate of 0.6 to 1.7 human resource employees (professional, technical, secretarial, and clerical) for every 100 employees in the company. The smaller the company, the higher the ratio; the larger the company, the smaller the ratio. The current trend is to use the term *human resource* rather than *personnel* to designate the function, organizational units, and titles.

In very large companies, the human resource function is more complex. In addition to the standard work to be done, factors such as the following have to be taken into account: higher degrees of specialization, number of geographic locations, globalization, unionization, and decentralization.

Positioning Consulting Services

Every consulting practice—whether a national firm, a smaller firm, or an individual practitioner—must portray an image of services or products that compares favorably with competing services or products in the marketplace. This concept is referred to as positioning and requires deliberate short-range and long-range decisions:

- Will you attempt to be a market leader? a market follower? a market nicher?
- Will you offer generalist or specialist services?
- Will you serve big businesses or small businesses?
- Which business sectors will you serve?
- Will you compete in the local, regional, national, or global marketplace?
- Will you compete on the basis of uniqueness, quality, cost, focus, and other distinguishing factors?

Some generalizations about positioning are possible. It is difficult for an individual consultant to be a generalist unless the consultant's primary focus is on guiding small, fast-growing businesses toward the internationalization of a human resource function or on contracting with small companies to handle human resource practices until the function can be internalized. Larger consulting firms with a regional or national presence are in the best position to provide generalist services through subspecializations within the firm. However, the market for human resource consulting lends itself to successful niche marketing—that is, to niche services such as: outplacement, employee leasing, temporary personnel services, benefits planning, management training, technical training, performance management, legal compliance, employee assistance programs, career assessment and planning, executive search services, organizational development, and corporate day care.

Table 25-1 shows some common human resource management functions with examples of deliverable services or products that can be provided through a consulting process.

Consulting Services to Meet Newer Needs

As in other business-related functions, human resource managers must respond to many new trends, events, and developments because of changes in the larger environment. Entrepreneurial consultants will see

Table 25-1. Human Resource Management Functions and Examples of Deliverables in the Consultation Process

Human resource management function	Examples of deliverables
Policy development	Legal issues in human resource management Policy and procedure manual Employee handbook Affirmative action plan
Personnel recruitment, selection, and employment	Labor market information Interviewing techniques Selection criteria Executive search services Processes and forms for employment, promotion, transfer, and demotion New-employee orientation Cost-benefit analysis of recruitment Turnover analysis
Wage and salary administration	Job descriptions and questionnaire Job evaluation system Salary surveys Salary scale and matrix
Benefits administration	Benefits trends Benefits surveys Benefits plan Flexible benefits plan Benefits Methods for communicating value of benefits to employees
Performance review	Review process Review instrument Plan for the review interview Pay-for-performance systems
Training and development	Training needs assessment Training systems Course development and delivery Career assessment and counseling Succession planning
Organizational development	Employee surveys Organizational climate assessment Organizational design Job design Management by objectives (MBO) Quality management

Table 25-1. Human Resource Management Functions and Examples of Deliverables in the Consultation Process (*Continued*)

Human resource management function	Examples of deliverables
Programs to attract and retain employees	Employee assistance Flextime Child care Wellness Retirement planning
Human resource information system	Hardware Software
Termination	Levels of disciplinary action Documentation requirements Grievance policy Termination process Guidelines for a termination interview Outplacement services

these changes as opportunities for new services. Recent editions of *The Human Resource Yearbook*[2] have focused on these and other trends and issues. For example:

- *Mismatch between job available and worker skills.* The demand for high-level technical skills is greater than the supply of skilled workers. Seventy-five percent of new jobs created will require some college education and good technical skills, yet one-half of the population will have only completed high school.

- *Immigration.* Immigrants have made up one-fourth of the U.S. population growth since the 1990s. The United States benefits significantly from immigrant labor, but not without surfacing tough human resource issues.

- *Overseas flight.* U.S. companies are moving their operations overseas, with a resulting loss of jobs at home. Anger among unemployed workers in the United States is rising.

- *Foreign competition at home.* More Americans are working for foreign companies in the United States. Mixed results are accruing for American workers.

- *Need to revive employee loyalty.* The wave of takeovers, mergers, and downsizings in recent years has left the work force disillusioned, cynical, and reluctant to become loyal, hardworking employees again.

- *Training and retraining the work force.* Because technology is changing so fast, workers will have to be trained and retrained several times during their working life.

- *Employee pressures for corporate social responsibility.* Workers and consumers want to be a part of and do business with socially responsible companies.

- *Shifting patterns of work and family life.* Over 70 percent of women in America now work. This participation raises the following issues to new levels: child care, elder care, parental leave, flexible work schedules, and family health care.

- *Human resource strategies for a global workplace.* Human resource planning for many companies is no longer local, or even national, but global. This creates many differences in business culture, business practices, and legal systems that must be responded to.

The Hay Group, an organization of international human resource consultants, has announced some of its next-generation products and practices. The ways that the group is responding to the marketplace are indicative of innovative approaches to compensation management. Here are examples:

- *Broadbanding.* As organizational structures flatten, jobs have become more multifocused, and employee growth is more lateral than vertical. Companies are beginning to rethink what they are paying for. Broadbanding is the concept of paying more for the person than the position—a new idea of salary ranges without midpoint and a way to focus more on personal growth and development.

- *Variable pay plans.* New plans emphasize systems that support quality and empower employees.

- *Development-focused compensation.* Competency-based pay programs respond to the changing nature of work and the implications of these changes for corporate pay practices.

Packaging of Consulting Services

Packaging is often the key to reaching the market. Quality management, for example, uses the organizing principle of continuous improvement to empower employees to make decisions and solve problems at new levels. Self-management training prepares employees to manage themselves and each other in the pursuit of productive results. An emphasis on performance management asks the larger question: What has to happen for our organization to develop and support employees as peak performers?

Figure 25-1 provides a checklist of human resource management practices organized around the creation of a work environment that supports employee peak performance, along with examples of deliverables in the consultation process.

Effective Performance Management Practices: Creating an Environment for Peak Performers	Y	N	Examples of Deliverables
A. Hiring employees with the potential to be peak performers			
1. Does our organization have a job description for each employee?	___	___	Job descriptions
2. Do we establish basic minimum requirements when employing new people?	___	___	Job requirements
3. Do we know our market for finding qualified applicants?	___	___	Job market information
4. Do we follow a thorough employment process when hiring each employee (résumé analysis, interviews, reference checks, and so on)?	___	___	Candidate-screening procedures
5. Do our managers develop a list of selection criteria and plan interview questions before interviewing job applicants?	___	___	Interview preparation
B. Orienting for performance			Orientation design
1. Do we have a plan to orient new employees?	___	___	
2. Do managers plan a new employee's schedule for at least the first day on the job?	___	___	Schedule for a productive first day on the job
3. Do we have basic human resource policies in place?	___	___	Policy manual

Figure 25-1 Human resource consulting services with performance management as the organizing principle.

Effective Performance Management Practices: Creating an Environment for Peak Performers	Y	N	Examples of Deliverables
C. Establishing accountability for performance			
1. Do our job descriptions clearly specify the work required in doing the job?	___	___	Job description
2. Do managers establish job objectives or standards with each employee?	___	___	Performance objectives and standards
3. Do managers delegate to the maximum capacity of each employee?	___	___	Delegation plans
D. Supporting and reinforcing performance	___	___	
1. Are managers thoroughly familiar with the performance level of each person reporting directly to them?	___	___	Observing and listening skills
2. Do managers regularly identify performance strengths in each employee and provide positive feedback to reinforce performance?	___	___	Positive feedback and skill building
3. Do managers spot performance weaknesses as they occur and provide corrective feedback?	___	___	Corrective feedback and skill building
4. Do managers have a systematic way to analyze performance problems and use dependable strategies for solving them?	___	___	Performance problem-solving strategies and skills

Figure 25-1 (*Continued*) Human resource consulting services with performance management as the organizing principle.

Effective Performance Management Practices: Creating an Environment for Peak Performers	Y	N	Examples of Deliverables
5. Do we have a formal review and documentation of job performance with each employee at least once a year?	___	___	Performance review system
6. When all else fails, do managers know how to handle a performance-related termination?	___	___	Termination policy and procedures
E. Rewarding performance			
1. Do we have an equitable system to determine the relative value of jobs within our organization and within the marketplace?	___	___	Job evaluation system
2. Do we have a salary and wage scale that establishes the minimum and maximum earning potential of each job?	___	___	Equitable salary scale
3. Do we have guidelines for granting salary increases, and are these administered consistently?	___	___	Salary administration guidelines
4. Do we have a competitive employee benefits plan?	___	___	Benefits review and planning
5. Do we "pay for performance" (i.e., do peak performers earn more than mediocre performers)?	___	___	Pay-for-performance plan
6. Do we use a variety of techniques for rewarding and recognizing performance?	___	___	Recognition plans

Figure 25-1 (*Continued*) Human resource consulting services with performance management as the organizing principle.

Effective Performance Management Practices: Creating an Environment for Peak Performers	Y	N	Examples of Deliverables
F. Practices that help develop and retain effective employees			
1. Do we actively communicate our company's mission, vision, values, and goals to employees?	—	—	Communications plan
2. Do we encourage employees to share information across functions and departments?	—	—	Team building
3. Do we encourage employees to take initiative individually and collectively to improve products, services, and operating systems?	—	—	Quality management program
4. Do we obtain input from employees in making changes which directly affect their jobs?	—	—	Management training
5. Do we know what employees consider to be the best things about our company?	—	—	Employee surveys
6. Do we know what employees consider to be the worst things about our company?	—	—	Employee surveys
7. Have we ever changed a company policy, procedure, or rule on the basis of employee input?	—	—	Management training
8. Do we communicate with employees as a group periodically?	—	—	Communications plan

Figure 25-1 (*Continued*) Human resource consulting services with performance management as the organizing principle.

Summary

The Human Resources Yearbook points out that human resource management is one of the fastest changing and most highly regulated functions in business today. This trend places heavy demands on consultants to stay current in the field. It also means that human resource professionals must work closely with attorneys to ensure that practices are legally defensible. The ultimate success of the consultant, however, depends on having competitive products and services that meet the needs of the marketplace and that are securely tied to the business strategies of client organizations.

Notes

1. Roger Cooke and Michael Armstrong, "The Search for Strategic HRM," *Personnel Management*, Vol. 22 (December 3, 1990), p. 31.
2. Mary F. Cook, *The Human Resources Yearbook* (Englewood Cliffs, N.J.: Prentice-Hall, 1991–1994).

Bibliography

Arthur, Diane, *Managing Human Resources in Small and Mid-sized Companies*, AMACOM, American Management Association, New York, 1987.

Carrell Michael R., and Frank E. Kuzmits, *Personnel: Management of Human Resources*, Charles E. Merrill Publishing Company, Columbus, Ohio, 1987.

Cook, Mary F., *Human Resource Director's Handbook*, Prentice-Hall, Inc., Englewood Cliffs, N.J., 1984.

Cook, Mary F. (ed.), *The Human Resources Yearbook*, Prentice-Hall, Inc., Englewood Cliffs, New Jersey, 1991–1994.

Cooke, Roger, and Michael Armstrong, "The Search for Strategic HRM," *Personnel Management*, Vol. 22 (December 3, 1990), pp. 30–33.

Churden, Herbert J., and Arthur W. Sherman Jr., *Personnel Management: The Utilization of Human Resources*, South-Western Publishing Co., Cincinnati, 1980.

Famularo, Joseph J., *Handbook of Human Resources Administration*, 2d ed., McGraw-Hill Book Company, New York, 1986.

Hendry, Chris, Andrew Pettigrew, and Paul Sparrow, "Changing Patterns of Human Resource Management," *Personnel Management*, Vol. 20 (November, 1989), pp. 37–41.

Ulrich, Dave, Wayne Brockbank, and Arthur Young, "Beyond Belief: A Benchmark for Human Resources," *Human Resource Management*, Vol. 28 (Fall 1989), pp. 313–315.

26
Team Building

The Cadence Group
Toronto, Ontario, Canada

Teams have become an increasingly important part of organizational life. As a result, working on issues of team effectiveness is becoming an important part of management consulting.

Key Issues in Building Teams

As a consultant, you may be asked to deal with a number of team problems. You may be called in because a business process reengineering team, which has been meeting for months, hasn't produced any tangible results. Or there may be personality conflicts on the sales team. You may be asked to do team building with company executives who are not working as a team.

We will examine ways to deal with each of these situations in the final section of this chapter. First, the chapter presents a framework for consulting on teams and team building in organizations. The goal is to challenge your thinking and bring some clarity to a number of current solutions applied to teams, including team rewards and incentives, shared leadership, and self-managed teams. As you work with the ideas in this chapter, you should continually challenge your own concepts about teams and team building.

The Business Basis for Teams

Organizations today are changing in order to thrive—or merely survive! The drivers of these changes include:

Figure 26-1 The four building blocks for effective teams.

- Customers who switch to the products and services that best satisfy their needs and expectations
- Competition for customers from offshore companies and niche marketers, as well as traditional competitors
- Costs that must be reduced or controlled, while simultaneously adding value for customers
- Technological advances in products and processes that redefine both the business that companies are in and the way they do business

Customers, competition, costs, and technology are challenging organizations, and teams are part of the solution. Employees can work in teams across functions to become more effective at meeting customer requirements and more efficient at controlling costs. Teams can provide the synergy of multiple contributions that creates innovative and timely products and services. And teams are enabled by computer networks, shared databases, expert systems, decision support tools, and other advances in technology.

Of course, teams are only part of the solution. Yet many companies embrace teams, thinking they've found the solutions to all their problems. And teams are only as effective as their outputs. Telling people they're a team isn't enough.

Requisite Conditions for Teams

There are four basic building blocks for effective teams called *requisite conditions* (Fig. 26-1). Requisite means "required by the nature of things and necessary for success." The requisite concept and many others presented in this chapter are based on the work of Elliott Jaques.[1]

To be effective, teams must have:

- A clear, common purpose that is important to the organization
- Clear accountability for outputs and the authority required to accomplish the outputs
- Employee appraisal, reward, and incentive systems that support performance on an ongoing basis
- The leadership, technical, informational, and interpersonal skills required to accomplish the purpose

There is a natural order to these requisite building blocks. Accountability without a worthy purpose makes no sense. Effective performance appraisal mirrors clear accountability and authority. And skills build on this basic foundation.

To provide a framework for consulting on teams and team building, we will address each of these requirements—purpose, accountability and authority, performance support systems, and skills—in turn. Unlike skills, the first three requirements tend to be neglected, so these will be addressed in more detail. First, however, it is important to make a distinction between teams and teamwork, and to take a look at two very different kinds of teams.

Teams versus Teamwork

People use the word *team* to mean a number of different things. In our work as consultants, it's essential to know what we and our clients mean when we talk about teams. Here's one approach to providing clarity: A *team* is a small group of people (typically fewer than ten) whose work needs to be highly coordinated to achieve specific outputs.

People say things like "This company needs to be a team." The word *teamwork* refers to values like sharing, cooperating, and helping one another. The employees of a company are not a team unless their work needs to be coordinated to achieve the same, specific outputs. This would happen only in a very small company. Groups may require *teamwork* even when they do not need to work as a team.

Types of Teams

A good deal of consulting work is done within managerial hierarchies. Elliott Jaques describes a hierarchy as a system of roles in which a manager is held accountable for the outputs and actions of subordinates. Jaques contends that a hierarchy is the most effective form of organization for getting work done in a way that builds trust among the people in the organization.

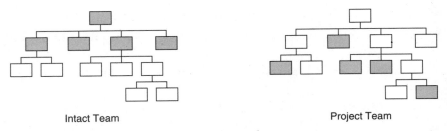

Intact Team   Project Team

Figure 26-2   Teams in the managerial hierarchy.

A managerial hierarchy has two basic types of teams called project teams and intact teams (Fig. 26-2). An *intact team* consists of a manager and all immediate subordinates. For example, the vice president of sales and her four regional directors are an intact team. Similarly, each director and his subordinates are an intact team. The work of the subordinates must be coordinated to achieve the output(s) for which the manager is held accountable.

A *project team* consists of a group of people with the particular mix of expertise required to produce specific outputs, who are not all subordinate to the same manager. Members of project teams often come from different functions. For example, individuals from sales, finance, administration, and service may work together to reengineer a specific process.

Project teams are sometimes called task forces, process teams, or cross-functional teams. They are usually temporary and may be part time. Occasionally, project teams exist on an ongoing basis. For example, the work of sales, service, and information technology might be tightly coordinated to meet the needs of one large customer. However, if a company has many permanent project teams, it may be better off reorganizing so that people whose work needs to be highly coordinated are subordinate to one manager.

Although a managerial hierarchy is an effective form of organization for getting work done. Different forms of organization may be needed when there's another important purpose. In a partnership, for example, the autonomy of the partners is also important. In a hospital, the accountability of physicians to their profession is also important. In a university, the free exploration of ideas is important, and in community associations, inclusion is important. The administration of a law firm, hospital, or university is, however, usually a managerial hierarchy.

Teams of partners, doctors, or professors and teams within community associations may not have a single individual with the authority to settle a dispute about who is accountable for what. When they don't, the requisite conditions of accountability, authority, and performance support systems become clouded, unlike the situation with teams in a managerial hierarchy. The requisite conditions of purpose and skills still apply, however.

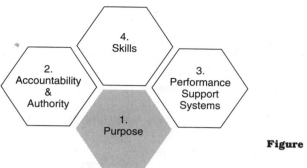

Figure 26-3

Purpose

With teams, as in life, if you don't know where you're going, any road will take you there. It may seem obvious that a team cannot be effective without a clear sense of purpose (Fig. 26-3). But time and again we work with teams whose members don't agree on where they are going. Occasionally, we encounter teams that don't really have a purpose. Sometimes each team member has a different opinion about what the purpose is. Often the team has a common purpose, but it isn't stated precisely enough to know whether it is achievable, or when it has been achieved.

Defining Team Purpose

Teams with a common purpose often describe that purpose in terms of a team vision or mission. Although a clear vision and/or mission is important, teams also benefit from a more specific definition of purpose. We find Jaques' definition of *task* useful in defining team purpose more specifically. Jaques defines a task in terms of four components:

Quantity	How much is to be accomplished
Quality	How well it is to be accomplished
Time	How long it is to take to accomplish the task
Resources	The budget, equipment, and people resources available to accomplish the task

A team may exist to accomplish one task, or a number of tasks. An intact sales team may, for example, have two tasks: achieving a quarterly sales target of $500,000 and improving customer retention by 100 percent within 2 years. The team manager may require additional resources, such as training, to accomplish one or both of these tasks. A project team may have one task: to reengineer the billing process, with a 50 percent reduction in errors and a 30 percent reduction in costs, within 12 months.

Resources required would include the authority to obtain information from individuals in the organization.

A task or tasks, expressed in terms of quantity, quality, time, and resources (QQT&R), can be a clear, concise way of stating a team's purpose. Although we refer to this as a "team task," it is really the team leader's task. Individual team members will have their own tasks, which are subtasks of the team leader's task. For example, a salesperson may have a quarterly sales target of $50,000. A member of the reengineering team may be accountable for mapping the process in her function.

When an intact team has a great many team tasks, it may make sense only to specify *key* tasks in terms of QQT&R. Although it may not be possible to specify exact quantity, quality, time, and resources at the beginning of a team project, estimating these parameters is useful both for the team manager or leader and for other team members.

A team can be effective only if the team purpose is important to the organization. When a team's purpose isn't important, the team members have little commitment.

Benefits of Purpose as QQT&R

Expressing the team's purpose in terms of quantity, quality, time, and resources ensures that all team members:

- Know why the team exists
- Know why they are on the team—understanding builds commitment
- Know whether the team's purpose is achievable and have a basis for renegotiating (for more time, more resources, less quantity, or less quality) if the purpose cannot currently be attained
- Know when the team has achieved its purpose

Questions to Assess Team Purpose

1. What is the team's purpose?
2. What specific task(s) is the team established to accomplish?
3. For each task:

   How much is to be accomplished?

   How well is it to be accomplished?

   How long do you have to accomplish this task?

   What resources do you have to accomplish this task?

   Can you accomplish this task within this time frame and with these resources?

Does this task warrant the resources required by the team?

4. Who are the members of the team?

5. Does each team member understand what the team is to work on?

6. How does each team member contribute to the team's task(s)?

We suggest that you question the team manager or leader, team members, and your client if he or she is not part of the team.

Accountability & Authority

When teams are a required part of an organization, they need to be integrated within the existing hierarchical structure (Fig. 26-4). Intact teams are a necessary part of hierarchy. Project teams can serve to strengthen an organization by integrating work across vertical, functional boundaries. Teams can be integrated within the existing structure through accountability and authority.

Accountability of the Team Manager or Leader

When teams are to be integrated within the existing structure, a key consideration is accountability for team task(s). Although people often talk about the importance of *mutual accountability* on teams, a better term is *shared responsibility,* since accountability cannot really be shared. Managers hold an individual accountable for a task when they appraise his or her performance on that task and, ultimately, remove that individual if warranted. Organizations don't hire teams, don't fire teams, and can really appraise only the work of the individuals on that team.

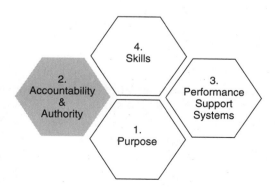

Figure 26-4

A team exists because some individual is accountable for a task which he or she cannot accomplish without the help of others. The team members are this individual's resources for the team's task(s)—the purpose of the team.

If an intact team is to be effective, it is the team manager who must be accountable for the team's task(s). Jaques defines a manager as someone who is accountable for:

- The outputs of subordinates (i.e., the team)
- Exerting leadership by setting a vision and having others follow it willingly
- Building a team by keeping subordinates clear about how they are to work with one another

On an effective project team, the team leader is held accountable by his or her manager for the work of the team. If the team is to be effective, this manager will hold the team leader accountable for team outputs, for team leadership, and for coordination of the work of the team. In other words, the team leader has the same accountabilities as a manager.

Accountability of Team Members

For a team to be effective, team members must also be accountable. They are accountable for their part in accomplishing the team's task(s). Team members' tasks are subtasks of the manager or team leader's task(s). On an effective intact team, members are held accountable by the team manager. On an effective project team, however, each member is held accountable both by the team leader and by his or her own manager. The team leader has the authority to remove the team member from the team if this work is not acceptable, while the manager appraises the team member on his/her team tasks as well as other accountabilities.

Benefits of Clear Accountabilities

Clarifying accountability on teams has a number of benefits.

- The team manager or leader knows that he or she is accountable for the team's task(s), and works with the team to produce results. Things don't fall through the cracks.
- Team members know that the manager or leader is accountable for the team's work, and understand why some decisions can be reached by consensus, while others cannot.
- Team members know the specific task(s) for which they are held accountable, and why they are on the team. Knowledge builds commitment.

- On a project team, team members don't find themselves trying to serve two masters. The team leader can assign tasks to team members only within limits prescribed by each team member's manager. The manager holds the team member accountable for nonteam tasks, and takes these other accountabilities into consideration when prescribing limits for team tasks.

Shared Team Leadership and Shared Responsibility

Although the team manager or leader is held accountable for team leadership, many aspects of leadership can be shared among team members. Any team member can take initiative to ensure that the team works well together. We will examine the leadership skills that all team members can use toward the end of this chapter.

Current books on team building that talk about the mutual *accountability* of team members go on to describe the importance of all teams members taking *responsibility* for the team's purpose. In essence, *taking responsibility* means holding oneself accountable by one's own conscience, as opposed to being *held accountable* by an external source. Shared responsibility does increase the effectiveness of teams. But it only builds on—and never replaces—the need for clear individual accountabilities in a managerial hierarchy.

In teams in which there is no hierarchy and no one is holding the team accountable for its results (teams of partners, for example), it is very important that each team member take responsibility for achieving the team's purpose. Once again, however, this is *shared responsibility*, and the distinction in terminology is important.

Team Decision Making and Consensus

The team manager's or leader's accountability for team tasks does not imply that this person is authoritarian or autocratic. Some decisions may be reached by consensus, and almost all decisions made by the manager or leader require input from individual team members or the team as a whole.

In fact, team decision making proceeds along a continuum, as illustrated in Figure 26-5. As we move from left to right along this continuum, participation of team members in the decision increases. Although this tends to take more time, participation may build commitment to the decision. Each method of decision making (A–D in the figure) is appropriate—under certain conditions. Teams, and especially new teams, can fall into the trap of wanting to reach consensus on everything.

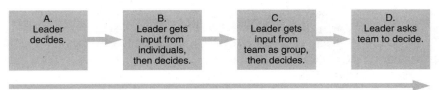

Time to make decision increases.
Participation in decision increases, which may build commitment for implementation.

Figure 26-5 The continuum of team decision making. (*Source:* Adapted and simplified from Victor H. Vroom and Arthur G. Jago, *The New Leadership: Managing Participation in Organizations*, Englewood Cliffs, N.J., Prentice-Hall, 1988).

Method A. The manager or leader may decide without team input, as long as he or she doesn't need participation to build commitment. For example, it's appropriate for the team leader to make quick, autocratic decisions in emergency situations if he or she has all the necessary information.

Method B. When the manager or leader needs information from team members, he or she may involve them one on one, as long as the leader knows exactly what information is required and doesn't need participation to build commitment. For example, the team leader may check with each person before scheduling an important meeting.

Method C. If the manager or leader needs information, and doesn't know exactly what information he or she lacks, it's important to bring the group together for dialogue. Dialogue is also important when conflict about alternatives is likely to arise among team members. Bringing the group together takes longer, but can build significant commitment. It's important, however, that the leader and team members are clear that the leader will make the final decision. Trust is undermined when team members assume that it's a group decision, only to discover it's not. Dialogue is an effective way of making many decisions that involve the team. The manager or leader, who is accountable for team output, is the decision maker, and the team has significant participation in the decision.

When the manager/leader is willing to support any decision the team makes, and commitment to implementing that decision is crucial, it is appropriate to ask the team to decide. Teams can decide by majority rule, or may take time required to reach consensus. Since majority rule tends to undermine commitment, consensus is preferable.

Because the manager/leader is accountable for any decision the team makes, he/she can only let the team decide when any alternative is acceptable. The team manager/leader can sometimes ensure this by providing parameters for an acceptable decision. For example, the manager/leader may ask the team to sort out the work schedule, by Friday, with the proviso that no overtime costs be incurred.

It's worth noting that reaching consensus on controversial issues takes considerable skill, and when a team is unable to reach agreement, the manager/leader, or a team member assigned by the manager/leader, must make the decision.

A skilled team manager or leader will involve team members to improve the quality of decisions and build commitment to the implementation of decisions, as it is appropriate. The manager or leader's accountability for team outputs does not lessen the need for team participation.

Self-Managed Teams

Many organizations make reference to self-managed teams, meaning teams in which members make a lot of the decisions. These decisions range from housekeeping issues to capital purchase decisions to compensation issues.

Vroom's work on participation can help teams and their leaders understand when team decision making is appropriate—and when it's not. And in this context the term *self-managed* is avoided. The reason is that, in a hierarchy, a team is always managed by someone. A team may indeed decide who will be appointed to the team and how bonuses will be divided. But if the team's performance falls to a point where an executive finds it worrisome, steps will be taken to ensure that the team stays on track and will find out who its manager has been all along. The term *self-managed* often raises unrealistic expectations and, eventually, can undermine trust.

Authorities of a Team Manager

As explained earlier, team managers and leaders of effective teams are held accountable for team outputs, exerting leadership and building the team. Jaques has found that a manager of an intact team needs four authorities in order to meet these accountabilities:

- The authority to veto the appointment of someone to the team
- The authority to remove someone from the team
- The authority to assign tasks to team members
- The authority to conduct appraisals of team members and assign merit increases in accord with company policy

On an effective project team, the authorities of the project team leader do not undermine the authority of the team members' own managers. Project team leaders need the following authorities:

- The authority to veto the appointment of someone to the team
- The authority to remove someone from the team
- The authority to assign tasks to team members *within limits prescribed by each team member's manager*
- The authority to call team meetings with reasonable advance notice

The project team leader does not conduct appraisals or assign merit increases. This is done by each team member's manager, with input from the team leader regarding work done on the team.

Questions to Assess Team Accountability and Authority

1. Who is accountable for the task(s) of the team?
2. What is the team manager or leader accountable for? Who holds the leader accountable?
3. What is each team member accountable for? Who holds the member accountable?
4. Do all team members understand the role of each member on the team?
5. What authorities does the team manager or leader have over team members? Are these sufficient?
6. Who makes decisions that affect the team?

   Are decisions based on sufficient information? Why or why not?

   Are decisions based on sufficient discussion? Why or why not?

   Which, if any, decisions are reached by consensus? Is this appropriate? Why or why not?

We suggest that you question the team manager or leader, team members, and your client if he or she is not part of the team.

Performance Support Systems

When the team leader or manager is accountable for the team's task(s) and other team members are accountable for specific subtasks, performance support systems become relatively straightforward (Fig. 26-6).

Performance Appraisal

The team manager or leader is appraised by his or her manager on the basis of the work of the team and the leadership and team building provided. In an intact team, team members are appraised by their manager

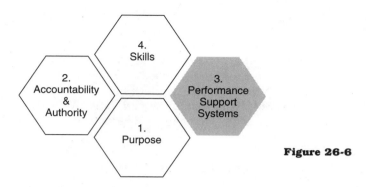

Figure 26-6

according to their individual accountabilities. For a project team, members are appraised by their line manager, with input from the project team leader regarding their project team accountabilities.

Team Incentives and Rewards

A popular team-building intervention today is to award bonuses according to team results. Thus, if sales to Acme Widgets are above quota, everyone on the Acme Widgets team receives a bonus. The intention is to increase the commitment of team members to the success of the team's work.

In many ways, this practice is not only unfair, but also counterproductive. It's unfair because each team member has control over only his or her behavior and not over the behavior of other team members. The practice tends to be counterproductive because the team may focus on short-term gains at the expense of the longer-term outcomes. Also, bonuses are usually based on something that's easy to measure, like volume of sales. Performance in other dimensions, including the subtleties of customer satisfaction, may be sacrificed.

Even though team incentives and rewards are ineffective in the long term, it is very important to recognize and compensate individual contributions to team outputs. Clear accountability for individual subtasks makes it relatively easy to do this.

Assessing Performance Support Systems

1. How does your organization's appraisal system influence the effectiveness of the team?

2. How do your organization's incentive or bonus system influence the effectiveness of the team?

We suggest that you question the team manager or leader, team members, and your client if he or she is not part of the team.

Skills Requirements

We have examined the first three requisite requirements—purpose, accountability and authority, and performance support systems—in some detail because they are not usually given the textbook attention they deserve. Once these requirements are in place along with performance support systems that reflect accountability and authority, we can turn to the skills requirements of the manager or leader and the team members (Fig. 26-7).

If the first three requisite conditions are not in place, the apparent skills requirements may be unrealistic. For example, a project team leader without the authority to assign tasks will need to be skilled at cajoling or manipulating team members. Members of teams in which accountabilities aren't clear will need to be very skilled at resolving—or avoiding—the many conflicts that will arise.

Consultants who are asked to do team building are not always given the mandate to ensure that the first three requisite conditions for effective teams are met. However, it is important that throughout the consulting process, they recognize the root causes of some of the symptoms they are faced with. It is also important that consultants discuss their insights with clients, so that both sides have realistic expectations regarding any interventions made.

In diagnosis and intervention with existing teams, skills are addressed after the first three requisite conditions have been met. Skills should, however, be addressed up front when a team is formed. Ideally, the team leader will have the leadership skills required, and team members are selected because of the varied technical or functional skills they bring to the team.

We will now turn to the skills needed by team managers and leaders—and members—when the other three requirements are in place. Because there are many good sources of information on these skills, we will address them in less detail and will focus on questions for assessing the skills required.

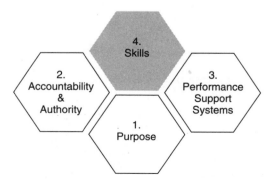

Figure 26-7

Four groups of skills are required for effective teamwork:

- Leadership skills
- Technical or functional skills
- Skills for gathering, organizing, and evaluating information
- Interpersonal skills

Leadership Skills

In an intact team, the manager is accountable for exerting leadership by setting a vision and having others follow it willingly. Such accountability may be required of a project team leader as well. Leadership skills also include coaching team members on fulfilling the requirements of their roles, encouraging team members in their work, and planning and facilitating productive team meetings. As noted earlier, any team member can demonstrate leadership. However, it is important that the leader model both leadership and interpersonal skills, and support other team members in developing these skills.

Questions to Assess Leadership Skills

1. Is the team manager or leader able to set a team vision which others follow willingly?
2. Does the team manager or leader coach team members effectively?
3. Are contributions of team members recognized?
4. Are team accomplishments celebrated?
5. Are team meetings well planned?
6. Are team meetings conducted effectively?

We suggest that you question the team manager or leader, team members, and your client if he or she is not part of the team.

Technical and Functional Skills

Technical or functional skills relate to a particular area of expertise—skills in information technology, accounting, sales, training, operating specific equipment, and so on. The technical or functional skills needed depend on the task of the team manager or leader. Technical or functional skills requirements need to be assessed when teams are formed. Team members are resources in part because they bring technical or functional expertise to the team. They may also bring the authority to commit functional resources.

Questions to Assess Technical or Functional Skills

1. What technical or functional skills are required to complete the team task(s)?

2. Which team members have these skills?

3. Which, if any, skills are not available on the team? How can these be obtained?

We suggest that you question the team manager or leader, team members, and your client if he or she is not part of the team.

Information Skills

Most team tasks require skills in gathering, organizing, and evaluating information. It is also important that teams have a common approach to dealing with information.

The actual skills required will vary with the task. Skills for gathering information may include techniques for generating creative ideas, interviewing, and conducting focus groups. Skills for organizing information may range from using total quality management (TQM) tools to implementing sophisticated methods for project management. Skills for evaluating information might include methods for finding root cause, for choosing among alternatives, and for analyzing risk.

Questions to Assess Information Skills

1. What information needs to be gathered, organized, or evaluated by the team, in order to accomplish the team's task(s)?

2. What skills are required to handle information?

3. Which team members have these skills?

4. Which, if any, skills are not available on the team? How can they be obtained?

We suggest that you question the team manager or leader, team members, and your client if he or she is not part of the team.

Interpersonal Skills

Interpersonal skills include listening, questioning, and discussion skills, as well as skills for surfacing and resolving conflict. These skills are required by team managers or leaders and, to varying degrees, by all team members.

Questions to Assess Interpersonal Skills

1. How well does the team manager or leader listen to team members?
2. How well do team members listen to one another?
3. How effectively do team members ask challenging questions?
4. How effective is team discussion? Why?
5. How does the team surface conflict?
6. How does the team deal with conflict? How effective is the process?

We suggest that you question the team manager or leader, team members, and your client if he or she is not part of the team.

Team-Building Situations

When our clients call us for team building, they never ask for help with accountability or authority issues. They usually ask us to fix issues of personality. Let's return to the three examples mentioned in the beginning of this chapter. We will take a look at the problem, and some possible causes and potential interventions, based on our four requisite conditions for effective teams.

The Problem: Team Not Producing Results

Your client calls because a team isn't producing results. The problem can occur with any kind of team, perhaps most frequently with cross-functional project teams. Your client may claim that team members "aren't committed" or can't "work as a team."

In dealing with this kind of situation, here are some possible causes to keep in mind:

- The team leader and members may either be unclear as to the purpose of the team, or they may not agree on the team's purpose.

- The team's purpose may not have been clearly defined, both in terms of the quantity and quality of specific outputs, and also in terms of resources and time required.

- The managers of project team members may not support team members' participation on the team by ensuring that work on the team, plus other accountabilities, is a manageable workload.

- The project team leader may not have the authorities required to be effective.

- The team leader may lack leadership skills.

- The team members may lack the functional or technical skills required to accomplish their tasks.

Here are some potential interventions:
Depending on the cause of the problem, the following interventions might be appropriate.

- Have the team leader meet with his/her manager to specify the team's task in terms of quantity, quality, time, and resources.
- Have team member's managers and the team leader work together to clarify team member's accountabilities for their team and nonteam tasks.
- Coach the team leader regarding leadership skills.
- Provide additional training in functional or technical skills for project team members.

The Problem: Personality Conflicts on the Team

"Personality conflicts" can be used to describe a whole spectrum of problems. For example, when you question your client about personality conflicts on his intact team, you may find that members argue with him about decisions, and with each other over who should do what work, who's not pulling their weight, and so on.

Based on our experience with clients, we would suspect the following possible causes in this situation.

- Team members believe that they, not the manager, are accountable for the team tasks.
- The manager has not clarified the specific tasks for which each subordinate is held accountable.

The following potential interventions might be appropriate.

- Have the manager clarify that he is accountable for the outputs of the team. This may require clarifying his accountabilities with his manager.
- Have the manager meet with each subordinate to clarify accountabilities, and with the team to identify and resolve any conflicts in resources.

The Problem: Members Not Working as a Team

Our clients experience this as a very real problem, on both intact and project teams at all levels. You may, for instance, get a call from a vice president wanting team building for her four directors who are "not working as a team."

Here are some possible causes we would keep in mind as we interviewed the directors.

- The directors may not be clear about the team's specific tasks, i.e., the tasks for which the VP is held accountable by her manager. The VP also may not be clear about her accountabilities.

- The team tasks, and the subtasks of the four directors may not be specific in terms of resources available, as well as time, quality and quantity. The VP may not have renegotiated with her subordinates, individually and as a team, regarding resources.

Depending on an analysis of the situation, the following potential intervention might be effective.

- Coach the VP with respect to negotiating clear accountabilities with her subordinates and meeting with her team of subordinates to identify and resolve potential conflicts among them.

Interventions with Teams in Nonmanagerial Hierarchies

In all three of these examples, we are dealing with accountable managers. Suppose, however, we're faced with a team of partners, or a team within a community association. Depending on our diagnosis of the cause of the problems, one or more of the following interventions might be appropriate:

- Work with the team to clarify its purpose, through creating a shared vision, and through specifying team task(s) in terms of quantity, quality, time, and resources.

- Work with the team to specify the tasks of individual team members in terms of quantity, quality, time, and resources.

- Hold a dialogue with the team about the importance of shared responsibility, and have each team member state what he or she is taking responsibility for.

- Provide coaching or training in leadership, technical, information, and interpersonal skills, as appropriate. Focus on skills for facilitating group discussion, making group decisions, and resolving conflict in a nonhierarchical structure.

Summary

Even though much is being written about teams these days, some basic, requisite conditions for effective teams seem to be ignored. To be effective, teams must have:

- A clear, common purpose that is important to the organization
- Clear accountability for outputs and the authority required to accomplish the work
- Performance appraisal, reward, and incentive systems that support performance on an ongoing basis
- The leadership, technical, information, and interpersonal skills required to accomplish the purpose.

It's important to distinguish between the two types of teams that exist in most organizations. Intact teams consist of a manager and his or her subordinates. Project teams, which are usually temporary and often cross-functional, consist of a team leader and team members who are not subordinates.

To be effective on an ongoing basis, teams need to be integrated within the existing structure of an organization. Teams exist because an individual is accountable for work that requires the coordinated effort of a group of people. The task(s) of that team manager or leader is the purpose of the team. The team purpose can be specified in terms of quantity, quality, time, and resources.

If the team is to be effective, team members must be assigned subtasks for which they, in turn, are held accountable. Performance support systems, such as performance appraisal and bonuses, must support the accountability structure of the team.

Once the basics of purpose, accountability and authority, and performance support systems are in place, we can turn our attention to team skills. All team managers and leaders require leadership skills, and good interpersonal skills are an asset to any team member. The technical, functional, and information skills required depend on the nature of the team's task(s). Leadership skills are important in the selection of team managers or leaders, whereas technical or functional skills are usually key in the selection of team members. All skills can, of course, be developed through training and coaching.

In consulting with teams, it is important to look beyond the presenting problem to determine whether symptoms are caused by a lack of one or more of the requisite conditions for effective teams.

Notes

1. Elliott Jaques, *Requisite Organization* (Arlington, Va.: Cason Hall, 1989).
2. Victor H. Vroom and Arthur G. Jago, *The New Leadership: Managing Participation in Organizations* (Englewood Cliffs, N.J.: Prentice-Hall, 1988).

27

Process Improvement

David J. Dyda
Senior Consultant, IBM Consulting Group
San Francisco, California

One of the most common themes in management and business books today involves the changing marketplace and prescriptions for enabling and addressing these changes. Hammer and Champy[1] discuss the reengineering of the corporation, Lipnack and Stamps[2] discuss how to take a team approach to organizing the organization, and Tapscott and Caston[3] discuss how a fundamental change is taking place in the nature and application of information technology in business. Tom Peters, in his book *Liberation Management*,[4] examines a wide range of issues, including moving away from a traditional hierarchical structure in what he calls the "necessary disorganization for the nanosecond nineties." Peters cites specific examples of how companies are changing the way they do business.

In order to address the changing marketplace, organizations are focusing on developing techniques that add value for the customer and eliminating those that do not. The approach that is receiving a great deal of attention today focuses on *total work processes*. The essence of this approach is to improve the processes that support what the organization does for customers and to add value in providing goods and services for them. Process improvement approaches are covered in more detail later in this chapter.

Relationship of Business Strategy, Process, and Information Technology

The business objectives of organizations are being shaped rapidly by the changing marketplace. The focus is on satisfying the customer or consumer. The values, mission, vision, business processes, and information technology infrastructure are all affected as the organization transforms itself to capitalize on these new opportunities. It appears that the major transformation emphasis is on organizational structure, teamwork, cross-functional views of work, and customer-oriented business processes.

Companies are moving away from the traditional hierarchical organizational structure, one that is oriented around departmental functions, to one that revolves around the processes of the business. The emerging view is that the organization has expertise, skills, and intellectual assets that should be focused on cross-functional lines—a focus that encourages the team approach. A *team* is a group of individuals who have a shared business mission and a similar set of values—in this case, customer satisfaction. In the traditional "inward" view of business, the emphasis was almost entirely on departmental processes, information, and the roles and responsibilities of personnel in the context of a departmental function. This approach resulted in the creation of "islands of information" that were disconnected from the rest of the business. In the emerging "process" view, the roles and responsibilities of people are focused on the processes that support the customer or consumer. This new attitude is driving the need for clearer definition of what processes are necessary, how to access information from other functions in the organization, and how to "integrate" the organization so it can become more responsive and competitive in the market.

Customer-oriented business processes provide the framework for determining whom the organization has to serve and satisfy, roles and responsibilities, accountabilities, and the requests that occur between the different parties that are a part of a business process. (See Fig. 27.1.) The fundamental question is: Who must be satisfied with the deliverables of a process? The roles and responsibilities of the different parties affect the location of data, business applications, and therefore the style of the information technology infrastructure. Clarifying the data and applications issue requires answering the following questions:

What data or information is needed?

Who needs the information?

When is the information needed?

Why is the information needed?

Where is the information needed?

Sample Business Process

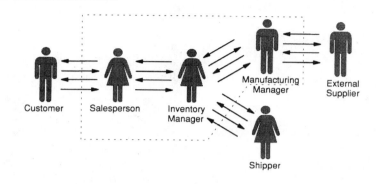

Checklist

- Why is this process/work being performed?
- Who is the customer of the process or work to be performed?
- What business logic (applications) are needed and where?
- What information/data is needed?
- Who needs the information/data?
- When is information/data needed?
- Why is the information/data needed?
- Where is the information/data needed?
- Do the process, data, application and I/T functions support the needs of the business?

Figure 27-1 Process and work flow evaluation. (*Source: IBM Corp.*)

Who has to create, read or view, update, and/or delete the information?

The answers to the questions address the architectural considerations of an information system that supports an organization's business processes. In order to provide front-line employees with the necessary tools and information to satisfy customers, business applications and data will be distributed across the organization in what is today known as as open, networked, or client/server environment. In the more traditional paradigm, by contrast, the information technology infrastructure was host-based and reflected the hierarchical, centralized command-and-control approach to running an organization.

The information technology infrastructure provides the enabling environment to support customer-oriented business processes that represent the organization's vision and strategy. The components of a business process support infrastructure include:

- Graphical user interface (GUI) software
- Networking hardware and software
- Systems management software

- Network management software
- Database software
- Transaction processing and management software
- Application development tools software
- Process and work flow enabling software
- Business applications software

The open, networked, or client/server infrastructure can be characterized as a "lego style" environment consisting of many pieces and parts that must interoperate to create the necessary infrastructure to support business processes. This pieces and parts environment is moving toward a technology based on standards. The standards-compliance approach will aid in assembling the pieces and parts and increase the likelihood that the components will be interoperable. The standards to which most vendors seem to be seeking or obtaining compliance include the Open Software Foundation (OSF) and X/OPEN. There are literally dozens of standards organizations that are government-, vendor-, and customer-based. The specific pieces and parts selected to create a process support infrastructure will affect the degree of integration responsibility that will be required to ensure that the infrastructure performs. This integration responsibility in turn will affect the skills and resources required to perform the job.

Therefore, clients must look at various partnering options to increase their odds of success. Partnering options include outsourcing, insourcing, and a shared arrangement in which the client provides part of the team and the supplier provides a complementary set of skills.

Business strategies are executed through business processes. George Stalk and his associates, writing in the *Harvard Business Review*, noted that "the building blocks of corporate strategy are not products and markets, but business processes. Competitive success depends on transforming a company's key processes into strategic capabilities that consistently provide superior value to the customer."[5] The open, networked, or client/server infrastructure represents the information technology enabling environment for business processes.

Process Improvement Approaches

Two views are emerging on how to go about improving business processes. The first approach falls into the category of major business transformation through business reengineering. This approach consists of analyzing and radically redesigning the work flow associated with the business functions of an organization. According to a J. P. Morgan research study[6] completed in September 1993, the market for business process reengineering services is growing at an annual rate of about 22 percent. Thus the market, estimated to be about $1.5 billion in 1994, should grow to over $2.13 billion by 1996.

The second approach focuses on changing and enhancing business processes incrementally. This particular approach is also growing rapidly, for a couple of reasons. First, it steers away from the notion of major redesign or transformation. Second, a number of techniques and tools have emerged that allow organizations to take the incremental approach in ways that are viewed as less risky than major reengineering projects. This emerging approach is known as *work flow analysis*. The term *business process reengineering* has also loosely been used.

Work flow analysis addresses problems related to how "work" actually takes place. This is accomplished by evaluating, designing, and automating the interactions between people and the sharing of information. The market research firm of IDC/Avante[7] estimates that the work flow software market alone is growing at over 100 percent per year. The market in 1993 was estimated at about $0.7 billion and is expected to reach about $2.5 billion by 1996. Other market research studies forecast that the services and consulting opportunities associated with work flow analysis range from $1 to $3 for every dollar spent on work flow software.

Collaborative Strategies, based in San Francisco, describes *groupware* as "a term loosely used to describe a group of technologies that mediate interpersonal collaboration through the computer." Groupware includes the following categories of products that organizations are using:

Category	Example
Work flow	IBM's FlowMark
Document image management	FileNet
Work group utilities	Microsoft Workgroup for Windows
Groupware development tools	Oracle Office
Shared-screen products	ShowMe
Shared-memory products	Lotus Notes
Calendaring and scheduling	IBM's Time and Place/2
Group decision support systems	Ventana's Group System V
Group editing	Face-to-face

Work flow is commonly lumped into the groupware category. How is it different from other groupware? Work flow automates the information flows and the processing of business tasks within an organization. True work flow automation manages not just the organization and presentation of information but its intelligent routing, processing, and tracking. This category of software technology does not try to eliminate paper transactions altogether. Rather, it focuses on electronically capturing the information flow involved in processing transactions.

Work flow management has a number of major functions. In particular, it:

- Notifies each user that a required step or action is to be completed
- Provides each user with the proper tools to complete tasks
- Allows each user to see where each work task fits into the overall process
- Manages the specific reminders, alerts the user to them, and follows up to keep the process moving in a timely fashion
- Automatically initiates regular process steps
- Integrates itself easily with the user's existing systems and procedures
- Routes work items in a parallel flow
- Provides cycle times and individual worker productivity statistics to help management eliminate bottlenecks
- Readily identifies the person responsible for each part of a process

Work flow software solutions have been categorized into three groups, according to the kinds of tasks being undertaken. *Administrative tasks* include such items as expense reports, sales proposals, purchase requests, and check requests. This software environment often employs an E-mail architecture, is geared to simple processes with minimal structure, and is highly distributed in nature. *Ad-hoc tasks* include strategic planning, product design reviews, and project-oriented functions. This environment is characterized by a document database architecture which is not highly structured, but is complex. *Production environment tasks* include loan applications, insurance underwriting, and mortgage processing. The production environment often uses relational database architectures and tends to be highly complex and structured.[8]

The number of participants in the work flow market is increasing rapidly. These competitors all tend to concentrate on certain aspects of the market. A general categorization of the primary vendors is given below.[6] Keep in mind that individual vendors' products positioning is dynamic.

Vendor	**Focus**
Action Technologies, Inc.	Development tools, work flow manager, and process modeler
AT&T/NCR	Development tools and work flow manager
Beyond Incorporated	Forms

Bull HN Information Systems, Inc.	Document and image
Delrina Corporation	Forms
Digital Equipment Corporation	Ad hoc work flows
Edify Corporation	Development tools
FileNet Corporation	Image, data, and text
Hewlett-Packard	Product data management for manufacturing
Image Business Systems	Documents and image
IBM Corporation	Development tools, work flow manager, and process modeler
Jetform Corporation	Forms
Lotus Development Corporation	Document sharing
Microsoft Corporation	Forms
Portfolio Technologies, Inc.	Documents
Quality Decision Management, Inc.	Forms
Reach Software	Development tools and process modeler
Recognition/Plexus International, Inc.	Process modeler, development tools, and work flow manager
Siemens-Nixdorf Information Systems	Work flow manager
Staffware	Work flow manager
UES, Inc.	Process modeler and work flow manager
Verimation	Forms
ViewStar Corporation	Development tools and work flow manager
Wang Laboratories, Inc.	Development tools and work flow manager
WordPerfect Corporation	Forms
Workflow, Incorporated	Documents
XSoft, division of Xerox	Process modeler and work flow manager for documents

Work flow automation is becoming a significant technology because it is comprised of a set of software products that provide an open platform for enabling work flow processes across the entire organization. The work flow metaphor goes beyond the traditional view of how to go about capturing and analyzing business processes. Today's view is more holistic in that it elevates the "people" part of business processes to a greater level of importance than do the traditional information engineering, object-oriented, and data modeling approaches. The work flow paradigm puts the focus on getting the right information at the right time to the right people. This is the very core of its philosophy and product design. The objective is to provide a way to enable business processes so that internal as well as external customers are satisfied with timely service, support, and products.

How is this done? Depending on the choice of technology, it often starts with a process model. What does a process model do? It consists of tools to capture and provide a graphical depiction of current and/or proposed processes. These process maps or models are used to analyze the flow of work in an organization, including the identification of who is doing what work (roles and responsibilities). In addition, some tools allow the user to run an animation of the process to determine where and if any bottlenecks can occur. Other work flow products identify work flow and process cycle times so that the cost or value of each process can be estimated.

Once a process map or model is created, an application builder can be used to build business applications on the basis of models or maps. The builder usually consists of tools for identifying and describing the forms and information used by the performers of the process. The builder also defines other relationships among the work flow, the interface to external systems, and the main functions of data that are specific to the business process. The work flow manager allows existing hardware and software to be integrated into a work flow system. During the execution of processes, users are presented with lists of activities they are to perform. Work flow managers are designed to support the separation of process logic and application logic and application data. Some work flow managers, such as IBM's FlowMark, are based on object-oriented technology. Many work flow managers can manage work flow not specific to any application area. They can be used to manage processes in many business areas—including forms, images, text, and data—and in many industries.

As business processes become more and more complex, planning and managing all the activities and resources involved in getting the job done become more challenging. Controlling the flow of work in a company requires time, diverse skills, and knowledge. Some critical issues for clients to consider include the following:[9]

1. Defining processes is a complicated exercise. The goal is to expend the effort once, and then have only to maintain and improve the processes.

2. Complex processes easily become hard to deal with. Managing complex processes can require large amounts of money, time, and expertise. Moreover, even the best-run processes can falter when a key person, who knows the details, is away.

3. Keeping track of processes is vitally important. Documenting process-es is necessary and it is an effort above and beyond the "real work" of a company, its revenue-producing activities.

4. As processes evolve, bottlenecks can arise that were not there before. Or a change to a complex process can create a deadlock. Fixing a process after it is broken is time-consuming and expensive.

5. Once a process has been developed, it may become apparent that con-siderable effort might be saved if parts of the process could be used in other areas of the company. Duplication of effort is expensive, and it often seems unavoidable, or sometimes is even unrecognized.

6. ISO 9000, British Standard 5750, and U.S. government requirements for defined processes require complete and thorough documentation of a company's processes—documentation that is available for inspection. Such documentation is expensive to produce and hard to maintain.

7. As business conditions change, a company needs to react quickly. It will need to refine existing processes, invent new ones, and try them out. This can be difficult, especially if current processes are not fully under control.

Figure 27-2 summarizes the key issues in process and work flow eval-uation.

Consulting Opportunities

There are many types of consulting opportunities available in conjunc-tion with process improvement. They generally fall into four categories:

- Content-based consulting, or providing advice on the basis of conclu-sions from data gathered within and outside the client organization
- Expert advice, or providing assistance on the basis of conclusions from experiences
- Facilitation consulting, or assisting the client in reaching its own con-clusions
- Educational consulting, or providing skills or knowledge transfer to the client

For most clients, process problems fall into one or all of the following categories:

What business do they want to be in and what should they do?

Where are they or how are they doing what they are doing today?

1. Business Issues
   a. How are reengineering or process improvement projects now being handled? How will they be handled?
   b. How is bureaucracy being handled?
   c. What is your client doing to focus on the needs of the customer?
   d. Is the focus of the work efforts of your client around the customer and providing value?
   e. How are productivity gains or improvements going to be addressed and improved?
   f. How are the business functions going to be integrated across different organizational units geographies to minimize duplication?
   g. What techniques are being used to identify key issues and how work processes are currently being performed?
   h. How will the desired work processes be documented and converted to executable processes?

2. Customer Issues
   a. Does your client clearly understand what the criteria are for satisfying customers regarding products and/or services, e.g., pricing, terms and conditions, delivery time, response time?
   b. How is the identification and documentation of the roles and responsibilities of employees established so that it maps to the customers' needs?

3. Process and Work Issues
   a. Who are the business processes and work being performed for?
   b. What is accomplished in a process or the work that is performed?
   c. Is the work performed in a process adding value for the customer?
   d. Who has to be satisfied by the work that is performed in the process?
   e. Are the criteria for satisfying the customer (internal and/or external) clearly understood?
   f. Is there a need for the business processes, that is, the rules and guidelines in use or proposed, to be documented and analyzed, e.g., ISO standards, US government standards?

Figure 27-2 Process improvement checklist.

g. How are the roles of the employee linked to the business processes or work to be performed, the data, the business applications and access to the information systems? How is this documented and put into action?

4. User Issues
   a. Do the employees or users clearly understand the entire work process and why they are doing what they do?
   b. Do the employees clearly understand the expectations of their internal and/or external customers and the work they have to perform for them?
   c. Do the employees have access to the right information anywhere, anytime to satisfy internal and/or external customers so they are empowered to perform their job?
   d. How is work coordinated across a team or group of users so that each team member knows who is responsible for what, by when, etc.?

5. Application Rules
   a. Are traditional business information systems inadequate in handling functional applications such as accounting and order processing?
   b. Are personal productivity tools like spreadsheets not improving contributions of individuals?
   c. How are employees supported in doing their work? Are they assisted in being more productive? Is status information provided on current work either automatically or on request?
   d. How are business rules and guidelines provided and complied with in an application?
   e. How is information about the work to be done, in process, or completed provided and communicated to the employees performing the work?

6. Data Issues
   a. How are the people who perform work, the programs, and data they use, coordinated so that workers can perform these jobs well?
   b. How is data accessed, integrated, and managed for spreadsheets, word-processing, databases, forms, electronic mail, images, documents, and line of business applications, etc.?

Figure 27-2 (*Continued*) Process improvement checklist.

---

7. Information Technologies

   a. Are departmental and enterprise-wide multinode business processes, applications, and data handled today? How in the future?
   b. How are business rules-based procedures, no matter how complicated handled? How well?
   c. How do current information systems coordinate or handle other external objects, such as documents, forms, and images, deciding when they are needed and invoking them accordingly?
   d. How do current information systems apply timescales to each stage of business procedures and then issue reminders to workers?

Figure 27-2   (*Continued*)   Process improvement checklist.

Once they know where they want to go, how do they do it or enable it to happen?

Who has the skills to make the change happen?

How do you know where your clients are in their business decision-making process and what the content of your conversation ought to be? It helps to find out if they are pondering business strategies, process strategies, information technology strategies, or implementation strategies. Once you've identified what stage they seem to be, you can determine if their needs mesh with your firm's business capabilities and skills.

Notes

1. Michael Hammer and James Champy, *Reengineering the Corporation* (New York: Harper Collins, 1993).

2. Jessica Lipnack and Jeffrey Stamps, *The TeamNet Factor* (Essex Junction, Vt.: Oliver Wright Publications, 1993).

3. Don Tapscott and Art Caston, *Paradigm Shift: The New Promise of Information Technology* (New York: McGraw-Hill, 1993).

4. Tom Peters, *Liberation Management* (New York: Alfred A. Knopf, 1992).

5. George Stalk et al., "Competing on Capabilities," *Harvard Business Review,* March–April 1992.

6. Client/Server Technology Study, September 1993, J. P. Morgan, New York, NY.

7. IDC/Avante Workflow Study, 1993.

8. For a detailed listing of work flow technology providers, see *New Tools for New Times: The Workflow Paradigm* (Alameda, Ca.: Future Strategies, 1994).

9. Introducing IBM FlowMark for OS/2, GH19-8215-00.

28

Change Management

Victor Bond

President, ChangeNet
Rancho Santa Fe, California

Our world now seems defined more by varieties of chaos and change than by varieties of stability. From the demise of the Soviet Union and the sweeping changes in South Africa, to the troubles facing General Motors, IBM, and Sears, to the chaos and confusion of our individual lives, it seems that change is overwhelming our ability to cope emotionally, to manage our affairs, and to plan for our future.

Speaking of the risks and opportunities facing the Times Mirror Company, vice president of strategic development Efrem Zimbalist III noted, "We're trying to predict demand for products that haven't been developed yet for people who in some cases haven't been born; other than that, we're sure of what we're doing." Add to this all the change taking place in the consulting industry itself and it becomes clear that this is a time of great promise and great peril for those who would consult on the management of change.

The Good News...and the Bad

The promise lies in part in the fact that there is greater expressed client need than ever for guidance in coping with, managing, and planning for change. There is even greater unexpressed, inchoate need for help in this area, lying just under the surface for employees who are frustrated, projects that aren't working, and strategies that never quite jell. The opportunity in this area is much greater that it seems, and it seems enormous.

Simply put, modern institutions are in states of constant turmoil, driven by ruthless competition and even more ruthless consumers of services and products, as well as rapidly shifting social and regulatory environments. A cursory scan of business literature reveals that the incidence of key phrases like *change management* and *business transformation* has risen virtually exponentially over the last 5 years. Further, this phenomenon shows no signs of abating, unlike many other briefly popular management fascinations like *corporate culture* and *intrapreneuring*.

The promise of change management is also driven by the crisis-induced willingness of business and other institutions to actually take the risks of applying radically new approaches to the organization and management of their enterprises. By far the most significant development in this area is the concept of reengineering: the radical redesign and reimplementation of institutional processes. Whether the buzzword or phrase is *reengineering* or *process innovation* or *business transformation*, the points are always the same: Discard outmoded, inappropriate, and dysfunctional ideas and methods in favor of thoroughly new perspectives on the job at hand. Then, because time is short and resistance is great, rigorously and aggressively apply these perspectives to the solution of fundamental institutional problems.

All this, of course, is much easier said than done. Also, because many businesses and institutions have tried radical change and failed, many potential clients realize that they need help with the change process itself, not only with the organizational processes that they sought to transform. This realization is occurring at the same time that another problem is increasing: the general crisis of management and leadership in complex organizations. This problem has been exacerbated by the fact that there are many opportunities for managers to experience institutional change but very few opportunities—academic or otherwise—for managers to learn about change itself, and thus become better prepared to deal with changes that they have not yet seen. There has simply never been a greater need for insights, guidance, and training in this critical area.

This is the good news. The bad news is that the very chaos and confusion that drive the need for change management services make the creation and delivery of such services tougher than ever. There are too many questions chasing too few answers, and there are too many insights, theories, techniques, and approaches chasing too little management attention, absorptive capacity, or application skill.

The irony is that virtually every manager needs—and very many realize that they need—solutions to their complex change management problems, but most of them absolutely require that these answers be simple, straightforward, and easy to apply. Many would also like these answers to be predictable (even algorithmic), reliable, and readily transferable to different groups and different types of problems. These needs—coupled with the serious institutional circumstances from which they arise—often produce client environments for which few consultants are prepared to deal: maximum latitude to respond, minimal margin for error.

It seems that there are virtually unlimited definitions for change management—from managing change in technical systems like communications networks, to managing change in human attitudes, behaviors, and organization. And there are as many or more discrete disciplines which are relevant to the management of change: from applied psychology to social anthropology to project management. Finally, there are as many approaches to applying these combinations of definitions and disciplines as there are consultants and clients: from top down to bottom up, from directive to participative—and everything in between, sometimes all at once. There are no generally accepted standards for the successful application of any of this. In fact, it is often not at all clear when a change effort has truly succeeded or failed. Though there are usually measures of success established at the beginnings of these efforts, these may no longer be relevant or effective measures at the ends.

The results of substantial change efforts are rarely those outcomes which are projected at the beginning, and, even when these outcomes do occur, they are never the only significant ones. And, in this world of "white water," when are the beginnings and endings anyway? In this field, it can sometimes seem that anything goes, everything is possible, and nothing important can be measured with finality. This can be as frustrating for consultants as it certainly is for clients.

The intention of this chapter is to address the interests and requirements of the widest possible range of change management consultants. The chapter will first describe the three key segments of the market for change management services and then identify and discuss issues and tools which apply to the basics of change management.

Market Segmentation

The market for change management services may be segmented into three nonexclusive areas:

- Managing stress
- Transforming structure
- Creating strategy

Virtually all change efforts include some component of all these segments. However, each segment typically addresses a different change management concern, has a slightly different target audience, requires different consulting and training skills, and has a different required scope within the organization.

Managing Stress

The stress management segment addresses the problems associated with human beings' efforts to cope emotionally and behaviorally with the rigors of organizational change. Stress reduction and emotional and physical coping strategies and techniques are regular requirements in this area, and are often offered as part of employee health and personal development programs. These approaches are relevant and appropriate for everyone in a changing organization, but the scope of such work need not be greater than a few people (or one person) at a time.

Stress management can significantly and directly involve the largest number of people. The target audience is everyone. It is therefore the most generalized of the segments. Managing stress and coping with change are defined more by the nature of human beings than by the particular industry or economic circumstances of a client. Insights into psychology and human behavior are important here, as is empathy: the ability to identify with and reflect the feelings of others.

For years, this segment essentially defined change management. Though change has been a constant in institutional life, change management often referred only to the management of the human consequences of change, after the fact. That is, until the next segment—structure—came to dominate.

Transforming Structure

The structure transformation segment addresses the problems associated with modifying the structure of activity in an organization. This effort may include process reengineering or innovation, organizational redesign and implementation, systems and network change management, personnel reductions, and mergers, acquisitions, or divestments. The activity may involve the entire institution, though it may be applicable only to a particular group or to a few groups within the institution. Changes in structure by definition apply to groups and not to individuals alone, though of course all the individuals in the restructured groups are affected.

Effective structural change requires analytical and intuitive insight into the dynamics of systems, whether they be process or work flows or the dynamics of corporate culture. This area also includes, as a necessary component, the management of stress and the other emotional consequences of change. The target audience for these efforts are primarily the relevant functional, departmental, and unit personnel, though senior, policy-level management is typically involved to provide guidance and support.

With the advent of process reengineering, process innovation, and business transformation, structure has emerged as the dominant change management segment. But even this area must be driven by decisions and actions from top institutional leadership if they are to be successful. This requirement has given rise to a shift in the methods and expectations of strategy development—leading logically to the next segment.

Creating Strategy

This segment of change management has emerged from the collapse of the *organizational action cycle,* illustrated in Figure 28-1. This cycle describes the series of activities that institutions (and for that matter, individuals) might go through to manage their affairs successfully. The

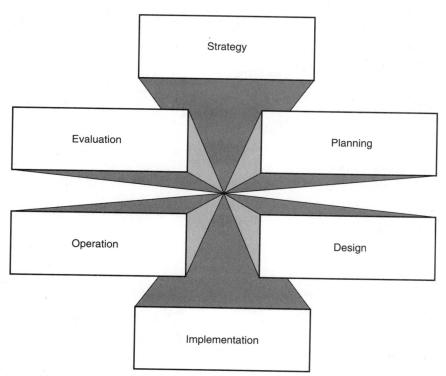

Figure 28-1 The organizational action cycle.

cycle takes time to complete, but in this relentlessly competitive and time-pressured world, it has become clear that the cycle is collapsing in on itself. There is simply not enough time to work through each step sequentially and remain organizationally relevant and effective. There are, for instance, numerous firms whose strategic horizon—the length of time *for which* they plan—is essentially equivalent to their strategic planning cycle—the time *within which* they plan. This means that, by the time their strategic plan is complete, it is almost immediately irrelevant and obsolete. The collapsing of this process means that strategic planning and implementation must take place essentially simultaneously.

The critical consequence of this is that both those who plan and those who implement and execute the strategy must be able to change fast enough to respond effectively to the very influences which caused the traditional strategic planning and implementation process to collapse. Conversely, and profoundly relevant to institutional survival, strategies must consider and reflect the capacity of the organization to generate and respond to change.

In corporate strategy, change capacity has become as important as financial capacity, and this insight, along with the tools to apply it, is slowly creeping into the executive suite. This change management segment has the broadest scope—the entire institution and all those associated with it—and the narrowest key audience—senior management. Finally, the strategy segment is by far the most institutionally specific. It depends utterly on an expert grasp of industry, financial, human resources, and environmental influences. It also requires the skills of the two other segments: stress and structure.

Present and Future Tense

Each of the segments discussed here has present and future incarnations. The change management consultant must always address the changes that are happening in the present—to both the client and the consultant—and those that may happen in the future, including those which are planned for, predicted by, or surprising to client and consultant. So there is always a balancing of present and future tenses in any discussion of the management of change.

Similarly, none of these segments ever exists as a phenomenon exclusive of the other segments, though each clearly may define a somewhat separate consulting requirement. Always remember, however, that each successive segment (as depicted here) includes the preceding one. So the management of stress begs the issues of structure and strategy, but does not require that they be addressed by the consultant. The development and management of strategy, however, requires consideration of both structural transformation and stress management to be effective.

The Basics of Change Management

There are four areas which concern any client and any consultant struggling with the management of change:

- Change readiness
- Power and sponsorship
- Transition
- Communication

Change Readiness

One of the most difficult challenges of dealing with major change is that neither the participants nor the leaders fully grasp the impact that the change is going to have on them as a group and as individuals.

The fundamental difficulty of assessing change readiness is that the transition from the present organizational state to the future *always* has significant unpredictable characteristics. Add this insight to the fact that it is extremely difficult to predict our or others' responses to *predictable* circumstances and we can imagine how suspect any pretransition state evaluations of readiness are likely to be. One phenomenon is apparent, however, and that is that serious consideration of the challenges of going through major change is itself beneficial to change preparation. This consideration must evaluate:

- The *competence* of the change team and the larger organization to implement the change
- The *commitment*—largely but not only emotional—of the change team and the overall organization to implement the change

The objectives of this process are to begin to assess the organization's readiness to realize its change project and, as a consequence of the discussions motivated by this assessment, to become better prepared for the change process. The question of change readiness is one of the most difficult to address.

Most people who do not actively oppose a given change project believe that they are "ready" for the change. Of course, many do in fact oppose change, and their opposition and resistance usually are revealed in the most cursory "change readiness" assessment. The same cannot often be said about many others who are involved in major change. Usually, people who think or feel unprepared for change actually are not ready. The biggest problem of "change readiness" is that many (even most) of those who feel or even "test" ready for significant change are not at all prepared.

In the first place, it is essentially impossible to predict the challenges that will confront the participants in major change efforts. This is, after all, one of the major reasons that many of us avoid change in the first place. Human beings typically want less uncertainty, not more. In the second place, there is the subtle but dangerous euphoria that can often result from *eagerness* for change, regardless of actual preparation. Senior managers, who are more removed from the practical implications of major change, are often particularly vulnerable to this euphoria.

These phenomena in combination are among the deadliest threats to significant change. When confronted by change realities, uncertainty and euphoria usually result in disillusionment, and often are the bases for retrenchment (retreating) or, even worse, project revisionism (declaring victory and then retreating).

So there are two goals of this change readiness activity, one straightforward and one deeper and far more complex. They are:

1. Identification of those who are clearly not ready for the change, in terms of either their competence or their commitment.

2. Deeper consideration, on the parts of those who seem ready, of the actual possible consequences of the change effort. This is particularly important for the leaders of the change effort, who are (ironically) often more vulnerable to the underestimation of their readiness. Evaluation of consequences is the most effective route to accurate self-assessment and the development of individual change *resilience.*

The first of these goals is fairly straightforward and can be addressed by thoughtful application of the *change readiness matrix,* illustrated in Figure 28-2. Note that this is a "two-quadrant" matrix, since the vertical axis has no negative component. This axis represents *competence* to achieve the change and runs from "incompetent" through "barely competent" to "highly competent." The horizontal axis represents *commitment* to achieve the change and runs from "committed opposition" through "indifference" (0) to "committed support."

This matrix may be applied to individuals or to groups, such as facilitators or salespeople. The workshop group should first identify the group or groups to which the matrix should be applied. They may then:

- Privately assess and position individuals or groups on the matrix

- Display their assessment on a public matrix, perhaps using adhesive dots color-coded to the appropriate groups or individuals

- Discuss anomalies or surprises

The second change readiness goal—deeper consideration of the actual consequences of the change effort—is much more difficult and is intensely personal. Your own judgment is the most important guide in this sensitive area. Beware of efforts to quantify the readiness of individuals or

Figure 28-2 The change readiness matrix.

organizations to change. Change readiness is a highly subjective condition, and should be approached as such.

Encouraging change participants to discuss the following key questions can be very effective:

"What risks do you feel that you are personally taking with this change effort?"

"What are the worst things that can happen to you if this change effort fails?"

"What are the worst things that can happen to you if the change effort succeeds?"

"Have you ever actually *witnessed* the kinds of change that will be necessary in order for the effort to succeed?"

"If you have not, why do you believe these changes are possible?"

"What if they are not?"

"Is this change effort worth risking your job or your career for? Why or why not?"

"What events or circumstances (including the attitudes of others) would cause you to quit the project, actually or emotionally?"

This kind of questioning and discussion will encourage serious consideration of the question of readiness, which is far more important than any effort to measure—and quantify—the extent to which an organization and its individuals are ready to change.

Power and Sponsorship

Power—the ability to act—is one of the most misunderstood and confusing concepts of organizational life. *Sponsorship*—the willingness and ability to act in support of specified goals, organizations, or individuals—is similarly misunderstood. The objectives of this section are to:

- Clarify the nature of power and sponsorship in organizations
- Evaluate the power and sponsorship available to the workshop organization and the change effort in particular
- Develop approaches to maintain and enhance the power and sponsorship available to the change effort

We will first examine organizational power and then relate that discussion to sponsorship, one of the key applications of organizational power.

The Dimensions of Power.   The following model, based on the acronym POWERR, describes the critical dimensions of organizational power:

Personality power: Who you are, your individual characteristics.

Organizational power: Where you are in the power structure of an organization. This is power invested in you by the organization, and it generally correlates with your hierarchical position or your function(s) in the organization.

Will power: What you believe, and how you believe it—the power of conviction.

Expert power: What you know—the power of knowledge or expertise.

Relationship power: Who you know—the power of your relationship(s) with other people.

Resource power: What you have—your control over specific resources (related to, but not limited to, organizational power).

It should be noted that *physical coercion* is not included here, because this power is generally applicable only in the context of police, military, penal, or illegal organizations.

Organizational power is the aggregation of individual power for specific ends. Total organizational power may be *greater or less* than the sum of the powers of its individuals' power. Relationship power—as in the case of collective action—is often *greater*, whereas Expert power—

because it can be difficult to identify, coordinate, and apply collective knowledge—is often *less*. Therefore, organizational power can, and often must, be assessed on an individual basis.

The Individual Power Assessment. The *individual power assessment* is a scale that enables change participants to evaluate and discuss their individual and organizational power. This is a straightforward individual assessment of the ability to act in support of a change—or any other—effort. Participants should respond to each dimension on a scale of 1 to 10, where 1 is "highly negative," 10 is "highly positive," and 5 is "don't know" or "neutral."

This tool is most effective when it is applied to a specific set of proposed or required actions. It is much less meaningful and can be frustrating to apply in a general or overall fashion. Here are the key questions, by dimension. Each should be given a 1 to 10 rating.

Personality power: "What impact do your personal characteristics have on your ability to act?"

Organizational power: "What impact does your organizational position or function have on your ability to act?"

Will power: "What impact does your personal conviction about the change effort have on your ability to act?"

Expert power: "What impact does your knowledge or expertise have on your ability to act?"

Relationship power: "What impact do your relationships with others have on your ability to act?"

Resource power: "What impact does your control or resources have on your ability to act?"

There are a number of ways that clients can use this assessment. First, they can perform brief personal assessments to stimulate group discussion and individual development. Second, clients may follow up the assessment by responding to these additional questions:

"How effectively is my personal power applied to the change project?"

"Is my impact sufficient to ensure the success of our efforts?"

"How can I increase my impact on the project?"

"How can I increase the power of others on my team or those in a position to help my team?"

Finally, clients may discuss the change effort as a whole by responding to the following questions:

"Do we have sufficient power to successfully complete our project?"

"If not, in what areas and in what ways can we sufficiently increase our power?"

"What can we do to increase the power of others who are or might be able to help us?"

Again, it is most effective to focus these assessments as specifically as possible on the *actual tasks* that the client must perform. It can be very frustrating to discuss these issues "in general."

The Role of Sponsorship.   The question of increasing the power of others introduces the concept of *sponsorship* and the identification and evaluation of those who can assist the change effort. *Sponsors* are those who are motivated and able to act in support of goals, the organization, or individuals. Thus, the critical dimensions of sponsorship are motivation and ability.

There will always be those who are motivated to help but cannot, and there will be those who can help but won't. There will also usually be those who are motivated, for whatever reasons, to obstruct a change. This is particularly so when the effort to change constitutes a threat to established interests, as significant change always does.

It is essential that teams evaluate the potential for sponsorship within their organization. The goals of sponsorship evaluation are to:

- Identify those who are able to significantly help (and therefore, by definition, also to significantly impede) the change effort
- Assess their motivations to help or impede
- Develop plans to maintain or enhance existing sponsor relationships and to create new ones where possible

This activity is important, because teams rarely spend sufficient time discussing their sponsorship relations. As a result, most team members are only vaguely aware of most of the critical sponsor relationships that already exist, and are even less sensitive to new sponsorship possibilities. Also, most teams leave sponsor development to the formal leadership of the organization. Sponsorship itself is often viewed in simple hierarchical terms. As a result of these common perspectives on sponsorship, opportunities to widen and strengthen support for the organization and the change effort are often completely overlooked.

Sponsorship is often an intensely personal relationship. Projects or organizations are rarely sponsored for their own sake alone, without some associated personal sponsorship of the leadership. Sponsors usually need to be comfortable, if not enthusiastic, about the people who are responsible for an effort. This dimension of sponsorship can be a delicate subject to discuss in a group environment.

Because of these factors, there is a tendency to conduct a rather formal review of the organization's hierarchical sponsorship. Formal evaluation can be a waste of the group's time, unless the group as a whole is unfamiliar with these issues, in which case the information sharing alone could be valuable.

When a consultant is called in to assist the process, he or she must exert great effort to encourage the group to "think outside the fishtank" for present or potential sponsors. There is usually a wide range of potential sponsors who are outside the normal hierarchy but who are able to give significant—often informal—support to the organization. Remember that indirect influence can be as important as or more important than direct action. The group should seek to cultivate both.

Finally, many people feel that attention paid to cultivating sponsorships is political and therefore is not related to "getting the job done." For these people *realpolitik* may seem like cynical manipulation, and they may therefore find it distasteful. The facilitator should be sensitive and responsive to these sentiments. After all, sometimes they reflect the truth.

The eternal truths of power and sponsorship, however, are that there are infinite requirements for the use of the very finite power in any organization and that life is not fair. Support does not always go to those who are "most deserving." It usually does go to those who are most diligent and thoughtful in its pursuit. A mechanism by which we can examine sponsor relations is the *sponsorship matrix,* illustrated in Figure 28-3.

The matrix is designed to organize the client's thoughts about the key characteristics of sponsorship: *ability to support* and *motivation to support.* The vertical axis—ability—runs from "no potential impact" to "high potential impact" (there is no negative component of this axis). The horizontal axis—motivation—runs from "negative motivation," through "indifference" (0), to "positive motivation." The task is to identify individuals who are able to affect the change effort significantly and to put plans in place to get those people into, or keep them as far as possible into, the positive zone.

First, participants should list those individuals who are able to have a significant positive or negative impact on the change effort or the organization in general. This process will require a discussion about the individuals who can significantly affect the organization. The conclusions of this discussion will often be not at all obvious. Usually, in fact, team members will learn things about their sponsorship that they did not know before, and they will learn them *together.*

Do not underestimate the value of this discussion to the team. Often the team benefit is the most important reason for this exercise. Participants should discuss the nature of each individual sponsor's impact and

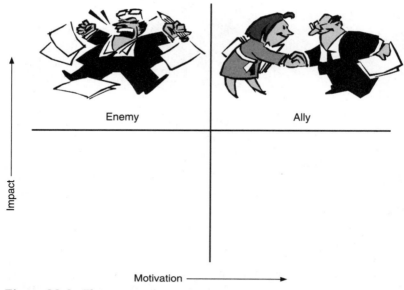

Enemy   Ally

Impact

Motivation ──────────►

Figure 28-3 The sponsorship matrix.

position his or her name appropriately on the matrix. Finally, if time and
circumstance allow, participants should discuss the methods by which
the individuals they have named might become more supportive or
maintain their present support for the organization. In particular, the
change team may assign the assessment and monitoring of sponsors to
members of the group.

Transition

A critical issue in change management is dealing effectively with the difficult and emotional transition from the present state of organizational
affairs to the future. One of the most important contributors to our
understanding of the human response to great stress and therefore resistance to change is Elizabeth Kubler-Ross. In writing on the human
response to impending death,[1] Dr. Kubler-Ross identified five stages
which have been found to describe the response to dramatic change:

- Denial and isolation
- Anger
- Bargaining
- Depression and resignation
- Acceptance

These five stages translate into the organizational arena as well. Simply put, organizational transformation is *traumatic,* both operationally and individually. These predictable stages are windows into the behavior of individuals and groups undergoing the trauma of change. *Organizational trauma* may be characterized by four types of loss that occur during times of organizational upheaval:

1. *Loss of the capacity to act* is caused by loss of power when organizations are destabilized and individuals are displaced.

2. *Loss of sensory input* results from changes in the amounts or types of information available to the individual.

3. *Loss of support* occurs when ties to valued subordinates, superiors, and networks are disrupted.

4. *Loss of love* in organizations involves the loss of familiar work relationships, products, and work settings.[2]

Individual reactions to these trauma seem to follow the Kubler-Ross stages of response.

Denial and Isolation. Denial is a natural outgrowth of the failure of most individuals to anticipate—and thus begin to emotionally prepare for—traumatic events in their lives. For most people "It could *never happen* to me" all too quickly transforms itself to "It *hasn't happened* to me" when disaster actually occurs. This denial is usually accompanied by isolation from any part of the environment which may tend to remind the individual that the traumatic change has in fact occurred.

Denial and isolation are emotional protection for the individual and thus are often not principled or thoughtful opposition to the change, though they are often mistaken for being so. This response is also analogous to the phenomenon of psychological *flight,* which is the tendency of individuals to flee from danger. The alternative (not necessarily exclusive) phenomenon—psychological *flight*—is analogous to the next Kubler-Ross stage.

Anger. Anger is a familiar but often misinterpreted response to traumatic change. As the veil of denial falls from the eyes of the individual, and the pain of the change begins to be felt, anger is an inevitable result. Feelings of unfair treatment, resentments about past injustices, and an infinite array of other motivations serve to fuel the angry emotion. All too often, this reaction is misunderstood and wrongly taken personally by others.

Bargaining. When denial and anger fail to make the change disappear, the next line of resistance to change is bargaining. This period is an effort by the individual, in every way possible, to mitigate the impact of the change and to "buy time." To some extent, it is an extension of the tendency to deny the change, but here the denial is selective: It accepts parts of the change phenomenon and denies others. In this stage, the individual wants to "make a deal" between the change factors which seem to be inevitable and those which do not.

Depression.   Depression is the final barrier to acceptance of change, and it comes in two types. The first is *reactive,* or depression over what has been lost. The second is *anticipatory,* or depression over what is expected to be lost.

Acceptance.   In the acceptance phase, reasonably rational action on the part of the individual usually begins. Acceptance is not necessarily either happy and satisfied or unhappy and dissatisfied. What it is, is *clear:* The individual finally "sees" the truth and is dealing with it—effectively or not—as a reality.

The Kubler-Ross model is a particularly important one because it helps explain many of the otherwise confusing behaviors of people going through transition. It also helps to guide the behavior of others who seek to effectively respond to the rigors of change, either personal or organizational.

People tend to view transition as essentially a traumatic period, whose difficulties must be overcome. This is because, most of the time, the obstacles—the resistance—during transition are the greatest dangers to the success of the change effort. But there is also emotional opportunity in the transition period. The excitement and euphoria associated with dramatic, positive change can be a significant motivational force and a major spur to creativity and innovation. These energies should not be ignored during the transition discussion, particularly if the entire team is present.

The negative, traumatic aspects of transition can be viewed as a protective emotional shell, the removal of which can liberate transition participants to find their positive, supportive motivations. In any case, each transition participant will respond differently to change, and these differences must all be addressed.

The Individual Transition Assessment.   As a consultant to an organization undergoing change, you can apply the *individual transition assessment* to aid team members. Ask five basic questions:

- What actual changes will be caused in the organizational environment by a given action, such as announcing a reorganization or even announcing an award?

- What individuals are likely to be affected in any way?

- How might they feel?
- How might they behave?
- How might the change team help them deal with their feelings?

This assessment should be applied to every person in the organization whenever potential trauma is introduced. Beyond that, it should become a periodic habit to simply run through the roster and ask "How's Susan? Jack? Pierre? Polly?" Exception reviews in departmental meetings can be a good discipline. Effectiveness in this area is as much a matter of additional *focus*, as of additional insight and sensitivity.

Communication

Most of us have two basic mental models of how communication takes place: the delivery model and the dialogue model. Further, the key communications concepts of content, context, and contact can assist us in developing effective messages.

The Delivery Model.   The guiding principle of the delivery model is that the sender assumes the recipient has both received and understood the message. A good image for this model is the subpoena. When an officer of the court delivers this critical communication—usually directly to the recipient—the court assumes that the recipient will read it, understand it, and respond to it. The sender assumes the message to be clear and unambiguous. There is not, nor is there intended to be, any discussion.

We generally associate this model with organizational communications. Whether it be interoffice memos or broadcasts over internal television networks, there is one abiding belief on the part of senders: "If we send it, they will hear; if they hear it, they will listen; if they listen, they will understand; and if they understand, they will act appropriately."

The delivery model assumes an attentive, discerning audience, but it does not actually need such an audience to succeed. It must simply "get the word out" to fulfill its mission. It has the great benefit of being familiar to most organizational members, so familiar that few organizations even consider that there might be a different way to communicate. Finally, the model is highly efficient, requiring primarily the energies of distribution, and only occasionally, when the system fails, the messy task of determining whether people actually received and understood the messages that were so efficiently sent. The problem here is that the system detects failure only when there is evidence of specific miscommunication traceable to the delivery. Thousands of *actually failed* communications are never found, and end up disrupting things later.

For this last reason, delivery is meaningfully less expensive than less organized and less predictable modes of transferring messages. The basic idea here is that communication is easy, as long as connection is made.

The Dialogue Model.   The dialogue model of communication is more like a successful conversation between two people. The guiding principle here is that both parties must listen as carefully as they speak in order to have any chance of understanding each other. (By the way, the delivery model is also alive and well in interpersonal communication, as any of us who have seen two or three people "talk at" each other can attest.)

Effective dialogue is a very simple concept that is extremely difficult to implement. Dialogue requires attentive and articulate participants who are motivated to understand. Significant dialogue is a rare occurrence. Few of us encounter it often, even when we think we do. It can be hard to tell if real dialogue is taking place, anyway.

Dialogue is highly efficient eventually, but highly inefficient in the short run. The sooner that product designers struggle to understand manufacturing and marketing, the more efficiently the product will be produced later. But those interminable meetings go on: "Can't anybody make a *decision* around here?" Dialogue is also much more expensive than other forms of communication, primarily because it takes so much more time. In short, dialogue is difficult no matter what we do, and in the best of circumstances.

Content, Context, and Contact.   The key communications concepts of: content, context, and contact can assist work groups in their efforts to send effective messages to their constituencies. Simply put, the content, or *explicit* portion, of a message is often far less important than the *implicit* component, which includes the context within which the message is communicated and the *way* that the message is communicated, or the contact.

The best-known illustration of this difference is nonverbal communication. It is generally believed that, in normal discourse, our actual noninflected words communicate less than 25 percent of what our audience understands. The rest of our message is conveyed through contact (the tone and inflection of our voice, our appearance, and the position of our body), and context (the situation in which we are communicating and our relationship with the recipient(s) of our message). And all of this is subject to *noise,* or the interference that results from other, conflicting messages or distractions in the communications environment. These implicit factors dominate our communication with others.

The problem is that we rarely take implicit communication into account when we are attempting to convey a message. Consider this example:

- There are at least four dictionary definitions of the word *fire*: (1) combustion, (2) employment termination, (3) shoot, as with a gun, and (4) harden, as with ceramics. This is *content*.

- When inflection and emphasis are added, "FIRE!!!" takes on a narrower meaning. Now the speaker probably means combustion, and maybe shoot, but not the others. This is *contact*.

- If someone says "FIRE!!!" in a crowded theater, the meaning is clear: The theater is on fire—get out! This is *context–situation*.

- If a child yells "FIRE!!!" and an adult says "There's no fire!" the message—to different people—will be entirely different: "Maybe there is a fire, but it's probably a joke." This is *context–relationship*. (The process can continue, with opposing messages from firefighter and police officer, or from hysterical person and calm person. Use your imagination.)

- If someone yells "FIRE" in a crowded theater, but there's a loud battle scene which completely overwhelms the voice, no message is communicated (except to those nearby who may see the person yelling). This is *context–noise*.

The Message Development Process. All the above concepts can be practically applied to real communications challenges in the *message development process*. If you are the facilitator of a team or work group, follow these steps:

1. *Identify the organization's key constituencies.* Specify the top five among them. (The exercise is valid for all constituencies, but in the interest of time, you may not want to cover more than five. Remember that part of the point of the exercise is to help the group *learn* the process.)

2. *Develop the "core" messages.* Determine which messages must be effectively communicated to each key constituency inside or outside the organization. Perform this step constituency by constituency. These messages should be crisply and explicitly stated.

3. *Discipline the process.* Many clients tend to create a rather long list of core messages—twenty to thirty, or more. Make it clear to participants that you will accept as many general messages in their initial brainstorming session as they'd like, but that they must settle for no more than *three* core messages.

4. *Encourage discussion and exploration of alternatives.* Do not allow the group to mechanically determine the core messages; the process should be put to a vote only as a last resort. With open discussion,

there may not be complete consensus on the core messages, but there will certainly be better understanding of those messages, even by those who disagree with their priority.

Flipcharts are useful for this exercise. Participants should be able to clearly see and read each suggestion as it is made. *Write clearly.*

- Headline this first chart, or series of charts, "Content."

- Consider the context within which the core messages must be communicated: the situation, the relationships between potential communicators and audiences, and the implicit messages and noise in the present environment that support, erode, or contradict the core message. Headline these charts appropriately: "Context–(Situation)," "context–(relationship)," "context–(noise)."

- Develop a "Communications Contact Envelope" for each constituency within which the group's messages can be effectively sent. This envelope should address the following message characteristics:

   Tone

   Style

   Source

   Environment

   Timing

   Coexistence with other messages

   Actions of leaders and other key communicators

This technique can be an effective and revealing method of developing (and teaching how to develop) a communications plan.

Conclusion

The management of change is perhaps the most difficult and universal of organizational challenges. Consulting on the management of change is, therefore, among the most daunting of assignments. This chapter has sought to provide the aspiring or practicing change management consultant with (1) an introduction to the marketplace for these services, (2) a discussion of the issues associated with the key areas of change management consultancy, and (3) a presentation of a few tools and techniques which have proved helpful to others.

You may consult on the management of stress, the transformation of structure, the creation of strategy, or all three together. In any case, thoughtful approaches to the challenges of change readiness, power and sponsorship, transition, and communication will ensure successful engagements and reinforce client relationships. Remember that the insights and skills discussed here are relevant and useful not only to the dedicated change management consultant, but to virtually any consultant whose work requires the client to change—and this includes virtually all management consultants.

Change management is a critical competence for management in the modern era. Change management consulting skills, therefore, are critical requirements for any management consultant. Keep in mind that organizations and individuals virtually always:

- Underestimate their readiness to change
- Fail to use all the power available to them to effect change
- Underestimate the trauma associated with major change
- Overestimate their ability to communicate effectively in the midst of change

Your clients and your practice will benefit if you develop and demonstrate first-class responses to these challenges.

Notes

1. Elizabeth Kubler-Ross, *On Death and Dying* (New York: Collier Books, 1969).
2. H. Levinson, "Easing the Pain of Personal Loss," *Harvard Business Review*, vol. 48 (1970), pp. 20–28.

29

Client Server: Evaluating System Architectures

Brian McDonald, Director
Lotus Consulting Services Group
San Francisco, California

Overview

In recent years, the role of a management consultant has expanded from identifying and solving business problems to implementing these solutions as well. This trend has accelerated in the 1990s as companies "downsize" their operations and shed staff and functions not closely related to their core business mission. At the same time, the increased importance of information systems within companies has meant that even nontechnical management consultants must have at least a working knowledge of information systems technologies, as these are frequently the platform on which their solutions are implemented. The rapid growth of the information systems practices within the largest management consultancies in the last 5 years shows the importance of this work within the management consulting industry. As a result, management consultants have found themselves in the role of system designers, in which they are doing work previously assigned to more technical people. This chapter explains how management consultants, when implementing business solutions through information systems technology, should be evaluating the system architectures that will eventually deliver these solutions to the business.

Information system designers in the modern corporate environment have a bewildering array of design choices to consider when constructing a new computer system. Although much attention has been paid recently to selecting the "best" software tools to use when planning a new system, many in the industry seem to overlook an even more fundamental requirement, which is to select the optimum system architecture on which to host the application.

It is important to look at the system architecture as consisting of two components: the physical architecture and the distribution of logical processing across it. The physical architecture includes mainframes or minicomputers, networks and communications, file or database servers, and PCs or terminals at the front end. The logical processing consists of the data, normally managed by some kind of database management system, the application logic, and the system presentation, or the user interface. How the system architecture is defined and how the processing is distributed across it can have profound effects on how well the system meets the delivery requirements of the solution for the business.

By "delivery requirements" we mean the way in which the system implements the solution and delivers it to the business. Depending on the application, and the business needs, certain architectures will be more appropriate than others for delivering a solution, *even if the application software provides exactly the same functionality*. Delivery requirements, although they may seem so obvious as to be dismissed as "apple pie and motherhood," are nevertheless frequently ignored when considering the configuration of the system architecture. As a result, they may have to be built directly into the system through software, resulting in a much more costly way of implementing them than if the actual architecture had been designed with them in mind. Over time, the author has defined the following delivery requirements and used them to design system architectures:

Availability. This refers to the percentage of time that the system is available to the user during the period when it is needed. Time when it is not available during required periods is referred to as *downtime*. Downtime can be due to hardware failures, software crashes, and communications breakdowns. Down time can also occur when the system must be shut down for system maintenance and administration procedures. It is important to note that availability approaching 100 percent is not required for all applications. For some, like electronic mail or document processing, occasional downtime will not have the same business impact that a loss of service for a trading system will have.

Efficiency. This measures the cost-effectiveness of the system in meeting user and corporate requirements. This can be evaluated by comparing the relative costs and benefits of a given system in meeting these needs as opposed to other systems. Spreadsheets, for example, can be delivered to end users on PCs or on mainframes, with differing measures of efficiency to the organization.

Performance. Performance is judged by the ability of the system to meet user and corporate processing and response time requirements. Performance is not just the sheer speed of the processor. Other factors can also impact overall system performance, such as the scalability of the system as more users are added, the peak-to-average load ratio and how the system is configured to support this, and other system bottlenecks (usually communications-related) such as LANs, WANs, and gateways. Performance requirements depend on the business solution they are fulfilling. A derivatives analysis and trading application will have much higher performance requirements than an electronic mail system.

Security. Security is implemented through the logical and physical protection of the system and its data. Logical security is implemented through passwords, automatic logouts for idle systems, and user- or role-based access control to application functionality, or data, or both. Business security is implemented through physical access control to work stations, or to remote logins to the system. Most businesses require a certain degree of security, either logical or physical, for their systems. Some systems, such as payroll and customer databases, require higher degrees of security than others, such as conference room scheduling systems.

Usability. Usability measures the ability of the user to learn and use the system. This depends not only on technological factors, such as what kind of user interface software the system is running (for example, Windows or a character-based interface), but also on what the user is used to working with, what the user will be doing with the system, and how much time the user can spare learning the system. Systems that require fast, simple, data entry of a repetitive nature will require very simple interfaces; others, such as graphics design systems, which require more complex functionality and are rarely used the same way twice, must provide a more complex interface in order to be considered usable.

Maintainability. This refers to the ease and efficiency by which the system can be operated and maintained by the system administrators. This includes such activities as batch and overnight processing, disk and processor management, capacity planning, backup and recovery, and user management.

Flexibility. This is the ability to adapt the system to meet changing business requirements. This could include adding new reports, customizing screens for particular users, changing system functionality, or linking to other systems. Some systems, such as payroll, change very little over time and have low flexibility requirements; others, such as customer support systems, are continuously evolving and must therefore be highly flexible.

Interoperability. This is a relatively recent requirement and refers to the ability of the system to integrate with new or existing technologies. This could include linking to other systems currently in place or the ability to incorporate new technologies into the architecture. Given the introduction of so many new technologies and architectures into most companies over the last 10 years, this should be looked at as an important requirement for all new systems regardless of the business requirement being fulfilled.

Scalability. This refers to the ability to change the number of users who are accessing the system with minimal cost and disruption. This can include scaling the system up for new users or scaling it down for a fewer number of users.

We will use the delivery requirements described above to evaluate different system architectures. Examining the requirements will illuminate the strengths and weaknesses of each and can be used by the management consultant to recommend the best system architecture on which to implement a solution. In each section, we will first define the architecture, then evaluate it against the delivery requirements we have described above. The three configurations we will be considering are terminal-host, client-server, and peer-to-peer.

Terminal-Host Configurations

Terminal-host is the oldest interactive processing model. It is essentially the practice of linking a number of terminals to a single logical processor at the host machine. Initially, these terminals did not have their own processing capability or memory but instead acted as remote monitors for the central computer. Until the arrival of the PC, this was the only processing configuration in use, and companies such as DEC, IBM, and Data General dominated the marketplace. It brings to mind massive air-conditioned data centers, with machines the size of London buses attended by minions of crew-cut programmers wearing horn-rimmed glasses. This is the image held by many of today's programmers, who have been weaned on PCs and Unix work stations instead of VT100s and 3270s. Although terminal-host may remind us of the olden days when the field was known as "data processing" rather than "information systems," it still is a valid architecture for many of today's systems.

Today, terminal-host systems are still used extensively in what are called "transaction-processing environments." This describes an environment in which operations against a database (transactions) are collected continuously from a number of sources. Common examples of this include airline reservation systems, banking and trading systems, and process control systems.

To understand how a terminal-host system is constructed, think of a business computer system as consisting of three basic components: presentation, application, and data. The presentation component is the user view of the system, in other words, the processing that delivers the screen view to the user. The application is the processing and logic of the software that delivers the system to the user and processes the data. Finally, the data are what the application processes and presents to the user.

In terminal-host systems, all data, application, and presentation processing occur at the back end (see Figure 29-1). Although the usual terminal-host configuration has a number of users running dumb terminals against mainframes or minicomputers, it is also possible to find terminal-host systems in which the PCs are running terminal-emulation software against a remote host. In this case, the PCs are acting as nothing more than dumb terminals, because all data, application, and presentation processing are still occurring at the back end.

Let's now look at the delivery requirements defined above to understand better the strengths and weaknesses of the terminal-host architecture.

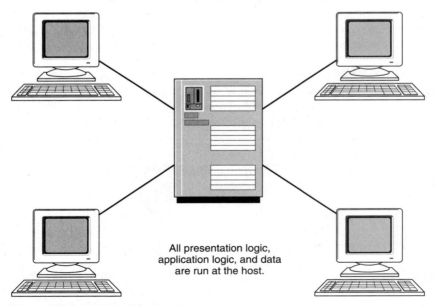

All presentation logic, application logic, and data are run at the host.

Figure 29-1 Terminal-host systems.

Availability.   Terminal-host systems are designed for high availability because of their traditional role as mission-critical corporate systems. They usually have fault-tolerance options available (such as clustered processors and mirrored disks), and the system software frequently allows on-line maintenance procedures to occur while the system is still functioning. In addition, because of their importance to critical corporate operations, such systems usually have short-reaction maintenance contracts and well-defined escalation procedures if a fault occurs.

Efficiency.   The efficiency of a terminal-host system depends on a number of factors: the kinds of applications running on the system, number of users, amount of new development required, and so on. For applications such as high-volume transaction-processing systems, terminal-host systems are very efficient. For the delivery of office automation functionality to end users, terminal-host systems are not as efficient. In general, the cost per user of a terminal-host system will be higher on a per-user basis than any other option once acquisition, development, and support costs are included. This is because of the increased competition from inexpensive midrange application servers that can offload some of their processing to front-end work stations.

Performance.   For certain applications, performance is very good. Transaction processing applications that use simple, consistent transactions can be optimized for very high throughput. Other applications such as decision support and complex transaction processing may not be as fast because the system cannot be optimized for what are essentially nonpredictable transactions.

Security.   Terminal-host systems are traditionally very secure, both physically and logically. Physical security is gained by basing all processing equipment in a single site, usually locked and in a halon-protected room. Terminals are hard-wired in a star network, and remote access through telephone lines is not allowed. Logical security is gained by controlling all system processing so that there is only a single point of entry into the system, i.e., through the operating system. Users with terminals cannot even begin to try to crack any security features until they have gotten past the operating system password. Further controls can be attached to databases and applications. In general, operating systems on traditional host systems tend to be more secure than in the Unix, OS/2, and Netware environment.

Usability.   Usability of these systems is generally thought to be lower than other systems, but it has to be noted that usability is strongly affected by the skills of the interface designer. In general, however, since all presentation processing occurs on the back end, the user interface has to be designed to address the lowest common denominator of user requirements. Otherwise, the configuration control of each user's interface would be extremely difficult to manage. In addition, the relatively higher development costs of mainframe software development and testing would make it prohibitively expensive to develop a different interface for each user or group of users. Finally, because the presentation logic must run on the host, thereby increasing network traffic and processing requirements, it is difficult to implement a mouse or graphical user interface (GUI) in a terminal-host environment.

Maintainability.   Maintainability poses an interesting dilemma. Terminal-host systems are highly maintainable, in that a number of performance parameters can be set and managed. These include memory, scheduling, tasking priorities, resource monitoring, and I/O tuning. As a result, however, it can take a small army of administrators to keep a mainframe system up and running on a regular basis. Other architectures may not have as many management features, but that is because they do not need them for most of the applications they support. The conclusion is that yes, these systems are highly maintainable, but the price paid in labor costs is commensurately high. The question to be asked is whether these costs are justified by the functionality of the system.

Flexibility.   Mainframe systems are not renowned for their flexibility. Given the complexity of a typical mainframe or minicomputer configuration, it is often difficult to replace one component of a system without replacing or modifying several others as well. In addition, since the software is usually designed for simple and homogeneous transactions, they are not best suited for a fast-changing environment. The high development and testing costs also tend to discourage a great deal of system modification. This is not an issue for a relatively static application—say, an accounting system—but it is not acceptable for sales and marketing systems or decision support systems.

Interoperability.   Since terminal-host environments—including all hardware, software, and communications—are normally purchased from a single vendor, they are not normally interoperable with other vendors' systems. Indeed, one vendor is even well known for a lack of interoperability across the successive generations of its own systems. The intent, naturally, is to lock the customer into the given vendor's products only, and even the trend toward open systems has been paid little more than lip service by most of the mainframe and minicomputer vendors.

Scalability.   Terminal-host systems are more easily scaled up than down. New users can be added with very little disruption until the processor is fully loaded. At that point, however, the system may require a processor upgrade, more memory, and new versions of applications software and operating systems. This is a very expensive and disruptive process. In addition, as the system scales down, it is difficult or impossible to scale the system back accordingly; upgrades tend to be nonreversible.

Appropriate Terminal-Host Applications.   Given these delivery requirements, what would be the best kind of system to use on this architecture? Given the relative strengths and weaknesses, we would have to say that the ideal architecture is one that has static requirements, implements a consistent set of transactions, requires a high level of security, requires high through-put, and has a fairly homogeneous user base. Typical applications would be accounting and payroll systems, inventory control, and high-through-put sales systems such as airline reservation or currency trading systems. In general, it is a safe rule of thumb to say that the most appropriate terminal-host systems are those that provide a company's data collection activities, have relatively unchanging requirements, and are far removed from the customer.

Client-Server Configuration

Client-server processing began appearing sometime after the first networks allowed intelligent work stations (such as PCs) to link directly to mainframes or minicomputers. Work stations downloaded data from the back-end machines in the form of files and processed them locally. Before long, some clever developers had discovered how to write programs that drew data directly off the back-end systems in real time. This was accomplished by remotely logging into the back-end system through the use of such software tools as remote procedure calls (RPCs). These allow software running on one platform to access and pass commands to another platform as though it were a local process. Using RPCs, client applications can pass data control statements (such as SQL) to a database running on the server, receiving the results directly back to the PC. This is a drastic departure from previous architectures, in that the application and display elements of the system are off-loaded to the PC at the front end (see Figure 29-2). The result of this is less network traffic, more flexible front-end systems, and, frequently, better performance. Although client-server systems have been implemented with mainframes acting as servers, the most common manifestation of these systems is to have a Unix-based minicomputer or high-end work station acting as the server.

A client-server architecture allows more customization of the front end at the point of presentation, while providing a consistent application across groups of users and a common data pool they could all share. Although we at Lotus are great proponents of client-server technology, it

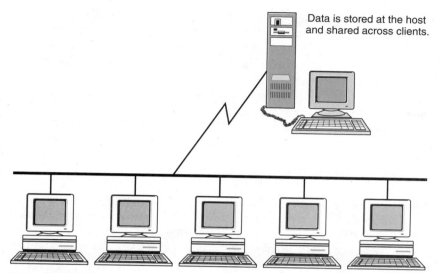

Data is stored at the host and shared across clients.

Figure 29-2   Client-server configuration.

must be noted that it is not without its limitations, and an unwary management consultant trying to implement her or his first client-server project would do well to read on and ensure that the right kind of technology has been targeted at the right business application.

Availability.   If very high availability is a delivery requirement for the system, it would be best to look again at terminal-host. The number of points of potential failure in a client-server architecture is so vast that data center managers get white-knuckled at the thought of trying to define service level agreements for this architecture. There are a number of ways a client-server system can go down in the middle of an important application:

The client application could crash because of a modification to the local environment (e.g., the AUTOEXEC.BAT, CONFIG.SYS, or WIN.INI files).

The client operating system could crash (such as Windows or OS/2, neither of which is as robust as a mainframe operating system).

The local (e.g., PC or work station) hard disk or memory could fail.

The network server or gateway could go down, or the physical connection could fail.

The database server software or operating system could crash (for any number of reasons).

The database server hard disk or memory could fail.

Of course, the likelihood of any of these occurring ranges from fairly high (especially in the case of client operating system crashes) to rather low (server memory failures), and any of these can be addressed in fairly short order. However, it is the large number of potential problems and the number of places in which they can occur that make it difficult to guarantee high-availability systems with today's client-server technologies. Having said that, developers have designed a number of high-availability trading systems by designing robustness into each component of the architecture, preparing comprehensive support plans, and, as much as possible, securing the operational system from any "adjustments" that can bring the entire system down.

Efficiency.   Client-server is increasingly seen as a highly efficient solution to many of today's system requirements. Client-server systems tend to be built with technologies such as relational databases and 4GLs that support very fast, very flexible systems development. This means that increased functionality is delivered more quickly and more cheaply to the user. This does not necessarily mean that the systems will be cheaper to maintain over their entire life cycle (see maintainability below), but it does reduce the cost of development. If the system is to be deployed in a business area in which user requirements are not homogeneous and are continuously changing, however, then the client-server architecture will be a much more efficient environment.

Performance.   As with terminal-host architectures, performance can be very good or very poor depending on the application. Client-server environments can be very good for decision-support applications in which the transactions cannot be anticipated and programmed beforehand. However, until recently, client-server architectures did not have the tools (such as transaction-processing monitors) that allowed the system manager to monitor and control through-put in high-transaction rate environments. Recent releases of products such as Tuxedo and CICS 6000 and features offered by RDBMS vendors such as Informix go some way toward addressing this issue, however. In the meantime, most companies will continue to use their mainframes for transaction processing and then download some of these data to a database server for use in client-server mode for decision-support applications.

Security.   Security is not an inherent part of a client-server architecture, which means it must be built into the systems that run on it. For example, one can design password control at the application level on the PC as well as setting database privileges on the back-end server. However, if a user accesses sensitive data and then stores them on a local hard disk, then the data may not be protected at all. This cannot happen in a terminal-host environment using dumb terminals. Physical security for client-server architectures also tends not to be very high. This is unfortunate, for although an application built on a client-server system may be just as business-critical as one built on a mainframe, we rarely see the servers stored in secured, halon-protected data center environments. If, therefore, security is a matter of paramount importance, one should be prepared to do at least the following when implementing a client-server architecture:

Establish password control at the front-end application, on the server database and the server operating system.

Ensure that data cannot be exported from the application or database into a file on the client or server hard disk.

Greatly restrict or eliminate external access to the system through telecomms lines.

Physically secure the server in a fire-protected room and back up the data, applications, and system configuration in a remote site.

Usability.   Increased ease of use is one of the arguments frequently advanced in favor of client-server architectures. This is to some degree a fallacious argument. First of all, client-server systems tend to be based on a graphical user interface (GUI) such as Windows, OS/2, or Macintosh, which is held to be more "usable" than a simple character-based interface. However, a poorly designed GUI system can be less usable than a character-based system. Users may also prefer one interface over another. (The author once reviewed a Windows-based prototype of a trading system with the currency traders at a large European bank and was told it was unacceptable because Windows was "too complicated," and they had neither the time nor the inclination to learn a new interface.) However, the flexibility of client-server does allow user interfaces to be targeted more toward individual classes of users than the mainframe would normally allow, resulting in different interfaces for, say, data entry clerks as opposed to financial analysts or managers. To summarize, we can conclude that, yes, the tools are available to make a more usable interface under client-server, but the ultimate result depends more on the quality of the design itself than the system architecture behind it.

Maintainability.   The jury is still out as to whether client-server systems are cheaper to maintain over the long term. Certainly, if we simply compare the costs of maintaining a Unix server with an IBM mainframe, the Unix server will be far cheaper. However, if we compare the costs of maintaining, say, two Unix servers, plus 200 PCs, plus the LANs to which they are attached, against a mainframe supporting 200 terminals, then the lower-maintenance argument of client-server can be questioned. (This is not entirely a complete comparison, as the PCs can provide additional benefits such as spreadsheets, word processors, and local databases, which the mainframe simply may not be able to provide.) However, bear in mind that support requirements in a client-server environment are no longer directly proportional to the cost of the box sitting at the back end but must take the complexity of the operating environment into account as well.

Flexibility.   One of client-server's strongest selling points is its flexibility. Its modular design allows developers to modify one part of the system, such as the presentation logic, without necessarily affecting the application logic or data structure. In addition, applications can be added and removed without affecting other components of the system. This modularity results in shorter development and testing times, which means that changes can be developed and implemented in a matter of hours or days rather than weeks. Finally, the fact that the presentation logic is running locally means that programs or interfaces can easily be customized for particular users or classes of users.

Interoperability.   Client-server would not exist today as we know it if it weren't for its interoperability. The typical client-server architecture can incorporate products from as many as half a dozen vendors as part of its essential infrastructure. Front-end applications can access numerous back-end databases, and these databases can be accessed from a large number of different front-end applications. The Windows environment can also allow links to host mainframes running in background, passing data to a local application or different back-end servers. An example of the different components of a client-server architecture, each of which could be from a different vendor, is given below:

Client hardware

Client operating system

Client front-end software

Network server

Network operating system

Application server

Application server operating system

Application server database management system

Routers and gateways

Scalability.   Client-server systems are more scalable than terminal-host systems. Since less processing power is required at the back end, servers tend to be cheaper than mainframes. In addition, this architecture supports multiple inexpensive servers supporting a given number of users, rather than a single expensive mainframe. Under client-server, new users can be added to a server until it is fully loaded; at that point, a new (and relatively inexpensive) server can be added to support more users. An incremental server can be added to the existing infrastructure with a minimum of disruption to existing operations. In addition, if the number of users on a system declines, some of the servers can be redeployed elsewhere.

Conclusions.   The foregoing discussion gives a perhaps confusing verdict on client-server architecture. However, many of its weaknesses are based on its relative immaturity relative to the mainframe world. Client-server does have real strengths for many applications, and we expect to see a large proportion of future systems development to occur in the client-server environment.

The most appropriate client-server application will probably be one with frequently changing requirements requiring very fast implementation. Such an application could have a number of different user types who use the system for different purposes. Examples include any decision-support system and many systems that are used in the sales and marketing environment. Systems that are very transaction-intensive and require high availability may not be appropriate for client-server at this time. In general, since these systems are more responsive and flexible, the closer the business user is to customers, the more likely that they will be better served by a client-server system than a terminal-host system.

Peer-to-Peer Processing

Peer-to-peer processing is actually a superset of the client-server model. In this model the presentation logic, application, and data all reside at each work station (see Figure 29-3). Strictly defined, peer-to-peer describes a model in which intelligent networked platforms can communicate to share files, data, and commands. As we all know, simple networks can allow us to share files across platforms, and client-server may allow us to share data (although this sharing must always go through the server), but only peer-to-peer will allow us to share commands between platforms.

The concept of "sharing commands" has not made its way into computer parlance yet, so it is worth explaining this further. Most computers support only a limited degree of integration between them; this includes, as noted above, the integration (sharing) of files and sometimes data. But what if the user is running a DOS machine on a network and needs to trigger a process running on another machine on the network? The user can access, say, a Unix or VAX box, or an IBM mainframe, through terminal emulation or a client front-end program (as described in the previous

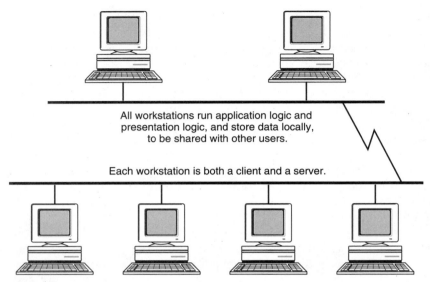

All workstations run application logic and
presentation logic, and store data locally,
to be shared with other users.

Each workstation is both a client and a server.

Figure 29-3   Peer-to-peer processing.

sections) but cannot directly trigger programs on other DOS or Windows
machines on the network. This is because DOS is not a preemptive multitasking operating system. This is a fancy way of saying that DOS can't
walk and chew gum at the same time. DOS—and, as of this date, we are
including Windows here as well—is a single-user, single-process operating system. It is all that DOS can do just to run local applications and
connect to the network. It cannot accept procedures from another
machine to, say, run Lotus 1-2-3 or even to do a DOS directory search.

Someday, a successor to DOS and Windows may be able to work in a
peer-to-peer environment. To do that today, you will need a more intelligent operating system, such as Unix or OS/2. What these can do is allow
other systems to "log in," as it were, to the work station to run procedures
or queries. This is of course not without risk, as particularly troublesome
users on the network could decide to delete others' files, use their disks
for all their own file storage, or run all their most complex programs on
someone else's machine so as to increase their local CPU performance.
Security features, however, can protect each machine from unauthorized
accesses or procedures from other users, while allowing users to share
selected files, databases, or applications with particular users.

Until now, peer-to-peer has sounded like an answer in search of a
question to many—interesting features, but so what? One reason that
client-server has developed as a common configuration today is because
of the inability of the large installed base of DOS/Windows machines to
run in preemptive multitasking mode. Peer-to-peer does have a number

of potential applications, and it is likely that as more robust software is deployed for client work stations, it will become the dominant computing paradigm in business.

What does peer-to-peer provide for the system designer? Just as with the early days of client-server, it is difficult to predict exactly how it will be used. Once the capability for peer-to-peer communication is made available to clients, there is no doubt that new classes of software will arrive that will take advantage of these features. What we can do is comment on how peer-to-peer is currently being implemented, either through emulation or on networks using Unix or OS/2 work stations that do support this capability.

Peer-to-peer processing is currently implemented in a simulated manner through a new class of software known as "groupware." This is programmable software that enables users to send, route, and share complex data and documents. Software such as Lotus Notes currently simulates peer-to-peer processing by enabling work stations to interact with other work stations through the intermediary of a server and through the Notes layer of software, which sits above the operating system. The success of Lotus Notes and the groupware model gives some indication of the potential of peer-to-peer processing.

On "true" peer-to-peer with Unix or OS/2 work stations, the need for centralized data stores and file servers goes away. The model begins to resemble the Internet, in which the routing of messages is flexible and the data is distributed. Any machine can access any other machine on the network for the files and data it needs without going through a central location. What takes true peer-to-peer beyond the Internet model is that each "server" in the Internet model would be a user work station. Users therefore not only share data and files, they can also run applications on the other work stations on the network. A distributed architecture such as this cuts down on bottlenecks in processing queries from a number of concurrent users who are trying to access the same database server or file server simultaneously. Data that need to be used locally can be collected and stored locally, along with other data that need to be shared with other users. The significance of this is that in the future, many if not most corporate computing environments will be greatly decentralized, with nothing more than large networks of intelligent work stations connected to each other. Although there will still be a need for an occasional mainframe, they will be used more in specialized applications, such as massive transaction processing, rather than everyday computing.

The peer-to-peer model will eventually give rise to truly integrated computer systems, in which all users are connected into a single logical system, which spans spreadsheets, databases, document processing, and communications applications. This will allow true data sharing across organizations, instant management information, and "everything-to-everything" connectivity, thus supporting the flat, highly integrated organizational structures that corporations will have to adopt for the 1990s and beyond.

Let's look at the delivery requirements defined above to understand better the strengths and weaknesses of the peer-to-peer architecture.

Availability. Peer-to-peer availability is hard to define. On the plus side is a much more resilient architecture; on the minus side are more potential points of failure. The resilience comes through spreading the processing across multiple CPUs. For example, if the machine normally used to access a financial application goes down, a user could access another on the network with the same program (assuming the user had an alternate store of that data). Thus if one machine goes down, it affects a smaller number of users than if the mainframe goes down or if the network server goes down. A greater number of potential points of failure means, however, that there may be less severe failures on a more frequent basis than before. The trade-off is between one occasional major failure that can affect the whole business and a number of more frequent failures that have less business impact. Looking at this from an organizational perspective, 99 percent availability on a peer-to-peer system means that at any given time it will be supporting about 99 percent of users, whereas 99 percent availability on a terminal host architecture means that 99 percent of the time all users have full functionality, whereas 1 percent of the time all users have no functionality at all.

Efficiency. The true efficiency of peer-to-peer systems is difficult to calculate because these systems are relatively new in the corporate world, and their value to the business is only now being realized. If we look at efficiency as the cost-effectiveness of meeting corporate and user requirements, and we say that in the 1990s these requirements require everything-to-everything connectivity, a high degree of flexibility, and full responsiveness to user requirements, then peer-to-peer will be the most cost-effective—if not the only—means of delivering this. This does not necessarily mean that these systems will be cheaper in absolute terms, but they will be more efficient when looked at on the basis of a cost-to-benefits comparison.

Performance. Peer-to-peer systems are not inherently higher or lower performance than other architectures. One can even design a terminal-host or client-server system over a peer-to-peer architecture. Depending on the application and how it is built, performance may be better or worse under peer-to-peer. For example, mainframes are well suited to transaction processing. However, transaction processing can be implemented over a peer-to-peer network with local data capture and storage and easily out-perform a mainframe-based system. Given the high-power work stations used in peer-to-peer systems, performance will probably not be an issue for the foreseeable future.

Security. Peer-to-peer is potentially the least secure kind of architecture. This is because there is not a single point of control on the system—there are potentially hundreds or thousands depending on the degree of connectivity. Furthermore, enabling everything-to-everything connectivity through peer-to-peer means that any user can potentially access any application, directory, or file on the entire network. Naturally, much of this can be addressed by building access controls into the software or network. Indeed, most peer-to-peer operating systems such as Unix provide access control at the file and even the process level, thus potentially addressing this issue if properly implemented and maintained. However, these access controls must be set up at each work station, rather than centrally as in the good old mainframe days. Security, then, can (and must) be implemented, but it is more difficult to administer and probably more porous than on a terminal-host system. At a minimum, the following procedures should be followed:

Establish password control for all work stations, and file protection procedures for each work station.

Establish password control at the application front end and on all databases.

Ensure that mission-critical applications and databases are either replicated across multiple work stations or kept on specially controlled work stations (e.g., physically secured and fire-protected if possible).

Prepare a backup and systems management strategy to minimize the possibility of loss of key data.

Continuously monitor and maintain user access controls.

Usability. Peer-to-peer systems (as with client-server systems) are neither inherently more nor less usable than other systems. As with client-server systems, a poorly designed peer-to-peer system can be every bit as unusable as a terminal-host system. However, the flexibility of peer-to-peer does allow user interfaces to be targeted more toward individual classes of users than mainframe systems would normally allow, resulting in different interfaces based on user preference or job function. This, plus the fact that users have simpler access to more applications under peer-to-peer architectures, would tend to indicate that peer-to-peer systems should generally score high in terms of usability provided the user interface is implemented well.

Maintainability. Currently, peer-to-peer systems are probably the least maintainable. This is because the technology is still fairly new, and the less glamorous features (e.g., housekeeping) have yet to be added to it. Indeed, the maintenance model for peer-to-peer systems does not seem to have been developed in full yet. In peer-to-peer, each user may also have to become his or her own system administrator unless better management utilities are developed for multiuser distributed systems. In internationally distributed systems, when systems operate across multiple time zones and languages yet share locally collected data, this becomes even more critical. For example, a large Japanese firm recently planned to roll out an international trading system based on a peer-to-peer network. A question arose as to who "owned" the system administration facilities: Tokyo, Hong Kong, New York, London, or all the sites. The solution finally arrived at was that each site would control its local operations during normal business hours, but central coordination came from a 24-hour support headquarters based in London. These are the problems that large organizations are just coming to grips with as they plan to roll out large peer-to-peer systems on a multisite basis.

Flexibility. Peer-to-peer systems are highly modular and so have a great deal of flexibility. This is because the databases, languages, operating systems, and configurations of potentially all the systems on the network can be changed. However, it must be remembered that such systems can also be highly interdependent, requiring the reconfiguration of components each time the architecture changes. This interdependency may actually limit the things that can be done on a given platform. For example, if a user wanted to change the data table structure on her or his local platform, she or he would have to take any other users into account who may be accessing the local database. Peer-to-peer development, by reason of its modularity, also permits shorter development times (as with the client-server model), thereby increasing flexibility, but the interdependence of these systems will also require more testing.

Interoperability. Peer-to-peer systems are designed to be the most interoperable of all architectures. As noted above, they can share files, data, and commands—something that no other architecture can do. They can allow a number of different front-end 4GLs to talk to a number of different RDBMSs simultaneously, and all platforms can act as both client and server.

Scalability. Peer-to-peer is the most scalable of all systems. Since each user runs his or her own "virtual mainframe," adding new users is simply a matter of adding additional work stations. There is no need to add another mainframe or Unix server to supplement additional users. This is the most fine-grained of the architectures for scalability planning, in that there should be only one machine per user for application purposes. (Of course, there may be a few additional machines on large networks to support utility functions such as communications gateways, but the requirement for these is usually minimal.) Conversely, if the number of users on a given system declines, then the work stations are simply deployed elsewhere.

Appropriate Peer-to-Peer Applications. The most appropriate peer-to-peer application, as with client-server, will probably be one with frequently changing requirements requiring very fast implementation. Such an application could have a number of different user types who use the system for different purposes. A peer-to-peer system would also be recommended for a system which requires large amounts of local data processing, such as a derivatives trading system, multimedia development tool, or computer-aided design system. In addition, systems that are geographically dispersed and do not require real-time data integration are also good candidates for a peer-to-peer architecture. This might include collaborative research databases and work group/work flow computing applications.

The astute reader may judge from the foregoing discussion that we are damning peer-to-peer with faint praise. This is possibly true, for today's applications and technologies. Peer-to-peer is still a young technology, but one with great potential. As processing and storage costs go down, all users will soon have the equivalent of a mainframe sitting on their desks, making the need for a mainframe less obvious than before. Peer-to-peer supports a new way of working that helps meet the increased challenges of the 1990s—data overload, accelerated timescales, a global economy, 24-hour operations—that are now only beginning to be addressed by revised business processes. As business cultures and organizations adapt and reorganize for performing in the 1990s, we believe that peer-to-peer processing will come into its own.

In the meantime, companies are experimenting with peer-to-peer. Some financial companies are using it for deal capture or decision support, engineering companies are using it for CAD, and it is being used in the entertainment industry to support multimedia and virtual reality. This is of course a far cry from running a general ledgers package, but the uses of computing are changing as technologies become more powerful.

Conclusions

The foregoing discussions give the management consultant some guidelines for recommending or validating system architectures on which to base recommended solutions. We can see that, although virtually any

	Terminal-Host	Client-Server	Peer-to-Peer
Availability	High	Low-medium	Medium
Efficiency	Low-high	High	High
Performance	High	Medium	Medium-high
Security	High	Low	Low
Usability	Low	High	High
Maintainability	High	Medium	Low-medium
Flexibility	Low	High	High
Interoperability	Low	High	High
Scalability	Low	Medium	High

Figure 29-4

kind of business application can be built on any of these architectures, the delivery requirements that these architectures support means that certain applications will be more appropriate on a given architecture than others.

Figure 29-4 shows a summary of these conclusions. It must be remembered that these are presented as general guidelines, and the consultant must consider the type application and its use within the organization when trying to select the most appropriate architecture.

Part 7

Specialized Consulting Services

30

Telecommunications

Charles E. Day, CMC
Arlington, Virginia

Introduction

In recent years, telecommunications has become a specialty in the field of management consulting for several reasons: (1) recognition that telecommunications (voice/data) is a specialized area that requires technical skills and planning similar to those for information systems; (2) increased willingness of commercial accounts to go outside their own organization for information systems and networking operations; (3) increased distribution of computing systems, local area networking, PC systems with dial-up capability, service bureau applications, and voice processing technologies; (4) availability of consulting skills from people˙ who had lost their jobs at companies such as AT&T and IBM; and (5) plans by common carrier and system manufacturers to include telecommunications and systems consulting for profit or to stimulate the acquisition of new technology by its users.

The maturity of voice and data communications—both as an industry and as an integral part of distributing automated application functionality—has contributed greatly to the prominence many consultants in the area now enjoy. Integration of voice and data technology is on the rise even in manually staffed customer service and order entry operations. Interactive voice response functions also assist the financial industry and public agencies in providing around-the-clock account and services information via telephone.

Whereas the growth in systems distribution and integration has brought about greater opportunities in telecommunications consulting, it has also challenged professional management consultants to match skills to assignments and to carve the kind of business niches that are conducive to acquiring relevant expertise and professionalism. In conducting assignments, it is critically important that you use proven project-management techniques and that you clearly understand the client's needs. Sections in this chapter will cover the process of conducting such engagements, a review of opportunities in voice and data communications, and a list of the ways to stay current in an ever-evolving field. In addition, there is a section on how marketing and sales development can lead to referrals that result in new business.

Understanding the Telecommunications Industry

Since the divestiture of AT&T and the Bell operating companies in January 1984, new telecommunications companies and services have created the need to determine how they meet an organization's needs. Figure 30-1 shows the results of the modified court decree that divested regional Bell operating companies from AT&T.

Voice and Data

Independent telephone companies are dispersed throughout the regional Bell operating company (RBOC) operating areas. Interconnect companies have sprung up to provide regional and national long-distance services to carry both voice and data, public and private. There are also aggregators, companies which represent such long-distance companies as AT&T, MCI, and US Sprint in negotiating bulk orders (for commissions) with common carriers. Aggregators sometimes compete directly with suppliers' internal staffs. The nationwide installation of fiber optics networks has provided expanded capacity for the major common carrier and regional operating companies, as well as for such specialized firms as WILCO, which can provide point-to-point voice and data communications connections for major users.

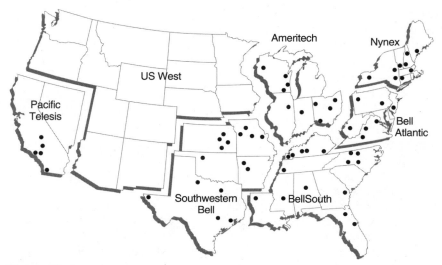

Figure 30-1

Distributed Systems

Another area of technological advance in recent years is that of distributed processing—the off-loading of major mainframe host computers to desktop work stations and PC processors. The distribution of information systems technologies with shared databases both on client server equipment and on mainframe database management systems has increased interconnectivity at employee work stations throughout organizations. Thus—in addition to normal telephone service—point-to-point connection to distributed processors or to local area networks will require additional planning and installation.

A major result of the AT&T breakup was the ability of organizations to purchase directly telephone equipment and systems for use on their own premises. This development immediately spurred major PBX (private branch exchange)/ACD (automatic call distributor) manufacturers, including AT&T, to increase the functional and technical capabilities of their systems. The RBOCs, by the way, are not permitted to develop such products, but, through the unregulated entities approved in the 1984 court decree, the RBOCs are able to distribute PBX/ACD and other premise-based equipment supplied by other manufacturers.

These changes resulted in such major developments as the ability to provide call detail statistics for comparative pricing of long-distance costs, management information reporting with automatic call distribution functionality, and the integration of digital systems technology with telephone line facilities for both voice and data. Associated with the shared use of wiring by computer terminals and telephones working concurrently at a work station is the capability for modem pooling to minimize an organization's dial-up computing costs.

Wide Area Network (WAN) and Local Area Network (LAN) Computing

With organizations having departmental autonomy and physically separated facilities, data networking facilities have been extended across larger groups of users within and outside of an office complex through local-area and wide-area networking technologies. Network protocols, developed to facilitate interconnections that use both coaxial and twisted-pair wiring, have become an increasingly popular way for organizations to get control of their own application functions and to have access to word processing spreadsheet software by electronic mail (E-mail) and other office/automation/business management applications. Availability of electronic mail applications through local area networks has also spurred increased use among organizations. This development has been precipitated by the lower cost of equipping an office work station and by the competitive development of software now viewed as essential for modern office management.

Broader application of two popular network protocols—Ethernet and token ring—benefited users with relatively simple installations of local area networking capabilities. Although these communication protocols have dominated local area networking, dissimilar protocols have given rise to routers, bridges, and interpretive network protocols such as transmission control protocol/internet protocol (TCP/IP).

Technological Integration

Because of the versatility of digital PBX/ACD switches and the increased need for distribution of information systems technology (while maintaining interconnectivity with host database system applications), voice and data technology applications increasingly have been integrated. For example, Figure 30-2 demonstrates a customer service call center which is equipped with lines and trunks terminating at a telephone PBX/ACD system that has access to voice messaging, voice recognition, and interactive voice response capabilities. The call center also affords direct access to distributed and customized systems and to mainframe host processors.

As illustrated in Figure 30-2, a customer service representative can access both telephone and customer record information through a single PC keyboard. The increased applications afforded by long-distance carriers in identifying the telephone numbers dialed and, in some cases, the number dialed from has provided a basis for even greater interconnectivity of telephone and information systems.

The Functional Parts of a Customer Service Systems Environment

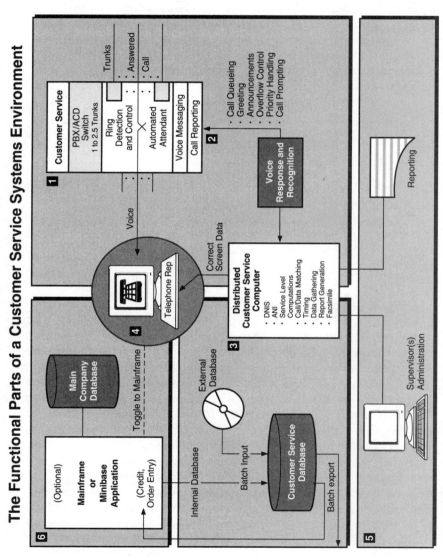

1 Customer Service

PBX/ACD Switch
1 to 2.5 Trunks

Ring Detection and Control

Automated Attendant

Voice Messaging

Call Reporting

Trunks
Answered
Call

2
- Call Queueing
- Greeting
- Announcements
- Overflow Control
- Priority Handling
- Call Prompting

Voice Response and Recognition

3 Distributed Customer Service Computer
- DNIS
- ANI
- Service Level Computations
- Call/Data Matching
- Timing
- Data Gathering
- Report Generation
- Facsimile

Voice

4 Telephone Rep

Correct Screen Data

Main Company Database

Toggle to Mainframe

6 (Optional) Mainframe or Minibase Application

(Credit, Order Entry)

Internal Database

External Database

Batch Input

Customer Service Database

Batch export

5 Supervisor(s) Administration

Reporting

Figure 30-2

30-7

Dialed Number Identification Services (DNIS)

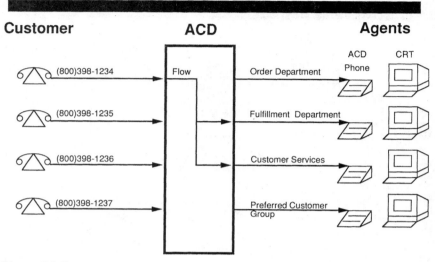

Customer   **ACD**   **Agents**

Figure 30-3

Figure 30-3 shows how integrated technologies can assist users who dial an 800 telephone number. The PBX/ACD system recognizes the number dialed and determines if the customer is calling to order a product or request a service. Before the system answers the call, it can also use the caller's number to access the associated customer service system and database. It can then queue the appropriate customer record for the staff representative terminal. Both the customer record and telephone call are directed concurrently to the employee's work station for servicing.

The effect of this is to reduce talk time for the caller, lower the network costs, and provide a fuller view for the organization's representative who is assisting the client. Further, credit card information can be obtained prior to physically answering a customer's call to improve customer service using telecommunications networks and systems functionality. A more sophisticated example of technologies working together would be the same scenario as described with the network and system automatically identifying the caller's number and finding through database look-up that the client has not paid his or her bill. The call may then be routed to the credit and collections department before it is routed to order services or customer services. New features are still being developed jointly between systems and switch manufacturers for computer-integrated telephony. Long-distance common carrier services are likewise involved and are still developing these information services digital network (ISDN) applications.

Interactive Voice Response

Similar to the integration of technologies discussed above is the new capability for more automatic servicing of customer calls through integrated voice response (IVR) technology. Such systems have heretofore been common to telephone usage in which callers interface with computers to direct their calls through automated attendant equipment. Callers press numbers on a keypad to select a department and/or extension. With the development of voice recognition systems, callers can speak the numbers "0" through "9," and such simple words as "yes" and "no" into the telephone handset for automatic system routing or other selections.

Current technology permits even more direct servicing of such calls, particularly in such businesses as banking, transportation information, and catalog order entry. For example, an interactive voice response system can lead a customer through certain prompts for encoding digits—such as account numbers and dates and amounts of last deposits—to query bank account status or make fund transfers. Similarly, one can determine next flight or train departure by accessing interactive voice response systems which use input from telephone touch pads to simulate agent transactions. Responses are then articulated electronically with such information as flight numbers, destination, and departing and arriving times.

Typical Client Engagements

It is important for consultants to understand the kind of assistance users need in this deregulated and fiercely competitive environment. Organizations usually decide to retain outside consulting assistance when they (1) don't have the technical skills to fully understand their needs in a specific area, (2) are short of staff and choose to contract short-term consultants instead of hiring new ones, (3) prefer a wider view of what similar organizations are doing and want to learn from consultants who know. Organizations seldom hire consultants to acquire cheap labor or to help build the management consulting profession.

It is important that a consultant have experience in either voice or data network systems technology and preferably in both. A primary area for recruiting outside consulting assistance is that of defining user requirements for internal systems; developing requirements and requests for proposals; and assisting with the evaluation, selection, procurement, and implementation oversight process type of counsulting. This applies to those organizations in need of new telephone switches, automatic call distributors, local area networks, office automation systems, or specialized applications in customer service, telemarketing, and information referral call centers.

At one time, organizations hired outside consultants primarily to compare common carrier alternatives. Such selection has become incidental, since users are now provided with other system procurement assistance. Some companies that the author does not consider management consultants review telephone bills to find errors and split the savings with the organizations that employ them. Here are some of the computer and communication assignments which are typically available to consultants, as well as other assignments that might assist manufacturers of computers and communication facilities:

For Users of Computers and Communications Systems

- Strategic and tactical planning of computer and telecommunications facilities
- Organization audits
- Project management of system changeovers
- Technical skills assessment and training
- Computer and telecommunications facilities selection
- Telephone traffic analysis and long-distance service selection
- Network configuration modeling and staffing analyses
- Call center users review and agent training
- Operational assessments
- System performance analyses
- Productivity analyses
- Disaster recovery planning

For Manufacturers of Computer and Communications Facilities

- Industry needs analyses
- Technology assessments
- Specific market studies
- Customer profiles
- Client surveys
- Market planning assistance

- Product and services critique
- Promotion/sales material assessment
- Product and service alliances studies
- Acquisition analyses

In general, users in need of new systems—telephone or computer—with which they are generally unfamiliar or have difficulty operating frequently require outside assistance. A major company move to reduce costs by reorganization or expansion may present an excellent opportunity for consultants who can help plan the move, engineer the network, and assist in acquiring the communications network and system components.

A consultant can also be invaluable in the start-up of an outbound telemarketing operation that requires contact management software, automated computer equipment, PBX/ACD capability, and long-distance services. Companies that need confirmation of a design plan or technical direction or advice about other decisions about systems design, selection, or implementation strategies are also ideal prospects.

Integration of voice and data systems can help an organization improve productivity and possibly downsize its staff. This is another opportunity for management consulting engagements.

Client Engagements Management

Engagement management among management consultants is typically directed toward these objectives: (1) clarifying expectations up-front, (2) establishing schedules for deliverables, (3) communicating the progress and problems of proposed resolutions, (4) identifying follow-on support opportunities, (5) submitting clear and valuable reports, and (6) recommendations. However, engagement management by technical consultants generally follows a more structured approach. Projects that extend beyond 3 months generally benefit from the development of a detail plan. Such a plan outlines scope and objectives, the approach to the project, major milestones and deliverables, responsibilities of both the client and the consulting team, and a detailed task list according to project area.

It is also customary for a consultant to hold regular project review meetings that involve all the relevant departments. Such meetings would also include information systems personnel and other technical support staff to ensure they understand the technical assistance provided. Progress reporting, action items summary, problem identification, and alternative solutions are customarily reported weekly or biweekly.

A number of things can go wrong in technical system projects. Many inside and outside factors need to be considered, including the danger of not understanding the technical discipline. And often confusion and misconceptions arise because of excessive use of acronyms and technical jargon.

The structured review approach and project management go a long way toward ensuring success in client engagements. There are also systems available to assist consultants in tracking project estimates in staffing and schedules—both through Gantt charts and Pert networks as well as through other more traditional dependency-oriented tracking methods. These two, through software products or a manual approach, can help illustrate changes in project direction and/or timing.

Since we are always affected by changes in the scope of systems development, manufacturers' component deliveries, and debugging schedules, there will probably always be trouble in meeting target dates. Therefore, allowances for delays should be built into the planning. Alternative planning to shorten developmental cycles and installation time and to defer noncritical efforts to later phases is both acceptable and desirable.

Projects that take longer than 6 months to complete will often benefit from a phased approach. Figure 30-4 shows one such project-tracking mechanism.

The following are some tips for engagement success:

Do's and Don'ts for Successful Engagements

- Do stay current on technology prescribed for client use.

- Do communicate in a clear language rather than in technicalese.

- Do use project management and a detail planning process.

- Do maintain independence from the manufacturers and providers of products and services.

- Do conduct user requirements definition with primary research versus favoring familiar products and offerings.

- Don't push technology onto users.

- Don't argue in philosophical and technical differences with vendors and clients, especially the information systems department.

- Don't forget to document the basis for all your equipment and system recommendations.

- Don't limit the recommendations to initial needs but plan for growth in capacity and complexity.

- Don't oversell your technical skills to clients and vendors if you lack such skills.

**BUSINESS COMPUTER
DEFINITION, EVALUATION AND SELECTION
PROJECT SCHEDULE**

Month #

	1	2	3	4	5	6	7	8

Requirements Definition

- Kick-off Meeting(s)
- Detail Plan Dev
- Data Collection
- Technical Interviews
- Admin Interviews

- Sys/Ntw Interfaces
- Database Architecture
- System Performance
- Other Busn Sys Rev

- Available Solution(s)
- Cost/Benefit Analysis
- Tech Spec Draft #1
- ABC Review/Approval
- Final Spec/RFP Dev/ Issuance

Evaluation and Selection (TBA)

- RFP Response Eval Grid
- Short List Dev
- Response Eval/Interviews
- Develop Benchmark Standards

- Proj Plan Implem Review
- Coord w/User Grps and Comm
- Verify Operations/References
- Coord Benchmark Test

- Evaluate Benchmark Results
- Update Cost/Benefit Analysis
- Recommend Supporting Products
- Obtain ABC Consensus
- Make Final Recommendation/Presentation

Figure 30-4

Sourcing Business

Many of the traditional ways management consultants secure client engagements also work well for those who specialize in telecommunications. However, some methods seem far more fruitful than others once a consultant establishes his or her credibility. Technical expertise, sound recommendations, and management success are all keys to finding new business. The following approaches are listed in the order of greatest benefit.

Referrals.   Your best chance of getting new business occurs when those who are acquainted with your skills and capabilities refer you to friends and business associates. As a new management consultant, you can first turn to friends, relatives, and acquaintances to identify opportunities. It is important that you be able to explain fairly specifically the telecommunications niche you consider your primary strength and interest. Many referrals will not be up to speed on technical needs but may recognize the correct business environment where your skills will count. You should consider all your existing clients as a primary source of referrals and strive to retain an average of 50 percent of ongoing business from your customer base.

Networking.   You should use business and technical organizations and specialized industry groups to cultivate relationships that will pay off in new accounts. You can draw attention to yourself and your services by seeking and accepting offices in trade and professional groups.

Presentations.   Develop interesting topics into presentations to industry officials and groups. If specialized industries are beginning to automate, for example, you can develop a presentation on the subject that will demonstrate your competence in a fairly technical and prevalent area.

Responding to Requests for Proposals.   Identifying potential client organizations and placing your name on their procurements lists and tracking public notices on requests for proposals are common but effective ways to acquire new business. Depending on your location, your rate of success will vary. The success rate for the average size firm that responds to requests for proposals is often quite low. Even when you use standard response forms, it still takes substantial time and money to submit proposals. It is good for you to know someone in the organization before you respond to a request for a proposal. The connection will ensure that your proposal has a ring of familiarity to it and thus increase your chance of being a finalist.

Direct Mail and Cold Call Follow-Ups.   This method should be moderately successful. Prospects may be moved to action when you introduce a business opportunity that could reduce their costs, increase revenues, or improve service level—even if they hadn't thought of acting before. Stimulating their thoughts may be your entry to developing yourself as a sole source opportunity for a new engagement.

Articles and Publications. You earn instant respect and credibility when you write articles and commentaries that are published in popular industry journals—and you reach a lot of readers who are potential clients. Similar exposure would be very costly if you had to obtain and service the journal's subscription list. If you do publish an article, it is important that you receive the right to include at least the name of the city where your company is located, and, if possible, the full mailing address and telephone number. Also, it is important for you to present topics and conclusions in your writing that are relevant but which do not solve the problems about which you consult.

Reference Material and Staying Current

Because telecommunications is one of the most rapidly changing technical specialties a management consultant could select, it is all the more important that you select readings and other materials that will guarantee your currency in the field. Listed below are some of the organizations, associations, periodicals, magazines, and conferences with which management consultants in telecommunications should be familiar.

Magazines

Data Communications

Datamation

Communications Week

Communications International

Communication of the ACM

Networking Management

Network Computing

Network World

Computer World and Datamation

Associations

Society of Telecommunications
  Consultants

Telecommunications
  Association

International Communications
  Association

Association for Computing
  Machinery

Communications Conferences

Supercomm '93

CIT, IVR, Voice Processing

Telecom Developers '93

ICA (International Communications
  Association)

COMNET

Competition

Who are the major management consultants that now specialize in telecommunications? First, there are large consulting firms: Booz, Allen & Hamilton, and Andersen Consulting hold a substantial portion of major contracts with large organizations and government. A number of smaller firms have evolved that specialize in telephone system type applications and use part-time consultants, drawing extensively from those who were previously employed full-time in the telecommunications industry.

Telecommunication companies and equipment manufacturers often provide consulting assistance to clients, and some have established separate organizations for call center consulting, disaster recovery, and similar specialties within the broader telecommunications area. These add to your competition, especially since the users regard these consulting services as free.

Companies that are not directly involved in telecommunications, including GE and IBM, either have or are establishing internal consultancies to assist clients as a business line. GE, for example, professes to be the world's greatest provider of customer service call center applications and training.

Another category of competition includes those in system integration who provide expertise in establishing local area networks and other telecommunication facilities as a by-product of delivering user applications. And, finally, in the 90s, with layoffs of thousands of specialists by such companies as AT&T and IBM, you can expect an avalanche of individual free-lance practitioners acting as consultants while they seek other employment.

The key to management consulting in telecommunications is to make your ability and consulting practice stand out through quality, understanding, and a focused marketing and sales approach. This will help you overcome the disadvantage of having to compete with large numbers of individuals.

31
Negotiation

Stuart Kliman

Jeff Weiss
Conflict Management, Inc.
Cambridge, Massachusetts

Introduction: Why a Chapter on Negotiation?

As we begin this chapter, the obvious first question to address is why a chapter on negotiation? The answer is really quite simple. Clients ask their consultants to help them with their negotiation challenges all the time. They ask their consultants for advice on negotiating purchase and sale agreements, on negotiating with regulatory agencies, on negotiating joint ventures and consolidations and, of course, on negotiating internally to implement the consultant's advice. The fact of the matter is that helping clients do well "at the table" is probably one of the most important and least understood ways that consultants can add value to their clients.

It should also be noted that consultants negotiate *with* their clients all the time. On any given engagement, consultants are required to negotiate over fees, scope, schedule, resources, access, and, of course, implementation. Thus, while negotiating *with* the client is not the major point of this chapter, it remains an important part of the consultant's life. As such, consultants using this handbook would be well advised to heed the advice we provide here not only as they coach their clients but also in planning their own negotiations.

To be clear, when talking about *negotiation*, we will not talk just about the things that happen when your clients sit down at the table and prepare to work out the terms and conditions of a deal. Rather, here we mean the act of *persuading* and *influencing*, moving parties closer to an agreement or a decision. Thus, we hope and expect that the ideas and concepts that we lay out for you in this chapter will be helpful to you, and therefore to your clients, in a myriad of situations.

In this chapter, we will introduce you to a framework you can use to help your clients think precisely about their negotiation goals, prepare carefully and systematically, and conduct their negotiations in a confident and strategic manner. We'll also talk some about how you can best coach your clients in the use of these concepts, and help them equip their organizations to get better negotiated results.

The Seven Elements of Negotiation: Toward a Clear Definition of *Success*

A wise person once said that if you don't have a clear sense of where your target is, you'll never be able to hit it. This is clearly the case with negotiation. All the time people—business people, lawyers, diplomats, and, yes, even consultants—jump into significant negotiations without a real sense of what an appropriate goal might be. Not surprisingly, without that clear sense of the target, they rarely hit it, getting pulled off track by various tactics and moves of the other party. Thus, the first question that must be addressed, prior to any discussion of how to best negotiate, is what is a good definition of *success* in negotiation?

We see lots of different measures of success as we work with clients throughout the world. Some clients think they have done well when they get lots of concessions from the other side as they negotiate; others feel they have done well if they "break" the other side's "bottom line"; others think that it is important to get the "last dollar" on the table; and others, particularly if they are in a relationship that they believe is very important, merely want to avoid confrontation and keep everyone happy. Obviously, although these ways of measuring success, and many like them, are commonly used, they generally do not lead to very good outcomes (for either party) and, for that matter, are not particularly helpful. For example, if your goal is to get the last possible dollar, how do you prepare? And can you ever *really* know if you have reached your goal? What about breaking the other side's bottom line? Can you ever really know where that is? And if you could have done better elsewhere or you paid too much as measured by some objective standard, is breaking their bottom line really a good sign of success?

It may be fair to say that these measures do occasionally work well when one is negotiating single-issue, single-party, one-shot deals. Clients generally call upon their consultants for help, however, when they are facing complex negotiations that involve many parties, many issues, and long-term relationships. In this context, a much more rigorous measure is called for. We have used a seven-element measure evolved out of the work of our partner, Roger Fisher, who coauthored the popular negotiation text *Getting to YES* (Roger Fisher and William Ury, Penguin Books, New York, 1983).

In negotiation, you will have reached a successful outcome if:

- Your agreement is better than the best *alternative* you have away from the table. *Alternatives* are those things that one could do *without* the agreement of the other side, away from the table, with another party, or by yourself. Thus, if you needed some fairly easy and reliable way to get to work, and were negotiating with a particular person for a used car, alternatives to an agreement with that person would include trying to buy a car from someone else, taking the subway, walking, stealing a car, and so on. Note, again, that each of these alternatives are things that you could do *without the agreement of the other side.* If you wanted to take the subway, the other party would not have to say "OK." Note, also, that out of all the possible alternatives, there is one that you would **prefer** to do if no agreement were reached. We call that most preferable alternative your *BATNA,* or your best alternative to a negotiated agreement.

- Your *interests* are very well satisfied. *Interests* are the aims, concerns, desires, and fears that motivate a party to negotiate. Thus, in the car-buying situation, your interests might include reliability, not getting wet or otherwise exposed to the weather, having the trip to work not take too much time, and maintaining a necessary cash flow in your checking account. Note that, in addition to wanting *your* interests well satisfied, you also need an agreement that satisfies the other negotiating party's interests at least acceptably if you want the party to say yes.

- Your agreement includes *options* that maximize and capture all of the possible value "at the table." *Options* are possible things the parties might agree to do together (as opposed to alternatives, which, as we said above, are things that one could do by oneself). For something to be an option, both sides would need to agree to it for it to happen. Thus, you and the car owner might talk about the possibility of your buying the car in cash immediately, your putting a nonrefundable deposit on the car and driving it for a time to decide if it is truly reliable before paying the rest, the owner's taking the car to get it inspected and painted lime green prior to your taking it, or even the owner acting as your chauffeur and driving you to work every day. Obviously, you couldn't make any of these things happen by yourself—you would need the other party to agree. That's why they are options and not alternatives.

- Your agreement has a strong sense of *legitimacy* in that it leaves both sides feeling appropriately treated and able to defend their agreement on the merits (based on some set of objective criteria). *Legitimacy*, therefore, can be defined as the extent to which the agreement relies on explicit logic, reason, or external criteria that lie beyond the simple will of the negotiating parties. In the car-buying situation, an agreement would *not* have a strong sense of legitimacy if the parties were unable to explain why the price was appropriate as measured by some external standard (the number seemed to come out of the air) whereas if the parties *could* explain it (by, for example, the average of the valuations given by three separate car dealers, or an automotive "blue book"), then one could say that the agreement seemed to be legitimate, defensible, and so on.

- Your final agreed upon commitment is clear and operational. *Commitment* here refers to the oral or written statements that define that which the parties have agreed to do. A good commitment is easy to understand, gives explicit instructions for what ought to happen next (people know what to do and how), and is clear about what is not included (it is not fuzzy or open to interpretation). With your car, you might want an agreement that specifies at what point title is to change hands, the form of payment, statements of warranty, and the like.

- Your final agreement was reached through an effective and efficient *communication* process. *Communication* refers to the ways you exchange messages, information, and so on back and forth with the other party. You would like that exchange to have been without confusion as to intent or meaning and to have occurred without waste of time. Thus, you and the used car owner might have agreed to communicate by fax, with offers and counteroffers, over the course of a day, and then to meet over drinks at a particular time to seal the deal—a reasonably effective and efficient communication/negotiation process.

- Your agreement was reached via a process that in and of itself enhanced the working *relationship* between the parties. *Relationship* here refers to how the parties treat one another and the extent to which they are able to do a good job of dealing with their differences. A good relationship tends to be a function of such things as mutual respect, trust, acceptance, and so on. Thus, you and the car dealer know that you have done well along this measure if, at the end of the negotiation, you think well of one another and believe that, should you ever have any dealings and/or disagreements with one another in the future, that you feel confident that you both can well handle any difficulties.

Thus, to put all this together, as you help your clients think about what a good negotiated outcome would be, it will be useful to get them to see that they will have a successful negotiation if they reach an agreement that is better than their best *alternative*, satisfies their *interests* very well (and the other side's at least acceptably), has in it value maximizing *options*, is viewed by both parties as *legitimate*, is a clear and operational *commitment*, is a result of an efficient and effective *communication* process, and is a result of a process that in and of itself enhanced the *relationship* between the parties. Once you have helped clients determine what exactly their alternatives are, what common interests they and the other party have, and so on, you will be able to construct a very precise target.

A Good Outcome

- Better than best *alternative*
- Satisfies *interests* very well
- Value-maximizing *options*
- Sense of *legitimacy*
- Clear, operational *commitment*
- Efficient *communication*
- Stronger *relationship*

If these seven elements define your client's measure of success, they should also help you guide your clients as they develop a strategy for negotiating.

Reaching Success: A General Strategy for Your Clients' Significant Negotiations

Armed with a definition of negotiation success, a target, the next logical question is how can your clients reach it? The answer, of course, has to do with what they actually do at the table. What they do at the table, in turn, is a function of the strategy they choose and the quality of their preparation to implement that strategy.

Thus, a diagram of this would look something like this:

PREPARATION   ⟹   **IMPLEMENT STRATEGY**   ⟹   **GOOD OUTCOME**
(CONDUCT)

Helping your clients with both strategy and preparation is critical, since one without the other will significantly reduce your clients' chances of negotiating well and getting the kind of results they would like.

As a general rule, many people find themselves, implicitly or explicitly, picking between one of two different general strategies—they choose either a "soft" strategy (designed to preserve the relationship with the other party, no matter what the substantive cost) or a "hard" one (designed to get as good a substantive result as possible, no matter the effect on the relationship). Although we caricature for effect here, as a general rule, in a hard strategy, parties take extreme positions (starting "high" or "low"), anchor in, making concessions only stubbornly (if at all), threaten to walk away if their demands are not met, mix up substantive issues with emotional and relationship ones (a "give me a concession or else I won't like you" tactic), and talk about all the things that they "won't" do. In a soft strategy (again caricatured), the parties take very reasonable positions, make concessions very easily (whenever the slightest confrontation occurs), never talk about the possibility of walking away, give in on substantive issues whenever the relationship is threatened, and talk a lot about what they are "willing" to do. Obviously, the choice between these two strategies is not an appealing one. The hard strategy sacrifices the kinds of long-term relationships that many of your clients want and more often than not need to have with their partners, their clients, their internal customers, their constituents, and so on. The soft strategy sacrifices the substantive value (e.g., the dollars and cents, terms and conditions) that your clients are striving to maximize. The challenge posed, therefore, is what kind of strategy can we design that will enable our clients to both build strong long-term relationships **and** maximize the value they are able to create in their agreement?

The answer is to design a strategy that does not ask you to choose—a strategy that has at its core an assumption that you can develop a negotiation process that enables you to be both soft and hard—soft on the people, hard on the problem. Not surprisingly, this strategy should be shaped by the definition of success we have discussed. Each of those seven elements can be used in a particular way to negotiate well. What follows is some advice for what you might coach your clients to do with each of the elements as they negotiate. Because of the linear nature of text, we have had to lay our advice out as if you did the first thing first, then the next, and so on. Unfortunately, that is not the case. Any negotiation involves at least two people, one of whom we have no control over. Thus, we cannot and should not try to script a negotiation. We can, however, prescribe some "rules of thumb" to use as a general strategy for reaching success. After running through advice about what to do with each element, we present a picture for you of what the strategy might look like in action (Figure 31-1).

Communication: Negotiate Explicitly over the Process First; Throughout the Negotiation, Question, Listen, and Adapt. In any negotiation, there are actually two negotiations going on—one over the substance (*what* we are negotiating about), one over the *process* (*how* we are negotiating). In most negotiations, the negotiation over process, however, tends to be implicit rather than explicit. Therefore, coach your clients to have a prenegotiation meeting over the process—to sit down with their counterparts and determine *how* they will move forward (by what process) to create the best agreement possible. This may include a conversation about, among other things, how each party will get prepared, when various types of information will be talked about, how they will start, what ground rules they will employ, how they will make decisions, what level of commitment they would like at various times throughout the negotiation, and who will be involved. Even if your client's negotiation is a simple one-time meeting, it is useful to still encourage him or her to begin with a quick conversation about how the parties will negotiate. As part of this, your client may want to talk with their counterpart about the definition of a good outcome we have discussed.

No matter how well parties negotiate over the process up-front, they will learn things as the negotiation proceeds that will suggest a need to adapt their strategy. Encourage your clients throughout the negotiation to ask questions of the other side and to really listen. We are all tempted to go in talking. Yet too many times when both parties have this attitude, they talk right past one another. Have your client keep in mind that there are two (smart) people in the negotiation, and that *both* need to be *persuaded*. If this were not the case, one could simply send a tape recording to the negotiation. "Share, question, listen, and reflect" is a very useful approach. Doing so will help your clients to strategically adapt their style and what they propose—not in a reactive manner, but in a thought-out and reasoned manner and for and with a purpose.

Interests: Consistently Work to Clarify Underlying Interests, Both Parties. Although it is a classic style of negotiating, few approaches that are more destructive of the ability to get to an optimal agreement than both parties' taking positions. When parties do this, they typically do not discuss what underlies those positions, their respective interests. Over the years, we have tried to illustrate the importance of the position-interests distinction through the use of a story, contained in

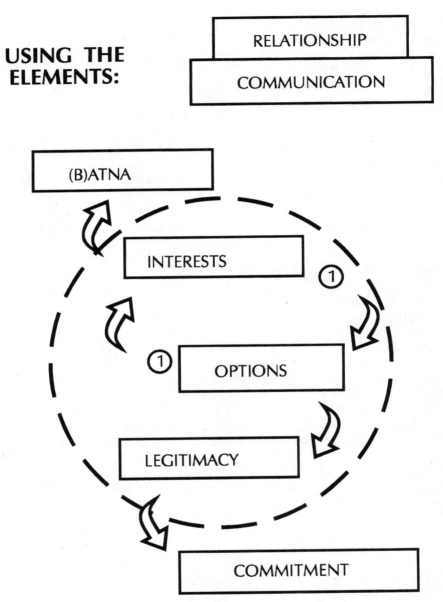

Figure 31-1 Integrated negotiation strategy.

Getting to Yes, of two sisters arguing over an orange. Each sister takes the position that she should get the whole orange, the last one left in the refrigerator. The sisters anchor into their positions, and as they negotiate, they get angrier and angrier, louder and louder, and more and more locked in. When their mother cannot stand the noise any more, she walks into the kitchen, takes the orange and cuts it in two, handing a half to each sister. The first sister peels the orange, throws away the rind, and walks out of the kitchen eating her half of the fruit. The second sister also peels the orange, but she throws away the fruit, and remains in the kitchen to bake half of an orange cake. The point of the story is evident—had each sister tried to explain *why* she wanted the orange (what her *interests* were in the orange), they both would have ended up with a better substantive result *and* a better relationship (they would not have engaged in an enraging battle of will and process of making demands back and forth). This may seem simple, but watch how many times your clients will get sucked into a positional game when confronted with the kind of demands, or positions, that they hear each day—"it must be done by the middle of next month," "it is only acceptable if we get it for 10 percent less," "do not come back without a 5 percent profit," "you must use these four people on this project," "I need the paperwork by the end of the day tomorrow."

When working with your clients, help them to be very clear with their counterparts about what they care about—*why* is it that they want what they want? This does *not* mean that your clients should lay everything they care about on the table. It *does* mean that they should question their assumptions about the cost and benefit of sharing various pieces of information, and that they should try hard to start by discussing needs, aims, and fears, rather than solutions. You should also coach them to push their counterparts to discuss their interests—why is it that their counterparts want what they want? To do this, your clients might get the ball rolling by first sharing some of their interest or suggesting a few of the counterparts' and ask what is missing, or tossing out a few possible solutions and asking what is wrong with the solutions. This latter tactic comes from the fact that, although most people do not like to talk about their interests in negotiation (for fear that they might be taken advantage of), most people do love to criticize. These criticisms are actually statements about the other side's *interests* (how they are not being met). Thus, if your clients ask for and really listen to their counterparts' criticism of a few possible ideas, your clients will learn a lot about their counterparts' interests. Further, since many people are afraid to talk about their interests (they fear they will get taken advantage of if they do), you might coach your client to put this directly on the table with a counterpart and have them each discuss how they can deal with those fears. Clearly, your client will also want to be able to articulate why it is so important to get interests out early—that doing so is critical to being able to get creative and create truly valuable solutions.

***Options:* Have Both Parties Jointly Generate a Number of Possible Options—Design Them to Meet Both Parties' Interests. Separate the Generating (Brainstorming and Inventing) Stage from the Deciding Stage.** The old saying goes that two heads are better than one, and most of us have experienced that the answers we come up with by ourselves, or with people who only look at the problem from the same perspective as we, are never as good as those we come up with when brainstorming with people who have a different set of views than we do. If one of the goals in negotiation is to be as creative as possible, in order to create the best solution possible, it is no surprise that "two heads" kind of thinking should apply just as well in negotiations. Unfortunately, few people ever really think about really putting their heads together with their counterparts' in negotiation. Instead, people tend to come in with "our" answer—the answer that we, from our more or less uninformed and one-sided perspective, believe to be the "right" one. Of course the counterpart does that as well, and the concession or haggling games begin. Creativity goes out the door, and, just as importantly, the process does not help build any sort of constructive relationship between the parties.

An alternative strategy is to coach your clients to try to engage those with whom they are negotiating in a process of jointly generating options *in the negotiation itself.* This is best done by using the ground rules of brainstorming, recording the ideas on a common piece of paper, and making it clear that inventing possible options at this point in the negotiation will be *separate* from either party *committing* to any one of them. It is critical that such brainstorming be targeted at the interests discussed, since the options that are invented should be attempts at meeting the various interests identified by both parties. Help your clients keep in mind that their job is to "expand the pie" and that this can only be done by getting creative. Doing this will mean that clients will need to restrain themselves from committing too early—many make the common mistake of being so concerned about reaching some sort of an agreement that they accept the first solution that gets put on the table that looks vaguely good for them.

***Legitimacy:* Use External Standards, Those That Are Not Determined by the Will or Strength of Either Party, to Make Joint Decisions about What Ought to Be Done.** There is nothing that is *harder* on the relationship, and that can get clients, and those with whom they negotiate, more and more entrenched in their positions, than arguing over what either of them "will" or "won't" do. At the same time, there is little that is *better* for a relationship and for reaching good substantive agreements than both parties striving to find good constructive ways to determine what they should agree to. Thus, encourage your client to focus the negotiation on what *ought to be done,* as determined by such things as objective criteria, external standards, industry precedent, analogous situations, what a third party would say. Help your clients to present standards and ask for them in return. Note that standards can be used as a "sword"—here's the data that explain why this makes sense—and as a "shield"—show me the data that explain why this makes sense. Help your clients provide their counterparts with the sound bites for explaining why your agreed-upon answer is defensible. Whether they want to admit it or not, each party knows that the other party needs to defend its negotiated agreement and its performance to both themselves and their ever-present constituents (bosses, colleagues, direct reports, and the like).

Just as important, of course, is the way that any such data are presented. If data, or criteria, are presented as justification for a previously taken position, their use will not be persuasive and will hurt the relationship. If, however, such data are presented fairly and even-handedly, if the presentation includes data that are "good" for both sides, if the data presented along with an invitation to mutually explore their validity (and with an openness to do the same with the other party's data), then presenting data is likely to result in a process that both enhances the relationship and leaves both parties feeling legitimately treated. This, of course, is very important. People in general have a need to feel fairly treated, and, in the business environment, clients and their negotiation partners need to be able to justify *why* they agreed to do something—why it makes sense, was appropriate, or was in line with the market. Thus, it is very important for you to help your clients use the element of legitimacy skillfully.

Alternatives: If They Threaten with It, Reality-Test Their BATNA; Discuss Your BATNA, If They Seem to Be Underestimating It; When Discussing It, Only Do So as a Possible Choice; Try to Avoid a "Whose BATNA Is Better/Worse" Discussion. Obviously, the ability to walk away from a deal is one of the most empowering things clients can take with them into a negotiation. When clients have this ability, however, they often use it foolishly. Instead of keeping their eyes on the seven-element definition of success, they begin to make threats about what they will do if their counterparts do not give in. They forget to talk about their interests, standards of legitimacy, and so on, and they forfeit any opportunity to have a constructive conversation about joint gains and creative solutions. Other times, when people don't really have walk-away power, they act as if they do, bluffing that they could walk away easily and informing their counterparts about how bad it would be if they did so. Yet other times, their counterparts will threaten first, to which your client's natural reaction will likely be to threaten right back. Each of these actions most often simply derails the negotiation. Sometimes a good well-founded threat helps, but rarely is this a useful first step.

It is critical that you help your clients to keep this in mind. If your clients have walk-away power, make sure they know it and that they don't agree to any deal that is not better than their BATNA (remember the 7-element definition of success). However, help them to use this power wisely. Encourage them to talk about their BATNA only as a last resort. They should push for interests, try to invent options, share some standards, and so on, all before they pull out their BATNA. Have your clients keep in mind that it is unlikely that their counterpart can take away their BATNA, so there is little incentive to using it early in the negotiation, especially since when it is discussed it tends to shut down the kind of joint invention process that can be so useful.

If your clients' counterparts to threaten with their walk-away power, encourage your clients to quite literally begin by taking a deep breath. Remind your clients that this is likely to simply be a tactic (the other parties will not walk away as quickly and easily as they say they are saying they will), and that even if it is not, their ability to walk away might not be as good as they believe it to be. Therefore, help your client to "reality-test" the other side's true ability to walk away. You might have your clients ask what they would achieve by going to their BATNA, push them for how doing so would meet the interests they have discussed, and try to show them that, although they obviously ought to make whatever business decision/choice is in their best interest, walking away might not truly meet their interests as well as they think (or at least not as well as the options that your clients might be willing to commit to). It is very important that in situations such as this you help your client stay calm and focused and, as much as possible, using language that feels collaborative. In particular, you might want to help your client say something like "obviously you could always walk away from this deal, that is of course your choice to make; it seems to me, however, that our purpose here is to see if we can come up with an option that makes better sense for both of us than walking away—so why don't we concentrate on trying to create that option, and leave our decisions around saying yes to each other or going elsewhere until later."

Obviously, this same type of advice holds true if your clients' counterparts are telling your clients how bad it will be if the former walk away. Have your client calmly explain why your client's walk-away is better than the other side believes (if it is), and that, in any event, your client thought that the purpose of this negotiation was not to talk about how bad each other's walk-away was but, rather, to try to *jointly create* something that is so good that walking away doesn't make sense for either party.

If and when your clients do feel it is useful to share their BATNA, they should do so in a way that allows the negotiation to continue. In other words, as your clients share their BATNA, they should do so in a way that truly encourages their counterparts to work with them to build a solution that would be better than this. If your clients simply put their BATNA out as a closed threat, they are far more apt to shut the negotiations down than to get what they want. Have your clients always keep their BATNA in mind, to share it cautiously and judiciously, and to always test the other side's threats, since it is too easy for people to overestimate their BATNA (especially when they perceive themselves to be in some sort of power position).

Commitment: Explicitly Set the Ground Rule That Both Parties Will Separate out Inventing a Possible Answer from Deciding What to Do, and Explicitly Make a Point of Leaving Any Commitments until the End of the Negotiation. Much of the strategy that we have laid out, above, will be hard for clients who fear that they will get locked into a particular brainstormed option or forced to do something that they talked about, or in any way get taken advantage of. It requires a fair degree of openness and confidence. In order for this to happen, your clients, when negotiating over the process (under the communication element, above), need to try to get their counterparts to agree that the first stage of the negotiation will be completely creative and designed to allow "out of the box" thinking and that no one will be forced to agree or otherwise be held accountable for an option that was created during the process. In other words, "inventing" options should be completely separate from deciding among them. As with the advice under the communication element, your clients will need to explain why they think this is a good idea, how the goal is to enable both parties to have their interests well met, create a no-waste solution, and so on, and that will never happen so long as they both fear saying anything or coming up with any idea that could potentially harm them.

Even if they cannot get the other side to agree to this ground rule, your clients can live by it themselves. Encourage your client to not commit too early, to invent before deciding. If your client is barraged by offers or requests for decisions, encourage your client to tell the other side that he or she will consider them as possible options to be improved upon and to be used to spark even better ideas. At some point, of course, some decisions need to be made. Have your clients do this with three thoughts in mind: (1) do so only after inventing (even if it is a 10-minute negotiation, taking the bulk of the time to invent is far more helpful than making immediate commitments); (2) carefully spell out and test their understanding of exactly what both parties are agreeing to do _prior_ to agreeing to it; and (3) do so only if what is being committed to is better than their BATNA.

Relationship: **Separate out Relationship Issues from Substantive Ones—Deal with Each Separately and on Its Own Merits.** To make their strategy for negotiation work for your clients, they will also need to have a strategy for dealing with the people issues, not just the terms and conditions, that crop up in negotiations. Have your client keep in mind a classic negotiation mistake—trying to fix a relationship problem with a substantive answer. Thus, when a party comes to your clients and says "I don't trust you," your clients will have two basic choices for how to respond. They could respond with a conversation around where the trust problem comes from (e.g., a dashed expectation) and come up with a plan to rebuild the trust, *or* they could respond by giving the other party some sort of substantive "bone" to try to make the party happy (e.g., some sort of price concession or a discount next time). Although it would be unwise to tell your client to never do the latter, the fact of the matter is that the former, trying to deal well with the trust problem, tends to work much better over the long haul. Trying to solve a relationship problem with a substantive concession almost never works; giving someone a price concession doesn't tend to make that person trust you more. It also teaches people that if they want a substantive concession, all they need to do is to threaten or complain about the relationship. Obviously, this is a dangerous precedent to set. Thus, encourage your clients to tackle relationship issues head on, noting them as such, explicitly indicating that an issue like trust or respect is different from what something like an appropriate fee might be, and coming up with some options that will deal specifically with the issue itself.

An equally important, and related concept, is to help your clients think about how best to deal with *appeals* to a "good relationship." We all of course will do special substantive favors for those with whom we have good relationships, but it is important not to allow your clients to get taken advantage of by those with whom they are closest. Your client will hear things like "good partners would cut their price" or "a team player would get this done by tomorrow." Help your client to resist these appeals. Here, again, they should deal separately with what partnership means, what the defensible price is, what a good teammate does, and the real need for and appropriateness of getting it done tomorrow. This is not easy to do, but it is critical to truly building strong relationships and to maximizing the value of the agreement.

Thus far, you have a set of tips for what you might coach your client to think about and do in significant negotiations. In short, help your client to do the following:

- *Communication:* Negotiate explicitly over the process first; throughout the negotiation, question, listen, and adapt.
- *Interests:* Consistently work to clarify both parties' underlying interests.

- *Options:* Have both parties jointly generate a number of different possible options—design them to meet both parties' interests. Separate the generating (brainstorming and inventing) stage from the deciding stage.

- *Legitimacy:* Use external standards, those that are not determined by the will or strength of either party, to make joint decisions about what ought to be done.

- *Alternatives:* If they threaten with it, reality-test their BATNA: Discuss your BATNA if they seem to be underestimating it; when discussing it, only do so as a possible choice; try to avoid a "whose BATNA is better/worse" discussion.

- *Commitment:* Explicitly set the ground rule that both parties will separate inventing a possible answer from deciding what to do, and explicitly make a point of leaving any commitments until the end of the negotiation.

- *Relationship:* Separate relationship issues from substantive ones—deal with each separately and on its own merits.

As to how your clients might put this advice together into an approach or strategy for negotiation, encourage them to think of negotiation as an exercise in *first* creating value and *then* claiming it. Have them consider Fig. 31-1 which represents an integrated strategy for doing this.

Reaching Success: Preparing to Implement Your Strategy

Your clients' ability to implement the advice we have just discussed is closely tied to how well they prepare. No matter how agile your clients are at the table, unless they are armed with useful information, they will not be effective. Our view is that power in negotiation comes mainly from preparation.

Just as our seven-element definition of success influenced the strategy your clients might employ, it can also help them systematically and strategically get prepared. To understand why this makes sense, it is useful to look at an example. If your clients are aiming to satisfy their interests, and their strategy therefore is to clarify interests with their counterparts, in their preparation they clearly need to have thought long and hard about what everybody's interests might be. Thus, your job, as you try to help your client negotiate well, will be not only to advise them on their strategy but also to assist them in getting well prepared. To do this, we would suggest you use the seven elements as a guide. The following are some tips to guide you.

First, Draw a Picture of the Situation. Negotiations, and negotiators, are constantly affected by the environment, other parties, other organizations, and in general other things that don't leap immediately to our consciousness. We have all been involved in negotiations in which we cannot understand why the other party is doing something, until we find out that someone or something else is actually driving or influencing that behavior. Other times the realization that another party or another factor is involved or has some interest in the negotiation unlocks our thinking and helps lead us to a new, creative solution (sometimes including that third party). For this reason, we have found the discipline of drawing a picture of the negotiation environment, including a broad range of potentially interested parties and entities, to be a very powerful tool. Thus, the first step to helping your parties get well prepared is helping them get a clear picture of the situation. Make sure that, among other things, you and your client include the key constituents and possible critics of both your client and their counterpart. As you help your client to take the following steps, make sure that you both keep the picture in mind. The array of parties represented in the picture should help you to expand your thinking as you assess interests, options, alternatives, and the like (Fig. 31-2).

Clarify Underlying Shared, Conflicting, and Common Interests of at Least the Main Parties. Use the following to help you focus on identifying *interests:*

- Clarify with your client what you believe to be the significant issues or questions to be addressed.

- List at least five to eight of your client's interests around each of the issues. Don't let your clients stop at too high a level—push them to really get at underlying interests by continually asking, "Why that?...and why that?" Consider prioritizing them.

- Repeat each of the above two steps from the viewpoint of your client's counterpart. Do not allow your client to caricature the other side; have clients really attempt to put the hat on of the counterpart. Consider a role reversal in which you play your client and your client plays the other party. Make sure clients think about their counterparts as people, and not as an organization.

- To the extent that you have time, repeat each of the above steps for other important parties or entities that you have identified in your picture.

Develop Options Designed to Meet Both Parties' Underlying Interests. Follow these guidelines in identifying *options:*

- Examine, with your client, the lists of interests you have recorded.

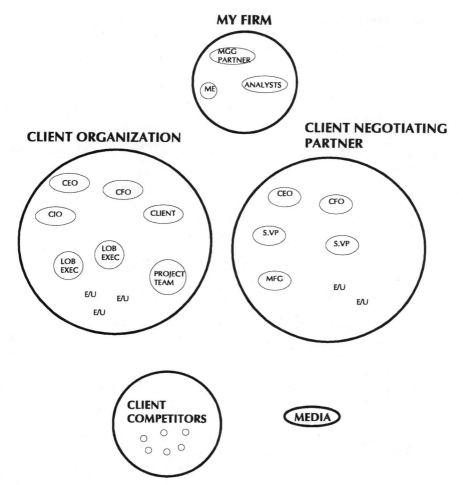

Figure 31-2 Negotiation environment.

- For each of the issues noted above, brainstorm possible options that your clients and their counterparts might agree to.

- Use the lists of interests to spark ideas. Use common interests and conflicting interests, and attempt to create possible options that meets various interests of both parties.

- Use your interest analysis as a checklist. If you have some interests that do not seem to be met by any of the options, try to come up with some additional options.

- After first inventing options (without evaluation), take the time to evaluate the various options in terms of their relative desirability to the parties, based on their interests.

Note that as you invent options, you may realize that the parties have additional interests. Go back and record these. This will happen as you work with each of the various elements, so make sure that as new ideas come up that you go back and record them under the appropriate element.

Determine a Set of Objective Standards That Might Serve as Reasonable Decision-making Criteria. Follow these guidelines to focus on *legitimacy* issues:

- For each of the various issues, brainstorm possible standards that might be used to decide which options or what details within an option are justifiable for both parties.

- Take the time to collect data, run numbers, get third-party opinions, find precedents or what was done in analogous situations, and so on. Get your clients to the point where they have facts, figures, third-party references at their fingertips.

- Identify which standards are likely to be most persuasive to your clients' counterparts. Collect data that speak their language, are based on the kind of reasoning that they tend to use, come from the kinds of environments that they are used to dealing with or looking to.

- Make sure your clients' standards are persuasive to themselves and their constituents.

Identify and Attempt to Improve Your BATNA; Identify and Examine Ways of Worsening Theirs. Focus on *alternatives* through these activities:

- Help your clients to brainstorm and record at least five to eight possible things they might do to meet their interests if they had to walk away from this particular negotiation. Among these, select the ones that seems to meet clients' interests best (their BATNAs).

- Brainstorm with your clients some things they might do to either make their BATNA even better or make it easier for clients to resort to.

- List at least five alternatives the other party may have, analyze how well each alternative may meet the party's interests (as you understand them), and select its most likely BATNA.

- List any actions that your clients might be able to take that would make their BATNAs either actually become less attractive to them or make it harder for them to resort to them. Also consider what data, questions, or the like that your client might be armed with at the table to help challenge a counterpart's perception of how good the counterpart's BATNA is.

- Looking at your picture, list any third parties that may have some information concerning the other parties' alternatives. See if there are some questions you should be asking those third parties about the counterparts' BATNA. See if there is anything you can say or do to those parties that might cause them to take some action designed to negatively influence the counterparts' perception of their BATNAs or their ability to resort to them.

- Help clients compare the relative strength of their and their counterparts' BATNAs. Ask yourselves: Are they both good? Are they both bad? Is there an imbalance here? Does it seem like there ought to be a broad or narrow zone of possible agreement?

Develop a Possible "Framework Agreement"; Determine the Purposes and Products (the Levels of Commitment You Want to Get to by the End) of Your Next Few Meetings. These activities will help you establish your *commitment:*

- Develop a draft framework agreement by first outlining what the headlines of a basic agreement might be (look at the issues you have identified and been using). As the negotiation evolves, you can help your client to add increasing levels of detail to the framework agreement. The trick here is to leave the nitty-gritty detail of exact prices and dates, for example, out. You will need to reach closure on these eventually. Yet it is often useful to start by hammering out what the agreement might look like overall (issues, best options, etc.) before getting at the details.

- Assess what level of authority your client has to make commitments in the negotiation. Try to do the same for the counterpart.

- Identify what you will need to accomplish along the way to a final agreement and break down the product (the tangible objective) of each negotiating session into a reasonable step along the way. For example the first session might have the purpose of setting the ground rules and schedule for the negotiation, the next might be aimed at getting a list of our interests recorded and some options and standards written down, the next might be aimed at narrowing options down to a select few, and so on.

- Consider how to make sure that any commitments made are understood by each party and are realistic and operational.

- Consider working with your client to invent some procedures your client might suggest to a counterpart for when the unexpected occurs during the implementation of any agreement. Keep in mind that even the best crafted, best understood, most realistic, and operational agreements will not be able to take every contingency into account.

Plan a Clear Possible Process and Some Strategies for Promoting Good Two-way Communication. Follow these guidelines to plan for good *communication:*

- Given the framework agreement, above, begin to explore the process your clients might best use to fill it out and get to agreement (or decide to go to their BATNAs). Think about the following: what sets of meetings and types of discussions will they need to have to put the strategy (as described above) into action? Should there be a prenegotiation meeting over the process that will be used? What will the aim (both purpose and product) of each session be?

- Consider what key questions your client might want to ask. Keep in mind that the work you have done with your client thus far (as to interests, alternatives, and the like) is speculative.

- Consider what messages your client might want to deliver and when. Think about how they should be delivered—in other words, how they should be framed.

- Lay out some possible communication protocols/ground rules for how your clients and their counterparts will communicate between them and among themselves and their constituents as the process moves forward. For example, if it is a team negotiation, will "time outs" for team caucusing be allowed? How will we recap commitments that seem to be made? What ideas will we record and who will do this?

- If communication between your client and counterpart has been difficult to date, consider diagnosing the causes for this and using the diagnoses to spark possible strategies/solutions. Help your clients to see when they might be falling into partisan perception traps—help them to at least view and understand (not necessarily agree with) their counterpart's perspective.

- Consider with your client how the counterpart likes to negotiate. Whether your client decides to play the "game," it is still useful for your client to think through the counterpart's preferred style.

Develop a Proactive Plan for Building the Relationship between your Clients and Their Counterparts. Use the following as a guide for building relationships:

- Help your client to describe the qualities of the relationship (how they will deal with one another) that your client would like to have with the counterpart at the end of the negotiation (e.g., trust, peer-to-peer, reliability, understanding).

- Describe the current relationship.

- Analyze the reasons for the gap between the current and desired relationship.

- Select the most important reasons and use them to spark ideas for some actions, inside or outside of the negotiation, that will help your client proactively move the current relationship toward the desired one.

- Consider inventing some strategies for putting any relationship issues (such as dislike for the style the counterpart is using or for how the counterpart is treating the client) that might get in the way of the negotiation on the table.

- Consider some approaches for setting a tone and approach of joint problem solving from the outset.

Interests: Clarify underlying shared, conflicting, and common interests of at least the main parties.

Options: Develop options designed to meet both parties' underlying interests.

Legitimacy: Determine a set of objective standards that might serve as reasonable decision-making criteria.

Alternatives: Identify and attempt to improve your BATNA. Identify and examine ways of worsening theirs.

Commitment: Develop a possible "framework agreement"; determine the purposes and products (the levels of commitment you want to get to by the end) of your next few meetings.

Communication: Plan a clear possible process and some strategies for promoting good two-way communication.

Relationship: Develop a proactive plan for building the relationship between client and counterpart.

As we have said, if you go through the seven elements as we have described with your clients, they ought to be pretty well prepared to enact the strategy. Note, however, that being prepared does not mean that they will know exactly what they are going to say at each point, at every juncture. Being well prepared in negotiation does not, in fact cannot, mean that your client knows the exact path through the woods. Rather, your client should know the terrain (accomplished through good preparation), have a set of ways to get started down or not go down a variety of paths (the rules of thumb and basic strategy), and maintain a clear sense of where she or he is going (the definition of *success*). If you can help your client get each of these three things, you have done your client a tremendous service.

The Twists along the Path to Success: Some Basic Tips on Dealing with Difficulties

No matter how ready your clients are to negotiate, because there are always at least two people in a negotiation, your clients are highly likely to come upon barriers along the road to success. As this happens, your role shifts from advisor to coach. As you try to coach the client, go back to the general strategy, as described above, diagnose what is getting in the way of it working (e.g., interests are not being explored, committing is occurring before there has been any inventing, lots of threats are being tossed around without any explanation of what they might or might not make sense to resort to), and consider how you might use the elements to overcome the barriers (e.g., start discussing some of the interests underneath the proposals that have been discussed thus far, suggest a 15-minute brainstorming session on new options, dig underneath the threats that have been made to see if resorting to them will truly help either party).

To give you a feel for how you might think this way and to get you jump-started, consider a few classic difficulties that occur in negotiations and some classic ways to use the elements and the strategy to help your client get out of those difficulties. As you review this, note how we use the elements as a list of prompts for ideas for "changing the game." For example, if the counterpart is locked into positions (stuck on making offers, or what we would call "commitments"), your client might move the conversation to "interests," asking "what can I do with 'interests' to 'change the game'?" Using interests as a prompt, the client might recognize that he or she could ask what needs the counterpart has underneath her or his position; the client might share his or her own interests and how the position meets and misses them. Your client could use any one of the other elements as prompts for new ideas for changing the game, as well, and as described below—this should also serve as a useful review for some of the concepts we have been discussing throughout the chapter.

Problem: Negotiators on the other side are locked into their position, refusing to budge.

Advice: (1) Have your client move to "interests" and "options." Tell your client to put a new option on the table and to ask the other side to criticize it. Few people can resist the temptation to criticize. Their criticism will in fact be statements about their interests. Use that information to create new options, put them on the table, ask for criticism, and so forth. Before you know it, the conversation will have re-begun.

(2) Have your client move to "communication." Tell your client to explicitly explain how each side's taking positions is not likely to help either move forward and explain how an alternative process (the one we have been talking about here) is likely to be more productive. Have your client explain the story about the two sisters and the orange.

Problem: The other side is taking a hard position, spending a lot of time talking about what he or she *will* or *won't* do.

Advice: Remember "legitimacy"; have your client suggest that they both take a step back and, instead of talking about what both of them will or won't do, that they talk perhaps about what they ought to do. Have your client suggest a number of different (and unbiased) decision-making criteria and processes and then ask for criticism around which one is most appropriate.

Problem: The other side is continually threatening to walk away, implying that that is OK for her or him but bad for your client.

Advice: (1) Move to "options" and "alternatives." Have your client explain that he or she understood that the purpose of this meeting was to see if the two parties, working together, could come up with an idea or option that was better for both of them than going to their respective walk-aways, that your client hoped that they could continue to try to do just that, that spending the short time they have together making threats is probably a bad use of time, and that obviously going elsewhere was always a choice that the other party was free to make, but one best made after both parties explore what they might be able to do together.

(2) Have your client move to "interests" and "alternatives." Have your client calmly and rationally explain his or her interests, what he or she sees as the best alternative, and why those interests seem to be reasonably well met by that alternative. Have your client explain what he or she believes to be the other side's interests, what the other side's walk-away is, and how that does not seem to be as good as the other side is implying. Counsel your client that it probably also makes sense, given the "hardness" of this move, to make all the points in the first piece of advice on this problem.

Problem: The other side is continually referring to the relationship that it has with your client, telling your client what good friends they are and how close they or their organizations are, in an effort to get your problem to agree to give them a better deal. Your

| | client feels guilty, and wants to give the other side the concession because she or he fears hurting such a good relationship. |

Advice: Remind your client of the strategic advice under the relationship element—separate relationship from substance. Have your client explicitly and proactively affirm how much she or he values the relationship and how it is incredibly important. Have client explain that it is precisely because the relationship is so strong that your client wants to make sure that both parties leave any deal feeling fairly treated, and that it is therefore very important that the parties come up with an agreement (price, deal structure, and so on) that they can both easily justify on the merits.

Problem: The other side is telling your client about a relationship problem (problems around trust, reliability, and the like) and that your client therefore needs to give a substantive concession.

Advice: As above, move to separating relationship from substance. Have your client try to deal with the relationship issue on its own merits, separate and distinct from pricing and other structural issue. Thus, if it is a trust problem, have your client explain that, if there is on the merits a problem that relates to price or whatever, that he or she will be happy to discuss that on the merits; if there is a trust or relationship problem, the client should explain that they need to deal with that on its own terms (i.e., how will we regain trust, what is appropriate recompense, if any, for dashed expectations, what can we do in the future to make sure such trust problems will not arise again, and so on).

Conclusion: Helping Your Clients Reach Success

As you move ahead and attempt to help clients with significant negotiations that they face, keep in mind the role you can play as advisor and coach. As you do this, consider what we have laid out above as some very systematic ways you can help your clients achieve more value from their important negotiations. To be clear, we believe that *value* comes in two forms: (1) *substantive value*—that which comes from the terms and conditions of the deal or, in other words, how well the parties' interest are met; and (2) *relationship value*—that which comes from the ways that both sides are left feeling about each other and how they dealt with their differences, and the resulting effect on their abilities to work well together in the future. Both forms of value are extraordinarily important in the kinds of complex negotiations in which your clients will get involved over time. These forms of value will be particularly important where long-term relationships with their counterparts matter and where the environment is rapidly changing so that working closely together and being able to adapt an agreement over time is critical.

As you attempt to help your clients, consider two additional things you might do. If you really want to help your clients do well in their negotiations, you may need to do a little negotiating with them yourself. Many clients already feel they are pretty good negotiators. If you face this, consider role playing a bit with them. This is often the best way to show clients that they do not know the kinds of traps into which they could fall. Of course, once you have prepared and strategized, role playing is a great way of practicing what the client might do at the table as well. Second, help your clients to learn from their negotiations over time by briefly reviewing with them. Ask them what worked well or what they might do differently next time. Ask them where they got stuck and how they got unstuck. If you can build with them a list of lessons for dealing well with their counterparts, you will really be able to help clients improve their approach and skills and develop customized ways of negotiating better.

Finally, keep in mind that all of what we have discussed above is equally applicable to you and your negotiations with clients. Make sure to help yourself. Define success, think through the strategy and advice we have recommended, get prepared, and have some various ways of adapting at the table and changing the game if necessary. As you do this, you will achieve better results for you, and, if you really are able to "stay in the circle," you will be able to achieve better results for your clients too.

32
Public Utilities

Jeff Kasschau
1st Approach, Inc.
Carlsbad, California

Introduction

Public utilities, long considered local or regional monopolies, typically offer essential services to the public in accordance with specific legislation controlling the utilities' territories, services, profit, prices, service quality, and ownership.

Falling within the category of public utilities are services for telephone, gas, water and electricity, as well as public transportation and refuse disposal. This chapter generally deals with the consulting opportunities in the primary group of telephone, gas, water, and electric public utilities. As a whole, this group represents a significant percentage of the total assets of nonfinancial businesses in the U.S. economy, following only the manufacturing sector of the U.S. group of businesses in total asset value.

In theory, the monopolistic offering of services provides a more efficient utilization of resources and thus lower cost to the public than would multiple locally competing companies. From that theory, it followed that a public utility operating as a natural monopoly would produce services to the public at a decreasing cost per unit as units of services increased with a growing local population and related escalating need for the services.

As such, public utilities traditionally have been different in form and substance from manufacturing or financial industries. Consequently, these traditional differences made the consulting practice for public utilities different. The consulting practice for public utilities involves a strong focus on the application of regulatory standards, an understanding of the effects of the decisions of state and local public utility commissions, an understanding of "rate base" accounting, and the business decision effects of providing the public utility shareholders with a predictable rate of return on their investments.

Trends in Public Utilities

The traditional business objective in public utilities involved maximizing capital projects to expand asset base following a normal cycle of:

- Project planning
- Project engineering
- Project construction
- Project operational start-up and operational testing
- Operations

These ongoing project cycles offered a full-service consultant the potential for continuous project engagements with the utility and a long-term relationship with the public utility for the life of the project operations (often 30 years or more). The types of consulting services within each project cycle included:

Project Cycle	Consulting Services
Project Planning	Demographic studies, feasibility studies, environmental impact studies, regulatory requirements services, cost-benefit studies, project scope, and scheduling services
Project Engineering	Engineering drawings, design specification development, material and equipment requirements planning, drawing and document control, quality assurance
Project Construction	Project management, project scheduling, budgeting, performance tracking, accounting services, records management
Project Operational Start-up and Operational Testing	Property accounting, master equipment lists, procedure development, training programs

Operations	Maintenance support programs, accounting, training, short- and long-term planning

Each of the above cycles and consulting support activities required personnel with a high degree of interpersonal and technical skills and, more often than not, a high degree of computer automation to manage a large volume of data. Frequently, the public utility had neither the staffing levels nor all the necessary technical expertise, thus providing a fertile ground for the use of consulting services.

Unfortunately, recent trends have retarded the degree of expenditure on large capital projects, ultimately shifting the focus from new construction to maximizing the utilization and extending the life of the existing facilities. The foundations of the natural monopolistic theory—an increasing population and demand for services and efficient utilization of resources by a single provider—have been disrupted by a decreasing rate of population growth, conservation, and deregulation.

The trends today point toward more regulation, more competition, and the need for public utilities to control and reduce costs and increase overall performance efficiencies.

Regulatory pressures from public utility commissions, local, state, and federal environmental protection agencies, Nuclear Regulatory Commission, Institute of Nuclear Power Organization, Federal Electric Regulatory Commission, and others impose a tremendous organizational and reporting burden on public utilities. Unfortunately, the pressures from regulatory mandates often become the primary focus in decision making, diverting attention from the objective of maximizing performance.

The trends have been to downsize staff, introduce more computer automation, diversify into related (property acquisition and development, cogeneration, equipment manufacturing) and unrelated (financial services, consumer goods, exporting) business activities, and pursue mergers to achieve additional economies of scale.

Why Public Utilities Use Outside Consulting Services

Public utilities have traditionally used outside consulting services to a significant degree. The reasons for this have been:

1. *To augment staff for defined projects.* Public utilities are often measured and regulated by public utility commissions on the number of permanent staff and are often constrained in hiring additional full-time staff. Therefore, as peaks occur in the work load, the use of outside services becomes necessary.

2. *To augment staff for extended periods.* Approved permanent "head count" is a key factor measured by regulators. Therefore, base-load work levels can be satisfied by outside sources who perform activities similar to those performed by the full-time staff.

3. *To acquire technical expertise/skills.* As with any other industry when a particular technical expertise does not exist internally, it is necessary to contract for this knowledge. In addition, project management and coordination expertise provide a valuable resource to the public utility during large-scale projects.

4. *To acquire industry expertise.* Outside consultants, by nature of their wide breadth of experience, often possess specific industry expertise not found internally within the utility's permanent staff.

5. *To achieve cost control.* Fixed-fee projects regularly occur with the use of outside consultants. This selection by the public utility is used to control risks associated with project overruns.

6. *To allocate capital costs.* Often the use of capital projects provides a public utility with an accounting/rate base advantage. The pure allocation of consulting support labor is more likely to be unquestioned by the public utility commission and is therefore used where appropriate.

Forms of Outside Consulting Services

As diverse as the business functions are in public utilities, it is not surprising to find a wide diversity of forms of outside consulting services for public utilities. There are two general but distinct forms of outside services. These are (1) contractors and (2) consultants.

Services by contractors to public utilities typically take the form of augmenting the staff. Because public utility commissions monitor the permanent "head count" of public utilities, a need is created to staff positions with contractors. The contractors may take positions at various levels in an organization and within virtually any business function of the public utility. Contract labor of this sort, by numbers, far exceeds the number of consultants used for outside services.

Contract labor is used for both short-term peak needs as well as long-term continuous need. Contract labor is typically provided by firms through multiyear contracts which are negotiated with a primary objective of least costs with a reasonable level of service and quality. Contractor services can include:

- Security and transportation services
- Facility management and warehouse staff services

- Bookkeeping and records management services
- Word processing and clerical services
- Computer software programming and data entry services
- Engineering drawing and drafting services

These services are usually provided by local services companies that can perform large-scale recruiting and provide timely results to the public utility's personnel.

The competition in this area of services includes:

- Large, well-organized staff services firms with local offices
- Local firms that have personal contacts with the public utility and the ability to control overhead costs

Consultants, however, provide outside bid services to public utilities for a number of reasons. These reasons include:

- The public utility has a defined project with defined deliverables but does not have the staff to conduct the project.
- The public utility does not have particular technical skills or does not have significant number of specialized technical skills on staff.
- The public utility does not have wide industry knowledge.
- The public utility would like to direct risk on a project or activity to an outside services firm.
- The public utility recognizes that the economics of using outside services on capital projects are favorable in the rate-based methods used by public utility commissions.

Consultant services of this nature are usually contracted as a result of competitive bid processes that consider each consultant's experience, reputation on similar projects, availability of staff, demonstrated ability in project management and project quality assurance, and cost. Consulting services can include:

- Feasibility studies
- Environmental impact studies
- Design and construction services
- Rate and regulatory affairs case preparation support services
- Demographic and service demand forecasting services
- Organizational review and staffing level services
- Distribution planning services

- Training
- Computer system planning, design, and development

These services usually are provided by firms that have focused on developing a particular expertise of value to public utilities. These services are not necessarily available only through large regional or national firms. A large share of this type of work is conducted by small- and medium-sized specialty firms that develop a reputation of offering high-quality services in a particular area.

The competition in this area of services includes:

- *Large public accounting firms with consulting practices.* These firms are often the only firms capable of providing a large number of personnel for software projects demanding large staffs and strong project management.
- *National or regional consulting firms.* Some of these firms can demonstrate numerous human-resource assessment studies and/or rate case/prudency audit expertise.
- *Large architect/engineering firms.* Firms that have demonstrated design and construction expertise are competitors.
- *Local or regional specialty consulting firms.* These firms can offer the same or greater level of specific technical knowledge than that offered by a large national or regional firm at more competitive rates.

Areas of Outside Consulting Services

Consulting within public utility industry groups offers a wide variety of opportunities. As with other industry groups (for example, the manufacturing or financial sector) some very traditional functional business areas exist, including:

- Finance and accounting
- Human resources
- Administrative support
- Purchasing and materials management
- Customer service
- Computer systems development and computer operations

Within these traditional functional areas, public utilities have unique attributes that need to be considered when offering consulting services.

In the area of *finance and accounting*, public utilities are large users of open market capital resources and are therefore extremely sensitive to fluctuations in interest rates and their bond ratings. As a result of large capital projects, the cost of capital contributes significantly to the utilities' abilities to meet regulatory pressures for providing reasonable or least-cost services to the public. The accounting functions within public utilities are complicated through the application of Federal Energy Regulatory Commission (FERC) accounting requirements and the necessary translation of accounting transactions and records to generally accepted accounting principles (GAAP) used for traditional financial reporting standards to the public, investors, and taxing authorities.

The area of *human resources* may vary from those of other industry sectors because of the large number of employees found within public utilities and the myriad of job classifications necessary to address the diversity of functions performed within the utility. Groups of public utility employees are often represented by collective bargaining units, thus requiring negotiation with multiple unions, singly and across specific union boundaries. Human resources typically is dealing with the trends of permanent staff downsizing, job reclassification, and training. Furthermore, more stringent health and safety laws are typically administered within this area.

The area of *administrative support* introduces unique attributes resulting from complexities in legal areas dealing with land (deeds, rights-of-way, leases) and water rights. Public utilities are typically large real estate holders of such property as administrative buildings, production facilities, and distribution/transportation facilities. Because a utility must manage and safeguard these assets and perform coordinating activities, administrative support is a significant business function within the typical public utility.

The functional aspects of the area of *purchasing and materials management* correlates with other industry groups. However, the volume and variety of materials and services causes the activity to be generally incompatible with those of other businesses. Whereas a manufacturer procures materials for use in the production of a product, a public utility procures materials for use in the generation of a service. The huge value of real assets invested for the production of service by public utilities demands considerable effort in the procurement of replacement parts, spare parts, consumables, and tools. Furthermore, as a result of the geographical disbursement of production and delivery facilities, sound materials management requires the use of widespread satellite warehousing facilities and the application of sound internal distribution methods.

The area of *customer service* can be found in such other industries as banking, consumer goods, and insurance. The uniqueness of the area in public utilities is due to the large degree of personal contact required in handling such matters as telephone or gas hookups, reading of meters, and resolving trouble calls. Customer service is often considered to be the most important function within a public utility. Its activities significantly impact capacity planning and future facility construction requirements planning and scheduling.

The area of *computer systems development and computer operations* is responsible for systems planning, systems development, systems implementation, and maintenance. Computer systems within public utilities tend to differ to some degree from similar areas in nonutilities, however, in that process computer applications are as common as business applications.

Functions that exist within public utilities which often do not exist within other industries include engineering and construction, rate and regulatory affairs, service generation, and transmission. The engineering and construction function mainly focuses on the design of new facilities and the design of improvements of existing facilities and on the construction of facilities or the management of construction contractors utilized in facility construction/improvements. The rate and regulatory affairs function plans, prepares, and presents rate cases, performs cost of course studies, analyzes rates and rate structures, prepares cost adjustment factors for regulator-approved rate relief, and administers the regulations imposed on the public utility.

Opportunities in Public Utilities

Although some of the trends in public utilities are negative trends (such as reduced construction and expansion, unfriendly actions by public utility commissions, declining rates of population growth, downsizing of public utility organizational staffs), the pragmatic observer should recognize opportunities for consulting in the public utility industry. The primary impetus for public utilities is or should be cost control (i.e., providing the same or better service at a lower per-unit cost). If the public utility cannot produce its service at a lower cost, competition will erode its ability to distribute maximum efficient capacity and will ultimately result in a higher unit-of-service cost. (The higher unit-of-service cost is based on the capacity/utilization formula, which states that the capacity divided by the cost equals the unit cost/capacity.) Opportunities clearly exist for consultants to assist public utilities in becoming more cost efficient, partly due to the downsizing which many have undertaken. Opportunities related to price and gross margin improvement also exist, but they are generally secondary to those involving cost containment.

The areas of greatest opportunity for consultants, often related to the goal of cost control, include the following.

Computer Automation. Applications involving computer-aided design, computer-aided engineering, and process computing can aid in improving, maintaining, and operating the facilities of public utilities. Hand in hand with these applications, the consultant is typically requested to assist in the evaluation of emerging technologies including hardware platforms (e.g., client/server architectures), telecommunication and local area and wide area networks, and software tools (e.g., CASE tools, designer workbenches).

Data Collection, Verification, and Consolidation. Traditionally, public utilities have decentralized functions and data. Current trends, however, point toward centralization as a means of effecting consistency in programs and gaining the ability to withstand staff downsizing. Therefore, the firms that can efficiently evaluate, merge, and consolidate data should be well poised for success.

Work Process Analysis. More efficient ways of conducting business should be the goal of public utilities. Studies, evaluations, and improvements in work processes will aid in reaching this goal. Consultants with strong industry experience will be best suited to support the public utilities with these tasks.

Regulatory Compliance. Defining methods to ensure compliance while reducing the effort required to track and report regulatory key factors should be a significant new opportunity for consulting firms.

Training. Whenever change occurs, training is needed to ensure that changes result in the anticipated benefits. The ability of consultants to provide training in work procedures, environmental and safety regulations, computer applications, and customer service should be valued by public utilities.

Positioning the Practice

As with any consulting practice, one emphasizing service to the public utility industry needs to define the type and level of service that the firm wants to provide. It is not wise to profess to be capable of providing all types of services to all public utilities. Your firm should focus on certain types of public utilities (e.g., electrical production and transmission, gas distribution, telecommunications, transportation) or it should focus on certain functional areas (e.g., finance, engineering and construction, human resources, customer service, computer services). Regardless of the services selected, your firm needs to recognize and exploit its capabilities, the skills of its personnel, and the experiences that it has had in dealing with specific problems.

Any firm currently building a consulting practice with public utilities or anticipating entering this area must be cognizant of industry trends (e.g., effects of deregulation, regulatory pressures, corporate downsizing, pressures of cost control and needs for efficiency gains, and current market position of the various public utilities).

Obtaining information on specific public utilities and the industry in general is an easy task because many of the industry's decisions, plans, and financial information is a matter of public record. Also, establishing contacts within the industry is possible because your consulting organization can join or attend numerous industry-related professional organizations and related conferences.

As with any industry group, there are promising candidates to whom you can market your consulting services. Key factors to evaluate as you look for suitable public utility candidates include:

Financial Health.   The selected public utility should be financially sound. Its ratios of capitalization and rate of return should exceed those of the industry averages. Bond ratings are also an important ingredient to evaluate. Sound bond ratings are an overall reflection of the company and have a significant bearing on the ability of the utility to obtain funds at an attractive rate.

Management Capabilities.   A stable, skilled, and innovative management team is a key factor. The management team should be capable of adroitly handling environmental, consumer, competitive, and cost pressures.

Mature and Sound Management Processes.   The utility should have developed a clearly defined and well understood set of management processes, which are supported by a core of effective information management systems.

Regulatory Track Record.   The public utility's past record with regulators is another key factor to consider. A sound track record should be a good indicator that regulators will not aggressively contest the practices of the utility, thus causing the management of the utility to devote excessive time in devising defensive measures.

Public Opinion. The public opinion factor will often provide a good indication of where a public utility stands relative to recent/past performance. Thus, by learning the level of respect that a public utility has earned with the public can provide a basis for identifying the suitability of the utility as a potential client.

Service Territory and Market Share. To be a suitable candidate, a public utility should serve a large territory in which the customer base is growing. Furthermore, the utility should be in a position to expand its territory and market share through potential mergers, acquisitions, and technological innovations. The public utility should also be supporting a rate structure which would dissuade the introduction of non-regulated competition.

Diversified Corporate Goals. The public utility industry previously has existed in an environment that has been essentially stable and unchanging. Unfortunately, significant changes occurred during the 1980s that have adversely affected the market positions of public utilities, and growth rates in primary business services have declined. A suitable candidate for consulting services should be willing to modify its corporate goals. For instance, it should accept diversification into innovative new markets to maintain or improve its rates of return.

The well-positioned consulting firm that maintains a public utility practice should have or seek to obtain long-term relationships with leading public utility clients. It should also be prepared to take advantage of the following opportunities.

Escalating regulatory pressures. Consulting solutions that ease these pressures should be a skill the consultant can provide to its public utility clients.

Escalating operations and maintenance costs. This is a prime target area within which the consultant can provide cost-cutting solutions. This area is also particularly well suited to the use of computer-based tools.

Permanent staff downsizing. This is an obvious opportunity for the use of qualified staff augmentation services.

Increasing information needs. Consultants that offer system integration services, particularly between production/operating units systems and corporate systems, should be well-positioned to assist in satisfying increasing information needs.

Demands for higher skills. Due to the need for skilled employees, consultants that can provide ongoing support in technical training to public utility personnel should be in a position to take advantage of this opportunity.

Conclusion

Public utilities have traditionally been heavy users of outside consulting services. This trend will probably continue, but with a more selective approach. The predominate needs will be in the area of specialized skills: environmental, computer, engineering, and design. The consulting firms which excel in these areas will be those that recognize the opportunities presented by the public utilities and be capable of responding to their needs with a full range of results-oriented solutions.

33

Health Care Organizations

Valerie Norton Downs

Senior Consultant
Skills Management and Transformation
IBM

Introduction

This chapter introduces you to the fast-growing health care industry and prepares you to begin practicing in this field. First, we'll discuss where to learn about the industry through professional associations, regulatory agencies, and publications. Then we'll examine the various types of health care organizations, their structures, people, issues, and trends. Last, we'll discuss special operational and practice management considerations in serving this industry.

Where to Learn about Health Care

There are several ways to get to know the health care industry. Total immersion in the industry via an internship or mentoring program is an ideal start. Here are some additional ways to learn about the industry.

Professional Associations

Professional associations provide a quick way to learn about the industry and are a great source of potential clients. Pick a few of the best in your practice's area of competency and become involved in their activities. Some associations require certain educational background or business experience for entry, but many do not. If your practice has multiple medical professionals in it, each person can join associations in his or her area of expertise, and the practice will achieve broad coverage. Most membership dues are very reasonable, and the benefits are well worth the investment. Many national associations have local chapter meetings and shows that provide excellent opportunities for networking with others in your geography. Volunteering for committees or becoming an officer or board member of the association can accelerate your learning and your exposure to others in the industry. Some organizations also offer credentials or a certification program. These may be awarded after oral or written examinations, paper writing, etc. Some consulting firms require industry certification as a prerequisite to promotion to management.

Here are some top associations we have found useful. There are also associations to serve the departmental, clinical, and quality areas. A complete listing of over 200 health care associations with detailed descriptions of each can be found in the *Encyclopedia of Associations*, 27th edition—1993, published by Gale Research Company, Detroit, Michigan.

The American Hospital Association (AHA), 840 N. Lake Shore Dr., Chicago, Illinois, 60611, (312) 280-6000, provides a wealth of information and includes many specialty organizations. Corporations and individuals can join. The association promotes the welfare of the public through its leadership and assistance to its members in the provision of better health services for all people. It does research, conducts educational programs, maintains a library, collects and analyzes data, presents awards, and represents hospitals in national legislation.

Affiliated associations of the AHA include the American Organization of Nurse Executives, the American Society for Health Care Human Resources Administration, the American Society for Health Care Marketing and Public Relations, the American Society for Health Care Risk Management, the Health Care Information and Management Systems Society, and many other specialty organizations. Each of these holds its own meetings, conducts education and publishes related journals.

The American College of Health Care Executives (ACHE), 840 N. Lake Shore Dr., Ste. 1103W, Chicago, IL, 60611, (312) 943-0544, is a professional society for hospital and health service administrators. It works to:

- Keep members abreast of current and future trends, issues, and developments

- Shape productive and effective organizational strategies and professional performance

- Increase the visibility and recognition of the health care management profession

- Act as an advocate for health care management in legislative activities and with government agencies

- Develop cooperation among professional societies and other health care associations

- Strengthen and encourage the profession's code of ethics

- Maintain professional standards

ACHE also grants awards, operates a library, provides education, offers student loans and scholarships, conducts research, keeps a database and operates committees and task forces.[1]

The Health Care Financial Management Association (HFMA), Two Westbrook Corporate Center, Ste. 700, Westchester, IL, 60154, (800) 252-4362 or (708) 531-9600, is a leading professional membership organization for financial management professionals including CEOs, CFOs, controllers, patient accounts managers, accountants, physicians, and consultants. It addresses the needs of health care financial managers through educational programs, providing networking opportunities, communicating news and information on key issues and technical data, and representing members in health care policy matters before government officials and others. HFMA also provides a significant amount of regulatory and tax and reimbursement update information to members.

The American Association of Health Care Consultants (AAHC), 11208 Waples Mill Rd., Ste. 109, Fairfax, VA, 22030, (703) 691-AAHC, is a professional association for individuals devoted to health care consulting. It acts as a resource for health care providers, provides education for consultants, and maintains a speaker's bureau, standards, and a professional code of ethics for health care consultants.

The Medical Group Management Association (MGMA), Denver, CO, 80256-0444, (303) 799-1111, serves those interested in physicians' practice management. It conducts national and regional meetings, offers continuing education classes and specialty programs for particular interest areas, maintains a library for research, operates a certification program including a fellowship program for medical office managers; and represents its membership in regulatory issues. An MGMA officer represents

---

[1]*Encyclopedia of Associations,* 27th edition—1993, published by Gale Research Company, Detroit, Michigan.

MGMA's interests to the Health Care Financing Administration or HCFA (see below).

State and county hospital associations and medical societies also provide a great source for your research about health care in a particular geography.

Government and Regulatory Agencies

Government and regulatory agencies have a tremendous impact on the health care industry. By keeping in close touch with their activities and rulings, you can spot trends and resulting consulting opportunities. The three major agencies we'll discuss here affect the hospital, physician, and managed care organizations.

Joint Commission on Accreditation of Health Care Organizations (JCAHO), Oakbrook Terrace, IL, establishes standards and conducts voluntary accreditation programs for hospitals, psychiatric facilities, substance abuse treatment and rehabilitation programs, community mental health centers, organizations providing services for the mentally retarded and developmentally disabled, long-term care facilities, hospice programs, and ambulatory health, managed care, and home care organizations.[2] Since maintaining JCAHO accreditation is key to receiving funding from Medicare, health care organizations must comply with JCAHO standards. One such key standard indicates that a health care organization must be able to demonstrate its progress toward continuous quality improvement (CQI) by 1994 to receive accreditation. Since many health care organizations have only recently begun their CQI efforts, this represents a significant opportunity for quality consulting. The JCAHO will also have information systems management standards as part of its review process in 1994. The JCAHO publishes, sponsors continuing education programs, and maintains a speakers' bureau.

Health Care Financing Administration (HCFA), a U.S. government agency, Washington, D.C., oversees the administration of Medicare and Medicaid programs. Medicare directs program administration through working relationships with contractors, providers, physicians, the Social Security Administration, regional offices, the office of the Inspector General, and other local and national organizations and individuals. Medicaid plans, manages, and provides federal leadership to state agencies in program implementation, maintenance, and regulatory review of state Medicaid program management activities under Title 14 of the Social Security Act. The Division of Health Standards and Quality

---

[2]Ibid.

ensures that health care services provided under the Medicare and Medicaid programs are furnished in the most effective and efficient manner, consistent with recognized professional standards of care.

The Omnibus Budget Reform Act (OBRA) of 1989 addresses payment reform for physicians and has created new issues for physicians' practice management. Doctors must now provide the service of submitting Medicare claims for the patient. The doctor can be charged penalties for failure to comply with this regulation. Other details of this act will be discussed in a later section. HCFA actions are having a significant impact on how the physician manages his/her practice and on the profitability of the practice.

Office of Prepaid Health Care Operations and Oversight (OPHCOO), a U.S. government agency, Washington, D.C., decides which health maintenance organizations (HMOs) are federally qualified. To receive Medicare payments, an HMO must be federally qualified or be deemed a "qualified Competitive Medical Plan" by the OPHCOO. The same inspection is required for both categories. The latter category is primarily intended to allow commercial, for-profit companies to receive Medicare payments without meeting all the requirements of the federally qualified HMO. Individual states can license HMOs, but many large employers prefer to work with a federally qualified organization.

State health departments or health agencies are different in each state and can have a significant effect on health care organizations. For example, in the state of New York, hospital rates are regulated by the state, regardless of the payor. The state also imposes penalties on hospitals with low occupancy rates. Since each state differs in how it establishes health policy, consultants need to learn about these differences to consult effectively.

Publications

Beyond national business reading sources such as *The Harvard Business Review, Fortune, Forbes,* and *Finance World,* there are a variety of sources of information about the health care field. Health care articles appear on the front page of almost any major newspaper any day of the week, and the major news services, such as Dow Jones News Retrieval, Compuserve, and Prologue allow you to set up standard retrieval searches that can give you the latest news in health care. The *Wall Street Journal* has a series titled "Pricing Health Care" that appears approximately monthly on the editorial page. There are also some excellent health care publications available.

The American Hospital Association publishes *Hospitals* magazine biweekly and *AHANews* weekly. Their annual publications include the *Guide to the Health Care Field* and *Hospital Statistics.* The JCAHO publishes

JCAHO Perspectives bimonthly, which covers changes in accreditation standards, policies, and procedures. JCAHO's *Home Care Bulletin* is a quarterly newsletter covering home care accreditation programs. An excellent source of information in health care quality trends is the JCAHO's *Quality Review Bulletin: Journal of Quality Assurance*, which is published monthly and provides information about quality assurance approaches, activities, theory, and research and related aspects of quality care in hospitals.

Another valuable magazine is *Modern Health Care*, which covers current health care trends, issues, and news. Excellent publications are also available from pharmaceutical firms, such as Merck Merrill Dow, and from Aspen publications, which offers quarterly journals targeted to specific interest areas. Other magazines targeted at particular interest areas include *The Health Care Forum Journal*, published by the Health Care Forum in San Francisco, which is an excellent source of information on quality trends; *Health Care Informatics* and *Computers in Health Care*, good sources for news about the use of information systems in health care; and *Medical Group Management Journal*, a good source for trends in the physicians group practice area. Other specialty areas publish niche journals.

Education

There are many sources of formal education in health care. Many local colleges and universities offer a bachelor's program via their health sciences schools and a master's in health care administration. Some allow students not pursuing a degree to take individual courses. Professional associations offer extensive continuing education programs (e.g., HFMA and ACHE offer courses that anyone can attend), and many hospitals provide continuing education locally. The American Society for Quality Control (ASQC), IBM's Education and Training Division, and many other consulting and education companies offer courses commercially in the health care field.

One of the best ways to learn about a health care organization's operation is to perform an internship there. After a week or two of working in the operation, you will have a far greater appreciation of the client's environment, pressures, and needs than you could ever gain from a textbook. You may even be able to establish a mentor/protege relationship with a health care executive or physician. An ideal internship might mirror the flow of the patient through the health care system. For example, an intern could start in admitting or the emergency room, then move to bed assignment, nursing and physician diagnosis and care planning, through the various ancillary departments, then through discharge, medical records, and billing.

Other Consulting Firms

To learn about your competition, you can get information from many sources. Reading the *Standard and Poor's* reports at your local business library is a start. *Consultants News*, by Kennedy Publications is a good source for news on other firms. The research departments of the AHA and other professional associations also can be sources. Talking with executive recruiters, reading magazine advertisements, attending trade shows, and picking up competitive literature provide additional information. If you lose an engagement, ask the client why he or she chose your competitor, and you may learn a great deal about your competitor's strengths.

Health Care Organizations, People, and Issues

There is a broad and growing variety of health care organizations in the United States. In this section we'll describe the most common organizations, their structures, and their people. We'll also examine health care issues that might provide potential consulting engagements.

Types of Organizations

The 1992 AHA *Annual Survey of Hospitals* indicates that there were 6539 hospitals in the United States, 6214 of which were nonfederal. Of these, 5292 were community hospitals that provided short-term, general care. We will look at the various types of health care institutions, but we will concentrate on the nonfederal environment. Additional details about specific hospitals and statistics about groups of hospitals can be found in two AHA publications: *Hospital Statistics—1993–1994* and the *AHA Guide to the Health Care Field—1993*. These are available by calling the AHA or by visiting most business or medical libraries. New annual data are published in November each year.

Government nonfederal hospitals include state, county, city, city/county, and hospital districts or authorities. Government hospitals must deal with issues such as a large indigent population, a high percentage of Medicare/Medicaid patients, and a higher acuity (sicker patients) than private hospitals. Many are also affiliated with universities and serve as teaching hospitals. Teaching hospitals are usually very large, complicated organizations. They conduct research projects and, therefore, need to take on the toughest cases. These intensive cases require more health care workers (full-time equivalents, or FTEs) per patient than an average case, causing costs per patient day to increase.

Nongovernment, not-for-profit hospitals include those with a religious affiliation and other not-for-profit hospitals. These hospitals are concerned with cost control, but their major focus is on providing high-quality health care. The church-operated hospitals' mission statements tend to reflect the religious heritage and affiliation of the hospital. Many church-operated hospitals are members of groups that provide centralized services and increase their buying power and negotiation strength with vendors. Examples include Catholic groups such as The Daughters of Charity and The Sisters of Charity, The National Jewish Center for Immunology and Respiratory Medicine (NJCIRM), and St. Jude's Children's Research Hospital.

Investor-owned, for-profit hospitals can be owned by individuals, partnerships, or corporations. They are focused on providing high-quality care in a competitive, profitable way. Many are part of chains and operate in the suburban communities. An optimum size for operational efficiency seems to be 150 to 250 in-patient beds. Examples of chains include Ornda, NME, and Columbia/HCA.

Government federal hospitals include Air Force, Army, Navy, and Department of Justice facilities. Also included are public health services such as the VA hospitals and the Indian Health Service.

Osteopathic hospitals can be religious-affiliated, not-for-profit, or investor-owned (by an individual, partnership, or corporation). Osteopathic hospitals began because schools of osteopathic medicine needed places for their students to practice. Many regular hospitals didn't accept D.O. students.

Service organizations, such as the Voluntary Hospitals of America (VHA), headquartered in Dallas, Texas, provide services and programs to improve members' competitive position. Services to member hospitals include education and development, management of health insurance plans for hospitals, consulting, and purchasing benefits.

Other large health care organizations include the fifteen major clinics in the United States, such as the Mayo Clinic, and the growing number of health maintenance organizations (HMOs), such as Kaiser Permanente, CIGNA, Champus, Blue Cross/Blue Shield, and the Group Health Cooperative. Almost all health care insurance companies now provide some type of managed health care program. The HMOs are most active in California, Arizona, Minnesota, and Florida, but they are growing rapidly as employers and individuals seek to cut their health care costs. HMOs focus on health promotion and disease prevention versus the more traditional hospital model which focuses on illness and outcomes.

Ambulatory care facilities are growing quickly in the United States today. These facilities can be free-standing or affiliated with another health care organization such as a hospital. They provide primary care and some day surgery. Advances in medical technology, cost reduction, and increasing consumer knowledge of health care have all contributed to the growth of these organizations.

Another growing organization type is the medical group practice. As physicians try to cut their overhead costs by joining in larger and larger group practices, new issues of practice management emerge. Physicians are learning how to run their practices as businesses, and most groups are hiring professional business managers to run their offices.

People

In this section, we'll give a thumbnail sketch of the health care executives you will be working with in your consulting engagements. We'll describe their typical backgrounds, issues on their minds, and the length of their planning horizons. In many hospitals there is a continual three-way balancing act going on in the power structure among administration, physicians, and nursing.

Chief executive officers (CEOs) usually have a master's degree in health administration (M.H.A. or M.S.). Some MBAs and MDs are also becoming CEOs. They spend about 60 percent of their time in community relations and about 40 percent of their time in the hospital. CEOs have a global view across the organization and the community, and their planning horizon is typically 2 to 3 years or greater. Many major cities have hospital councils and/or business coalitions that are working together to drive down health care costs. CEOs participate in these organizations and are involved with health policy issues at the local, state, or federal levels. They have a strong business orientation and are concerned with quality, organizational structure and dynamics, staffing, employee benefits, profitability or cost control, and physician relationships.

Chief operating officers (COOs) may have clinical backgrounds or they may have a CEO-type background. They have a strong business focus that is more tactical than that of the CEO, with a planning horizon of approximately 6 months to 2 years. Most have multiple departments (usually those that generate revenue) reporting to them.

Chief nursing officers (CNOs) are also sometimes called chief nursing executives (CNEs) or VPs of nursing. They are responsible for all nursing service provided by the institution. Most have at least their R.N. degree, and many CNEs now have master's degrees (MSNs) or doctorates (PhDs) in nursing. Their planning horizon is tactical—less than 1 year. CNOs are involved in the annual budgeting process. They are likely to be evaluated on patient care measurements such as the number of nursing hours per patient day and quality of care.

Chief financial officers (CFOs) are usually CPAs by background and are concerned with the management of the cash flow, revenue stream, and expenses. In small organizations, they may have a tactical planning horizon. In large institutions, where they are likely to have a controller reporting to them, they tend to have a longer strategic planning horizon. CFOs many be involved in bond issues and strategic financial planning and funding issues. They typically manage the accounting, medical records, information systems, and (sometimes) materials management departments. They are very interested in reducing expenses, improving cycle time, and making operational improvements. Many will need to see a financial justification before investing in quality improvement activities. CFOs are interested in the availability of information for the special reports that they must make periodically to the board of directors.

Chief information officers (CIOs) are sometimes called directors of information systems (I/S) in small facilities. Many CIOs, even in large facilities, still report to the CFO. In some organizations, however, the CIOs now report directly to the CEO. In a small facility, a director of I/S or a CIO is likely to have a technical background, possibly as a programming or operations manager. In larger facilities, CIOs tend to have more business background and be more user-focused. Some new CIOs are MBAs, but they still stay in touch with the technical trends in the I/S industry. CIOs are typically measured on down time, response time, availability of information, integration of systems, user satisfaction, and, sometimes, profitability.

Department heads participate in annual planning efforts but typically have a tactical focus of under 1 year. Many department heads have 2- or 4-year degrees in their areas of expertise, and in some states department heads must be licensed. Lab, pharmacy, and radiology departments in many health care organizations are beginning to share information across the three departments. Many department heads are measured only on the expenses and revenue of their individual departments and are not usually focused on information sharing.

Physicians care about providing high-quality health care for their patients and about the profitability of their practices. The medical chief of staff represents the interests of the physicians as a member of the executive team. Although many physicians are not hospital employees, they sometimes act like employees and sometimes like customers.

As we mentioned earlier, recent legislation is making physicians' profitability more challenging every day. The Omnibus Budget Reform Act (OBRA) of 1989 establishes payment reform for physicians. There are three major parts of OBRA:

1. The resource-based relative value scale (RBRVS) establishes fixed payment amounts paid to physicians for various procedures and services based on a complex set of factors including geography, number of years the physician attended medical school, patient risk, amount of insurance available, type of illness, etc.

2. The balance due for medicare patients will be reduced. Medicare currently pays 80 percent of the usual and customary fees for physicians' services. The physician then bills the patient for the remaining 20 percent. OBRA reforms will drive the amount due from the patient down, thereby reducing the doctor's revenue.

3. Volume control is the third aspect of the OBRA reforms. The objective of this portion of the legislation is to ensure that the physician does not try to make up for the reduced revenue from Medicare payments by increasing his or her volume of patients. Medicare is establishing acceptable limits for volume that the physician must not exceed.

These reforms along with the rising costs of malpractice insurance and other factors are driving many physicians to join group practices to cut costs. Others are choosing to get out of private practice and go to work as salaried professionals on the staffs of HMOs or other institutions. More physicians than ever before are seeking help from information technology to streamline their practices and improve the quality of the care they deliver.

Issues and Opportunities

Several major trends and issues in health care today can create consulting opportunities. The community, consumers, and employers are increasing their involvement in health care planning and management to reduce or control costs. A collaborative community model is replacing the traditional competitive model. This can yield opportunities for strategic planning engagements. Health care organizations are increasing their focus on running like businesses, with a keen eye on profitability and cost control. Engagements are increasing in the financial management area and in improving treatment protocols and outcomes. Many institutions are working to determine their strengths and to become more competitive by building on those strengths. Product line management and marketing might be potential engagement opportunities.

The increased emphasis on quality due to (1) JCAHO guidelines and (2) the need to reduce costs, offers a broad area of opportunity for consulting. The trend toward becoming more patient-centered, in both the in-patient and the growing out-patient areas, will yield opportunities for market research on customer wants and needs, definition of new services, and process improvement engagements. Because of our aging U.S. population, we'll see the long-term care and home health care markets growing in the 1990s. As these new businesses grow, they also will need consulting services in the areas of market analysis and planning, information technology strategy and planning, and quality.

As physicians work to cut costs and automate their offices, they will have a growing need for information systems selection consulting for medical groups. Both physicians and hospitals will continue to need help with systems integration and implementation management. Other potential engagement types include disaster/contingency planning, operational or organizational right-sizing, and business transformation.

Operational and Practice Management Considerations

This selection discusses operational and practice management issues that are unique to health care. General operational and practice management issues are covered in other chapters of this book.

Fees

Because most health care organizations do not have the financial resources to invest in large consulting contracts, it is wise to break proposed consulting work into smaller, phased engagements. In the 1990s, we may see a change in the fee structure from flat fees to fees based on a percentage of the benefit attained by the client as a result of the consultant's work. For example, a client might pay the consultant a percentage of additional revenues generated or a percentage of expenses reduced by the consultant's efforts. This sort of profit and risk sharing is already being done in some areas, such as accounts receivable. A consultant today may receive a percentage of the enhanced A/R collections that result from his or her involvement.

Legal

As in any industry, it is wise to obtain legal counsel for your consulting practice. In health care, because decisions can affect patients' lives, it is especially advisable to do so. If your consulting reports give opinions, ensure that you have substantial data behind them. Ensure that your stated opinions are limited to your area of expertise. If you sense that a potential engagement involves a very high risk, your best move may be not to bid on that engagement. Your reputation will suffer more from an unsatisfactory job than from not bidding on the job at all. A good question to ask yourself might be: "If an investigative news crew showed up at the door of my firm and wanted to look at *everything*, would there be anything that I would not want them to see?"

Practice Structure and Development

There are many consultants working in the health care field today, so it is important that you differentiate yourself by establishing a niche. Decide via your market analysis which key areas you will focus on, for example, managed care or quality. You need to hire or affiliate yourself with experienced professionals who are knowledgeable in your chosen areas. The competition will have clinical professionals such as nurses and physicians on its teams, where appropriate. If you don't have the same type of strong credentials in your proposal, you simply won't get the business.

Depending on the size and budget for the engagement, you may need to bring in a nationally recognized expert, someone who speaks frequently at association meetings and is a published, respected authority in his or her field. Degrees and credentials are very important in the health care field, especially with physicians.

Development of Staff and Alliances

Stay connected! Health care is a tightly knit industry. This is positive because it makes it easier to get to know people and organizations. It is also challenging because one must establish one's credibility to become accepted. Investing time and energy in professional associations and community work can help you to establish yourself. Participate in internships, continuing education, and advanced degree work to keep in touch with the latest trends and issues. Look for opportunities to write, speak, or teach in your area of expertise. Talk with the regulatory agencies and universities. Stay current with your health care reading. One of your greatest assets in building your practice is your ability to build networks with good people in the health care field.

Business Development

To establish a relationship with a client, a consultant may wish to perform a small engagement first, with the hope of acquiring follow-on work. These investment marketing activities must be well-managed. You must rely on the strength of your reputation and on creative prospecting to find new opportunities. Satisfied clients will invite you back for follow-on engagements, and you probably will find opportunities through your work with associations. Public speaking and publishing articles or books also will provide exposure to new clients. As you build your network within the health care consulting community, you will receive references from other consultants or be invited to participate with them on engagements. If you and your practice are viewed as the thought leaders or experts in your niche, word of mouth will bring you new business.

Summary

This brief introduction to the health care industry can help you start practicing in this exciting field. Consulting in health care is challenging but rewarding. By consulting in this field, you can make a contribution to improving the quality of health care that is delivered in the United States today—and that is a valuable endeavor!

34

Government Agencies and Authorities

Dwight W. Clark
Industry Consultant—Justice
Public Sector Industry
IBM Consulting Group

The Potential Client Base

To assess the potential government client base you need to determine (1) which levels and types of governmental clients you want to target and (2) whether a sufficient client base exists from which to draw customers. In 1992, there were nearly 86,700 government agencies and authorities in the United States.[1]

In the U.S. government, entities are found at the national, state, and local levels. The people depend upon governments to make laws and provide services that keep society running smoothly. Some functions belong to the national government, and other functions are under the jurisdiction of the state or local government.

There is one national entity commonly referred to as the federal government. Excluding the military, there were over 3,019,000 civilian employees in the federal government in 1986.[2] There are 50 state government entities within the United States. State governments employed over 4,068,000 persons in 1986.[3] Every state in the United States has a state government operation.

In 1992, there were 86,692 local government entities in the United States.[4] These local governmental units included county/parish/borough,[5] municipal, township, school districts, and special districts. The count does not include semiautonomous agencies such as state institutions of higher education or certain authorities. Of the 48 states in which county governments operate,[6] the number of counties per state varies from a high of 254 in Texas to 3 in Delaware. In local government operations, 9,846,000 persons were employed in 1986.[7]

Statistics relating to federal, state, and local governments are compiled by the Bureau of the Census. In years ending with a 2 or a 7, the Bureau conducts the census on government units including their number, finances, and employment. Tables 34-1, 34-2, and 34-3 present the numbers for three separate local government entities by population and the distribution of population for each group. These tables contain 1987 census data, since the 1992 distribution of population statistics was not available at the time of publication. The local government entity count for 1992 is shown in each table.

State constitutions establish local government operations to handle government programs at the local level. These programs include local roads, courts, corrections, tax assessment and collection, human services, health services, transportation, and fire protection. Some functions are provided by overlapping authority and responsibilities shared by local and state governments. These may include education, public safety, sanitation, parks, and zoning.

Municipalities and townships are established under state law and are granted specific powers. The power may include the authority to tax, spend, and adopt local laws to manage local government affairs.

Table 34-1.[8] Number of County
Governments by Population

Population group	Number	Percent of population
250,000 or more	167	52.1
100,000 to 249,999	231	16.4
50,000 to 99,999	387	12.6
25,000 to 49,999	616	10.0
10,000 to 24,999	943	7.2
9,999 or less	698	1.9
1987 Total	3042	

The 1992 total is 3,043.

Table 34-2.[9] Number of Municipal
Governments by Population

Population group	Number	Percent of population
250,000 or more	61	29.4
100,000 to 249,999	122	11.9
50,000 to 99,999	285	13.0
25,000 to 49,999	561	13.0
10,000 to 24,999	1,303	13.6
5,000 to 9,999	1,544	7.3
2,500 to 4,999	2,151	5.1
2,499 or less	13,173	6.7
Total	19,200	

The 1992 total is 19,296.

Table 34-3.[10] Number of Township
Governments by Population

Population group	Number	Percent of population
250,000 or more	4	3.4
100,000 to 249,999	29	7.7
50,000 to 99,999	74	9.6
25,000 to 49,999	233	15.1
10,000 to 24,999	706	20.9
5,000 to 9,999	1,005	13.5
2,500 to 4,999	1,775	11.9
2,499 or less	12,865	17.9
Total	16,691	

The 1992 total is 16,666.

Such local governments often share power with county, state, and the federal governments.

In addition to the federal, state, and local government units, semiautonomous institutions and authorities also use consulting services. In 1992, there were 47,687 school districts, special districts, and special government authorities. The figures are shown in Table 34-4. There are approximately 1270 community and junior colleges and approximately 3000 universities in the United States.

The governing boards of the special government districts or authorities are either elected or appointed. The governing board members may be called commissioners, trustees, directors, or regents. They set policy and normally appoint the administrative officer. These governing boards function like a board of directors of a private corporation.

Table 34-4.[11] Number of Special
Government Districts and Authorities

Group	Number
School districts	14,556
Special districts and authorities	33,131
Natural resource	6,564
Fire protection	5,354
Utilities	4,054
Sewage and waste	3,728
Housing and development	3,663
Transportation	1,409
Hospitals and health	1,393
Park and recreation	1,212
Other	3,821
Total	47,687

With thousands of government entities, institutions, and authorities, the potential client base exists. Potential clients are those who have a problem, want to change, or need the assistance that an expert can provide. Identify your target client base and the prospects for consultant services.

The Need for Services

Time is an important resource for you, the expert. Before investing time in marketing to the public sector,[12] you should determine if the services you offer are of value to this client market. In other segments of this book, you have been introduced to the types of consulting services, attributes, and knowledge needed by consultants. You have been introduced to a skill assessment and can determine the type of consulting services you offer.

There are hundreds of ways that expert services are of value to the public sector as a client. In the public sector, you will be dealing with clients who face a very complex set of challenges. Those challenges include a public that wants increased services and services without user fees, taxpayers who demand decreased costs, and the uncertainties of the political and the economic environments.

In the past, this client base has utilized consultant services for training, automation, strategic planning, reorganizing, work flow documentation, analysis, changing service delivery, improving efficiency, consolidating operations, management auditing, operations auditing, designing processes, and assessing alternative solutions.

Recently, public sector entities have contracted for consultant services with privatization, implementing technology, development of alternative services, integration of information systems, and reengineering the business. There is more. David Osborne and Ted Gaebler in their book on reengineering government state:

> We use the phrase entrepreneurial government to describe the new model we see emerging across America. This phrase may surprise many readers, who think of entrepreneurs solely as business men and women. But the true meaning of the word entrepreneur is far broader. It was coined by the French economist J. B. Say, around the year 1800. "The entrepreneur," Say wrote, "shifts economic resources out of an area of lower and into an area of higher productivity and greater yield." An entrepreneur, in other words, uses resources in new ways to maximize productivity and effectiveness....When we talk about the entrepreneurial model, we mean public sector institutions that habitually act this way—that constantly use their resources in new ways to heighten both their efficiency and their effectiveness.[13]

Osborne and Gaebler build a case for why government cannot be run like a private business.[14] However, government can become more entrepreneurial even if public sector operations may not be run just like a private sector business. This author firmly agrees with the observations of Osborne and Gaebler. Contacts with clients and customers eventually move to a discussion on changing the operations to be more entrepreneurial. This signals a change in public management concepts and practices in the operations of government agencies. It is a paradigm shift for government operations, even government itself.[15]

> Each of us has a mental image of government, a set of assumptions that guide our perceptions....But many practitioners, particularly in state and local government, needed something more than a nineteenth century paradigm if they were to deal with the new realities. They had little choice: they had to grapple with the tax revolt, the sad state of public education, the runaway cost of prisons....Suddenly, the field of government was brimming with new catch phrases: "public-private partnerships," "alternative service delivery," "contracting out," "empowerment," "Total Quality Management," "participatory management," "privatization," "load shedding."[16]

From the creative use of processes for management[17] to the generation of creative thinking for an employee, one can find a number of entrepreneurial methodologies published in business and management literature.[18] The terminology may be focused on private sector business, but the theme is applicable to the public sector. Public sector managers are finding opportunities for the application of those entrepreneurial methodologies in their organizations.

The financial situation will become tighter for public sector managers, elected officials, and special district authorities. Government entities will not be able to assume the delivery of more services simply by adding staff or increasing the tax and revenue base or assessing service fees. The tax revolts in California, Illinois, Maryland, Oregon, and Colorado indicate that citizens are less willing to support tax increases. With rising costs, it will even be difficult for the public sector to maintain the current level of services. In this unfavorable climate for raising taxes and fees, government leaders will need to rethink and change their way of doing business.[19]

The downsizing, tax revolts, and recessions of the 1980s have also generated a new reality for management in the public sector. In a number of states,[20] public sector managers are facing the constraints of limited budget increases or reduced budgets with increased demand for services. These managers and administrators are finding that they can no longer just add staff resources to handle the service demands. Like their counterparts in the private sector, they are looking for ways to meet the service demands with fewer resources. Even the much heralded potential of the Information Age will be only part of the new realities for running the business of the public sector tomorrow.[21]

As elected or appointed officials, public sector managers and administrators come face to face with the external forces of change; they will seek advice, counsel, and decision support. A vast majority will want to respond with an entrepreneurial spirit. Others will follow in order to survive. Responding to this need for change is where the opportunity lies for consulting to government entities.

Obtaining the Business

There are ways to ensure that the target client base becomes aware of you and your services. Public sector clients from the same segment[22] are not in direct competition with each other. Therefore, information is frequently exchanged between agencies. This underscores the importance of becoming known within particular public sector segments. News of outstanding work spreads rapidly. Equally, news of poor quality or deficient work of a consultant spreads rapidly.

An easy way to become known within a particular public sector segment is through associations. There are over 23,000 associations at the national level and approximately 100,000 associations at the state and local level.[23] By consulting one of the major directories on associations,[24] you can identify the associations to which a particular client group belongs. These directories are available in most public libraries. If eligible, you may want to join the association and become an active member. The objective is to become known to the membership. The more they are aware of you, the better your chances for a consulting opportunity or a referral. Many associations have local chapter meetings and hold conferences where speakers or presentations are needed. Offer to speak or make a presentation at such meetings. One of the best methods to generate business is personal contact. Again, association conferences provide a number of possible contacts. Making the client aware of you and your services will lead to opportunities and business.

There are other ways to become known. Write an article for an association journal or a professional periodical. You can establish a newsletter or write a book. Speaking engagements with target audiences is another way to make the target client base aware of you. These activities will broadcast your name as well as enhance your credibility.

Public sector managers and administrators have a tendency to keep material for reference. Therefore, a brochure about you and your services may lead to future opportunities. Another way to find potential contacts is to utilize electronic bulletin boards, or "on-line" resources. Public databases, commercial databases, and electronic mail services may lead to opportunities.[25]

In large metropolitan areas, private firms act as brokers in the placement of specific services including consulting. Bidders' lists are another source for leads on consulting work. Bidders' lists are maintained by procurement and contracting offices. Talk with the procurement and contracting office to obtain information and register for bidders' lists.

Cultivating referral sources is very important to the consultant who provides services to the public sector. Unless those in the public sector know about you and the services you offer, you will not have the referrals or opportunities you need to be a successful consultant.

The Procurement Process

The process used by the public sector to purchase goods and services is frequently referred to as "procurement." Because most purchases are made with public funds, numerous rules, regulations, and procedures ensure an open, impartial, and competitive procurement. Between federal, state, and local governments, there are differences in a procurement. It is important to understand the process for each one, know the procedure you are expected to follow, and where to find the leads.

Several criteria influence which procurement tools are used—dollar value, technical skills needed, regulations, and timing. The most frequently used procurement process for obtaining professional services is the request for proposal, or RFP. An RFP is a request for an offer (a proposal) to complete the scope of work identified in the RFP. An RFP does not necessarily require advertising or awarding the contract to the lowest bidder. The evaluation or selection criteria in addition to price are frequently identified within the RFP. When responding to an RFP, follow the proposal instructions closely.

Sole source and unsolicited proposal procurements are also used to obtain a consulting contract. A sole source procurement may be used where the needed skills are very specialized and technical—only one source available. An unsolicited proposal process may occur when an offer (a proposal) is accepted to complete specific work without a competitive procurement process.

Most federal purchasing is done by an individual agency using its own staff and procurement process. Federal agencies use a classification of goods and services groups. There are nearly 100 classifications with about 18 classifications that identify services which a consultant may provide. However, consultant opportunities may also be published in the product categories such as "70" for data processing or "69" for training. Become familiar with the classifications and then regularly scan notices under selected categories for consulting opportunities.

You will want to obtain a copy of the Application Bidders List Standard Form 129. Complete the form and make multiple copies. Then file a copy with each federal purchasing office which will process a procurement that interests you.

The *Commerce Business Daily* is published by the federal government to announce contract opportunities and awards.[26] The *Commerce Business Daily* is available by subscription and is in most major public libraries. It can provide leads for potential clients as well as leads for a consultant subcontract. Most agencies that do their own purchasing also publish a guide to their particular procurement process. There are other government publications that contain valuable information on the procurement process. Several of those documents are the *Federal Procurement Regulations, Government Contract Principles, Procurement Law, Guide for Submission of Unsolicited Proposals, Code of Federal Regulations, Title 41, Public Contracts and Property Management,* and *Doing Business with the Federal Government.*[27] Another way to learn about federal procurement is to request literature from a nearby General Services Administration Business Service Center. Check the telephone directory under government listings for the "General Services Administration Business Service Center."

State governments tend to centralize the procurement process. In larger states, however, it is more likely you will find state agencies handling the procurement. States have laws and regulations regarding government procurement and contracting. You need to know these regulations and procedures. Frequently, agencies will maintain bidders' lists and notify those on the bidders' list of a procurement. Major state offices will have guidelines for doing business with them.

In general, state laws determine how local governments may purchase services. In addition, local ordinances usually establish threshold dollar amounts for a formal procurement. Usually, contracts under $5000 do not require a formal bid process. The smaller the local government, the more likely purchasing will be centralized for the local government departments. In larger counties and cities, the purchasing is done at the department level. In order to do business, you need to know the regulations governing how that government unit purchases services. Many local governments have the option to use the products and services available under a state contract.

Typically, educational institutions, school districts, special districts, and authorities will provide their own procurement support. It is important that you know the particular rules, policies, and procurement laws for these types of governmental entities. Direct contact with the particular institute's, district's, or authority's purchasing department will provide you with the necessary information.

When you receive an RFP through a bidders' list, respond even if you are not bidding. Failure to respond may lead to deletion from the bidders' list. Learning about the public sector procurement process can be overwhelming. But it is very important to your success for you to know the procedure you are expected to follow and where to find the leads.

If you have a public sector client base, your skills match the client's needs, and you can handle the complexities of the public sector environment, you will find many opportunities and success as a public sector consultant.

Notes

1. Data for this table came from *1992 Census of Governments,* U.S. Department of Commerce, Bureau of the Census, GC92-1(P), November 1992.

2. Data for this table came from *City and County Data Book,* U.S. Department of Commerce, Bureau of the Census, 1988, Table No. 479, "Governmental Employment and Payrolls: 1970–1986." See *San Francisco Chronicle,* Tuesday, December 15, 1992, p. A3, "Government Keeps Hiring Despite the Recession."

3. Data for this table came from ibid.

4. Data for this table came from *1992 Census of Governments,* U.S. Department of Commerce, Bureau of the Census, GC92-1(P), November 1992. *City and County Data Book,* U.S. Department of Commerce, Bureau of the Census, 1988, Table No. 468, "Number of Local Governments, by Type—States: 1982–1987."

5. In the state of Louisiana, a similar government entity is called a parish. In the state of Alaska, a similar government entity is called a borough.

6. The states of Connecticut and Rhode Island do not have a county type of government operation.

7. Data for this table came from: *City and County Data Book,* U.S. Department of Commerce, Bureau of the Census, 1988, Table No. 479, "Governmental Employment and Payrolls: 1970–1986." See *San Francisco Chronicle,* Tuesday, December 15, 1992, p. A3, "Government Keeps Hiring Despite the Recession."

8. Data for this table came from: *City and County Data Book,* U.S. Department of Commerce, Bureau of the Census, 1988, Table No. 469, "County, Municipal,

and Township Governments, 1987, and their Population, 1986, by Population-Size Group." Since the differences in totals between 1987 and 1992 were small, the distribution would be similar for 1987 and 1992.

9. Data for this table came from ibid.

10. Data for this table came from ibid.

11. Data for this table came from: *1992 Census of Governments*, U.S. Department of Commerce, Bureau of the Census, GC92-1(P), November 1992. *City and County Data Book*, U.S. Department of Commerce, Bureau of the Census, 1988, Table No. 468, "Number of Local Governments, by Type—States: 1982–1987."

12. Throughout this chapter, public sector includes those government entities, districts, institutions, and special authorities discussed as part of the potential client base.

13. David Osborne and Ted Gaebler, *Reinventing Government* (New York: Addison-Wesley Publishing Company, Inc., 1992), p. xix.

14. Ibid., pp. 20–22.

15. See Joel Barker, *Discovering the Future: The Business of Paradigms* (Minnesota: ILI Press, 1989) for a discussion on paradigms and paradigm shift. Also see Walter Wriston, *The Twilight of Sovereignty* (New York: Charles Scribner's Sons, 1992). Wriston writes about the change of capital worth from material resources to intellectual resources, the global implications of the massive information revolution that is in progress, and how these factors are transforming private and public institutions.

16. Osborne and Gaebler, *Reinventing Government*, pp. 322–323.

17. See Charles Kepner and Benjamin Tregoe, *The New Rational Manager* (New Jersey: Princeton Research Press, 1981).

18. See Peter Drucker, *Innovation and Entrepreneurship: Practice and Principles* (New York: Harper & Row, 1985). Peter Drucker, *The New Realities in Government and Politics/in Economics and Business/in Society and World View* (New York: Harper & Row, 1989). See Gerald Nadler and Shozo Hibino, *Breakthrough Thinking* (California: Prima Publishing & Communications, 1990). Nadler and Hibino identify seven principles that are consistently used by effective problem solvers to convert information and knowledge into creative solutions. The seven principles identified and explained are uniqueness, purposes, solution-after-next, systems, limited information collection, people design, and betterment timeline. See Peter Senge, *The Fifth Discipline* (New York: Doubleday Currency, 1990). Senge writes about generating a continuous metanoia for self, team, or business using the essence, principles, and practices of five learning disciplines—systems thinking, personal mastery, mental models, building shared vision, and team learning. See Michael Michalko, *Thinkertoys* (California: Ten Speed Press, 1991). By examples the author presents specific linear and intuitive techniques for generating ideas—becoming more creative or continually practicing creativity. See Michael Hammer and James Champy, *Reengineering the Corporation* (New York: Harper Business, 1993). See Robert Tomasko, *Rethinking the Corporation* (New York: American Management Association,

1993). See Gifford Pinchot and Elizabeth Pinchot, *The End of Bureaucracy and the Rise of the Intelligent Organization* (San Francisco: Berrett-Koehler Publishers, 1993).

19. See Al Gore, *From Red Tape to Results: Creating a Government that Works Better & Costs Less*, Report of the National Performance Review (Washington, D.C.: U.S. Government Printing Office, 1993).

20. Budget constraints are not affecting all levels of government or geographic areas in the same ways. In nearly half of the states, some sort of tax revolt has placed constraints on government budgeting. However, the number of government workers has increased nationwide in the last few years. In a newspaper article, Jonathan Marshall quoted Samuel Brunelli, executive director of the American Legislative Exchange Council in Washington, D.C.: "Public employment continues to rise at a faster rate (than the private) economy....In the private economy, waves of downsizing and belt-tightening have pared payrolls to the bone....Federal job rolls remained flat....But state and local governments have hired 1.3 million new workers since Bush became President. Total government employment [is] at 18,678,000....Education represents nearly half of all state and local employment." Source: *San Francisco Chronicle*, Tuesday, December 15, 1992, p. A3, "Government Keeps Hiring Despite the Recession."

21. See Wriston, *Twilight of Sovereignty*. See also Thomas Davenport, *Process Innovation* (Cambridge, Mass.: Harvard Business School Press, 1993). Davenport presents six key messages about process change and the application of information technology for defining organizational change and utilization of human resources. See Don Tapscott and Art Caston, *Paradigm Shift* (New York: McGraw-Hill, Inc., 1993). Tapscott and Caston reveal how the application of information technology is enabling, in some cases forcing, businesses to rethink their success and survival. See Daniel Burrus, *Technotrends* (New York: Harper Business, 1993).

22. The same segment identifies agencies that are the same type, for example—health, law enforcement, controllers, school districts.

23. Source is the *Association FACT BOOK*, published by the American Society of Association Executives (ASAE), 1575 Eye Street, NW, Washington, D.C. 20005-1168, 202-626-ASAE.

24. There are several directories. *The Encyclopedia of Associations* (Gale Research Company; Detroit, Michigan; (313) 961-2242) is frequently referred to as Gale's *Association Directory*. Another source is the *National Trade and Professional Associations in the United States and Canada*, Columbia Books, Inc., Washington, D.C., (202) 737-3777. A third resource is *Who's Who in Association Management/Allied Societies Directory*, American Society of Association Executives, Washington, D.C., (202) 626-ASAE.

25. See *The Bulletin Board Book*, by Tom Scott (New York: M&T Books, 1992). There are other directories on bulletin board and electronic resource databases.

26. For subscription, contact the Superintendent of Documents, U.S. Government Printing Office, Washington, D.C. 20402, (202) 783-3238.

27. For more information about these documents, contact the Superintendent of Documents, U.S. Government Printing Office, Washington, D.C. 20402, (202) 783-3238.

Bibliography

Bevers, Charles, Linda Christie, and Lynn Price: *The Entrepreneur's Guide to Doing Business with the Federal Government* (Englewood Cliffs, N.J.: Prentice-Hall, 1989).

Block, Peter: *Flawless Consulting,* San Diego, CA (University Associates, 1981).

Greiner, Larry E., and Robert Metzger: *Consulting to Management* (Englewood Cliffs, N.J.: Prentice-Hall, 1983).

Holtz, Herman: *The 100 Billion Market* (New York: AMACOM, 1980).

MacManus, Susan: *Doing Business with Government* (New York: Paragon House, 1992).

Steele, Fritz: *Consulting for Organizational Change* (Amherst: University of Massachusetts Press, 1975).

U.S. General Accounting Office: *Government Consultants* (Washington, D.C., 1988), GAO/G6D-88-99FS.

35
Family Business

Mary Ann Kipp

Kipp & Associates
Nashville, Tennessee

Happy families are all alike: every unhappy
family is unhappy in its own way.
——LEO TOLSTOY

This chapter will look at family business issues, examining the merits
and drawbacks of family business systems. As a consultant to family
businesses, you will need to consider some important elements which
stretch beyond the day-to-day concerns of any enterprise. Most of these
revolve around maintaining the delicate balance between family interests
and practices in conjunction with sound business interests and practices.
Specifically, we will focus on growth cycles of family businesses, the
influence of family dynamics, and the pitfalls and strengths of family-
owned enterprises. Those areas which are common to all businesses, that
is, marketing, systems development, etc., will not be covered.

The Dimensions of Family Business

Family business is big business. Family businesses make up 90 percent of
the 15 million businesses in the United States. Fifty percent of all wages
paid occur within family businesses, and 40 percent of the gross national
product is family business generated. Many such businesses are household names—H&R Block, Hallmark Cards, and Marriott Corporation. Of

the *Fortune* 500 companies, one-third are family owned or controlled. Others are not so well known but are part of everyday business and service. Everyone has experienced the benefits of family business whether it is at the corner grocery, local specialty restaurant, or clothing establishment. The backbone of agricultural development in the United States stems from a strong tradition of family business.

Family business is a U.S. tradition which we expect to be upheld. After World War II, there was a tremendous surge in the establishment of family enterprises to meet the demands of a growing population and economy. Today, in a very different environment, new businesses must evolve to meet the demands for new products, new services, and new technologies. Changes in corporate structures and the increase of women in the work force will influence family business development. Many middle managers, no longer part of organizations because of downsizing, will establish businesses of their own. Women have discovered that establishing their own businesses allows them to compete and succeed equally with men in the world of free enterprise.

Family businesses come in all shapes and sizes. Some are small and involve the owner directly in the day-to-day operations. Others are larger and reflect less direct involvement. But in the main, a family business is an organization designed as a proprietorship, a partnership, or a corporation and is privately owned by the family or is one in which the family holds the controlling interest.

Almost 70 percent of family businesses do not survive into the second generation. Of those that continue into the second generation, half will not sustain into the third generation. The typical family business has a life expectancy of only 24 years. This grim statistic substantiates the cliché "shirtsleeves to shirtsleeves," but more importantly it validates the belief that family businesses need outside expertise.

Phases of Family Business Development

Family businesses go through three phases of development. Each requires a particular style of operation and has specific talent and system demands.

Phase I: Start-up and Entrepreneurship

Family businesses begin in the spirit and vision of the founder. The founder is generally an individual who has decided to "build a better mousetrap"

Figure 35-1 Characteristics of development in family business.

and to escape or abandon the confines of larger corporate structures. The entrepreneur is willing to take risks, finds stimulation in innovation, and has a strong desire to develop a dream into reality. The founder seeks control over his or her own destiny based upon his or her own skills, ability to make decisions, and capacity to act quickly. This individual is fiercely independent, dedicated, and motivated by a sense of vision.

In this phase, the important goal is survival. It involves long hours, a mixture of talents, and a great deal of flexibility and is often characterized by extreme highs and lows. Meeting financial obligations is a constant preoccupation and worry. Finding the means or individuals to patch through from one task or one contract to the next is both a thrill and a threat. There is very little true management during this phase. Control of all aspects remain with one central figure, the founder, through what is very much a hands-on approach.

Phase II: Stabilization and Professionalization

During this phase the company begins to take on and realize a definite identity. Both customers and the company know its market niche. Financial unpredictability is replaced with a known level of income and growth. Responsibility and control within the organization are shared, and there is a professional level of management which is recognized and practiced. Systems are developed and established. Employees have more traditional jobs and job descriptions and less overlap in roles. Growth is less sporadic because there is real planning. It is no longer a "one-man show." Controls are in place.

At this stage, the founder has much less of a hands-on approach. The founder's vision or dream begins to be recognized as a viable entity which will continue into the future. The entrepreneur now functions more as a manager, and he or she must manage for consistent, gradual growth. At the same time, although not directly involved in every detail, the owner/founder maintains a firm grasp on what is going on in all areas of the organization.

Phase III: Succession and Expansion

At this point the future of the business is its main consideration. It is accepted by now that the leadership of the organization has changed or will. The future of the business and areas of potential growth or expansion become the focus. Change in leadership can work in conjunction with a change in direction. The company is professionally managed and requires discernible skills and abilities at all levels of the organization. The original vision or dream may look quite different, either in scope or configuration, than originally conceived.

The founder/entrepreneur is clearly on the sidelines and probably is not directly involved with the company in any way. This is the retirement stage for the entrepreneur—at least from this particular enterprise. At this time, the pursuit of other interests, whether recreational or business, becomes the founder's main focus. The management of the family business at this point may be in the hands of other family members or professional managers or some combination of the two.

Transitions

Between each phase is a period of transition. It is the effective execution of these transitional periods that determines the ultimate success and stabilization of any family venture. Although these phases have been described in the context of the founder/entrepreneur, phases II and III can cycle throughout the life of the organization. It is possible that an offspring can assume leadership of the business and result in a revisit to phase I with new directions being taken and tremendous expansion occurring. This has similar elements to phase I whereby the "new" leader sees the enterprise as his or her "baby." This leader is likely to have difficulty transitioning, just as the founder might have had.

The periods of transition are vital and probably the most difficult. It is generally a time when a consultant's services and more objective view are sorely needed. Transition from phase I to phase II requires the first true assessment of the skills of those current and potential members of the organization—specifically family members. Phase II involves the complicated process by which the fiercely independent entrepreneur needs to acknowledge that he or she depends on the talents and commitment of others to sustain the enterprise. This is compounded by the need to assess the strengths and weaknesses of employees, which may include offspring or other family members, and to assess appropriate levels of responsibility and involvement. The founder is required to acknowledge limitations and adopt the very structure of corporate life the venture was designed to escape. And for the first time the founder/entrepreneur must recognize mortality as a part of life.

Christie Hauck, president and founder of Christie's Cookies, captures the difficulties and requirements of a successful phase I to phase II transition in an interview published in *The Tennessean,* October 11, 1992:

> In its early days, the company was driven by sales from a single outlet....
>
> It was not unusual for Christie to be baking and selling cookies himself. The stores [now] account for about 40 percent of sales. He said he regrets the company's growing pains, which has seen it lose some of the early management team.
>
> "Sometimes, the company takes a turn and needs skills that people don't have," he said.
>
> Hauck, who started the company after a lengthy personal search to create "the perfect chocolate-chip cookie," said he misses the earlier days when he baked and watched people smile as they tasted his cookies.
>
> "The most fun that I've had ever is being behind the counter selling cookies," he said. "I love the interchange, the interplay. The desire to do that is very strong."
>
> "But this whole goal from day one...[was]to become a national company. And you don't do that by putting an apron on and standing behind the counter."

Phase III can easily make the headlines. The boss is passing the torch, and the quality of planning and implementation involved in this stage becomes profoundly apparent. It is a time when the foundation of the organization is reinforced and strengthened or else becomes weak enough to threaten the whole enterprise. Sam Walton, founder of Wal-Mart, had geared his organization toward this phase in an expert manner. When he died recently, the company showed no sign of disruption. The passing of the torch had been firmly implanted in the minds of all concerned, including the employees, the customers, the investors and the family. The negative publicity the Beaman family of Nashville and the Bingham family of Louisville incurred during their transitions attests to the problems of faulty succession or phase III planning gone awry. The headlines reached scandalous proportions, and the lawyers received a fair share of the business profits.

Transitions are obviously laden with many personal, professional, and business decisions and issues. It is during these phases that many organizations appear in the daily headlines with one sensational report after another. These moments of change require shifts in power which profoundly affect all elements of the founder's life because the outcome affects both the survival of the family and the business. The stakes are high, and it is during these periods that the potency of the mix of power, money, and love becomes apparent. It is not the three phases themselves that create difficulties for businesses but the character of the transitions, their anticipation, their acceptance, and their execution which can make or break a successful outcome.

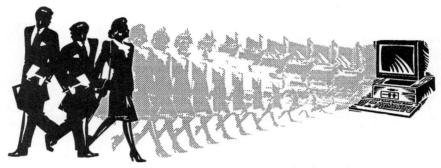

Figure 35-2 Blurring of family systems and business systems.

If the Family Business Represents the Family's Livelihood, Why the Problems?

Family systems and business systems have very different purposes. The priorities of each and the basis of each are in opposition to one another. There can be conflict between the values of each. Conflict and problems occur when the distinction between the two becomes blurred or when the boundaries overlap to such an extent that the balance of each system is not maintained. The blurring of these systems and their opposing purposes can bring either system to the point of destruction or, at the very least, serious imbalance.

Conflicting Values between Family Structures and Business Structures

In some vital areas, both family systems and business systems have values which are at opposite ends of a continuum. The owner/founder must balance and effectively monitor the tension that exists between the two systems. With a foot in both "camps," it is the owner who establishes and sustains the environment in which both systems will coexist. He or she sets a tone that becomes policy, whether formal or informal, which is understood and practiced in both systems.

Family Values	**Business Values**
Lifetime membership	Membership is role- or job-related and temporary
Entitled through birth	Hired based on skills and experience

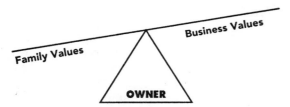

Figure 35-3 Balancing family and business values—a pivotal requirement.

Need-based finances	Income based on skills and performance
Emotion-based structure	Reason-based structure
Members treated equally	Hierarchy, status, and position rewarded
Parents have total authority	CEO/board are authority
Individual growth and development	Growth and training meet company needs
Primary purpose is care and nurturing	Primarily provides profit, goods, or services

There will be problems when the values in one realm are altered or abandoned to take on the values of the other. If a family sacrifices its value base in the areas identified, there will be tremendous conflict and upheaval. Basic needs will not be met. The same is true if family values, as identified in this list, become operating principles within the business environment. If positions are rewarded based on the needs of the individual rather than those of the organization, the void or imbalance will create problems in functioning, operations, profits, etc. The differentiation between these two systems and the maintenance of these distinctions limit the amount and severity of conflict in each. The challenge for all family businesses is to sustain a healthy integration of the interest of the business, founder and family.

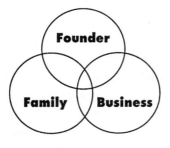

Figure 35-4 Integrated interests of three dimensions with appropriate balance.

Family Culture and Its Strengths

In the business community in general, the culture of an organization can have an enormous impact on its success and ability to compete. There are many examples of enterprises that succeed because of their ability to sustain a competitive edge based on the values which are sustained through the culture of the organization. The culture of family businesses are often unique and demonstrate the positive nature of families and business working together.

There are aspects of combining family and business which are difficult for other organizations to duplicate and which can provide the business with a distinct competitive advantage. In the most recent edition of Levering and Moskowitz's *The 100 Best Companies to Work for in America*, the number of privately held companies listed has increased to 31. In 1984 that number was 20. Speculation has it that family businesses are able to plan for and commit to the long term and do not have to be influenced by the whims of the stock market. The implementation of business decisions in the present can be agreed upon with the understanding that the payoff may not be immediate. These decisions will be implemented with an eye toward future successes and long-term results.

Family characteristics that exert a positive influence are:

- A strong commitment and sense of loyalty among members
- Shared values and common understanding of "the way things work"
- Diminished need to play politics; limits and strengths are known quantities
- High trust level based on relationship which increases openness and security
- Customers perceive a greater measure of integrity and commitment
- Members are "owners" and take an interest in customer needs
- A company "in the family" provides a sense of continuity to its members
- High flexibility in responsiveness and planning; not limited to quarterly fluctuations
- Shared pride and sense of history
- Because of the genuine caring, work can be a real labor of love
- Willingness to share the good times and make necessary sacrifices in bad times

Caterpillar understands, very well, the attributes of working with family businesses. Caterpillar is known to have a superior, global dealer network for its construction equipment. Its network is outstanding in the industry. The company's strategy is not only effective, it is unique. Caterpillar believes in a dealer mix made up entirely of family-owned operators. The assumption, borne out through results, is that family operators are more committed to their business than salaried managers. The determining factor seems to be that as on-site operators, owners take a special interest in their business, as opposed to absentee owners who see the venture strictly as an investment. A family-owned dealership has as the bottom line the owner's name and reputation.

Intergenerational Career Paths

When family members are seeking to fulfill career development strategies within one organization, there can be moments of bliss and contentment because the stages are compatible. But there can also be constant tension when there are divergent aspirations. Most career stages can actually be viewed as a constant search for identity or fortune. Each stage, although somewhat unique, has as its main focus one area or the other. Family members may be on paths that inhibit the career path of other members. When this is a strong dynamic within the organization, an assessment of the individual's stage is appropriate to allow for a reasonable adjustment and modification of existing conditions.

Six Stages of Career Development

Career stages divide roughly into six developmental areas. As with all developmental models, it is possible for any one individual to linger in one stage or to revisit it at a later age based on the need to deal with "unfinished business" before being able to move on effectively.

Search Stage—Ages 18–27 During this stage, nothing is permanent. The main focus is on experimentation and education and learning. It involves a search for identity as well. Experiencing different roles, using different skills, exposing oneself to a variety of work settings and indi-

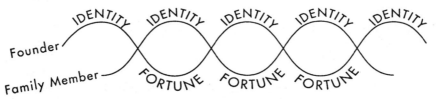

Figure 35-5 Cross-purposes and conflicting career agendas.

viduals are the intents of people at this stage. There is no expectation that any of these positions will endure. It is a trial-and-error period, a time to try one's wings.

Initial Settling-in Stage—Ages 27–36 This is the first attempt to take on an identity in a serious way and the age to show evidence of early management talents and responsibilities. The need to be recognized and to have independence is very strong. The influence of a mentor becomes pronounced. It is also a time when there is a desire to take risks. And it is usually the time when entrepreneurial characteristics come into play. The individual begins to look seriously at issues of "fortune," which include current and potential worth.

Expansion Stage—Ages 36–45 At this point, one's identity is either agreed to or abandoned. It is a point at which people reexamine their lives and decide whether to become further entrenched in a position or profession or to abandon it and "do something else with my life." There is a summing up, and there can also be a great deal of turmoil when it becomes clear how the years of life, education, and work have or have not added up to fulfill one's initial expectations and dreams. The identity issue is generally resolved, but the identity may not be acceptable. Also, there can be a strong thrust toward expanding the base of power—a need to be seen as a force to be reckoned with.

Stability Stage—Ages 45–54 An identity has by now been established. Most serious decisions about "what will I be when I grow up?" have been answered. Parenting, family, and work issues have reached a point of clarity. A confidence emerges, and there is a decrease in the need to compete. The ability to manage effectively and to keep priorities has stabilized, and a sense of balance emerges. The shift at this point is usually to a focus on "fortune" and to take a true look at one's net worth. Matters of retirement and financial status become increasingly important. A desire to contribute in a significant way and a wish to promote the growth of others through mentoring are parts of this stage.

Winding-down Transition Stage—Ages 54–63 Here, one continues to focus on fortune and financial standing. Some definite decisions have to be made about the world of work and how much longer it will remain a primary part of one's life and identity. There can be some "last ditch" efforts to compensate for anything that is lacking by way of position, reputation, or significant contribution. This can be seen as the final "make it or break it" opportunity intensified by the pressures of limited time and resources. The transition can also involve a plan for a peaceful exit from the world of work and for a more vigorous pursuit of other interests. These interests can be recreational, professional, spiritual, and/or familial.

Retirement Stage—Ages 63–72   At this stage, one leaves the world of work and its challenges, adventures, triumphs, and tragedies to the next generation of managers, leaders, and workers. Walking away from a place which has consumed the better part of one's life and energy and finding a new place to put that energy is the route taken now. If the balance of other aspects of life have not been attended to during the earlier stages, this can be a time of struggle, bitterness, and despair. If there is a sense of "a job well done" when this stage arrives, the richness of the opportunity to pursue other interests in conjunction with the time to develop those interests will be cherished. This period can involve expanding one's identity or enhancing aspects of that identity. Individuals may make high-profile contributions to the community. Formerly busy parents can now become nurturing and indulgent grandparents.

Compatibility and Conflict: Intergenerational Issues

Compatibility is possible when the individual needs of one generational stage combine to meet the needs of another individual in a different stage. If, however, the needs of one generation cannot productively combine with the needs of the other, there will be conflict:

- If the offspring has a need to try a lot of things, to take on risk and responsibility (initial settling in) and the founder/parent is in need of expanding the base of power and control (expansion), there will be conflict.

- If the offspring is in the initial settling-in stage and the founder in a stage where mentoring is the key element, the two will experience compatibility. The offspring is not seeking to take control but to learn through guidance and modeling.

It is useful to identify the precise stages the founder and the offspring or family member involved in the business have reached. Looking for evidence of the essential elements within each stage will help to discern whether the individuals are experiencing career progression and satisfaction. Beyond that, areas of natural compatibility and conflict become immediately apparent. It is possible, for instance, if an offspring desires a mentor and if the parent needs to focus on a stage of winding down, that a mentor within or outside the organization can be chosen. This ensures that there will be appropriate training and that the parent can address his or her own developmental needs.

Some family businesses agree to train members of other families through a mutual exchange agreement. This can expand experience and knowledge in ways which are mutually beneficial. In Japan, this has been a traditional way of doing business.

Built-in Problems

There are times when an organization will experience problems because its founder or leader is stuck at the in-between point where the ability to accommodate the predicament of the offspring/family member is eclipsed by the founder's overriding needs and desires. This phenomenon will fuel conflict and inhibit the ability of the family member to contribute and grow. Eventually it lessens the organization's capacity to be responsive.

Conflicting Needs

Founder	Offspring
Spontaneous, last-minute decisions	Needs area of definition and responsibility
High need to control	Independence and freedom to develop
Security conscious; preserve resources	Desire to risk and grow company
Founder and company's identities fused	Need for identity as leader/manager
Parental role dominates relationship	Seeks to go beyond limitations of family roles.

Systems, Strategy, and People: A Crucial Balance

There are three main components to consider when examining a family business. When these areas are in balance and monitored effectively, the

Figure 35-6
Founder/owner needs eclipse family member and diminish capacity.

business will prosper. Relationships, although complex, must have certain characteristics which demonstrate healthy work practices. The management team must be strong and interdependent and fueled by sufficient talent and systems. It is essential that there be consistent effort to plan and execute accordingly. Two-thirds of all family businesses have no written strategic plans, and 63 percent have no annual budget. Often the business is run "family checkbook" style—pay the bills, give an allowance to members with the rest. When there is an unexpected windfall, the business is likely to engage in extravagances. Little thought is given to long-term considerations.

Healthy relationships show evidence of:

- An atmosphere of free and open communication
- Information available to all members equally
- An atmosphere that promotes rapport and trust
- Mutual respect among members of the family
- Relationships built upon mutual goals and interdependence

Healthy systems have the following characteristics:

- Job descriptions are clear and accessible.
- Training and adequate supervision are available and required.
- Management is aware of and adheres to the overall goals of the business.
- Appropriate controls are in place to monitor inventory, budgets, expenses.

A healthy strategy exhibits these characteristics:

- The business plan is developed by and adhered to by the management structure with appropriate attention to results.
- A plan is in place for management of the business: who will fill what positions under what conditions and timetables are identified; succession planning to transfer the ownership and assets of the business

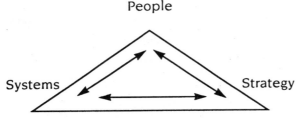

Figure 35-7 Systems, strategy, and people.

has been developed and is in place; these things are known to family and managers.

- Family meets regularly (once or twice a year) to discuss and evaluate the business, important values, expectations, etc., and to plan the future of the business and the individual part each member will play.
- Plans demonstrate adequate flexibility to be modified or amplified to meet unanticipated threats or opportunities.

Signs of Trouble

Any business which is not operating effectively will show danger signs that can be read fairly easily. Sometimes in family businesses these signs or areas can be hidden or ignored for prolonged periods because of the closed nature of the family network. Often, when trouble does begin to stir, families are isolated from markets and external indicators or input and can postpone taking a long hard look at what is exactly happening to the business and what factors are at the core. There are some indicators which, when looked at alone or in combination, can assist in evaluating a family business in trouble. These fall into three broad categories: the market or outside indicators, the company or internal indicators and, finally, the family. Outside indicators include:

- Ability to sustain its competitive edge is eroding
- A pattern which shows consistent losses of market share—a loss of quality or an increase in customer dissatisfaction—an increase in competitors

Inside indicators include:

- Profits (margins) shrinking in spite of steady or increased sales
- Cash-flow problems that are chronic or recent but not temporary in nature
- High employee turnover
- Persistent low morale among employees
- Environment that promotes fear
- Tolerance of aberrant family work habits involving substance abuse, absenteeism, low performance, and high compensation
- Emotionally charged climate with unpredictable flare-ups

Familial indicators include:

- Denial that problems are there or that they seriously influence the business

- History of poor problem-solving or coping mechanisms within the family over generations such as physical illness from stress (ulcers, insomnia) or substance abuse
- Multiple divorces and remarriages
- Family feuds that carry from one generation to the next; use of money to demonstrate or hold power and affection

Assessment

When assessing family businesses, the following tool provides a guideline when considering which areas are to be examined and specific features identified. This tool can be used as a checklist with a "yes" or "no" column. It can also be used as an "always, sometimes, or never" frequency check. Finally, it can be administered using a scale of 1 to 9 to evaluate the effectiveness in each of the delineated areas and activities. It is possible to use this instrument at all levels and to compare perceptions at the various levels.

Organization

There is a written strategic plan.

Priorities are established and acted upon.

Management responsibility is shared.

The management team is cooperative and effective.

Management decisions are made at the appropriate level.

Information is accurate and accessible to management.

There is a marketing plan which is utilized and reviewed.

The budget is reasonable, accurate, and followed.

Communication flows easily—vertically and horizontally.

Effective systems are apparent in the organization chart and daily activity.

Clear lines of authority exist at all levels.

People

Low turnover at all levels of the organization.

Job descriptions are in writing and followed.

Performance appraisals are conducted regularly.

Compensation and performance are aligned.

Employee training is directed and focused.

Individuals make decisions appropriate to tasks and responsibilities.

Communication is open; information is accessible.

Problem-solving and responsible decision making are encouraged.

Appropriate risk-taking is allowed.

Feedback is constructive, frequent, and encouraged at all levels.

Recruitment is according to procedures and anticipated needs.

Work is in an atmosphere of pride and mutual respect.

Hiring and firing practices are performance based.

New ideas are encouraged, discussed, and adopted.

The mission and goals of the organization are known and valued.

Owner

Seeks opinions of employees throughout the organization

Encourages decision making at appropriate levels

Mentors and fosters the development of employees

Evidences a sense of balance in lifestyle

- Seeks the advice of others in the industry
- Takes time off from the business with vacations and holidays
- Has access to formal or informal outside board for guidance and input
- Attends meetings to stay current on business practices and trends

Has clear grasp of organization direction and goals

Can communicate effectively and openly with employees

Planning is an integral part of thinking and activity; few crises

Shows minimal signs of overwork, high stress, or substance abuse

Has integrated approach to family and business, which is constructive to both

Has interests and activities that provide recreation, hobbies, or diversions

Has a succession plan, in management and ownership, that is current and viable and known and accepted by the owner, family, and company

The next section of the instrument will provide perspective on problems or areas which will not necessarily surface through other means but which are important for a comprehensive view of the business and its potential for success and change. These questions will provide clues which will enable the consultant to discover "the way things are done around here" and will also surface values which drive many decisions and practices. Often in a family business, there will be positions or processes or other factors which do not make sense at first glance. A deeper look into family history intertwined with the business will often be very enlightening.

History

How was the business established?

Who was the founder and what was he or she noted for?

What is the long-standing reputation of the business? The family?

Traditionally, how have family members been brought into the business? What was the outcome (effective leaders, turmoil, short stay, etc.)?

What has been the financial history of the company and the financial standing of the family? How are the two related?

Are there any notorious characters in the family? Notorious feuds? Outcasts?

What is it that the family prides itself for?

Finally, examining the phases of the organization according to the information provided previously and looking at the career needs of the various family members should round out the profile of the entire organization and its inner workings. Finding phase shifts which have not occurred or career transitions which have been inappropriate will help identify areas that need attention. Also, the strengths of the organization and family members can be identified through these devices and used as a foundation for sound growth and future direction.

Role of the Consultant

The dilemma for the consultant when entering the realm of the family business involves discovery of the appropriate role and the manner in which that role is expressed. The owner, the business, and the family are all part of the client package. The challenge is to be able to discern the areas of common concern and mutual goals, to uncover the areas which conflict and to evaluate objectively the entire system. It is only in family businesses that the consultant has to concern him or herself with the influence of family dynamics.

The consultant is obligated to have a foot in both camps. What is good for the business is not always good for the family and vice versa. A son or daughter may need a job and seek a level of involvement which exceeds his or her abilities or value to the company. A parent does not always share this view. Also, a parent may go to the other extreme and attempt to underpay an offspring (more often the case) in an attempt to deny favoritism or because the owner feels it is the son or daughter's obligation to suffer and contribute beyond the average employee.

The role of the consultant might best be identified as that of a "Dutch uncle," that is, one who can evaluate honestly and speak directly, in the spirit of a mentor or critic who seeks to guide constructively. The consultant must be able to understand what it means to be a member in a particular family and to "read" the dynamics of that system. The consultant's role further necessitates evaluation of the founder/owner as a leader, family person, and business manager. It finally includes the assessment of the business itself in all the usual ways—markets, profits, customers, products, distribution, controls, etc.

Eventually, the needs, strengths, and weaknesses of all these aspects must combine to create an accurate picture. It is a picture that may need to be fine-tuned or adjusted in some ways to permit appropriate change and growth. The consultant must partner with the enterprise in a way that permits the family, business, and owner to carry on a tradition which not only is a vital part of the country's free enterprise system but also allows the family to claim ownership with pride.

Index

About the Editors in Chief

SAM W. BARCUS III received his B.B.A. degree from the
University of Texas and his M.B.A. degree from the
University of Houston. He joined Price Waterhouse in
Memphis as a consultant, working on a variety of computer-
related projects, including system design. He joined Touche
Ross in Nashville to establish a management consulting practice serving businesses throughout the Southeast. Today he
is a partner in Barcus Britt Leiffer Consulting, which provides information management consulting, education/train-
ing, and technology implementation. Mr. Barcus is a certified
public accountant and has held leadership positions in a
number of professional and community organizations. He
conducts workshops and seminars in North America, Asia,
Europe, and South Africa.

JOSEPH W. WILKINSON is professor of accounting at Arizona
State University, where he teaches courses in accounting
information systems, systems analysis and design, financial
modeling, and management consulting. Before earning his
doctorate at the University of Oregon, Dr. Wilkinson worked
as an industrial engineer, systems analyst, and accountant in
such organizations as Price Waterhouse and Hughes
Aircraft. Dr. Wilkinson is the author of numerous articles
and four textbooks, including *Accounting and Information
Systems.* He also was the founding editor of the *Journal of
Accounting Systems.*